# A HISTORY OF PSYCHOLOGY
## Main Currents in Psychological Thought

THOMAS HARDY LEAHEY

*Virginia Commonwealth University*

# A HISTORY OF
## Main Currents in

# PSYCHOLOGY
## Psychological Thought

What a chimera then is man!
How strange and monstrous!
A chaos, a subject of contradictions, a prodigy.
Judge of all things, yet a stupid earthworm;
depository of truth, yet a cesspool of uncertainty and error;
the glory and the refuse of the universe.
Who will unravel this tangle?

Blaise Pascal, *Pensées*

**PRENTICE-HALL, INC.**, Englewood Cliffs, New Jersey 07632

*Library of Congress Cataloging in Publication Data*

Leahey, Thomas Hardy.
   A history of psychology.

   Includes bibliographies and index.
   1.   Psychology – History.        I.    Title.
BF81.L4            150'.9            79-24332
ISBN 0-13-391755-X

A History of Psychology: main currents in psychological thought

Thomas Hardy Leahey

©1980 by Prentice-Hall, Inc., Englewood Cliffs, N.J. 07632

editorial/production supervision: Scott Amerman and Cathie Mick Mahar
interior design: Scott Amerman
cover design: Saiki/Sprung Design
manufacturing buyer: Edmund W. Leone

Printed in the United States of America

10   9   8

Prentice-Hall International, Inc., *London*
Prentice-Hall of Australia Pty. Limited, *Sydney*
Prentice-Hall of Canada, Ltd., *Toronto*
Prentice-Hall of India Private Limited, *New Delhi*
Prentice-Hall of Japan, Inc., *Tokyo*
Prentice-Hall of Southeast Asia Pte. Ltd., *Singapore*
Whitehall Books Limited, *Wellington, New Zealand*

Elizabeth, who came in the middle,

and

Grace, who helped through it all

# Contents

## Fifteen
Prospect, 387

# Preface

Human beings make history—political, military, social, and scientific. In the history of science, ideas are especially important, for science is a changing collection of ideas to which short-lived human beings make contributions. This is not to deny that human personalities and institutions play a role in shaping science; but it is to say that the history of science can be written and studied in more than one way. One may choose to study the history of a science as a succession of great scientists and their major contributions to the field. Or one may study the history of a science as an institution, recording the founding of laboratories and the intellectual genealogies of the generations of scientists. Or, finally, one may study the history of a science solely as a collection of scientific concepts which evolve over time, paying relatively little attention to the personal histories of the scientists who formulate the concepts or the laboratories which put them to the test. Since any historian has only limited space at his or her disposal, the historian cannot practice all three kinds of scientific history, no matter how desirable that might be. This book contains practically no institutional history, which is probably the least developed aspect of the history of psychology. Instead, we will focus our attention on the leading psychological *concepts* as they have evolved since the earliest days of recorded human history. To help organize our study of these concepts and how they have changed, I have chosen to consider the leading exponents of different psychological systems during each historical era. Although little will be said about the personal backgrounds of these people, concentration of them will help pull together concepts into competing viewpoints on the nature of human nature and will prevent us from diffusing our efforts.

Another important option is open to a historian of science. Older histories of the sciences were generally *internal* histories considering the development of the technical ideas of each science independent of the broader intellectual and social context in which the science operated. More recently, histories of the sciences have tended to be *external* histories considering the outside intellectual and social context and its effects on the development of the science. For the most part, this book tends to be externalistic. Psychology is a young science, with only a short history of technical concepts: before the nineteenth century, psychological ideas were always part of some other field—philosophy, biology, or politics. Moreover, since psychology studies human nature—on which everyone has opinions—it is particularly subject to influence by larger social and intellectual currents. Such is not the case in other sciences. For example, physics has over its long history become so abstruse that society has little *intellectual* influence on it, although both physics and psychology are profoundly affected as institutions by the degree of support given by society at large.

No historian can be neutral to the subject matter. Historians must care about it enough to want to understand it and to make it come alive for others. Historians must be fair; they must weigh argument and counterargument; and finally, they must choose. Historians must choose some facts over others, for they cannot record everything. They must choose to discuss some thinkers and not others, for not all are equally great—although greatness is hard to define. Historians must choose some concepts over others, for some have survived while others have become extinct. They must choose some interpretation to put on the facts, events, people, and concepts written about, for history is an understanding of the past.

It is therefore the duty of the historian to state at the outset where he or she stands, what ideas he or she accepts or rejects. In short, the historian's point of view must be examined and communicated to the audience. What follows is an attempt to do this for myself.

I stand more in the rationalist tradition than in the empiricist. In philosophy I sympathize with Plato more than Aristotle, with the Stoics more than the Atomists, with Descartes and Kant more than Locke and Hume. I came to psychology by way of Freud and later was trained as a cognitive psychologist. I admire Wundt and Piaget, Tolman and Chomsky, more than Titchener and Watson, Hull and Skinner. My views on science have been shaped by Einstein, Popper, Toulmin, Kuhn, Feyerabend, and Suppe more than by Carnap, Feigle, Mach, Bridgmann. My approach to history has been conditioned by Hegel and Carlyle, Kendall and Cantor.

The purpose of this book and of the course for which you are using it is to give you a chance to work out your own point of view. The concepts and issues you learn about in content courses do not exist in a vacuum. They arose and exist in a particular historical context. The questions asked in today's research are the outcome of a historical process and the answer given contributes to that process. The opportunity that *history* and *systems* gives you is a chance to see the historical context and the historical process, to reflect on psychology as it is—and on your own experiences as a student of psychology.

Erik Erikson describes adolescence as a search for identity, a necessary prerequisite to a productive adult life. Identity is achieved through reflections on one's past and present, and through making a decision on where to go and what to do with one's life. Your reflections on psychology's past and present state is an important part of finding your identity within psychology. You should bring away from your experience not a list of names, dates, and events, but an understanding of what psychology is and of your own relation to it. You should not be a passive recorder of a monotonous march of years, but rather an explorer of the past and of great minds. The first task is dull and bloodless; the second is an adventure and full of life.

I would also like to acknowledge the helpful, if not always agreeable comments of the usually anonymous pre-publication reviewers, all professors of psychology: Dr. Richard Blanton, Vanderbilt University; Dr. James Brennen, University of Massachusetts-Boston, Dr. Darryl Bruce, Florida State University, Dr. Patrick Capretta, Miami University (Oxford, Ohio), Dr. T. S. Krawiec, Skidmore

College (Saratoga Springs, NY), Dr. Richard Morris, Trent University (Peter-borough, Ontario, Canada), Dr. Barbara Ross, University of Massachusetts-Boston, Dr. E. L. Saldanha, University of Southern Maine (Portland), Dr. Anthony Walsh, Chairman of Psychology, The Newport College-Salve Regina (Newport, RI), Dr. Michael Wertheimer, University of Colorado at Boulder. It is especially important to point out that I remain solely responsible for whatever virtues and flaws are in this book.

My most important acknowledgement goes to my wife Grace. She read every word, compiled the index and made numerous improvements, large and small, to the writing of the book. Without her efforts the manuscript would have been awkward and unclear. She also typed several of the chapters. And above all she endured the trials of pregnancy and raising an infant through it all. My second acknowledgement is to William Brewer, my mentor in graduate school, who never demanded technical specialization to the detriment of broad philosophical and historical ideas about psychology. His own unpublished analysis of behaviorism is central to the statement of the behaviorist paradigm in Chapters 10 and 11. Two other teachers, Frederick Suppe and Don Dulany, taught me philosophy of science, and some of their ideas helped shape Chapter 1. Finally, however, the responsibility for everything in this book is mine.

# 1

# Introduction
## Psychology, Science, and History

In this chapter we will develop some general concepts that define the course we will follow and that serve as tools in our attempt to understand the development of psychology. We will define psychology, explore the natures of science and history, and finally sketch the history of psychology in a broad outline that will be developed in more detail in the following chapters.

## PSYCHOLOGY IS HUMANITY'S ATTEMPT TO UNDERSTAND THE SELF

> And all our Knowledge is, OURSELVES TO KNOW.
>
> Alexander Pope, *Essay on Man*

What is psychology? This question is a natural starting point for any general study of psychology. The usual answer given today is that psychology is the science that studies behavior and mental processes. Just a few years ago psychology was described most often as the study of the behavior of man and the other animals, while shortly after its founding, psychology was described by William James in *The Principles of Psychology* as "the science of Mental Life." The nature of psychology has changed several times in its short one-hundred-year history.

This book is about those changes, about why they happened, and about the people who caused them. As Ebbinghaus reminded us, however, psychology has a long past but a short history. Our concern with self-understanding is not just 100 years old. Humanity has wondered about motives, language, thoughts, knowledge, and memory at least as long as thoughts have been recorded in writing. Broadly construed, then, psychology goes far beyond the bounds of the definitions just quoted. Psychology is humanity's attempt to understand the self, to find order in people's own affairs. Even when psychologists study animals, they hope to illuminate some aspect of humankind. In examining the history of psychology, therefore, we must press our search back to the beginnings of human records, written or archeological. People's speculations about their own nature, even when nonscientific, have shaped the course of scientific psychology. The ideas of Plato and Aristotle, of Descartes and Locke, can be found in the research of Wundt and Watson, of Chomsky and Skinner.

Introductory textbooks define psychology and then present it. The aim of this book is to understand what psychology is and what it has been. To do this, we will examine the psychological work of philosophers, doctors, astronomers, and one possible charlatan. Psychology, in the broad sense, is not the exclusive province of psychologists, and—even in the narrow sense—all these people have made important contributions to psychology.

The course for which you are using this book is probably called something similar to "History and Systems of Psychology." In coming to understand psychology, we will consider two important topics. On the one hand, psychology has a long past in the hands of philosophers and other thinkers. To understand what psychology is today we must understand the historical forces that have molded psychology into its present form. On the other hand, psychologists have always had systematic differences over such issues as the subject matter and scope of psychology and its permissible methodology and experimental procedures. These two topics have typically been treated in isolation. Writers have discussed either the historical flow of psychology from Plato to Descartes to Herbart to Wundt to Watson and so on, or they have discussed the kinds of systems built by different scientific psychologists and examined the nature of these different systems, such as structuralism, functionalism, and behaviorism.

This is an artificial dichotomy. Any field goes through a conceptual evolution over time and to reach a thorough grasp of any science, we must examine the historical causes as well as the systematic reasons that have shaped this evolution. The history of psychology is more than an ordered collection of names, dates, places, and achievements. It is the history of people's attempts to find order in themselves, and it results from a complex interplay of historical causes and arguments justifying various systems. As the subtitle of this book indicates, we will examine psychology as an evolving conceptual system. We will examine both the historical causes and the justificatory arguments that shape psychology. We will consider both history and systems.

## SCIENCE

### Science Is an Effort by Humanity to Bring Order Out of a Chaos of Sense Perceptions

When psychologists debate the nature of psychological theory, explanation, subject matter, and methodology, the one phrase that recurs in all definitions of psychology is "Psychology is the science of . . .". Regardless of the particular point of view, psychology is always seen as a science. To understand the evolution of psychology, then, we must determine what science is.

One old and reasonable answer is: "Science is an effort by humanity to bring order out of a chaos of sense perceptions." Scientists do try to produce theoretical accounts that will explain a range of disparate phenomena. Physicists, for example, show that all falling objects, from raindrops to missiles, follow the same mathematical laws. Our experience is of a continually changing world. Out of the flux of experience the scientist extracts regularity and order; the scientist's theories are the tools that accomplish this task. This definition, therefore, does describe science.

Yet the definition is too broad. The painter orders experience, the sculptor imposes form on matter, and the jurist seeks regularities in human affairs. These, however, are not sciences—though our definition is true of them. What can we add to this definition to make it fit science more exactly? There are several ingredients that distinguish science from other ways people try to order their experience.

One way art and science differ is that an artist may hope to make a permanently enduring contribution, while a scientist may not. The works of Shakespeare are still appreciated by modern audiences. For all that the theater has changed in 300 years, Shakespeare's plays are just as great today as they were when written. In science, however, the work of any scientist, no matter how great, is transcended in time. Modern physicists read Newton, for example, only as a historical exercise. They expect to learn nothing from Newton in the way we can still learn from Shakespeare. Although the arts may progress, they do not progress in the same way the sciences do.

Another way science differs from art is that science is a collective, public enterprise, and the scientist must submit his or her ideas to the challenge of colleagues. This process of give and take enables science, as a collective enterprise, to partially determine what is right and what is wrong. The painter and the sculptor are free as artists to pursue their own vision of reality. Artists do not try to find a single, authoritative vision of reality. Scientists do. Scientists must make their vision explicit, public, and arguable. The artist is not required to do this. There is beauty in art, but there is seldom objective truth. Scientists on the other hand, seek the truth, and sometimes produce beauty. Thus, science is a collective effort by man to bring a public, authoritative order out of the chaos of sense perception.

A final distinguishing feature of science is that it accepts observation as the final arbiter of truth. Scientists must submit their ideas to the challenge of reality, asking nature questions that find their answers in experimental results. This is not true of art, nor of myth and religion; they change—if at all—to meet human and social needs, not to fit nature, which they do not even question. It is sometimes, but not always, true of law; law creates order where there may be none and enforces this order with sanctions. The scientist, however, cannot enforce the laws of nature; the scientist can only uncover such laws. Finally, then, science is a collective effort by man to bring a public, authoritative order out of the chaos of sense perception, an order that is continually judged by careful observation.

In all of this, nothing has been said about the so-called "scientific method." There is no uniform scientific method which, if scrupulously followed, will produce scientific knowledge. Scientific discoveries have been made in many ways, some of which are highly subjective, such as dreams. Scientific theories have been built both on flashes of insight and on plodding fact-gathering. Creativity in science cannot be put into a methodological straightjacket. Science progresses as it can. The responsibility of the scientist is not to an abstract method, but to the phenomena being studied as well as to the scrutiny of colleagues. In passing judgment on a scientist's work, colleagues may use methodological criteria. These, however, change from age to age, and a challenged scientist may finally convince others that they are wrong and he or she is right. There is no unchanging, timeless scientific method—only the twin arbiters of collective reason and pertinent experiment.

Is psychology a science? This question is often answered in the negative by philosophers, natural scientists, laypersons, and sometimes even psychologists themselves. They say psychology is too disorganized, or that the subject matter is too broad, or that psychology is just common sense, or that psychology can be reduced to biophysics. We will consider these objections in more detail after we have examined psychology in conceptual and historical depth. Broadly speaking, however, we can say that psychology is at least scientific, even if it is not a single, unified science. Psychologists do try to find order in the behavior, thoughts, memories, and motives of human beings; psychologists do communicate their ideas and results in print and at meetings in an effort to make this order collective and public; and psychologists do submit their theories to experimental test. We will see later that this conclusion must be qualified by questions about psychology's scientific unity, but that its scientific status remains unaltered.

### Science as a Human Enterprise

The conventional image of the scientist, for good or ill, is that of a cold, logical, completely objective collector of facts who pursues knowledge for its own sake. The image is positive in *Star Trek's* Mr. Spock, negative in Dr. Frankenstein. The resulting image of institutional science is architectural, seeing science as a cumulative, progressive enterprise, with each scientist adding a new brick to the edifice.

These images of science and scientists have been effectively challenged recently by a number of historians and philosophers of science, including Kuhn, Feyerabend, and Lakatos. Science is a human enterprise carried out by individual scientists who are members of a larger scientific community concerned with a particular subject matter. Therefore, to fully understand science, we must examine not only well-articulated theories and methods, but also the frequently hidden human and social factors that affect the functioning of the scientist and of the scientific community. What has been most intensively analyzed are the pre-theoretical assumptions on which a science rests.

For scientific research to be progressive, the scientific community in a particular research area must agree on certain basic issues. Its members must agree on the goals of their science, on the basic characteristics of the real world relevant to their subject, on what counts as a valid explanation of phenomena, and on permissible research methods and mathematical techniques. Given agreement on these issues, scientists can proceed to analyze nature from a collective, unified standpoint; without such agreement, each researcher would have his or her own standpoint, and there would be much fruitless discussion at cross-purposes. The traditional architectural metaphor may be modified to clarify this point. A building must be constructed according to a plan and on a firm foundation. Until the blueprints and the foundation have been decided on, there can be no construction, no progress. Only when the plans are agreed on can construction begin.

In science, the basic set of assumptions that provides the framework within which scientists work has been called a *paradigm*. A paradigm has two components: the *disciplinary matrix* and the *shared exemplars* (Kuhn, 1970). The disciplinary matrix consists of a set of fundamental assumptions that are usually unstated, often unconscious, and are typically not subject to empirical test. These assumptions, however, provide the basis for specific hypotheses that are subjected to empirical tests. Consider, for example, atomism, the idea that psychological behaviors can be reduced to assemblages of simple behaviors. This assumption has been part of many psychological systems. It is an untestable, metaphysical concept in that it is impossible to prove that all behavior is so reducible. Once atomism is assumed, however, the scientist can explore particular, specific hypotheses about how specific complex acts are compounded out of specific simpler acts. Thus, the unproved assumption of atomism makes much research possible. A disciplinary matrix is an organized structure of assumptions such as atomism. As we consider each major psychological system, we will try to discover what its disciplinary matrix is.

The second component of a paradigm is a set of shared exemplars. These are models (or—as scientists ordinarily use the term—paradigms) of good research which provide agreed-upon methods for the investigation of new problems. They are examples held up to scientists in training as patterns for their own research. Consider, for instance, the standard operant conditioning paradigm. A rat is placed in a small chamber with a bar at one end. When the rat accidentally presses the bar it is rewarded with food for doing so. After several such experiences the rat will press the bar regularly to get food. This paradigm provides a model for many other kinds of research. A psychologist trained in this (Skinnerian) tradition will approach any problem in these terms. For example, how do children learn mathematics? By assumption, it must be by the acquisition of certain "correct responses" to specific problem situations. As a result of this approach, many schools are filled today with step-by-step teaching machines and behavior modification techniques derived from the shared exemplar of rat-in-Skinner box. Each major psychological paradigm will hold up one or more shared exemplars that the psychologist trained in the paradigm will automatically apply to any research problem. We will try to discover what each paradigm's exemplars are.

If a scientific community must, often unconsciously, agree on a paradigm, then paradigms must be learned in some way. They are rarely, if ever, specifically taught; rather a student picks up a paradigm almost by osmosis. The shared exemplars are learned by example with the student participating in research that follows the exemplars so that they become the natural approach to any problem of the student's own. The disciplinary matrix is learned by indirection. The student is exposed to theories and hypotheses that embody the assumptions, and therefore, the student's thoughts come naturally to fall into certain tracks. The student learns to think in the established ways largely because these ways are embodied in everything studied and alternatives are rarely presented. The neophyte Skinnerian, for example, does not need to be told "there is no soul," for the hypothesis that there is a soul is never considered. Because paradigms are learned in such indirect ways, it is not surprising that the individual scientist is usually unaware of them.

What are the effects of a paradigm? The first effect is wholly positive. The paradigm, by answering the metaphysical questions, frees the researcher to get on with the puzzle-solving work of science. The researcher knows from the paradigm approximately what nature is like; thus all that remains is to work out the details. For example, once we assume that learning is caused by reinforcement, we can proceed to investigate exactly *how* reinforcement works: what happens if we vary amount of reinforcement, frequency of reinforcement, or quality of reinforcement? Such specific questions cannot be thought of without the basic assumptions of a paradigm or investigated without its shared exemplars. The assumptions make possible the invention and testing of specific theories about the details of nature's workings.

It is important to understand that such experiments do not test the paradigm; rather they are attempts to answer puzzles posed by the paradigm. If a scientist fails to solve a puzzle, the failure is the scientist's, not the paradigm's. Consider what happens in your own laboratory courses. You follow all the instructions, but the "correct" results do not always occur. When you inform your instructors, they do not tear their hair and cry, "All our theories are wrong!" On the contrary, they assume that you must have erred at some point, and they give you a poor grade. This reaction is typical of what happens in "normal science," the puzzle-solving research guided by a paradigm. The scientific community recognizes certain puzzles as ripe for solution, and—except in extraordinary circumstances—when a scientist tackles one of these problems it is the scientist and his or her theories that are on trial, not the unstated paradigm.

This may seem a restrictive and unromantic view of science. Yet it is the possession of paradigms and the ensuing puzzle-solving that makes scientific progress possible. This becomes clearer if we return to our architectural metaphor. The most creative part of building is when an artist-architect makes the plans. Yet if artist-architect and colleagues and clients get too involved in this stage in debating large issues of aesthetics and function, no progress on the building can be made. It is only when the blueprint, or paradigm, is agreed on that constructive puzzle-solving can begin. Agreement on basic assumptions is always necessary if progress is to be made.

There is a psychological consequence of acceptance of a paradigm that is also necessary for progress, but which is perhaps less fortunate. The scientist in acquiring a paradigm is learning to see the world in a certain way. The physician learns to see an x-ray correctly; the physicist must learn to read bubble chamber tracks. Neither source of data is comprehensible without training, yet once the scientist learns to interpret them, he or she will see them in those ways and no others. Thus training can act as a set of blinders, keeping the scientist from seeing things in new ways.

All observation and perception—whether scientific or not—is a matter of interpretation, as numerous psychological experiments have shown. The simple drawing of Figure1-1a, a Necker cube, illustrates this point. If you look at it a while, you will find that two precepts are possible, two cubes of different orientation. Your mind must give some interpretation to the figure, yet since two interpretations are available and equally valid, it vacillates between the two. At no point do you see the figure with no interpretation, for your mind naturally attempts to make sense of all it perceives.

Another example, Figure 1-1b, is even closer to what happens in scientific observation. The crucial stimulus is the last in each row. If subjects are shown the four top stimuli and then the fifth, they see the fifth as a face; if shown the bottom four stimuli first, they see the fifth as a rat. There is only one set of data in the last stimulus, but two interpretations of it; and which interpretation is adopted depends on the "training" of the subject. Paradigms have exactly this effect. The scientist learns to see in certain ways, and what he or she sees in the data depends on the

**FIGURE 1-1.**
(a) The Necker cube (From Gregory, R. L. *The intelligent eye.*
New York: McGraw-Hill, 1970). (b) Experience and perception.
(From Bugelski, B. R. & Alampay, D. A. The role of frequency in
developing perceptual sets. *Canadian Journal of Psychology,*
1962, *15,* 205-211. Copyright © (1966)
Canadian Psychological Association.
Reprinted by permission).

The Necker cube. This is the plane projection of a cube as seen from a great distance. There is no perspective size change. The figure is seen in spontaneously reversing depth. Evidently, there are two equally probable solutions to the perceptual problem: "What is the object out there?" The brain entertains each of its hypothetical solutions in turn —and never makes up its mind.

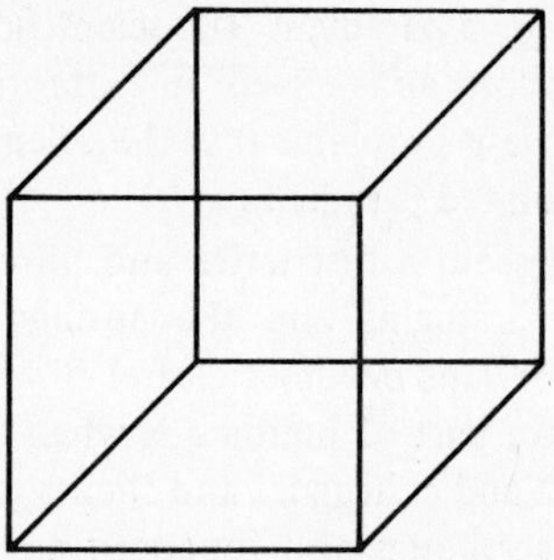

a.

b.

Man or rat?

paradigm the scientist has acquired. Neither face nor rat is a truer interpretation than the other; they are simply different. The stimulus, like nature, is one unchanging reality, yet the meaning and explanation of that reality depends on one's background and paradigm. It is futile to ask if it is *really* a rat or a face. One paradigm construes it as a face, another as a rat. That the meaning of the world depends on paradigms is of great consequence in disputes between paradigms. When psychics fail to perform in the laboratory, for example, the materialist sees a disconfirmation of psychic phenomena, while the believer sees the destruction of fragile psychic abilities in the cold, sterile research environment. The materialist and the spiritualist thus have a paradigm clash that cannot be resolved by the data, since each will persistently interpret the data according to his or her paradigm.

Finally, a paradigm defines limits on what science is—limits that can be crossed only if the scientist is willing to risk criticism, ostracism, and even ridicule. Such cases have occurred. Imagine a young scientist getting up before an audience of Skinnerians and attributing operant learning to the workings of a rat's immortal soul! The paper would be greeted with shouts of disbelief, because the scientist had stepped outside the acceptable bounds of psychological science. If persistent in such beliefs, the scientist would surely be exiled from the Skinnerian community. And correctly so—the builders cannot tolerate a worker who refuses to follow the blueprints. However, it remains possible for the rebel to convince others of the correctness of his or her views, and so lead a scientific revolution establishing a new paradigm, a new way of looking at the world as valid as the old.

Whether psychology has a paradigm is a much-debated question which we will consider in more detail later. Now, only this much need be said: Each system of psychology—structuralism, behaviorism, cognitivism, and so forth—constitutes a paradigm. However, unlike the physical sciences, which typically possess only one paradigm at a given time, in psychology there are several.

### Theory, Method, and Data

Holmes then (descended) into the hollow . . . (and) stretching himself upon his face and leaning his chin upon his hands he made a careful study of the trampled mud in front of him.

"Halloa!" said he, suddenly, "what's this?" It was a wax vesta (a sort of match), half burned, which was so coated with mud that it looked at first like a little chip of wood.

"I cannot think how I came to overlook it," said the Inspector, with an expression of annoyance.

"It was invisible, buried in the mud. I only saw it because I was looking for it."

"What! You expected to find it?"

"I thought it not unlikely."

Sir Arthur Conan Doyle, *The Memoirs of Sherlock Holmes*

The role and value of good theory are well illustrated in the preceding passage from Sherlock Holmes. Theory tells the researcher what to look for. Holmes found the match because he had formed a theory of the crime that led him to expect the presence of a match, while the police—who had no theory—failed to find the match despite their meticulous search procedures. Crude fact-gathering is never as powerful as theoretically guided research. To the fact-gatherer, all facts are equally meaningless and meaningful. To the theoretically guided researcher, each fact assumes its proper place in an overall framework.

Around the basic assumptions of a paradigm scientists construct a "protective belt" of specific, testable theories. It is these theories that are proposed, refined, or discarded as the research program progresses. They form a "protective belt" in that experimental failures lead to modification in the protective belt of specific theories, not in the basic assumptions of the hard core (Lakatos, 1970). For example, an important behaviorist, Clark Hull, proposed some specific mechanisms for reward learning based on drive reduction in 1938. He had to substantially modify these by 1953, but he never abandoned the assumption that all learning is based on reward and drive reduction.

From a theory, the scientist constructs a *model* of reality. Models are highly idealized, partial simulations of the world. They describe what the world would be like if the theory were completely true, if the variables found in it were the only ones involved in behavior, and if these variables act as the theory claims. The physical theory of particle mechanics, for example, describes a block sliding down an inclined plane as a system of three frictionless, dimensionless, point-masses—one each for the block, plane, and the earth. In the real world, these bodies are extended in space and there is friction between block and plane; in the model, such irrelevant or complicating factors disappear. Thus the model is a simplified, idealized version of reality which is all a theory can cope with. It is important to realize how limited a scientific theory is. It purports to explain only some phenomena, and only some aspects of these. A scientific theory is not about the real world as we experience it, but about abstract, idealized models. The real world, unlike the model, is much too complex to be explained by a theory. To take a psychological example, a theory of paired associate learning describes an ideal learner as untroubled by neurosis or motivational factors—which of course are determinants of the memory-performance of actual subjects.

These models give science enormous power. First, they free the scientist from the impossible task of describing all of reality which, because of its infinite complexity, will never conform to theory. By using models of reality, the scientist can ignore "the *actual* counterexamples, the available data . . . [and can refuse] to be drawn into observation. He will 'lie down on his couch, shut his eyes and forget about the data.' Occasionally, of course, he will ask Nature a shrewd question: he will then be encouraged by Nature's *YES*, but not discouraged by its *NO*" (Lakatos, 1970). The scientist cannot apply his or her theory to the whole world, but can apply it to the model. Science does not progress by the mere accumulation of data, but by asking careful, theoretically pertinent questions of nature. Models allow the scientist to imagine how the world is, and to try out and refine theories before coping with the world. Many of the greatest experiments in physics were thought-experiments never carried out in actuality. Einstein built his theory of relativity on many such experiments.

Second, these idealized theories and models enable the scientist to make powerful and wide-ranging explanations of observed phenomena. The model embodies certain *ideals of natural order*, descriptions of an idealized world (Toulmin, 1961). These descriptions, while not observed, provide the basis for explaining that which is observed.

Newton's theory, for example, provides as an ideal of natural order the idea that all natural motion of objects through space is in a straight line which continues forever. Such motion cannot be observed. Motion that does not conform to this ideal is explained as being a result of other factors. For example, a ball rolling across grass quickly comes to rest, but we say the motion would have gone on forever except for friction. The scientist does not *explain* the ideal of natural order, but rather uses it and other factors to explain phenomena that do not conform to the ideal, such as the stopping ball. Scientific explanation is always indirect and metaphorical. The scientist can only describe what the world would be like if a theory were true, and then explain why the world is not really like that.

How does the scientist go from theory and idealized model to real-world phenomena, or data? The usual picture is that the scientist derives a prediction from a theory and tests it with an experiment. If the data agree with the prediction, the theory is confirmed; if they do not agree, the theory is disconfirmed. However, Lakatos' statement about the value of models has already indicated that the picture is too simple, and an example will make it clearer: Scientist A proposes a theory; Scientist B runs an experiment and finds data that appear to refute the theory. Does Scientist A say, "Boy, was I wrong! Back to the drawing board."? Almost certainly not. Scientist A will examine the experiment, not the theory, and query Scientist B's methodology. A may accuse B of using the wrong subject population, the wrong statistics, the wrong response measure, or of making incorrect inferences from the theory. The protective belt of conditions surrounding a theory is thick indeed, for it includes not only theories, but important methodological ideas as well.

The route from theory to data and back again is long and complex, not the three-step process of theory → prediction → experiment. Figure 1-2 shows the hierarchy of steps that intervene between theory, model, and observed phenomena. The center column names each step, the right-hand column describes the step in general scientific terms, and the left-hand column gives some psychological examples of each level.

At the top we have the theory itself and its associated model, which together describe the world in its idealized form. In psychology, we might have a theory of memory, which will contain such theoretical terms as short-term memory, long-term memory, and rehearsal. The theory would describe an ideal memorizer (the model), untroubled by the things that trouble real subjects, such as lack of sleep, boredom with the experiment, or dislike of the experimenter. The memory model is thus idealized and counterfactual. The abstract theory must be translated into a specific situation that can be created in an experiment. The scientist must select

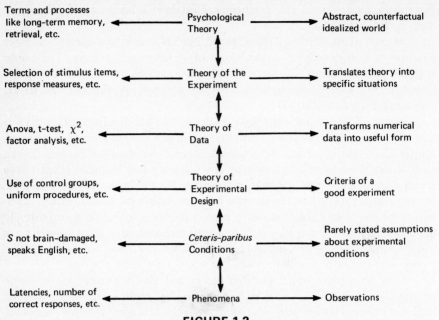

| Terms and processes like long-term memory, retrieval, etc. | ← | Psychological Theory | → | Abstract, counterfactual idealized world |
| Selection of stimulus items, response measures, etc. | ← | Theory of the Experiment | → | Translates theory into specific situations |
| Anova, t-test, $\chi^2$, factor analysis, etc. | ← | Theory of Data | → | Transforms numerical data into useful form |
| Use of control groups, uniform procedures, etc. | ← | Theory of Experimental Design | → | Criteria of a good experiment |
| *S* not brain-damaged, speaks English, etc. | ← | *Ceteris-paribus* Conditions | → | Rarely stated assumptions about experimental conditions |
| Latencies, number of correct responses, etc. | ← | Phenomena | → | Observations |

**FIGURE 1-2.**
Hierarchy of theories (after P. Suppes, 1962).

particular items to be remembered, a measure of the subject's memory (such as trials-to-criterion), and any other pertinent variables, such as the ages of the subjects. Further, the scientist must derive specific predictions about what ought to happen in such a situation or experiment. In this way the scientist produces an empirically testable version of the idealized model derived from the theory.

The test of the theory involves deriving from the phenomena another model that as far as possible describes an idealized model based on the data. In various ways the researcher must purge from the data those variables and influences that are not part of the theory, such as motivation in the case of our memory experiment. This is done in a series of steps rising from the phenomena.

The phenomena are the actual raw observations made during an experiment, such as trials-to-criterion or response latency. The conduct of the experiment that collects these data is predicated on certain tacitly understood assumptions called *ceteris-paribus* (all other things being equal) assumptions. These are never stated by a researcher in the "Method" section of a report unless some special reason compels the researcher to do so. To continue our example, it would be assumed that the subjects in the memory experiment were not brain-damaged, were not retarded, and spoke English. These assumptions will be made explicit only under special conditions. If the researcher were interested in memory in split-brain subjects, for instance, the use of such subjects would be stated.

A good experiment also must conform to the sophisticated demands of experimental design. The researcher, for example, must use appropriate control and experimental groups, uniform procedures for all subjects, and so forth. Next, the mass of raw data collected during an experiment must be analyzed by sound statistical procedures appropriate to the theory under test. Masses of data are useless until summarized and digested into a form that makes possible a test of the theory via analysis by statistical methods, such as t-tests and correlations. Finally, at all levels the theorist or researcher relies on auxiliary hypotheses which are not part of the theory under test. For instance, should the researcher pay the subjects according to the number of correct responses, it will be assumed that this reward will affect behavior in ways described by operant learning theory, which is not the theory under test, but rather an auxiliary theory used to help test the memory theory.

Each of the levels—beginning with phenomena—is designed to produce data that reflect the variables with which the theory under test is concerned, and so produce an evaluation of the theory. Theory says, "The perfect world (model) of my theory behaves just so." Experiment says, "Here is a model based on the theory's variables." The crucial question is, "Do these models act the same?" If they do, the theory is supported. If they do not, something must be changed.

The theorist may alter a theory if the data are not consistent with predictions. However, since error may occur at each step of the hierarchy, the theorist may question something else, saying, for example, that the wrong response measure was used, the wrong age subjects were run, the wrong control group used, the wrong statistical test applied, or the predictions were wrongly derived from the theory. There is no scientific method that produces truth automatically. Science is a creative enterprise. The scientist must ask nature the right questions in the right way and must carefully interpret the answers. The scientist must know when to accept disconfirming data and alter a theory, and when to reject data and retain a theory.

Sometimes, too, the scientist must know when to abandon a research program. Program change and revolution are our next concern.

## HISTORY

### What Is History?

Just asking this question may cause astonishment. We all know what history is; the usual question today is, "Is history relevant?" Yet history, like science, is more complicated than it appears at first glance. The obvious answer to the first question is "history is the record of past events." Yet history is more than this. To borrow Jacob Bronowski's comment on science: "History does not record the past, it tackles it." The goal of the historian is to make sense of the past, not just place events on a time line. For example, it is not enough to say "the American colonies declared their independence in 1776" or "Napolean was defeated at Waterloo in 1815." The goal of the historian is to understand the importance of these events, to understand how and why they came about, and to understand their influence on the future.

Similarly, it is not enough to say "Wilhelm Wundt founded psychology in 1879" or to hypothesize that "behaviorism began to disintegrate in 1959 because of Chomsky's work." We shall try to understand the importance of these events, how they fit into the conceptual evolution of psychology, how they came to be, .why they happened, and what effect they have had on the past.

Understood this way, history is necessarily relevant. Today we participate in psychology in a given slice of time. We pursue the activities of a human science; we are part of a historical process. The events of today are influenced by the historical past and will influence the historical future. To understand what we are doing and why we are doing it, we need to understand what psychologists did before us as well as the nature of historical change. To ignore the past is to cut off a source of self-understanding. (Why, for example, is the nature-nurture debate so central to psychology? Part of the answer is that this has been a central concern of philosophy, psychology's parent field.)

To understand the present, we must understand the past. This has become a truism. We have all heard: "He who is ignorant of the past is condemned to repeat it." What is less often understood, however, is that the sense we make out of the past depends on our current affairs, on our present. Our vision of the present is affected by our knowledge of the past; the reverse is also true. Americans used to think of the opening of the West as a liberating, progressive step in the ascent of the United States. Today this view makes us uncomfortable. This "progressive" step crushed many healthy native cultures and can even be seen as an act of genocide. Our experience in Vietnam and elsewhere has changed our perceptions of the past.

And so it is in the history of science. For example, in the arch-empiricist, post-Newtonian period of the eighteenth and nineteenth centuries, Galileo was seen as a sound empirical researcher, and he was mis-translated to show that he actually carried out experiments which in fact he only hypothesized. In the last decade, Galileo was pictured quite differently as one who knew to such a degree of certainty what was true that he felt no need to experiment. His laws of nature were thought to have been discovered by pure ratiocination. Finally, in the last few years, this excessively rationalistic picture has been challenged in its turn. Such revisionism is not always or necessarily a matter of distortion. Galileo did experiments and reasoned mathematically; which was more important? An empiricist age will emphasize experimentation; a rationalist age will emphasize mathematical reasoning.

Psychology is equally bound to its own culture. Any history will naturally emphasize those men and those ideas that resonate with the men and ideas of today. A behaviorist age will look for past behaviorists, a mentalist age for mentalists. The study of history, then, has two aspects. Understanding the flow of past events will aid our understanding of our present position. Yet, as we look back, our vision of the past will necessarily be affected by our present position.

## Historical Change

The analysis of paradigms and theories describes science at one moment in time. We now turn to the question of change. How do research programs change over time? How does one paradigm replace another? Scientific change is a type of historical change, so concepts and issues that apply to the latter also apply to the former.

The oldest debate involving historical explanations is over the degree to which individuals, as opposed to large impersonal forces, make history. The sides in this debate are usually called the Great Man and the *Zeitgeist* theories of history. The Great Man theory was popular during the European Romantic period and was stated concisely in *On Heroes, Hero-Worship and the Heroic in History* by Thomas Carlyle when he wrote that universal history "is at bottom the History of Great Men." This approach holds that historical change is created by Great Men ("movers and shakers," in slang terms), such as Julius Caesar, Napolean, and Hitler; and scientific change is created by figures such as Galileo, Newton, and Einstein. The view is that these people, by force of genius and personality, imposed their wills on history. History is thus seen as the story of the behavior of people, primarily of the great ones. Thus, the history of psychology would be made up of the biographies of Plato, Aristotle, Wundt, Freud, Watson, Skinner, and Chomsky.

Our own age, however, leans away from the Great Man theory, favoring instead the zeitgeist theory, which was first influentially stated by G.W.F. Hegel. *Zeitgeist* is a German word meaning spirit (*geist*) of the times (*zeit*), and those who hold this view believe that history is determined not by the actions of Great Men but by large impersonal forces that transcend individuals. Advocates of the zeitgeist theory would say that if Freud had been strangled in his cradle, someone else would have invented psychoanalysis, for the ideas were all there in the nineteenth century zeitgeist.

The best-known example of an extreme zeitgeist approach to history is Marxism, which owes much to Hegel. The Marxist believes that the character of an era is determined by the economic relations of the time—in particular the ownership of the means of production—and that historical change is the story of change in the ownership of the means of production.

The zeitgeist approach is inherently more difficult than the Great Man approach. The Romantic historian need only recount the great deeds of great men and then step back and say: "That is History." The zeitgeist historian must go beyond great deeds to analyze the forces thought to create the pattern of events and the texture of a period, often by analyzing seemingly trivial data. So the Marxist must carefully analyze the economic situation of a period in order to understand it. Many kinds of zeitgeists have been proposed, some of which are believed to pervade the behavior of all people, while others are assigned more limited influence. At one extreme, the Marxist sees all of history as the succession of only a few economically defined stages which determine the behavior of everyone. At the other extreme, paradigms can be seen as small-scale zeitgeists that determine the research and theorizing that take place within them by shaping the assumptions held by a few scientists—who often belong to a small and esoteric specialty. In both instances, the zeitgeist dominates peoples' activities, but in the former view, the scale is large; in the latter, the paradigm view, the scale is small.

Our approach here will be a judicious mixture of the Great Man and zeitgeist views. The history of a science is a history of ideas rather than a history of events or a series of biographies. In particular, we will try to determine the paradigm or paradigms prevalent in psychology at a given time, and we will attempt to determine why one paradigm disappears and another takes its place. We will also try to discover the larger intellectual zeitgeist within which particular paradigms and research programs operate. To do this we will employ the concept described by Michel Foucault as an *episteme,* the set of basic assumptions underlying all the sciences of a given era (Foucault, 1970). *Epistemes* are wholly unconscious and difficult to bring to light.

We will not neglect, however, the minds and personalities of those creative individuals whose ideas contributed to psychological progress, for they each left a stamp of their individuality on at least the details of their theories. Although something like psychoanalysis might have come into being had Sigmund Freud died as a child, for example, it would almost certainly have been different in detail. It is true that the central concepts of psychoanalysis were all available in the late nineteenth century; Freud did not invent them. His genius was to weld them into a powerful and coherent synthesis, a synthesis that would have been different had another mind performed it, that is, the same concepts might have been used, but they would have been used differently.

As well as distinguishing between Great Men and zeitgeists, we must also distinguish between reasons and causes in historical explanations. When someone performs an action, the person can usually give a set of rational justifications for that action; these are the *reasons* for the action. An action is also conditioned by nonrational personal and social factors that do not justify an action but do *cause* it. This distinction is especially important in science. When a scientist proposes a theory or concept, the scientist must persuade colleagues of the theory's value by presenting rational arguments in its favor, such as, the theory explains more data than its rivals; it is simpler; it has more heuristic value; and so forth. These are the reasons for the theory or concept. However, it may also have been presented for a variety of nonjustificatory causes, such as, the scientist might have a feud with a rival theoretician; the scientist might feel the theory is politically superior to that of rivals; the scientist might be desperate for tenure, and so on. These factors neither add to, nor detract from, the rational scientific value of an idea, but they do condition its proposal—and sometimes its acceptance or rejection.

Any historical event, to be fully understood, must be explained from both points of view. It has become fashionable since Freud to focus on unconscious causes and to view reasons as mere rationalizations of no more than symptomatic value. This view, however, is too narrow, especially in its application to science, for it is through reason that a scientist persuades self and others of the value of particular ideas. Whatever may be the personal causes that impel a scientist to propose some idea, they play little role in the process by which the scientist persuades others to take it seriously and adopt it. Persuasion requires the articulation of effective reasons to support the idea, and without them the idea will die a quiet death, having no impact on the course of science no matter how fervently the scientist personally believes in it. Therefore, we must look for both the personal and historical causes of an event as well as the rational justificatory reasons for that event.

## Scientific Change

The issues discussed so far are applicable to any analysis of historical change. Now we must examine in more detail the special processes of scientific change which have received much attention from philosophers and historians of science since the early 1960s.

### Evolution of Concepts

According to Stephen Toulmin, a science can be viewed as a collection of concepts that change over time (Toulmin, 1972). How is this change to be explained? It has been proposed recently that concepts evolve very much as Darwin theorized animal species evolve. Darwinian theory has three key concepts: variation, selection, and retention. All can be applied to scientific change (Figure 1-3).

We begin our study at a given time with the science consisting of a cluster of initial concepts. Four initial concepts are shown in Figure 1-3. Just as nature constantly scrutinizes organic species to weed out the unfit and select the fit, so scientists constantly scrutinize their concepts by rational analysis and empirical test to weed out useless concepts and preserve useful ones. Weak concepts, like weak species, are abandoned, as is concept $C^V$ in Figure 1-3. Sometimes the value of a concept is a matter of intense debate, as is concept $C^W$ in the figure. During such periods of debate, variants of the concept are proposed and evaluated, just as species produce variations subject to evaluation by natural selection. In the case of concept $C^W$, all variants of the concept are abandoned and are referred to as abortive variants. In other cases, however, debate produces viable variants of a concept, as is the case for concept $C^X$. These are successful variants and are subject to the continuing evolutionary process.

Debate also occurs when a novel concept such as $C^Z$ is proposed. Variants of the concept are put forward and are subject to empirical and rational evaluation. In the case of $C^Z$, the original variant is retained, while alternatives are abortive.

According to this view, then, concepts evolve over time just as species do. Variant concepts compete with one another for acceptance by the scientific community. Those that succeed are *selected* by the community to be *retained* in the science and passed on to the next generation of scientists. The process of variation, selection, and retention is continuous and never ending. It accounts for much of

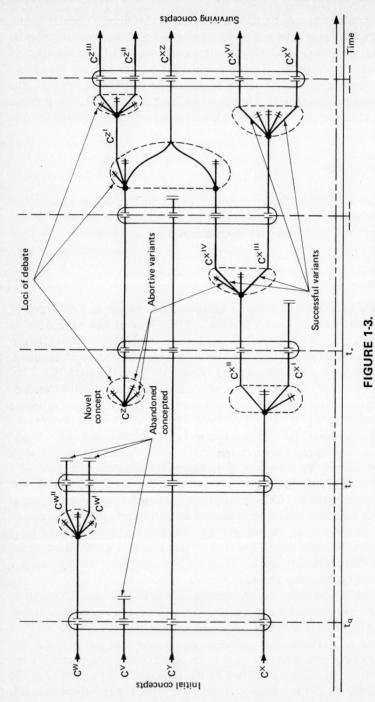

**FIGURE 1-3.**

The evolution of scientific concepts. (From Stephen Toulmin,
*The Collective Use and Evolution of Concepts*, Vol. I of *Human Understanding*
[copyright © 1972 by Princeton University Press], Fig. C, p. 205.
Reprinted by permission of Princeton University Press).

scientific change, just as variation, selection, and retention explain natural evolution. Figure 1-3 shows a science at time $t_q$ as consisting of the initial concepts $C^w$, $C^v$, $C^y$, and $C^x$. At each successive moment of time, $t_r$, $t_s$, and so forth, we find a different constellation of concepts, until at the end we find that the science consists of the five concepts $C^{z^{III}}$, $C^{z^{II}}$, $C^{xz}$, $C^{xVI}$, $C^{xV}$. The field looks very different than it did at $t_q$, but change has been gradual and continuous.

### Revolution of Paradigms

Scientific change, however, is not always gradual and continuous. There are times when a science undergoes radical change in a short period of time—change so radical that those who were great individuals beforehand often become forgotten antiques, and concepts and issues that previously occupied scientists minds simply disappear. Such change seems to constitute revolution rather than evolution and depends on principles beyond those of variation, selection, and retention.

The cluster of concepts that change by evolution is generally in the protective belt surrounding the hard core, or paradigm, of a research program. Since much of the paradigm is unconscious, and since it is explicitly guarded by the protective belt, it will not be subject to the usual conscious processes of scientific selection. The assumptions of a paradigm are seldom debated and seldom subjected to empirical test. Indeed, many cannot be tested, for they are often metaphysical as we have seen. Paradigms then do not—indeed cannot—endure, but must be overthrown in a process similar to political revolutions.

According to this view proposed by Thomas Kuhn, any science passes through a number of distinct stages, as shown in Figure 1-4. Every science has its beginning in a pre-scientific period called the pre-paradigm period. During this time, individ-

**FIGURE 1-4.**
The revolutionary character of paradigm shifts, and the cyclical nature of science. (A schematicization of Kuhn, T.S. *The structure of scientific revolutions.* Chicago: University of Chicago Press, 1970).

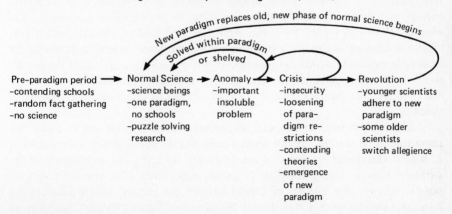

uals concerned with a given subject matter, proto-scientists, do not all agree on a set of paradigmatic assumptions. Rather they are divided into a number of rival camps or schools, each of which attempts to impose its views on the field, to vanquish its competition. Research is undertaken as part of this competition rather than to solve puzzles posed by the paradigm, or to establish basic variables and facts on which to erect a paradigm. Taken as a whole, this kind of research is nothing but random fact-gathering, rather than a concerted attempt to understand nature. In this stage, there can be no scientific progress and, indeed, no science. According to our architectural metaphor, this period would correspond to various architects squabbling over building plans, perhaps even each going off alone to build his or her own building, pausing to throw bricks at the opposition. There is no concerted, unified, and constructive effort, for energies are dissipated by infighting and random fact-gathering.

Eventually one school gains control of the field and ousts its competitors—who may be relegated to pseudo-scientific status. This ushers in an era of normal science working under a paradigm, as described earlier. In our architectural metaphor, during this period the basic plans are agreed upon and building proceeds, as concrete puzzles are solved and the edifice is erected. No time is wasted in fighting with rival paradigms, for there are none.

However, scientists inevitably find problems that resist solution. In a strict sense, every research program is faced with data that are inconsistent with it, and we have seen that scientists typically do not take these data too seriously, especially if in other respects research is going well. The orbit of Mercury, for example, was never reconciled with Newtonian physics, yet this did not concern early nineteenth century physicists, for otherwise Newtonian physics proceeded from success to success until the late 1800s. Such inconsistent findings are anomalies, unexplained phenomena that are not generally considered important.

Some anomalies, however, are perceived to be important, and it is on them that a research program may founder. Although Newtonian physicists were untroubled by Mercury's anomalous orbit, the late nineteenth century failure to find evidence of ether-drift was deeply troubling, and the ability of Einstein's theory to explain it was an important factor in its eventual acceptance. The anomaly shown in Figure 1-4 is this serious, second kind of anomaly, and it provides the opening wedge for a scientific revolution. Most anomalies, however, are eventually explained within the paradigm by making adjustments within the protective belt. It also sometimes happens that an anomalous problem resists solution and is shelved for future attention; it thus is shifted to the nonserious category of anomaly.

However, it may happen that an anomaly resists solution and is simply too important to be shelved. At this point a crisis ensues during which normal science is largely abandoned in favor of extraordinary research. The restrictions of the paradigm loosen, freeing scientists to pursue approaches otherwise forbidden. In normal science, the burden of failure to find the correct results falls on the scientist; now the burden may shift to the paradigm. Various theories are proposed to account for the anomalous findings, and these may differ more radically than the alternative hypotheses proposed during normal science. Indoctrination of young scientists into the prevailing paradigm weakens, accelerating the blurring of the paradigm and the proliferation of rival approaches. In short, it is a time of acute crisis, especially for older scientists, when scientists feel depressed and sometimes find it hard to continue.

Sometimes a crisis is resolved by solution of an anomaly within the old paradigm. However, during a crisis an alternative paradigm may emerge, usually in the work of young scientists, and if it succeeds in solving the anomaly, there may be a scientific revolution. This is an especially difficult time for a science. The effects of a paradigm are great, extending even to the observation of facts. Thus the adherents of the old paradigm and the advocates of the new frequently do not see the same things in their data. This means that the scientists talk at cross-purposes. Such paradigm clashes cannot be rationally resolved. ESP (extrasensory perception) experiments, for example, illustrate this lack of communication between paradigms. For the believer in ESP, its failure to occur in the laboratory shows merely that it cannot occur in sterile, hostile surroundings. The nonbeliever, on the other hand, sees the experiment's failure as evidence that there is no ESP. This dispute cannot be resolved, for the data mean one thing to one group, something else to the other.

A revolution is therefore won less on the basis of data than on other considerations; causes become more important than reasons. The new paradigm will be attractive to young scientists who flock to its banner. The old paradigm is left with scientists past their productive primes, some of whom may switch allegiances to the new paradigm. Eventually, the new paradigm triumphs.

After the revolution the science is radically transformed. Issues that were once important are no longer so; scientists once revered are dismissed, while previously obscure figures may gain ascendency as precursors of the new order. A new disciplinary matrix and set of shared examplars are adopted, and a new period of normal science ensues, with scientists tackling a new set of puzzles. If the last shape in Figure 1-16 was formerly thought of as a face, it now becomes a rat.

A revolution may not entail scientific progress precisely because the puzzles change, in other words, precisely because the new paradigm is a change in point of view rather than an addition onto the old one. In terms of our architectural metaphor, what happens is that the builders of a building abandon it in favor of erecting a new one. There was progress at the old site, and there will be progress at the new site, but the resulting structures may very well be merely different, neither being necessarily better than the other. The history of science in this view would resemble a landscape dotted with the ruins of previous research programs, some in an advanced state of construction, others abandoned at the foundation, while work proceeds on the most recent. There is activity; there is, or was, progress at each site; but there need be no progress when we change sites—only alterations in the approach to architecture.

Both views of change outlined here are controversial, for they contradict our common sense view that science is always, not just periodically, cumulative and progressive. The view of scientific change as being a result of the evolution of concepts describing scientific change in the protective belt implies that even normal science is not progressive, only adaptive. Concepts do not change as we march toward truth, rather they respond solely to local selection pressures. The monkey is not "more advanced" than the dinosaur, only better adapted to the current environment; should the ecology change, the monkey might disappear to be replaced by something else. Just so are concepts. They adapt to the demands of the scientific community; should these change, new concepts will replace the old.

As we consider the history of psychology we will ask if it fits these patterns, which provide useful tools for understanding historical change. However, we will also ask if the tools may be improved. The history of psychology cannot be distorted to fit these accounts of change, but rather, psychology's history provides data to which the theories of change must conform. We may in the end be led to modify or reject the theories of change advanced earlier. In any case, the effort will tell us about psychology, history, and science.

## OVERVIEW

### The Plan of this Book

In this chapter we have examined a number of general meta-scientific concepts that we shall apply to psychology in the next 14 chapters. We will not just catalog the doings of a few great psychologists, but rather we will attempt to analyze the conceptual evolution and paradigmatic revolutions that make up the conceptual history of psychology.

In Part I, we will discuss the conceptual background of psychology as laid down by philosophers from Thales to John Stuart Mill, and by physiologists and scientists from Alcmaeon to Charles Darwin.

In Part II, we will examine the great founders of psychology in Germany, England, and America, beginning with Wilhelm Wundt, the founder of academic psychology, and including Sigmund Freud, William James, and the *Gestalt* movement.

In Part III, we will consider the most important movement of twentieth century psychology, behaviorism, which dominated experimental psychology until the 1950s. We will also look at psychology from 1950 to the present. This was a period in which behaviorism was vigorously challenged by a number of competitive paradigms, especially cognitive psychology which in many ways returned to the original psychology of the science's founder, Wilhelm Wundt, whose ideas had been so vehemently rejected by Behaviorism.

In Part IV, we will reflect upon psychology's long past to then assess its future and consider its status as a science alongside the science of astronomy, physics, and chemistry.

## SUGGESTED READINGS

The most influential work in recent philosophy of science has been Thomas S. Kuhn's *Structure of Scientific Revolutions* (University of Chicago Press, 1970), which proposed the theories of paradigms and revolutions discussed in this chapter. Also important has been the work of Stephen Toulmin, who has applied evolutionary concepts to scientific change, first in his *Foresight and Understanding* (Harper & Row, 1961) and most recently in *Human Understanding* (Princeton University Press, 1972). An outstanding, although technical, discussion of the history of the philosophy of science can be found in Frederick Suppe's "The Search for Understanding of Scientific Theories," the introduction to his edited volume *The Structure of Scientific Theories* (University of Illinois Press, 1974), which contains papers by important philosophers of science, among them Kuhn and Toulmin.

## REFERENCES

Bugelski, B. R., & Alampay, D. A. The role of frequency in developing perceptual sets. *Canadian Journal of Psychology,* 1962, *15,* 205-211.

Foucault, M. *The order of things.* London: Tavistock, 1970.

Gregory, R. L. *The intelligent eye.* New York: McGraw-Hill, 1970.

James, W. *The principles of psychology.* New York: Holt, 1890.

Kuhn, T. S. *The structure of scientific revolutions* (enlarged ed.). Chicago: University of Chicago Press, 1970.

Lakatos, I. Criticism and the methodology of scientific research programmes. In I. Lakatos & A. Musgrave (Eds.) *Criticism and the growth of knowledge.* Cambridge, England: Cambridge University Press, 1970.

Suppes, P. Models of data. In E. Nagel, P. Suppes, & A. Tarski (Eds.) *Logic, methodology, and philosophy of science.* Stanford: Stanford University Press, 1962.

Toulmin, S. *Foresight and understanding.* New York: Harper & Row Pub., 1961.

Toulmin, S. *Human understanding,* V. 1, The collective evolution and use of concepts. Princeton, N.J.: Princeton University Press, 1972.

# 1

# Background
# to Psychology

## PHILOSOPHY, SCIENCE, AND PSYCHOLOGY

Plato observes that philosophy begins in wonder. Science also begins in wonder, and all sciences, including psychology, were originally part of philosophy. The early Greek philosophers were really philosopher-scientists who wondered about the essential nature of the universe. Gradually, over the centuries, each science, beginning with astronomy, separated itself from philosophy to become an independent science. Psychology remained within the fold of philosophy until the nineteenth century. The first scientific psychologists, such as Wundt, Külpe, and James, were also philosophers, often using their philosophical positions to support their psychological research and vice versa. In Part I we will trace the philosophical and scientific background from which psychology grew.

The first philosophical inquiries into the world were physical. Philosophers from Thales to Democritus wanted to know what the universe was like, what were its basic constituents and its laws. They laid the foundation for modern natural science; indeed, remarkable parallels exist between ancient Greek atomism and modern physics. As psychology is a science, it owes a debt to these thinkers who started science.

The nature of philosophy changed, however, in the second half of the fifth century B.C. Philosophers stopped asking the questions of physics and began asking the questions of psychology. The primary physical question is: what is the universe that people can know it? The primary psychological question is: what is a person that he or she can know the universe? No longer did philosophers seek to know the fundamental characteristic of matter, seeking instead to understand knowledge itself. What is knowledge? How do we acquire knowledge? What is knowledge about? This field of philosophy is called *epistemology*, from the Greek words *episteme,* knowledge, and *logos*, account or discourse. Epistemology is naturally related to psychology, for it is people who know and people who learn. Plato made epistemology the central concern of philosophy for two millennia. Psychology, at least as it was founded, is an attempt to wed science to epistemology, to provide scientific answers to philosophical questions. The founders of psychology, such as Wundt and James, were aware of this as are many psychologists of today, such as Piaget and Norman. The important psychological issues were originally philosophical, and so it is impossible to understand psychology historically without knowing about philosophy, especially epistemology.

We must not forget, however, that psychology wedded *science* to philosophy. The first psychologists were philosophers; they were also physiologists. Human beings as thinking, knowing creatures cannot be considered apart from humans as biological organisms. Humanity knows, but humanity's knowledge is the outcome of physiological sensation and central cortical processes. Psychologists from the beginning have been aware of that, and so we cannot understand psychology without knowing about biology. However, more space is given here to philosophy because with the exception of evolution—which has been of supreme importance in shaping twentieth century psychology—the important concepts, issues, and questions of psychology have come from philosophers, not from biologists.

# 2

# The Classical World
## Origins of Philosophy, Science, and Psychology

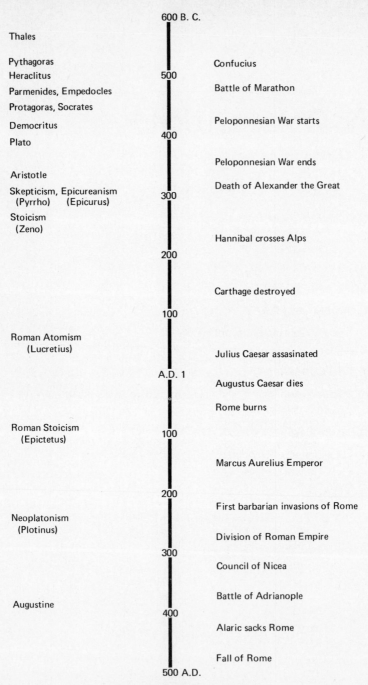

**FIGURE 2-1.**
Chronology 600 B.C.—A.D. 500.

## BEFORE PHILOSOPHY

Even before human beings began to make written records of their ideas, they took a lively interest in the universe. Archeological investigations suggest that early people made records on incised bones that represented important astronomical regularities such as the phases of the moon. These systematic observations could make possible accurate calculation of eclipses and changes in the seasons. The most dramatic, but by no means the only, evidence of early humanity's astronomical sophistication is Stonehenge, which served as both observatory and calculating machine.

Stone monuments and incised bones, however, tell us nothing about man's earliest views on human nature, or psychology. For that we must consult myths, stories preserved in oral tradition for decades or centuries before being written down. Myths serve various functions. They often justify the structure of a society and its moral code, as well as meet deep human needs both for faith and for knowledge. Myths described and explained the universe before science was invented. Tales of natural events are physics-to-be; tales of human nature are psychology-to-be.

One famous pair of myths are the *Iliad* and the *Odyssey,* which are a collection of oral tales synthesized not long before the Golden Age of Athens and which were then inscribed by the poet Homer. The *Iliad* and the *Odyssey* concern themselves with human action and contain the common sense psychology of pre-philosophic Greece.

The Greeks had no word corresponding to "personality," but they did have names for what we would call different components of personality. First, there was *psyche,* the "breath of life" from which "psychology" derives, that leaves a person at death; we may interpret *psyche* as the vital principle of life that separates the organic from the inorganic. Another part of personality was *thymos,* which seems to mean a motivational principle underlying both action and feeling. Our own word *(e)motion* also expresses the idea that behavior must result from motivational arousal. Finally, there was *nous,* the psychological organ for the clear perception of truth.

A remarkable thing about the Homeric heroes was how little control they often had of the various parts of their minds. In the *Iliad* the gods often cloud a warrior's *nous* and plant madness in his *thymos,* causing him to act irresponsibly. Indeed, Agamemnon's theft from Achilles, which opens the *Iliad,* is such a divinely controlled act. The concept of personal responsibility and the attribution of behavior to entirely internal causes did not appear until approximately 500 B.C. in the works of the Greek dramatists. Consequently we usually find it easier to appreciate Greek tragedy than the *Iliad,* for the tragic characters act out of what we recognize as deep human passions rather than at the whim of the Olympian gods.

One important philosophical distinction appears in the *Iliad* when Homer appeals to the divine knowledge of the gods who "know all things" to correct errors in his own human opinion based on "rumor." The division between truth, or reality (divine knowledge), and appearance (opinion) is a profound one in Western thought, even today. A table appears to human eyes and hands to be solid, but physics tells us it is really a swarm of infinitely small particles. Philosophers have always wrestled with the problem that appearances can be deceptive and have looked for ways humanity can know reality. We shall see that psychology, too, shares the problem of how unreliable sensory information produces our stable picture of "reality." It is the oldest problem of reflective human thought.

The *Iliad* and the *Odyssey* record for us the common sense psychology and philosophy of the ancient Greeks. Common sense, however, is seldom self-critical; it engages in no attempt to improve itself. All that changed in the sixth century B.C. when philosophy was invented.

## PHILOSOPHY BEFORE PLATO

### The Pre-Socratic Philosophers

#### The Critical Tradition

It is difficult for people to accept criticism of their ideas or to reflect critically on them. Consequently, many systems of thought are *closed,* that is, they do not criticize themselves, but rather defend themselves against criticism. We frequently find closed systems of thought in religion, for believers adhere to some great revealed Truth beyond human criticism; critics are called heretics and are often persecuted. Political systems, too, may be closed. Communist nations often reproach each other for "deviation" from the Truth of Marx, and persecute critics as if they were religious heretics.

Closed systems, therefore, are profoundly conservative, accepting change slowly if at all. Sometimes good can result. Chinese society was largely run by intellectual Mandarins who subscribed to a uniform Confucian ideology. Consequently China enjoyed a political stability unknown to Europe. The Mandarins' job was to preserve what they felt was a fundamentally sound society. Stability, however, can also be stagnancy. Chinese science, what there was of it, made little progress under the Mandarins. The technological feats of inventing gunpowder and building the Great Wall were accomplished by artisans, not by the educated Mandarins.

In Greece, however, the intellectual life took a different turn. The ancient Greek philosophers were the first thinkers to progress by employing criticism.

There, beginning with Thales of Miletus (flourished* 585 B.C.), a tradition of systematic criticism whose aim was the improvement of ideas, came into being. As the philosopher Karl Popper wrote (1965): "Thales was the first teacher who said to his pupils: 'This is how I see things—how I believe that things are. Try to improve upon my teaching.'" Thales did not teach his ideas as a received Truth to be conserved, but as a set of hypotheses to be improved. Thales and those who followed him sought change. They knew that ideas are rarely right, that only by making errors and then correcting them can we progress. Dogma enshrines error in concrete and makes progress impossible. The critical attitude is fundamental to both philosophy and science, but it requires overcoming intellectual laziness and the natural feeling of hostility towards critics. Founding a critical tradition was the major achievement of the Greek inventors of philosophy.

### The Physicists and Naturalism

The specific problem Thales addressed was the nature of reality. Thales proposed that although the world appears to be made up of many different substances (wood, stone, air, smoke, and so forth), there is in reality only one element—water—which takes on many forms. Water can be liquid, gaseous, or solid, and was, Thales proposed, the essential constituent of all things. The name for the single element out of which all things are made was *physis,* and so those who followed Thales in searching for some such universal element were called *physicists.* Modern physics continues the search, asserting that all the substances of common experience are really composed of a few elementary particles.

Besides inaugurating a critical tradition, then, Thales also began a line of physical investigation. In doing so he moved away from religious or spiritual interpretations of the universe toward naturalistic explanations of how things are constituted and how they work. Thus Thales asserted that the world is within human understanding, for it is made up of ordinary matter and does not reflect the capricious whims of gods. Critically he recognized that his hypothesis was fallible human opinion, but he held out hope that divine knowledge might eventually become human knowledge.

Thales' tradition continued with his student Anaximander of Miletus (fl. 560 B.C.) who accepted the concept of a *physis* but criticized Thales' hypothesis that it was water. Anaximander asked how one ordinary element could change into others. Instead, he proposed the existence of an element that was not any recognizable element, being instead something less definite that could take on many forms. He called his proposed *physis* the *apeiron,* best translated as "the Indefinite." In his turn Anaximander was challenged by his student Anaximenes of Miletus (fl. 546 B.C.) who proposed that the *physis* was air.

Anaximander also deserves notice for his shrewd observations on evolution.

---

*flourished will be given as fl. A person "flourishes" at age 40.

He argued that since human babies are so fragile and require such prolonged nursing, human beings' original, primeval form must have been different, sturdier and presumably more quickly independent, as are animal infants. Anaximander appealed to fossils of unknown creatures to support his notion of evolution. This is one of the rare instances of a Greek philosopher appealing to empirical data to buttress an opinion. As we shall see, most Greeks preferred abstract argument to empirical research.

While he was a poet rather than a philosopher, Xenophanes of Colophon (fl. 530 B.C.) broadened the critical and naturalistic traditions by his open assault on Greek religion. Xenophanes maintained that the Olympian gods were simply anthropomorphic constructions, behaving just like human beings, even lying, stealing, murdering, and philandering. Xenophanes argued that if animals had gods they too would make them in their own images, inventing lion gods, cat gods, dog gods, and so on. Xenophanes' critique is the beginning of the ancient struggle between scientific naturalism and religion that reached its greatest crisis when Darwin proposed the theory of evolution in the nineteenth century.

More directly influential on later philosophers, especially Plato, was Pythagoras of Samos (fl. 530 B.C.). Pythagoras was an enigmatic figure, both a great mathematician and a religious leader. He is most famous for the Pythagorean theorem, and he also formulated the first mathematical law of physics, expressing the harmonic ratios of vibrating strings of different lengths. Mathematics, however, was more than just a tool of science for Pythagoras. It was also a magical key to the cosmos. Pythagoras founded a secret religious sect devoted to numbers which believed: "Everything that can be known has a number; for it is impossible to grasp anything with the mind ... without this [number]" (Freeman, 1971). The Pythagorean sect was complete with secret rites and dietary laws, and it long outlived its founder.

In psychology, Pythagoras drew a sharp distinction between soul and body. Not only could the soul exist without the body, but, going further, the Pythagoreans considered the body a corrupting prison in which the soul was trapped. An important part of Pythagorean religion was directed toward purifying the flesh so the soul could more easily attain truth.

Plato was greatly influenced by the Pythagoreans. He too viewed the soul as a pure knowing entity thrust into a corrupting body. His theory of knowledge held that sense perception, depending as it does on the corrupt body, is inherently untrustworthy. Instead, the soul's reason should seek abstract knowledge of mathematical purity.

Finally we must mention Alcmaeon of Croton (fl. 500 B.C.), because he foreshadows the founding of psychology. Alcmaeon was a physician who practiced the first dissections. He was also interested in philosophy and directed his attention to understanding perception. He dissected the eye and traced the optic nerve to the brain. Unlike later thinkers, such as Empedocles and Aristotle, Alcmaeon correctly believed that sensation and thought occur in the brain. Alcmaeon's work hints at the founding of psychology, the attempt to answer philosophical questions about reason by using scientific methods borrowed from physiology. In most founding psychologists, including Wilhelm Wundt, Sigmund Freud, and William James, we will find the figure of Alcmaeon, the physician turned empirical philosopher.

### Being vs. Becoming

An important intellectual polarity in Western thought has been, and remains, the tension between philosophies of being and of becoming. Advocates of *being* maintain that beyond the flux of the changing world there are eternal truths and values that exist apart from humanity, truths we should seek and use to guide our lives. These truths exist in a realm of pure Being; they exist changelessly apart from the changing physical world. Advocates of *becoming,* on the other hand, deny that any such truths, or realm of pure being, exist. Instead, the only constant in the universe is change; things never simply *are,* but are always *becoming* something else. For such thinkers even moral values can change as the world changes. In the Pre-Socratic period the great spokesmen for becoming and being were respectively Heraclitus of Ephesus (fl. 500 B.C.) and Parmenides of Elea (fl. 475 B.C.).

Heraclitus was a difficult philosopher, known even to his contemporaries as "The Obscure." He asserted that the *physis* was fire, which has change as its most obvious characteristic. This idea led him to the conclusion that there is even less permanence in the world than there seems to be. What looks like a stone is really a condensed ball of ever-changing fire, a reality not unlike the modern physicists' swarm of particles. His most famous aphorism was that no one ever steps in the same river twice. The statement aptly sums up his philosophy, in which nothing in the universe is ever the same twice. Nevertheless, Heraclitus also believed that although change is the only constant, it is lawful rather than capricious. Regulating change is a dynamic universal harmony that keeps things in an equilibrium of balanced forces. Thus what truth philosophy and science may attain will be truth about change rather than about static things.

Although Pythagoras' worship of eternal numbers expressed a philosophy of being, his cult's secrecy limited its influence. The philosophy of being was first stated by Parmenides, like Heraclitus an obscure writer, who set his philosophy down in a poem. Parmenides sharply distinguished a Way of Seeming (appearances) from a Way of Truth (reality). Since, for Parmenides, Truth was eternal and unchanging, the philosopher concluded that change is an illusion based on our faulty senses. In reality there is no change. This changeless reality had to be grasped by reason and logic, and Parmenides was the first philosopher to present his arguments as logical deductions from intuitively plausible premises. Parmenides is thus the founder of rationalism.

Since the time of Parmenides the struggle between being and becoming has been fought by many thinkers. Through his admirer Plato, Parmenides' philosophy of being dominated Western thinking, although not without challenge, until modern times. Neoplatonism was the philosophical cornerstone of medieval Christian thought. It was not until the breakdown of the Middle Ages that becoming began to ascend. With Darwin's theory of evolution by random mutation and natural selection, becoming triumphed in science. This triumph is evident not only in the biological sciences but even in physics. Thus quantum theory asserts that we can never know where a particle is with certainty, only where it might be.

There was one revealing early reaction to Parmenides in the Way of True Opinion advanced by the physician-philosopher Empedocles of Acragas (fl. 450 B.C.), who may be regarded as the founder of empiricism. Building on the ideas of Alcmaeon, Empedocles tried to develop a theory of perception that would justify our common sense reliance on our senses. Empedocles stated that objects emit effluences that are sense-modality specific copies of themselves. Today we know that smell works this way; our noses respond to certain molecules given off by some things. Empedocles thought this true of all kinds of perception.

Unlike Alcmaeon, Empedocles believed that the effluences get in the blood-stream where they meet and mix in the heart. The agitation of the effluences in the beating of the heart, Empedocles argued, was thinking. His theory, although it sounds absurd today, was an important step for naturalism, since it proposes a purely physical basis for mental activity, which was usually attributed to a soul.

Empedocles' views are characteristically empiricist, claiming that we know reality by observing it, specifically by internalizing copies of objects. Thought can create nothing new, being able only to rearrange the atoms of experience. And Empedocles' conclusions show why empiricists have generally contributed more to psychology than rationalists have. The empiricist must show how the senses work in order to justify our using them in seeking the truth. This necessarily requires developing psychological theories of sense-functioning. The rationalist, on the other hand, simply denies the validity of sensory information, and so can ignore problems of empirical psychology as philosophically irrelevant.

### Socrates' Contemporaries

#### The Last Physicists: Atomism

The last classical philosophers to be concerned primarily with the nature of physical reality were Leucippus of Miletus (fl. 430 B.C.) and his better-known student, Democritus of Abdera (fl. 420 B.C.). After them, philosophers turned to questions about human knowledge, morality, and happiness. As the name of their school implies, the *atomists* proposed an idea that has proven immensely fruitful in physics: that all objects are composed of infinitesimally small atoms. For physics, this has meant that the complexity of substances we find around us can be analyzed as collections of a few particles interacting in mathematically precise ways.

Atomism can be metaphorically extended to psychology, where it has proved to be the most durable of psychological assumptions. Psychological atomism says that complex ideas such as "cathedral" or "psychology" can be analyzed as collections of simpler ideas, or even of sensations, that have been associated together. This assumption has been an integral part of empiricist theories of the mind and it still, in some form, underlies all psychological systems except Gestalt psychology.

The atomists pushed their hypothesis to its limit. They supported materialism, determinism, and reductionism. A favorite motto of Democritus was that only "atoms and [the] Void exist in reality." There is no God and no soul, only material atoms in empty space. If only atoms exist, then free will must be an illusion. Leucippus said, "Nothing happens at random; everything happens out of reason and by necessity." The soul and free will are illusions that can be reduced to the mechanical functioning of our physical bodies. Democritus wrote, "We know nothing accurately in reality, but only as it changes according to the bodily condition and the constitution of those things that impinge upon [the body]" (Freeman, 1971).

Like Empedocles, Democritus proposed a materialistic account of perception and thinking. Indeed, Democritus' theory is only a modification of that of Empedocles. Democritus said that every object gives off special kinds of atoms called *eidola,* which are copies of the object. When these reach our senses we perceive the object indirectly through its copy. Thus our thought processes are restricted to putting together or taking apart the *eidola*-images in our brains. Democritus did see the fatal flaw in this theory: We have no way of knowing that the *eidola* are accurate and precise copies of the objects that emit them. If they are inaccurate, our "knowledge" of real objects is in error. We will later see how this problem became a sticking-point for the eighteenth century empiricists, Locke, Berkeley, and Hume.

Democritus also maintained an ethical doctrine that came to trouble eighteenth century ethical philosophers deeply. A consistent materialism, denying as it does God and the soul, can only offer one guide to the conduct of life: the pursuit of pleasure and the avoidance of pain. This doctrine is called hedonism. We find Democritus saying, "The best thing for man is to pass his life so as to have as much joy and as little trouble as may be" (Copleston, 1962). This is the logical outcome of naturalism, for it reduces values to our natural bodily experiences of pleasure and pain. To many, however, it is morally offensive, for if an individual's pleasure is the sole criterion of the good, what right has anyone to condemn the happy and successful criminal or tyrant? Such questions were at the heart of Socrates' and Plato's thinking, and Plato once suggested burning Democritus' books. Democritus' own answer to this moral dilemma strikes most people as lame: The greatest pleasure is philosophising—greater than the obvious physical pleasures—and the happy (good) life is a philosophical one.

### The Sophists: Attitudes of the Modern World

Philosophy's shift of focus from the nature of physical reality to the nature of man was expressed most forcefully by the Sophists. Their famous motto was enunciated by the greatest Sophist, Protagoras (approximately 490-420 B.C.): "Of all things the measure is man, of things that are that they are, and of things that are not that they are not" (Sprague, 1972). The center of concern became man and his needs rather than the physical world or the gods.

The Sophists maintained no fixed philosophical doctrine. They were primarily teachers of rhetoric who offered—for a fee—to teach the ambitious young men of Athens how to argue well in court and in assembly. Their aim was thus the process of effective arguments, not true arguments. They have been likened in this respect to modern advertising agents whose first concern is to sell a product or a politician, regardless of merit.

Protagoras' motto reflects a humanistic relativism: man is the measure of all things. This aphorism has a range of meanings. The narrowest interpretation says that one is the best judge of one's own experience. Two people may enter the same room, yet one may experience the room as warm, the other cool, if the former has been out in a blizzard and the latter downstairs stoking the furnace. Neither perception is incorrect; each is true for its perceiver. Generalizing this perceptual relativism brings us to a broader meaning of Protagoras' idea: cultural relativism. The Sophists tended to be materialists like Democritus, considering pleasure and pain to be the only guide to conduct. Pleasure and pain are individual sensory experiences, so it follows that ethically each person is the only judge of what is right for her or him. Any attempt to lay down general rules of conduct is necessarily arbitrary, for the law-giver knows only his or her own pleasures and pains. Nevertheless, the Sophists recognized that law was necessary for the survival of human communities and accepted a cultural relativism by which any person living in one culture had to live by the rules of that culture but should not attempt to impose that culture's rules on people from other cultures.

Finally, at its greatest level of generality, "man is the measure of all things" is a statement about the universe. There is no permanent, enduring Truth, no divinely sanctioned law, no eternal transhuman code of values. The measure of things is not God or abstract, scientific truth, but human beings, their needs, and their search for happiness. This view is central to humanism and offers a philosophy of becoming quite different from that of Heraclitus.

Like Democritus' hedonism, the Sophists' humanistic relativism is offensive to those who see in it a recipe for moral anarchy and a denial of enduring Truth. In dialogue after dialogue, Plato's Socrates defeats the Sophists, who appear as characters in many of Plato's dialogues. Out of Plato's attempt to refute relativism came a powerful philosophy of being, classical rationalism.

## THE TWO CLASSIC STATEMENTS OF WESTERN PHILOSOPHY

### Socrates and Plato: The Philosophy of Rationalism and Being

Socrates (470-399 B.C.) was a wondering teacher who inquired about the meaning of such general terms as Truth, Beauty, and Justice. His greatest pupil was Plato, who provided positive answers to the provocative questions Socrates himself did not answer. Plato (428-348 B.C.) wrote dialogues in which Socrates discusses various issues with the Athenians. The early dialogues show us the early, inquiring Socrates. In the later ones, Plato has Socrates propose Plato's own rationalism.

The Sophists and Socrates were contemporaries and antagonists. Socrates, who concentrated on ethics, believed that the Sophists would undermine all morality with their relativistic teachings. In opposition to them he sought to discover the general meaning of the Good, the Just, and the Beautiful. Plato extended the search to encompass all of knowledge.

Plato did accept, however, one aspect of Sophistic relativism: their argument that all sensations are relative to the state of the observer. Plato provided a powerful argument in support of this position, in the example of the two men entering a room from different backgrounds and therefore perceiving the room differently (as in the preceding example). You can arrange another demonstration, proposed centuries later. Take three buckets of water—one hot, one cold, one lukewarm. Place the left hand in the hot water, the right in the cold. Then plunge both hands into the lukewarm water. The left hand will feel cold, the right hot. The water, of course, is at one temperature, yet you feel it at two temperatures. Your experience of the water is relative to the state of your hands. Plato argued from this relativity that in fact you do not *know* what the temperature of the water is; you can only form some belief about it.

Plato also accepted the Heraclitean doctrine of flux, arguing that all objects are constantly changing. To Plato this meant that objects cannot be known. We cannot have eternal, unchangeable knowledge—essential characteristics of knowledge for Plato—about things that are constantly changing. Plato concluded that perception gives a highly imperfect, relativistic picture of an everchanging world of objects, a picture that cannot be called knowledge.

Plato did not question the existence of knowledge, however, but sought to show how knowledge can be achieved. If we cannot know reality, what can we know? Knowledge cannot be of nothing, of what does not exist, for then it would not be knowledge. Knowledge is eternally true and unchangeable, so the objects of knowledge must be eternal and unchangeable. Plato called these objects of knowledge Forms (or Ideas). There is a Form for every class of objects to which we give a general name, such as "cat," "bed," "man," "just," or "good." Plato believed that perceived objects are imperfect copies of these Forms, imperfect because they are ever-changing and relative to the perceiver.

The best expression of this idea comes in the metaphor of the line in Plato's *Republic*. Imagine a line (Figure 2-2) divided into four unequal sections. The line is divided into two large sections, standing for the world of perceived Appearances and opinion and the world of abstract Knowledge, the intelligible world. The former section is shorter, indicating its imperfection. The world of Appearances is further divided, in ratios equal to that of the whole line, into worlds of Imagining and of Belief. Imagining is the lowest level of cognition, dealing with mere images of concrete objects, such as images cast in water. Plato also relegated art to this realm, for when we see a portrait of a man we are seeing only an image, a shadow of a shade. Plato banished art from his Utopian Republic.

| | Objects | States of Mind |
|---|---|---|
| **Intelligible World** | The Good | Intelligence or<br>D  Knowledge |
| | Forms | |
| | Mathematical objects | C  Thinking |
| **World of Appearances** | Visible Things | B  Belief |
| | Images | A  Imagining |

**FIGURE 2-2.**

Plato's metaphor of the line. (From F. M. Cornford, trans., *The Republic of Plato.* New York: Oxford University Press, 1941, p. 222.)

Our apprehension of images is the most imperfect way of knowing. We are on surer ground when looking at the objects themselves; Plato called this Belief. With the next section of the line, Thinking, we achieve knowledge, beginning with mathematical knowledge. The mathematician can prove theorems about right-angled triangles or quadratic equations without reference to actual triangles or numerical equations. The mathematician has knowledge of these things. Plato was greatly influenced by Pythagoreanism, as is evident in the stress he placed on mathematics as a form of knowledge.

The ideal world of geometry is very similar to that of the Forms. In geometry you might prove, for instance, that the sum of the square of the hypotenuse of a right-angled triangle is equal to the sum of the squares of the sides (Pythagorean theorem). In establishing this you might draw a right-angled triangle, yet your proof is not about that triangle, but about all right-angled triangles, or, more Platonically, The Right-Angled Triangle. Any triangle you might draw would be an inferior copy of the perfect Right-Angled Triangle, but your proof is about the Form of this Triangle. We accept this as a commonplace of mathematics and geometry, which are not about collections of numbers or drawn figures but about ideal variables and figures. Plato, however, believed that the relation of copy to form was true of everything, not just of drawn triangle to Ideal Triangle, but also of Plymouth Rock to the Ideal Rock. This must be so in order to make knowledge of rocks (geology) possible, since perceived rocks are in flux and only relativistically experienced.

Today we might agree with Plato that mathematics is knowledge. It is rigorous, and its proofs are necessarily true. The greatest advances in modern physics have come from pursuing elementary insights with formal mathematical logic to their necessary conclusions. Yet Plato believed the highest form of knowledge, in the last section of the line (Intelligence or Knowledge in the figure), to be more than this. Mathematics, or at least the geometry of Plato's time, relied on perceived images such as triangles, circles, and squares. This reliance on images rendered geometry imperfect. More seriously, mathematics argues rigorously from certain assumptions which it leaves unquestioned. Euclidean geometry, for example, starts with fundamental axioms and works out the consequences, but these axioms remain unproved. In the nineteenth century, forms of geometry radically different from Euclid's were discovered by altering only one or two of his axioms. Although Plato was of course unaware of this development, it would have demonstrated to him that he was right—mathematics produces knowledge within its system of assumptions, but it cannot know which assumptions are correct. Therefore, mathematics is not true knowledge, for its assumptions may always be questioned.

To attain knowledge, then, we must mount still higher to the realm of the Forms themselves, not being satisfied with their mathematical replicas, their concrete replicas, or images of these replicas. We must ascend from mere assumptions to first principles, from the world of visible Appearances to the world of intelligible Forms. How is the journey to be made? How are we to attain knowledge of the Forms? On this question Plato's views evolved over the years. He always believed that we must turn away, to some extent, from sense perception and enter into philosophical dialectic out of whose give-and-take true knowledge would arise. The exact nature of his idea of dialectic, however, changed as he grew older.

In the earlier dialogues Plato believed that experience of concrete objects stimulated remembrance of the innate knowledge of the Forms acquired between incarnations. Perceived objects do resemble the Forms, although imperfectly, and so may provide an effective stimulus to awaken our knowledge of the Forms. In his middle dialogues, Plato denied any valid role to sense perception and put the entire burden of learning on abstract, philosophic dialectic. Finally, in his late dialogues and unpublished lectures (which we know through Aristotle), he returned to his earlier belief in the potential value of sense perception. At the same time he elaborated his notion of dialectic into a tool for carefully classifying all things, a tool Aristotle was to perfect and make the basis for his entire philosophy. At the same time, Plato's conception of the Forms also became increasingly mathematical and Pythagorean.

The problem Plato addressed with his theory of the Forms is one that has exercised thinkers from the Middle Ages up to modern research in concept formation. For example, if one uses the term "cat," one is not referring to one's own cat, or to any particular cat, but rather to some general notion of "catness." Each physical cat is a mixture of features, some essential to its being a cat, such as meat-eating, and some not, such as the length of its fur or its color. The essential "catness" is defined by the first kind of features. This universal "catness" was for Plato the Form of the cat, and physical cats were imperfect replicas of this Form precisely because of their accidental, unessential features. This problem of general terms as opposed to specific instances came to be called the problem of universals. It is still a lively question in learning and developmental psychology. How does a person, especially a child, learn to separate general concepts such as "triangle," "cat," or "lie" from her or his experiences of specific triangles, cats, and lies? Plato believed that the person had to remember these concepts as recollections of the Forms seen between incarnations.

### Psychology

Plato's overriding interest in the otherworldly Forms led him to place little importance on an empirical study such as psychology. Only one dialogue, the *Timaeus,* is given over to scientific matters. Here we will glean from various dialogues Plato's opinions on a variety of psychological topics.

**Nature of the Soul.**   Plato divided the soul, or mind, into three parts. First there is the immortal, rational soul, located in the head. The other two parts are mortal. The spirited or courageous soul, oriented to winning honor and glory, is located in the chest, and the passionate or appetitive soul, concerned with bodily pleasure, in the belly. The rational soul is akin to the Forms and to knowledge; the perishable (mortal) souls are tied to the body and hence are only capable of opinion. It is the duty of the rational soul to control the desires of the other two, as a charioteer controls two horses. The passionate soul was viewed by Plato as particularly troublesome and requiring great restraint by reason. Centuries later, we find a similar idea in Freud who also stressed the "primacy of the reason" over instinctual drives. Plato was clearly a mind-body dualist who said that a person is defined by his rational mind, the body being a disturbing tomb in which the soul finds itself incarnated and which it operates like a puppet.

**Motivation.**   As might be expected, Plato, especially in his early and middle works, takes a dim view of pleasure. Seeking pleasure and avoiding pain, man's obvious drives, are things of the body that serve only to debase the rational mind and hinder its contemplation of the Good. All forms of sensation, including pleasure, were seen as unavoidable evils. In his later writings, however, Plato modified this extreme view. Some pleasures, such as the aesthetic joy found in beauty, he now considers healthy and he rejects the purely intellectual life as too limited. His view of motivation becomes Freudian: We have within us a stream of passionate desire which can be channeled to any of the three parts of the soul, into the pursuit of physical pleasure, honor, or philosophical knowledge and virtue. Our drives can motivate either the pursuit of transitory pleasure or the philosophical ascent to the world of the Forms.

**Physiology and Perception.**   Plato's physiology is quaint to our ears. He said, for instance, that the function of the liver was to display images sent by the rational soul to the passionate soul; these images were later erased by the pancreas. Since Plato distrusted perception, he said little about the empirical science of physiology. He often just records traditional Greek views. Of vision, for example, he said that we see because our eyes throw out visual rays which strike objects in our line of sight. This idea persists in modern language in such phrases as "he threw her a glance," and this theory dominated optical thinking for centuries after Plato.

**Learning.**    Plato was the first great nativist, for he believed that all human knowledge is innate, that is, present at birth. In his more extreme moments, Plato believed that this knowledge can be revived only through dialectic and contemplation, giving no role to sense perception. Elsewhere, however, Plato proposes an account of learning—his theory of recollection—that resembles certain modern theories, for example, Noam Chomsky's nativist account of language acquisition. Perceived objects, of course, resemble the Forms they partake of, and the resemblance, especially if aided by teaching, can stimulate our rational soul to remember what the Forms are like. Put in modern terms, perceptual input arouses and develops innate cognitive mechanisms. At the same time, Plato provides the basis for the doctrine of associationism, later a fundamental part of empiricist philosophy. Sensible objects remind us of the Forms either because they are similar to the Forms, or because the two objects or ideas have been frequently associated in our experience. These are two of the fundamental laws of association—resemblance and contiguity—central to many later psychological systems.

**Development and Education.**    Plato believed in reincarnation. At death the rational soul is separated from the body and attains a vision of the Forms. Then, depending on the degree of virtue present in one's previous life, one is reincarnated somewhere on the phylogenetic scale. When the soul is thrust into a new body full of animal sensations and desires, it becomes completely confused and must adapt. This confusion explains why knowledge of the Forms is not present in infants. It is the purpose of education to help the rational soul gain control of the body and of the other parts of the soul. Education has three phases. First, infants must be soothed and rocked to master their inner chaos. Then elementary education in gymnastics, rhetoric, and geometry gives the child mastery of the external world. Finally, for those who are capable, higher education in philosophy leads one to knowledge of the Forms. This education is especially rigorous and exacting and was meant to produce the rulers of society.

Plato's psychology is fragmentary and incomplete. The first systematic psychology was worked out by his student Aristotle, who had a higher regard for perception and empirical science than had his teacher.

### Aristotle: The Philosophy of Empiricism and Growth

Aristotle was the first professor. Plato wrote dramatic dialogues in which Socrates' flashes of insight illuminated philosophical and moral problems. Aristotle wrote prosaic treatises. He was the first to systematically "review the literature" of earlier thinkers. Instead of being led by intuitive insight, he was guided by order, method, and the syllogistic logic he invented. Plato's rationalism forced him to adopt fantastic ideas, such as the Forms, which do violence to common sense. But Aristotle's careful, empirical attitude never strayed far from common sense, and his errors were usually simple and factual, such as his belief that the heart was the seat of the soul, which includes the mind. Plato created a magical world of disembodied Forms and mysterious forces of participation. Aristotle's world was one founded on common sense, in which heavy objects fall faster than light ones.

Even though Aristotle was for twenty years Plato's student, they represent outlooks so different as to be antithetical. Plato was a pure philosopher whose approach bordered on mysticism and who so distrusted sense-perception that to him the visible world was not real. Aristotle was above all else a scientist who believed in the reality of the sensible world and in the worth of sense perception and the joy to be found in it. The body was not a tomb to Aristotle. His fundamental error was the opposite of Plato's. He believed mathematics to be useless in science because it does not deal directly with what is observed. Despite their years together, it seems that to a large extent they did not communicate. In his writings, Aristotle frequently criticized Plato, but his objections were seldom telling. They only persuade those who share Aristotle's own empirical orientation, but do not touch a true Platonist. This was, perhaps, the first Kuhnian paradigm clash in which proponents of different views argued without persuading each other.

### Epistemology

Aristotle naturally rejected the doctrine of the Forms. His specific points of criticism are usually acknowledged to be weak, but his general standpoint was that the Forms do not explain anything. They are just glorified individuals—perfect, heavenly individuals, it is true—but individuals nonetheless. To introduce a new set of particulars into the universe gains nothing. In modern terms, to Aristotle Plato was rather like a child at Piaget's preoperational stage of thinking who cannot conceive of classes of objects, only particular, concrete objects. Plato attempted to answer the problem of universals by positing glorified, perfect, individual, concrete objects. Aristotle advanced to the next stage of thinking—concrete operational—characterized by class logic and exemplified by the syllogism, a form of argument Aristotle created.

What had primary existence for Aristotle was the sensible world of things. He begins his philosophy by considering "this thing here." From our experience of objects we abstract the essence of classes of things, or species. The goal of science is to understand the essence of permanent species. We begin with sensations of particular, perishable objects and ascend by the processes of the mind to knowledge of immutable species.

Universals to Aristotle are not products of the mind, however, as some later thinkers have maintained. We know universals through the mind, but we do not create them. Aristotle believed that universals exist in nature and that we discover them. There is a universal essence of what it means to be a cat, quite apart from our thinking about cats. Universals are not separate Forms, nor are they just useful labels, for they exist as the essences of naturally real species of concrete objects.

### Psychology

**Philosophy of Nature.**   For Aristotle, psychology was an empirical science, more specifically a part of biology. Hence we begin by looking at Aristotle's approach to natural explanation.

*The Four Causes.* Aristotle believed that there are four kinds of natural cause —formal, final, efficient, and material. The material cause refers to the matter of which something is made. So, for example, the material cause of the Venus de Milo is marble. The efficient cause refers to an immediate source of change or motion. If you drop a vase on a concrete floor, the efficient cause of its shattering is the sharp impact of the vase on the floor. The final cause refers to the purpose of an object or of a change. For example, in response to the question "Why did you go to the store?", you answer: "To buy this book." This answer appeals to a final cause, since it refers to the purpose of the trip. The formal cause is the essence of an object, what makes it what it is, or defines it. It refers most obviously to the shape of the object, its form. What distinguishes the Venus de Milo from other marble statues is its precise form. However, formal cause need not refer to external shape, but it always refers to the defining essence of a thing, as separate from its accidental features. Finally, it should be noted that although the causes can be discussed separately, it is possible for a single thing to function simultaneously as more than one cause. This is the case for the soul, as we shall see.

*Potentiality and Actuality.* Although there are various kinds of visible change recognized by Aristotle, the form of change he was most concerned with was qualitative change, an emphasis which colors his analysis of all change. How does an acorn become an oak, a child become an adult, or a ball of wool become a sweater? These questions concern qualitative change. Aristotle's answers would be that the acorn is potentially an oak, the child potentially an adult, the ball of wool potentially a sweater. This potentiality must actualize itself or be actualized—the oak is actually an oak, the adult actually an adult, the sweater actually a sweater. Qualitative change is thus explained by an appeal to *teleology,* to purpose in nature. The purpose of an acorn is to become an oak, to actualize itself as an oak. Aristotle's system is frankly and thoroughly teleological. Aristotle often said that nature does nothing to no purpose, and the scientist explains change by discovering and appealing to these purposes.

*The Scala Naturae.* This striving for actualization creates a grand hierarchy among all things, from perfectly unformed, neutral matter in a state of pure potentiality up to God who is pure actuality, and who moves the universe because of the universe's desire to ascend to God—to perfect actuality (hence Aristotle's God is the Unmoved Mover, Unmoved because perfect actuality cannot change or move). Of particular interest for psychology is Aristotle's scaling of living species from the simplest (such as, al gal) to the closest to God (humans). Thus, although Aristotle denied evolution, being a believer in the fixity of species, he produced something like a phylogenetic scale, his *scala naturae,* with the result that his psychology is in part a comparative psychology.

**Definition and Types of Soul.**     The soul is the form (or formal cause), essence, and actuality of the person. The soul is what defines an animal—a cat is a cat because it has a cat's soul and behaves like a cat. A human being is human by virtue of possessing a human soul and hence acts human. In sum, each creature is defined by its soul, and, although Aristotle is not clear on this point, each individual is defined by her or his individual soul, what we would call the self. Hence the soul is the formal cause of the person, for it defines what kind of living thing it is. The soul is thus the essence of the animal. Finally, it is the actuality of a body which potentially has life. Without soul a body is dead; with soul there is life. The potential for life in a creature, therefore, is actualized by tne soul. In addition, the soul is the efficient cause of bodily movement, for it causes movement to happen. It is also the final cause, for the body serves the soul. To summarize, of any animal the material cause is the body of which the animal is made, while the soul is efficient cause of motion, formal cause that defines the animal's essence, and final cause, the purpose of the body.

What is the relation of soul and body? Aristotle, a biologist, took a naturalistic view of the mind-body problem. The soul, with the exception of one part, is inseparable from the body. His view resembles what is today called the dual aspect position: there is only one material reality, body, but it has two aspects, physiological and mental. Soul is the form of body and can no more be separated from its material embodiment than the form of the Venus de Milo can be separated from the marble it is made of, although we can discuss them separately, considering either the marble or the shape alone. Aristotle put it this way in *De Anima*: "That is why we can wholly dismiss as unnecessary the question whether the soul and the body are one: it is as meaningless to ask whether the wax and the shape given to it by the stamp are one. . . ." Aristotle was not a dualist. He rejected Plato's dualism and would have rejected Cartesian dualism. He is not a materialist reductionist, however. Soul cannot be reduced to body, even though there is only one matter, for we can separately discuss physiological and psychological functioning.

As a teological biologist, Aristotle asked about the soul as about any organ: what is it for, what is its purpose? He believed that the soul has several powers, such as nutrition, movement, and reason. Most philosophers call Aristotle's a faculty psychology, speaking of the faculty of reason, for example, but it would be better described as the first functional psychology, an approach congenial to a biologist. When, in the nineteenth century, American psychologists under the influence of Darwin again adopted a biological perspective, they formed a school called functionalism, emphasizing, as did Aristotle, the biological value of mental functioning.

It is obvious that not all living things exhibit the same functions, and Aristotle distinguished three levels of soul appropriate to different levels on his *scala naturae*. At the lowest level there is the *nutritive* soul, possessed by plants, serving two functions: the maintenance of the individual plant through nutrition, and the maintenance of the species through reproduction. Animals possess a more complex, *sensitive* soul, which subsumes the nutritive soul's functions while adding others. Animals, unlike plants, are aware of their surroundings. They have sensations, hence "sensitive soul." As a consequence of sensation, animals experience pleasure and pain, and so feel desire either to seek pleasure or to avoid pain. There are two further consequences of sensation: first, imagination and memory (since experience can be imagined or recalled), and second, in some animals, movement as a consequence of desire. Highest in the scale of souls comes the human soul, subsuming the others and adding mind, the power to think. This is the *rational* soul.

**Structure of the Rational, Human Soul.**  According to Aristotle, gaining knowledge is a psychological process that starts with the perception of particulars and ends with general knowledge of universals. Aristotle is in a sense the first information processing psychologist: we receive information from the senses, process and store this information, and act on it to yield knowledge, solve problems, and make decisions. Aristotle's analysis of the soul can be represented by an information processing flow-chart, showing the faculties of the soul and their interrelationships (Figure 2-3). The five primary senses send information to common sense, which unifies sensations into conscious perception and passes this processed information on to the passive mind, which is imprinted with the objects of perception. These perceptions may persist, creating images. Memory for Aristotle was a species of imagination, for our memories are always concrete images. Material passes into memory as we learn and can be recalled to consciousness later, hence the flow of information goes both ways. Finally, the contents of the passive mind are acted on by the active mind to produce universal knowledge. We will now consider these functions in more detail.

**Sense Perception.**  The special senses passively receive sensations of external objects. Their power is the potential to absorb the form of external objects, actualized by reception of a sense impression. To each special sense correspond certain qualities that only it can perceive. For instance, only by vision can we sense color, only by taste, sweetness. This aspect of perception is infallible. One cannot be wrong in saying that one sees a red spot or tastes sweetness. What can be in error is perception of the "incidental sensibles," which requires judgment. What one senses as a red spot may incidentally be a lady bug. But if one says, "I see a lady bug," one may be in error, for this requires a judgment. One may be

**FIGURE 2-3.**
Structure of the soul in the *De Anima.*

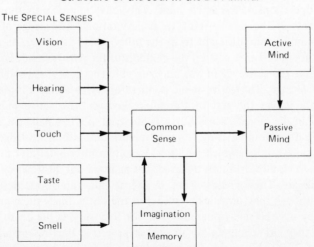

seeing a spot of paint. There are also sense qualities which are perceivable by more than one sense. One can see that an object is moving, or one can feel it move. One can see that there are two books on the desk, or one can find this out by touch. These qualities of movement (or rest), number, shape, and size, are called *common sensibles* because they are common to more than one sense.

Perception of the incidental and common sensibles is a result of common sense, which unifies data from the special senses into coherent, conscious experience. We do not live in a world of red patches, isolated sounds and tastes, but in an experienced world of objects (incidental sensibles) with important common properties (common sensibles). This apparent contradiction between what our sense organs detect and the conscious "lived experience" of which we are aware becomes (and remains) a vexing problem for twentieth century psychology when the Gestalt psychologists opposed Wundt's apparent reduction of experience to bundles of sensations. Aristotle was the first to try to deal with this question by postulating this common sense which unifies color patches, touches, and other sensations into conscious experience. Common sense is also responsible for self-awareness, and it is the inactivity of common sense that causes us to lose self-awareness in sleep.

**Mind.**   The rational part of the soul Aristotle called *mind*. It is unique to human beings and is capable of acquiring knowledge of abstract universals, as opposed to the knowledge of individuals given in perception. As we experience different members of the same natural type, we note similarities, and so form an impression of a universal, which Aristotle believed was always an image. As one experiences a multitude of cats, one eventually forms an idea of what the essence of a cat is.

Within the mind there must be, as Aristotle believed there to be throughout nature, a difference between potentiality and actuality. The passive mind is potentiality. It has no character of its own, for it can take on the form of experienced objects. Knowledge of universals in the passive mind is actualized, or made manifest, by the operations of the active mind. The active mind is pure thought, acting on the contents of the passive mind to achieve rational knowledge of universals. This active mind is quite different from the other parts of the soul. As actuality, it is not acted upon, rather it acts on the contents of the passive mind. For Aristotle, this meant that the active mind was unchangeable and hence immortal, for death is a form of change. The active mind is, therefore, separable from the body and survives death, unlike the rest of the soul. However, the active mind is not a personal soul in the modern sense, for it is identical in all human beings. It is pure thought and carries nothing away from its sojourn on earth. Knowledge is realized only in the passive mind, which perishes. A modern interpretation can be put on this thesis of Aristotle's. It is now believed that many of our information-processing abilities are innate. These processes are, in a sense, pure thought because they have no content although they provide knowledge of the world. Since these processes are inherited, they may be said to be immortal, for they survive the death of any one person, and they are common to all. These processes thus resemble Aristotle's active mind.

**Imagination and Memory.**    Aristotle believed that thought without images was impossible, therefore we should expect considerable discussion of imagination in his works. However, there is very little. His comments on imagination describe it narrowly as the persistence of a percept after the object originally causing it has gone. He does not discuss the active use of imagination, although he seems to be aware it exists. The only place imagination is important for Aristotle is in memory. To Aristotle, the act of memory consists of having an image and being aware of it as an image of something past.

Memory as a repository appears to consist of a set of images that represent past experience. Aristotle distinguishes simple memory—the recognition of an image as a representation of a past moment—from recollection, which involves a search among the memory images. Recollection is based on the fact that memory is organized, and Aristotle notes the fact (rediscovered by modern psychologists) that material inherently organized, such as mathematics, is easier to remember than that which is less organized.

This organization is based on association, as described in many modern psychological theories. Plato, as we have seen, hinted at laws of association, but Aristotle was the first systematically to exploit them. Aristotle discusses three laws of association—similarity, contiguity, and contrast. Similar images are associatively linked, images of contiguous experiences are linked, and opposite images are linked (that is, "hot" usually elicits the association "cold"). He also hints at the law of causality—causally linked experiences remind us of one another.

**Motivation.**    Movement is characteristic of animals and thus is a function of the sensitive soul, which can experience pleasure and pain. All action is motivated by some form of desire, which Aristotle believed involved imagination. In animals, motivation is directed by an image of what is pleasurable, and the animal seeks only present pleasure. Aristotle calls this type of motivation *appetite*. Man, however, is capable of reason and so can conceive of right and wrong. Therefore, man can be motivated by desire for what is good or for long-term future benefits. This type of motivation is called *wish*. Animals experience simple motivational conflicts between opposing appetites, but man has in addition the problem of moral choice. Aristotle's view of motivation resembles Freud's, distinguishing between the innate, animalistic pleasure principle, which cares only for immediate pleasure, and the acquired, uniquely human reality principle, which calculates long-term gain.

## PHILOSOPHY AFTER ARISTOTLE

### Philosophies of Happiness

Aristotle was the last great philosopher of the Classical Age. After him thought took new directions. Empires, first Alexander's and then the Romans', replaced the old city-states. Civilization was spread around the Mediterranean Sea and into Europe and Britain by these empires. This culture, however, did not produce many philosophers or scientists. Empires tend to be pragmatic, and we find in the Romans great engineers and practical politicians rather than great thinkers. Science flourished for a time at Alexandria, the capital of post-Alexandrian Egypt. Under Alexander's successors, the Ptolemies, research institutions were established and important advances were made in mathematics, astronomy, physics, and medicine. A great library was established in Alexandria, and one of the tragedies of history was its destruction in the early Christian era. Our knowledge of the early philosophers became fragmentary with the burning of the library.

What philosophical movements there were in the Hellenistic and Roman periods differed greatly from those that went before. Instead of investigating questions of science or epistemology, philosophers now sought recipes for human happiness. We may call the period from Aristotle and Alexander (both died in 323 B.C.) to the Middle Ages the period of happiness philosophies. Most of their names are still household words.

Epicurus (341-270 B.C.) accepted atomism, though not determinism, and like Democritus he advocated hedonism. But Epicurus' formula for pleasure was not what we associate with the name of his school, epicureanism. He stressed the avoidance of pain over the active pursuit of pleasure and counseled his followers to lead quiet lives withdrawn from the strife of the outside world. His warnings strike home to an energy-conscious age: To depend on the pleasures of life is to risk pain if they are withdrawn.

The Cynics not only withdrew from the civilized world but also attacked it. They felt that the doings of society were full of hypocrisy encompassing greed, envy, and hate. The Cynics flouted social conventions. The most famous Cynic was Diogenes (who died in 324 B.C.); he lived a life of poverty, called himself a citizen of the world, and advocated free love and communal families. It is said that Alexander the Great visited Diogenes at the cave where he lived. Standing in the entrance, Alexander asked what he could do for the renowned philosopher. "Get out of my light," was Diogenes' reply. This story epitomizes Cynicism.

Skepticism was a related but more intellectual movement, founded by Pyrrho of Elis (360-270 B.C.) and developed by several later heads of Plato's academy. Like Plato, the Skeptics distrusted sense perception. They did not believe in any world of the Forms, however. Therefore they held that any general conclusions one might reach on the basis of experience might turn out to be wrong in the light of new experience. Since being refuted is a painful experience, the Skeptics believed we should accept no general conclusions so as to avoid the unhappiness of being wrong.

More widespread than any of these philosophies was Stoicism, which counted among its adherents both a slave (Epictetus, A.D. 50-138) and an Emperor (Marcus Aurelius, A.D. 121-180). Its founder was Zeno of Citium (333-262 B.C.), who taught at the painted collonade, or *Stoa*, in Athens. Today a Stoic is someone who accepts misfortune "philosophically"—quietly and without complaint. Ancient

Stoics behaved this way because they believed that the universe was rational and good, often likening it to a living, semi-divine being present in everything. The Stoics were also determinists, holding that whatever happens to a person *must* so happen because of the causal ordering of the universe. Happiness, then, lies in placing one's own reason in harmony with that of the universe, accepting one's fate as part of a greater, divinely rational whole.

The most influential happiness philosophy was Neoplatonism, whose best spokesman was Plotinus (A.D. 204-270), an Egyptian Greek. Plotinus fully developed the mystical aspects of Platonism, very nearly turning that philosophy into a religion. He described the universe as a hierarchy, beginning with a supreme and unknowable God called *The One*. The One "emanates" a knowable God called *Intelligence*, which rules over Plato's realm of the Forms. From Intelligence serially emanate more divine creatures until we reach humans, whose divine souls are imprisoned in degrading, material bodies. The physical world is an imperfect, impure copy of the divine realm.

Plotinus' concern was to turn his followers eyes away from the corrupting temptations of the flesh and toward the spiritual world of truth, goodness, and beauty in the realm of the Forms. In his *Enneads* Plotinus wrote: "Let us rise to [the] model . . . from which [the physical] world derives. . . . Over [it] presides pure Intelligence and incredible wisdom. . . . Everything there is eternal and immutable . . . [and] in a state of bliss." The last phrase makes the change from Platonic philosophy to the ecstatic vision of the religious and points toward the most successful happiness philosophy, which was a religion.

### Early Christian Philosophy

The happiness philosophies gained the adherence of various Greek and Roman intellectuals, but as the Roman Empire began to disintegrate, more and more people needed something stable to believe in. The old Olympian gods were no longer plausible, and in the later Empire many religions of Eastern origin attracted Roman converts. These faiths were usually centered around some religious mystery and were called *mystery religions.* There were several strong ones. *Mithraism,* for example, based on the death and rebirth of Mithras, was a complex religion with at least one temple as far away from its Persian birthplace as Roman London. It almost became the official religion of Rome. The long-run victor among these mystery religions, however, was based on the death and rebirth of an obscure Jewish teacher named Jesus. It was known as Christianity and gained many converts, including emperors. It became the Roman state religion in the fourth century A.D.

An important problem for Christian believers was how to deal with classical philosophy. Should it be condemned as pagan and necessarily heretical as St. Jerome (345-420) contended, or should Christians accept those elements of philosophy compatible with faith as St. Ambrose (340-430) argued? The latter position emerged victorious, and its greatest representative, one of the two greatest teachers of Catholic philosophy, was St. Augustine (354-430). Augustine is the last classic philosopher and the first Christian one, combining Stoicism, Neoplatonism, and Christian faith.

Stoicism, with its emphasis on divine wisdom and human submission, has elements that can be assimilated easily to Christian belief. Even more compatible, however, was Neoplatonism, which was a philosophy evolving into a religion. In the fourth century, Christianity was a simple faith, lacking a supporting philosophy. Augustine integrated faith and philosophy into a powerful Christian world view that would dominate all aspects of medieval thought until the thirteenth century. The following passage illustrates Augustine's Christian Platonism:

> God, of course, belongs to the realm of intelligible things, and so do these mathematical symbols, though there is a great difference. Similarly the earth and light are visible, but the earth cannot be seen unless it is illumined. Anyone who knows the mathematical symbols admits that they are true without the shadow of a doubt. But he must also believe that they cannot be known unless they are illumined by something else corresponding to the sun. About this corporeal light notice three things. It exists. It shines. It illumines. So in knowing the hidden God you must observe three things. He exists. He is known. He causes other things to be known.
>
> St. Augustine, *Soliloquies I*

Augustine assimilated a sophisticated if mystical philosophy and created basic Christian theology. In the next chapter we will look at Augustine's distinctively Christian medieval ideas, for with Augustine we have reached the beginning of the Middle Ages.

## CONCLUSION

> I shudder when I think of the catastrophes of our time. For twenty years and more the blood of the Romans has been shed daily . . . the great cities have been sacked and pillaged and plundered by Goths . . . Huns and Vandals. . . . The Roman world is falling; yet we hold up our heads instead of bowing them.
>
> St. Jerome, "The Roman World is Falling"

The fall of Rome is dated officially as A.D. 476. All forms of culture, art, philosophy, and science went into a sharp decline around A.D. 300, a decline that began, however, about 200 B.C. There was a brief renaissance under Charlemagne in the middle of the ninth century, but European civilization did not really revive until the twelfth century. At this point, therefore, we will pause to consider the achievement of the classical world.

**Conceptual Summary:**
**The Essential Tensions of Western Thought**

As the Roman Epicurean Lucretius said, the Greeks have been before us. In this chapter we have briefly inventoried some of the ideas that the classical world created and bequeathed to their intellectual successors. There are few modern concepts that cannot be traced to Greek roots. The ideas of such men as Plato, Aristotle, Democritus, and Thales are an integral part of the texture of modern intellectual life.

There are two important intellectual tensions that emerge from the Greek period and are intertwined throughout the subsequent centuries. The first tension is that between rationalism and empiricism. The rationalist, from Parmenides on, denies that true knowledge comes from perception and so turns inward to reason and innate ideas in the search for truth. The empiricist, from Empedocles on, looks outward, believing that a way of true seeming can be built on the material of sensory experience. The rationalist fears the illusions of sense; the empiricist fears the delusions of reason.

The other tension is between being and becoming. The advocate of being, often a rationalist, believes in eternal and transcendent truths and values, which exist apart from us and which we must seek. The advocate of becoming, often an empiricist, denies the existence of eternal truth and immutable being, finding in the changing flux of experience the only truth—that everything is constantly changing. The interplay and struggle between these two intellectual tensions has motivated intellectual life ever since the Classical Age.

## SUGGESTED READINGS

An excellent short work that spans the entire classical period is Giorgio de Santillana's *The Origins of Scientific Thought* (Mentor Books, 1961). On the pre-Socratics, see Drew Hyland, *The Origins of Philosophy* (Putnam, 1973). Plato and Aristotle have received many valuable studies; for these and for works on the post-Aristotelian period, consult the bibliography.

## REFERENCES

Copleston, F. *A history of philosophy,* V. 1., Greece and Rome. Garden City, N.Y.: Doubleday, 1962.

Cornford, F. *The Republic of Plato.* Oxford: Oxford University Press, 1945.

Freeman, K. *Ancilla to the presocratic philosophers.* Cambridge, Mass.: Harvard University Press, 1971.

Popper, K. Back to the presocratics. In *Conjectures and Refutations.* New York: Harper & Row Pub., 1965.

Sprague, R. *The older Sophists.* Columbia, S.C.: University of South Carolina Press, 1972.

# 3

# Spirituality and Individualism
## The Middle Ages and the Renaissance

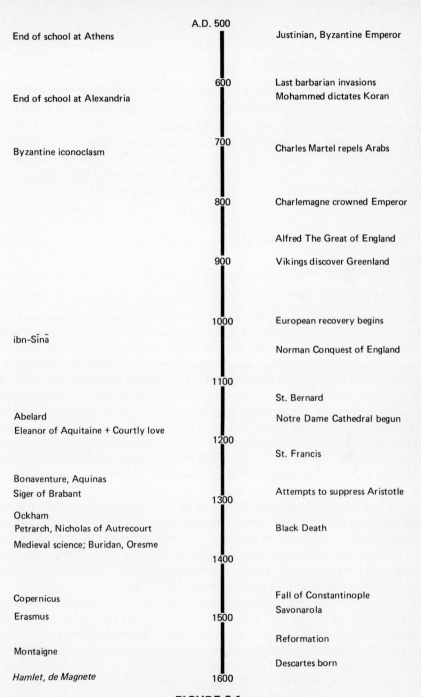

**FIGURE 3-1.**
Chronology 500–1600.

The Middle Ages was the crucible in which our modern world was formed; the Renaissance was the first self-consciously modern period. The medieval (Middle Ages) period saw the beginning of constitutional democracy, romantic love, individualism, and experimental science. During the Renaissance learning and scholarship left the confines of the Church to become again the property of lay society concerned with humanity's nature and needs rather than God's.

## THE MIDDLE AGES (A.D. 476-1453)

### The Medieval Context

#### The Nature of Society

Although tradition sets the date of the end of Classical civilization at A.D. 476, something like the medieval way of life began during the Roman Empire in the late third and fourth centuries. Because of an economic decline, small farmers became legally tied to the land, a state which evolved into serfdom. As the control of Rome over her provinces loosened, local autonomous leadership grew which led to feudalism. The breakdown of the Roman world was evident as barter economy began to replace the money economy of the Empire, communication broke down, the Imperial army became more and more a mercenary army of barbarians rather than a voluntary army of Roman citizens, populations declined, and the Eastern Empire with its own Emperor and capital at Constantinople leached treasure and resources from the European, or Western Empire to preserve its own superior way of life.

These crises were compounded by an extraordinary movement of barbarians into the empire. Early settlers had often come peacefully into the Empire, but later invasions were bloody and destructive. Rome itself was sacked in Augustine's time; the Emperor Romulus Augustulus who fell in 476 was himself only a barbarian usurper. The movement of northern peoples from Goths to Vikings, which finally tore the Empire asunder, continued to almost A.D. 1000.

This extended period of transition from classic to medieval times, from before 475 to about 1000, is sometimes still called the Dark Ages, but is better called the Early Middle Ages. Although creative thinking declined, there were periods of intellectual development, most notably the Carolingian Renaissance under Charlemagne (768-814, not to be confused with the Italian Renaissance of the fifteenth and sixteenth centuries). New political forms were developed to replace the husk of Imperial government. It was even a period of technological advance. For example, the heavy plow and the modern horse-harness were invented, opening new lands for farming and improving the yield from old. Although this period saw economic, demographic, and intellectual decline, a new, creative society was arising from the Imperial ashes.

The economy and population began to rise again around 1000, ushering in the High Middle Ages, which lasted to about 1300. This was an enormously creative period in Western civilization. Many Greek works, especially those of Aristotle, were recovered, and philosophical thinking resumed in the twelfth century renaissance. The magnificent Romanesque and Gothic churches were constructed. Modern political forms, especially in England, were developing, as was the concept of romantic love and the interest in individuality.

This fertile European culture ended between 1277 and 1350 in the rise of nationalism and in the wake of wars between the embryonic nations, the increasing dogmatism of the Church, and the Black Death of 1348-1350, which killed no less than one-third of the population of Western Europe. Friedrich Heer calls this the "closed" Europe of the Late Middle Ages, in contrast to the intellectually and politically "open" Europe of the previous period. The Late Middle Ages lasted into the Renaissance Period which began in Italy as early as 1300, but which took about 200 years to reach the north of Europe.

It is against this background of loss and recovery, decline and innovation that we must understand medieval thinking.

### The Shape of Medieval Mentality

**Reason:**    What, then, do you want to know?
**Augustine:**    The very things for which I have prayed.
**R:**    Summarize them concisely.
**A:**    I want to know God and the soul.
**R:**    Nothing else?
**A:**    Nothing else at all.

St. Augustine, *Soliloquia*

Augustine (354-430) was the last great classical philosopher; he was also the first great Christian philosopher. His attitudes dominated medieval philosophy until about 1300. Philosophy was carried out in a context of Christian faith. Augustine wanted only to know God and the soul, and used faith to justify belief. Medieval humanity turned away from the observable world, full of pain and turmoil, and concentrated on heaven and the soul, both of which could be known through introspection.

The soul could be known by introspection by seeking within oneself that divine illumination that comes from God, so that to know the soul was to know Him. And just as the soul was the representative of God within the self, so spiritual truth could be found in all things. In Neoplatonic fashion nothing—no word, no animal, no event—was as it seemed, but had to symbolize something supernatural and beyond human experience. Just as Plato found in every class noun the symbol of a Form, medieval man found symbols in every aspect of life. The medieval thinker did not want to understand the mind or the world in its own terms, but only as clues to the invisible reality of God in heaven.

Science and philosophy as we (or the Greeks) know them are impossible in such a context. The medieval thinker did not freely use his mind to seek the truth whatever it might be, but rather to justify what he knew to be true from faith. Few found this restriction onerous, for they did not seek to overthrow faith but to support it. Most medievals who found themselves in heresy simply concluded they had erred, and rethought their views. However, as the Middle Ages progressed—especially after 1277—the boundaries of dogma became more rigid, the hand of censorship more oppressive, and the spirit of many thinkers rebelled, helping to dissolve the medieval synthesis.

The Middle Ages sought a grand synthesis of all knowledge. Since all knowledge was of God, the soul, and the spiritual world, it was believed that knowledge, tradition, and faith could be synthesized into a single grand authoritative picture of the universe. The summit of such efforts was the *Summa Theologica* of St. Thomas Aquinas (1225-1274). This belief, too, broke down after 1300.

It should be pointed out that not all Christian thinkers in whatever time have accepted the rule of reason in seeking Godly truth. Augustine had to struggle against ideas of those like Tertullian (160-230) who rejected the classical philosophers. St. Bernard (1091-1153) decried excessive "curiosity" about Christian beliefs. Savonarola (1452-1498) burnt heretical books. All these people emphasized the mystical aspects of Neoplatonism, the immediate inward confrontation of man with God, either through contemplation or reading His word. They rejected reason as at best unnecessary, at worst heretical. Fundamentalism and mysticism were important elements not only in Christianity, but in medieval Islam and Judaism, where they triumphed and extinguished philosophical thought. In the Christian West, the thinkers of the Later Middle Ages finally drew a line between the ideas of faith and the ideas of reason and observation. This separation of science and philosophy from theology, while destroying the medieval synthesis, opened the way to autonomous thought.

Neoplatonism colored every aspect of medieval thinking. All things were symbolic of God's invisible world, and visions, prophecies, astrology, and witchcraft were everyday parts of life. The medieval mind also saw hierarchy everywhere. Just as there was a universal hierarchy from God to angels to man to animals to matter, so was the Church a hierarchy from Pope to archbishop to bishop to priest to laymen, as was society, from king to vassal and sub-vassal to serf. In psychological theory, Aristotle's picture of the soul was made hierarchical, from active mind to passive mind to common sense to special sense. So all the world was doubly structured—every thing, every event was symbolic of the invisible world and found its exact place in a hierarchically structured universe.

This magical outlook was enhanced by the nature of learning in the Middle Ages. Literacy was the preserve of the Church. To be literate was almost without exception to be a cleric, and the language of learning was Latin. The Church forbade the translation of the Bible into vernacular language, and services were conducted in Latin. The religion of the common man, therefore, was a barely modified paganism. One of the most revolutionary developments of the Later Middle Ages was unauthorized translation of the Bible and the rise of vernacular literature.

Thus, medieval knowledge was priestly knowledge. The monasteries carefully preserved past learning and kept historical chronicles. Many priests became the first governmental bureaucrats, bringing order, reason, and literacy to the rule of near barbarians. The seeds of the future, however, lay in the schools attached to the cathedrals of the twelfth century renaissance. These became the first universities, with regularly scheduled courses, lectures by masters, textbooks, and even student riots. It was also there that the most progressive thinkers, such as Peter Abelard, were to be found. It was from them that the rule of reason produced heresies to be suppressed by the Church, and it was from them that learning began to spread beyond the close confines of the Church. One of the most important developments of the Renaissance was the increase in the numbers of literate secular people.

We must not overestimate the oppressiveness of the religious framework of thought, especially in the High Middle Ages, nor underestimate its achievement. It was the crucible of the modern mind. A modern person would be an alien in those times, but modern thought could not have developed without its medieval predecessors. Before discussing medieval achievements, however, we must consider the achievement of peoples outside the circle of Western Christendom: the Jews and Muslims.

### The Contributions of Judaism and Islam

Relations between European Christendom and its two great rival religions were, to say the least, ambiguous. It was against Muslims that the Crusades were directed, while in the Early Middle Ages Islam nearly engulfed Europe. Christendom's relations with the Jews were even more unpleasant. Jews were persecuted with a ferocity rivaling that of the Nazis: they were expelled from England and France; they were forced to live in ghettos and wear distinctive clothing; they were often killed *en masse* by burning down their homes with the inhabitants inside. Yet, without Judaism, Christianity is unthinkable. Jesus was, of course, a Jew, and his teachings reflect the concern of Jewish rabbis of the first century B.C. It was largely because of the gentile St. Paul that Christianity did not remain a Jewish sect.

Both Muslims and the Jews who lived among them made major contributions to the intellectual development of the West. They preserved, and later translated, the works of the ancients, forgotten in Europe. In the Early Middle Ages only the *Timaeus* of Plato and the *Categories* of Aristotle (not their most representative works) were known. By 1200 much of Plato and almost all of Aristotle were available to Christian scholars. The works of Aristotle revolutionized the thinking of the West, substituting Aristotle for Plato as *the* philosopher. Thus both the Jews and Muslims greatly enriched the knowledge of European Christendom by preserving and translating the Greek philosophers. This new knowledge was disseminated to

European Christendom through Spain and Sicily, where, within Muslim culture, Jew and Muslim lived together in peace.

Both Jews and Muslims also made important philosophical contributions of their own, and their influence often rivals Aristotle's. Maimonides, the greatest Judaic philosopher, was treated with the utmost respect by Thomas Aquinas. Islamic thinkers also contributed to mathematics and science as well as philosophy. The two most important Muslims for our purposes were ibn-Sina, whose psychological system we will examine later, and ibn-Rushd, whose purified Aristotelianism provoked an intellectual crisis that marked the end of the High Middle Ages.

We should also note that both Judaic and Islamic philosophy failed to escape the fate so narrowly avoided in Latin Christendom. The conservatives among Jewish and Islamic leaders found the free inquiry of philosophy too dangerous to revealed "truth" to be tolerated. Philosophy and its works were prohibited, so that after the time of ibn-Rushd (died 1198) there was no independent, nontheological philosophy among Jews or Muslims. As we shall see in a later section of this chapter, a similar persecution just failed of its object in fourteenth century Europe. In unified, absolutist Islam, thought control could succeed; in politically diverse Europe it could not.

### Medieval Psychology

He who knows his soul, knows his creator.

                    Proverb of the Muslim Brethren of Purity

### The Early Middle Ages

This proverb could stand as the motto of early and high medieval psychology. Augustine, as we have seen, wanted to know God and the soul. He believed that by turning inward and inspecting the soul one could come to know God, who is present in every soul. Augustine saw a unity of Creator and Creation so that the three mental powers—memory, understanding, and will, mirror the three beings of the Holy Trinity as any three related things were thought to.

Introspective psychology characterized the earliest years of Christian philosophy. A philosopher looked inward to his own soul in order to know God—not to understand himself as a unique human being but only as a vehicle for divine illumination. It was not until the High Middle Ages that true individualism appeared, and then largely in popular culture rather than philosophy.

However, outside of European Christendom an ultimately more fruitful and naturalistic faculty psychology based on Aristotle was developing. This psychology was originally worked out in a Neoplatonic framework within which Aristotle was interpreted, and combined an elaboration of Aristotle's psychology with late Roman and Islamic medicine. Over the next two centuries, as Aristotle became better known in Europe, this naturalistic faculty psychology completely replaced the older, Augustinian Neoplatonic psychology.

In the Neoplatonic scheme of things, humans stand midway between God and matter. As a rational animal, a human being resembles God, while as a physical being a human resembles animals and other purely physical creatures. In this view, when allied with Aristotelian faculty psychology, a human's mind itself reflects this ambiguous position: the five corporeal senses are tied to the animal body, while the active intellect—pure reason—is close to God. A person is a microcosm reflecting the greater Neoplatonic macrocosm.

Various writers elaborated on Aristotle's psychology inserting various *inward wits*, or internal senses, between the rational soul and the corporeal senses. These became the exact transition point between body and soul in the chain of being. Such a scheme appears in Islamic, Judaic, and Christian thought in the Early Middle Ages. Muslims made the special contribution of placing the discussion in a physiological context. Islamic medicine carried on the classical medical tradition, and Muslim doctors looked for brain structures that hosted the various aspects of mind discussed by philosophers. The most complete statement of the Aristotelian medical view was made by Abū Ali al-Husain ibn-Sina (980-1037), known in Europe as Avicenna, who was both a doctor and a philosopher and whose works were influential in constructing high medieval philosophy and psychology.

Different lists of mental faculties had been drawn up before ibn-Sina. The five corporeal senses and intellect were not considered mental faculties, a status reserved for the *interior senses.* Aristotle had proposed three faculties—common sense, imagination, and memory—although the lines between them were not sharply drawn. Later writers proposed three to five faculties, but ibn-Sina produced a list of seven faculties that became the norm. This list presented a Neoplatonic hierarchy from the faculty closest to the senses (and the body) to the faculty closest to divine intellect, and is outlined in Figure 3-2.

Beginning with the parts of the mind closest to the body, ibn-Sina discusses the *vegetative soul*, common to plants, humans, and animals (which he treats as did Aristotle), saying that it is responsible for the reproduction, growth, and nourishment of all living things.

Next comes the *sensitive soul*, common to men and animals. At its lowest level it comprises the five external or *corporeal senses* (which again follows Aristotle). The second level of the sensitive soul comprises the *internal senses,* or mental faculties, which are at the border between man's animal and angelic natures. They, too, are hierarchically arranged. First comes *common sense* which, as in Aristotle, receives, unites, and makes conscious the various qualities of external objects perceived by the senses. These perceived qualities are retained in the mind by the second internal sense, *retentive imagination*, for further consideration or later recall. The third and fourth internal senses are the *compositive animal imagination* and the *compositive human imagination,* which are responsible for active, creative use of mental images, for they relate together (compose) the images retained by the retentive imagination into such imaginary objects as unicorns. In animals this process is simply associative, while in man it may be creative, hence the distinction of two faculties. The fifth internal sense was *estimation,* a kind of natural instinct for making judgments about the "intentions" of external objects. The dog avoids the stick because it has learned the stick's punishing "intentions."

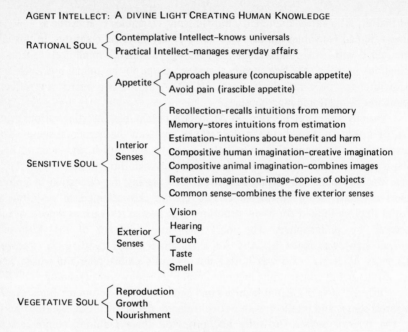

AGENT INTELLECT: A DIVINE LIGHT CREATING HUMAN KNOWLEDGE

RATIONAL SOUL
- Contemplative Intellect–knows universals
- Practical Intellect–manages everyday affairs

SENSITIVE SOUL
- Appetite
  - Approach pleasure (concupiscable appetite)
  - Avoid pain (irascible appetite)
- Interior Senses
  - Recollection–recalls intuitions from memory
  - Memory–stores intuitions from estimation
  - Estimation–intuitions about benefit and harm
  - Compositive human imagination–creative imagination
  - Compositive animal imagination–combines images
  - Retentive imagination–image-copies of objects
  - Common sense–combines the five exterior senses
- Exterior Senses
  - Vision
  - Hearing
  - Touch
  - Taste
  - Smell

VEGETATIVE SOUL
- Reproduction
- Growth
- Nourishment

**FIGURE 3-2.**
Ibn-Sina's faculty psychology.

The wolf seeks the sheep for it knows the sheep is edible. This power, similar to the simple conditioning of modern psychologists, "estimates" the value or harm of objects in the animal's world.

The highest internal senses are memory and recollection. Memory stores the intuitions of estimation. These intuitions are not sensible attributes of the object, but rather simple ideas of the object's essence. Recollection is the ability to recall these intuitions at a later time. The material stored by memory and recalled by recollection are thus not copies of objects, for this function is performed by the retentive and compositive imaginations. Instead, the material is a set of simple but abstract ideas, or general conclusions, derived from experience. They are not, however, true universals, for only the human mind has the power to form universals.

Ibn-Sina was a physician, and he tried to combine his explication of Aristotle's philosophical psychology with the traditional, though erroneous, Roman medical tradition stemming from Galen. By speculation, without resort to forbidden dissections, ibn-Sina located the internal senses in different parts of the brain. His proposals became standard medical teaching until in the sixteenth century Vesalius again practiced dissection and proved ibn-Sina's ideas wrong.

Figure 3-3 shows a simple figure of a head from a medical textbook of about 1420, which shows the location of four internal senses. Although the figure combines some of ibn-Sina's senses (as he himself often did), it follows his teaching. Four "cells" of the brain are shown. The first one contains common sense, which

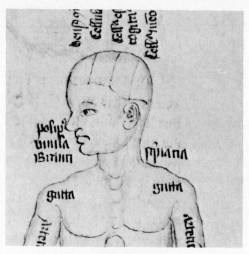

**FIGURE 3-3.**
Head of a man from a medical textbook of about 1420
showing the locations of four internal senses. From front to back
the cells contain *common sense, imagination, estimation,* and *memory.*
(From Clarke & Dewhurst, 1972.)

here includes retentive imagination. The second cell contains human and animal compositive imagination. The third cell holds estimation. The fourth and rearmost cell contains memory, including recollection.

The final aspect of the sensitive soul treated by ibn-Sina is motivation. As Aristotle had pointed out, what sets animals apart from plants is that they move themselves. Ibn-Sina, following Aristotle, calls this motive power *appetite,* and it has two forms. Animals sense pain or danger, and flee; this may be called avoidance. On the other hand, animals sense or anticipate pleasure, and move toward it; this is approach.

The mental powers and senses so far considered by ibn-Sina are tied to the body and brain and are held in common by man and animal. However, man surpasses the animals in the ability to form universal concepts. This is the unique power of the human soul that alone transcends the material body and brain. Ibn-Sina distinguished two faculties within the human soul: *practical intellect* and the *contemplative intellect.* The lower practical intellect concerns itself with everyday affairs. It regulates the body, maintains good behavior, and protects the contemplative intellect so it may fulfill itself.

The fulfillment of the contemplative intellect is knowledge of universals abstracted from particular sense experiences. In this ibn-Sina follows Aristotle, as he does in further distinguishing active and passive intellect. The contemplative intellect of the human soul is entirely passive (Aristotle's *passive mind*) and has the potential for knowledge, which is actualized by the active intellect, or *agent intellect.* However, ibn-Sina sets the agent intellect outside the human soul, as

Aristotle had not done. It is a kind of angelic intellect next up in the Neoplatonic hierarchy which illuminates the contemplative mind and leads it to knowledge of the Forms, as in Plato and Augustine. As we shall see, the doctrine of a separate agent intellect is un-Christian and its entry into Europe via the Muslim philosopher ibn-Rushd precipitated the intellectual part of the crisis that ended the High Middle Ages.

### The High Middle Ages

The High Middle Ages saw an intellectual renaissance as the works of Aristotle and his Muslim commentators, such as ibn-Sina, and other Greek works poured into the West through Spain, Sicily, and Constantinople. Aristotle's philosophy was naturalistic and as such was restricted by the reigning, mystical Augustinian establishment of the time. Aristotle brought a fresh, unreligious approach to knowledge and humanity, an approach that was reconciled with Christian faith only with difficulty. Thomas Aquinas, who synthesized faith in God's word and reason as found in Aristotle's philosophy, only narrowly escaped the charge of heresy. This union of Christ and Aristotle, impressive though it was, was relatively sterile. The future belonged to those who, like William of Ockham, divorced faith from reason and pursued only the latter. We will therefore only briefly summarize the psychology of the High Middle Ages, for it rarely surpassed Aristotle or ibn-Sina and was itself surpassed by fourteenth century science.

In the twelfth and thirteenth centuries there was a great increase in education, and philosophers abounded. We will limit our consideration to the twin peaks of high medieval Christian philosophy: St. Bonaventure (1221-1274) and St. Thomas Aquinas (1225-1275). They stand for the two great medieval approaches to knowledge, humanity, and God: the Platonic-Augustinian mystical way, and the Aristotelian-Thomistic way of natural reason.

**St. Bonaventure.**    St. Bonaventure was the great voice of the older conservative Platonic-Augustinian philosophy that resisted the introduction of Aristotle into Christian thinking. He took a sharply dualist, Platonic view of soul and body, as did Augustine. Although the soul is the form of body, as Aristotle maintained, to Bonaventure it was much more. The soul and body are two completely distinct substances, and the immortal soul merely uses the mortal body during its earthly existence. The essence of a person is the soul.

The soul is capable of two sorts of knowledge. First, as united with the body, it can have knowledge of the external world. Here Bonaventure follows the empiricism of Aristotle by denying innate ideas and arguing that we build up universal concepts by abstraction from experienced individual objects. However, like Aquinas, Bonaventure asserts that abstraction alone is insufficient and must be joined to the divine illumination from God for there to be any true knowledge.

The second source of knowledge belongs to the soul alone and is knowledge of the spiritual world, including God. The source of this knowledge is introspection, which discovers the image of God illuminated in the soul, and so knows Him through interior reflection without recourse to sensation. The idea of God is thus innate. We should emphasize again that this Augustinian introspection is meant only indirectly to yield knowledge of self or of human nature; its goal is a vision of God, not humanity.

Bonaventure distinguishes four mental faculties: the vegetative faculties, the sensitive faculties, the intellect, and the will. However, Bonaventure speaks of other "aspects" of the soul which he refuses to call faculties, but whose inclusion makes his system resemble ibn-Sina's. For example, he distinguishes a "higher" aspect and a "lower" aspect to the intellect which resembles ibn-Sina's contemplative and practical intellects.

Bonaventure's Platonism was destined to be overtaken and overshadowed by Aquinas' Aristotelianism, which became the official doctrine of the Catholic Church. However, it lives on in Protestantism which stresses the word of God over reason, and individual communion between each person and God over ritual.

**St. Thomas Aquinas.**    As Aristotle became known in the West, many thinkers struggled to reconcile his scientific naturalism with the teachings of the Church. The greatest and most successful of these was St. Thomas Aquinas. He saw Aristotle as The Philosopher, the thinker who showed the limits of human reason, demonstrating all that could be known without the word of God. Aquinas adopted Aristotle's system and showed that it was not incompatible with Christianity. In doing so he stood Aristotle on his head. Where Aristotle stays close to nature and is silent on God, Aquinas reorients everything to depend on and reveal Him.

To reconcile philosophy and theology, Aquinas distinguished sharply between them, limiting a person's reason to knowledge of the world of nature. Aquinas thus accepts Aristotle's empiricism and the consequence that reason can know only the world, not God. God can be known only indirectly, from His work in the world. This is an important moment in the evolution of Western thought. Aquinas is saying that philosophy and religion are separate, that while they are not incompatible, they do not connect. This division finally destroyed the medieval synthesis Aquinas worked so hard to achieve. However, Aquinas' philosophy and theology are, in practice, if not in theory, intertwined; reason and revelation do make contact. But later thinkers pursued his division of reason and faith to its logical conclusion and destroyed theological metaphysics while giving birth to science.

Aquinas sets out to consider all topics, including psychology, philosophically, that is, independent of revelation. In his psychology he closely follows Aristotle, but also gives weight to the opinions of Islamic writers, especially ibn-Sina. He makes no original contribution to Aristotelian psychology, but he refines and extends the classification of mental aspects given by The Philosopher and his Islamic commentators. Figure 3-4 summarizes Aquinas' picture of mind. As can be seen, most of it is similar to ideas of Aristotle and ibn-Sina, and most of the new points are self-explanatory. It will be necessary only to comment on a few unique points.

Aquinas, more than Aristotle or his non-Christian commentators, was concerned with distinguishing persons, who have souls, from animals. This comes out

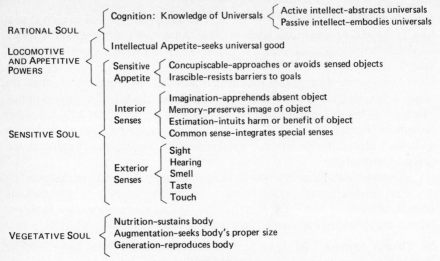

**FIGURE 3-4.**
Aquinas' conception of mind.

most clearly in his discussion of the faculties of estimation and appetite or motivation. Unlike ibn-Sina, Aquinas held that there are two kinds of estimation. First there is *estimation proper,* characteristic of animals, and not under voluntary control: the lamb *must* flee the wolf it sees to be dangerous; the cat *must* pounce on the mouse. The second kind of estimation is under rational control. Aquinas calls it *cogitava,* and it is found only in humans: we flee the wolf, or choose to approach it. One's estimative power is under the control of one's free will, for one chooses and makes judgments instead of simply responding blindly to animal instinct. Just as there are two kinds of estimation, so there are two kinds of motivation or appetite. Sensitive, animal appetite is an unfree, natural inclination to pursue pleasurable objects and avoid harmful ones, and to overcome obstacles to that pursuit. A human being, however, has intellectual appetite, or will, which seeks the general good under the guidance of reason. The animal knows only pleasure or pain; the human knows right and wrong.

Three other changes from ibn-Sina may be noted. First, Aquinas drops compositive imagination as unnecessary additions to retentive imagination and rational thinking. Second, by making *cogitava,* human estimation, a rationally guided faculty concerned with the outer world, the need for ibn-Sina's practical intellect vanishes. Finally, Aquinas makes the mind whole by returning the active intellect to the human soul. Knowledge is an active product of human thinking, not a gift of divine illumination via the agent intellect.

Despite some Neoplatonic remnants, such as the hierarchic organization of faculties, Aquinas' views are in sharp contrast to Bonaventure's. Aquinas rejects the radical dualism of soul and body of the Platonic-Augustinian tradition. The body is not a tomb, prison, or punishment; nor is it a puppet operated by the soul.

A person is a whole, a mind *and* a body. Although the soul is transcendent, its natural place is in a body, which it fulfills and which fulfills it.

Aquinas also adopts a consistent empiricism. The human mind can have direct knowledge only of what was once in the senses, as there are no innate ideas. All thinking requires images. Bonaventure had upheld the Augustinian notion of direct self-knowledge through introspection, which revealed an innate image of God. Aquinas rejects this. All knowledge of the soul or God, and of all things invisible, must be indirect. Direct communion with God or with the essence of ourselves is impossible. We can know God only by examining the world, which is His work; we can know ourselves only by examining our acts, which are our work. Nothing else is possible.

Aquinas is here at a bridge point between the old medieval world view and the modern view, and he places himself in a dilemma. He said that only philosophical knowledge is possible, yet he continued to be a theologian. He acted as if his distinction between philosophy and theology had not been made. His philosophy was *not* an unfettered search for truth, but a Christian science, bound by the limits of belief. On these grounds Bertrand Russell denied that Aquinas was a philosoper.

Perhaps this criticism is true. What is important about Aquinas, however, is that his work was not only the summit of the medieval synthesis, but also a harbinger of the future, when reason and revelation became completely separated. Aquinas brought a fresh naturalism to the traditional Platonic Christian framework, but he accepted that framework, and worked within it. The resulting edifice is a monument to human thought. A monument, however, commemorates the past. The future of science and psychology belonged to more radical men.

### The Late Middle Ages

The summer of the medieval synthesis was in the thirteenth century, the greatest of centuries as later scholars called it. The fourteenth century is usually seen as a period of decline and decay, which in some ways it was. Society began to go through the transition to the modern age. Medieval institutions became irrelevant or baroque, while around them the new world of cities and capitalism was being born. The Black Death of midcentury carried off about a third of the population of Europe, including many scholars. The Papacy was corrupt and worldly, paving the way for the Reformation. Yet in philosophy, especially in the first half of the fourteenth century, it was a creative time, during which modern science was born. At present, we will briefly examine the most influential late medieval thinker, William of Ockham (1290-1349, approximately), whose contribution was to open up for psychological analysis what had previously been reserved to metaphysics.

Medieval philosophers confused psychology and ontology, the study of the nature of being or existence. As did Plato, most medieval thinkers believed that there must be something real corresponding to each mental concept. For Plato they were the Forms; for Aristotle they were real essences; for medievals they were Ideas in the mind of God.

For the Greeks and medievals, the only real knowledge was knowledge of universals; indeed, it was asserted that the rational soul, or intellect, had knowledge *only* of universals, not of particular things. Following Aristotle, they held that the only certain knowledge was what could be deduced from universal propositions. This attitude persisted even in Aquinas. Although he described the process of abstraction as the way to universal knowledge, and although he held that the intellect knows only what is derived from the senses, he still maintained that the abstracted essences were metaphysically true, that they corresponded to holy Ideas.

Ockham changed all this by substituting psychology for metaphysics. He asserted that all knowledge begins with "intuitive cognition," which is direct, infallible acquaintance with some object in the world. The intellect is not restricted to knowing only abstract images; what it knows first is objects and their qualities. Intuitive cognition does not yield mere opinion, as Plato held, but yields knowledge of what is true and false. From such knowledge it may go on to "abstractive cognition" of universals. But these universals exist only as mental concepts, having no existence outside the mind. These abstract concepts may be either true or false; for example, one may form the concept of a unicorn, which does not exist. Abstractive cognition is thus wholly hypothetical. The touchstone of reality and truth is intuitive cognition. Ockham discarded the metaphysical problem that bedeviled Plato, Aristotle, and the medievals, namely how can each individual participate in a transcendent essence or form, and substituted the psychological question, how do we form universal concepts given that we have certain knowledge only of individuals? His answer was that the mind notes similarities among objects, and, based on the similarities, it classifies objects. Thus, universals are logical terms that apply to some objects and not others and which indicate relations among objects. For Ockham, universals are a psychological problem rather than an ontological one.

Up to this point, Ockham was the truest empiricist of the Middle Ages, for he made the test of knowledge become that which is revealed by intuitive cognition, or observation. However, Ockham was a Franciscan, and there is an important Augustinian element in his view of the soul. Like Bonaventure and unlike Aquinas, Ockham held that we have direct, introspective, intuitive knowledge of the soul, rather than mere reflection on our acts. The soul can know itself directly, not just indirectly.

Unlike Aquinas and other faculty psychologists, Ockham denied the distinction of soul from its faculties. According to Ockham, the soul does not *have* the faculty of Will or Intellect. Rather, what we call a faculty is simply a name for a certain kind of mental act. *Will* describes the soul in the act of willing; *Intellect* describes the soul in the act of thinking. Ockham always sought to simplify accounts as much as possible, ridding them of nonessentials, which is why we speak of "Ockham's razor," although the idea is Aristotle's. Ockham saw faculties as unnecessary reifications of mental acts into mental entities apart from the mind.

Habit was crucial to Ockham's view of the mind. For him, concepts were learned habits, ideas derived from experience. Since he rejected the world of universals, whether Platonic Forms or divine Ideas, the status of universals was reduced to habit. These habits are what make possible a person's thinking independent of actually sensed objects. We cannot think about the Forms, for they do not exist. We think instead about derived, habitual concepts; without them we would be animals, reduced to simple responses to external stimuli. Ockham was the first thinker, but not the last, to put such a burden on habit; but he was not a behaviorist, for to him habits were mental concepts, not bodily responses. Ockham drew a radical distinction, far more radical than Aquinas', between faith and reason. Ockham pointed out that there is no ground in experience, or intuitive cognition, for believing we have an immaterial, immortal soul. As far as reason, or philosophy, goes the mind may be a perishable entity dependent on the body. It was only from faith that knowledge of the immortal soul comes. This separation of faith and reason greatly weakened theology and metaphysics, but helped bring science into being.

Ockham's views were revolutionary, widely taught despite attempts by the Church to silence them, and influential. Ockham was not as skeptically and radically empiricist as the later British empiricists, especially David Hume, but he is the origin of modern empiricist philosophy.

### Romance and Individualism:
### Psychological Aspects of Popular Culture

The Middle Ages saw many social developments that came to define the modern world: the primacy of law over personal rule; capitalism; the growth of cities. Two closely related developments command our attention, for they express important popular psychological attitudes that provide the setting for later theories about human motivation and society. These movements are particularly important to our understanding of Freud. When one speaks of "popular culture" in the medieval context, of course, nothing like the modern meaning is intended, for few people were literate outside Church. However, there was a popular vernacular literature and a common set of ideas evident in both educated clerical society and lay society that can be considered a kind of limited "popular culture."

#### Women, Sex, and Romantic Love

Medieval Christianity did not invent misogyny. Europe's antifeminist attitudes come from the Romans and even from Aristotle, who considered female infants as suffering from a sort of birth defect. Christianity, however, intensified the Classic hatred of women, linking women to sexuality as the foundation of sin and temptation, and instituting a schizophrenic attitude toward good women (virgins) and ordinary women, who were at best mothers. As St. Thomas Aquinas said, "Woman was created to be man's helpmate, but her unique role is in conception . . . since for other purposes men would be better assisted by other men." (Heer, 1962).

In early Christianity women were full participants in religion; they preached and often lived in chaste, mixed-sex monastaries. The Early Middle Ages were full of strong female figures as capable and powerful as any man. However, as

Christianity absorbed classical culture, it absorbed Roman misogyny and Platonic aversion to sensual pleasure. Marriage was forbidden to priests; women were forbidden to preach or even approach holy relics. They were reduced to second class status, as, at best, helpers of men, as the quotation from Aquinas shows.

One especially strong source of Christian misogyny was St. Jerome (340-420), a Neoplatonist who linked womanhood to the temptation of the flesh. Medieval Christianity looked upon sex in all its manifestations as the worst sin, whether inside marriage or out; compared to the purity of Christ's body, all sexual inter-course was seen as unclean. By the fourteenth century sexual intercourse was forbidden by the Church on 220 days of the year. As St. Jerome said ". . . woman is the gate of the devil, the path of wickedness, the sting of the serpent. In a word a perilous object . . ." (Erickson, 1976). Thus the onus of sexual guilt fell much more heavily on women than on men. Even pregnant women were viewed with distaste. A woman who had given birth bore the stigma of the "filth of sin," for a child is the product of sex. She could not return to church for thirty-three days following the birth of a son, or for sixty-six days following the birth of a daughter. Should a pregnant woman, or a woman who had recently given birth, die (as was common), she could not be buried in consecrated ground and was thought to be denied entrance to heaven.

At the same time, virginity was exalted; the immaculate Virgin Mary was contrasted with Eve the temptress. As the oppression of women grew, the cult of the Virgin spread throughout the Middle Ages until well into modern times, as is evident from the number of churches and schools named "Notre Dame." This created a schizophrenic attitude toward (and within) women. Women at their best were seen as holy vessels of God, yet most women were cesspools of corruption. (Menstrual blood, for example, was thought to wilt crops.)

These ideas did not die out as the Renaissance approached. Boccaccio, a great early Renaissance writer, called woman "an imperfect animal, obsessed with a thousand revolting and abominable passions." (Erickson, 1976).

Most Medieval women lived lives of quiet desperation, but there were two important responses to their oppression. Many women became actively involved in heretical movements. Albigensianism, for example, which was more a rival religion than a heresy, put many women in positions of power and influence.

The other response was more subtle, more influential, and tied to wider developments in Christendom. It was the invention of romantic love. Medieval people certainly were not unaware of sex. It was the major topic of many folk tales, bawdy stories, and *fablioux*. It was also the main topic of the goliards, student poets and singers of the High Middle Ages. The most famous collection of their songs is the *Carmina Burana,* which often presents a blasphemous glorification of the pagan goddess of love, Venus. She is described in terms such as "Rose of the World" that usually referred to the Virgin Mary. (The rose, incidently, was widely used as a symbol of both the vagina and the Virgin.) Romantic love was to have tremendous popular influence down the ages; today's popular love songs are echoes of the twelfth century troubadors. Love is thought to form the basis of all enduring male-female relations. It is thus an important element in popular consciousness and psychology. Theories of motivation must reckon with the romantic love which we think is natural, but which was invented in the Middle Ages.

Ultimately, romantic love undermined the corporate nature of medieval society, for it made the basis of relationships personal feeling rather than appointed status. Gottfried von Strasbourg, in his *Tristan and Isolde,* one of the most enduring romantic love stories, wrote about the lovers' union this way: "Man was there with Woman, Woman there with Man. What else should they be needing?" Gottfried dispenses with Church, State, and society in favor of the romantic, spiritual, and carnal union of two individuals.

### The Growth of Individuality

Gottfried von Strasbourg's statement in a popular thirteenth century poem stands in total contrast to the rest of medieval society and philosophy. There was no conception of the individual in most of the Middle Ages. The concept was invented during the Middle Ages, but did not become deeply ingrained in thought until the Renaissance. This is not to say that there were no individuals in the Middle Ages, for it was full of strong and distinctive men and women. What is true is that there was no *conception* of the individual as an important object of concern or study. This lack is part of the Neoplatonic *Zeitgeist* that dictated that the human intellect knows only universals, not individuals. The rational mind of each person thus knows another only as an essence—humanness—not as an individual defined by the characteristics that make each person unique. A person's status as Emperor, Pope, King, or serf was far more important than status as an individual human being distinct from all others.

Medieval philosophical psychology, even Ockham's, expresses this attitude. The philosopher-psychologist was interested in *the* sensitive soul, *the* will, *the* imagination, *the* intellect; medieval theorists had no interest in, and seem to have been unaware of, individual differences in psychological makeup. This Platonic attitude has a long and durable history; it is not until the nineteenth century that we find a systematic interest in individual differences. The founder of psychology, Wundt, was himself interested only in *the* human mind. The value of studying individual differences is still debated.

Thus, we cannot look for the birth of a conception of individualism in academic philosophy or theology, but must look rather in popular culture and religion, as our study of courtly love shows. The concept of the individual blossoms forth in many areas during the High Middle Ages: biographies and autobiographies are written; portraits reflect the individual, not merely the person's status; close friendship is encouraged; and literature is increasingly concerned with individual thoughts and feelings rather than with an external narrative of action.

In two areas only does individualism make its way into academic culture—ethics and mystic religion; and even here to movement begins in popular culture. Before the twelfth century, sin was acknowledged, but not felt as something personal. Penance was a mechanical procedure for expiating sin. In the twelfth century, however, people begin to weigh personal intention in judging transgressions. This attitude was formalized in Peter Abelard's (1079-1142) *voluntaristic* ethics, the motto of which was "know yourself." Abelard held, contrary to other thinkers, that sin was entirely a matter of intention, not of action. An act is not right or wrong; what is right or wrong is the intention behind the act. Intentions are, of course, intensely personal, so Abelard's ethics were part of the growth of the individual.

Mysticism begins in popular religion rather than scholastic theology. Mysticism emphasizes the personal relationship of a worshipper to God. The end result of religion, according to the mystic, should be a private, direct communion between God and man; the way to God is contemplation, not ritual. St. Francis of Assissi (1182-1226), the greatest medieval popular preacher, shunned the trappings of the world in favor of communing with God through nature. St. Francis' teaching was thus individualistic and was perceived, correctly, as subversive by the Catholic Church. He narrowly escaped persecution as a heretic instead of canonization as a saint. Poverty was not an ideal that a worldly-rich Church wished to support, while solitary contemplation threatened the complex of rituals the Church claimed brought salvation. Only by absorbing St. Francis and his followers (the Franciscans) could the Church avert the threat of the rising consciousness of the individual inherent in mysticism. Thus the idea of the individual, which would grow to great prominence in the Renaissance, was born in medieval popular culture.

### Analysis and Science:
### The Dissolution of the Medieval Synthesis

By the fourteenth century the factors that would bring about the end of the Middle Ages had coalesced. The growth of cities, capitalism, and the nation-state eroded feudal life, which finally ended in empty playing at chivalry. A severe economic depression began. Population declined. Crime and violence increased. The death blow to the medieval synthesis was probably the Plague of 1348 which carried off about a third of Europe's population, including such scholars as William of Ockham. People became cynical and pessimistic.

The Church was distrusted and divided by schism, while popular preachers emphasized man's sinfulness and helplessness before God. It was a period when the medieval confidence in man's ability to find a total explanation of the world in unified terms was abandoned and the limits of human reason were acknowledged. We will focus on two intellectual movements that undercut the medieval world view: analytic philosophy, which demonstrated the shortcoming of human knowledge; and science, which offered an alternative to the religious conception of the universe.

#### Analysis and the Limits of Reason

Most medieval philosophers believed, as did the Greeks, in the power of human reason to know eternal Truth. They went further in asserting that God's truth and philosophical truth were one and could be synthesized, as in Aquinas' *Summa Theologica*. The idea was rejected by some mystical clergymen, such as

St. Bernard of Clairvaux who denied that philosophy could say anything about God, who is known through faith alone. Despite the mystics, the general trend of thought before 1300, however, favored the Greek view.

We saw this previously in this chapter when we touched on the problem of universals. Most medievals held to some form of *realism,* the belief that universal human concepts correspond to some enduring Form or essence, conceived by medievals as an Idea in the mind of God. This view was held by Plato, Aristotle, and Aquinas, despite their other differences. A few thinkers, called *nominalists,* maintained that universals were mere puffs of air emitted when we speak names (hence nominalism). They have no transcendent reality, being nothing more than verbal behaviors. Nominalism was held by a small minority of thinkers.

It was the analysis of the problem of universal human knowledge that led fourteenth century philosophers to put severe limits on what man may know. The first step was taken by Peter Abelard, the greatest medieval philosopher before the High Middle Ages when Aristotle's works were recovered. Abelard saw the absurdity of the metaphysical-realist approach, predicating one thing of another thing. According to realists, to say "Socrates is a man" is to relate two things, the living individual Socrates and the heavenly Form of man. Abelard saw that *man* should be considered a label, or better a *concept* that we apply to some individual. *Man* is a mental concept applied to Socrates, not a separate thing, or transcendent Form. For Abelard, concepts were purely mental images or labels, and when we discuss universals we are discussing these mental entities, not eternal Forms. Abelard's account of universals was thus logical and psychological rather than metaphysical. This position is best called *conceptualism,* and was a forerunner of Ockham's views discussed earlier.

An interesting point is that Abelard was attacked and ultimately convicted of heresy by St. Bernard, his contemporary, for excessive curiosity about God. Abelard thought that philosophy and theology could be harmonized, while St. Bernard saw them as necessarily separate. The irony is that the fourteenth century analytic and scientific movements took Bernard's view, not Abelard's, even though Abelard's conceptualism and Ockham's are quite similar. Abelard's innovation lacked influence in its own time, partly because of his condemnation, but primarily because of the acceptance of Aristotle's abstractive realism by later philosophers such as Aquinas.

So, in the High Middle Ages it was thought that human knowledge and Holy Truth were coordinate, that human universals corresponded to the divine Ideas. William of Ockham, whose psychological analysis of universals we have examined, destroyed this self-confidence. He posed a whole new set of questions about the bases of human knowledge. If universals do not reflect the divine ideas, and if they rest upon knowledge of individuals, how do we justify our knowledge and show its truth? Before Ockham's time, knowledge was taken for granted; after his time knowledge had to be justified. Philosophers now had to show how knowledge and opinion can be distinguished without reference to God or Forms. It is a problem that lives today: Jean Piaget, the great Swiss psychologist, for example, takes as his explicit task the description and explanation of knowledge as the result of child development.

Interestingly, it was their belief in God's omnipotence that forced this critical attitude on fourteenth century philosophers. All Christian thinkers must believe that God is omnipotent, that He can do anything that is not self-contradictory. Therefore, if you are looking at a tree, God could destroy the tree, but maintain in you the experience of the nonexistent object. If this is so, Christian thinkers must ask how can we be certain of any perception, of any piece of knowledge?

This problem fostered a thoroughgoing critique of human knowledge by all fourteenth century philosophers. The most interesting of them, one who resembles the eighteenth century British empiricists—was Nicholas of Autrecourt (born 1300), a follower of Ockham. Like Ockham, he did not see psychology as metaphysics, saying that there are only acts of understanding and volition, not separate faculties of Understanding and Will. Like the atomists before him, (he, in fact, proposed an atomistic theory of nature) and the empiricists after him, Nicholas argued that certain knowledge lies in staying as close to appearances as possible. All we can know is what our senses tell us, so knowledge is grounded in experience, and the best knowledge is that which remains closest to experiences. To infer from sense perception to Forms, essences, or divine Ideas, he considered illegitimate.

Nicholas of Autrecourt rejects the possibility of divine intervention to maintain an illusion of perception and bases knowledge on an assumption shared with Ockham: that whatever appears is true. This belief is necessary to any empiricist theory of knowledge, and Ockham held it implicitly. By making it explicit, Nicholas had to ask whether it is justified, as did Hume 300 years later. Nicholas concluded that we cannot be certain of this assumption, only that it is probably true since it seems more likely than the contrary assumption that whatever appears is false. Nicholas did not become a total skeptic, but he came close.

Nicholas and others worked out the complications of Ockham's psychological account of universals by close analysis of the grounds of human knowledge. The search for a justification of man's knowledge of the external world has continued ever since and is a root problem for any cognitive psychology.

Ockham's new approach also had another consequence, perhaps the single most momentous revolution in human thinking since Greek rationalism. By dividing faith and reason, and by limiting human knowledge to this world, excluding it from the next, Ockham destroyed theology, which he denied was a science. No one after Ockham, save the Medieval-Renaissance transition figure, Nicholas of Cusa, again attempted to synthesize divine and human knowledge. Theology became an empty pursuit compared to the study of appearances, of nature; in a word, science.

### The Medieval Foundations of Modern Science

We are not discussing God's miracles; what we have to do is to discuss what is natural in a natural way.

Siger of Brabant (1240-1282)

Science has displaced religion as the centerpiece of the modern world. Scientific knowledge is taken as the model for all knowledge. The beginnings of this trend are apparent in William of Ockham and Nicholas of Autrecourt, who tell us to study appearances rather than the divine mind. Thus began, in the Middle Ages, the scientific revolution that was to completely remake humanity's image of the self and the world.

The watershed date in ending the Middle Ages is 1277. In that year, the Church condemned a school of thinkers at the University of Paris led by Siger of Brabant who went too far in accepting Aristotle's naturalism in place of Christian dogma. Some of the condemned doctrines were held by Thomas Aquinas. The Church was challenged by Aristotelianism, for it was an un-Christian, naturalistic, and complete account of nature that did not depend on God's word. Aquinas struggled to reconcile The Philosopher with Christ, but the Church did not accept his synthesis until it became necessary to the very survival of the Church in the modern age. The Church's first response was to reject Aristotle and restrict his works. It tried to do this in 1210, 1231, and 1272. Despite its attempts, however, thoroughgoing Aristotelians were to be found at the University of Paris, and the Church finally could not tolerate them; they were condemned, and Siger was arrested. (He was murdered by a madman while under detention in Rome.) Naturalist philosophers were regularly attacked afterward. Nicholas of Autrecourt had to recant and burn his own books.

It was in this climate that Siger and others after him, like Ockham, began to separate the domains of faith and reason. Only by asserting that the two were separate, that one did not bear on the other, could naturalism be defended as innocuous to Christianity. It was a move that failed in Islam, where philosophy and science were stamped out after promising starts. Europe, however, with its many nations and kings, was too heterogeneous to succumb to dogmatic repression. Ockham's analysis of knowledge successfully separated Reason and Revelation. But precisely because Revelation was not something known by Reason, minds turned to study the natural world, and religion became less and less important to European intellectuals, until, by the Age of Enlightenment, Revelation was openly rejected and deism or atheism adopted.

The immediate result of Ockham's ideas in the fourteenth century was an increased interest in science. Scientific interests had, in fact, been present before the fourteenth century. We can trace the modern scientific attitude back to Robert Grosseteste (1168-1253) and Roger Bacon (1214-1292), both English Franciscans like William of Ockham. Grosseteste and Bacon both conducted experiments in optics because of their Platonic-Augustinian belief in the primacy of light among the world's elements. Both also stressed the role of mathematics in reaching an understanding of nature. This belief is most important, for mathematization has been the touchstone of science from Galileo through Newton to Einstein. Immanual Kant was to deny psychology scientific status partly because he believed the mind could not be studied mathematically.

Roger Bacon is interesting for several further reasons. He ridiculed those who based ideas on authority rather than experience. In accordance with this belief,

Bacon venerated the vital medieval craft tradition. Even in the early middle ages, important technical advancements were made over the ancient world, and this technological tradition continued. Technology and craft is empirical and practical in orientation, for value is placed on what is seen to work, rather than on what authorities say is true, as in scholastic philosophy. Bacon valued this practical outlook, and based his empiricism on it. Combined with his mathematical emphasis, Bacon pointed the way to the Newtonian future, in which the universe was pictured as a divinely crafted machine, rather than a series of divine emanations. In the eighteenth century the mechanical view of the universe was applied to humanity, to be ultimately embodied in the behaviorist and information processing theories of behavior.

Bacon also practiced alchemy. Although alchemy is often pictured as a naive and rather silly search for the ability to make gold, alchemists were the only systematic experimenters before Galileo. Alchemy was pre-paradigm chemistry; it is to be criticized not for its goals but for its lack of a consistent theoretical structure. The alchemists' fundamental empirical attitude was valuable and scientific.

One attitude Grosseteste and Bacon shared that marks them as distinctly medieval was their desire to harmonize faith and science. Their researches grew from religious belief; their optics, for example, derived from metaphysical-religious beliefs about light. After Ockham, however, medieval scientists began to take the claims of religion less seriously, and to assert the claims of science more forcefully.

This new attitude emerges in Jean Buridan (approximately 1300-1358) and Nicholas Oresme (1320-1382), the greatest cleric-physicists of the fourteenth century. Both of them worked on the problem of motion, and Oresme nearly formulated the law of inertia. In this they challenged the authority of Aristotle and laid the groundwork for Galileo. They also argued that the earth rotated, contrary to the prevailing belief that the earth was motionless and circled by the stars, moon, and planets, which were each pushed by an angel. They pointed out that experience did not support the received view that the earth is stationary at the center of the universe. They believed in the power of mathematics and in the possibility of conceiving of the universe mechanically.

It was to be nearly 200 years before Buridan and Oresme's work would bear fruit. There was a long hiatus during which science did not advance. As medieval society broke down from economic depression, the Black Death and the end of feudalism, there was no room for science, and even Renaissance humanists did not value abstract scientific research. It remained for Galileo to found modern physics. There is also an important paradox in post-Ockham empiricism. Although Ockham argued that all general knowledge was rooted in particular experience, fourteenth century medieval scientists did not apply their physical theories to experimental data. Rather they preferred to argue from everyday experience, from Nicholas of Autrecourt's appearances. They were, in short, *too* empiricist to do good science, for they tried to account for all aspects of the world, an impossible task, as shown in Chapter 1. Galileo took a more Platonic view of experience—he isolated crucial aspects of reality for experimental investigation. He saw, as the fourteenth century empiricists did not, that science is built on a selective and idealized, not a comprehensive, treatment of experience.

Such is the medieval contribution to philosophy, science, and psychology. The medieval world is not one we recognize as our own, for it was deeply religious and fostered a symbolic mentality. The medieval mind was focused on God and universal truth, not on nature and individual experience. This religious-symbolic orientation began to change in the fourteenth century, inaugurating an intellectual crisis that helped bring about the consciously modern world view of the Renaissance. Because of radical thinkers such as Ockham and Nicholas of Autrecourt, and because the feudal system was no longer viable, society and the life of the mind had to reorganize on a new basis, the individualistic capitalistic world with which we are familiar.

## RENAISSANCE AND REFORMATION (1453-1600)

### The Renaissance

What a piece of work is man, how noble in reason,
How infinite in faculty,
In form and moving how express and admirable,
In action how like an angel,
In apprehension how like a god;
The beauty of the world, the paragon of animals.

Shakespeare, *Hamlet,* II,ii,300-303

The idea of the Middle Ages was invented by the Renaissance. Renaissance thinkers divided world history into three ages: the classical period of Greece and Rome, which was viewed as a Golden Age of philosophy and art; a Middle Age of ignorance and superstition, which was the Dark Age; and the third age, their own era. The Renaissance was a self-consciously "modern" period that saw itself breaking sharply with the past. This judgment was reaffirmed by the German historian Jakob Burkhardt, who defined the Renaissance as a special creative period crucial to the formation of contemporary society.

Ever since, historians have disputed Burkhardt's acceptance of the self-evaluation of the Renaissance. Today, continuity with the Middle Ages is stressed and historians speak of a Carolingian renaissance and a twelfth century renaissance. It has become apparent that Western society has been renewing itself since A.D. 1000, if not earlier.

However, when all this is said, there is unquestionably something historically new, but immediately familiar about the Renaissance. One has only to compare a painting by Leonardo da Vinci or Michelangelo with any medieval work to feel the difference. One feels far more at home reading Pico della Mirandola or Michel de Montaigne than Thomas Aquinas or William of Ockham. We understand Shakespeare far more easily than medieval mystery plays. The Renaissance does usher in the modern world.

The date of the Renaissance is hard to pin down. A traditional starting point is 1453, when Constantinople fell and Greek speaking scholars fled to a West that knew only Latin. However, it would be more accurate to date the beginning of the Renaissance to around 1300 in Italy. The first Renaissance man was Francesco Petrarch (1304-1374), most famous today as a poet, but also active in the distinctive Renaissance activities of classical scholarship, education, and history. The Renaissance reached its peak in Italy around 1500, by which time it had spread to Northern Europe. Although the Renaissance is the beginning of modern history, it shares its world view with the Middle Ages, a world view that begins to be weakened by the Reformation and is dissolved by the Scientific Revolution around 1600.

The nature of the Renaissance is most elusive. It contributed nothing to philosophy: there is no first rate philosopher between Ockham (died 1348) and Descartes (born 1596). It is doubtful how much it contributed to science; for which Renaissance thinkers had little use. Its enduring achievements were in art and politics, made by such men as Shakespeare, Leonardo da Vinci, and Machiavelli.

What is most important about the Renaissance is a broad mutation of values, usually called humanism. Humanism is a word much overused in the twentieth century; today everyone from Rogers to Skinner is called a humanist. If everyone is a humanist, however, no one is. It would be better to define humanism in the present context by its secularization of life. In all spheres, thinking became more human-centered and less God-centered, although religion was never abandoned, and in the sixteenth century, the Reformation dominated all else.

This secularization started modestly with the increased reclamation of the classics begun by Petrarch. *Humanism* originally meant the recovery of classical thought and its application to contemporary human problems. We have seen that the recovery of the past began in the twelfth century, but its pace accelerated in the fourteenth, and its outlook changed. The first and most obvious contribution of the humanist efforts was in the recovered works themselves. The whole of Plato became known for the first time, for example. Renaissance scholars also sought to edit the works, to separate text from commentary, to ascribe to each author the correct treatise, and to discover forgeries.

What the Renaissance scholar wanted was to understand the mind of each classical writer in itself, and in its own historical context. This is the first manifestation of the secularization of philosophy and of an important Renaissance attitude which we have not seen since the Sophists, that truth has many perspectives. Medieval philosophers held to one truth, known perfectly by God, that must be sought by humans. Although they used the classics, medieval philosophers did not want to understand Plato or Aristotle as individual thinkers. They wanted to find God's truth in the ancient writings. Accurate texts were, therefore, unimportant, as it did not matter whether the words were those of the original writer or of a later commentator, as long as God's Word could be found.

The Renaissance humanists sought human truth rather than divine truth. They wanted to converse with the ancients (to whom they wrote letters), not rummage through works in search of support for revelation.

Although the humanists believed in God and truth, they believed that truth can be seen in many ways, from many individual perspectives. During the Reformation, the northern humanist Disiderius Erasmus (1466-1536) held to this belief despite the fanaticism of Protestant and Catholic alike. He would commit himself to neither camp, despite his initial sympathy for Luther, and he found himself condemned by both sides.

The shift from God-centeredness to human-centeredness appeared in many spheres of life. The State increasingly resisted the temporal claim of the Pope to a secular power. Higher education became open to lay people, not just to clerics. Even religious movements were occasionally led by the laity; Anabaptism, a radical protestant movement, was started by a German weaver.

What we meet in the Renaissance humanists is a figure we last met in Greece, the Sophist. Like the humanists, the Sophists were practical educators, interested in individual perspectives rather than divine truths. The most important belief of the Sophists was that humanity is the measure of all things. The humanists could not go so far without abandoning Christianity, which none did, but they came close. Shakespeare's expression of man's worth is typical, found in every humanist writer. Petrarch quotes Seneca's ". . . nothing is admirable besides the mind . . . ." Pico della Mirandola (1463-1494) writes "Who is there that does not wonder at man?" Human beings were placed at the center of God's creation, lords over nature, and in intellect like the angels and even like God himself. There is an optimism about a person's potential and a faith in a person's powers that separate the humanists from their medieval predecessors.

One might have thought that in an age which glorified humans there would have been an outpouring of psychological studies, but there was none. Authors wrote to exalt humanity, to establish humans' proper place in nature, but not to study them. Even the most scientifically oriented of all Renaissance philosophers, Sir Francis Bacon, simply modified the faculty psychologies of the middle ages.

Just as there was no advance in psychology in the Renaissance, there was no philosophical progress. Humanists concentrated on human needs, rather than on abstract philosophy. The other strain of Renaissance thought, Platonism, was more sympathetic to the medievals, but likewise failed to create anything new in philosophy. What the Renaissance contributes to Western thought was an attitude, humanism, not a coherent philosophy or psychology.

However, we should note three related harbingers of the post-Renaissance age. Of most relevance to psychology was the idea of physiological mechanism, the tendency to see the body as a machine. We see this clearly in Leonardo da Vinci, an acute observer of human and animal anatomy. The Renaissance was also a time of renewed medical research and dissection. As physiological knowledge grew over the years, the mechanistic attitude increased until mechanism extended naturally to the brain and, hence, to human thinking.

The second forward-looking development is what is called Renaissance *nature philosophy*. These nature philosophers revived the Greek habit of speculation about the universe. They were not scientists, but they were influenced by science, especially by Copernicus, as well as by magical and alchemical traditions. The greatest of them, Giordano Bruno (1548-1600) speculated that there were many solar systems besides our own, and that life might be found on them. These naturalistic speculations took Bruno to the stake. These men are transition figures. They are medieval because they engage in pure speculation, but they point the way to the scientific revolution by their interest in nature rather than in God.

In the works of Sir Francis Bacon (1561-1626), we find the third way the Renaissance foreshadows the modern world—the beginning of English empiricism. Bacon died, characteristically, of pneumonia caught while stuffing a chicken with snow to study the effects of refrigeration. He believed that philosophy should investigate nature in a wholly naturalistic and mechanistic way, eschewing theology and teleology equally. He was the first to deny that Aristotle's final cause was legitimate. He believed that scientific study should be wholly inductive, that one should carefully collect facts unguided by any biasing hypothesis, until one could cautiously draw some simple generalization. Although science was not actually studied this way, as Galileo would show, Bacon was articulating anew the fundamental thesis on which empiricism rests, the primacy of experience over reason. Bacon died for his belief.

### The Reformation

Although the Reformation is outside our purview, we cannot pass the sixteenth century without taking note of it. It officially began in 1517 when Martin Luther nailed his 99 theses to the door of Wittenberg Cathedral and challenged the Catholic hierarchy. There was, however, already religious unrest in the air and other rebels, many socially far more radical than Luther, were active.

The Reformation pitted Augustine against Aquinas. Luther wanted a personal, intensely introspective religion, an Augustinian religion, deemphasizing ritual, priesthood, and hierarchy. The Catholic response was to make Aquinas' philosophy official Catholic dogma to which all believers must adhere.

The Reformation divided Europe into two warring camps and encouraged intolerance. Bloody wars were fought in a futile attempt to extinguish the Protestants, who fought back successfully. Both sides felt that whoever was not wholeheartedly with them must be against them, and the victim was dispassionate thought. Philosophers were caught in the middle and in the seventeenth century, charges of heresy haunted Descartes and Spinoza, and the Reformation outburst of God-centeredness undermined Renaissance humanism.

### The End of the Renaissance

Tomorrow, and tomorrow, and tomorrow
Creeps in this petty pace from day to day,
To the last syllable of recorded time,

And all our yesterdays have lighted fools
The way to dusty death. Out, out, brief candle!
Life's but a walking shadow, a poor player
That struts and frets his hour upon the stage
And then is heard no more. It is a tale
Told by an idiot, full of sound and fury,
Signifying nothing.

Shakespeare, *Macbeth,* V,v,17-28

For all its creativity, the Renaissance was a time of tremendous social disloca-
tion, misery, and anxiety. Lynn White (1974) has written that the Renaissance
was the "most psychically disturbed era in European history." The Hundred Years
War and later the Thirty Year Wars raged, bringing destruction to much of France
and Germany, as mercenary armies alternately fought each other and pillaged the
countryside when they were not paid. The Black Plague that began in 1348 had by
1400 halved the population of Europe. Tremendous famines struck beginning in
the fourteenth century. Syphilis was brought back from America by Columbus and
ravaged Europe. The Church was corrupt, the feudal order crumbling.

Everyday life reflected the anxiety engendered by stress. Europe was obsessed with death. Picnics were held under the rotting corpses of the hanged. The
image of the Grim Reaper was born. Scapegoats were sought; mobs attacked Jews
and witches. At the same time that humanity was being glorified by the humanists,
human mortality and suffering were reaching new lows, and the dark side of human
nature was everywhere in evidence.

The later sixteenth century was a time of doubt and skepticism. Ambiguity
about humanity is found dramatically in William Shakespeare (1564-1616). The
quotation from Hamlet that headed the Renaissance section in the chapter sums up
the optimistic humanist view of humans as noble, infinite, admirable, and godlike.
Yet Hamlet goes on immediately to say, "And yet to me what is this quintessence
of dust? Man delights not me . . . ." The quotation from Macbeth is a powerful
statement of disdain for humankind and life in the face of mortality, a statement of
the absurdity of life that would delight any existentialist. Shakespeare's dramatic
genius sees both the positive side of humans stressed by the humanist and the negative side evident in history.

A more philosophical thinker also felt and articulated the limits of humanity,
Michel de Montaigne (1533-1592). In stark contrast to the earlier humanists,
Montaigne wrote: "Of all creatures man is the most miserable and frail, and there-
withal the proudest and disdainfulest." The humanists made the human the paragon
of animals with a unique and godlike intellect. Montaigne here denies the uniqueness of humans. People are not the lords of creation, they are part of it; they are
not the highest of animals, they are on a par with them. Animals as well as humans
have knowledge. Montaigne decries reason as a weak reed on which to base knowledge, and argues instead for experience. But he then goes on to show how deceptive and untrustworthy are the senses. In short, Montaigne topples humans from the
special place given them by medieval and Renaissance thinkers. This view continued
to grow, culminating in Darwin, Freud, and Skinner.

Montaigne pointed to the future, to a skeptical and naturalistic theory of humanity and the universe. Montaigne was, in fact, denying the world view that held sway in Europe from classical times. Polished and refined in the Middle Ages and Renaissance, it was ultimately to be shattered and replaced by science and an increasingly secular philosophy. We now will summarize the old world view that Montaigne challenged.

## CONCEPTUAL SUMMARY

### The Classical-Medieval-Renaissance Episteme

The World's a book in Folio, printed all
With God's great works in letter Capital:
Each creature is a Page, and each Effect
A fair Character, void of all defect.

du Bartas, *Divine Weeks*

According to the French intellectual historian, Michel Foucault, every age is characterized by an *episteme,* a largely unconscious world view—rather like Kuhn's paradigm—that provides the basis for all forms of knowledge during that period. The Renaissance perfected an episteme implicit in classical culture and developed by the Middle Ages. Fundamental to this episteme was the idea that all things in the Universe are linked in a grand order that we can decipher through resemblance. So, for example, the Renaissance physician thought skull and brain damage could be cured by the administration of walnuts, for the walnut shell resembles the skull and the nut resembles the brain.

As the poet du Bartas writes, the world is like a book, any being is like a word, in that it has signs which indicate its secret meaning to what else it is linked. Nature is to be understood by deciphering these signs, not through experiment but by close observation, seeking out similarities and relationships. Hence, the Medieval-Renaissance scrutiny of the classic writers: just as the world is a book revealing nature's symbolic order, so are books collections of words, signs that should reveal universal order. This order is not the scientific order of natural law, but an order built on sympathies and analogies between things, sympathies and analogies signified by resemblance, as between walnut and brain.

Man occupies the central place in this orderly web of analogies. Annibale Romei's seventeenth century *Courtier's Academy*: "the body of man is no other than a little model of the sensible world, and his soul an image of the world intelligible (Plato's world of the Forms)." The human body is a summary analogy of the physical world, the mind a summary analogy of the invisible world. The human is a microcosm reflecting the natural and supernatural macrocosm. The human is at the exact midpoint of the universe. The human body is worldly flesh and the bodily passions tie humans to the animals. The human's rational soul is angelic, for angels are rational souls without bodies. In between, mediating between rational soul and worldly body are human faculties, such as imagination and common sense. These faculties in the brain are subtle animal spirits, the purest of earthly substances, which link body and soul.

This Neoplatonic conception of humankind was a medieval and Renaissance commonplace. But it stands for a broader and deeper existence which orders the universe—sympathy and resemblance. No individual thing stood outside this natural order; some link, some resemblance could always be found. Such an existence precludes scientific specialization. The order of nature is truly universal, for the laws of resemblance in one domain are the same for all domains; there is only one universal science of order.

This episteme was shattered in the seventeenth century and brushed away in the eighteenth. Montaigne pointed the way: the human is not the center of creation, but one animal among many. So also did Sir Francis Bacon: Nature is to be investigated by experiment and explained mechanistically. Soon Galileo would show that the world is to be understood not by the decipherment of signs, as in language, but by the application of mathematics, which transcends particular observation.

### Historical Trends

We conclude this chapter in 1600. In that year William Gilbert published his *de Magnete (On magnets)*, the first systematic experimental study of any topic. Shortly after 1600 the Scientific Revolution took off under Kepler, Galileo, Newton, and others. They brought to the study of the world a new conception of the world as a great machine, understandable by simple mechanical-mathematical laws. In the nineteenth century the mechanical analogy overthrows the angelic view of human reason and mechanizes psychology.

In philosophy, after the dissolution of the old *episteme*, philosophers attempted to start afresh, to ignore the teaching of the Church and the old philosophers, to seek truth unencumbered by the confusion of the past. But the old duality of rationalism and empiricism, which the Medieval-Renaissance episteme had nearly overcome, reasserted itself. In France, Rene Descartes found the source of truth in his own native reason, and so founded modern rationalism. In England, John Locke found truth in unbiased observation, and so founded modern empiricism. By 1800, both systems ended in nearly identical absurdities and Immanual Kant attempted a synthesis, only partially successful.

These developments and others are the subject of the next two chapters.

## SUGGESTED READINGS

Numerous works on the Middle Ages, Renaissance, and Reformation are available. A recent radical work on the Middle Ages which attempts to make it relevant today is Norman Cantor's *The Meaning of the Middle Ages* (Allyn & Bacon, 1973). The classic, though now dated, work on the Renaissance is Jakob Burkhardt's *The Civilization of the Renaissance in Italy* (original edition, 1862; available in paper from Mentor, 1960). For the Reformation, see Roland Bainton, *The Reformation of the Sixteenth Century* (Beacon, 1956).

## REFERENCES

Clark, E. C. & Dewhurst, K. *An illustrated history of brain function.* Berkeley: University of California Press, 1972.

Erickson, C. *The medieval vision.* New York: Oxford University Press, 1976.

Heer, F. *The medieval world.* New York: Mentor, 1962.

Spencer, T. *Shakespeare and the nature of man.* New York: Collier Books, 1966.

White, L. Death and the Devil. In D. S. Kinsman (Ed.) *The darker vision of the Renaissance.* Berkeley: University of California Press, 1974.

# 4

# The Mechanization of the World Picture, 1600-1700

**THE SCIENTIFIC REVOLUTION**

**REMAKING PHILOSOPHY**

The Continental Rationalist Tradition

The British Empiricist Tradition

**THE SEVENTEENTH CENTURY: SEEDS OF CHANGE**

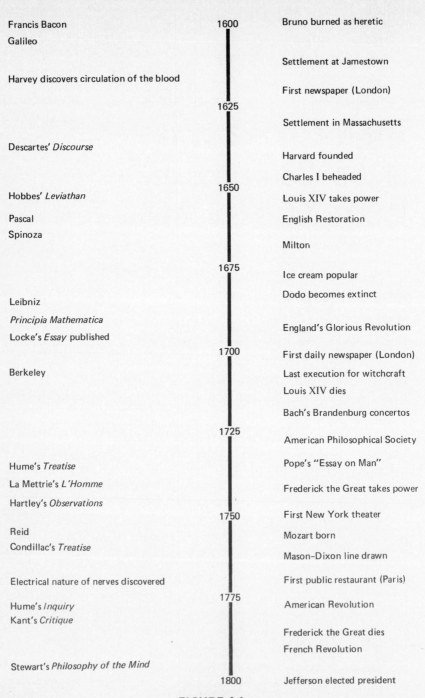

| | 1600 | Bruno burned as heretic |
|---|---|---|
| Francis Bacon | | |
| Galileo | | |
| | | Settlement at Jamestown |
| Harvey discovers circulation of the blood | | |
| | | First newspaper (London) |
| | 1625 | |
| | | Settlement in Massachusetts |
| Descartes' *Discourse* | | |
| | | Harvard founded |
| | | Charles I beheaded |
| | 1650 | |
| Hobbes' *Leviathan* | | Louis XIV takes power |
| Pascal | | English Restoration |
| Spinoza | | |
| | | Milton |
| | 1675 | |
| | | Ice cream popular |
| | | Dodo becomes extinct |
| Leibniz | | |
| *Principia Mathematica* | | England's Glorious Revolution |
| Locke's *Essay* published | | |
| | 1700 | First daily newspaper (London) |
| Berkeley | | Last execution for witchcraft |
| | | Louis XIV dies |
| | | Bach's Brandenburg concertos |
| | 1725 | |
| | | American Philosophical Society |
| Hume's *Treatise* | | Pope's "Essay on Man" |
| La Mettrie's *L'Homme* | | |
| Hartley's *Observations* | | Frederick the Great takes power |
| | 1750 | First New York theater |
| Reid | | Mozart born |
| Condillac's *Treatise* | | Mason–Dixon line drawn |
| Electrical nature of nerves discovered | | First public restaurant (Paris) |
| | 1775 | |
| Hume's *Inquiry* | | American Revolution |
| Kant's *Critique* | | |
| | | Frederick the Great dies |
| | | French Revolution |
| Stewart's *Philosophy of the Mind* | | |
| | 1800 | Jefferson elected president |

**FIGURE 4-1.**
Chronology 1600-1800.

The two centuries after 1600 were literally revolutionary. The period begins with the Scientific Revolution of the seventeenth century and closes with political revolutions in colonial America and monarchical France. The scientific and philosophical revolutions laid the basis for the political. In broad historical terms these centuries witnessed the crystallization of the Western world we know today. The nascent nation-states of the Renaissance began to be consolidated by tyrants of more or less enlightened dispositions such as Louis XIV (1638-1715) of France and Frederick the Great (1712-1786) of Prussia. Ideologies of liberty and revolution, so much a part of modern politics, were first articulated by Age of Enlightenment philosophers. The modern economy of industry and capitalism were born in the Industrial Revolution of late eighteenth century England.

One general trend may be extracted from all these changes, which has enormous import for psychology. To the medieval and Renaissance thinker the world was a somewhat mysterious place, organized in a grand hierarchy from God to human to material world, in which each event had a special meaning. The world was profoundly spiritual. In the seventeenth century this view was attacked and replaced by another one: scientific, mathematical, and mechanical. Natural scientists demonstrated the mechanical nature of heavenly and earthly phenomena and then of the bodies of animals. Finally, the mechanical approach was extended to humanity itself. Thus the study of humankind, from politics to psychology, could be subjected to the scientific method, and laws of nature could be sought in the human mind as well as in the heavens. By 1800 both the universe and humanity were believed by most to be machines subject to natural law. In the process, the older view of the world and its relation to humankind as a pattern of mystically meaningful symbols disappeared.

We will divide our study of this period in two parts. The first runs from about 1600-1700 and sees the establishment of modern science and the reconstruction of philosophy on new (yet familiar) lines. The second period, from 1700-1800 is commonly known as the Enlightenment. In this era, the principles of science and reason were applied to human affairs, including the study of human mind and behavior.

## THE SCIENTIFIC REVOLUTION

The Scientific Revolution outshines everything since the rise of Christianity and reduces the Renaissance and Reformation to the rank of mere episodes, mere internal displacements, within the system of medieval Christendom. (Butterfield, 1965)

The importance of science in the modern world cannot be doubted, and the Scientific Revolution can be passed over by no history of the West—especially a history of a science—although psychology was not part of the revolution. The outcome of that revolution is unquestioned. It displaced the earth from the center of the universe and made of the universe a grand machine quite independent of man's feelings and needs. It overthrew the philosophic attitudes of scholasticism and the secretive magical attitudes of alchemy, substituting a public search for precise mathematical regularities confirmable by experiment. It also proposed that man could improve his lot by the application of reason and experiment rather than prayer and devotion (Rossi, 1975). However, the roots of the scientific revolution and its means of progress are monstrously confused, becoming more so with each new piece of historical research.

It is all too easy—and used to be traditional—to write the early history of science as if it were an unrelenting step by step progression to modern science in which prototypical materialist scientists rejected superstition and alchemy for mathematics, experiment, and mechanism. However, this comfortable story is no longer tenable. Far from rejecting alchemy, Newton spent more time on it than on physics (Westfall, 1975). Some fathers of the Catholic Church saw mechanism as vindicating God, not destroying Him. Galileo was greatly influenced (as was Newton) by Renaissance Neoplatonism, and he drew on medieval philosophers for a number of his scientific ideas.

Francis Bacon may be taken as a convenient figure to represent the swirls of controversy over the formation of modern science. Bacon is conventionally taken to be one of the great figures of early science because of his rejection of scholasticism, Aristotle, mystical Neoplatonism, and all other forms of received and preconceived authority. In their place Bacon urged the authority of observation against all hypotheses, anticipating Newton's later disregard for speculation. Bacon was also important for calling attention to the value of craft and technology. Craftsmen work directly on the world and have no room for superfluous hypotheses, so their wisdom may serve as a model for science and a means to humanity's improvement. Bacon is therefore modern in calling for observation and application as basic parts of science.

However, Bacon was sometimes a rather Aristotelian conservative. He did not accept Copernicus' sun-centered world system because it was too hypothetical and mathematical. Similarly, he rejected Galileo's physics, for Galileo studied movement by restricting himself to a few mathematically treated variables. Like Aristotle and the medieval scientists, Bacon distrusted mathematics and wanted to explain all aspects of every phenomenon. It has also been argued that despite his attacks on magic and alchemy, Bacon's desire that science be useful derives from alchemy's practical goals, that is, the transmutation of lead into gold (Rattansi, 1972). Finally, Thomas Kuhn (1976) has argued that Bacon was outside the Scientific Revolution altogether. The only sciences revolutionized during the seventeenth century were the "classic," already mathematicized sciences of astronomy and physics in which Bacon was uninterested. Instead, Bacon stands at the head of more purely empirical, "Baconian" sciences, such as chemistry, which were not mathematicized until the nineteenth century.

Today's historical scholarship has demonstrated that not only Bacon, but every figure in the Scientific Revolution, can be made to look modern or medieval, and—with a few exceptions—crucial or trivial.

We must conclude that the Scientific Revolution took a long time, and no single figure was a thoroughgoing spokesman for modern science. The revolution may be said to begin in 1453 with the publication of Nicholas Copernicus' *Revolution of the Heavenly Orbs* which proposed that the sun, not the earth, was the center of the solar system. However, Copernicus' physics was Aristotelian, and his system was no better supported by the data than the old Ptolemaic one, although some found its simplicity attractive. Galileo Galilei (1564-1642) was the most effective spokesman for the new system, supporting it with his new physics, which helped make sense of the sun-centered proposal, and producing telescopic evidence that the moon and other celestial bodies were no more "heavenly" than the earth. However, Galileo, like Copernicus, could not shake the old Greek assumption that the motion of the planets had to be circular, even though his friend Johann Kepler (1571-1630) showed planetary orbits to be elliptical. The final unity of celestial and earthly physics, and the ultimate victory of the new world view of science, came from Isaac Newton's *Principia Mathematica,* published in 1687.

Newton's laws of motion put the capstone on the idea that the universe was a grand machine. The machine analogy was proposed by Galileo and René Descartes, and quickly became a popular view of the universe. Originally, it was put forward as a support for religion against magic and alchemy: God the master engineer constructed a perfect machine and left it running. The only operative principles are, therefore, mechanical, not occult; magical machinations cannot affect machines. However, implicit in the mechanical view is the possibility that God is dead, and has left behind a cold, impersonal universe. Newton himself seems to have suspected this, for in his own mechanical world there are various imperfections, requiring God to be ever-present, ever-vigilant, and ever-active to keep things running smoothly. Unfortunately for God, the image of Him as a Cosmic Tinkerer flitting about keeping the planets steady is absurd. The more consistent mechanism of Descartes and Galileo triumphed, supported by Newton's physics. The view was deadly to the old medieval conception of God as an ever-present being who manifested himself in signs and portents.

Two important views of knowledge became separated in the seventeenth century, with important later implications for psychology. Should science be pure and abstract, or applied and useful? The old Platonist tradition upheld the former view: in the words of Platonist Henry More, the value of science is not to be measured by "what help it can procure for ye back, bed, and board" (Rattansi, 1972). Wundt and Titchener upheld this view for psychology. In the seventeenth century, however, a tradition that science should be useful arose, expounded most forcefully by Bacon, although whether its inspiration came from magic, the craft tradition, or the Puritan zeal for good works is unclear. By the eighteenth century the latter tradition was well established in England and America, and was drifting toward anti-intellectualism. The English entrepreneur Richard Arkwright wrote: "It is well known that the most useful discoveries that have been made in every branch of art and manufactures have not been made by speculative philosophers in their closets, but by ingenious mechanics . . . practically acquainted with the subject matter of their discoveries" (Bronowski and Mazlish, 1960). William James upheld this tradition for psychology.

An important epistemological distinction emerged during the Scientific Revolution, reviving an old atomist idea. Some sensory qualities of objects are readily measurable: their number, weight, size, shape, and motion. Others are not: color, texture, smell, taste, sound. If science is to be a quantitative, mathematical undertaking (as Galileo and Newton desired), then it could only deal with the former sorts of qualities, called *primary qualities,* which the atomists had attributed to atoms themselves. These objective qualities are to be contrasted with the subjective *secondary qualities,* which exist only in human perception and are the subjective outcome of atoms striking the senses. So, for example, color is a secondary property, for totally color blind people see only greys. Color is a property of vision's response to light waves, it is not really in a colored object.

Psychology was founded as the study of consciousness, and therefore included all sensory properties. However, when the behaviorists revolted against introspective psychology, they deliberately modeled themselves on physics and took the subject matter of psychology to be behavior, an organism's motion in space. Behavior as motion is an objective, primary quality. Such primary qualities, so the behaviorists believed following Newton and Galileo, were the only suitable data for science. Subjectivity was banished first from physics in the seventeenth century, and from psychology in the twentieth.

The change in world view wrought by the Scientific Revolution cannot be underestimated. Science provides the basis for almost all thinking in the twentieth century, from political science to philosophy to physics. It has given man a powerful technology that has changed the face of the earth and taken men to the moon. Psychology, as a science, came to the Revolution late, but was nonetheless affected by its assumptions of mechanism, technological progress, and objectivity. It is because of the Scientific Revolution that the Medieval-Renaissance world view is so alien to us. A distinguished philosopher, E. A. Burtt (1954), contrasts the two views this way:

> The scholastic scientist looked out upon the world of nature, and it appeared to him a quite sociable and human world. It was finite in extent. It was made to serve his needs. It was clearly and fully intelligible, being immediately present to the rational powers of his mind; it was composed fundamentally of, and was intelligible through, those qualities which were most vivid and intense in his own immediate experience—colour, sound, beauty, joy, heat, cold, fragrance and its plasticity to purpose and ideal. Now the world is an infinite and monotonous mathematical machine. Not only is his high place in a cosmic teleology lost, but all these things which were the very substance

of the physical world to the scholastic—the thing that made it alive and lovely and spiritual—are lumped together and crowded into the small fluctuating and temporary positions of extension which we call human nervous ... systems .... It was simply an incalculable change in the viewpoint of the world held by intelligent opinion in Europe.


## REMAKING PHILOSOPHY

The Renaissance worshipped the classical writers, even claiming at times that the modern world would never attain the perfection of the classical world, so mighty did the ancients seem. Modern science, however, showed that the ancients were not perfect. Furthermore, the sixteenth century voyages of exploration had discovered strange and wonderful things unknown to the ancients. In 1636, Tomasso Campanella wrote: "The exploration of the globe having resulted in discoveries that have destroyed many of the data on which ancient philosophy reposed, a new conception of things will inevitably be called for" (Hazard, 1963). Although familiar themes continued, two avowedly new philosophical conceptions were shortly to be provided. The first philosophy to dispense with the ancients was René Descartes' rationalism; the second, John Lockes' empiricism.

### The Continental Rationalist Tradition

*Truth from Doubt: René Descartes (1596-1650)*

Descartes was a Renaissance man: soldier, tutor, scientist, mathematician, philosopher, speculative psychologist. In three areas his influence has been deep and lasting: in his reformulation of rationalism, in his mechanical concept of the world, and in his dualist concept of humans. We shall examine each in turn.

As it was for Plato's rationalism, the immediate philosophical background for Descartes' program was skepticism. The late Renaissance produced a herd of skeptics, such as Montaigne. Like the Sophists, they were uncertain that humans could attain absolute Truth. Unlike the Sophists, Renaissance skeptics did not consider humanity to be the measure of all things, however. On the contrary, human senses were considered so weak, human reason so frail, that people needed faith in God to achieve anything. Like Plato, Descartes did not accept either the skeptics' belief in the unattainability of knowledge or their low estimation of human reason. For Descartes, proper use of the divinely implanted light of reason was the way to truth.

While serving in the army of the Emperor of Germany, Descartes spent one day in a stove-heated room meditating on his own thoughts and formulated the basic principles of his philosophy. Setting aside the ancients as hopelessly confused, and taking a leaf from the skeptics, he resolved to systematically doubt everything until he found something so self-evidently true that it could not be doubted. Descartes found he could doubt the existence of God, the validity of his sensations, the existence of his body. He continued in this way until he found one thing he could not doubt, his own existence as a self-conscious, thinking being. One cannot doubt that one doubts, for in doing so, one realizes the very action supposedly in doubt. Doubting is an act of thinking, and Descartes expressed his first indubitable truth as the famous *"Cogito, ergo sum"*: I think, therefore I am. Descartes then erected his philosophy on this simple truth. From his own existence Descartes established the existence of God by arguments whose validity, cogency, and even sincerity have been doubted since he first stated them. Having established God, the rest was plain sailing. Descartes established the existence of the world and his own body, and the general accuracy of perception.

We will sidestep the vexing questions of Cartesian metaphysics to look at important features of the philosopher's approach. In the first place Descartes firmly believed that the correct method of reasoning can discover and prove what is true. Descartes' first published philosophical work was *Rules for the Direction of the Mind, on the Method of Rightly Conducting The Reason and Seeking for Truth in the Sciences* (1637). Descartes held that there is but one proper way to search for the truth, namely the discovery by reason of intuitively obvious truths, and the deduction from them of other truths. This method is the opposite of Bacon's method of induction, for it is a rationalist method. Descartes' faith in reason was to have long lasting and revolutionary consequences. Many later thinkers decided Descartes erred in his specific conclusions, but had total respect for his method of accepting as true only what was evident to reason, cutting through sophistry, superstition, prejudice, propaganda, and the divine right of kings. While Descartes professed to believe in God and the Church, his sword of reason served the cause of freethinkers everywhere. It should also be pointed out that in elevating reason, Descartes did not wholly condemn the senses as Plato did. Part of his method involved collecting all observations relevant to a question at hand. Descartes simply insisted that facts were of little value until rightly ordered by reason. Certainly Descartes did not value facts as ends in themselves, but as aids to finding more general truth.

Descartes was not the first to prove his own existence from mental activity. St. Augustine had said, "If I am deceived, I exist," and Parmenides had said, "For it is the same thing to think and to be." So we may place Descartes in the intro-spective rationalist tradition: truth is primarily evident in me, in my self-conscious-ness, my thinking. After Descartes, however, introspection became the major philosophical tool of rationalist and empiricist alike. Philosophers differed about what they found in the mind, but they all looked to it for truth. After Descartes, therefore, philosophy became increasingly psychological, seeking to know the mind through introspection, until in the nineteenth century psychology is founded as the *scientific,* rather than armchair-philosophical, study of consciousness known through introspection.

The method was more widely revolutionary as well. No longer was philosophy to be practiced by poring over ancient texts, whether the *Republic,* the *de Anima,* or the Bible. Instead, philosophers begin with an analysis of mind, or experience, or will, as they understand them. This is a decisive break with the scholastic and

Renaissance tradition of studying texts and marks a return to the more freely speculative philosophizing of the Greeks. The break is underlined by noting that by and
large the modern philosophers were not academic professors; Descartes, for
example, supported himself for a time by soldiering. Furthermore, these philosophers
abandoned Latin in favor of their native tongues as vehicles for writing and publication. Increasingly, philosophers did not care to persuade established scholastic
academics, but sought the wider audience of all literate people. Philosophy and
science gradually escaped the control of Church and State by publishing widely in
the vernacular.

   Finally, Cartesian philosophy is rationalist in its nativism. Plato had thought
knowledge of the Forms innate in the human soul. For the Forms, Descartes substitutes clear and distinct ideas we immediately know are true, and moreover, these
ideas come not from the senses but from "certain germs of truth which exist
naturally in our souls." Thus the indubitable principle truths are innate. As for
Plato, they are potential ideas only, requiring activation by experience. Descartes
held the idea of God to be innate (certainly we never see God), but obviously
infants do not have the idea yet. Descartes draws an analogy with certain inherited
diseases: they are not present at birth, but the disposition to develop them is.
Descartes also speaks of innate ideas in another sense, not as concepts, such as
the concept of God, but as certain innate ways of thinking. For example, we know
that if A=B and B=C, then A=C. We did not learn this through experience, so it
must be innate. It is an innate way of thinking, and so our minds are thus disposed
naturally to conceive things in certain set ways. This kind of nativism will be
developed with great force by Immanual Kant; rejection of the first kind was the
beginning of Locke's empiricism.

   Descartes  first work was in science, not philosophy, but his account of it,
*The World,* he suppressed upon hearing of Galileo's condemnation by the Church
in 1632. Some of his scientific ideas were later published in 1644 in the *Principles
of Philosophy.* In its details, Descartes' physics is reminiscent of the pre-Socratics.
His description of the world is largely speculative, founded sometimes on out-of-
date information and ignorant of current developments, such as Kepler's laws of
planetary motions. It relies more on abstract argument than on empirical proof,
as one might expect from a rationalist. If its details were wrong, however, its basic
conception was triumphant. With Newton's help it has given us our modern view of
the world. Descartes was from his earliest education impressed with mathematics,
and his world view became mathematical. He conceived the world, the entire
material universe, to be one complex machine obeying deterministic, mathematical
laws knowable to the mind. In the material world there was nothing but extended
matter; there were no colors, no tastes, no angels, no demons. God had created
the perfect machine and set it running. Man's reason could understand the natural
laws and use them to his advantage, but they are fixed and remorseless. Descartes'
own account of the world machine was unsatisfactory, his speculative nature
playing loose with the facts. It remained for Newton to truly grasp the machinery
of physics. His success and Descartes' vision have guided science ever since. To a
large extent the subsequent history of all the sciences has been to formulate each in

mechanical terms, beginning with physics, then chemistry, and in our own times, biology. Nor has man escaped Descartes' vision, which brings us to his psychology.

If the material world as it objectively exists possesses the single primary property of extension, it is obvious that the world as we subjectively experience it possesses many other secondary properties—color, smell, taste, sound, joy, pain, fear. There is therefore, in addition to a material world which includes the body, a subjective world of consciousness and mind. Perhaps this second world is spiritual as well, for God and the soul are not material. In any case, as far as human knowledge is concerned there are two worlds, an objective, scientifically knowable, mechanical-material world—the world as it really is—and a subjective world of human consciousness known through introspection—the world of a person as a thinking being.

Thus Descartes proposed a dualism of mind and body seen as quite distinct entities, one physical (the body), the other nonphysical (the mind). These two entities interact: the mind acquires information about the material world through the senses; the desires of the body are felt in consciousness, while the mind may direct the actions of the body. The exact nature of Descartes' dualism has been long debated. To many of his contemporaries Descartes seemed to have eliminated the Christian soul, for the only property he definitely assigned it was consciousness or thinking, not immortality. Moreover, his proofs of God seemed weak. Descartes himself asserted his orthodoxy, but his own suppression of his first scientific works indicate heterodoxy. The question is unsettled. Some argue that Descartes was a sincere Christian whose system contained seeds of materialistic atheism. Others contend that Descartes was himself a thoroughgoing mechanist who believed subjective consciousness to be only a brain process, but that he tried to conceal his true beliefs from the authorities of Church and State.

In any event, the most important consequence of his psychology was its mechanism. As a material entity, Descartes conceived the body as a machine, and he gave detailed mechanical accounts of how sensation and action occurred as body and mind interacted through the pineal gland, the seat of the mind. As with his physics, Descartes' physiology was speculative and incompatible with already existing information on the nervous system. What is important is Descartes' view of the human body as a machine incorporating many faculties previously assigned to the soul. Like Aristotle and the medieval faculty psychologists, Descartes wrote about memory, imagination, and common sense. However unlike them, Descartes assigned these faculties to the body, implying that although they appear to be mental activities, they may be explained as bodily activities. Therefore, Descartes sought to account for as much of the mind as possible on materialist, mechanical terms within the sphere of science, reserving only self-consciousness at most to philosophy. Hence, whether or not he intended to give a completely materialist and mechanical account of human mental activity, Descartes gave great impetus to the assimilation of mind to mechanical science. In the eighteenth century we will find complete mechanistic psychologies.

Descartes also suggested the possibility of comparing human and animal minds. Descartes looked on animals as nothing but mechanical automata lacking self-conscious souls, using the uniqueness of human language to support his view. Human beings, no matter how otherwise unintelligent, possess a creative language capable of expressing reflective rational thought. Animals, in contrast, possess at best vocal signals which indicate simple bodily states such as fear. In the 1950s language became a special problem for psychology, and at least one linguist would follow Descartes in treating language as an innate, uniquely human ability.

Descartes is finally a paradoxical figure. In his emphases on reason as opposed to perception, on innate ideas as opposed to experience, on absolute truth as opposed to relativism, he is a rationalist. However, in his mechanical view of the world and the human body his psychology would ultimately support empiricism and behaviorism.

### The heart has its reasons which the reason does not understand: Blaise Pascal (1623-1662)

If Descartes prefigures the confident rationalist of the Enlightenment, Pascal prefigures the anguished existentialist of recent times. For Descartes, doubt led to the triumphant certainty of reason; for Pascal, doubt led to worse doubt. Wrote Pascal: I am "... engulfed in the infinite immensity of spaces whereof I know nothing and which know nothing of me, I am terrified ...." (Bronowski and Mazlish, 1960). Pascal detested Descartes' excessive rationalism and derived solace and truth from his faith in God. For Pascal, what is essential in humans is not natural reason, but will and the capacity for faith, that is, the heart. Pascal thus resembles earlier Christian skeptics such as Montaigne. But Pascal is Cartesian in the value he places on self-consciousness, as shown by his statement in the *Pensees*: "Man knows that he is wretched. He is wretched, then, because he is wretched; but he is great, because he knows it, .... Man is only a reed, the frailest thing in nature; but he is a thinking reed." Pascal doubted a person's capacity to fathom nature or to understand self—man is wretched. Yet a human's unique self-consciousness lifts her or him above nature and the animals, offering salvation through faith in the Christian God. Pascal's anguish and need for faith echoes through all modern existentialists, not excepting atheists such as Sartre.

At the same time, Pascal was a scientist and mathematician who investigated the vacuum and helped found probability theory. As a mathematician he was a child prodigy. At 19, he constructed the first mechanical calculators, some of which still exist. Although its purpose was humble—to help his father, a tax official, do calculations—its implication was profound. Pascal wrote: "The arithmetical machine produces effects which approach nearer to thought than all the actions of animals." (Bronowski and Mazlish, 1960). Pascal was the first to sense that the human mind could be conceived as an information processing machine capable of being mimicked by computer, a concept central to contemporary cognitive psychology. In Pascal's time, and to someone with his sensibilities, the implication was frightening, for it meant that reason—which Descartes exempted from his mechanical system—could not be so exempted. Perhaps animals, wholly mechanical creatures according to Descartes, *do* reason. Pascal then declared that a human's free will, not reason, is what distinguishes humans from animals. It is the heart, not the brain, that makes a human, human.

### Determinism Extended: Baruch Spinoza (1632-1677)

Spinoza was a thinker out of step with his own time. Born a Jew, but excommunicated for his disbelief in Yahweh, he articulated a philosophy that identified God with nature, and saw the State as merely a revocable agreement among men. He was spurned by the people of his birth, denounced by Christians, and his works were suppressed even in the liberal state of Holland where he lived. In the Enlightenment, he was admired for his independence but rejected for his pantheistic philosophy. Later, the Romantics venerated his apparent mysticism, while scientists saw in him a naturalist.

Spinoza's philosophy begins with metaphysics and ends with a radical reconstruction of human nature. Spinoza argued that God is essentially nature. Without the existing natural world, nothing would exist, so that God (nature) is the supporter and creator of all things. But God is not a separate being apart from nature; all things are a part of God without exception, and God is no more than the totality of the universe. Hence Spinoza was thought to be an atheist. Furthermore, nature is entirely deterministic. Spinoza argued that to understand anything means to unravel its efficient causes. Spinoza denied the existence of final causes, believing teleology to be a projection of humanity's feelings of purpose onto nature, applied only to events we cannot explain with efficient, that is, deterministic causes.

Spinoza extended his deterministic analysis to human nature. Mind is not something separate from body, but is produced by brain processes. Mind and body are one, but may be viewed from two aspects, as physiological brain processes or as mental events—thoughts. Spinoza did not deny that mind exists, but did see it as one aspect of a fundamentally material nature. Thus for Spinoza mental activity is as deterministic as bodily activity. Spinoza rejected Cartesian dualism, and so for him there is no problem of interaction. We feel we are free, but this is only an illusion. If we properly understood the causes of human behavior and thinking we would see we are not free. Just as no blame may be attached to the river that floods and destroys a town, so no blame can be attached to a multiple murderer. Society may act to control the river or the killer to prevent future devastation, but this is a pragmatic consideration rather than a moral one. Spinoza's account of responsibility thus calls for a psychological science to unravel the causes of human behavior, and bears a striking resemblance to B.F. Skinner's. Spinoza's account of memory, which says that ideas experienced together become mechanically linked, also resembles later conditioning theories which associate stimulus and response.

Spinoza, however, went on to describe an ethics of self-control that transcends materialistic determinism, and which to some degree conflicts with the rest of his thought. He argued that right action and thinking depend on the control of bodily emotions by reason. The wise person is one who follows the dictates of reason rather than the dictates of the momentary and conflicting passions arising from the body. Reason will lead one to act out of enlightened self-interest—helping others as one would want to be helped. Spinoza's ethics and his view of humanity are quite Stoic. The physical universe is beyond our control, but our passions are not. Thus wisdom is rational self-control, rather than a futile effort to control nature, or God. Spinoza also argued that states should allow freedom of thought, conscience, and speech, for each person should be free to order his or her mind as he or she sees fit. For all this, Spinoza was reviled even by the most advanced thinkers of his day.

### Levels of Consciousness:
### Gottfried Wilhelm Leibniz (1646-1716)

Leibniz was a mathematician, logician, and metaphysician. He independently invented calculus, and dreamed of a formal conceptual calculus that would do for verbal reasoning what mathematics had done for the sciences. His metaphysics is extremely difficult. Briefly, he conceived of the universe as composed of an infinity of geometrical-point entities called *monads,* each of which is to some extent living and possesses some degree of consciousness. Animals and people are made up of monads that subserve a most conscious, and hence most dominant, monad. Thus, unlike Descartes, Leibniz ascribed souls to animals.

Leibniz' theory of monads led to a solution to the mind-body problem that became increasingly popular over the next two centuries. Descartes had said that mind and body interact. However, it was unclear how spirit could act on matter and vice versa, leading to a view called *occasionalism* in which God saw to it that when a bodily event occurred, so did a mental event and vice versa. This, too, has its difficulties, with God running around keeping mind and body coordinated. Leibniz proposed an answer which has since been called mind-body (or psychophysical) *parallelism.* Leibniz argued that God had created the universe (the infinitude of monads) such that there is a pre-established harmony between the monads. Leibniz used an analogy of two clocks. Imagine two identical and perfect clocks, both set to the same time and started at the same moment. From then on the clocks would always agree with, and mirror, one another, but they would not be causally connected. Each would run identical but parallel—not interacting—courses of development. Just so mind and body. Consciousness (mind) mirrors exactly what happens in the body, but only because of God's pre-established harmony, not because of a causal connection. In fact, Leibniz extended this scheme to the whole universe, holding that monads never interact but stay coordinated in their pictures of the universe because of God's perfect harmony. Although the metaphysical basis of psychophysical parallelism was dropped later, the doctrine itself caught on as physiological knowledge of the body and the growth of physics rendered both interactionism and occasionalism implausible.

Leibniz also reintroduced final causes into philosophy. The material world is governed by efficient causes, as Spinoza argued, but since Leibniz believed in his immaterial monads, a second kind of causation was needed. Leibniz postulated that monads have a tendency to perfect themselves, to actualize their potentiality, a view that recalls Aristotle. In fact, since monads do not interact, the only way they can change (and so reflect changes in the universe) is through inner development. Thus monads are purposeful and develop toward an end: their own perfection. This development is natural and spontaneous; it is not caused by anything outside the monad. Again, with the metaphysics dropped the idea has been influential, especially in developmental psychology. Some developmental psychologists, notably Jean Piaget, believe child development to be a spontaneous, natural progression relatively unaffected by the environment. This is, of course, in contrast to empiricist views which see the child as being extensively molded by the environment.

Also in contrast to the empiricists, Leibniz upheld innate ideas. Like Descartes, Leibniz believed many ideas, such as God and mathematical truths, were impossible to derive from experience for they are too abstract. Such ideas must be innate. Leibniz expressed his conception by his famous statue metaphor. The mind at birth is likened to a block of marble. Marble is veined, and it may be that the veins outline the form of Hercules in the marble, for example. Certain activities are required to bring out the statue, but in a sense Hercules is "innate" in the marble. Similarly, an infant's innate dispositions to certain kinds of knowledge must be activated, either by experience or by the infant's own reflection on mental life.

Finally, we will consider Leibniz' account of perception, for here Leibniz laid the ground for both psychophysics and Wundt's founding psychology (McRae, 1976). First, Leibniz distinguished *petite perceptions* from *perception*. *Petite perception* is a stimulus event (to borrow a modern term) so weak it is not perceived. To use Leibniz' most usual metaphor, one does not hear the sound of a single drop of water hitting a beach; this is a *petite perception*. Yet a wave crashing on the beach is but thousands of drops hitting the beach, and this we do hear. Thus our perception of the wave's crash is made up of many *petite perceptions* each too small to be heard but together making a conscious experience. This doctrine points the way to psychophysics, the systematic study of the quantitative relation between stimulus intensity and experience, which we will discuss in Chapter 6. Leibniz' account also implies the existence of the unconscious, or as Leibniz writes, "changes in the soul itself of which we are not conscious." As modified in the nineteenth century and adopted by Freud, the concept of the unconscious had momentous impact on psychology.

Leibniz also distinguished perception from *sensation*. A perception is a raw, confused idea, not really conscious, which animals, as well as humans, may possess. However, a person can refine and sharpen perceptions, and become reflectively aware of them in consciousness. They then become sensations.* This refining process is called *apperception*. Apperception also seems to be involved in uniting petite perceptions to become perceptions. This uniting process, stressed Leibniz, is not a process of mere aggregation. Perceptions, rather, are emergent properties coming from masses of *petite* perceptions. If we combine blue and yellow lights, for

---

*Leibniz' usage is roughly the opposite of modern psychological usage. Today, a sensation refers to a sensory receptor process, while a perception is a central brain or mental event.

example, we do not experience separately blue and yellow but instead green, an emergent experience not present in the simpler constituent lights.

Attention is the major component of apperception for Leibniz, and he distinguished two types, passive and active. If you are absorbed in some activity, you may not notice another stimulus, such as a friend speaking to you, until that stimulus grows so strong that it automatically draws your attention. Here the shift in attention is passive, for the new stimulus captures attention. Attention may also be voluntary, as when you focus it on one person at a party to the exclusion of others. Sometimes Leibniz tied apperception closely to voluntary attention, for he saw apperception as an act of will. This is also how Wundt used the term apperception.

Memory is also involved in attention, for when we attend to something it must be fixed in the mind by memory. Leibniz cites a simple example used in twentieth century research on echoic memory and attention. If a friend speaks to you while you are otherwise absorbed, it sometimes happens that your first response is "What?" but that you can then answer your friend's question. This shows that the question was at first unattended, but somehow stored in memory so you could attend to it subsequently; similarly once your attention is caught, you can usually remember having heard a noise earlier, if only dimly.

We will later see all these ideas refined and elaborated in Wundt's theory of apperception.

### The British Empiricist Tradition

On the other side of the English Channel modern empiricism was being founded. In England there was a very different atmosphere, less heavy with metaphysics and more concerned with things as they are. The empiricists are more descriptive in their approach to the mind. Descartes, Spinoza, and Leibniz all wanted to improve the mind by propounding some method to escape error. The empiricists were more interested in how the mind ordinarily works rather than how it ideally should work.

### The Laws of Social Life: Thomas Hobbes (1588-1679)

Hobbes' importance derives from being the first to comprehend and express the new scientific view of humans and their place in the universe. Hobbes wrote: "For seeing life is but a motion of limbs . . . why may we not say, that all *automata* . . . have an artificial life? For what is the *heart*, but a spring; and the *nerves,* but so many strings; and the joints, but so many *wheels,* giving motion to the whole body." (Bronowski and Mazlish, 1960). Hobbes' contemporary, Descartes, believed animals, but not humans, to be entirely machines. Hobbes went considerably further, claiming that spiritual substance is a meaningless idea. Only matter exists, and the actions of people, no less than those of animals, are fully determined.

On one point Hobbes and Descartes agreed: that philosophy should be constructed after the model of geometry. Indeed, it was Hobbes' accidental exposure, at age 40, to the elegant proofs of Euclid that led him to philosophize. Otherwise, Hobbes is very much an empiricist. He believed that all knowledge is ultimately rooted in sense perception. He upheld extreme nominalism, seeing in universals no more than convenient names grouping remembered sense-perceptions. He dismissed arguments over metaphysics as scholastic wrangling about meaningless concepts. He rigidly separated philosophy, which is rational and meaningful, from theology, which is irrational and meaningless. His most interesting psychological doctrine is that language and thinking are closely related, perhaps even identical. In his major work, *Leviathan* (1651), Hobbes wrote: "Understanding is nothing else but conception caused by speech." Further, he states that "Children are not endowed with reason at all, till they have attained the use of speech." Hobbes was the first in the long, and still living, line of British philosophers who equate right thinking with right use of language. For psychology, this is an old and unresolved issue: whether thinking is overt or covert speech, or whether speech merely dresses up abstract concepts. Hobbes clearly argued the former.

However, Hobbes' real interest was political science, which he claimed to have invented. Hobbes believed that if man is a deterministic machine like the stars and planets, then a science of human affairs ought to be as attainable as astronomy and physics.

As one who had endured the English civil war, he desired to put government on a sound rational footing to avoid such horrors in the future. In *Leviathan,* Hobbes begins with a commonplace of modern liberalism, that persons are created roughly equal in physical and mental powers. However, were there no government, each person would seek his or her own interest against fellow humans. Outside of organized society, Hobbes wrote: *"There is always war of every one against every one . . .* and the life of man is solitary, nasty, brutish, and short." The solution is for men to recognize that their rational self-interest lies in a regulated state which will provide security, the fruits of industry, and other benefits. This means recognizing the existence of Laws of Nature, for example that each person should give up the total liberty and equal right to all things that breeds war, and "be contented with so much liberty against other men, as he would allow other men against himself." The best state for securing such liberties, Hobbes went on to argue, is an absolute despotism, in which all members of society contract their rights and powers to a sovereign, whether king or parliament, who will then rule and protect them, uniting their many wills into one will.

Hobbes' idea that Natural Law would apply to people is of considerable importance to psychology. He said that there are regulations inherent in nature, existing apart from humanity's recognition of them, that govern everything from the planetary machine of the solar system to the biological machines of the animals, including humans. Hobbes' attitude however, is not fully scientific, for he says that we rationally consent to follow Natural Laws. Only in times of security must we follow them; they may be broken should government or other persons try to compel anyone to personal ruin. The planets cannot choose to obey or not obey Newton's laws of motion, and in this respect Hobbes' Natural Laws are not like the laws of physics. As time passes, other thinkers would make them more similar.

John Locke was a friend of the scientists Isaac Newton and Robert Boyle (in whose laboratory he assisted), a member of the Royal Society, adviser and tutor to noble politicians, and at times a practicing physician. As we might expect, therefore, Locke brought a practical and empirical bent to his philosophy. His major work was *An Essay Concerning Human Understanding* (1690), which he started writing in 1671. Unlike the rationalist Descartes, who sought ultimate Platonic Truth, Locke wanted to understand how the human mind actually works —the sources of its ideas, and the limitations of human knowledge. Thus Locke's epistemology is really a psychology, for his emphasis is on *how* the mind knows rather than on *what* it knows. Locke thus brought the scientific spirit to philosophy, shearing off metaphysics, to say what can be empirically known about the human mind. In the history of psychology, then, Locke is an important turning point. Now the inspection of the human mind itself becomes important, replacing metaphysical speculation on what cannot be known.

What, then, may humans know? Locke stated: "Since the Mind, in all its thoughts and Reasonings, hath no other immediate Object but its own *Ideas* . . . it is evident, that our Knowledge is only conversant about them." The mind does not know Forms or Essences, but its own ideas only. Where do our ideas come from? Locke wrote: "To this I answer, in one word, From *Experience*: In that, all our knowledge is founded and derives itself. Our Observation employed either about *external, sensible objects; or about the internal Operations of our Minds . . . is that which supplies our Understandings with all the materials of thinking.* These two are the Fountains of Knowledge, from whence all the *Ideas* we have, or can naturally have, do spring."

Locke thus states the empiricist principle that knowledge derives from experience alone. Elsewhere, he uses the famous simile for the mind of the *tabula rasa,* or piece of white paper, on which experience writes ideas. However, we must note some important qualifications to Locke's thesis, for he was not a radical empiricist. To begin with, experience is of two types: sensation of external objects and reflection on the working of our minds. Thus we may know about both the external world and our own inner, mental world. Direct knowledge about the mind is therefore possible through introspection. Furthermore, Locke does not say that the operations of mind are acquired through experience. The powers of thinking, memory, perception are all innate, as they were for Descartes. Locke's later followers reject both these theses.

Now it is well known that Locke attacked innate ideas, spending the first book of his *Essay* arguing against them. However, he was not attacking Descartes, as is usually assumed. What Locke opposed were a large number of English writers who believed in innate *moral principles,* seeing in them the foundation of Christian morality. Thus they could say that it was God's law implanted in the soul that a person should believe in Him; anyone who did not believe was depraved and as much a moral monster as a three-legged baby would be a physical monster. Indeed, Locke himself was widely denounced as a dangerous atheist for denying innate moral truths. Locke attacked them because he believed the idea of innate moral and metaphysical truths to be pillars of dogmatism. The schools of his day used maxims as the basis of teaching. Students were to accept them and then prove them. Locke advocated a discovery principle. Students should keep open minds, discovering truth through experience and following their own talents, instead of being forced into the straightjacket of scholastic maxims. To see in Locke, as many do, the father of structured education, is wrong.

Locke's arguments against innate ideas make no headway against Descartes' or Leibniz' nativism, as he recognized. They believed in innate ideas activated by experience, which Locke believed was only trivially different from his own doctrine of innate mental abilities. In fact, one finds a great deal of innate active mental machinery in Locke's "empty mind." Like Descartes, Locke indicates that language is a human, species-specific trait. He wrote in *Essay*: "God having designed Man for a sociable Creature . . . furnished him also with language . . . . Parrots, and general other Birds, may be taught to make articulate sounds distinct enough, which yet, by no means, are capable of Language." Only humans can use articulate sounds to represent ideas. In his work on education, Locke holds that much of a child's personality and abilities are innate. Man's basic motives, to seek happiness and avoid misery are likewise "innate practical principles," although of course having nothing to do with truth.

For Locke the mind was not merely an empty room to be furnished by experience, but was rather a complex information processing device prepared to convert the materials of experience into organized human knowledge. Direct experience provides us with simple ideas, which are then elaborated and combined by the mental machinery into complex ideas. Knowledge comes about as we inspect our ideas, and see how they agree or disagree. The bedrock of knowledge for Locke, as for Descartes, was intuitively self-evident propositions, although for Locke they are self-evidently experienced truths instead of truths found in the soul. For example, you know directly and intuitively, without possibility of error, that the colors black and white are not the same (they "disagree"). More complex forms of knowledge arise as we deduce consequences from self-evident propositions. Like Descartes, Locke believed that in this way all human knowledge, even ethics and aesthetics, could be geometrically systematized.

We may conclude that the differences between Locke the empiricist and Descartes the rationalist were primarily differences of emphasis. Both wanted to transcend sterile scholastic philosophy; both tried to do so by examining the human mind. Descartes was more the captive of the past, still searching with pure reason for transcendent truth. Locke points more to the empirical future. He recognized the limits of human knowledge and reason; indeed one reason for writing the *Essay* was to show what humanity could hope to know so that only fruitful questions might be pursued. In some ways, Locke was less empiricist than his predecessor Hobbes. Hobbes said we think in our acquired language, that words *are* ideas. Locke insisted that words are only signs of ideas. Thus for Locke reason comes first, and then is framed in conventional words. For Hobbes, more radically, one cannot think without acquiring language; reason comes second.

Locke was usually a very clear and common-sensical writer. However, on one crucial point he was ambiguous, fueling the radical empiricism of his British successors, and agonizing his modern commentators. As we have seen, Locke states that human knowledge is only about ideas. However, what is an idea? Two interpretations are possible. The first was adopted by Locke's first commentator, Bishop Berkeley, with radical implications we will come to in the next chapter. According to this view, ideas are mental objects, furniture of the mind, and our knowledge is limited to them. So when one says "A snowball is white," one is referring only to the mental picture of a snowball. Although it is clear Locke believed ideas to correspond to things in the world, Berkeley showed that this cannot be proven, so we have no guarantee that our knowledge is "real" knowledge. Skepticism results. On the other hand, most, but not all, modern commentators follow the Scottish philosopher Reid and reject Berkeley's interpretation. They hold that Locke meant *idea* to be a kind of mental act, specifically an act of perception by which the mind contacts the outside world. Thus when one says, "A snowball is white," one is referring not to some mental image, but to real snowballs.

This dispute affects how we place Locke in the history of psychology. In the nineteenth century there were two major European academic psychologies, each of which is compatible with one interpretation of Locke's *idea*. One was the psychology of content, whose best spokesman was E. B. Titchener. In this psychology, sensations were believed to be irreducible atomic constituents of consciousness—the elementary content, or furniture, of the mind. This account follows Berkeley. The other psychology, whose spokesman was Franz Brentano, was the psychology of *act,* in which any mental event was construed as a mental act referring to something in the outside world. This account follows Reid. Titchener saw that here are two rival ways of viewing the mind. Locke's ambiguous use of "idea" can be related to either system.

In any case, what is most important about Locke is his empirical attitude regarding the mind. Locke wanted to know how it works, and this is a psychological question unencumbered by metaphysics. Locke did not practice a scientific psychology, collecting data and designing research programs; he believed the mind could know itself through reflection. But he opened the way for a science of mind.

## THE SEVENTEENTH CENTURY: SEEDS OF CHANGE

The seventeenth century laid the foundations for the Enlightenment of the eighteenth. The Newtonian-Cartesian mechanical universe rationalized God, world, and humankind. It had no room for miracles, oracles, visions, and metaphysical dogmatism. It proposed theories of humanity, society, and ethics that discounted the heavenly nature of humans but held out hope of happiness here on earth. In the seventeenth century Locke abandoned metaphysics for psychology, and Leibniz proposed ideas basic to later scientific psychology. In the eighteenth century these seeds would come to fruition as science and reason replaced religion as the chief intellectual institution of modern society. Man would be proclaimed a soulless machine, and societies would be overthrown in the name of material happiness.

By 1700 the medieval world order was finished. Three dates seem especially portentous. In 1686, a popular French writer, Fontenelle, brought science to the literate public of France, dazzling his readers. Although humans were reduced to a mechanical speck in a mechanical universe, knowing this secret was uplifting. Science and mathematics became all the rage. In 1687, Newton's *Principia Mathematica Philosophiae Naturalis* appeared, the triumph of the mathematical view of the world-machine. Soon Natural Law would be extended to human beings and governments with revolutionary impact. In 1688 came England's Glorious Revolution, the peaceful deposition of James II and the installation of William of Orange. In this revolution was born the modern liberal state: Kings are not divinely appointed agents whose will is absolute law. They are instruments of the people, replaceable at the people's will. The revolution was philosophically justified by John Locke in terms that were similar to the American Declaration of Independence 90 years later. Reason had prevailed over tradition and faith.

The triumph of reason in the Age of Reason was at hand. Yet, a different undercurrent lurked just below the surface. The voyages of discovery had found strange primitive cultures. To Hobbes and Locke these wild men represented man in an uncivilized and unhappy state of Nature. Locke wrote in his *Second Treatise on Government*: "In the beginning all the world was America." Yet were the Indians unhappy? They lived close to nature, unfettered by artifice, living according to natural instinct. Perhaps happiness lies in giving up reason, with its abstract, artificial ways, and returning to the instinct of the happy savage. A reaction against reason was about to set in. The poet Chalieu wrote in 1708 that reason is an "inexhaustible source of errors, poison that corrupts the natural feelings." Jean Rousseau wrote that reason "feeds our mad pride . . . continually masking us from ourselves." Asked Rousseau: "Which is the least barbarous . . . reason which leads you astray, or instinct which guides [the Indian] truly?" Chalieu said he comes "to destroy the altars which have been raised to thee [Reason]." Here the seed is sown for the Romantic Rebellion against reason and for the coming of the Noble Savage. The tension between the individual and society, so poignantly felt by Sigmund Freud, was increasing as reason demanded more and more of men and women.

## SUGGESTED READINGS

For the Scientific Revolution, see Richard Westfall, *The Construction of Modern Science* (John Wiley, 1971). For the Rationalist and Empiricist philosophers, see Frederick Copleston, *A History of Philosophy,* Volume 4 (on the continental Rationalists) and Volume 5 (on the British Empiricists) (Image Books, 1963 and 1964).

# REFERENCES

Bronowski, J. & Mazlish, B. *The western intellectual tradition.* New York: Harper & Row, Pub., 1960.

Burtt, E. A. *The metaphysical foundations of modern science.* Garden City, N.Y.: Doubleday, 1954.

Butterfield, H. *The origins of modern science 1300-1800.* New York: The Free Press, 1965.

Hazard, P. *The European mind 1680-1715.* New York: New American Library, 1963.

Hobbes, T. *Leviathan.* New York: Collier Books, 1962.

Kuhn, T. Mathematical vs. experimental traditions in the development of physical science. *The Journal of Interdisciplinary History,* 1976, 7, 1-31.

Locke, J. *An essay concerning human understanding* (Variorum edition). (Peter Nidditch, Ed.). Oxford: Clarendon Press, 1975.

McRae, R. *Leibniz: Perception, apperception, and thought.* Toronto: University of Toronto Press, 1976.

Rattansi, R. The social interpretation of science in the seventeenth century. In P. Mathias (Ed.) *Science and Society 1600-1900.* Cambridge: Cambridge University Press, 1972.

Rossi, P. Hermeticism, rationality, and the scientific revolution. In M. Bonelli, & W. Shea (Eds.), *Reason, experiment and mysticism in the scientific revolution.* New York: Science History Publications, 1975.

Westfall, R. The role of alchemy in Newton's career. In M. Bonelli & W. Shea (Eds.) *Reason, experiment and mysticism in the scientific revolution.* New York: Science History Publications, 1975.

# 5

# Reason and Reaction
## The Eighteenth Century Enlightenment

The seeds of the Enlightenment were planted in the seventeenth century. The most important sources were Newton and Locke, whose empiricism overcame rationalism across Europe. Newton was the hero of the new age. He showed that restrained empirical enquiry, shorn of unprofitable speculation, could work wonders in understanding and controlling nature. Locke, who by his own statement was Newton's "under laborer," brought the empirical approach to the human mind, considering it without speculation and with due regard for facts. In his efforts Locke had many followers who wanted to be Newtons of the mind. Psychology replaced metaphysics as the central philosophical concern of the eighteenth century, with questions about the mind's power to know replacing speculation about ultimate truth. In the Enlightenment, psychology became a mania if not a science.

Newton and Locke also sowed the seeds of revolution. Newton showed that if Nature could be understood, we could hope to bend it to our will, as Bacon had foreseen. In denying innate ideas, and therefore innate depravity, Locke asserted that people may be educated and perfected and consequently, society enlightened and perfected. So the Scientific Revolution, and what we may call Locke's psychological revolution, implied social and political revolution.

Locke himself participated in the first and mildest revolution, the Glorious Revolution of 1688, and partly laid the philosophic foundation for the second bloody, but not vicious revolution—the American Revolution of 1776. The Enlightenment may be said to have ended with the third, bloody, vicious, and finally unsuccessful revolution, the French Revolution of 1789.

In this period psychological treatises explode in number, although most are inspired by Locke. In this section we will first treat the great eighteenth century philosophers Berkeley and Hume, who extended and purified Locke's empiricism, and Kant, who reasserted the primacy of metaphysics. Then we will turn to the less original thinkers who chart the tendency of the age toward an empirical, empiricist, associationistic psychology.

## THE MAJOR PHILOSOPHERS

### Empiricism Perfected

#### Mind over Matter: Bishop George Berkeley (1685-1753)

Like Locke and Descartes, Berkeley as a philosopher wanted to refute skepticism, while as a deeply religious man he wanted to refute the Newtonian materialism that imperiled faith in God. He admired Locke deeply, and felt Locke had taken the correct road, empiricism, toward both knowledge and religion. However, he thought that Locke had said that our knowledge is about ideas ultimately rooted in sensation. Berkeley, interpreting and agreeing with Locke that ideas are mental objects, not acts, saw an opening for skepticism. Locke believed in the existence of "real" objects that exist beyond our perception and which have unobservable properties. But the skeptic may ask, if *ideas* are the objects of our knowledge, if in fact what we perceive are ideas of objects, how can we be sure our ideas truly correspond to the "real" material objects? In Berkeley's view, Locke was helpless to refute the skeptic.

Berkeley saw the problem to be Locke's belief in matter as something apart from perception. For example, as I am sitting here writing, I know my pen exists because I sense it. But when I lay it down and leave the room, what grounds have I for asserting that it still exists? All I can say is that if I went back I would see it, or if someone else looks for it, he or she will see it. Ultimately then, I know the pen exists only because I see it. And in fact, said Berkeley, the pen exists when it is perceived. Berkeley's famous motto is *"Esse est percipi"*: to exist is to be perceived. Berkeley thus refuted skepticism by an astoundingly simple assertion. As Locke said, all we know are our ideas, but Berkeley adds that there is no permanent material reality apart from our perceptions. The question of how ideas correspond to "real objects" does not arise if there are no "real objects" at all. Furthermore, Berkeley's philosophy refutes atheism, for God may now be introduced as the omniscient perceiver who sees all things and so continues their existence.

The arguments Berkeley adduced to support his immaterialism or idealism (the view that there is no matter and that only ideas are real) are complex and con-troversial. What is psychologically important about Berkeley is that as part of his arguments he gave a persuasive empiricist account of perception—especially vision—that was widely accepted until the twentieth century.

Berkeley focused on the problem of distance perception. We see the world in three dimensions, yet the retinal image—the immediate (or "proper") object of vision—is only two-dimensional, lacking depth. So, for example, as a friend walks away from you, you see him or her getting farther and farther away, but if we examine your retinal image, we would find only that the image of the friend gets smaller and smaller. Of course, you may observe that indeed your friend looks smaller, but your subjective experience is that he or she is getting farther away. So the problem arises, how does one perceive three dimensions when all one can see (on the retina) are two dimensions?

Berkeley's answer was that other sensations are available which do give cues about distance. For example, as an object approaches, you move your eyes close together as you follow it; as it recedes, you move them apart. Thus there is a regular association between an object's distance, and the degree to which you cross your eyes to focus on it. (Berkeley and others found many additional distance cues). So far, Berkeley's analysis of how we see depth is uncontroversial, and is the foundation of modern analyses. However, Berkeley goes on to make the empiricist claim that the association must be *learned*. The infant would not know that a person was receding as the person walked away; the infant would simply see the figure shrink. Berkeley's claim that depth perception must be learned was countered later by Immanual Kant who asserted depth perception to be innate. Although the controversy between the nativist and empiricist views continued for decades, it was not until the 1960s that experiments with infants showed Kant to be reasonably correct (Bower, 1974).

The real force of Berkeley's argument becomes clear if we generalize the problem to all visual experience. You hold a blue book at right angles to your eyes. What do you see? The naive answer is to say a book, yet as Berkeley would argue, all you really see is a rectangular patch of blue, the retinal image. You rotate the book to a 45° angle. What do you see now? Again, you want to say "a book," and in fact you would still believe the book to be a rectangle. But Berkeley would say that what you are really seeing is a blue patch which now has the shape of a truncated pyramid. Berkeley's argument is that all anyone ever sees is a collection of colored patches on one's retina. One must *learn* to "see" them as books, people, cats, cars, and so on. One must *learn* to believe one is still seeing a rectangular book when in fact one is seeing a truncated-pyramid blue patch.

Berkeley's analysis of vision supports his idealism. One's sensory and ideational world is just a collection of sensations, and one believes in the permanence of objects only because certain collections of sensations are regularly associated. Belief in matter is therefore a learned inference only, for matter is not directly perceived. For Berkeley, if something, even matter, cannot be directly perceived it is a metaphysical fiction to be eliminated.

Two important psychological systems branch off from Berkeley's psychological analysis of vision and his philosophy. Berkeley constantly appeals to introspection as evidence for his conclusions and implies that we should try to describe conscious experience without making inferences. That is, psychology should strive to describe only color-patches and shapes, the true objects of perception. This is later the approach of E. B. Titchener's structuralism. He taught his subjects to report their experiences only as sets of sensations, the basic Berkeleyan building blocks of experience. Titchener also tried to show how we learn to associate stimuli together into complex ideas, such as a book or a person, in line with Berkeley's associative psychology. Berkeley thus set Titchener's empirical problems.

The second system, the radical behaviorism of B. F. Skinner, appears at first wholly unrelated to Berkeley, and it is certainly hostile to structuralism. Yet Berkeley asserted the fundamental tenet of the positivism that underlies radical behaviorism: If something cannot be perceived, it is a metaphysical relic to be expunged from science. Berkeley said that substance is only inferred from experience, and so is unreal. Skinner says that mind is likewise an inference from experience, but that we never perceive mind itself. It, too, is a metaphysical, unobservable entity to be expunged from science. Of course, Skinner is a materialist, not an idealist. The fundamental similarity between Berkeley and Skinner is in restricting inquiry to that which is immediately perceived.

It is evident that all the sciences have a relation, greater or less, to human nature. . . . To explain the principles of human nature, we in effect propose a complete system of the sciences, built on a foundation almost entirely new, and the only one upon which they can stand with any security . . . and the only solid foundation we can give to this science itself must be laid on experience and observation.

So Hume wrote in his *Treatise on Human Nature.* Locke began the attempt to replace metaphysics with psychology as the foundation for the other sciences, and Hume carried out the task in a rigorously Newtonian and empiricist manner. Hume analyzed human nature as he found it in his own introspection and in the behavior of others. As with Locke, Hume's intention was to fix the limits of human knowledge, to sort out the knowable from the unknowable so that inquiry could be profitably fixed on the former. Precisely because science is a human enterprise, psychology, not speculative metaphysics, is the foundation for all science.

Hume began his inquiry into human nature by categorizing the contents of our minds somewhat as Locke had. Locke had spoken of the contents of our minds as "ideas" for which Hume, following the Scottish moral philosopher Francis Hutcheson (1694-1746), substituted "perceptions." Perceptions are then divided into two types, *impressions* and *ideas.* Impressions are essentially what we today call *sensations,* and ideas were for Hume less vivid copies of impressions. Thus you have an immediate impression of the book before you, an impression you may recall later on as an idea, a pale copy of the actual experience. Both impressions and ideas come either through sensation of external objects, or through reflection, by which Hume meant our emotional experiences (or what Hume also called the *passions*). Passions are of two sorts: the violent passions, such as love and hate and the other emotions we ordinarily call passions. However, Hume also included *calm passions,* such as aesthetic and moral feelings. The diagram (Figure 5-1) adapted from Smith (1941) summarizes Hume's categories; remember, however, that the distinctions under *impressions* apply also to *ideas.*

Finally, Hume distinguished *simple* and *complex* perceptions. An impression is a single, unanalyzable sensation, such as a blue spot of ink. Most impressions are complex, since our senses are usually exposed to many simple sensations at once. Simple ideas are copies of simple impressions, and complex ideas are aggregates of simple ideas. This means that complex ideas may not exactly correspond to some complex impression. So, you may imagine a unicorn, which of course you have never seen. However, complex ideas may always be broken down into simple ideas which are copies of simple impressions. So, your complex idea of a unicorn simply combines the impression or idea of a horse with the impression or idea of a horn, both of which you have experienced. Before considering how complex perceptions are formed, two important conclusions may already be drawn from Hume's category of mental content. First, Hume gave priority to impressions over ideas. Impressions bring us directly in touch with reality by perception, while ideas

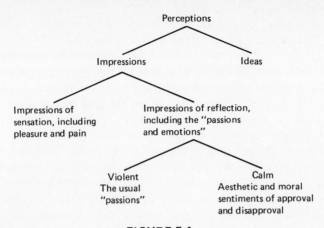

**FIGURE 5-1.**
Hume's categorization of the human mind. (Adapted from N. K. Smith
*The philosophy of David Hume,* reprinted by permission of
Macmillan, London and Basingstoke).

may be false, corresponding to nothing (such as, the unicorn). The truth is to be determined by tracing ideas to impressions, and whatever ideas are found to have no empirical content, such as the ideas of metaphysics and theology, are to be expunged. Thus Hume asserted a positivism—the claim that all meaningful ideas must be reducible to something observable. The second important conclusion is that Hume assigned priority to simple perceptions over complex ones. All complex perceptions are built up from our experiences of simple ones and may be completely analyzed into simple components. Thus Hume was a psychological atomist, holding that complex ideas are built up out of simple sensations.

When we turn to how complex perceptions are built up out of elementary ones, we come to what Hume himself thought was his central contribution to the science of human nature: his doctrine of the association of ideas. The concept of association was not new with Hume. We find it in Hobbes, Spinoza, and Berkeley; the phrase "association of ideas" was coined by Locke. However, they had used it in only a limited way—Locke, for example, seeing in association an obstacle to clear thinking and sound education. What Hume prized was his use of association to inquire into fundamental philosophical and psychological questions. It was the chief theoretical tool of his new science.

Hume wrote in his essay *An Inquiry Concerning Human Understanding* (Hume, 1962), "To me there appear to be only three principles of connection among ideas, namely, *Resemblance, Contiguity* in time or place, and *Cause* [and] *Effect*." In his *Abstract of a Treatise of Human Nature* (Hume, 1962), Hume exemplified each: " 'resemblance'—a [portrait] naturally makes us think of the man it was drawn for; contiguity—when St. Denis is mentioned, the idea of Paris naturally occurs; 'causation'—when we think of the son we are likely to carry our attention to the father ... [T]hese are the only links that bind the parts of the universe together or connect us with any person or object exterior to our-selves . . . ." At least, said Hume, "so far as regards the mind."

The influence of Newton is strong here. Gravity is the attractive force that binds the atomic parts of the universe together. For Hume association "is a kind of *attraction* which in the mental world will be found to have as extraordinary effects as in the natural," (Hume, 1817) and the laws of association "are really *to us* the cement of the universe" as experienced. Thus for Hume complex human experience (complex ideas) is at root simple ideas (derived from impressions) united together by the principle of association. As Newton did with gravity, Hume thus made association into an ultimate principle that could not be reduced further.

Hume then proceeded to investigate human knowledge in light of these three (soon to be two) laws. Cause and effect is the most important law, underlying most everyday reasoning. You will lift your arm; it rises. You knock one billiard ball into another; the second one moves. You turn off a light switch; the light goes out. Moreover, cause and effect even lies at root of the inference that, contrary to Berkeley, a material world exists, for one assumes the world acts on the senses so as to cause one to perceive it. However, whence comes our knowledge of causation? Causes are never directly perceived. Rather we perceive a regular conjoining of two events: the feeling of intention with the subsequent movement of the hand; the flipping of the switch with the subsequent extinguishing of the light; the motion of one ball with the subsequent motion of the second; the opening of the eyes with the appearance of things. Furthermore, no rational argument can be produced to prove causation. Hume argued that belief in causes is learned through experience. As a child experiences many regular conjunctions of events, a "propensity" of the child's mind leads to the firm conviction that the first event caused the second. This propensity also brings along a feeling of necessity. Causation is not simply correlation for Hume, it is a *feeling* of necessity between two events. This means, of course, that cause-and-effect is not a basic principle of association, since it is reducible to contiguity plus the feeling of necessity.

Hume generalized his argument to all generalizations. When one claims "All swans are white," it is on the basis of experiencing a number of swans, all of which were white; so one assumes that future swans in one's experience will also be white and one therefore draws the conclusion. It is quite like assuming—based on past experiences—the light will go out when one flips the switch. In neither case, how-ever, can the generalizations be given a rational justification, for they are based on experience, not on reason. No principle of reason underlies empirical generaliza-tions. But we do make them and Hume wanted to explain how we do so, in order to have a complete theory of human nature.

The principle Hume employed is the principle of *custom* or *habit*. In the *Inquiry* (Hume, 1962), Hume wrote: "For whenever the repetition of any particu-lar act or operation produces a propensity to renew the same act or operation without being impelled by any reasoning or process of the understanding, we always say that this propensity is the effect of *custom*. . . . All inferences from experience . . . are effects of custom [habit], not of reasoning."

It was, and is, frequently assumed by Hume's readers that by reducing causation and inductive generalization to habit he is denying their validity, and that he must have been a total skeptic, surprised each morning to find that the sun had risen. This is wrong (Smith, 1941). Hume was only trying to find out *how* we reach causal and inductive conclusions; he was not concerned with validity. He discovered that reason is not involved; but he did not therefore have to deny the validity of causation and induction. In fact, Hume wrote (1962), "as this operation from the mind, by which we infer effects from causes and, *vice versa* is so essential to the subsistence of all human creatures, it is not probable that it could be trusted to the fallacious deductions of our reason, which is slow . . . appears not, in any degree, during . . . infancy, and, at best, is . . . extremely liable to error and mistake." Further, the "wisdom of nature" has implanted in us this "instinct or mechanical tendency" that is "infallible in its operation" and appears at birth. Thus the ability to form general conclusions, or habits, is founded on association, on our propensity to generalize from limited instances, and on our propensity to feel causes necessarily linked to effects. This ability to generalize is innate, "infallible," and of its operations we are "ignorant." Habit is a surer guide to the world than reason.

In support of this, Hume noted that the same generalizing tendency is present in animals whose practical knowledge of the world is nearly faultless, yet who do not possess reason. Animals learn habits, and according to Hume (1962) "any theory by which we explain the operations of the understanding . . . in man will acquire additional authority if we find the same theory is requisite to explain the same phenomenon in other animals." Other philosophers had stressed man's uniqueness, but Hume here stressed man's similarity to animals, implying the value of a comparative approach to human and animal mind.

As a consequence of his views, Hume made a statement that seems startling coming from a philosopher in the Age of Reason. He writes in *A Treatise of Human Nature*: "Reason is, and ought only to be the slave of the passions, and can never pretend to any other office than to serve and obey them." This is quite natural, given Hume's position. Reason is helpless to know reality, it must serve experience and the instinct for generalization, which reflect the world as it is. For Hume, morality is a matter of feeling (passion). We approve and disapprove the actions of ourselves and others according to how we feel about them and reason must thus serve our moral sentiments.

Hume thus resisted skepticism by relying on human nature. As he and others pointed out, the most extreme skeptic never behaves according to his beliefs; he always assumes there will be a tomorrow. Hume wrote in his *Inquiry* (1962): "[N]o durable good can ever result from *excessive* skepticism," nor can it hope that "its influence will be beneficial to society." Hume preferred a moderate skepticism, which accepts the limits of reason, properly values animal nature, and knows that general conclusions may be false (after all, there *are* black swans). Such a skepticism is practical (for it does not doubt the accumulated wisdom of experience) and useful (for it preaches toleration and provides a science of human nature for the proper founding of the other sciences).

In Hume's work we see the first glimmerings of the psychology of adaptation.

At bottom, human knowledge is habit, whether mental as with Hume, or behavioral, as with the behaviorists. Hume stressed the practical knowledge of the everyday world that lets us adapt to our environment, as would post-Darwinian American and British psychologists. Hume appealed to human continuity with animals, as would psychologists after Darwin, especially the behaviorists. Hume viewed feeling —the passions—as an essential part of human nature. A person is not pure rational soul locked in a material, passionate body. So, too, would Freud and the behaviorists stress the emotional, or motivational, side of humans. Finally, in preferring one theory to another because of its social and practical utility, Hume also anticipated those American psychologists for whom one defect of structuralism was its avowed practical inutility.

Before leaving Hume, we should mention that he may be viewed as a faculty psychologist (Stern, 1971), although his faculties were not those of Aristotle and his medieval followers or of the later Scottish faculty psychologists. Hume distinguished five faculties. There are two *rational faculties:* abstract reason and experimental reason. *Abstract reason* is properly concerned with the nonempirical, tautologous fields of pure mathematics and logic. *Experimental reason* deals with empirical matters of fact. Experimental reason draws its material from the first of three *irrational faculties:* perception (which includes memory and imagination). *Perception* is the faculty concerned with impressions and ideas of all sorts. The last two irrational faculties are *taste,* whose sphere is moral and aesthetic value judgments, and *faith*, whose sphere is theology (and in which Hume placed little value). In Hume's view, confusion and error result when faculties are applied to problems outside their appropriate sphere. Thus the illusions of metaphysics arise when abstract reason constructs logical systems about ideas such as "God" and "being" and then thinks they exist. Knowledge of what exists is reserved to experimental reason.

Although Hume's philosophy was not widely read (his history of England was) he roused two important responses to his skeptical empiricism. One response became the common-sense psychology of American colleges; the other was the critical philosophy of Immanuel Kant.

### Responses to Hume

#### The Reassertion of Common Sense: The Scottish School

Although Hume endorsed only a limited skepticism, many who read him thought he was a radical skeptic—and a hypocrite to boot—since he did not live as a skeptic. Hume himself, along with Adam Smith, the economist, was a Scot, and it was some of his fellow Scots who reacted most strongly to his apparent skepticism. These philosophers asserted the claims of the common man against the abstruse speculations of philosophy. "I despise philosophy, and renounce its guidance—let my soul dwell with Common Sense," Thomas Reid, the founder and best philosopher of the movement, wrote. In addition to Reid (1710-1796), other members of the Scottish School were James Beattie (1735-1803), popularizer and polemicist against Hume, and Reid's student, Dugald Stewart (1753-1828).

As we have seen, Locke's "Way of Ideas" is subject to two interpretations, as act or content. Reid found the latter view in both Locke and Hume, and traced it to Descartes. According to Reid, Locke claimed there were four elements to any perceptual act: the perceiver, the act of perception, the idea which is the immediate object of perception, and the real object which the idea represents. Reid claimed that Hume had simply worked out the skepticism inherent in Locke's account, driving his skeptical wedge between object and idea.

Reid found Hume's conclusion offensive to common sense, as simply too absurd to be believed. We all have secure knowledge of our world and never become skeptical unless prodded by abstruse philosophy. Reid adopted common-sense beliefs as his philosophy. He explicated common-sense by an analysis of the ordinary language which embodies it. This approach is similar to that of modern ordinary-language philosophy. For our purposes, two points of Reid's common-sense philosophy are important.

First, Reid repudiated the way of ideas, or as he called it, idealism. He maintained that there are only three elements in perception: the perceiver, the act of perception, and the real object. Our perceptual acts made direct contact with objects, not with just their representative ideas. We know the world in a direct, unmediated way, consistent with what each of us believes common sensically. Reid formulated the *act psychology* version of Locke's "idea." In the nineteenth century, act psychology was the chief European rival to Wundt's and Titchener's psychology of content. Reid stated the fundamental tenet of act psychology, that perceptions imply something seen and known directly: "I cannot see, without seeing something." The founder of act psychology, Franz Brentano, would call this principle *intentionality*.

Reid also anticipated two related ideas that grew out of act psychology and are later found in the *Gestalt* movement. First, Reid said, experience is not a compound of simple sensations. Our primary experience is of complex impressions, to use Hume's term. Reid acknowledged that one can analyze complex impressions into simple ones, but denied that the complex ideas are formed by learned associations. As the Gestalt psychologists would say, a triangle is composed of three lines, but we always experience it as an organized whole—the triangle. Reid derived from this observation the conclusion that perception is always meaningful. Concepts are mental symbols that stand for something real. Perception is thus like language. As believed the medievals, Reid said we get knowledge by reading the "book of the world" which tells us the meaning of reality as surely as reading a book tells us its meaning. Complex experience cannot be reduced to atomic sensations without robbing it of something vital—its meaning.

The second general point central to Reid's philosophy, and it will also be found in Gestalt psychology, is his nativism. According to Reid, we are naturally endowed with certain innate faculties and principles of mind which allow us to know the world accurately and which furnish us with essential moral truths as well. Reid wrote: "Such original and natural judgments are, therefore, a part of that furniture which Nature hath given to the human understanding. They are the inspiration of the Almighty . . . they serve to direct us in the common affairs of life, where our reasoning faculty would leave us in the dark . . . and all the discoveries of reason are grounded upon them. They make up what is called *the common sense of mankind*. . . . When a man suffers himself to be reasoned out of the principles of common sense, by metaphysical arguments, we may call this *metaphysical lunacy*. . . ." (Reid, 1975). Thus knowledge of the world is secure because of our innate constitution which delivers it. We are so constructed as to know. Reid's claims for the existence of innate mental faculties sometimes causes his school to be called faculty psychology, but they clearly did not invent the concept, they only popularized it.

What Reid said really only restated what Hume actually argued, and Hume never took Reid seriously. We have seen how Hume, too, subordinated reason to innate powers of association and propensities to generalize. Reid exceeded Hume in the number of principles he believed are built into the human constitution, including such moral "first principles" as the worship of God.

The root difference between them was religious. A curious aspect of the nativism-empiricism debates of the eighteenth century often escapes the modern eye. We today assume that native constitution is the arbitrary product of natural selection. Our ability to see depth is basically a genetic accident based on a favorable mutation in some early creature. However, most philosophers before Darwin believed in God, and assumed that since God made man, whatever ideas or principles He implanted must be *true,* unless God is a deceiver. Thus Locke, staunch opponent of innate truths, never used the best counter claim to so-called innate principles—namely to show that they may not be true—for Locke assumed that whatever God did implant must be true. Hume, however, was an agnostic (if not an atheist) and his moderate skepticism was an inevitable result. Our faculties, not being God-given, may err. Reid, however, avoided any skepticism whatsoever by dogmatically asserting that the Almighty implanted in us first principles, necessarily valid because of their source. Thomas Reid was a clergyman—perhaps a clergyman first and a philosopher second.

We may ask if he was a psychologist. Reid, like Hume, wanted a science of human nature conducted along Newtonian lines. However, his extensive nativism coupled to his claim that the God-given first principles cannot be revised, puts his system outside psychology as a science. The hypotheses of any science must be open to proof, test, and revision. They cannot be enshrined as God's immutable truth. A similar criticism may be directed at Hume. By replacing metaphysics with psychology, he made psychology into a metaphysics, a set of necessary principles underlying the other sciences. Again, there could be no revision; Hume opened no paths for scientific investigation. Both Reid and Hume elevated psychology to a central place among human concerns; both enunciated general principles and embodied certain attitudes that shaped psychology later; but neither was really a psychologist. Both used psychology to pursue philosophy, their first concern.

Among the Scots, a step toward psychology was taken by Reid's student, Dugald Stewart. Stewart was more reconciled to Hume than was Reid, abandoning the term *common-sense* and using association extensively. His basic work, *Philosophy of the Human Mind* (1792) reads like an introductory psychology text based on everyday experience instead of laboratory experiments. There are sections on attention, association (learning), memory, imagination, and dreaming. Stewart wrote charmingly about magicians, jugglers, and acrobats to illustrate his points. His discussions of attention and memory have a contemporary air about them, with Stewart making some distinctions found in modern information processing psychology, citing everyday experiences to support them. Stewart followed Reid in dissecting the mind into component faculties, each of which is assigned its role in mental life and knowledge. Stewart spent 62 pages showing the practical value of the study of psychology.

In all, Stewart's work is engaging and attractive. Through Stewart especially, Scottish philosophy became quite influential in some places. It was especially important in America. Some of America's earliest college founders were adherents of the Scottish School, as were some important college presidents in the nineteenth century. In the hands of later writers (beginning with Stewart), Scottish philosophy became a readily acceptable psychology, intuitively appealing and consistent with Christianity. Most American colleges were (and many still are) religious, and in the nineteenth century Scottish faculty psychology was part of the "moral sciences" taught to their students. We will find that a large part of the inspiration to Watson's behaviorism was a revolt against this tradition of religious psychology.

### The Reassertion of Metaphysics: Immanual Kant (1724-1804)

Kant himself tells us that Hume's skeptical empiricism roused him from his "dogmatic slumbers." Before reading Hume, Kant had been a follower of Leibniz through his teacher Christian Wolff (1679-1754), though Kant was not without originality. However, Hume upset Kant's Leibnizian "dogmatism" by his psychological analysis of human knowledge. Kant saw Hume's empiricism as undermining certain knowledge and as threatening the absolute achievement of Newton's physics. As a result, Kant tried to rescue metaphysics. He realized that the old speculative metaphysics about God and man's spiritual substance was dead, and in fact Kant proved that it had always been an illusion. However, Kant could not accept Hume's merely psychological analysis of knowledge, for it only said we have a tendency to form general conclusions based on association. Kant wanted to prove the validity of human knowledge quite apart from any empirical facts about human habit formation. He thus reasserted the claim of philosophical metaphysics over psychology to be the foundation of the other sciences.

Kant's answer to Hume bears a strong resemblance to Reid's. What we have knowledge of, in Kant's term, is *phenomena*. The objects of science, such as planets or balls rolling down inclined planes, are found in human experience. Kant argued that experience is organized by the inherent nature of human perception and thinking. For example, in our experience every event has a cause. Why? According to Hume, belief in causation is something learned, primarily by association. But for Kant, Hume's account undermined the absolute truth of causation; a mere habit cannot be absolutely true, as required by the Newtonian physics Kant took as his model of human knowledge. Belief in causation therefore cannot derive from habit, but from something inherent in human thinking. The world as we experience it, phenomena, *must* be such that every event has a cause, for this is the only way we can conceive the world. Our experience will never violate causality because we are so constructed that every experienced event has a cause. The Newtonian assumption of universal causality can never be falsified, and it is therefore absolutely and necessarily true—at least as regards phenomena.

Outside phenomena are what Kant called *noumena,* or things-as-they-are. In the noumenal world there may be uncaused events, and in fact Kant assigned human moral freedom to the noumenal realm. However, as noumena affect us to produce phenomena, all events are perceived to be caused. Thus, according to science all behavior is caused, for science rests on phenomena; but man may very well be noumenally free—in fact must be free if moral responsibility is to have any meaning. Kant built in many inherent principles of understanding which structure our phenomena—from time and space as preconditions of sensation to concepts of causality and existence.

What Kant tried to do, in his own words, is to carry out a "Copernican Revolution" in epistemology. Previous empiricist philosophers assumed that humans have knowledge because objects impose themselves on understanding, which conforms itself to them. Hume's philosophy is the end point of this assumption. For Hume, events in the real world are regular because of the laws of nature, and these regularities register themselves in our mind as habits. But Hume's view leads to at least moderate, if not total, skepticism, which Kant (like so many others) found appalling. So, Kant decided to "revolutionize" philosophy by a new assumption—that objects conform themselves to our understanding. The following example may help clarify Kant's view (Copleston, 1964). If a person wears red glasses, every object of his or her understanding will be red. Now the person will probably assume, if he or she has worn them all his or her life, that all objects are red, that is, that understanding conforms itself to objects. However, it is possible (and in fact true in this instance) that objects have many colors, but that something about the perceiver (the glasses) imposes redness on all objects of knowledge, and for the wearer it is phenomenally true to say "Everything is red." Kant argued that something like this is true of human knowledge as it is. We are endowed with certain qualities of perception and thinking which impose themselves on experience to create the objects of knowledge about which science makes true statements. For the empiricist, the mind is passive in registering the qualities of objects; but for Kant the mind actively structures experience into an organized, knowable shape. Only thus can human knowledge be rescued from skepticism. Of course, only phenomena are rescued from skepticism; noumena may or may not be always caused or always organized in time and space. Illusory metaphysics arises when human reason applies its inherent concepts to noumena, to which they do not apply. Thus attempts to prove the existence of God are futile, for God is never known phenomenally, and so the empirical, if innate, concept of "existence" simply cannot apply to God. Of course, God cannot be proved not to exist either.

Kant's philosophy is extremely difficult, and its influence in pure philosophy has been very great. However, from the psychological standpoint we may question whether Kant departs in any essential way from Hume or Reid. Hume gave a psychological analysis of knowledge as founded on man's propensity to form habits. Reid proposed an involved nativism in which common-sense beliefs are implanted by God and therefore correspond to the material world. Kant also proposed that human innate principles so structure experience that knowledge is necessarily true of phenomena, though not of noumena. Kant thought he had *proved* the transcendental validity of his innate concepts, but from a modern perspective these concepts, if they exist, are evolutionary accidents, and Kant's explanation is just as psychological as Hume's or as physiological as Reid's. In other words, what applied to Reid as against Hume applies to Kant as well. The major difference between Hume, on the one hand, and Reid and Kant on the other, is the amount and nature of innate equipment humans come with. The verdict of history is mixed on this score. Kant has been supported by findings that perception of three-dimensional space is innate, but has been undermined by modern quantum physics (in which not all events have causes) and the construction of non-Euclidean geometries (which Kant implied were inconceivable).

Given his disdain for Hume's psychological account of knowledge, Kant cared little for psychology. Kant believed that psychology, defined as the introspective study of the mind, could not be a science. It is usually said that Kant said this because he believed psychology could not be mathematicized, but that is only a part of the reason. According to Kant, any science has two parts—the empirical part, involving observation and research, and the rational or metaphysical part, comprising the philosophical foundations that justify the empirical science's claim to produce knowledge. Kant believed that he had provided the metaphysical grounding of physical science in his account of human experience, the *Critique of Pure Reason*. There he showed that the basic assumptions of physics, such as universal causality, were necessarily true of human experience. Hence physics is a complete science.

Kant argued, however, that rational psychology is an illusion. The object of rational psychology is the thinking substance, or soul—Descartes' "I think." According to Kant, the soul is pure thinking; it has no content, and there can be no science without a subject matter. Kant held that since our experience is unitary —we do not experience disjuncted sensations—we assume that there is a self or ego, the soul, behind this unity. However, we do not experience the soul—or what Kant called the *Transcendental Ego*—directly for it has no content, being pure thought, and has only noumenal, not phenomenal, existence. To apply our inherent empirical categories of understanding to the Ego, for example, to say that it exists and that it has a spatial location, is illusion and bad metaphysics. There is an empirical ego, however, the sum total of our sensations or mental content, and of course we can study it through introspection. However, this empirical psychology, unlike empirical physics, cannot be a science for it lacks its rational counterpart, and so Kant thinks little of it.

Nevertheless, Kant believed in a science, or at least a discipline, concerned with humanity; he called it anthropology, the study (*logos*) of humans (*anthropos*).

As Kant practiced anthropology, however, it bears much greater resemblance to psychology than to anthropology as we know it, for Kant's anthropology studied human intellectual faculties, human appetite, and human character, but was not the cross-cultural study of societies. Kant delivered a very popular series of lectures published as *Anthropology from a Pragmatic Point of View*. If Kant's philosophy is similar to Reid's, his *Anthropology* is similar to Stewart's psychology, complete with an enumeration of faculties. Kant's lectures are accessible, full of shrewd observations of everyday behavior, charming and even funny anecdotes, and popular prejudice. In short, *Anthropology* is Kant's common-sense psychology, and bears some attention.

Kant distinguished physiological anthropology, concerned with man's body and its effect on mind, and pragmatic anthropology, concerned with man as a morally free agent and citizen of the world. The goal of pragmatic anthropology was to improve human behavior and so was grounded not in the metaphysics of experience, but in the metaphysics of morals. Pragmatic anthropology's methods were many. First, we have some introspective knowledge of our own minds, and by extension, of other's minds. Kant was aware of the pitfalls of introspection, however. When we introspect we change the state of our minds, so what we find is unnatural and of limited value; the same holds for trying to observe our own behavior. Kant even went so far as to say that excessive reflection on one's own mind may drive one insane. Similarly, when we observe others, they will act unnaturally if they know we are watching. Anthropology must be an interdisciplinary study embracing these methods—but using them with care—and also calling on history, biography, and literature for information about human nature.

*Anthropology* is a rich work. Kant discusses everything from insanity (which he felt was innate) to the nature of women (they are weaker but more civilized than men) to how to give a dinner party for philosophers (Kant wrote: "Dinner music . . . is the most tasteless absurdity that debauchery could have devised," because it prevents conversation.) Just one of Kant's many topics will be presented here, however, for it occurs in Wundt's psychology in much the same form.

Kant discussed "ideas that we have without being aware of them." If we examine our awareness, we will find that some perceptions are clear—the ones we are attending to—while others are obscure. As Kant put it, "our mind is like an immense map, with only a few places illuminated." This view of consciousness as a field with clear and obscure areas is identical to Wundt's, as we will find later. The obscure ideas are those we are not clearly aware of, so obviously Kant's doctrine is not Freud's view of repression into the unconscious. However, Kant does say we can be subtly affected by obscure ideas. He observes that we often unthinkingly judge persons by their clothes without directing conscious attention to them. Kant also offers pragmatic advice to writers: make your ideas a little obscure so that when a reader clarifies them you will make him feel clever.

In addition to his conception of consciousness, many other ideas of Kant's influenced Wundt, the founder of the psychology of consciousness. By Wundt's time, ways to experiment on and quantify mind had become available, and so Wundt was able to show that a scientific empirical psychology was possible without

a rational companion. Wundt thus could abandon the Transcendental Ego altogether. However, it still lived in Wundt's system in modified form. Wundt
emphasized how apperception gives unity to conscious experience, a role Kant
assigned to the Transcendental Ego. In addition, Wundt put thinking beyond the
reach of introspection, as did Kant, holding that it could be investigated only
indirectly through a study of man in society, similar to Kant's *Anthropology*.
Wundt's psychology had two parts: the laboratory study of experience via introspection (Kant's empirical psychology made into a science despite him), and the
study of the higher mental processes via the comparative study of culture similar to
Kant's *Anthropology* (although Wundt did not use the label). Wundt also modified
Kant's view of introspection. Wundt said good, scientific introspection was not the
intense scrutiny of the soul Kant found dangerous, but only the self-observations of
one's experiences, which even Kant said was possible.

We have noted here only some of Kant's influence on Wundt, but Kant's
overall influence on Western thinking was profound. He is frequently viewed as the
greatest thinker since Plato, and all philosophy after him was shaped by his
philosophy—either through elaboration on his system or by provoking alternative
answers to the problems he raised. His thought thus influences psychology directly
(as in Wundt's case) or indirectly (as in behaviorism, which discarded the ego altogether), for it emerged out of philosophy. His most direct intellectual successors
were the German speculative idealists Johann Fichte (1762-1814), Friedrich
Schelling (1775-1854), Arthur Schopenhauer (1788-1860), and G. W. F. Hegel
(1770-1831), who all in one way or another dispensed with the things-in-themselves
so that the Transcendental Ego, or alternatively the World-Spirit, constitutes the
world via its own ideas. In America, Kant's transcendental philosophy was a vital
influence on transcendentalism, an important intellectual movement in the first
part of the nineteenth century. The value of Kant's influence is much debated. True
empiricists, such as Bertrand Russell in his *History of Philosophy*, maintain that
Kant is refutable by Hume, and that through his influence on Hegel, he is responsible for modern totalitarian governments that purport to serve transcendent truth.
Others claim that Kant's influence on psychology was a disaster, because of its
exclusive emphasis on introspection and a radical dualism between self and world
(Wolman, 1968). It may be replied, however, that Kant did not invent introspection, and indeed warned against it, and that the dualism of self and world has been
part of Western thought at least since Plato. It is true that the categories of human
understanding he thought necessarily true have proven unnecessary, but Kant was
trying to reconcile human nature—including morality and the concept of freedom
that it requires—to the mechanical Newtonian-Cartesian world view that seemed
about to engulf and alienate humanity.

## THE PHILOSOPHES AND OTHERS

The eighteenth century swarmed with would-be Newtons of the mind. Few of them
had such long-term effects on Western thought as to rival the major philosophers,
but they are admirable barometers of the general current of psychological thinking

during the Enlightenment when the possibility of a scientific psychology was first seen and debated.

### Associationism

The association of ideas was not new in the eighteenth century. We have found it in Plato and Aristotle, and later in Locke. What was new in the eighteenth century was the extensive use to which the idea was put. Hume considered his widespread employment of association to be his main achievement, while others as diverse as Spinoza, Reid, and Kant recognized association as a force in human thinking. However, in the hands of the great philosophers it was used philosophically, either as a key to human knowledge or as an example of bad thinking.

Associationism as a distinct psychological program was founded by a British physician, David Hartley (1705-1757), whose major work was *Observations on Man* (1749). He worked out a complete associationistic account of human mind *and* behavior from simple sensation to sexual activity. Although Hartley's work appeared some years after Hume's *Treatise on Man,* Hartley had been working at his system for many years, and Hume was not one of his sources.

Hartley acknowledged his debt to John Gay (1699-1745), a clergyman who developed a moral associationism, inspiring Hartley's more extensive work. Hartley, like so many proto-psychologists, was a physician, and one of Hartley's aims was to establish the physiological basis of association. Hartley's greatest influence, however, as with the other "Newtons of the mind," was naturally Isaac Newton. Hartley attempted to follow Newton's methodological rules, indulging in no hypotheses and attempting to deduce phenomena from propositions already rooted in observation. In good Newtonian fashion, Hartley at one point admitted his proposed physiological laws of association were probably fictions, but were valuable because they explained so much. Additionally, unlike Hume, Hartley also adopted some of Newton's ideas on the physiological operation of sensation as given in Newton's *Opticks.*

Hartley believed in a close correspondence between mind and brain, and he proposed parallel laws of association for both. He was not a parallelist like Leibniz, however, for he made clear that mental events causally depend on neural events, although he could not explain how. The door to later parallelistic associationism remained open, nevertheless.

Beginning with the mental sphere, Hartley built up the mind from simple atomic units of sensation, as did Hume. Our sensory contact with a perceivable quality (what Hartley called an *impression*) causes a *sensation* (similar to Hume's impression) to arise in the mind. If the mind copies the sensation, this constitutes a simple *idea of sensation* (comparable to Hume's simple ideas) which may be compounded via association to form complex *intellectual ideas* (comparable to Hume's complex ideas). Like everyone else we have looked at so far, Hartley assumed the mind possessed certain faculties which could transform mental elements, although association remained the basic mental operation.

Turning to the physiological substrate of elements, Hartley adopted Newton's theory of nervous vibrations, which said that the nerves contain submicroscopic particles whose vibrations pass along through the nerves and constitute neural activity. An impression started the sensory nerve-substance vibrating and this vibration passed to the lower brain where it brought a sensation to the mind. Repeated occurrence created a tendency in the cortex to permanently copy this vibration as a smaller vibration, or *vibratiuncle,* corresponding to an idea. Thus vibratiuncles are weak copies of vibrations, and ideas of sensations are weak copies of impressions, just as in Hume's account.

Hartley distinguished two fundamental forms of association: successive and simultaneous. Successive associations are built up when trains of ideas regularly follow one another and so get bound up together. For example, a sentence could be analyzed as a string of words associated together in sequence. We will see the same kind of view in the work of James Mill and then in that of John B. Watson, founder of behaviorism. Simultaneous associations are bonds built up between ideas that regularly occur together at the same time. So, for example, a child's face is made up of many atomic features, all of which naturally occur together in consciousness. The elements become united by association so that if you see only a few features, you mentally fill in the rest of the face. Hartley stated only one law of association, that of contiguity. Sensations, and their consequent ideas, occur either in regular temporal order or together at once, and are associated by sheer closeness in time, that is, by contiguity. Hartley went on to apply these principles to the whole of the mind and also to behavior, claiming that motor responses, too, could be associated together and with ideas. This is one of the rare attempts to include actual behavior in a philosophical system.

Hartley's associationism was quite popular. It was propounded to the public and defended against critics by Joseph Priestley (1733-1804), a great chemist and co-discoverer of oxygen. Because Hartley said pleasure and pain accompanied sensations and so affected thought and action, it worked its way into utilitarianism, which we will consider in the next chapter. It was also quite influential in aristic and literary circles, deeply affecting the critical sensibility of turn-of-the-century artists, especially the romantics. Coleridge named his eldest son  David Hartley. And of course in the long-run, associationism eventually gave rise to analysis of behavior in terms of associated habits (Clark Hull's S-R bonds) or events in time (Skinner's account of reinforcement).

Among the many later eighteenth century associationists, Thomas Brown (1778-1820) deserves mention. Brown was a pupil of Dugald Stewart, and is often accounted a member of the common-sense school. However, he was severely critical of Reid, noting that Reid failed to differ from Hume. Brown also was much more an associationist than Reid or even Stewart. He also seems to have been influenced by Kant, for Brown discarded Hartley's physiological substrate of association, and possibly even its dependence on real-world regularities, in favor of a purely phenomenal account of association. Brown preferred to call association *suggestion* on the rather Humean grounds that *association* implies an unobservable bond between ideas. According to Brown, one idea simply suggests another, but there is no substantive link between them.

Brown offered three laws of suggestion which he felt were variations on the basic principle of proximity. The three laws were: resemblance (compare with Hume), contrast (*white* suggests *black*), and nearness in time and space (essentially contiguity). Brown took a step toward a more fruitful, empirical associationism with his enumeration of secondary laws of suggestion. They are nine in all and represent specific conditions which affect the operation of the basic law or laws. So, for example, memory of associated events is facilitated by long duration of the original ideas, liveliness of ideas, frequency of association, and closeness of ideas in time. Other secondary laws cover learned and constitutional individual differences in memory and association-formation. The step forward here is that these secondary laws suggest obvious experiments: what are the exact effects of frequency, of duration, of contiguity? It would be some years before anyone would actually do the experiments, but Brown points the way to an empirical and experimental psychology of mind.

By the middle of the eighteenth century associationism was surely an idea whose time had come. What started with Locke as a modest suggestion for how the mind errs in thinking became to various thinkers the real key to the science of human nature. So far, the British associationists were not radical associationists, leaving other mental forces in their theories, such as Hartley's faculties. When we turn our attention to the French philosophes however, we shall meet thinkers in whom Locke's empiricism and association of ideas took a more extreme form.

### The Philosophes

The Enlightenment was led by a diverse collection of thinkers now called philosophes; as the name implies, they were largely French. Few philosophes were academic philosophers, except in Germany. Their interests were eclectic, and they debated among themselves every topic of human knowledge. What united them was hostility to the established Church and the feudal governments it supported. They believed that the Christian religion was founded on superstition and myth, and that by enforcing belief in theological dogma it robbed man of intellectual freedom. When we speak of the Age of Reason, reason should be understood to be in contrast to Christian faith and revelation, rather than in contrast to emotions. The great enterprise of the French philosophes was Denis Diderot's *Encyclopedia,* meant to be a compendium of human knowledge and achievement, declaring to the world man's independence from God. The *Encyclopedia* embodied reason; the Bible embodied revelation. The philosophes wanted to be able to inquire freely into all matters without censorship or the threat of condemnation.

Although the philosophes opposed Christianity, few were atheists. Most followed Voltaire in believing in a Supreme Creator, while rejecting the ritual and accumulated dogma of Christianity.

What the philosophes tried to do was reconstruct society and philosophy on a new and natural basis, inspired by Newton's physics. For medieval and even

Renaissance thought, the natural and human worlds were given meaning by God: God created the world and everything was ultimately related to Him through the Great Chain of Being. In particular, man was a spiritual creature, possessing an immortal soul. However, as the medieval world view collapsed, it became necessary to give a new account of man and the universe. Newton's physics seemed to accomplish this task for the physical universe. Newton gave a complete account of the material world based only on the application of reason and observation. The philosophes, rejecting Christianity, wanted to complete Newton's work, that is, to provide a rational account of man and his relations to the world. We may call the philosophes' orientation *naturalism,* an understanding of man in natural rather than supernatural terms. Man was conceived to be part of nature, not forever outside it in a spiritual world of God, angels, and souls.

There were two major sources for the philosophes' naturalism (Vartanian, 1953). One was John Locke's empirical psychology. In eighteenth century France there was a mania for things English, especially Newton's science and Locke's psychology. The supreme philosophe, Voltaire, wrote in his *Philosophical Letters*: "So many philosophers having written the romance of the soul, a sage has arrived who has modestly written its history. Locke has set forth human reason just as an excellent anatomist explains the parts of the human body. He everywhere takes the light of Newton's physics for his guide." The other source of naturalism was native to France, Descartes' speculative physiology. As there were so many philosophes, major and minor, sometimes anonymous, we will focus our attention on two representatives of each tradition, beginning with the Cartesian.

Immediately after Descartes proposed that animals are simply machines (the beast-machine), but that humans were not machines by virtue of their souls, many of his religious opponents saw the trap he had set. For if animals, which behave in such diverse and often sophisticated ways, are but machines, is not the next logical step to say that a person, too, is but a machine (the *human*-machine)? They believed that Descartes was a secret materialist who only intimated what he hoped others might later say openly. They also spotted an interesting flaw in Descartes' *cogito*. If I know I exist as a thinking, spiritual substance only through introspection, how may I know other people are not machines and myself the only soul? This remarkable insight lies at the heart of behaviorism two centuries hence, for it was exactly by denying the validity of introspection that behaviorists re-made psychology into an objective, deterministic discipline concerned with movement, not mind. Of course Descartes said language was the sign of the soul in other people, but his opponents countered that one can certainly imagine language produced by some clever mechanical device. The religionists said these things to ridicule Descartes' system as subversive of faith, but in the irreligious eighteenth century there were those who said them in earnest, proclaiming materialism.

Although materialists can be found at least as far back as the seventeenth century [for example, Pierre Gassendi (1592-1655)], their number multiplied in the eighteenth century. They spoke up first in anonymous pamphlets, fearing persecution, but they soon grew bolder. The most outspoken and complete extension of Descartes' beast-machine into the human-machine was made by Julien

Offray de La Mettrie (1709-1751), whose major work was *L'Homme Machine* (*The Man-Machine*) of 1748. Interestingly, La Mettrie, too, thought Descartes was a secret materialist, but praises him for it. La Mettrie wrote: "He was the first to prove completely animals are pure machines" a discovery of such importance that one must "pardon all his errors." La Mettrie takes the step feared by religionists: "Let us boldly conclude that man is a machine. . . .", that the soul is but an empty word.

La Mettrie was a physician, and stated that only a physician may speak on human nature, for only he knows the mechanism of the body. La Mettrie went into some detail to show how the state of the body necessarily affects the mind, for example in the effects of drugs, disease, and fatigue. Against Descartes' insistence on the uniqueness of human language, La Mettrie suggested that apes might be made into "little gentlemen" by teaching them language the way the deaf are taught. In the 1960s, La Mettrie's proposal of teaching apes language was carried out with some success. La Mettrie remained a Cartesian, however, in asserting that language is what makes a person human. He only denies that language is innate, claiming that we can make the ape human, too, via language.

In general La Mettrie gives the impression not of lowering humans to the level of animals, but of raising animals to near-human status. This emerges most clearly in his discussion of natural moral law. La Mettrie argued that animals share moral sentiments such as grief and regret with humans, so that morality is inherent in the natural biological order. Having said this, however, La Mettrie leaves the door open to sheer hedonism by stating that the point of living is to be happy.

La Mettrie adopts an uncompromisingly scientific, anti-Aristotelian attitude to his subject. He denies finalism or any Godly act of intentional creation. For example, the animal eye was not made to see, but is a natural outcome of physical law. La Mettrie here was stating a doctrine called transformism, increasingly popular in the later eighteenth century, which marks the beginning of evolutionary thought. According to transformism, the universe was not created by God, but emerged from primordial matter as a result of the action of natural law. The development of the physical, and La Mettrie implies, biological, universe is a necessary consequence of the way nature is organized. Voltaire's Creator is no more necessary than the Christian God.

However, La Mettrie looked at the universe differently from Newton, Descartes, or the atomists and Epicureans. For them, matter was dead, incapable of spontaneous action. Hence, Descartes' dualism of dead matter and living but immaterial soul. However, La Mettrie advocated a new doctrine, just then coming into prominence in biology, that is later called *vitalism.* He thought biological matter at least to be capable of self-generation and motion. La Mettrie cited recent physiological research to prove his point. Polyps cut in two regenerate their missing halves; muscles of a dead animal still move when stimulated; the heart may beat after removal from the body. Matter is alive; it is vital, not dead; and it is precisely this natural vitality that made La Mettrie's human-machine plausible. In the twentieth century, vitalism became the great enemy of scientific biologists, but it was a necessary step in the founding of biology as a coherent field apart from physics. La Mettrie's vitalism again attests that his materialism was not meant to degrade humanity, to make of a human being a cold, metallic machine (the image we have today of the machine), but rather to make of a human a vital, living, dynamic machine, an integral part of a living nature.

We should conclude this summary as La Mettrie did his book. Like a good philosophe, and like B.F. Skinner today, La Mettrie urged the progressive nature and moral goodness of accepting materialism, of giving up vain speculation and religious superstition to live pleasurable lives. Recognizing ourselves to be part of nature, we can then revere, honor, and never destroy nature. Our behavior to others will improve. Wrote La Mettrie: "Full of humanity we will love human character even in our enemies . . . in our eyes they will be but mismade men . . . we will not mistreat our kind. . . . Following the natural law given to all animals we will not wish to do to others what we would not wish them to do to us." "Such is my system, or rather the truth, unless I am much deceived. It is short and simple. Dispute it now who will." Thus La Mettrie closed *L'Homme Machine.* Although his "truth" was not acceptable to all philosophes in its extreme form, and of course Christians hotly disputed it, materialism was a growing doctrine. It was reluctantly and partially accepted by Voltaire himself, by Denis Diderot, conceiver of the *Encyclopedia,* and espoused in extreme form by Baron Paul d'Holbach (1723-1789), who worked out its deterministic and atheistic implications. Its deeper implications we will see shortly.

The other route to naturalism was from Locke's empiricism. We have already seen how Hartley derived naturalistic psychology from Locke, Newton, and associationism. In France, too, there were *soi-disant* "Newtons of the mind." The general tendency of their thought was toward *sensationism,* deriving the mind entirely from sensations, denying the existence of the automous mental faculties and the power of reflection found in Locke's psychology. The French commentators thought they were improving on Locke.

The outstanding French empiricist was Etienne Bonnot de Condillac (1715-1780). Although he knew and influenced the philosophes he was never one himself. He shied away from the controversy they reveled in; he was a Catholic priest, albeit inactive, in the midst of anti-Christians.

Condillac dismissed everyone but Locke: "Immediately after Aristotle comes Locke. . . ." and he subtitled his first book, *An Essay on the Origin of Human Knowledge* (1746), "Being a Supplement to Mr. Locke's Essay on the Human Understanding." Like Berkeley, Condillac believed Locke had not pursued his own empiricism far enough, but in his *Essay* he followed Locke closely. It is only in a later work, *Treatise on Sensations* (1754) that Condillac really fulfilled his earlier promise to "reduce to a single principle whatever relates to the human understanding." That principle is sensation.

Locke had allowed the mind certain autonomous powers: the power of reflection on itself, and mental faculties or acts, such as attention and memory. Condillac strove to see the mind in a more passive, purely empiricist way. He denied the existence of reflection, and tried to derive all mental acts or faculties from simple sensation. His motto might have been "I sense, therefore I am." Condillac asks us to imagine a statue which we will endow with each sense in turn, starting with smell. Condillac then endeavors to build up complex mental activity from these senses. For example, memory arises when a sensation is experienced for a second time and recognized. We should observe that here Condillac cheats, for he assumed an inner power or faculty to store the first sensation, an innate power indistinguishable from memory. Attention is reduced to the strength of one sensation to dominate the mind over other weaker sensations. In his *Essay*, Condillac had followed Locke and said attention was a mental act (as will Wundt a century later), but in the *Treatise* his sensationism is consistent, and he anticipates Titchener's identical sensationist revision of Wundt's theory.

In short, Condillac attempted independently of Hume to work out a complete empiricist theory of mind, leaving as innate only the senses, the passions, and (implicitly) memory. In this he may be contrasted to La Mettrie, who left in his human-machine a rich and vital natural structure. In one respect, Condillac is more Cartesian than La Mettrie, for Condillac opposed materialism, accepting Descartes' dualism of spiritual soul and dead matter. However, since the soul always remained outside Condillac's actual discussions of the growth of understanding, when we strip the soul away, his system is more coldly mechanical than La Mettrie's. Condillac's statue-person is an inorganic, but intelligent, automaton, not a living piece of vital flesh.

The stripping away of the soul was performed by Claude Helvetius (1715-1771), who accepted Condillac's sensationism and a mechanical version of La Mettrie's materialism. Helvetius consequently proclaimed a complete environmentalism, in which humans have neither a divine soul nor a complex biological structure. The human possesses only senses, a passive mind able to receive sensations, and a body capable of certain actions. This mind is passively built up through watching the effects of a person's own and others' actions and observing the ways of the world. For Helvetius, then, the mind at birth is both blank and powerless; everything a person becomes is the result of the environment. Helvetius found cause for optimism in the malleability of the mind, holding out the hope that improved education can lead to improved people. In this he presaged the radical behaviorists who believe human behavior is similarly malleable. Such beliefs, however, have a negative potential as well—the possibility that an effective dictatorship can be founded on brainwashing.

Helvetius also presents the crucial problem of the Enlightenment: If we are going to conceive of humans as part of the natural world, on what basis can we erect a system of ethics? Ethics depend on rational control of passions, and the philosophes, far from glorifying reason, reduced it to the slave of the passions. La Mettrie said pleasure is the natural cause for our existence; nature made us to pursue pleaure. Condillac, too, reduced reason to desire, or need. If each sensation produces pleasure or pain, then our thinking, built up out of our sensations by association, is determined by their affective quality and directed by our momentary, animal needs. Hence, empiricism undercuts the autonomy of reason. For the rationalist, reason is prior to, and independent of, sensation, so hedonism is only a temptation to be overcome. The empiricist, however, constructing reason out of affectively charged sensations, makes hedonism the directing force behind all thought.

Condillac tried to elude the obvious hedonism in such a view by appealing to God and His transcendental moral order, but Helvetius, the materialist, did not. Like Freud, Helvetius postulated a pleasure principle as man's fundamental drive, and he reduced all feelings, including love and altruism, to the egotistical pursuit of pleasure or avoidance of pain. La Mettrie maintained much the same position. Helvetius, however, differed in asserting that this pleasure principle could be harnessed through education, a position La Mettrie did not accept.

Here we see the fundamental crisis of naturalism, first confronted by the philosophes, and which became acute after Darwin. If we are only machines, destined to pursue pleasure and avoid pain, what can be the ground of moral value and of meaning in our lives? The early philosophes assumed, as humanists, that the world was made for humans by a beneficent, if non-Christian, Creator. As the century progressed, however, it became evident that this optimism was unjustified. The great Lisbon earthquake of midcentury, for example, blotted out thousands of lives. Newton's universe seemed to be a machine indifferent to human life, which was a mere speck of no consequence. Moreover, the extension of materialism, determinism, and hedonism to human beings, while intellectually persuasive, was hard to accept emotionally. Diderot, for example, wrote in a letter, "I am maddened at being entangled in a devilish philosophy that my mind can't help approving and my heart refuting" (Knight, 1968). The whole dilemma, thus comes down to a question of our feelings—our feelings of freedom and dignity versus our natural desire to seek pleasure and avoid pain.

But how can life be given meaning by the hedonistic pursuit of pleasure? One solution was given by romanticism, which glorified the emotions, especially love. Another solution was to make pleasure and pain reasonable and prudent, to seek general happiness rather than personal happiness. This was the way of English utilitarianism, already implicit in Hume and Hartley. It tried to found society on a naturalistic ethic of calculating pleasure rationally and balancing diverging needs. Both these solutions become important in the nineteenth century.

However, one darker solution was offered at once. There is a remarkably existentialist sentence in La Mettrie's *L'Homme Machine*: "Who can be sure that the reason for man's existence is not simply the fact that he exists?" He continued: "Perhaps he was thrown by chance on some spot on the earth's surface, nobody knows how or why, but simply that he must live and die, like the mushrooms which appear from day to day...." La Mettrie states the possibility of a meaningless world, the abyss of moral nihilism that every philosophe saw and tried to avoid.

However, one man cheerfully jumped into that abyss, proclaiming the autonomy of pleasure, the illusion of morals, and the rule of the strong. The Marquis de Sade (1740-1814) wrote in *History of Juliette*

The weak is then right when, trying to recover his usurped possessions, he purposely attacks the strong and obliges him to make restitution; the only wrong he can have is to depart from the character of weakness that nature imprinted in him: she created him to be poor and a slave, he doesn't want to submit to it, that is his wrong; and the strong, lacking this wrong, since he preserves his character and acts only according to it, is equally right when he tries to despoil the weak and obtain pleasure at his expense. Let both now look for a moment into their hearts; the weak, in deciding to attack the strong, whatever his rights may be, will experience a slight struggle; and this resistance to satisfying himself comes from his trespassing against the laws of nature by assuming a character which is not his; the strong, on the contrary, in despoiling the weak, that is to say in enjoying all the rights he has received from nature, in giving them the greatest possible extension, finds pleasure in proportion to this extension. The more atrociously he harms the weak, the more voluptously he is thrilled; injustice is his delectation, he enjoys the tears that his oppression snatches from the unfortunate wretch; the more he grieves him, the more he oppresses him, the happier he is. . . . Besides, this necessary gratification which is born from the comparison that the happy man makes between the wretch and himself, this truly delicious gratification never establishes itself better for the fortunate man than when the misery he produces is complete. The more he crushes that wretch, the more he intensifies the comparison and consequently the more he nourishes his voluptousness. He has then two very real pleasures in the wrongs he inflicts upon the weak: both the increase of his physical resources, and the moral enjoyment of the comparisons which he makes all the more voluptuous in proportion as his injuries weaken the unfortunate wretch. Let him pillage then, let him burn, let him ravage, let him not leave the wretch more than the breath to prolong a life whose existence is necessary for the oppressor to establish his laws of comparison; whatever he does will be in nature, whatever he invents will be only the active use of the forces which he has received from her, and the more he exercises his forces, the more he will experience pleasure, the better he will use his faculties, and the better, consequently, he will have served nature.*

If the only goal in life that naturalism can find is pleasure, then we should each seek it uninhibited by morals or the opinions of society, according to Sade. In doing so, we will be fulfilling natural law. The strong must triumph over the weak. Sade extended comparative psychology to morals. The animals prey upon one another without compunction; they have no moral law. Since we are animals we should act in the same way. Moral law is a metaphysical illusion. The philosophes first struggled with the problem of a world ruled only by efficient causes and hedonism and tried to avoid Sade's logical extrapolation of naturalism. In the twentieth century the problem remains unsolved, and in our own time we have seen moral nihilism proclaimed again, while modern existential humanists seek to restore man's dignity. The problem became acute in the nineteenth century

*Quoted and translated by Lester Crocker, *An Age of Crisis,* Baltimore: Johns Hopkins University Press, 1959, pp. 212-213.

when Darwin cut away all reason for believing that humans transcend nature. In Darwin's universe, too, the strong destroy the weak. And Sade was a harbinger of the moral nihilism that would stare every Victorian in the face.

### Enlightenment and Anti-Enlightenment in Germany

The Enlightenment took a different turn in Germany than in France or England. German thinkers were generally academic philosophers rather than amateur philosophes; the movement failed to widely penetrate German consciousness. It was here too that a counter-movement arose against the Age of Reason.

The German Enlightenment may be said to start with the philosopher Christian Thomasius (1655-1728). Thomasius valued French more than German philosophy, believed philosophy should be useful, and rejected metaphysics for empiricism, all Enlightenment beliefs. Most interestingly, Thomasius seems to have conducted the first empirical psychological research of all time (McReynolds and Ludwig, 1977). Thomasius used a four-dimensional rating scale to define individual personalities. He did not conduct experiments, but based his ratings on conversations with his subjects, plus background information on occupation and personal habits. Thomasius even used multiple raters to increase his scales' reliability. In his attention to individual differences Thomasius was out of step with the Platonic tradition of German psychology we will see in Wundt, and Thomasius' pioneering researches appear to have exerted no influence on the history of psychology. The time was not yet ripe for empirical, scientific psychology.

With Christian Wolff (1679-1754) German philosophy returned to rationalist Leibnizian metaphysics. Wolff propounded a systematic metaphysical philosophy that dominated German thinking for many years, keeping out more empiricist Anglo-French thinking. So it was that Kant was slumbering in Wolff's dogmatism when he was aroused by Hume's radical empiricism. After Wolff there were a number of philosophe-like "popular philosophers" of limited influence.

More important for psychology was Johann Nikolaus Tetens (1736-1807), the first German to propose a systematic empirical psychology. Like Hume, Tetens wrote an essay on human nature, but his approach was different. Tetens rejected the empiricist view, manifested most clearly in Condillac's sensationism, that the mind was no more than a collection of sensations. Following a more rationalist line, Tetens maintained that the mind was active and autonomous, uniting sensations by its own activity, not merely registering passively regularities in sensation. The mind to Tetens did not rest content with empirical generalizations, but actively sought scientific and aesthetic ideals. Psychology, then, should not study only the content of the mind, to which an empiricist would be limited, but also the energetic activities of the mind that unify and process sensations. We will find Tetens' endeavor to explain nonsensational mental processes in Wilhelm Wundt, while Wundt's English student, E. B. Titchener, reverted to sensationism.

In Germany there arose a revolt against the Age of Reason, founded on the cultivation of history. Enlightenment philosophes were fond of genetic analysis.

Thus, Condillac tried to explain the mind by reducing it to its origins in sensations, and many philosophes, including Hume and Voltaire, wrote histories. However, Enlightenment history tended to be abstract and polemical, not really historical. Condillac's statue-person was entirely hypothetical and ideal, giving no concrete evidence for Condillac's genetic account of mind. The philosophes wrote history primarily to expose the evils of the Middle Ages, to extol the near perfection of their own age, and to predict the rosy future of enlightened humanity. Although they claimed to detest metaphysical systems, the "geometric spirit" of Descartes lived on in the philosophes' ideal system of mind and in their vision of the ideal society. The mathematical perfections of physics were applied to humankind and society by these would-be Newtons.

An Italian thinker, Giambattista Vico (1668-1744), had already spoken out against the extension of the Cartesian-Newtonian viewpoint to humanity and its products. Vico drew a sharp distinction between natural and human sciences. Humans observe nature, but create society, art, and self. Therefore, the methods applicable to nature, which humans only observe passively, ought to be different from the methods used in the human sciences. History was the most important social science for Vico, for it studies humanity's construction of self in different times and places. Vico denied that there is an essential, transcendent, universal human nature. Each society and historical period should be understood in its own terms, not dismissed as "barbaric" or "superstitious." For Vico, each historical epoch is characterized by its own unique pattern that conditions all the activities of its people. In short, Vico held a *Zeitgeist* view of history. His special respect for historical understanding went against the intellectual current of his time, however, and his work had no general influence in Europe for well over a century. In the 1970s he was rediscovered by a wide spectrum of social scientists.

Tremendously influential, however, was Johann Gottfried Herder's (1744-1803) similar historically-minded rejection of the extension of the geometric spirit to humans. Herder's views are remarkably similar to Vico's, although they were formed in ignorance of Vico's works. His motto "We live in a world we ourselves create" could have been said by Vico. Herder, too, stressed the absolute uniqueness of each living or historical culture. We should strive to fulfill ourselves and our own culture, not slavishly follow classical styles and attitudes of a bygone age. Herder is modern in his belief that each person should try to fulfill his or her potential as a total person instead of being an alienated collection of roles. Herder even opposed faculty psychology for its fragmentation of the human personality. For both the individual and the individual's culture, Herder stressed organic development.

Because each culture is unique, Herder opposed any attempt to impose one culture's values on any other. He detested the tendency of the philosophes to caricature the past and hold out their own times as a universal model for humanity. Herder even went so far as to imply the degeneracy of the Age of Reason. It was artificial; it aped the Greeks and Romans; it was too reasonable and insufficiently spiritual.

Herder's views were highly influential, especially in Germany. The intellectual framework in which Wundt founded psychology was permeated by the idea of the unique historical development of each cultural group, or *Volk*. The contrast of "degenerate" Anglo-French Enlightenment "civilization" with vital German *Kultur* was also popular, as was an opposition to mechanism and a belief in organic development. Half of Wundt's psychology, his *Völkerpsychologie* was an attempt to grasp humans' inner nature through the study of history and human cultural products, such as language and myth, both of which Herder valued highly. Also like Herder, Wundt stressed the organic unity of the human mind against the faculty psychologists. We should note in passing that the authoritarian, militant German nationalism in Wundt's milieu would have been rejected by Herder himself, although it partly grew out of his philosophy.

More generally, Herder helped lay the foundation for romanticism. He passionately opposed the mock-classical art of his time, calling modern critics "masters of dead learning." Instead he advocated "Heart! Warmth! Blood! Humanity! Life!" Descartes had said, "I think, therefore I am." Condillac implied, "I sense, therefore I am." Herder wrote "I feel! I am!" Thus ended the rule of abstract reason, the geometric spirit, and reasonable emotion. Instead, organic development led by emphatic emotion was the base of the new romanticism.

### Two Others: Rousseau and Smith

Two important thinkers of the eighteenth century need to be considered, although they fall outside the Enlightenment.

#### Jean-Jacques Rousseau (1712-1778)

To place Rousseau outside the Enlightenment may seem unusual, since he, along with Voltaire, is popularly thought of as a paradigmatic philosophe. However, in significant ways Rousseau, like Herder, rebelled against the Age of Reason. Rousseau is best known as the incipient revolutionary. In *Social Contract* he wrote: "Man is born free, and everywhere he is in chains." When Marx and Engels wrote, "The proletariat have nothing to lose but their chains," their call to revolution echoed Rousseau's *Social Contract*. Rousseau is also famous for his idea of the Noble Savage, a picture of humans before the coming of the society that put people in chains. It is, however, an image we have met before, inspired by the voyages of discovery.

In many ways Rousseau's complaints about the Enlightenment parallel Herder's, although Rousseau was less conscious of history than was Herder. Rousseau said "To exist is to feel," and, "the first impulses of the heart are always right," sentiments which recall Herder and point to romanticism. Like Herder, he rejected mechanism because it cannot explain human free will. Both Rousseau and Herder felt that language is what makes man unique in the world.

Rousseau became famous, not to say notorious, with his first works, which, in opposition to the Enlightenmanet spirit, denied that humanity has benefited from scientific and technological advances. Like Herder, Rousseau felt contemporary French civilization was artificial and excessively rational; it had put humans in chains. Rousseau's invented Noble Savage was not intended to describe a primitive Eden to which we ought to return, but to reveal human nature. Rousseau believed that people are inherently sociable and that primitive isolation is neither desirable nor possible. Still, Rousseau argued that the present state of society corrupted and degraded human nature. Instead of a return to primitivism, Rousseau advocated building a new, less alienating society, and it is in this that his revolutionary potential lay.

He was a friend of Condillac and was similarly empiricistic and interested in education. His greatest influence has been on educational psychology. Rousseau described his ideal educational program in *Emile,* in which a child and his tutor retire from corrupt civilization and return to nature for education. After his education is complete, Emile returns to society. Rousseau advocated a kind of nondirectional education, believing that a child should be allowed to express his or her native talents, and that a good education is one that cultivates the natural growth of these talents. The tutor should not impose views on the student. Nevertheless, behind the apparent freedom is firm control. At one point Rousseau described what we would call open education: "It is rarely your business to suggest what he ought to learn; it is for him to want to learn." However, earlier, he had written: "Let him always think he is master while you are really master. There is no subjection so complete as that which preserves the forms of freedom. . . ." For Rousseau the empiricist, the corrupt state of civilization may be overcome by a proper education which perfects the potentialities of each person. Herder, too, believed in self-fulfillment, but was less individualistic, seeing fulfillment in the larger context of the person's culture which the person helped perfect while perfecting self.

Rousseau's influence has been wide. His affinities with romanticism and political revolutionaries have been alluded to. In education he inspires those who support open education of the "whole child" against those who prefer highly structured teaching of separate basic skills. He is also behind those who want to reform society through education. In his belief in human malleability and perfectability, he foreshadows B. F. Skinner, who advocates a carefully controlled society whose goal is human happiness, although Skinner openly disbelieves in human freedom.

### Adam Smith (1723-1790)

1776 saw not only the birth of a new nation, but of a new social science—economics—with the publication of Adam Smith's *Wealth of Nations.* Smith's economics was perhaps the first fruit of Hume's science of human nature, for Smith put economics on a scientific basis. Smith extended to human economy the idea of natural law, and in particular, the law of self-interest. Each person naturally seeks his or her own self-interest, and out of everyone's interactions general benefit will accrue. Smith described nature as an "invisible hand" which promotes the general interest out of each person's desire for personal benefit. It follows that a good political economy will be one which interferes with the "invisible hand" as little as possible.

One interesting point of Smith's theory is its anticipation of Darwin's theory of natural selection. In economics, according to Smith, each individual seeks his or her own good, but nevertheless the general good of society is served by the competition of interests. According to Darwinian biology, each member of a species seeks only its own survival, but the good of the species is served as the weak are weeded out by individual competition.

## CONCLUSION

### Conceptual Summary

The major theme of the period 1600-1800 was the triumph of science, in particular Newtonian science, over the old medieval theological world view. In the seventeenth century Galileo, Kepler, Descartes, and Newton demonstrated the power of a new kind of understanding of nature. The new scientific view substituted the idea of universal mathematical order for the older idea of universal meaning in nature. Humanity's view of nature changed greatly. Nature had been a book of signs revealing the invisible world beyond. Now it became an indifferent machine that could be known only in a limited way, via mathematics. Nature lost its meaningfulness, but humanity gained power over it from mathematically precise predictions.

The viewpoint of science was something fundamentally new in human history. Heretofore, thinkers had merely speculated about the nature of reality—speculations that were comprehensive in scope but lacking in detail. Newtonian science substituted detailed analysis of concrete cases for vast speculations about cosmic order. Since Newton's time, of course, science has grown in comprehensiveness until for many it has entirely supplanted religion as a world picture.

No sooner had Newton propounded the new anti-metaphysical science of physics, than philosophers began to see the possibility of extending it to human nature. The enterprise began with Locke, and occupied almost every eighteenth century thinker. The keynote was sounded by Hume in his call for a science of human nature to be as fundamental to science as metaphysics had been thought to be. Of course it has emerged that natural science can get along quite well without psychology, and the average physicist would laugh at Hume's proposal. Still, the eighteenth century did move significantly toward creating a science of human nature. The philosophes believed in Hume's science, but showed no more unanimity on the nature of human nature than psychology shows today.

One consequence of the growth of empiricism and its substitution of psychology for metaphysics was the virtual death of rationalism. The empiricists, especially Hume, today still have a large following, while Descartes, Leibniz, and Spinoza do not. Their rationalist attempt to found human knowledge on purely rational first principles derived without observation and to erect complete systems of nature on those first principles is now seen as futile. Elements of rationalism survived, especially in Germany, where the Enlightenment did not penetrate deeply and where voices of protest were strong, and they played a part in Wundt's founding psychology. But rationalism was too medieval and too scholastic to long survive in the modern era.

There is no doubt that the Enlightenment finally marks the beginning of modern times. The philosophes wrestled with the problem of understanding human nature apart from God and faith. They generally agreed that man could be improved, but they did not agree on what man was like underneath the social veneer. Their optimistic hopes seemed upheld by the American Revolution, which seemed to put the new world view into motion in the new world. The French Revolution was greeted at first as the triumph of reason over feudal oppression. But the new triumph quickly went sour. The change may be marked in one revolutionist, Robespierre, who began as a foe of capital punishment and upholder of democracy, and ended as a tyrant who executed the entire family of one girl suspected of thinking about assassinating him. It is easy for persons who believe they know human nature to go on to think they know what "the people" want better than the people do themselves. So the modern world witnesses despotism in the name of liberty and murder in the name of enlightenment. The Reign of Terror in France seemed to show that Sade's vicious ideas were right, and we still have not resolved the crisis of naturalism.

A poet, Alexander Pope (1688-1744) caught the spirit of the age in his *Essay on Man.* In the following lines he begins in good Enlightenment fashion by telling humanity to study people, not God, but ends by despairing of the possibility of such knowledge. He writes:

> Know then thyself, presume not God to scan;
> The proper study of Mankind is Man.
> Placed on this isthmus of a middle state,
> A being darkly wise, and rudely great:
> With too much knowledge for the Sceptic side,
> With too much weakness for the Stoic's pride,
> He hangs between; in doubt to act, or rest,
> In doubt to deem himself a God, or Beast,
> In doubt his Mind or Body to prefer,
> Born but to die, and reas'ning but to err;
> Alike in ignorance, his reason such,
> Whether he thinks too little, or too much:
> Chaos of Thought and Passion, all confused;
> Still by himself abused, or disabused;
> Created half to rise, and half to fall;
> Great lord of all things, yet a prey to all;
> Sole judge of Truth, in endless Error hurled:
> The glory, jest, and riddle of the world!
>
> Go, wondrous creature! mount where Science guides,
> Go, measure earth, weigh air, and state the tides;

Instruct the planets in what orbs to run,
Correct old Time, and regulate the Sun;
Go, soar with Plato to th' empyreal sphere,
To the first good, first perfect, and first fair;
Or tread the maze round his follow'rs trod,
And quitting sense call imitating God;
As Eastern priests in giddy circles run,
And turn their heads to imitate the Sun.
Go, teach Eternal Wisdom how to rule—
Then drop into thyself, and be a fool!

### Historical Trends

From our standpoint the major historical trend begun by the Scientific Revolution and the Enlightenment was the move toward founding a science of human nature or psychology. In the next century we will inch closer to that goal, until it is reached by Wilhelm Wundt around 1879. There are three important specific trends rooted in the present period: materialism and mechanism, which extend the Cartesian-Newtonian machine-universe to humankind; faculty psychology, which became a popular psychology universally opposed by the scientific psychologist; and, above all, associationism, which provides a plausible vehicle for empiricist theories of mind, and which will prove serviceable to mentalists and behaviorists alike.

Three further trends that began during the eighteenth century in a small way, would grow in importance during the nineteenth century. One is romanticism, a revolt of feeling against a sterile and profitless reason. Another is utilitarianism, the attempt to ground ethics and society on the pleasure principle. The third, and by far the most important, was evolution. As biology became naturalistic, as attempts were made to explain the origin of things without a Creator, as paleontological and geological knowledge was accumulated, the theory of evolution became inevitable. The first evolutionary speculations began in the eighteenth century and formed the background for Charles Darwin's crisis-making book, *The Origin of Species,* which would bring the crisis of naturalism to a painful head.

## SUGGESTED READINGS

On the Enlightenment, see Peter Gay, *The Enlightenment, An Interpretation*— especially the second volume, subtitled *The Science of Freedom* (Knopf, 1966 and 1969. Paperback editions are available from Norton).

## REFERENCES

Bower, T. G. R. *Development in infancy.* San Francisco, Calif.: W. H. Freeman & Co., 1974.

Condillac, E. B. de *An essay on the origin of human knowledge.* New York: AMS Press, 1974.

Copleston, F. *A History of Philosophy* (V. 5). Garden City, N.Y.: Image Books, 1964.

Crocker, L. *An age of crisis.* Baltimore: Johns Hopkins University Press, 1959.

Hume, D. *A treatise of human nature.* London: Thomas and Joseph Allman, 1817.

Hume, D. *David Hume on human nature and the understanding* (Anthony Flew, Ed.). New York: Collier Books, 1962.

Kant, I. *Anthropology from a pragmatic point of view* (trans. M. J. Gregor). The Hague: Martinus Nijhoff, 1974.

Knight, I. F. *The geometric spirit: the Abbe Condillac and the French Enlightenment.* New Haven: Yale University Press, 1968.

La Mettrie, J. O. de *Man a machine.* La Salle, Ill.: Open Court, 1961.

McReynolds, P. & Ludwig, K. Psychometrics in the seventeenth century: the personology of Christian Thomasius. Paper presented at the annual meeting of CHEIRON, Boulder, Colorado, 1977.

Reid, T. *Thomas Reid's Inquiry and Essays* (K. Lehrer & R. Beanblossom, Eds.) Indianapolis: Bobbs-Merrill, 1975.

Rousseau, J. *Emile.* New York: Dutton, 1974.

Smith, N. K. *The philosophy of David Hume.* London: Macmillan, 1941.

Stern, G. *A faculty theory of knowledge.* Lewisburg, Pa.: Bucknell University Press, 1971.

Vartanian, A. *Diderot and Descartes: A study of naturalism in the Enlightenment.* Princeton, N.J.: Princeton University Press, 1953.

Wolman, B. Immanual Kant and his impact on psychology. In B. Wolman (Ed.) *Historical roots of contemporary psychology.* New York: Harper & Row, 1968.

# 6

# To the Threshold of Psychology
## The Nineteenth Century

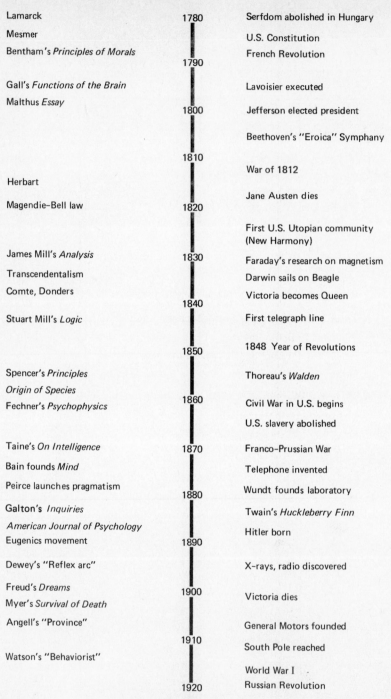

| | | |
|---|---|---|
| Lamarck | 1780 | Serfdom abolished in Hungary |
| Mesmer | | U.S. Constitution |
| Bentham's *Principles of Morals* | 1790 | French Revolution |
| Gall's *Functions of the Brain* | | Lavoisier executed |
| Malthus *Essay* | 1800 | Jefferson elected president |
| | | Beethoven's "Eroica" Symphany |
| | 1810 | |
| | | War of 1812 |
| Herbart | | Jane Austen dies |
| Magendie–Bell law | 1820 | |
| | | First U.S. Utopian community (New Harmony) |
| James Mill's *Analysis* | 1830 | Faraday's research on magnetism |
| Transcendentalism | | Darwin sails on Beagle |
| Comte, Donders | | Victoria becomes Queen |
| | 1840 | |
| Stuart Mill's *Logic* | | First telegraph line |
| | 1850 | 1848 Year of Revolutions |
| Spencer's *Principles* | | Thoreau's *Walden* |
| *Origin of Species* | | |
| Fechner's *Psychophysics* | 1860 | Civil War in U.S. begins |
| | | U.S. slavery abolished |
| Taine's *On Intelligence* | 1870 | Franco-Prussian War |
| Bain founds *Mind* | | Telephone invented |
| Peirce launches pragmatism | 1880 | Wundt founds laboratory |
| Galton's *Inquiries* | | Twain's *Huckleberry Finn* |
| *American Journal of Psychology* | | Hitler born |
| Eugenics movement | 1890 | |
| Dewey's "Reflex arc" | | X-rays, radio discovered |
| Freud's *Dreams* | 1900 | |
| Myer's *Survival of Death* | | Victoria dies |
| Angell's "Province" | | General Motors founded |
| | 1910 | South Pole reached |
| Watson's "Behaviorist" | | World War I |
| | 1920 | Russian Revolution |

**FIGURE 6-1.**
Chronology 1780-1920.

# THE WORLD OF THE NINETEENTH CENTURY

The Enlightenment consensus ended with the French Revolution, which was at first welcomed as the dawn of a greater Age of Reason, but later feared and hated for its Reign of Terror. The real implications of the geometric spirit became clear, and nineteenth-century thinkers had to come to grips with naturalism. This task was made more pressing by Darwin's theory of evolution, which not only made man into an ape but also took all purpose and progress out of history. Throughout this period, then, the problem of human nature was considered by many philosophers, physiologists, writers, and revolutionaries. The second half of the century saw the founding of scientific psychology and the formulation of its three variants: the study of consciousness, of the unconscious, and of adaptation.

A student of the nineteenth century, Franklin Baumer (1977), has suggested a useful conceptual division of the period, finding it too complex for chronological treatment. He proposes four nineteenth-century worlds, which we will roughly follow here. The first is the romantic world, which reacted strongly against the naturalism of the philosophes. The second world is the New Enlightenment, which carried on, in somewhat altered form, the program of the philosophes. The third is the world of Darwinism and evolution. The fourth world Baumer calls the *fin de siècle* (end of the century), a world of anxiety born of despair over nature, humanity, and the future.

## The Reassertion of the Transcendental: The Romantic Revolt

Although we usually think of romanticism as a movement in the arts that emphasized human feeling, it was much more. It established a general revolt against the Cartesian-Newtonian world view. The first romantic poet, William Blake (1757-1827), for instance, in the hope that humanity could escape the scientific outlook, wrote: "May God us keep/ From Single vision and Newton's sleep."* Where the Enlightenment writers had valued mild and moral "passions," the romantics were inclined to worship all strong emotions—even violent and destructive ones. Above all, the romantics wanted there to be something more in the universe than atoms and the void. In a certain sense, romanticism reasserted a rationalist belief in something transcending material appearance.

It is appropriate, then, that the romantic movement, at least in philosophy, began with Kant. We have already noted how his idealist successors made material

*Blake taunted the philosophes: "Mock on, Mock on, Voltaire, Rousseau:/ Mock on Mock on: 'tis all in vain!" As did other romantics, Blake detested the Industrial Revolution, whose "dark Satanic Mills" defiled "England's mountains green."

reality the expression of something spiritual that manifested itself in appearances. The romantic poet Coleridge adapted and elaborated Kant's distinction of *Verstand*, the limited process of understanding described by Locke, and *Vernuft,* an intuitive faculty capable of transcending appearances and grasping noumenal truth.

Several concepts important for psychology are evident in romanticism. One was the unconscious. Conscious, discursive thought was the tool of the Enlightenment in both art and philosophy. Romanticism, however, in its search for the infinite, held the unconscious to be more important. Poets, for example, hoped to write automatically in an ecstatic transport so that the Infinite was recorded directly on paper. In philosophy, Schopenhauer posited Will as the noumenal reality behind appearances. Schopenhauer's Will, specifically the will to live, pushes man on to endless, futile striving for something better. This description of the Will foreshadows Freud's id. Schopenhauer wrote in *Parerga* "In the heart of every man there lives a wild beast." Intelligence tries to control the Will, but its raging inflicts pain on the self and others. Also prefiguring Freud were those writers who saw in dreams the language of the unconscious needing only to be decoded to reveal the secrets of the Infinite.

In Schopenhauer's Will (the core of mental life) we find another important and complex romantic concept—that of mental activity and freedom. The Will is a wild beast, but while that wildness implies pain, it also implies freedom of choice. Schopenhauer's philosophy thus was voluntaristic, a romantic reaction against Enlightened materialistic determinism. Generally, this led the romantics to worship heroes, geniuses, and artists—those who asserted their Wills and did not bow to the way of the world. Thomas Carlyle, for instance, revered heroes who ranged from Odin to Shakespeare to Napolean. Psychologically speaking, this new form of voluntarism did away with the *tabula rasa*. Such a willful mind as the romantics envisioned would hardly be a mere passive receptacle for external stimuli. Coleridge, for instance, likened the mind to a lamp that casts intellectual light. Schopenhauer's effect is also evident in Wundt's psychology of consciousness, for Wundt lays great stress on the mind's ability to organize its own content, a form of voluntarism that contrasts sharply with the passivity of associationism.

Not only did the romantics reject the idea that a person is a machine, they also rejected the idea that the universe is a machine. They were vitalists and teleologists for whom nature was not dead matter—mere atoms in the void—but something organic, growing, improving itself with time. Biology, not physics, should be the model for thinking about things, the romantics said. Herder expressed this sentiment in Germany. In England, it was forcefully stated by the conservative thinker Edmund Burke (1729-1797) who said that human nature and society develop slowly over the course of centuries. He decried the attempt of the French Revolutionists to erect a society based only on pure, geometric reason, ignoring the wisdom of history. This romantic conception of nature was progressive and optimistic, but was soon to be shattered by Darwin's theory of natural selection. The romantics already believed in evolution, but it was not the randomly directed process of Darwinism.

Romantic vitalism meant that although we may see in romanticism a reassertion of the rationalist search for transcendent Truth, the romantics were not advocates of Being. Carlyle, for instance, insisted that Truth is always becoming, it never simply is. Truth is not a static collection of Forms, but something alive, something always perfecting itself. This belief, at least, would be quite compatible with Darwinian evolution.

There was one Enlightenment concept that inspired the romantics, and which they enriched. Hartley's associationism was an important part of romantic critical theory. Classical poetry was full of capitalized abstractions such as "Beauty," but the romantics wrote about the concrete, individual beautiful things out of which we form our idea of Beauty. In associationism, aesthetic and moral judgments are sentiments, subjective emotional reactions relatively separate from discursive reason. The romantics elevated the subjective and passionate and sought to use the associative analysis of mind as a way to evoke emotional responses in their readers. They enriched associationism by stressing the concept of coalescence, that is, the active imagination may synthesize atomic elements into a creation that is more than the sum of the atomic units themselves, as when elementary colors are mixed to make a qualitatively different one. Wundt made much of the power of the mind to synthesize mental elements, while the Gestalt psychologists became even more holistic.

We may conclude by saying that the romantics opposed mechanism in every field and promoted rival concepts such as individual freedom, voluntarism, holism, vitalism, and teleology. Although romanticism was subdued by subsequent developments in science, especially Darwinism, it played a role in forming psychology—especially in its birthplace, Germany—and in one form or another, romanticism has always appealed to those discomfited by the geometric spirit and its products.

### The New Enlightenment

Of course, not everyone was disenchanted by naturalism. There were many important thinkers who carried on the spirit and ambitions of the Enlightenment, especially in England and France. Several movements in the New Enlightenment are important to psychology.

### Utilitarianism and Associationism

Utilitarianism and associationism are inextricably intertwined doctrines. *Utilitarianism* describes the dynamic motivational aspects of mind; *associationism* describes the cognitive mechanics of mind. Utilitarianism was implicit in the teachings of the eighteenth-century associationists from Hume onward who said that sensations are either pleasant, which we desire to repeat, or unpleasant, which we desire to avoid. Utilitarianism simply tried to apply this motivational system to society as a whole.

The motivational doctrine of utilitarianism was most completely worked out by the English reformer Jeremy Bentham (1748-1832). He opened his *Intro-duction to the Principles of Moral Legislation* (1789) with a forceful statement of utilitarian hedonism: "Nature has placed mankind under the governance of two sovereign masters, *pain* and *pleasure*. It is for them alone to point out what we ought to do, as well as to determine what we shall do. . . . They govern us in all we do, in all we say, in all we think." The individual should conduct her or his life, therefore, by choosing those courses of action that will maximize personal pleasure and minimize pain; this is the only scientific ethics. The legislature—Bentham's target as a reformer—should follow the same standard, seeking to promote the greatest happiness of the greatest number in all acts of government. Bentham saw government as naturally oppressive; he assumed, as did the first economist, Adam Smith, that minimal government would let each individual seek his or her own happiness.

The laws of Bentham's principle of pleasure resemble the laws of association proposed by Hume, Hartley, and Brown. The value of pleasure and pain is deter-mined by the intensity, duration, certainty, and propinquity of the corresponding sensation. Bentham sought to quantify both pleasure and pain, so that moral decisions could be made by summing up the net pleasure or pain to be expected to follow from a selection of possible acts and choosing that which satisfied the principle of utility. Also following the associationists, Bentham distinguished simple pleasures or pains and their compounds, complex pleasures and pains. He goes on to give an elaborate enumeration of the kinds of pleasure, giving a much longer list than a post-Freudian modern would expect. There are sensual pleasures and pains, to be sure, but there are also the pleasures of wealth, power, piety, and benevo-lence, to name only a few. Bentham also discussed individual and racial characteris-tics that modify the workings of the utility principle according to personal disposition. His major effort was then to devise a program of good government based solely on the rational principle of utility, disregarding any considerations of historical context or human rights. It was an exercise in the geometric spirit and the mechanistic philosophy to make Edmund Burke or any romantic shudder.

One of Bentham's most enthusiastic followers was James Mill (1773-1836), a politician turned philosopher. He ardently expounded Benthamism, but is best known in psychology for his mechanistic associationism. In no way did Mill really add to associationism; rather he represented its ultimate form. He follows Hume and Hartley in distinguishing sensations and their copies—ideas—and follows Condillac in trying to reduce all mental activity to association. Mill adopts what one might call the tinker-toy theory of mind. In this view, the mind is a passive, blank slate, receptive to simple sensations (the tinker-toy nodes) out of which complex sensations or ideas are compounded by forming associative links (the sticks linking the nodes) between atomic units. Associative links are built in two ways. Some sensations always occur together, or *synchronously,* and become linked. Smelling a rose suggests its other attributes with which the smell is regularly associated in our experience. Other sensations regularly occur in sequence, or *successively,* and Mill follows Hume in reducing causation to regular associative trains. Mill analyzes speech as a train of associated atomic words, wholly ignoring a sentence's meaning's control of discourse. His mechanical associationism is widely taken as a *reductio ad absurdum* of the associative psychology. For example, in *Analysis of the Phenomena of the Human Mind* Mill describes the idea of a house as compounded out of a huge number of simpler units such as nails, boards, and pieces of glass. He then concludes: "How many more [ideas make up] the idea called Every Thing?" One imagines the mind filled with a colossal and unwieldy tinker-toy arrangement.

Mill's associationism dispenses with the mental faculties retained by Hartley and other associationists. Combined with utilitarian hedonism, the result is a completely mechanical picture of mind in which idea follows idea automatically with no room left for voluntary control. The exercise of will is an illusion, Mill maintained. Reasoning is no more than the associative compounding of the ideas contained in syllogisms. Attention is no more than the fact that the mind is preoccupied with whichever ideas are particularly pleasurable or painful. The mind does not direct attention; its attention is mechanically directed by the principle of utility. Like Bentham and many others who wrote on the mind, Mill expounded his psychology for purposes of reform. He was not a psychologist. Influenced by Helvetius, as Bentham also was, Mill was especially interested in education. If the person is entirely passive at birth, it is the duty of education to correctly mold the person's mind. Mill put his ideas into practice by the rigorous education he gave his son, teaching him ancient Greek at three and Latin at eight. This son wrote a history of Roman law at ten.

The son, John Stuart Mill (1806-1873), did not become the perfect utilitarian his father had expected, however. Although an early adherent of Benthamism, he experienced a nervous breakdown during which he came to find Benthamism sterile, narrow, and excessively calculating. He even went so far as to call Bentham's program "evil." He eventually tempered Bentham's hedonistic principles with Wordsworth's romantic vision of nature and human feeling. He even endorsed the romantic preference for the grown or natural over the manufactured, and denied that the human being is a machine. He saw people as living things whose autonomous development and growth should be nurtured.

J. S. Mill's version of associationism was tempered by the romantic penchant for synthesis. This combination led to his idea of mental chemistry. Earlier associationists, including his father, had recognized that certain associative links became so strong that the linked ideas appeared inseparable. J.S. Mill went further, maintaining that elementary ideas could fuse into a whole idea not reducible to its elements. The elements generate the new idea, they do not merely compose it. He offered colors as an example of such a process. Spin a wheel divided into wedges, each colored with a primary color, and at a certain speed the experience will be of whiteness, not of spinning colors. The atomic colors on the wheel are generating a new color, a different kind of experience.

We must emphasize, however, that although Mill tempered his father's associationistic Benthamism with the broader conceptions of romanticism, he still sought to improve utilitarianism and empiricism, not to refute them. He always detested the mystic intuitionism of Coleridge, Carlyle, and the other romantics. He returned to Berkeley's analysis of matter, although without God, allowing for no noumenal reality beyond appearances. Matter is no more than the permanent possibility of sensation for J. S. Mill. The pen in one's room, for example, exists only because it always may be perceived, whether or not it is being perceived at the moment. Nor did Mill accept romantic voluntarism. His mental chemistry, although it recognized the possible coalescence of sensations and ideas, remained a passive description of mind. It is not the mind's autonomous activity that brings about the qualitative chemical change, but the way the sensations are associated in experience: one can not choose to see or not to see the white spinning disc, for the experience is forced on one's perception by the conditions of the experiment.

John Stuart Mill was the last great philosophical associationist. His associationism arose in the context of logical and metaphysical—not purely psychological—discussions. Mill did believe in the possibility of Hume's science of human nature and in fact tried to contribute to its methodology. Later associationists became more distinctly psychological; therefore we will postpone them to a later section.

### Positivism

We have already met philosophers such as Berkeley, Hume, and Newton who are at least partially positivistic, favoring an epistemology that restricts human knowledge to what is immediately observable. However, as natural science and technology marched from success to success, a general attitude called *scientism* spread through Europe, a faith in the ability of science to answer all questions, to solve all problems. It was natural, then, for science, based since Newton and Bacon on a positivist epistemology, to be elevated to a new religion—a world view intended to supplant an already embattled Christianity. Such was the undertaking of Auguste Comte (1798-1857). Comte named *positivism,* which embraced an epistemology, philosophies of science and history, and a religion.

As an epistemology, positivism adopted a radical empiricism. Metaphysical speculation and explanations of nature in terms of unobservable entities were to be abandoned. Instead, human knowledge would confine itself to collecting and correlating facts to yield an accurate description of the world. Such was the method and proper philosophy of science, according to Comte. With the ability to predict nature comes the ability to control nature. Hence, when a science of humanity emerges, society and individuals will likewise be subject to control.

Comte gave a sweeping picture of history as inevitable upward progress in three broad stages. The first step is the theological, in which man explains natural events by positing invisible gods and spirits responsible for them. The second stage is the metaphysical, in which the gods and spirits become abstractions of other unobservable causes thought to explain nature. The third stage is the scientific, in which explanation is given up for description, prediction, and control, and in which The Religion of Humanity supplants Christianity. Comte gives elaborate descriptions of his new religion. It is complete with a scientific elite of priests, a revolutionary manifesto for the scientific control of society, and a flag. Some of Comte's views are quaintly Victorian—for instance, his belief that worship of Woman was the first part of worship of humanity.

Comte's interest was not in science as such but in how science might be used to improve humanity. His epistemology and his philosophies of science and history are all subordinate to the construction of a new scientific society. His real audience was composed of women and working people whom Comte believed were oppressed by the vested interests then ruling society. He believed it was through their efforts that the positivist revolution would come about. Although a scientific elite would rule the new society, Comte wanted first to persuade the masses.

Comte's views on psychology are interesting. He lists a hierarchy of sciences, from most basic (and first developed) to most comprehensive (and last to develop). This hierarchy is: mathematics, astronomy, physics, chemistry, physiology and biology, and sociology. He is usually credited with being one of the founders of sociology, which was to be the science that would make his new, scientifically managed world possible. Psychology, however, does not appear on the list. Comte disapproved of introspective psychology, which he regarded as muddled and metaphysical. He held out some hope for phrenology, which tried to tie personality traits to distinct areas of the brain. Hence he divided psychology in two, destroying it as a coherent field. The study of the individual he assigned to physiology and biology, as in phrenological psychology. The study of man as a social animal belonged to sociology. Moreover, Comte seems to have found contemporary philosophical psychology too intellectual. He emphasized over and over that human beings are creatures of feeling first and intellect second.

Comte's positivism and his Religion of Humanity inspired many people all over Europe. Some tried to carry on his religious-revolutionary program, founding positivist societies and even opening positivist churches. More serious thinkers, however, found Comte's religion distasteful, preferring instead his epistemology. Such, for example, was the attitude of John Stuart Mill, who carried on extensive correspondence with Comte. Consequently positivism became more and more a purely philosophical movement, and finally a philosophy of science. Two figures deserve recognition in this connection, Claude Bernard (1813-1878) and Ernst Mach (1838-1916).

Bernard was a French physiologist who wrote an influential work in the philosophy of science, *Introduction to the Study of Experimental Medicine* (1865). Although he rejected Comte's system and religion for displaying the same vices as other metaphysical systems and religions, his account of science is eminently positivistic. Only the rigorous testing of objective scientific hypotheses with objective methods could yield knowledge. Any question not subject to such treatment is regarded as meaningless. The world is to be viewed as a perfectly deterministic system, for only on such a view is science possible. The first goal of science is prediction and control.

Ernst Mach was a great German physicist who put forward a radical version of positivism as a philosophy of science in an attempt to explicate the true foundations of science. He admired Berkeley, and like Berkeley he saw human consciousness as a collection of sensations beyond which we cannot penetrate without committing the crime of metaphysics. The goal of science is the economical ordering of sensations and nothing more. So, for example, Mach refused to believe in the existence of atoms because no one had ever seen one. Theory was to be avoided except insofar as it correlated experiences and was useful for making predictions. Knowledge for Mach ultimately served a pragmatic, biological function. Organizing our experience helps us to adapt to our environment; it penetrates no reality beyond appearance. Mach also introduced a critical, historical method to the study of science. He believed that many scientific concepts had incorporated metaphysical accretions in the course of their development, and that the best way to strip off the accretions and reduce the concepts to their sensory base was to study the development of the concepts. Echoing Comte, Mach noted that early science had grown up in the theological atmosphere of the seventeenth century and consequently concepts such as force had acquired "divine" attributes as something transcending mere experience.

The influence of positivism in one form or another was very great, embracing physicists and realistic novelists alike. In psychology, it affected the English and American schools more than the European schools. Wundt, for example, was very critical of Comte. Although his individual psychology in some ways resembled Mach's science in that both were analyses of immediate experience, Wundt postulated unperceived mental processes to explain experienced mental events. Mach's philosophy had more influence on Wundt's English student Titchener, who took science to be a descriptive, not explanatory, enterprise, and on the Gestalt psychologists who studied objects as given immediately to experience. Freud's explanation of the unconscious, which is unobservable by definition, is certainly not positivistic, giving another example of the German's relative immunity to this view of science.

In America, however, the influence of positivism was great. William James was a great admirer of Mach whose concept of knowledge as a practical adaptation to life is quite consistent with James' pragmatism. Mach was a source of inspiration to the twentieth-century logical positivists who had considerable influence on behaviorism. The clearest influence of positivism is on B.F. Skinner. Although Mach's psychology was introspective, that is, a psychology of the subject, once behaviorists decided to treat human beings as objects of observation, Mach's philosophy led directly to radical behaviorism. Skinner maintains that the single goal of science is to find lawful relations between independent and dependent variables, leading to prediction and control. Reference to unobservable "mental" processes is as much illegitimate metaphysics to Skinner as it was to Mach. Furthermore, Skinner's call for a scientifically managed, nondemocratic utopia is secular Comtism. Both believe in the perfectability of man through scientific control.

### Marxism

It is impossible to pass over the thought of Karl Marx (1818-1883) in any account of the nineteenth century. Marxism, in one form or another (many of which Marx would have disowned) has been one of the most important philosophies of modern times. Furthermore, Marx erected his system not just on considerations of economic history, but also on a particular view of humanity. Marx maintained that, although human consciousness is determined by the economic structure of a given era, there is a real underlying human nature whose needs are stifled by all historically existing forms of society. Hence, people are alienated from their true selves, and this alienation is the motive force for human improvement and political revolution. Only in a genuine communist society (nowhere achieved in Marx's or our own time) would humans no longer be alienated from their true selves.

Given Marx's fame and general influence, it is remarkable how little impact his thought has had on psychology outside the Soviet Union, where it is, of course, official dogma. We must suspect the reason for his lack of influence is political. After 1848, communism was a spectre haunting Europe, a spectre rendered frighteningly concrete in the Russian Revolution of 1917, and in subsequent revolutions.

In the early days of psychology, Marxism was probably a dangerous philosophy to study, let alone espouse, and neglecting this theory could be rationalized by its apparent irrelevance to psychology. Few Western psychologists are sympathetic to Marx; of those who are, most prominent are the humanist psychologist Erich Fromm and the developmental psychologist Klaus Riegel, both of whom are widely viewed within psychology as distinctly eccentric. Yet Marx's thought is perfectly compatible with other accepted influences on psychology. His stage view of history and his revolutionary call to the masses resemble Comte. He accepted naturalism and materialism. He studied the influence of the environment on the human personality, yet held a rather humanistic view of human nature. However, the other revolutionary thinker of the nineteenth century was quieter, happily bourgeois, and much more influential.

### Heraclitus Triumphant: The Darwinian Revolution

#### Background

The Newtonian-Cartesian mechanical world was changeless. God, or some Creator, had constructed a marvelous machine perfect in conception and endless in time. Each object, each biological species, was fixed for eternity, changelessly perfect in obedience to fixed natural laws. Such a world view was equally consistent with Plato's Forms, Aristotle's essences, and Christian theology. On this view, change was something unusual in nature. Even the geological doctrine of uniformitarianism, which helped Darwin invent his theory of evolution, was anti-evolutionary in tracing the continuum of natural forces back over millions of years. In biology the Aristotelian belief that species were fixed and immutable was a dogma supported by the highest scientific authorities right up until Darwin's time. Given the Cartesian-Newtonian concept that Matter is inert, incapable of acting, and passive only, spontaneous change the origin of new species, the mutation of old seemed impossible. Once the supreme Intelligence had acted creatively, dead matter could effect nothing new.

In the atmosphere of progress characteristic of the Enlightenment, however, this static view of nature began to change. Evolutionary ideas go back at least to Anaximander (see Chapter 2), but in the eighteenth century they really began to take hold. One old Aristotelian-theological concept that helped evolution along was the Great Chain of Being, or Aristotle's *scala natura.* The Chain was viewed by medievals as a measure of a creature's nearness to God and consequently its degree of spiritual perfection. To the naturalistic thinkers, on the other hand, it became a record of the ascent of living things toward nature's crowning perfection, human-kind.

To accomplish the change from a stable but perfect universe to a changing, striving one, a different view of matter was needed; dead, stupid matter can neither change nor strive. In the eighteenth century, precisely the necessary conception arose. Matter—for some thinkers, even inorganic matter—was now endowed with vitality and a tendency to progress. It was thus possible for many writers to assert that the universe had evolved from simple beginnings, and that species had changed and progressed since the beginning of time and could go on changing and progress-ing forever. This view was embodied in one form or another in French transformism and German nature philosophy. It certainly does not abandon naturalism, for it enables one to eliminate God altogether and give a thoroughly natural account of the origin of the earth and its inhabitants. This concept of evolution is not mechan-ical, however, for it endows matter with God-like attributes. For the Newtonian, stupid matter was set in mechanical motion by an intelligent, purposeful Creator. For the vitalist, matter itself is intelligent and purposeful. Vitalism is thus a romantic view of Nature—self-perfecting and self-directing, progressively unfolding itself throughout time.

Charles Darwin's signal contribution to the concept of evolution was to mech-anize it, to de-romanticize nature and capture evolution for the Newtonian world view. However, before examining Darwin's theory, we should first consider the major romantic alternative whose appeal is strong even today—and which even Darwin himself could not entirely resist—the evolutionary theory of Jean Baptiste Lamarck (1744-1829). Lamarck, being a naturalist well-known for his work in taxonomy, was the most scientific exponent of the romantic-progressive view of evolution. There were two important aspects of Lamarck's theory. The first said that organic matter is fundamentally different from inorganic, that each living species possesses an innate drive to perfect itself. Each organism strives to adapt itself to its surroundings and changes itself as it does so, developing various muscles, acquiring various habits. The second part of his theory claimed that these acquired characteristics could be passed on to an animal's offspring. Thus each individual's striving for perfection was recorded and passed on, and over generations species of plants and animals would improve themselves, fulfilling their drives for perfection. Modern genetics has destroyed Lamarck's vision. Organic matter is now said to be merely complexly arranged inorganic molecules; DNA is a collection of amino acids. The DNA chain is unchanged by modifications to an individual's body. (Certain external influences, such as drugs or radiation, can affect genetic information, but that is not what Lamarck meant.) In the absence of genetics, however, the inheritance of acquired characteristics is plausible and even Darwin from time to time accepted it, although he never accepted the vitalist view of matter. Later, both Wundt and Freud believed that acquired habits and experiences were capable of being passed through heredity.

So, by Darwin's time evolution was a widespread concept, disbelieved only by firm religionists and the biological establishment, which still accepted the fixity of species. A naturalistic but romantic conception of evolution was in place. The phrase "survival of the fittest" had already been coined in 1852 by Herbert Spencer, an English Lamarckian. And in 1849, a decade before the publication of Darwin's *Origin of the Species,* Alfred, Lord Tennyson wrote in his greatest poem, *In Memorium,* lines that foreshadowed the new view of evolution, in which the individual sacrifices for the species in the struggle for survival, a view of which Tennyson disapproved:

Are God and Nature then at strife,
That Nature lends such evil dreams?
So careful of the type [species] she seems,
So careless of the single life.

Later in the poem, in a widely quoted line, Tennyson calls nature "red in tooth and claw."

### The Victorian Revolutionary: Charles Darwin (1809-1882)

Evolution could not long remain a poetic effusion, although Darwin's own grandfather, Erasmus Darwin, anticipated his grandson's theory in a scientific poem, *Zoonomia.* Nor could it remain a romantic fancy, inspiring but finally implausible. Darwin's achievement was to make evolution into a scientific theory by providing a mechanism—natural selection. Then a campaign to convince scientists and the public of the fact of evolution was needed. Darwin never campaigned himself. He was something of a hypochondriac—the biographer (Irvine, 1959) called him "the perfect patient"—and after his trip on the *Beagle* he became a recluse, rarely leaving his country home. The struggle for the survival of natural selection was carried on by others, most spectacularly by Thomas Henry Huxley (1825-1895), "Darwin's bulldog."

Darwin was a young naturalist who had the good fortune to be included on a round-the-world scientific voyage aboard *HMS Beagle* from 1831 to 1836. Darwin was impressed, especially in South America, by the tremendous variation within and between species. Darwin noted there are innumerable distinct natural forms, each of which is peculiarly suited to its particular habitat. It was easy to imagine that each subspecies had descended from a common ancestor, and that each subspecies had been selected to fit some part of the environment.

Then, sometime after his return to England, Darwin began to collect data on species, their variation and origin. In his *Autobiography,* he said that he collected facts "on a wholesale scale," on "true Baconian principles." Part of his investigation centered on artificial selection, that is, on how breeders of plants and animals improve their stocks. Darwin talked with pigeon fanciers and horticulturalists and read their pamphlets. One pamphlet he read, "The Art of Improving the Breeds of Domestic Animals," written in 1809 by John Sebright, indicated that nature, too, selected some traits and rejected others, just as breeders did: "A severe winter, or a scarcity of food, by destroying the weak and unhealthful, has all the good effects of the most skillful selection" (Ruse, 1975). So, by the 1830s Darwin already had a rudimentary theory of natural selection: Nature produces innumerable variations among living things, and some of these variations are selected for perpetuation. Over time, isolated populations become adapted to their surroundings. What was entirely unclear was what maintained the system of selection. Why should there be improvement in species? In the case of artificial selection, the answer is clear. Selection is made by the breeder to produce a desirable kind of plant or animal. But what force in nature parallels the breeder's ideal? Darwin could not accept Lamarck's innate drive to perfection. The cause of selection must reside outside the organism, he insisted, but where?

Darwin got his answer in 1838 while reading Thomas Malthus' (1766-1834) *Essay on the Principle of Population as it Affects the Future Improvement of Society* (1798). Malthus attacked the utopian fantasies of certain writers by arguing that population growth necessarily exceeds growth in the food supply, with the consequence that life is a struggle of too many people for too few resources. The mass of humanity is necessarily kept at a subsistence level economy, at best. In his *Autobiography*, Darwin stated he had at last "got a theory on which he could work." It was the struggle for survival that motivated natural selection. Too many creatures struggled over too few resources, and those who were "weak and unhealthful" could not support themselves and died without offspring. The strong and healthy survived and procreated. In this way, favorable variations were preserved and unfavorable ones eliminated. Struggle for survival was the engine of evolution.

Darwin need not have gone to Malthus for the concept of individual struggle for survival. As William Irvine (1959) points out, "In her evolutionary aspects nature is almost tritely mid-Victorian." Darwin's theory "delighted . . . mid-century optimists" who learned that "nature moved forward on the sound business principles of laissez-faire." Natural selection may have offended the pious, but not the Victorian businessman of the industrial revolution, who knew that life was a constant struggle that rewarded failure with poverty and disgrace. The improvement of the species from the struggle of individuals was merely Adam Smith's "invisible hand" all over again.

Darwin had formulated the essentials of his theory by 1842, at which time he first set them on paper with no thought of publication. His theory may be summarized as a logical argument (Vorzimmer, 1970). First, from Malthus, Darwin holds that there is a constant struggle for existence resulting from the tendency of animals to outgrow their food sources. Second, nature constantly produces variant forms within and between species. Some variants are better adapted to the struggle for survival than others. Consequently, organisms possessing unfavorable traits will not reproduce, causing their traits to disappear. Finally, as small adaptive change follows small adaptive change over eons, species will differentiate from a common stock as each form adapts to its peculiar environment. Furthermore, environments will change, selecting new traits for perpetuation, and as environment succeeds environment, species will diverge ever more from their parent forms. Thus the observed diversity of nature can be explained as the result of a few mechanical principles operating over millions of years, as species evolve from species.

The theory as it stands is deficient. Without our knowledge of genetics, the origin of variations and the nature of their transmission could not be explained. Darwin was never able to overcome these difficulties and was in fact pushed closer and closer to Lamarckism as he defended his theories against critics. It is an irony of history that while Darwin was writing and defending his *Origin of Species,* an obscure Polish monk, Gregor Mendel (1822-1884), was doing the work on heredity that eventually supplied the answer to Darwin's difficulties. It was not until 1900 that Mendel's work, published and ignored in 1865, was rediscovered and hailed as the foundation of modern genetics. By the time Darwin died he had earned burial in Westminster Abbey, and his thought had revolutionized the Western world view, but it was not until the twentieth century that evolution seriously affected biology.

Darwin set his ideas down in 1842, but he did not publish his *Origin of the Species* until 1859. Why? It appears that even for its discoverer, evolution was too threatening a thought. In a letter Darwin said that admitting that species are not fixed "is like confessing a murder" (Irvine, 1959). It has been suggested that Darwin's hypochondria and various physical symptoms resulted from a neurotic crisis over the enormity of the idea of natural selection. In any event, Darwin pursued other things, spending eight years, for example, studying barnacles. Then, on June 18, 1858, Darwin was shocked to discover that someone was about to publish his theory. Evolution was truly in the air. Alfred Russell Wallace (1823-1913) had also been to South America, had been impressed by natural variation, and had read Malthus. Younger than Darwin, he was less hesitant to publish his conclusions. In fact, in later years Wallace was faithful to natural selection after Darwin retreated to Lamarckism.

It was arranged that Darwin and Wallace would each write a paper on natural selection. These were read on July 1, 1858, in their absence, to the Linnean Society of London, thus establishing Darwin and Wallace as co-discoverers of natural selection. Darwin rushed through a short verson of his projected work on evolution, which appeared in 1859 as *The Origin of Species by Means of Natural Selection or the Preservation of Favored Races in the Struggle for Life.* It presented his theory backed by a mass of supporting detail. It was revised until its sixth edition in 1872, as Darwin tried to answer his scientific critics—unsuccessfully as it turned out—in ignorance of genetics. Darwin wrote numerous other works, including two on the descent of humans and the expression of emotion in humans and the animals. The latter two works form part of the founding of the psychology of adaptation, and therefore will be considered in Chapter 9.

### Reception and Influence

The world was well prepared for Darwin's theory. The idea of evolution was already around well before 1859, and when the *Origin* was published it was taken seriously by learned men in all quarters. Biologists and naturalists greeted the work with varying degrees of criticism. Part of Darwin's thesis, that all living things descend from one common ancestor in the remote past, was scarcely novel and was widely accepted. Great difficulties were seen with the theory of natural selection, however, and it was not until 1930 that the new knowledge of genetics put natural selection on a sound scientific footing. It was still easy for scientists to hang on to some form of Lamarckism, to see the hand of God in progressive evolution (as did Charles Lyell, the great geologist, even though he was a powerful proponent of Darwin's ideas), or to exempt man from natural selection (as did nearly everyone).

If the reception of the *Origin* was so calm, how can we speak of a Darwinian revolution? To begin with, an appearance of revolution is given by the vituperative reception given evolution by Christian fundamentalists. Beginning with Bishop Wilberforce and continuing with William Jennings Bryan, defenders of the Bible attacked evolution, only to be crushed by such powerful personalities as T.H. Huxley and Clarence Darrow. Such clashes are the stuff of drama and give an appearance of revolution to the situation. The Biblical literalists, however, were already well behind the times. The Bible had received two hundred years of historical scrutiny and had been found wanting as a historical document. Even the Catholic *Dublin Review* was not shocked by Darwin's ideas.

To consider Darwinism as an intellectual revolution we must distinguish Darwinism as a scientific hypothesis and Darwinism as a new metaphysics in the tradition of the Enlightenment. Darwin himself cared only for the first, his intellectual child, but was alive to the possibilities of the second. Darwinism as a naturalistic metaphysics was the creation of others. Herbert Spencer, who had believed in the survival of the fittest before Darwin and applied it ruthlessly to man and society, was one forceful proponent of metaphysical Darwinism. Another was T.H. Huxley who used evolution to batter the Bible, miracles, and the church generally.

Huxley did much to popularize Darwinism as a metaphysics. Darwin's theory did not begin the modern crisis of conscience. Profound doubts about the existence of God and about the meaning of life go back to the eighteenth century. Darwinism was not the beginning of the scientific challenge to the old Medieval-Renaissance world view. It was the culmination of this challenge, making it most difficult to exempt human beings from immutable, determinate natural law. In his *Man's Place in Nature,* Huxley carefully related mankind to the living apes, lower animals, and fossil ancestors, showing that we did indeed evolve from lower forms of life, that no Creation was needed. In the hands of people like Huxley, science then became not just the destroyer of man's illusions, but also a new metaphysics offering a new kind of salvation through science itself. Huxley wrote that:

This new nature begotten by science upon fact . . . [constitutes] the foundation of our wealth and the condition of our safety . . . it is the bond which unites into a solid whole, regions larger than any empire of antiquity; it secures us from the recurrence of pestilences and famines of former times; it is the source of endless comforts and conveniences, which are not mere luxuries, but conduce to physical and moral well being.

More effusively, Winwood Reade wrote in *The Martyrdom of Man*: "The God of Light, the Spirit of Knowledge, the Divine Intellect is gradually spreading over the planet . . . Hunger and starvation will then be unknown . . . Disease will be extirpated . . . immortality will be invented . . . Man will then be perfect . . . he will therefore be what the vulgar worship as a God" (Houghton, 1957). This hope is similar to Comte's positivism, which Huxley called "Catholicism *minus* Christianity." Clearly for some, the new religion of scientific humanity was at hand. Huxley also boasted of sciences' practical fruits: "Every chemically pure substance employed in manufacture, every abnormally fertile race of plants, or rapidly growing and fattening breed of animals. . . ." This immediately brings to mind today's cancerous chemicals, tasteless tomatoes, and steroid-stuffed steers.

Darwinism did not instigate modern doubt, but it did intensify it. Darwin effected a Newtonian revolution in biology, robbing nature of her capital *N*, reducing evolution to random variation and happenstance victory in the struggle for survival. The beginning of the reduction of biological nature to chemical nature that was completed with the discovery of DNA had begun. In psychology, Darwinism leads to the psychology of adaptation. Assuming evolution, one may ask how mind and behavior, as distinct from bodily organs, help each creature adapt to its surroundings. Behaviorism is the ultimate heir to Darwinism in psychology; Skinner carefully modeled his account of animal learning on Darwinian variation, selection, and retention. Darwinism contributed also to the mechanization of human nature. In one of his more effusive moments, Huxley proclaimed that he would willingly be a clockwork mechanism if it were set to think and act correctly. Just such an image of man becomes the justification for Skinner's projection of a scientific Utopia.

Many, however, could not accept naturalism or were depressed by it. Huxley himself in his last writings said that man was unique among animals, for by his intelligence he could lift himself out of the natural Cosmic Process and transcend organic evolution. Sentiments such as this were not at all uncommon among both scientists and laymen, and help account for the popularity both before and after Darwin's time of various semi- or pseudo-scientific trends based on the uniqueness of man.

### On the Fringes of Science and the *Fin de Siècle*

We now come to three movements that at first seem unrelated: *mesmerism,* the belief that an imponderable fluid, which permeates the universe, can be manipulated to cure certain illnesses; *phrenology,* the belief that bumps on the head correspond to well-developed mental faculties manifested as highly developed parts of the brain; and *spiritualism,* the belief that there is a plane of existence apart from material appearances that can be known through certain occult experiences and practices. In fact, however, these three beliefs are historically interconnected; adherents of one were frequently adherents of the others. They were presented in various combinations in nineteenth-century popular self-help psychology. Two of these movements, mesmerism and phrenology, ultimately contributed substantially to psychology, and the third, spiritualism, was taken seriously by numerous men of science, most notably William James. All three are intimately related to the way science gradually filled the popular void left by the weakening of religion. Faith in science was replacing faith in the Church. At the same time, all three, but most particularly spiritualism, often consoled those who were distressed by naturalistic materialism. This distress intensified after 1859 in the *Fin de Siècle* period, and thoughtful people, among them philosophers and scientists, turned to the occult for spiritual comfort.

### Mesmerism: The First Popular Science

The term *mesmerism* comes from the name of the movement's founder, Franz Anton Mesmer (1734-1815), a Viennese physician who attributed numerous bodily diseases to an impalpable fluid penetrating the entire universe. Mesmer believed that this fluid was vital to the nervous activity of the body and that physicians could cure various diseases by manipulating the fluid in a patient's body. Mesmer began by using magnets to draw the fluid away from the afflicted areas, but soon decided that the fluid was really susceptible to animal magnetism rather than to mineral magnetism. Mesmer devised a complicated and outré therapy for his patients involving, among other things, striking the diseased parts of the body with his hands or a magic wand, tubs of water with iron rods focused on a patient's symptoms, and a "crisis room" lined with mattresses in which Mesmer's cures were effected during a kind of seizure. He specialized in what we now call "functional" illnesses, those that come from purely psychological causes. Although it was suggested at the time that at least some of the cures were a result of the patient's suggestibility, Mesmer firmly resisted any such hypothesis, insisting on his theory of animal fluids.

No single element of mesmerism was new. The curing of apparently physical diseases by inspired individuals goes back at least as far as the time of Jesus. It was also practiced by such contemporaries of Mesmer as Valentine Greatraks in England and Johann Gassner in Germany. Greatraks' speciality was scrofula, or the King's Evil, so-called because the touch of the monarch was said to cure it. If Mesmer's practice was not new, neither was the hypothesis of an ineffable universal fluid. Central to Newton's universe was the *ether,* a subtle fluid that carried electromagnetic waves and defined absolute space. A whole line of alchemical doctors had believed in a universal fluid essential to health, and even such a modern chemist as Robert Boyle attributed Greatraks' cures to invisible particles passing from doctor to patient.

Mesmer's novel approach was to try to put such cures and theorizing on a scientific basis. He attempted to convince the medical establishment, first in Vienna and later in Paris, that his cures were genuine and that animal magnetism was real. Over and over again, physicians admitted that Mesmer had seemingly effected great cures, but they found his methods too bizarre, his theory thoroughly unscientific. Some even intimated that he was a fraud. Mesmerism was too close to the occult —using trances, magical passes, and the trappings of the seance—to satisfy any Newtonian doctors. Mesmer was eventually worn down by these repeated rebuffs and by what he felt were betrayals by some of his followers, and in 1784 he left Paris to live the rest of his life detached from the movement he had started.

That movement was enormously popular. In the years before the French Revolution it was an absolute mania, garnering far more attention from the French public than the issues of the Revolution. Mesmeric lodges sprang up all over France in the 1780s. Mesmer enlisted the Marquis de Lafayette as a patron and corresponded briefly with George Washington. Mesmer and mesmerism seemed to fill perfectly a gap left by religion's receding influence. Science was all the rage in the late eighteenth century, and its influence grew in the nineteenth. People were hungry for a new set of certainties to replace the old. Mesmer offered at least the trappings of science—a reasoned theory about why his cures worked, an explanation that also covered the ancient miracle workers. Yet at the same time Mesmer's practice was served up in mystical and magical dress, more interesting than the austere rationalism of Newton's science. In short, Mesmer offered exactly the right pseudo-science to appeal to the times. It was scientific enough to appeal to the new rationalism, but spiritual enough to appeal to latent religious needs as well. Whether or not Mesmer himself was a charlatan is an extremely difficult question. Certainly he demanded absolute obedience from his followers, lest they betray his invention. But so did Freud. His treatment sessions were lurid seances, with Mesmer attired in mystic robes and wielding an iron wand. In his later life, Mesmer drifted into genuine occultism, using animal magnetism to explain clairvoyance, telepathy, and precognition. Yet Mesmer always did try to convince the medical establishment even when it brought him nothing but ridicule. Mesmer was at once a charlatan and a pioneer in abnormal psychology.

There was at the center of mesmerism a useful tool for the treatment of neuroses. Mesmer did cure many people of a great range of hysterical symptoms, from hysterical blindness to mysterious pains. He obscured the sources of his cures with the trappings of the seance and the theory of the universal fluid. What was central to Mesmer's cures, however, was the trance he could induce in his patients. In this trance he could command their actions and effect a cure. Although Mesmer attributed the trance to animal magnetism, it became apparent even to some of his followers that something simpler was involved. The trance was due to the psychological control of one person over another rather the passing of an invisible fluid from one body to another.

Once this insight was obtained, it became possible to extract the mesmeric trance from the mystical context Mesmer had given it and make it into a tool for the ordinary physician. Mesmerism was transformed into hypnotism.

This transformation occurred in France, scene of Mesmer's greatest successes and greatest denunciations, and in England, little touched by Mesmeric mania. In 1825 the French Royal Academy of Sciences decided to look into animal magnetism again, and their report, delivered in 1831, was far more favorable than any Mesmer had received in his lifetime. Without Mesmer's abrasive personality and occult theory, the magnetic trance could be viewed more objectively as an unusual but real mental state of possible use to doctors and meriting further investigation.

In the late 1830s animal magnetism was brought to England by the Baron Dupotet de Sennevoy who conducted a series of magnetic demonstrations. They caught the attention of a young, radical, and innovative physician named John Elliotson (1791-1868). He began to use magnetism both as a cure for various diseases and as an anesthetic drug during surgery. Like Mesmer, Elliotson was eventually drummed out of established medicine for his beliefs. He founded a journal devoted to animal magnetism and phrenology and encouraged other physicians to use magnetism in their practices. James Esdaile (1808-1859) was another persecuted English physician who tried to use mesmerism, especially as an anesthetic. Despite his popularity with the natives of India where he worked, the government denied support for his mesmeric hospital. In one respect, Esdaile stayed too close to Mesmer, maintaining in *Natural and Mesmeric Clairvoyance* that "the essential condition of the mesmeric state is the transmission of foreign nervous matter [according to Esdaile, a fluid] to the brain of the patient from the brain of the agent." Mesmer's old fluid theory, however, was becoming less and less plausible in the mid-nineteenth century, as the electrical nature of nervous conduction became known.

The transformation of mesmerism was completed by James Braid (1795-1860) who named it neuro-hypnotism, or more briefly hypnotism, derived from the Greek *hypnos*, meaning sleep. Braid considered the hypnotic state to be "nervous sleep." He began as a skeptic of mesmerism, but his own investigations convinced him that the phenomena were real enough, but that the theory of animal magnetism was incorrect. In *Neurypnology,* Braid wrote: "The phenomena of mesmerism were to be accounted for on the principle of a derangement of the state of the cerebrospinal center . . . induced by a fixed stare, absolute repose of the body, [and] fixed attention. . . ." The hypnotic state, Braid wrote, depends "on the physical and psychical [mental] condition of the patient . . . not at all on the volition or passes of the operator, throwing out a magnetic fluid, or exciting into activity some mystical universal fluid or medium." Braid rescued hypnotism from the occult surroundings of mesmerism and gave it to scientific medicine. But Braid himself encountered resistance from the medical establishment. The development of chemical anesthetics rendered the use of hypnosis in surgery unnecessary, and even today hypnotism has not completely shed its occult image.

In France, hypnotism advanced as a treatment for hysteria. In this connection, two theories arose as to the nature of the hypnotic trance. A.A. Liebeault (1823-1904) began one school of thought in Nancy, France, which was carried on by his student Hippolyte Bernheim (1837-1919). The Nancy school held that the hypnotic state was an intensification of certain tendencies in ordinary sleep or wakefulness. Some actions, even sophisticated ones, are automatic: we all respond impulsively to some suggestions; we all hallucinate in dreams. According to the Nancy school, in hypnosis the conscious will loses its usual close control over perception and action, and the orders of the hypnotist pass immediately and unconsciously into action or hallucinatory perception. The rival school of the Salpêtrière hospital in Paris maintained that since hypnotic suggestion could be used to remove hysteric symptoms, the hypnotic state must be a completely abnormal one, found in hysteric patients only. Hypnosis and hysteria were both seen as evidence of a pathological nervous system. The leading spokesman for the Salpêtrière school was Jean Martin Charcot (1825-1893), under whom Freud studied for several months. With the coming of Freud, the study of hypnotism became part of the psychology of the unconscious, for Freud used hypnosis in his early activities as a psychotherapist. It may be maintained that subsequent developments have supported the Nancy school's concept of hypnosis, but that today the exact nature of the hypnotic state, including its existence is a distinct mental state, still remains unclear.

If we return to Braid, we find hypnotism linked to another of our three fringe sciences—phrenology. Braid practiced what he called phreno-hypnosis, believing that in a hypnotic trance one could differentially manipulate the various mental faculties located, according to phrenology, in the different parts of the brain.

## The First Physiological Psychology: Phrenology

So far in treating the history of psychology we have found it to be part of philosophy. Even the occasional physician-psychologists generally founded their psychologies on philosophical, not physiological, principles. Hartley is a case in point. He erected his psychology on the principles of associationist philosophy and only buttressed it with Newton's speculative account of nerve function. The separation of the physiological and philosophical portions of Hartley's psychology was so complete that his follower Priestley could issue an edition of Hartley's *Observations on Man* that omitted all the physiology. Hartley wanted to create a psychology that combined philosophy and physiology, but philosophy clearly came first.

It was the achievement of Franz Joseph Gall (1758-1828) that reversed this relationship. Gall was unusual because he took seriously the idea that the brain is the seat of the soul. The idea was hardly new: Plato believed it; the Hellenistic scientists of Alexandria demonstrated it; the medieval faculty psychologists located each faculty in a different portion of the brain. However, beyond encouraging materialism, the concept had little effect on psychological thought. The locations assigned to the medieval faculties were based on prior analysis of mind, not brain, and philosophical psychology had done nothing to change this. Gall, however, stated that the brain was the specific organ of mental activity, in the same way that the stomach is the organ of digestion and the lungs the organ of respiration. Therefore, the study of human nature should begin with those functions of the brain that give rise to thought and action, rather than with abstract and introspective inquiries into mind.

The philosophical background of Gall's work was French empiricism, especially Condillac's sensationism. Gall offered several reproaches to the philosophical approach to psychology (Young, 1970). To begin with, the empiricists claimed that experience was the proper basis of science, yet their own psychology, Hume's science of human nature, was wholly speculative, having no reference to objective behavior or to the brain that controls it. Furthermore, the categories of analysis used by the philosophes were "mere abstractions." None of the faculties listed by philosophers—such as memory, attention, and imagination—were specific enough to explain actual human behavior and concrete individual differences. In *On the Functions of the Brain*, Gall wrote: "How are we to explain, by sensation in general, by attention [etc.] . . . the origin and exercise of the principle of propagation; that of the love of offspring, of the instinct of attachment? How explain by all these generalities, the talents for music, for mechanics, for a sense of the relations of space, for painting, poetry, etc." The philosophers' faculties exist but "they are not applicable to the detailed study of a species, or an individual. Every man, except an idiot, enjoys all these faculties. Yet all men have not the same intellectual or moral character. We need faculties, the different distribution of which shall determine the different species of animals, and the different proportions of which explain the differences in individuals" (Young, 1970). In short, the philosophers' concepts are useless for the specific empirical investigations that science requires.

Gall's ideas brought him into conflict with the empiricist philosophers in a final way. Condillac had attempted to derive every faculty of mind from sensation. Gall, however, believing the brain to be the organ of the mind, went on to conclude that each of his faculties was innate, based in a particular region of the brain. Gall's approach also implies a comparative psychology. Since the brains of species differ up and down the Great Chain of Being (Gall wrote before Darwin), so should the corresponding faculties differ. In fact, Gall and his followers carried out comparative studies to support this argument.

The problem for Gall, then, was to correlate specific behavioral functions with particular regions of the brain. Although he carried out detailed anatomical studies of the brain and nervous system, he found the techniques of his time too crude to answer the questions he posed, and he had moral scruples about experimenting on living but "martyrized" animals. Gall's method, therefore, was different. He assumed that well-developed faculties would correspond to well-developed parts of the brain. Those "organs" corresponding to the well-developed faculties in the brain would be larger than those organs corresponding to less developed faculties, and their relative size would be registered on the skull as bumps overlying the developed organ. Empirically, then, Gall's method was to show that people possessing certain striking traits would possess skulls with bumps over the corresponding organs of the brain, and that weak traits would go with undeveloped brain-organs and skull-regions. Although Gall's specific hypothesis was new, the idea that personality traits reveal themselves in physique and face was as old as antiquity.

Gall's theory has been schematized by Young (1970) as in Figure 6-2.

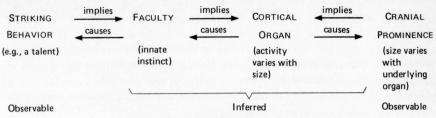

**FIGURE 6-2.**
Gall's theory of mind, brain and behavior.
(Adapted from R.M. Young, *Mind, brain and adaptation*
*in the nineteenth century,* Oxford University Press, 1970, p. 36.)

Thus Gall could observe people's unique behaviors and correlate them with cranial prominences. On the basis of such observations Gall drew up a long list of faculties, including such faculties as destructiveness, friendship, and language, each located in a particular region of the brain. Destructiveness, for example, was located just above the ear. Later followers of Gall expanded his list to include such faculties as Veneration, whose existence was believed to show that God must exist to be the object of veneration.

Certain conceptual features of Gall's approach have been mentioned: it was nativistic; it compared humans with other animals; it was materialistic, although Gall himself struggled against this tendency. Gall's psychology was also behavioristic rather than introspectionistic. His system rested on the observation of behaviors, and of bumps on the skull rather than on the introspection of his own mind. Gall's psychology was therefore the first objective, rather than subjective, psychology. More broadly, Gall's was a functional psychology concerned with how the mind and its organ, the brain, actually adapt a person or animal to everyday demands. Philosophical psychology was more concerned with grand problems of epistemology. Finally, Gall's psychology was a psychology of individual differences. He explicitly rejected the study of the generalized adult mind in favor of a study of how people differ.

Gall's conception points in two directions, one scientific and one occult. Scientifically, it inspired more experimentally minded physiologists to investigate the localization of behavioral functions in particular parts of the brain. At the hands of these men Gall's system suffered badly. His specific locations were found to be faulty. Worse, the basic assumptions that size of brain organ corresponds to strength of faculty and that bumps on the skull conform to the shape of the brain, were found to be without foundation. The entire system was violently rejected as a pseudo-science, appealing like astrology only to the credulous lay society.

The appeal to the lay society was the other direction—occult direction—taken by Gall's ideas. His close associate, Johann Caspar Spurzheim (1776-1832) who coined the term *phrenology* that Gall refused to accept, popularized the concept by turning it into a general and optimistic philosophy of life. In Spurzheim's hands, phrenology became the new popular psychology, and Spurzheim aimed to reform education, religion, and penology. His missionary activities carried him to the United States where the ground was most fertile for phrenology. He died shortly after arriving, but his work was carried on by the English phrenologist George Combe. The story of phrenology in the United States belongs to the chapter on the psychology of adaptation, where we will find that precisely those features in phrenology that appealed to ordinary Americans were also those that ensured the success of evolutionary psychology in America.

### Revolt Against Materialism: Spiritualism and Psychic Research

The doctrine of materialism and the religion of positivism may have inspired enthusiasts of scientism, but many people were unsettled and even repelled by them. The crisis of naturalism got worse after Huxley proclaimed humans to be only well-developed apes. Religion seemed dead; the prospect of the immortal soul annihilated. So, especially after 1859, many thoughtful people, including well-known scientists, turned to science itself for assurance that there was more to human life than the bodily and cerebral machines.

"The discovery that there was a life in man independent of blood and brain would be a cardinal, a dominating fact in all science and in all philosophy." So wrote Frederic Myers (1843-1901), the leading psychical researcher of the nineteenth century. Myers was horrified even as a child with the thought of not living forever. This fear was intensified when, like many Victorians, he lost his religious faith during his education. He met the philosopher Henry Sidgwick, who encouraged Myers to search scientifically for evidence of immortality. Sidgwick, too, had lost his faith, but deeply believed that ethics required personal immortality for the rectification of evil on earth. Myers took up Sidgwick's challenge and gathered an enormous amount of relevant data. Sidgwick and Myers founded the Society for Psychical Research, and in 1882 their journal published Myers' findings. These were also published posthumously in two volumes in 1903.

Simply as a catalogue of unusual psychological phenomena, Myers' *Human Personality and Its Survival of Bodily Death* won the respect of no less a psychologist than William James, himself once president of the Society for Psychical Research. Although from its title one might expect a collection of ghost stories, Myers in fact surveys the whole realm of abnormal psychology, from sleep and hysteria to messages from departed spirits. Myers' approach to his problem is psychological. He was the first English writer to disseminate Freud's early studies of hysteria. Hysteria was an important phenomenon for Myers, for it demonstrated the power of purely mental activity over the body when physical symptoms are caused by psychological disturbances (see Chapter 8).

Indeed, Myers fixed on exactly what Freud found most instructive in his early cases, that a hysteric's symptoms express unconscious desires that the patient does not want to admit to consciousness. Like Freud, Myers formulated a theory of the unconscious, which Myers called the *subliminal self.* In Freud's hands, the unconscious was an affront to human pride, revealing the irrational, impulsive, frightening depths that underly rational, discursive conscious thought. Myers' conception of the subliminal self, however, was romantic, Platonic, optimistic, and progressive. True, the subliminal self is irrational, said Myers, but it enables us to communicate with a spiritual world that transcends the material one. The existence of the subliminal self demonstrated for Myers the separability of soul and matter. It opened up the prospect of not just material evolution in which the individual plays a brief part, but also of spiritual, cosmic evolution in which each soul perfects itself forever, actualizing mental powers hindered by our animal bodies. We must conclude that although Myers scientifically investigated spiritualistic phenomena—and he was as skeptical of mediums as anyone could wish—his scientific searching was really guided by a Neoplatonic and occult view of the cosmos.

Myers could sound like a Huxleyan naturalist, as when he wrote: "The authority of creeds and Churches will be replaced by the authority of observation and experiment." Psychical research, however, was not well received in Huxley's circle. Huxley (1871) himself was sarcastic, likening "the talk in the spiritual world" to "the chatter of old women and curates," saying of both, "They do not interest me." Despite this hostility, the intellectuals of the Society for Psychical Research carried on, and at the popular level spiritualism approached a mania around the turn-of-the-century. As quickly as debunkers, such as the magicians Harry Houdini and John Maskelyne, exposed fake mediums, new ones sprang up. The dialectic of paranormal claim and skeptical counter-claim continues today, as illustrated by the controversy over persons such as Uri Geller. Psychical research, now called parapsychology, continues in scholarly journals and research programs today, while college courses in the subject proliferate. Nevertheless, it is an even more suspect subject than hypnotism, and its very mention makes most psychologists uncomfortable. Its existence and appeal, however, are undeniable.

### Disquiet at the End of the Century

It is unsurprising that the three movements we have examined belong together. Each has something of science about it—mesmerism as a medical tool; phrenology as a chart of brain faculties; psychical research as a study of abnormal mental states. At the same time, each has something of religion about it: mesmerism duplicates the ecstatic trance of the saint or mystic; phrenology offered a guide to moral life; mediums offered proof of a life beyond the physical. In 1852 an anonymous writer linked the three movements with homeopathy, vegetarianism, and hydropathy as "Physical Puritanism" in an "age of physiological reformers." Science offered a new morality. Nothing could better illustrate the weak state of orthodox religion and the effect of science in the nineteenth century than these occult movements. Atheistic materialism was too great a burden for most people. They feared Sade's amoral abyss and the meaningless world of the existentialist. They reached out, therefore, to science for reassurance upon matters about which Christianity was no longer plausible (Webb, 1974).

That all three movements could exist together in an eminent Victorian and renowned scientist is proved by Alfred Russell Wallace, co-discover of evolution

As a young man Wallace had been exposed to phrenology and mesmerism. Later, he used phrenology to argue that mankind's evolution was no longer physical, but was now mental. He also thought phrenology would be the psychology of the twentieth century. Wallace practiced mesmerism, which he believed enhanced telepathic and clairvoyant powers. Around 1865 Wallace attended a seance and was converted to spiritualism, writing a series of books reporting his investigations of mediums and promulgating a new philosophy of life. He finally concluded that a godlike mind was directing evolution, a conclusion that left Huxleyans wondering about Wallace's mental health.

Wallace was not alone in the dismay he felt at the new world of naturalism. Myers (1903) summed up the feelings of many around the turn of the century when he spoke of "the deep disquiet of our times. Never, perhaps, did man's spiritual satisfaction bear a smaller proportion to his needs. The old world sustenance, however earnestly administered, is too unsubstantial for the modern craving." There is, said Myers, an "underlying *Welt-Schmerz,* the decline of any real belief in the dignity, the meaning, the endlessness of life." Both occult movements and aggressive socialism were responses to the crisis. A particular variety of psychology was strengthened by the late nineteenth-century malaise, the psychologies of the irrational. The dark side of human nature became apparent to philosophers, sociologists, and psychologists. We therefore owe the origins and popularity of psychoanalysis, the psychology of the unconscious, to the same feelings that made people fasten onto mesmerism, phrenology, and spiritualism. Like these movements, psychoanalysis offered insight into the human unknown, practical advice, and hope of salvation—at least in this world.

## TOWARD THE SCIENCE OF PSYCHOLOGY

Within the general intellectual climate of the nineteenth century, certain specific developments in various areas made important contributions to the nascent science of psychology.

### Progress Outside Philosophy

#### A Contribution from Astronomy: Chronometric Analysis of Mental Processes

An important function of astronomy is to precisely map the stars. Until the advent of modern mechanical and photographic methods in which an astronomer rarely looks through a telescope, accurately locating stars depended on the ability of an astronomer to note the exact moment when a star passed directly overhead, marked by a single cross-hair in the telescope's field of vision. In one common early method, the astronomer noted the exact time on a clock as the star entered the field of vision, and then counted as the clock beat seconds until the star crossed the cross-hair. Accurately noting the exact moment of transit was critical, for slight errors would be translated into immense interstellar distances in calculating the exact positions of stars in the galaxy.

In 1795 an assistant astronomer at Greenwich observatory lost his job when his superior discovered that his own transit-times were about 0.5 seconds faster than his assistant's. Of course, the head astronomer assumed his own times to be correct and his assistant's in error. Years later, this event came to the attention of the German astronomer F.W. Bessel (1784-1846) who began to systematically compare the transit-times of different astronomers. Bessel discovered that all astronomers differed in the speed with which they reported transits. To correct this grave situation, Bessel constructed "personal equations" so that the differences between astronomers could be canceled out in astronomical calculations. For example, the "personal equation" of the two Greenwich astronomers would be Junior – Superior = 0.5 sec. The observations of any pair of astronomers could be compared by these equations reflecting their personal reaction times, and calculations of star positions could be corrected accordingly. Unfortunately for astronomers, use of the personal equations assumed that individual differences were stable, which proved to be false. Indeed, experiments with artificial stars with known transit-times, showed that sometimes observers "saw" the star intersect the cross-hair before it occurred. Only the increasing automation of observation was able to eliminate these problems.

Meanwhile, the reaction time experiment had been independently invented by the great German physicist Hermann von Helmholtz in response to a very different problem, that of the speed of nerve conduction. In 1850 Helmholtz stimulated the motor nerve of a frog's leg at points near and far from the muscle itself, measuring the time it took for the muscle to respond. Before Helmholtz's investigation, it had been widely assumed that nerve impulses traveled at infinite or at least immeasurably fast speeds. Helmholtz estimated the speed to be only 26 meters per second.

These two lines of research on reaction time came together in the work of F. C. Donders (1818-1889), a Dutch physiologist. Donders saw that the time between a stimulus and its response could be used to objectively quantify the speed of mental processes. Helmholtz had measured the simplest sort of stimulus-response (S–R) reaction, while astronomers had, for another purpose, investigated mental processes such as judgment. It was Donder's especial contribution to use reaction time to infer the action of complex mental processes. So, for example, one could measure a person's simple key-press response to a single stimulus—a mild shock to the foot. This is *simple reaction time.* However, one might ask the subject to press a key with the left hand when the left foot is shocked and with the right hand when the right is shocked. Obviously, a simple reaction is involved, but in addition the subject must discriminate which foot is shocked and choose which response to make. If simple reaction takes, for example, 150 msec to complete, and the discrimination and choice experiment takes 230 msec to complete, Donders reasoned then that the mental actions of choice and discrimination inserted into the simple reaction must take 230 msec – 150 msec, or 80 msec. This seemed to offer an objective way of measuring physiological and mental processes and was called mental chronometry.

The method was early taken up by Wundt and extensively used by the early mentalistic psychologists. Precisely because it was a quantitative method, it helped assure the scientific stature of experimental psychology as apart from qualitative philosophical psychology. It took the mind out of the armchair and into the laboratory. Unfortunately, numerous difficulties in the application of mental chronometry cropped up, and it ran into a dead end early in the twentieth century. One of the difficulties was implicit in its original discovery by astronomers—the problem of individual differences. They greatly troubled Wundt, the psychologist of the general mind, but fascinated his American student, J. M. Cattell. With the advent of behaviorism, psychologists largely turned away from reaction time experiments in their attention to learning. However, when cognitive psychology arose in the 1960s, mental chronometry was reborn, for cognitivists wanted ways to infer the temporal nature of inferred mental processes such as judgment, reasoning, memory, and pattern matching.

### Psychophysics: Psychology's First Research Program

The dean of historians of psychology, E. G. Boring, dates the founding of experimental psychology to 1860, the year in which a book called *Elements of Psychophysics* was published, written by a retired physicist, Gustav Theodore Fechner (1801-1887). Boring's claim rests on the fact that Fechner conceived and carried out the first systematic research in experimental psychology—research, moreover, that produced mathematical laws. Before Fechner, philosophers had widely assumed, following Kant, that the mind can neither be experimented on nor subjected to mathematical scrutiny. Fechner showed these assumptions to be false. The difficulties do at first seem to be immense. In physics, we can manipulate objects and observe what they d , and we can measure their position and momentum, writing mathematical laws interrelating these variables (such as, Newton's inverse-square law of gravitation). However, minds are private, and no instruments can be applied to conscious experiences.

Fechner's greatness was to overcome these problems. He saw that the content of consciousness can be manipulated by controlling the stimuli to which a person is exposed. This control makes mental experiment possible. We can have a person lift objects of known weight, listen to tones of known pitch and volume, and so on. Even so, how do we measure the resulting conscious experiences, or sensations? We can assign no number to a tone or weight sensation. Fechner perceived the difficulty and got around it by quantifying sensations indirectly. We can ask a subject to say which of two weights is heavier, which of two tones is louder. By systematically varying both the absolute values of the pairs of stimuli and the difference between them, and by observing when subjects can and cannot distinguish the pairs, sensation can be indirectly quantified. Hence, we can mathematically relate stimulus magnitude (R) with the resulting strength of sensation (S). One might expect that sensation would vary directly with stimulus, but Fechner found it did not. Instead, he found that $S = k \log R$ (where $k$ is a constant). That is, stimulus differences are easier to detect when both stimuli are of moderate absolute intensity than of high absolute intensity (for example, it would be easier to distinguish a 10-ounce weight from an 11-ounce weight than a 10-pound weight from a 10-pound, 1-ounce weight).

Fechner's approach was not without antecedents. The basic method of asking subjects to distinguish stimulus differences had been pioneered by the physiologist, E. H. Weber (1795-1878). The concept of treating sensations as quantitatively varying conscious states goes back to Leibniz's monads and his doctrines of *petite perception* and *apperception*. This line of thinking had been developed further by the German philosopher, Herbart (see the section on Progress in Philosophy). Fechner followed both in admitting the existence of unconscious, or as he called them negative, sensations which do not cross the threshold of consciousness. The immediate motivation of Fechner's work was the mind-body problem. Fechner held a dual aspect position, believing that mind and brain were simply two aspects of the same underlying reality, and therefore that physical stimuli and subjective sensations ought to be functionally related. Fechner hoped his psychophysics would solve the mind-body problem.

Fechner is not the founder of the science of psychology because, unlike Wundt, he carved out no societally recognized role for psychologists to take. Nevertheless, Fechner founded experimental psychology, for his methods, broadened to encompass more than sensations, was basic to Wundt's experimental psychology of consciousness. In Wundt's experiments, antecedent stimulus conditions were controlled, as in Fechner's, and data were provided as subjects reported the resulting conscious content. It was not Wundt's only method, but it was an important one, and it was the one most of his students carried away with them from his laboratory.

### Physiology Approaches Psychology: The Functions of the Brain

Gall, in his system of phrenology, had been the first to take seriously the idea that the brain is the organ of the mind. He therefore investigated the detailed relationship of brain organ and mental faculty. Gall's researches raised a storm of controversy in physiology, helping to push physiologists to experiment on the brain to discover exactly how it works and what it does. These experiments first led away from phrenology and then back to a "new phrenology" as physiologists discounted, and then discovered, the localization of brain functions.

Gall's major critic was a leading French physiologist, Jean-Pierre-Marie Flourens (1794-1867), a pioneer in experimental brain research. Flourens discovered the functions of the various lower parts of the brain, but when it came to the cerebral hemispheres, he parted company with Gall. Flourens ridiculed phrenology and argued on the basis of his own researches—which involved lesioning or ablating parts of the brain—that the cerebral hemispheres act as a unit, containing no specialized organs for special mental faculties. In his conclusions Flourens was more dominated by philosophical ideas than Gall was. Flourens was a Cartesian dualist who viewed the soul as residing in the cerebral hemispheres, and since the soul is unitary, the action of the hemispheres must be so too. He believed there was no organic connection between the sensory and motor functions of the lower parts of the brain and the cerebrum. Flourens' stature assured the success of his attack on Gall, and his view of the unitary action of the cerebrum remained orthodox dogma for decades.

In 1822 a discovery of momentous long-term implications was announced by Francois Magendie (1783-1855). Earlier, on the basis of postmortem dissections, the English physiologist Charles Bell (1774-1842) had distinguished two sets of nerves at the base of the spinal column. Bell suggested that one set carried information to the brain (sensory nerves) while the other carried information from the brain to the muscles (motor nerves). Previously, it had been thought that nerves work in both directions. Magendie discovered the same thing independently and more conclusively because he demonstrated the different functions of the nerves in the spinal column by direct experiment on living animals. The next decade in brain physiology saw the extension of the sensory-motor distinctions up the spinal column and into the cerebrum. Magendie, however, did not take this step. Like Flourens, his views on the functions of the cerebral hemispheres were controlled by a philosophy—in Magendie's case by a modified sensationism. For Magendie, all faculties were just modifications of perception, and he saw no role for the hemispheres in the direct control of behavior. The empiricist philosophy traces sensations and their associations as concepts are formed by the understanding but says little or nothing about human action. Magendie, therefore, went no further in his physiology.

Another breakthrough in the study of the functions of the cerebrum suggested that Gall was at least correct in asserting that different parts of the brain have specific behavioral functions. This discovery was made by Pierre Paul Broca (1824-1880), who observed that patients with speech disorders showed, when autopsied, damage to the same area of the left frontal lobe of the brain. Broca, who rejected the study of bumps on the head, viewed his finding as limited support for Gall, although the faculty of language had not been found where Gall had predicted.

Meanwhile, other researchers had been extending the distinction between sensory and motor nerves up the spine and into the cranium. Young (1970) reports that in 1845, one English physician wrote, "The brain . . . is subject to the laws of reflex action, and that, in this respect it does not differ from the other ganglia of the nervous system . . . [and] must necessarily be regulated . . . by laws identical with those governing the spinal ganglia and their analogues in the lower animals." That is, it was known that the involuntary reflexes of the lower nervous system work by sensory-motor reflex, and it is suggested here that the cerebrum works the same way.

Against this view was the observation that the cerebral hemispheres seemed insensitive. They had been poked, prodded, pressed, and pricked, but no movement resulted in living animals. This supported Flourens' view that the hemispheres were not involved in action. However, in 1870 two German researchers announced that electrical excitation of the cerebrum can elicit movement and that different parts of the brain, when stimulated, seem to regulate different movements.

This finding encouraged others to map out the brain, locating each sensory and motor function. Today, such maps are remarkably precise and allow tumors to be located with great accuracy. A "new phrenology" was thus born, in which each part of the brain was assigned a discrete sensory or behavioral function. But the new localizations were different from Gall's, for they resulted from an extension of the sensory-motor nerve distinction to the cerebrum. Some parts of the brain receive sensations, others govern specific actions, and the association of sensation and action produces behavior. In this view, the brain is a complex reflex machine. It should be pointed out here that not all neurophysiologists accepted then, or accept now, the localization of brain functions. Some maintain that the brain acts at least in some respects as a unit and that information present in one part of the brain is at least potentially present in others.

The formulation of the brain as a reflex device associating sensory input with motor action made possible the integration of British associationism with physiology and the extension of associationism and empiricism to action as well as understanding. This integration was the work of Alexander Bain.

### Progress in Philosophy

*England: Alexander Bain (1818-1903) and Association Psychology*

In 1851 Bain wrote to his friend and colleague, John Stuart Mill, "There is nothing I wish more than so to unite psychology and physiology that physiologists may be made to appreciate the true ends and drift of their researches into the nervous system." Bain fulfilled his desire in two massive volumes *The Senses and the Intellect* (1855) and *The Emotions and the Will* (1859), a comprehensive survey of psychology from the standpoints of associationism and physiology and embracing every psychological topic from simple sensation to esthetics and ethics.

Bain offers few new ideas. His associationism derives from Hartley and the Mills. His physiology was drawn from leading texts and lectures of his time. Even the idea of uniting physiology and philosophical psychology was Hartley's first. Bain's physiology, however, was based on experimental research, not on Newton's speculations. Bain's wish to unite psychology and physiology probably came from his early exposure to phrenology, which he later rejected in favor of Mill's associationism and Flourens' physiology.

What is most important about Bain is the attitude he adopted toward his material. The aim of the earlier associationists was to give an adequate empiricist epistemology. Bain, however, wrote as a psychologist. He assumed the associationist epistemology and inquired instead into how to account for human action, not just conception. Bain was not concerned to justify human knowledge, but to explain human thinking and behavior.

To this end Bain adopted the sensorimotor physiology of the German physiologist, Johannes Müller (1801-1858). In his *Elements of Physiology* (1842) Müller had already proposed that the role of the brain is to associate incoming sensory information with appropriate motor responses. Bain knew the *Elements* and incorporated Müller's conception of the role of the brain into his psychology. Thus, Bain united the philosophy of associationism with sensorimotor physiology to give a unified human psychology. Even today most general psychology texts are organized like Bain's, beginning with simple nerve function in sensation and working up to thinking and social relations. Bain's integration was quite influential. He wrote before the functions of the cerebrum were known, and his uncompromising associative view of physiology guided later English investigators to press their studies into the mysterious cerebral hemispheres.

Thus Bain had a considerable effect on psychology. The journal *Mind*, which he founded in 1874, is still in existence as an organ of philosophical psychology. He was, however, too philosophical in his outlook; his conception of mind was soon out of date. Despite his use of physiological data, he did no experiments, and while he recognized the importance of Darwin's work, his associationism remained pre-evolutionary. The future of association psychology lay more in its integration with evolution than with physiology.

### France: Ideology, Spiritualism, and Positivism

During and after the French Revolution, French philosophical psychology was carried on by the "ideologists" named by their founder, Destutt de Tracy (1754-1836). *Ideology* means here the study of ideas and of their origin, and it continued the Enlightenment tradition of French empiricism. De Tracy, however, rejected Condillac's radical sensationalism and returned to a conventional faculty psychology more consistent with Locke. As heirs to the Enlightenment, the real goal of the ideologists was social reform. They favored a moderate democracy based on personal property and were particularly interested in improving education as the foundation for the new society.

The best known of the ideologists is Pierre Jean Georges Cabanis (1757-1808), a physician who is sometimes called the father of physiological psychology. Cabanis is the epitome of Enlightenment empiricism and materialism. Stating what could have been Condillac's motto, Cabanis said, "We sense; we are." He compared the function of the brain to the function of the stomach. Wrote Cabanis (1824): "The brain digests the impressions; [and] organically produces the secretion of thought." Although Cabanis detested the Reign of Terror—when ideologists had been imprisoned—Cabanis used the "experiments" of the guillotine to argue that mental activity and action are multi-leveled: the body may twitch after the head is severed, but this is simply unconscious reflex activity. Consciousness resides in the brain and disappears at the moment of execution. Cabanis never performed physiological researches and avoided any precise speculation on the relation of nervous activity to mind, although he was clearly a materialist. Consequently, his ideas remain more philosophical than those of Gall or the later experimental physiologists, although he does tend in their direction.

One interesting figure began as an ideologist but then swam against the prevailing empiricist-materialist stream toward Catholicism. He was Francois-Pierre Maine de Biran (1766-1824). Although Maine de Biran was not afraid to take a physiological approach to the study of the mind—and always insisted that psychology should study the whole man—he felt that there was more to human nature than mere matter. He possessed an intensely introspective disposition and argued that the fundamental method of psychology should be reflection, or the scrutiny of one's own mind. Maine de Biran called this enterprise "experimental psychology." Upon such reflection, the central psychological fact he discovered was will, or the feeling of effort we experience as we carry out a voluntary action. Like Wundt, Maine de Biran was a voluntarist, with the important distinction that Maine de Biran's "experimental psychology" used an intense Cartesian form of introspection rather than Wundt's simple self-observation. Maine de Biran's one direct influence on psychology was on Freud, who knew of Maine de Biran's belief that many important influences on mental life are marginally conscious at best and that only careful reflection could reveal them. As Maine de Biran grew older, he moved further still from French naturalism and toward religion. He finally believed that man had a separate immortal soul whose relation to God needed investigation. This last direction of his thinking helped found the later French school of spiritualism, which opposed materialism and insisted on man's spiritual nature, but did not involve psychic phenomena. Maine de Biran completed his retreat from the naturalism of ideology by dying a Catholic. He represents an attempt, ultimately unsuccessful, to reassert the reflective Platonic-Cartesian rationalist psychology against the rising tide of naturalism and positivism.

The last French philosophical psychologist, Hippolyte-Adolphe Taine (1828-1893), expounded these new positions. Although most of his works are on history and literature, he was most proud of his psychological book, *On Intelligence* (1870). In *On Intelligence* Taine presents an integration of association psychology similar to Bain's, arguing that all ideas, no matter how apparently abstract, may be reduced to a collection of sensations associated with the idea's name. The business of psychology is, thus, similar to chemistry's—"to decompose [compounds] into their elements to show the different groupings these elements are capable of, and to construct different compounds with them" (Taine, 1875). Following Leibniz, Taine proposed that conscious sensations are simply aggregates of weaker, more fleeting sensations that are only marginally conscious at best. Thus Taine, like so many others in the nineteenth century, believed in the unconscious.

Taine then discussed the physiological substrate of sensation. He maintained a dual aspect psychophysical parallelism, holding that every event in consciousness has a corresponding neural event. According to Taine, the reverse is not true, for some neural events give rise only to unconscious sensations. Taine's neurophysiology presents the brain as an unspecialized organ associating stimulus and response: "The brain, then, is the *repeater* of the sensory centers. . . ." That is, the brain simply copies incoming neural information, as mental images copy sensations. Mind and brain are both seen in terms similar to Hume's or Hartley's.

Taine, then, may be regarded as a French Bain, although he had less systematic effect on later psychology than Bain since his later writings abandoned psychology. Nevertheless, he integrated physiology and philosophical association psychology and is followed historically by the earliest French psychologists. In his philosophy he even pointed beyond Bain toward behaviorism. His approach to science resembled that of the later logical positivists. In this view, the first task of a science is to gather firm observational data from which simple generalizations are drawn. Then, a logically organized, deductive, theoretical edifice is to be erected on the observational foundation. Finally, new phenomena may be predicted from the theoretical system and these predictions checked against observation. Biran had tried to return French psychology to reflective rationalism, but Taine put it back on course as an objective, empiricistic science integrated with biology.

### Germany: Struggle Toward Science

As we have seen earlier, the dominant philosophical system in Germany after Kant's time was idealism in one form or another. Certain concepts of the idealists found a place in early German psychology. Wundt studied individual consciousness, proposed a historical, genetic approach to the investigation of the higher mental processes, and stressed human will as the unifying force in mental life. All of these ideas are part of idealist philosophy. Freud, too, was influenced by Schopenhauer's concept of unconscious primitive forces lurking in the personality. Nevertheless, the German idealists, following Kant, took a dim view of psychology as a would-be science. Psychology studies only a concrete individual, or a set of individuals, whereas what the idealists sought was transcendent Platonic knowledge of a godlike Absolute Spirit, which they took to be the noumenal reality behind physical appearances and the individual mind. Although Wundt retained a bias toward the study of the general human mind, he did not believe in an Absolute Mind. Empirical research seems trivial in the idealist context, and the idealists—most forcefully Hegel—actively opposed the development of empirical psychology (Leary, 1978b).

However, there were those in Germany who did seek a scientific psychology, taking Kant's negative analysis of psychology as a challenge (Leary, 1978a). The most important of them was Johann Friedrich Herbart (1776-1841) who attempted to mathematicize psychology. Herbart viewed psychology as applied metaphysics. His extremely complex psychological system formed only a small part of an even more complex metaphysics, developed largely out of Leibniz's monadology.

Herbart pictured the mind as a collection of elementary ideas of varying intensity. Some ideas are strong enough to cross the threshold of consciousness; others reside in unconsciousness. In fact, Herbart prefigured Freud by maintaining that no idea is ever completely destroyed. Ideas struggle with one another for access to consciousness, as dissonant ideas repel one another and associated ideas help pull each other into consciousness or drag each other down into unconsciousness. Herbart's real aim was to formulate a Newtonian mathematics of the mind. Just as Newton described the mathematically exact interaction of objects in space, so Herbart tried to describe the mathematically exact interaction of ideas in the mind. In equation after equation Herbart proposed exact formulas for the mechanics of ideas entering and leaving consciousness.

The difficulty of Herbart's system was that there was no way to connect it to empirical reality. To begin with, Herbart himself argued that the mind could not be subject to experiment because each mind is unique and can shed no light on general mental functioning. Furthermore, he admitted that his calculations were wholly fictional, based on hypothetical assumptions incapable of proof. Finally, Herbart said that in his psychology for an idea to be "in consciousness" doesn't mean that its possessor is conscious of it! This seems to cut Herbart's psychology off from science as ordinarily understood, and Wundt continually attacked Herbart's metaphysical, unscientific psychology. It was a common criticism of Herbart that he failed to measure mind, as Fechner was able to do later.

We must bear in mind, however, that mental measurement and experiment were not Herbart's aim. It is best to view him as proposing a mental algebra or geometry in Plato's realm of mathematics. When you solve the quadratic equation or prove the Pythagorean theorem you are concerned wholly with abstract entities. Algebra and Euclidean geometry are, like Herbart's psychology, hypothetical systems based on *a priori* rules for manipulating symbols, rules that may be changed to create a different system (such as, non-Euclidean geometry). Algebra can be used to compute the price of apples or the force of gravity; geometry can be used to survey roads or map the stars. Each is also an autonomous study in its own right. So, Herbart would have thought his laws of the rise and fall of ideas could be applied equally to dissonant musical notes or dissonant Oedipal attitudes toward one's father.

Viewed this way, Herbart resembles the modern psychological school of structuralism, associated with Chomsky and Piaget (see Chapter 13). Piaget, for example, treats thinking as an abstract activity which can be described in the language of formal logic. *What* a child thinks about is less important to Piaget than the logical *structure* of his thinking. The Western child may think about classifying sports cars, the African child about classifying species of antelope, but the logic of classification is universal. Herbart seems to have held the same position. Each person's mind is absolutely unique, for the experiences giving us our ideas are unique; but common to all people are the mathematics of how ideas are related.

Herbart's direct influence was small, for he had no devoted students. His idea that ideas continuously vary in intensity helped Fechner formulate psychophysics, using a version of Leibniz's concept of apperception which was greatly stressed by Wundt. He contributed to the idea of the unconscious and, against the idealists, proclaimed psychology a science. Yet Wundt, Fechner, and all experimental psychologists repudiated Herbart's metaphysical, vaguely introspective, fictional mathematics of mind. They had to if they were to establish psychology as an independent science. Herbart was much interested in pedagogy, and several decades after his death "Herbartianism" enjoyed a vogue in educational circles. But Herbartianism was more the creation of others who picked up and reshaped Herbart's ideas, and even in modified form it exerted no long-term influence. Herbart's most lasting effect was his determination to make psychology a science despite the strictures of Kant and the opposition of the idealists.

Another important German philosophical psychologist was Hermann Lotze (1817-1881). Before he turned to philosophy, Lotze received his M.D., and he was Fechner's friend and physician. In one respect, Lotze appears to be German psychology's Bain or Taine. In his *Outlines of Psychology* (1881) Lotze proposed an empiricist view of consciousness, saying that depth perception is learned, not innate, and experience is compounded out of simple ideas. This empiricism he integrated with the growing sensory-motor concept of brain function.

However, Lotze was not wholly dedicated to empiricism and naturalism. He insisted that although physiology offered a valid approach to the material aspects of mind and behavior, man and the animals each possessed divinely given souls. As was typical of German philosophers, Lotze (and Herbart) emphatically rejected materialism in favor of Cartesian dualism. By insisting on the spiritual nature of man, Lotze earned the admiration of English-speaking psychologists dissatisfied with the associationistic and reductive psychologies they found around them. Among them were James Ward, the English psychologist who bitterly attacked naturalism (see Chapter 9), and William James, the tender-minded psychologist who took part in psychical research.

A more eminent and consistent exponent of naturalism and empiricism was Hermann von Helmholtz (1821-1894), probably the greatest natural scientist of the nineteenth century. For much of his career he was occupied with physiology. We have already learned of his measurement of the speed of nerve conduction; he also conducted definitive studies of physiological optics and acoustics. But he was also a leading physicist, formulating the law of conservation of energy when he was only 26.

Helmholtz's approach to the mind is essentially that of a Lockean empiricism in which ideas are interpreted as mental content. Helmholtz argued that all we know for certain are our ideas, or images of the world gathered by experience. He strikes a pragmatic note by acknowledging that we cannot know if our ideas are true, but argues that this does not matter as long as they lead to effective action in the real world. Science was an example of such effective action. Although he followed Kant in holding causality to be an innate principle, Helmholtz, like the empiricists, maintained that the other Kantian categories of knowledge are acquired.

Of particular interest to psychology is Helmholtz's theory of unconscious inference. If, for example, visual perception of space is not an innate intuition, then in the course of development we must learn to calculate the distance of objects from us, as Berkeley proposed. Yet we are not aware of performing such calculations. Helmholtz theorized that these kinds of calculations, or inferences, must be unconscious and moreover must be unconsciously learned, as happens in language acquisition. Like words, ideas (including sensations) are mental contents which represent reality. Just as a child learns language spontaneously and with no direct instruction, so too he spontaneously and unconsciously learns the meanings of ideas. Helmholtz's theory of the unconscious differs from other views. For Herbart, the unconscious was just a place where ideas reside when they are not conscious. For the romantics it was a repository of ancient and irrational forces. For

Helmholtz, it was an agency autonomous of consciousness, but essentially rational; unconscious inferences were of the same form as conscious ones.

As we would expect of a physicist and physiologist Helmholtz was a forceful advocate of the natural sciences. He welcomed their growth in the German universities and heaped scorn on the idealist philosophers for whom natural science was the trivial study of physical reality, which was of no consequence compared to the spirit behind physical reality. Furthermore, Helmholtz's own researches supported materialism. His physiological studies of sensation established the dependence of perception on mere fleshly matter. His theory of conservation of energy inspired some young physiologists to swear, as Helmholtz' friend Emil du Bois-Reymond put it in a letter, "a solemn oath to put in effect this truth: no other forces than the common physical-chemical ones are active within the organism" (Kahl, 1971). This attitude encouraged the young Freud to compose his first systematic psychology, one that was entirely materialistic.

Helmholtz, however, was aware of the dangers of too much materialism when he wrote in "Thought in Medicine": "Our generation has had to suffer under the tyranny of spiritualistic metaphysics; the younger generation will probably have to guard against materialistic metaphysics." He continues, "Please do not forget that materialism is a metaphysical hypothesis . . . If one forgets this, materialism becomes a dogma [compare this to the 'solemn oath' above] which hinders the progress of science and, like all dogmas, leads to violent intolerance." While he could not accept spiritualism or vitalism, neither could he accept extreme materialism. He preferred to maintain an open mind and let the facts decide.

## CONCLUSIONS

### Conceptual Summary: The Nineteenth Century Crisis

The nineteenth century was a century of conflict and its conflicts are our conflicts. It saw the Industrial Revolution bring unparalleled material progress and tremendous urban poverty. It witnessed widespread religious revival, while the foundations of belief were steadily eroded by science. It inculcated in its people acute and ferocious sexual morality, while allowing—or causing—prostitution and crime to be endemic. The sciences and humanities flourished as never before, but the practical businessman sneered at the ivory tower intellectual. Pessimism and optimism mixed in the same mind. Wrote Carlyle: "Deep and sad as is our feeling that we stand yet in the bodeful night; equally deep, indestructible is our assurance that the morning also will not fail" (Houghton, 1957).

To summarize the specific ideas of nineteenth-century thinkers would be merely confusing. It will be more useful to note that one conflict underlies all the others: the conflict between the new scientific naturalism and the older beliefs in a transcendent spiritual reality.

Naturalism, product of the Enlightenment, occasioned both hope and despair. It held out the hope of perpetual progress, of the perfectability of humanity, of useful and profound knowledge of the universe. Yet it challenged every prejudice from naive beliefs about physics to faith in God and in His highest creation, the human being. Science also threatened to dehumanize humans, reducing the individual to a collection of chemicals laboring in a vast industrial machine. It seemed to strip the world of meaning and each person of freedom and dignity.

Proponents of naturalism, of course, did not see the conflicts. They believed that technical, scientific solutions could be found for every human problem. Their problem was convincing society of their sincerity and efficacy. Science became a new religion, most clearly seen in Comte's positivism, but also present in popularizing scientists such as Huxley. The naturalists benefited from being united in a single Newtonian conception of nature, differing among themselves only in detail. Forceful, optimistic, successful, natural science came to dominate the intellectual world.

Arrayed against the naturalists were a motley group of people who felt poignantly the conflicts precipitated by naturalism. Their answers were diverse. Some clung to traditional religion; there was a significant Catholic revival in Protestant England, for example, and Maine de Biran died a Catholic. Some, like Wallace, found a faith in a Divine Intelligence guiding evolution. Some sought assurance of immortality through psychical research into the spirit world. Still others embraced philosophical idealism, transforming God into Hegel's Absolute Spirit.

Against united science, believers in these varied transcendental ideas could not prevail. But neither were they conquered. Science is today's orthodox belief, but the occult maintains an underground existence. Every newspaper has its astrologer. Every bookstore has its occult section, where one may find a bewildering variety of "secret" doctrines published in both cheap paperbacks and expensive hardbacks. Science has prevailed in that every doctrine wants to call itself a science, but it has failed in that popular science is pseudo-science ranging from mesmerism and phrenology to the *Chariots of the Gods*. The concept of God as an alien astronaut epitomizes the Victorian conflict of religion and science and shows us that it is our conflict still.

Psychology was, and is, caught in the middle. Nothing is harder for most to believe than that we are no more than chemical machines devoid not only of spirit but also of free will. Consequently, psychology became a battleground contested by the materialists who could believe it and by the many who could not. Bentham, Cabanis, and Darwin stood on one side; Herbart, Lotze, Maine de Biran, and Myers stood on the other. Nor is the conflict over in psychology. Materialism seemed to triumph in behaviorism, but this triumph was transitory and we will find in the last chapter that there are contemporary psychologies whose goal is transcendent awareness of a cosmic consciousness. Victorian conflicts are very much with us.

### Historical Trends: Founding Psychology

Out of the nineteenth century emerged the three founding forms of psychology. Wundt founded the psychology of consciousness. Freud founded the psychology of the unconscious. And various evolutionary psychologists founded the psychology of adaptation. All the concepts for each were in place, awaiting only the creative minds and forceful personalities needed to weld them into coherent psychological programs. Since we will explore the immediate background of each psychology in detail in later chapters, we need only briefly summarize them now.

### The Psychology of Consciousness

The ground was well prepared for the founding of experimental psychology by Wundt. Physiology and philosophy had been mated many times and with increasing frequency in the mid-nineteenth century. Wundt, too, made the journey from physiologist to philosopher, but he alone established psychology as an independent, experimental science.

The first component of Wundt's system, the experimental study of the individual consciousness, had already begun with Fechner and Donders. The definition of psychology as the study of conscious experience was virtually unanimous in the nineteenth century. Fechner and Donders showed that consciousness could be manipulated through experiment, and Wundt extended their techniques and invented others to furnish the raw data of an experimental, mentalistic psychology. Wundt's central concept, that of the voluntary control of mind through apperception, was present in thinkers as diverse as Leibniz, Maine de Biran, and Schopenhauer.

The other part of Wundt's psychology, the comparative historical approach to the development of mind and to the higher mental processes, was also ready to hand. The German idealist philosophers put great stress on studying the historical development of anything, and Wundt tried to do just that for the mind. Wundt held that laboratory experiment was helpless to reveal deep mental processes and hoped to reach them indirectly through their social and historical products, particularly language and myth. Only by combining the experimental and historical methods, Wundt believed, could a complete picture of the human mind be obtained.

### The Psychology of the Unconscious

It is sometimes said that if Freud had died in infancy, psychoanalysis would have been invented anyway. This acknowledges the strong historical trend toward a psychology of the unconscious. Like Wundt, Freud began his work in medicine and physiology. However, he came to consider psychological questions because of his clinical experience treating hysterics, rather than because of a desire to find scientific answers to philosophical questions. Psychoanalysis has always been strongly set off from academic psychology, finding its home in the clinic, not the laboratory.

The idea of the unconscious was present in much of European thought. Scarcely anyone denied its existence, although it took different forms in different philosophies. For Helmholtz it was a rational calculator of sense-data. For Herbart it was a repository of ideas. For the romantics it was a wild, untamed force. Freud combined Herbart's conception with the romantics', and added the mechanism of repression to create the psychoanalytic unconscious.

The other cornerstone of psychoanalysis, Freud's theory of motivation, was also available. Hedonism as man's basic need was proposed by the utilitarians;

the pleasure principle was nothing new. Wedded to the romantic unconscious it produced the psychoanalytic id, repository of irrational but vital forces motivating all activity and opposing the constraints of civilization.

### The Psychology of Adaptation

From Plato to Wundt, the aim of psychology was epistemological: how does *the* human mind arrive at general knowledge? Whatever particular answer was given, empiricist or rationalist, individual differences and the demands of the environment were viewed as mere nuisances. The focus was clearly on the abstract universal mind as it sought abstract, universal truths. This rather Platonic psychology was especially strong in Germany and created an intellectual gulf between Wundt and his Anglo-American students.

Once a theory of evolution is available, however, different kinds of questions arise. What is mind good for in the evolutionary scheme of things? How does mind help the individual creature adapt to his individual environment? The focus shifts from what the mind contains to how it works. Whether evolution is conceived in Lamarckian or Darwinian terms, these questions are natural ones to an evolution-minded thinker. The Darwinian theory also demands the scrutiny of individual differences in mental function, for such differences are the grist for the mill of natural selection. As evolutionary thinking penetrated European philosophy, especially in England and America, a new psychology concerned with how the individual adjusts to his environment naturally arose. Later, coupled to radical materialism and an aggressive positivism, the psychology of adaptation would become behaviorism. In one form or another, it was a psychology destined to dominate academic psychology for much of the twentieth century.

One logical question suggested by evolution was seldom raised, however. If the brain is the organ of the mind, it is reasonable to ask how evolutionary pressures have shaped that organ. What aspects of human thinking and behavior are innate? Although the question is reasonable, other forces eclipsed it until very recently. Both the association psychology, with its attendant empiricism, and the sensori-motor model of the brain naturally minimized the native structure of the mind, reducing it to a *tabula rasa*. Associationism sees the mind, and sensorimotor physiology sees the brain, as simply a device for linking incoming stimuli with outgoing responses. The only innate differences between individuals and species are in the number of possible connections, which still makes the environment responsible for qualitative differences. Given this conception of mind and brain, it is no surprise that the question of evolution's impact on the structure of the species' mind did not arise. However, when such questions were raised in the mid-twentieth century, they posed serious problems for behaviorism.

## SUGGESTED READINGS

No single source is adequate for the student of nineteenth-century psychology. A good survey of the nineteenth-century intellectual world may be found in Franklin L. Baumer, *Modern European Thought* (Macmillan 1977). Excellent and provocative special studies are: Frank M. Turner's *Between Science and Religion* (Yale University Press, 1974) which discusses the intellectual's reaction to naturalism; William Irvine's *Apes, Angels and Victorians* (Meridian, 1959) which discusses Darwin and the reception of evolution; Robert M. Young's *Mind, Brain and Adaptation in the Nineteenth Century* (Oxford University Press, 1970), which discusses the development of concepts of brain function and its integration with evolution and associationism; and James Webb's *The Occult Underground* (Open Court, 1974) which discusses beliefs resistant to scientific naturalism.

## REFERENCES

Baumer, F. *Modern European thought.* New York: Macmillan, 1977.

Bentham, J. *Principles of Morals and Legislation* (1789). Reprinted in *The Utilitarians.* Garden City, N.Y.: Doubleday, 1973.

Braid, J. *Neurypnology.* London: John Churchill, 1843.

Cabanis, P. Relations between the body and the mind of man (1824). Partially reprinted in S. Diamond (Ed.) *The roots of psychology.* New York: Basic Books, 1974.

Darwin, C. *The autobiography of Charles Darwin and selected letters* (F. Darwin, Ed.). New York, Dover, 1958.

Darwin, C. *The origin of species.* New York: Mentor, 1959.

Esdaile, J. *Natural and mesmeric clairvoyance.* London: Hippolyte Bailliere, 1852.

Helmholtz, H. Thought in medicine. Reprinted in R. Kahl (Ed.) *Selected writings of Hermann von Helmholtz.* Middletown, Conn.: Wesleyan University Press, 1971.

Houghton, W. E. *The Victorian frame of mind.* New Haven, Conn.: Yale University Press, 1957.

Huxley, T. H. Letter. In London Dialectical Society (Eds.) *Report on Spiritualism.* London: Longmans, Green, Reader & Dyer, 1871.

Huxley, T. H. *Man's place in nature.* Ann Arbor: The University of Michigan Press, 1959.

Irvine, W. *Apes, angels, and Victorians.* Cleveland: Meridian Books, 1959.

Kahl, R. K. (Ed.) *Selected writings of Hermann von Helmholtz.* Middletown, Conn.: Wesleyan University Press, 1971.

Leary, D. E. The philosophical development of the conception of psychology in Germany, 1750-1850. *Journal of the History of the Behavioral Sciences,* 1978a, *14,* 113-121.

Leary, D. E. German idealism and the development of psychology in the nineteenth century. Unpublished manuscript, University of New Hampshire, 1978b.

Mill, James. Analysis of the phenomena of the human mind. Partially reprinted in J. M. Mandler and G. Mandler (Eds.) *Thinking: From Association to Gestalt.* New York: John Wiley, 1964.

Myers, F. *Human personality and its survival of bodily death,* 2 vols. London: Longmans, Green & Co., 1903.

Ruse, M. Charles Darwin and artificial selection. *Journal of the History of Ideas,* 1975, *36,* 339-350.

Taine, H. *On intelligence.* New York: Holt, 1875.

Vorzimmer, P. *Charles Darwin: The years of controversy.* Philadelphia: Temple University Press, 1970.

Webb, J. *The occult underground.* LaSalle, Ill.: Open Court, 1974.

Young, D. *Mind, brain, and adaptation in the nineteenth century.* Oxford: Clarendon Press, 1970.

# Founding
# Psychology

Although psychologists traditionally revere one man, Wilhelm Wundt, as the founder of psychology, and one date, 1879, as the founding year of psychology, their faith is misleadingly simple. Wundt's long-term importance for psychology has proven to be institutional, for it was he who created a socially recognized and independent science and a new social role for its practitioners. Conceptually, psychology was founded three times, each founding giving rise to a distinctive way of thinking about psychology's problems. Each founding took place in the late nineteenth century.

The most traditional founding psychology was the psychology of consciousness, the introspective study of the normal, adult human mind. This psychology directly continued traditional philosophical psychology and made it more rigorous. Wundt stands at the head of this tradition, although many others took part. The most important rival psychology of consciousness was Gestalt psychology, which rejected many of Wundt's premises and which drifted into a kind of science of behavior. The psychology of consciousness proved to be the least durable form of psychology, notwithstanding Wundt's unique and momentous creation of institutional psychology.

The most famous, and in its own time notorious, founding psychology was Sigmund Freud's psychology of the unconscious. Freud attempted to plumb the hidden and threatening darkside of human nature, and what he found there offended some and inspired others. Freud's psychology of the unconscious is less a rival to Wundt's psychology than it is its complement. It has, however, been much more influential and durable than Wundt's psychology. Freud's ideas have profoundly affected Western thought in the twentieth century, and Freud's psychotherapy—psychoanalysis—has spawned innumerable variants into our own time.

Among academic psychologists, the most important founding psychology has been the psychology of adaptation. Its founding was the work of many hands, first among them being William James. The psychology of adaptation does not see the problem of psychology to be the philosophically motivated dissection of consciousness, or the therapeutic exploration of the unconscious, but sees it to be the biological study of the evolutionary utility of mind and behavior. The psychology of adaptation began as an introspective study of mental activity, but soon became the study of activity itself, that is, behavior. Out of this shift in perspective came behaviorism, the most important academic psychology of the twentieth century.

In the next three chapters we will describe each founding psychology in turn.

# 7

# The Starting Point
## The Psychology of Consciousness

| | |
|---|---|
| Wundt founds laboratory | A.D. 1879    Einstein born |
| Galton's *Inquiries* | Marx dies, Keynes born |
| *American Journal of Psychology* | Jack the Ripper |
| James' *Principles* | 1890 |
| Dewey's "Reflex Arc" | "Adventures of Sherlock Holmes" |
| | Safety razor invented |
| Titchener's "Structural Psychology" | Trans-Siberian Railroad |
| Freud's *Dreams* | 1900 |
| Pavlov's Nobel Prize | Wright Brothers fly |
| Angell's "Province" | Special Relativity proposed |
| Start of *Gestalt* School | 1910    China abolishes slavery |
| Watson's "Behaviorist" | Titanic sinks |
| | World War I |
| Final revisions of Freud's theory | 1920 |
| | Immigration to U.S. restricted |
| Beginning of Neobehaviorism | Hirohito becomes Emperor of Japan |
| | 1930    Stock market crash |
| | F.D. Roosevelt elected president |
| | Hitler comes to power |
| Skinner's *Behavior of Organisms* | Hindenburg disaster |
| | 1940    World War II |
| Hull's *Behavior System* | Atom bomb dropped |
| Tolman's "Cognitive Maps" | |
| Conference on Learning Theory | 1950    McCarthy attacks "Reds" |
| | Korean War |
| *A Study of Thinking* | Civil Rights movement starts |
| Chomsky reviews Skinner | First commercial jets |
| | 1960    John Kennedy elected president |
| Kuhn's *Scientific Revolutions* | |
| Collins & Quillian | U.S. troops sent to Vietnam |
| Skinner's *Beyond Freedom* | 1970    Moon landing |
| | Watergate |
| | Communists win in Vietnam |
| Simon's Nobel Prize | Jimmy Carter elected president |
| | 1980 |

**FIGURE 7-1.**
Chronology 1879-1980.

## WILHELM WUNDT (1832-1920) AND GANZHEIT PSYCHOLOGY

Although Wilhelm Maximilian Wundt is revered as the founder of scientific psychology, he is the most misunderstood of all psychology's major figures. His system is usually considered to be dualistic, atomistic, associationistic, purely introspective, and concerned only with describing the conscious contents of the normal adult mind viewed as the passive recipient of sense perception. It was none of these things. It is, however, often confused with E. B. Titchener's system which had all these characteristics except dualism. Titchener was Wundt's student, but he made Wundt's voluntaristic psychology into an experimental British associationism, abandoning along the way many Wundtian essentials. This alteration is one reason for Wundt's distorted image today. Another reason is that his psychology was swamped in the later behaviorist movement. Thus Wundt is remembered primarily as a ponderous old German introspectionist of no importance save as psychology's founder.

Contemporary scholars, however, have begun to demonstrate that Wundt's system was very different from the way it is usually presented and that it has contemporary relevance. Today, cognitive psychologists are returning to the study of the mind, if not of consciousness, and are rediscovering many of the basic mental phenomena first discovered by Wundt. They are also returning to topics, such as attention, that preoccupied him. Wundt's psychology and its fate provide a valuable lesson for both history and psychology.

### Personal and Intellectual Background

Wilhelm Maximilian Wundt was born on August 16, 1832, in Neckarau, Baden, Germany—the fourth child of a minister, Maximilian Wundt, and his wife Marie Frederike. Many ancestors on both sides of Wundt's family were intellectuals, scientists, professors, government officials, and physicians. At the age of 13 Wundt began his formal education at a Catholic *gymnasium.** He disliked school and failed, but transferred to a school in Heidelberg from which he graduated in 1851. Wundt decided to go into medicine, and after an initially poor start, he applied himself and excelled in his studies. His scientific interests emerged in physiological research. He got his M.D. in 1855, *summa cum laude,* and after some study with the physiologist Johannes Müller received in 1857 the second doctorate German universities required of lecturers. He immediately gave his first course in experimental

---

*The German gymnasium was a college-preparatory high school; entrance was generally restricted to the sons of middle class intellectuals.

physiology—to four students in his mother's apartment in Heidelberg.* These courses were interrupted by an acute illness from which he almost died.

During his convalescence, Wundt applied for and received an assistantship with Hermann von Helmholtz. Although Wundt admired Helmholtz they were never close, and Wundt rejected Helmholtz's materialism. While with Helmholtz, Wundt gave his first course in "Psychology as a Natural Science" in 1862, and his first important writings began to appear.

He worked his way up the academic ladder at Heidelberg while dabbling in politics, for the first and last time, as an idealistic socialist. He got married in 1872. His publications continued, including the first edition of his fundamental work, *Grundzüge der Physiologischen Psychologie,* in 1873 and 1874. This work in its many editions propounded the central tenets of his experimental psychology.

After a year in a "waiting room" position in Zurich, Wundt received a chair in philosophy at Leipzig, where he taught from 1875-1917. It was at Leipzig that Wundt won a degree of independence for psychology by founding his Psychological Institute. Beginning as a purely private institute in 1879, it was supported out of his own pocket until 1881. Finally in 1885 it was officially recognized by the university and listed in the catalog. It began as a primitive, one-room affair and expanded over the years; in 1897, it moved to its own specially designed building, later destroyed during World War II.

During the years at Leipzig, Wundt continued his extraordinary output—supervising at least 200 dissertations, teaching over 24,000 students, and writing or revising volume after volume, as well as overseeing and writing for the psychological journal he founded, *Philosophische Studien.* He trained the first generation of psychologists, many of them Americans.

In 1900 he began a massive undertaking, the publication of his *Völkerpsychologie,* which was completed only in 1920, the year of his death. In it Wundt developed what he believed was the other half of psychology, the study of man in society as opposed to man as an individual in the laboratory. Wundt's work continued to the last. His final undertaking was his reminiscences, *Erlebtes und Erkanntes,* which he completed only a few days before he died on August 31, 1920, at the age of 88.

During World War I, Wundt, like almost all German intellectuals, was feverently nationalistic. He, like many other "patriots of the lectern," wrote violently anti-English and anti-American tracts that can be read only with embarrassment today. They are interesting, however, as they reveal the gulf between the German and the Anglo-French-American world views. For Wundt and other German intellectuals, the English were—in the words of Werner Sombart—mere "traders" who regarded "the whole existence of man on earth as a sum of commer-

---

*The German university system in the nineteenth century was very different from the modern American system. One had to obtain the usual doctorate and then a second, higher level doctorate before one could teach—and even then one had no regular salary and could only give private, fee-supported courses. Only after years of private teaching and a life of relative poverty could one obtain a salaried professorship.

cial transactions which everyone makes as favorably as possible for himself" (Ringer, 1969). The English were excoriated by Wundt for their "egotistic utilitarianism," "materialism," "positivism," and "pragmatism" (Ringer, 1969). The German ideal, on the other hand, was "the hero," a warrior whose ideals were "sacrifice, faithfulness, openness, respect, courage, religiosity, charity and willingness to obey" (Ringer, 1969). The goal of the Englishman was seen as personal comfort while that of the German was seen as sacrifice and service. Germans also had a long-standing contempt for French "civilization," a superficial veneer of manners, as opposed to the true German, organic "culture."

Such polemics illustrate the German intellectual climate in the nineteenth century. The Germans as a whole, and despite Kant, followed Herder in openly rejecting the Enlightenment. They were romantic intellectuals who valued things of the heart, spirit, and soil rather than things of the cold intellect. They saw Germany as midway between the intellectualism of the countries west of the Rhine, and the anti-intellectual, religious culture of Holy Mother Russia to the east. They rejected the atomism and utilitarianism of British philosophy and were anti-individualistic. In place of atomism the German intellectuals constantly sought synthesis, to reconcile opposites into a higher truth. Thus, "psychological synthesis" was a key element in Wundt's psychology. Wundt and the other elitist intellectuals of the German "Mandarin" tradition perceived, maintained, and strengthened an immense intellectual gulf between themselves and the West (Ringer, 1969). Wundt held himself to be the heir of Kant, Fichte, and Hegel, and rejected the philosophies of Locke, the Mills, Spencer, and William James.

Underneath all this we can once more detect the division between rationalism and empiricism. The West was empiricist: associationistic, atomistic, utilitarian, and concerned with individual rights and happiness. Germany was nationalistic, and romantic, rejecting the narrow utilitarian rationalism of the West in favor of a spiritual romantic rationalism. Since Plato, there has always been a mystic, anti-individualistic aspect to rationalism. Ascent to the Forms is a sort of mystical union. People existed to serve Plato's Republic, not vice versa; rationalism easily tends toward totalitarianism. Hence, German thinkers were rationalists: anti-associationistic, searching for synthesis, avowedly impractical (the universities cultivated unworldly fields like philosophy and refused to recognize such practical fields as engineering), and statist (the individual is seen as the servant of the State).

Wundt's psychology shares this Mandarin tradition. It rejects association of static ideas and the tinker-toy theory of mind. It rejects atomism and reductionism in favor of psychological synthesis and an analysis of consciousness. It seeks no practical results, although it does not exclude them. Finally, it rejects the study of individual differences in favor of an almost Platonic investigation of *the* human mind.

This rationalism explains not only certain essential features of Wundt's system, but also its failure to gain a foothold in America. It was too alien. Wundt's American students happily got their degrees in Leipzig, but pursued a thoroughly American psychology, functionalism, when they returned home, and psychology quickly became an American science. In Germany, Wundt was attacked as an atomist by the even more "synthetic" Gestalt psychologists, and along with the rest of the German intellectual community, his ideas perished under the pressures of the Nazis and World War II.

All this tells us something of Wundt's background, but how did he come to found psychology? Psychology is a hybrid offspring of physiology and philosophy. Alcmaeon won the title of the first psychologist because he was a physician-philosopher. Bain and Lotze also combined physiology and philosophy. Yet none of them founded psychology. Wundt is the founder because he wedded physiology to philosophy and made the resulting offspring independent. He brought the empirical methods of physiology to the questions of philosophy and also created a new, identifiable role—that of the psychologist, separate from the roles of philosopher, physiologist, or physician. This was Wundt's professional achievement, but there were personal reasons as well as philosophical ones, behind it.

In the mid-nineteenth century, physiology "took off" as a science. It expanded rapidly, with new opportunities arising for individual advancement all over Germany. At the same time, philosophy was a nonexpansive field in which advancement was difficult. Wundt entered physiology during the boom period. Beginning as early as 1860, and certainly by 1870, however, the growth of physiology slowed down and competition for the existing positions became fierce. In philosophy, a period of growth began about 1860.

Thus, to an ambitious academic with the right interests, philosophy in the 1860s became an attractive field, and in accepting the Zürich and Leipzig posts in philosophy, Wundt switched from a closed to an open discipline. However, at the same time, the relative prestige of physiology was greater than that of philosophy, a situation which naturally placed Wundt in a state of cognitive dissonance. A resolution was possible by innovation—invent a new role, that of scientific psychologist, derived at least in part from the higher status field of physiology, but investigating the questions of philosophy (Ben-David & Collins, 1966).

Wundt's stature as a historical figure lies in this innovation. Others had combined philosophical and physiological interests, but it remained for Wundt to create something new and enduring, the hybrid science of experimental psychology.

In this section we have examined some of the personal and historical causes that were behind the founding of psychology. Next, we will examine Wundt's system to understand it as a rational science.

### Wundt's Psychology

#### General Standpoint

Wundt never gave a name to his school of psychology. As the founder, what he did was simply *psychology* without qualification. Later, his student Titchener, who opposed (and named) American functionalism, called his own system structuralism and this label became erroneously attached to Wundt's psychology. Wundt's German students who carried on his tradition later called it *Ganzheit* psychology, which means essentially "holistic" psychology. Although holism describes Wundtian psychology, the label became attached to subsequent movements unrelated to Wundt, so we shall retain the German term Ganzheit psychology.

For Wundt, psychology was the scientific study of immediate experience—and thus the study of human consciousness or the mind, as long as mind is understood as the totality of conscious experience at a given moment and not as a mental substance. The natural sciences are also based on experience, but of a kind Wundt called *mediate* experience, because the experience is regarded as dependent on external objects and all subjective elements are removed. Psychology studies all experience—including subjective elements such as feelings—directly as it is given in consciousness, and as dependent on the psychological state of the observer.

Wundt thus proposed an introspective psychology, but with important qualifications. According to Wundt, it is unnecessary to postulate a special inner sense to observe one's consciousness. One simply *has* experiences and can describe them; one does not have to observe the experiences happening. Wundt specifically rejected Locke's idea of reflection as a source of ideas. To Wundt, *all* experience is direct experience. A second way in which Wundt's psychology differed from philosophical introspective psychologies was that in the study of individual experience the method was to be *experimental*. To Wundt, the ordinary act of introspection is untrustworthy because it disturbs experience and because it applies only to some unique experience that has already passed. For this unreliable form of introspection, used in part by Titchener and the Würzburg psychologists, Wundt substituted a host of objective procedures involving measures of reaction time, emotional states, and other variables.

This kind of psychology was what Wundt (1896) meant by *physiological psychology*:

> In psychology we find that only those mental phenomena which are directly accessible to physical influences can be made the subject matter of experiment. We cannot experiment upon mind itself, but only upon its outworks, the organs of sense and movement which are functionally related to mental processes. So that every psychological experiment is at the same time physiological. . . .

Physiological psychology was thus just the experimental psychology of the individual and was physiological only in that the experimental approach was borrowed from Wundt's original field, physiology.

The final distinction between Wundt and other introspective psychologists and philosophers is that his work was not limited to experimental psychology. He considered the development of mind an important topic, which could be addressed partially by child and animal (comparative) psychology, but above all by the study of the historical development of the human species. Life is short, so our own experience is limited, but we can draw on the historical experience of humanity as written and preserved in existing cultures at different levels of development. This collective experience enables us to study the inner recesses of consciousness, those well removed from sensorimotor responses and hence not amenable, in Wundt's view, to experimental study. He called this his *Völkerpsychologie* (ethnic or folk psychology) embracing especially the study of language, myth, and custom.

Wundt was as antimetaphysical as any modern experimental psychologist. He rejected all forms of speculative psychology, both dualistic and materialistic. He refused to postulate the existence of a separate spiritual or mental substance as Descartes had done. To do so, he thought, would be inconsistent with modern science and unnecessary—psychology studies experience given in consciousness, not a separate, substantial mind. On the other hand, he rejected materialistic reductionism. He recognized that all mental phenomena have a bodily substrate, but thought that experience and physiology can be studied independently. Further, he believed conscious experience and physiological events to be so different that they cannot be causally related. This separation of the mental and physical into connected but separate realms, each with its own laws of causality, Wundt called the principle of psycho-physical parallelism. It is not, however, the same parallelism we have come across before. What Wundt perceived as parallel was not a body-substance and a mind-substance, but only bodily events and mental events. To Wundt, there is only one reality, but it can be examined from two points of view: the mental and the physical. His position is less a form of parallelism than it is a form of the dual aspect theory.

Wundt resisted any attempt to materialize the mind. Hence he rejected the view of the British associationists and Herbart that ideas are little billiard balls (Wundt used this phrase) connected by association that bounce in and out of consciousness; in short, he rejected the tinker-toy model of the mind. For Wundt ideas were active *processes*, not passive elements interacting via mechanical laws. Each experience is an *event*, not a *thing* appearing in consciousness and disappearing into unconsciousness. Memory is not the resurrection of a previous idea—which Wundt held to be impossible since consciousness is ever-changing—but is instead the use of rules for the reconstruction of previous experience.

For Wundt mind was active in even its simplest aspects, a doctrine he referred to awkwardly as the *actuality* of mind. Wundt also called his system *voluntaristic* to underline its emphasis on mental activity and the important role in mental events it assigned to feeling and will. In line with this, Wundt replaced atomistic reductionism with a doctrine of mental synthesis. Complex mental events are based on simpler ones, but according to Wundt the relation is one of active synthesis of elements into a higher unity rather than a reduction of the complex to the simple.

These are the fundamental tenets of Wundt's Ganzheit psychology. In the next two sections we shall review some of Wundt's theory and research, proceeding as he did—ascending upward from the simple by synthesis and arriving finally at the most complex higher mental processes. We will review first the experimental psychology of the individual, and then the collective, *Völkerpsychologie*.

### Experimental Psychology of Consciousness

A good way to begin to understand Ganzheit psychology is by looking at one of Wundt's most important experiments. His psychology was the study of consciousness, so a natural question is, "How many ideas may be present in consciousness at a given moment?" Simple introspection cannot answer this question. How many ideas do you have in consciousness right now? It is futile to try to hold for analysis a moment in the stream of consciousness in order to answer the question.

Therefore, an experiment is called for, one that complements and perfects introspection and will yield quantitative results. The following is an updated and simplified version of Wundt's experiment. Imagine sitting in a darkened room facing a projection screen. For an instant, about 0.09 sec, a stimulus is flashed on the screen. This stimulus is a 4-column by 4-row array of randomly chosen letters, and your task is to recall as many letters as possible. What is recalled provides a measure of how many simple ideas can be grasped in an instant of time, and so may give an answer to the original question. Wundt found that unpracticed subjects could recall about four letters; subjects who have practiced could recall up to six but no more. These figures agree remarkably well with modern results on the capacity of short-term memory.

Two further important phenomena can be observed in this experiment. First, imagine an experiment in which each line of four letters forms a word, for example, *work, many, room, idea*. Under these conditions one could probably recall all four words, or at least three, for a total of 12 to 16 letters. Similarly, one could quickly read and recall the word "miscellaneousness" which contains 17 letters. Letters as isolated elements quickly fill up consciousness so that only four to six can be perceived in a given moment, but if these elements are organized many more can be grasped. In Wundt's term the letter-elements are *synthesized* into a greater whole, which is understood as a single complex idea and grasped as one new element.

This phenomenon shows in what sense Wundt was an atomist and in what sense he was not. The word *work* is in fact made up of four simpler elementary idea-processes, *w, o, r,* and *k*, but it cannot be reduced to these elements. The word is a *synthesis* of the elements and the whole word functions as an element. Complex ideas derive from elements; they are not compounded out of them or reducible to them. Wundt rejected the atomism of the British associationists, including the mental chemistry of J. S. Mill.

There is a second phenomenon that can be observed in this memory experiment. The subject in the original experiment very easily notices that some letters— the ones the subject names—are perceived clearly and distinctly, but that other letters are only dimly and hazily perceived. Consciousness seems to be a large field populated with ideational elements. One area of this field is in the focus of *attention*, and the ideas within it are clearly perceived. The elements lying outside the focal area are only faintly felt as present and cannot be identified.

Attention, like synthesis, played a key role in Wundt's theory. In fact, attention was the process which could actively synthesize elements into larger units. Wundt's ideas on attention were derived from Leibniz, and Wundt used Leibniz's terms. An idea that enters the large field of consciousness was said to be *apprehended*, and one that enters the focal area of attention was said to be *apperceived*.

Apperception was especially important in Wundt's system. Not only was it responsible for the active synthesis of elements into wholes, but it also accounted for the higher mental activities of analysis (revealing the parts of a whole) and of judgment. It was responsible for the activities of relating and comparing, which are simpler forms of synthesis and analysis. Synthesis itself took two forms: imagination and understanding. Apperception was the basis for all higher forms of thought, such as reasoning and use of language, and so was central to Ganzheit psychology.

Finally, Wundt's emphasis on apperception displays the *voluntaristic* nature of his system. Since neither *mind* nor *self* referred to a special substance for Wundt, to what did he attribute our sense of self and the feeling that we have a mind? It is this *feeling* that provides the answer. Apperception is a voluntary act of the will by which we control and give synthetic unity to our mind. It is the feeling of activity, control, and unity that defined the self. Wundt wrote: "What we call our 'self' is simply the unity of volition plus the universal control of our mental life which it renders possible."

Wundt did not neglect feelings and emotions, for they are an obvious part of our conscious experience. He often used introspectively reported feelings as clues to what processes were going on in the mind at a given moment. Apperception, for instance, he thought to be marked by a feeling of mental effort. He also studied feelings and emotions in their own right, and his tridimensional theory of feeling became a source of controversy, especially with Titchener. Wundt proposed that feelings could be defined along three dimensions: pleasant versus unpleasant, high versus low arousal, and concentrated versus relaxed attention. He conducted a long series of studies designed to establish a physiological basis for each dimension, but the results were inconclusive, and other laboratories produced conflicting findings. Recent factor-analyses of affect, however, have arrived at similar three-dimensional systems (Blumenthal, 1975). While Wundt emphasized the active, synthesizing power of apperception, he recognized the existence of passive processes as well, which he classified as various forms of association or "passive" apperception. There were, for example, *assimilations,* in which a current sensation is associated to an older element. When one looks at a chair, one knows immediately what it is by assimilation, for the current image of the perceived chair is immediately associated with the older universal element *chair*. Recognition is a form of assimilation, stretched out into two steps—a vague feeling of familiarity followed by the act of recognition proper. Recollection, on the other hand, was for Wundt, as for some contemporary psychologists, an act of reconstruction rather than reactivation of old elements. One cannot re-experience an earlier event, for ideas are not permanent. Rather one reconstructs it from current cues and certain general rules.

Finally, Wundt did not fail to notice abnormal states of consciousness. He discussed hallucinations, depressions, hypnosis, and dreams. Of particular interest was his discussion of what we now call *schizophrenia*. He observed that this disease involves a breakdown in attentional processes. The schizophrenic loses the apperceptive control of thoughts characteristic of normal consciousness and surrenders instead to passive associative processes, so that thought becomes a simple train of associations rather than coordinated processes directed by volition. This theory was developed by Wundt's student and friend, the great psychiatrist Emil Kraepelin, and has been revived by modern students of schizophrenia and autism.

### Völkerpsychologie

Wundt believed that experimental individual psychology could not be a complete psychology. The minds of living individuals are the products of a long course of species development of which each person is ignorant. Therefore, to understand the development of the mind, we must have recourse to history. The study of animals and children is limited by their inability to introspect. History expands the range of the individual consciousness. In particular, the range of existing human cultures represents the various stages in cultural and mental evolution, from primitive, tribal to civilized, national man. *Völkerpsycholgie* is thus the study of the products of collective life—especially of language, myth, and custom—that provide clues to the higher operations of mind. Wundt said the experimental psychology penetrates only the "outworks" of the mind; *Völkerpsychologie* reaches deeper.

Emphasis on historical development was a legacy from Herder and was typical of German intellectuals in the nineteenth century. In the German view every individual springs from, and has an organic relationship with, his or her natal culture. Further, cultures have complex histories which determine their forms and contents. Thus, it was generally believed that history could be used as a method for arriving at an intuitive understanding of human psychology.

Wundt's remarks on myth and custom are unexceptional. He saw history as going through a series of stages from primitive tribes to an age of heroes and then to the formation of states, culminating in a world state based on the concept of humanity as a whole. It was, however, in the study of language (which early in his career Wundt almost pursued instead of psychology) that he made his most substantial contribution, articulating a theory of psycholinguistics that reaches conclusions being rediscovered today. Language was a part of *Völkerpsychologie* for Wundt because, like myth and custom, it is a product of collective life.

Wundt divided language into two aspects: *outer phenomena,* consisting of actually produced or perceived utterances, and *inner phenomena,* the cognitive processes that underlie the outer string of words. This division of psychological phenomena into inner and outer aspects is central to Ganzheit psychology and has come up before in the contrast between the "outworks" of the mind that can be reached by experimentation and the deeper processes that cannot. The distinction between inner and outer phenomena is easiest to understand with regard to language. It is possible to describe language as an organized, associated system of sounds which we speak or hear; this constitutes the outer form of language. However, this outer form is the surface expression of deeper cognitive processes that organize a speaker's thoughts and prepare them for utterance and enable the listener to extract meaning from what she or he hears. These cognitive processes constitute the inner mental form of speech.

Sentence production, according to Wundt, begins with a unified idea which one wishes to express, the *Gesamtvorstellung,* or whole mental configuration.* The analytic function of apperception prepares the unified idea for speech, for it must be analyzed into component parts and a structure that retains the relationship between the parts and the whole. Consider the simple sentence, "The cat is orange." The basic structural division in such a sentence is between the subject and predicate, and can be represented with the *tree-diagram* introduced by Wundt. If we let G = *Gesamtvorstellung,* S = subject, and P = predicate, then we have

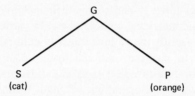

The idea of an orange cat has now been divided into its two fundamental ideas, and can be expressed verbally as "the cat is orange" with the addition of the function words (*the, is*) required in our particular language. More complex ideas require more analysis and must be represented by more complex diagrams. The entire process in all cases can be described as the transformation of an unexpressible organized whole thought into an expressible sequential structure of words organized in a sentence.

The process is reversed in comprehension of speech. Here, the synthesizing rather than the analytic function of apperception is called on. The words and grammatical structure in a heard sentence must be used by the hearer to reconstruct in his or her own mind the whole mental configuration that the speaker is attempting to communicate. Wundt supported his view of comprehension by pointing out that we remember the gist of what we hear, but only rarely the surface (outer) form, which tends to disappear in the process of constructing the *Gesamtvorstellung.* Wundt's theory of language processes closely resembles much modern psycholinguistic theorizing.

We have touched on only a small portion of Wundt's discussion of language. He also wrote on gesture-language; the origin of language from involuntary, expressive sounds; primitive language (based more on association than on apperception); phonology; and meaning-change. Wundt has a fair claim to be the founder of psycholinguistics as well as psychology. His ideas about how language works were central to Wundt's views, and as we shall see, are remarkably similar to many aspects of contemporary psycholinguistics.

*\**Gesamtvorstellung* was misleadingly translated by Titchener, Wundt's leading translator, as "aggregate idea," but Blumenthal (1970) has shown Titchener's error and proposed the phrase used here: "whole mental configuration." The mistranslation reveals Titchener's misperception of Ganzheit psychology.*

# EDWARD BRADFORD TITCHENER (1867-1927) AND STRUCTURALISM

Edward Bradford Titchener was an Englishman who brought German psychology to America. He thus played an important role in the founding of American psychology, for he was the foe of both functionalism and behaviorism, while on the European front he was the enemy of act psychology and of imageless thought. In this chapter we will examine his system, structuralism, and its relation to Wundt's Ganzheit psychology.*

Titchener has usually been taken by historians to be a faithful reflection of Wundt, the two systems being seen as identical. A recent history of psychology says this: "Titchener's system was so close to Wundt's and so much easier to describe, that we shall not here dwell on . . . Wundt. . . ." (Keller, 1973). This attitude naturally led American psychologists who rejected Titchener's system to reject Wundt's at the same time. We shall see to what degree this identification and simultaneous rejection was justified. Given the complexity of Ganzheit psychology, however, we should be suspicious of substituting Titchener for Wundt because the former is "so much easier." Much is bound to be left out.

## Background

E. B. Titchener was born in 1867 at Chichester, England. His ancestors included a mayor of Chichester, a school headmaster, and a distinguished lawyer. He attended a prestigious secondary school and went to Oxford from 1885 to 1890. His educational record was outstanding. During his Oxford years, his interests shifted from classics and philosophy to physiology. The conjunction of interests in philosophy and physiology naturally predisposed Titchener to psychology, and while at Oxford he translated the third edition of Wundt's massive *Principles of Physiological Psychology*. Titchener could find no one in England to train him in psychology, so in 1890 he went to Leipzig, taking his doctorate in 1892. Titchener was impressed by Wundt, but they were never close.

We must remember that as an Englishman Titchener arrived in Leipzig from the other side of the intellectual gulf separating Germany from the West. He was thoroughly versed in philosophy and was much impressed by James Mill, remarking that Mill's speculations could be empirically demonstrated. In his first systematic book, *An Outline of Psychology* (1897), he wrote: "The general standpoint of [my] book is that of the traditional English psychology." It is reasonable to expect, therefore, that Titchener may well have assimilated Wundt's German Ganzheit psychology into the "traditional English psychology" that Wundt rejected.

*Titchener adopted the label "structural psychology" to distinguish his position from functionalism (which he also named in the same paper). He later came to prefer the label "existentialism," but this term now stands for a very different approach to philosophy and psychology associated with people such as Sartre and Heidegger.

Titchener's personality was reputedly "German" but his psychology is more a mixture of German and English.

After a short stint as a lecturer in biology in England—a country not receptive to psychology—Titchener left for America to teach at Cornell, replacing his Leipzig friend, Frank Angell, who was going to Stanford. He remained at Cornell until his death in 1927. He transformed Cornell into a bastion of mentalistic psychology, even as America's focus went first functionalist and, after 1913, behaviorist. Titchener never compromised with these movements, despite his friendships with the functionalist J. R. Angell and with Watson, the founder of behaviorism. He published almost exclusively in the *American Journal of Psychology,* which he edited, shunning rival journals like *Psychological Review* and *Journal of Experimental Psychology*. He did not participate actively in the American Psychological Association, even when it met at Cornell, preferring instead his own group, the Experimental Psychologists, which he kept true to his version of psychology. It was clear that structuralism depended upon one man, Titchener, and when he unexpectedly died in 1927 the school collapsed.

### Structural Psychology

Titchener apparently possessed a mind in which everything had imaginal-sensational character. His mind even had an image for such an abstract word as *meaning*. Titchener (1909) wrote: "I see meaning as the blue-grey tip of a kind of scoop, which has a bit of yellow above it . . . and which is just digging into a dank mass of . . . plastic material." Even though he recognized that not everyone had an imaginal mind as he called it, he built his psychology on the premise that the mind was made up of sensations or images of sensation and *nothing else.* This led to his rejection of various Wundtian concepts such as apperception, which is not directly observed. Titchener's system was thus explicitly sensationistic, as opposed to Wundt's which was voluntaristic.

The first task of Titchener's sensationistic psychology was the discovery of the basic sensation-elements to which all complex processes could be reduced. As early as 1897 he drew up a catalog of elements found in the different sense-departments. There were, for instance, 30,500 visual elements, four taste elements, and three sensations in the alimentary canal.

Elements were defined by Titchener as the simplest sensations to be found in experience. They were to be discovered through the systematic dissection by introspection of the contents of consciousness; when an experience could not be dissected into parts it was declared *elemental*. Titchener's method of introspection was much more elaborate than Wundt's, for it was not a simple report of an experience but a complicated retrospective analysis of that experience. Wrote Titchener (1909): "Be as attentive as possible to the object or process which gives rise to the sensation, and, when the object is removed or the process completed, recall the sensation by an act of memory as vividly and completely as you can." Persistant application of this method would in Titchener's view eventually produce a complete description of the elements of human experience. It was an unfinished (and, as many thought, unfinishable) task when Titchener died.

The second task of Titchener's sensationistic approach was to determine how the elementary sensations are connected together to form complex perceptions, ideas, and images. These connections were not all associations, because for Titchener an association was a connection of elements that persisted even when the original conditions for the connection no longer could be obtained. Titchener rejected the label of associationism, not only for this reason but also because the associationists spoke of association of meaningful ideas, not of simple meaningless sensations, which was all that concerned Titchener.

The third task of Titchener's psychology was to explain the workings of mind. Introspection, according to Titchener, could yield only a description of mind. At least until about 1925, he believed that a scientific psychology required more than mere description. Explanation for Titchener was to be sought in physiology which would explain why the sensory elements arise and become connected. Titchener rejected Wundt's attempt to psychologically explain the operation of the mind. According to Titchener's system, all that can be found in experience are sensory elements rather than processes such as attention. Appeal to such an unobservable entity as apperception was illegitimate in Titchener's eyes, and betrays his positivism. He therefore sought to explain mind by reference to observable nerve-physiology.

How did Titchener treat a process such as attention that was so central to Ganzheit psychology? He rejected as wholly unnecessary the term *apperception*, which in Wundt's psychology gave rise to attention. Attention itself Titchener reduced to sensation. One obvious attribute of any sensation is clarity, and Titchener said that "attended" sensations are simply the clearest ones. Attention was not for him a mental process, but simply an attribute of sensation—clearness—produced by certain nerve-processes. What of the mental effort that Wundt says goes along with attention? This, too, is reduced to sensation. Wrote Titchener in *Experimental Psychology: A Manual of Laboratory Practice*: "When I am trying to attend I . . . find myself frowning, wrinkling my forehead etc. All such . . . bodily sets and movements give rise to characteristic . . . sensations. Why should not these sensations be what we call 'attention'."

Was Titchener a more comprehensible, English-speaking double for Wundt as is so often assumed? We must conclude not: Titchener is "so much easier" than Wundt because Titchener discounted so much of his teacher's teaching. He took the complex voluntaristic psychology of Wundt and filtered it through his own positivism and atomism to produce a reductive sensationism for which mind is nothing but complexes of elements found in experience. He had nothing similar to Wundt's *Völkerpsychologie*. Wundt's Ganzheit psychology has many resonances with modern cognitive psychology; Titchener's structuralism has none. However, as we will see it does have resonances with the most extreme form of behaviorism, B. F. Skinner's descriptive behaviorism.

A word should be said about the direction Titchener's thought was taking at his death. His last work was his *Systematic Psychology: Prologemena* which appeared posthumously in 1929. In this book he was becoming even more positivistic than before. He abandoned explanation as a goal of science in favor of pure description. He abandoned the notion of analytically discovered sensory elements in favor of phenomenologically described dimensions of sensory attributes. He departed even farther from Wundt's attempt to penetrate the hidden mental processes underneath the outer, sensory phenomena.

## CHALLENGES TO THE ANALYTIC
## PSYCHOLOGY OF CONSCIOUSNESS

Three assumptions were important to Wundt's analytic study of human consciousness. The first was that all the elements of consciousness derived directly or indirectly from sensation or bodily feelings; all the contents of thought were *images* of some sort. The second assumption was that all complex ideas were associative or apperceptive combinations of simpler elements, even when emergent properties resulted from the combination. The third assumption was methodological, that the higher mental processes, such as thinking, were too unstable, too subject to individual differences, and too far removed from outer mental phenomena to be studied in the laboratory. Wundt's *Völkerpsychologie* was intended to remedy this shortcoming. These fundamental assumptions did not escape criticism by other psychologists of conciousness.

### The Psychology of Thinking:
### The Würzburg School (1901-1909)

One of Wundt's most outstanding and successful students was Oswald Külpe (1862-1915). Although his early psychology was even more conservative than Wundt's, during his brief professorial tenure at the University of Würzburg, he helped develop a new approach to psychological experiment, one which claimed that thinking could be studied experimentally. Two important sets of results emerged from this research. The first indicated, contrary to Wundt, that some thoughts are imageless, while the second undermined associationism as an account of thinking.

Wundt's exclusion of the higher mental processes from the laboratory turned out to be merely a dogmatic prejudice. As early as 1879 Hermann Ebbinghaus undertook to study the higher process of memory, his results appearing in 1885. Shortly after leaving Wundt, Külpe seems to have decided that the highest mental process of all, thinking, could be experimentally studied and could be introspected —if only Wundt's methods were changed. Wundt's experiments were quite simple, involving little more than reaction to, or a brief description of, a stimulus. Fechner's psychophysics, Donder's mental chronometry, and Wundt's apperception experiments are examples of this procedure. Under Külpe (who never published an experiment from his Würzburg days but participated in others' experiments) the tasks were made more difficult and the job of introspection more elaborate.

During the years of the Würzburg school, the complexity of the experimental tasks increased from giving free associations to stimulus words to agreeing or disagreeing with difficult metaphysical theses or Nietzche's aphorisms. These tasks, whether simple or difficult, required thinking whereas Wundtian tasks did not. Subjects had to respond to the problem and then describe the thought-processes leading to the response. As the method developed, the subject would be asked to concentrate introspective attention on different parts of the subjective experience, that is, the subjects would focus on their mental state while awaiting the stimulus word, or on the appearance of the answer in consciousness. In these experiments the Würzburgers hoped to directly observe thinking as it happened.

The first results were a shock to almost all psychologists: thoughts can be imageless. This finding emerged in the first Würzburg paper by A.M. Mayer and J. Orth, published in 1901. In this experiment the subject was told to give a free associate to a stimulus word. The experimenter gave a ready signal, called out the stimulus word, and started a stopwatch; the subject gave a response and the experimenter stopped the watch. The subject then described the thinking process. Mayer and Orth reported that most thinking involved definite images or feelings associated with acts of will. However, wrote Mayer and Orth (1901), "apart from these two classes of conscious processes, we must introduce a third group . . . The subjects very frequently reported that they experienced certain conscious processes which they could describe neither as definite images nor as acts of will." For example, while serving as a subject, Mayer "made the observation that following the stimulus word 'meter' there occurred a peculiar conscious process, not further definable, which was followed by the spoken word 'trochee'." So Wundt was wrong, according to Mayer and Orth; non-imaginal events in consciousness had been found.

The Würzburgers refined their methods over the years, but the results remained: there are imageless thoughts. Moreover, the finding was made independently in Paris by Alfred Binet in his studies of children's thinking, and in New York by Robert Woodworth. Both studies were reported in 1903, but the investigators did not know the Würzburg work. In fact, Binet later claimed that the new method should be called the "method of Paris." In any event, the finding of imageless thought was a challenge to psychological orthodoxy and provoked a storm of controversy that aided and abetted the birth of behaviorism.

What was to be made of imageless thought? The Würzburger's own interpretation changed during the life of the school. Mayer and Orth did no more than discover imageless thoughts—vague, impalpable, almost indescribable "conscious states." Later on, they were identified simply as "thoughts" themselves. The final interpretation was that thought is actually an unconscious process, reducing the imageless thought elements to conscious indicators of thinking rather than thinking itself. However, on both sides of the Atlantic many psychologists found the Würzburg methods, results, and interpretations to be unacceptable or at least suspect.

Writing in 1907, Wundt tried to falsify the Würzburg results by attacking the method. He argued that the Würzburg experiments were sham experiments, merely reversions to unreliable armchair introspection that happened to be conducted in a laboratory. According to Wundt, experimental control was entirely lacking in the thought experiments. The subject did not know exactly what task would be set. The ensuing mental process would vary from subject to subject and from trial to trial, so the results could not be replicated. Finally, said Wundt, it is difficult if not impossible for a subject to both think about the set problem and to watch that process at the same time. Consequently, Wundt said, the so-called findings of imageless thought are invalid. Properly conducted experiments would show that, properly analyzed, "imageless" content was imaginal after all.

Wundt's methodological attack was taken up by Titchener as well. But he also undertook the experimental refutation of the Würzburg findings. Methodologically, Titchener echoed Wundt by claiming that subjects' reports of "imageless" thought were not descriptions of consciousness at all, but fabrications based on beliefs about how one would solve the problems set in the experiments. Experimentally, Titchener's students performed thought experiments and reported that they could find no evidence of imageless thought elements; they successfully traced all conscious content to sensations or feelings (Clark, 1911). Titchener concluded that the Würzburgers had failed as introspectors by declining to analyze a mental content and then calling it "imageless thought."

Other commentators offered alternative interpretations of the Würzburg results. It was suggested by some that certain types of minds possess imageless thought while others do not, reducing the Titchener-Külpe controversy to one of individual differences. This hypothesis was criticized as unparsimonious; why should nature create two types of mind to attain the same end—accurate thinking? The hypothesis of unconscious thinking was rejected on the grounds that what is not conscious is not mental but physiological, and therefore not a part of psychology. A similar criticism greeted Freud's hypothesis of the unconscious.

Perhaps the most important consequence of the debate about imageless thought was the suspicion that introspection was a fragile and unreliable tool, easily prejudiced by theoretical expectations. The Würzburg subjects believed in imageless thought, and they found it. Titchener's subjects believed only in sensations and feelings, and they found only those. R.M. Ogden, an American suporter of imageless thought, wrote (1911a) that if Wundt's and Titchener's criticisms of the Würzburg methods were valid, "may we not carry the point a step farther and deny the value of *all* introspection. Indeed, in a recent discussion among psychologists, this position was vigorously maintained by two among those present." Ogden himself suggested that the differential results from Cornell and Würzburg betray "unconscious bias" based on different training (Ogden, 1911b). The imageless thought controversy revealed difficulties with the introspective method and by 1911, the year of Ogden's papers, we find some psychologists ready to discard it altogether. Two years later, Watson, the founder of behaviorism, included this controversy in his indictment of mentalism.

The imageless thought results represent a budding anomaly for certain forms of mentalism. Woodworth wrote as late as 1938 that "the whole question may well be shelved as permanently debatable and insoluble." This is one fate of anomalies, according to Kuhn. The debate over imageless thought showed signs of developing into a Kuhnian paradigm clash. In 1911, J.R. Angell wrote: "One feels that the differences which divide certain of the writers are largely those of mutual misunderstanding as to the precise phenomenon under discussion. . . ." However, the anomaly and paradigm clash were incipient only; their development was cut short by the advent of behaviorism. Woodworth found the problem being shelved in 1938 not because the problem had been exhausted, but because no one cared anymore. By the second (1954) edition of Woodworth's *Experimental Psychology*, this controversy which had occupied many pages in the 1938 edition had shriveled to four paragraphs.

The Würzburgers' second shock for the psychological establishment arose when they studied the process of thinking. Their results led them to reject traditional associationsism as an adequate account of mind. Their problem was this: what makes one idea rather than another follow a given idea? For free association, as in Mayer's and Orth's experiment, associationism has a plausible answer. If the stimulus word is "bird" the subject may respond "canary," then the associationist can say simply that the bird-canary bond was the strongest in the subject's associative network. However, this situation is complicated if we use a method of constrained association, as Henry J. Watt did in 1905. In this method we set a specific task for the subject to carry out, such as "give a subordinate category" or "give a superordinate category." To the former task, the subject may still reply "canary." To the second task the correct response cannot be "canary" but instead should be "animal." However, these tasks are no longer free associations, but rather are acts of directed thinking that produce propositions that may be true or false—unlike free association. So, the simple associative bond, bird-canary, is overridden in directed thinking.

The Würzburgers argued that associationism fails to explain thinking, for something must direct thought along the proper lines in the associative network in order for a subject to respond correctly to such tasks as Watt's. The Würzburgers proposed that it was the task itself that directed thinking. In their later terminology they said that the task establishes a mental set—or determining tendency—in the mind that properly directs the subject's use of his or her associative network. It was these experiments that suggested unconscious thinking, for subjects found that given the task "Give superordinate to canary," the response "bird" popped into their heads with little experienced mental activity. The Würzburgers concluded that the mental set accomplishes thinking even before the problem is given; the subject is so prepared to give a superordinate that the actual response occurs automatically.

Their investigations of the process of thinking took the Würzburg psychologists toward a psychology of function instead of content. They found that laboratory work could reveal something about how the mind functions in addition to what it contains. We will find that American psychology was predominantly functional, and the reception of the idea of the mental set was much more favorable in America than the reception given imageless thought. While the discussion of imageless thought in Woodworth's authoritative *Experimental Psychology* shrank between 1938 and 1954, index references to *set* increased from 19 to 35, with more extended discussions. The concept of set made sense to American functional psychologists interested in mental operations, and the behaviorists found that they could reinterpret *set* as establishing determining tendencies in behavior instead of in mind.

Although Würzburg-inspired work was continued after 1909, especially by Otto Selz who had worked there, the school essentially dissolved when Külpe left for the University of Bonn. No systematic theory based on the Würzburg studies was ever published, although there is evidence Külpe was working on such a theory when he died. It is puzzling that from 1909 until his death Külpe said almost nothing about the dramatic Würzburg results. Therefore no alternative paradigm arose from the Würzburg school to challenge the dominance of Wundt or Titchener in a systematic way. Their methods were innovative, their findings stimulating and anomalous, and in the concept of the mental set they made a permanent contribution. But the Würzburg school remained a school, a research program cut off prematurely. The other challenge to traditional psychology was more sustained, systematic, and memorable.

### Against Atomism: The Gestalt Movement

Atomism is a useful dimension on which to classify psychologists. The most atomistic psychology was James Mill's tinker-toy theory, and Titchener's catalog of sensory atoms is not much different. Moving toward holism, we find John Stuart Mill's mental chemistry and Wundt's theory of apperceptive synthesis. Both recognized the emergence of new properties as mental elements combine, but both still believed psychology should analyze complexes into elements, just as chemists do. More holistic still was Thomas Reid who maintained that complex ideas are not built up out of elements by any process, but are immediately given in experience as meaningful wholes. Introspection can break them down into elements, but this is artificial and does not imply that the mind starts with atoms and forms wholes; according to Reid the wholes are there from the beginning.

The *Gestalt* psychologists went even further, arguing that decomposing wholes into parts is not only artificial, but pointless and scientifically sterile, revealing nothing about the mind whatsoever. The philosophical root of their protest was *phenomenology*, whose proponents argued that experience should be simply described as given, never analyzed. Presented with a triangle, a good Titchenerian introspector would report "I see three lines;" the report would contain only meaningless sensory atoms. The phenomenologist would say "I see a triangle," reporting a meaningful mental whole transcending the atomic elements.

Even some elementalists were moving in this direction. Christian Ehrenfels (1859-1932) discussed "Gestalt qualities" in 1890. Ehrenfels wanted to know how certain experiences maintain their character despite sensory changes. This is most apparent in hearing tunes. Despite transposition of keys, and thus its sensory elements, we always hear the same tune as the same. Ehrenfels was dealing with the problem of organized perceptions, not elements, and arguing for a new mental element. A tune is made up of sensory elements—its specific notes—but it possesses in addition a Gestalt (or form) quality that represents the organization. Similarly, in the case of the triangle it is made up of three sensory elements, the lines, plus a form-quality element of triangularity. Ehrenfels' former teacher, the philosopher Alexius Meinong (1853-1920), tried to specify the source of the form-quality. Sensory elements are given by experience, and then the mind in a mental act adds the structuring form-quality. This theory of an additional mental act derived from the act psychology of Franz Brentano, whom we shall consider in the next chapter. Both Ehrenfels' and Meinong's theories remained elementalistic, merely adding a mental element of organization to the accepted list of sensory elements.

Both atomistic elementalism and the act interpretation of form-qualities were rejected by the phenomenologically oriented Gestalt psychologists, as is shown by the following Gestalt experiment. A subject is seated in a darkened room and two spots of light are flashed off and on alternately. When the interval between flashes is more than 0.2 sec, the subject sees two flashing lights; but when the interval is less than 0.2 sec the subject sees one light in continuous motion. The subject perceives apparent motion where in fact there is none. This phenomenon underlies our experience of movies, which are actually a rapidly displayed series of still photographs. Such experiments indicated that more than a mental element was needed. Such apparent motion undermines the atomistic account of consciousness, for sensational "atoms" given on the retina are not perceived, but instead give rise to a qualitatively different experience. Apparent motion is an experience that emerges from simple sensations but cannot plausibly be reduced to them. It is, in short, a perceptual whole (*Gestalt*, in German), given immediately to consciousness and deserving direct study. The Gestalt psychologists advocated a holistic psychology based on the mind's perception of complete forms.

This experimental demonstration (called the *phi phenomenon*), which shows that conscious experience is not usefully reducible to bundles of discrete sensations, was the starting point of the Gestalt movement. Its inspiration, however, had deeper and more general sources. We have already seen how German culture rejected the tide of associationism, atomism, and mechanism that flowed from traditional British and French philosophies. Wundt's psychology was a partial reaction to this tide, but the young men of the next generation reacted even more strongly. Even more than Wundt they looked for wholeness and transcendence as a way out of the post World War I crisis of German culture. They fought against all philosophies or sciences that saw creatures or cultures as machines, as no more than collections of simpler parts.

The leader of this movement in psychology was Max Wertheimer (1880-1943) who carried out the phi phenomena research in 1912 using the other two great Gestalt psychologists, Wolfgang Köhler (1887-1967) and Kurt Koffka (1887-1941), as the main subjects. Wertheimer was by nature a prophet for whom the idea of the Gestalt was "not only a theory of perception or of thinking, or a theory of psychology, or even an entire philosophy; it was, rather, a *Weltanschauung,* indeed an all encompassing religion. The core of this religion is the hope that the world is a sensible coherent whole, that reality is organized into meaningful parts, that natural units have their own structure" (Michael Wertheimer, 1978).

The phi phenomenon demonstrated a faith that Wertheimer held before 1912. Despite being a Jew, Wertheimer received an education "typical of the elite of his day" including studies with von Ehrenfels at Prague and Külpe at Würzburg (Michael Wertheimer, 1978). In all his studies he was immersed in the reaction against traditional atomism and traditional psychology, but Wertheimer moved in a more holistic direction than either of his teachers. His Gestalt ideas appeared first in a 1910 paper on the primitive music of a Ceylonese tribe in which he concluded that their compositions were organized by "*Gestalten* that are rhythmically and melodically strict" (Michael Wertheimer, 1978).

Wertheimer condemned traditional—Wundtian—psychology for containing what he called (1925) an abundance of "things arid, poor and inessential" and for having "alien, wooden, monstrous" implications. He argued that traditional psychology rested on two erroneous assumptions. The first is "*the mosaic or bundle hypothesis*" which is Wertheimer's term for sensationism. The second is "*the association hypothesis,*" by which Wertheimer means the tinkertoy theory. Nor could Wertheimer accept Wundt's idea that the mind's power of apperception unites elements into greater wholes, for this still concedes the fundamental status of sensational elements. Wrote Wertheimer (1922): "Gestalten" are not "the sums of aggregated contents erected subjectively upon primarily given pieces. . . . Instead, we are dealing with wholes and whole-processes possessed of inner intrinsic laws. 'Elements' are determined as parts by the intrinsic conditions of their wholes and are to be understood 'as parts' relative to such wholes." This is the central formula of Gestalt psychology.

Two important new concepts were used by the Gestalt psychologists to put their formula into practice. The first is the concept of the psychological field, consciously borrowed from field theory in physics. Gestaltists deny that experience is like a mosaic, a collection of inert, noninteracting, discrete units, or sensations. Instead, they see experience as a field of dynamically interacting parts. In the phi phenomenon the "parts" of the field, the two flashing lights, interact to give rise to the perception of motion. Thus, a visual illusion such as the Müller-Lyer is produced by interactions among the visual elements. The central lines are the same size, but because of the context in which they are viewed (the arrowheads) they seem to be different lengths.

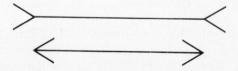

The Gestalt psychologists extended the field concept to refer not only to the phenomenal field of immediate experience involved in the phi phenomenon or illusions, but to the behavioral field in which our actions take place. For the Gestalt psychologists, a problem to be solved defined a behavioral field in stress. An animal or child, for example, might be prevented from reaching visible food by a barrier. The "stress" in such a field is obvious. The problem is resolved when the field is reorganized by "insight," that is, when the subject sees that the barrier may be walked around. The solution allows access to the food and relieves the stress in the behavioral field; the problem no longer exists. An important implication is that the subject must be aware of all elements in a problem situation before a real psychological problem exists. Should the subject not be able to see the food, no problem would exist, for no psychological field-stress would exist, even if the subject were hungry. For this reason the Gestalt psychologists criticized animal learning experiments, such as E. L. Thorndike's, in which the animal could not perceive all elements of the situation. How can an animal exhibit its intelligence unless the relevant factors are available for intelligence to consider? According to Gestaltists, animals are reduced to trial-and-error conditioning if this is the only kind of behavior allowed in an experiment.

The field concept proved capable of indefinite extension to psychological problems. Not only could it be applied to simple visual experiences and problem solving, but was also applied to creativity (by Wertheimer himself) and social psychology (by Kurt Lewin, 1890-1947). However, the concept of the experiential field was insufficient. The two flashing lights do not by themselves create apparent motion; it is a psychological phenomenon. Problems do not solve themselves, they only pose themselves. The Gestalt psychologists, however, were unwilling to posit an active mind "which is able to grasp intrinsic relations and utilize such understanding," just as they did not recognize active apperception as a unifying force behind the creation of whole ideas. In their view this alternative would lead to "vitalistic or spiritualistic dualism which we . . . have refused to accept." (Koffka, 1935). Instead. he said, "the dynamics of the process (of perceiving or thinking) are determined by the intrinsic properties of the data."

These "intrinsic properties" must act on the organism to produce experience or behavior. If there is no mind to act on, the action must be directly on the nervous system. This leads us to the second important concept of Gestalt psychology, the principle of *isomorphism*. This principle has given rise to numerous misconceptions.The Gestalt psychologists held that the brain is not the sensormotor association machine that most believed it to be, but instead is a complex electrical field. The idea of isomorphism is that the structural relationships in the behavioral field create in the individual who experiences them a pattern of brain-fields isomorphic to themselves. So in the phi phenomenon the flashing lights create two brain-fields that overlap and create the experience of motion. In a problem situation, the stresses in the behavioral field are represented in the brain as stresses in its electrical field. Insight is the resolution of the brain-field stresses that leads to resolution of the real problem.

The concept of isomorphism is difficult to grasp. The best analogy was suggested by Woodworth (1938). Functional isomorphism exists between the United States and a map of the United States. The two things are not the same, but structural relations in the former are directly related to structural relations in the latter. So, the problem of driving from Chicago to Los Angeles can be experienced and solved through the map. The "stresses" of the trip can be seen and resolved on the map. But Woodworth's analogy is simplified. The Gestalt psychologists did not maintain that a picture of the behavioral-field exists in the brain. Exactly what they did mean remains obscure; it is only certain that they maintained a functional isomorphism between behavioral and brain-fields. It was only through isomorphism and the electric field picture of the brain that the Gestalt psychologists could uphold their holistic dynamic-field explanations of experience and behavior without falling into dualism.

The Gestalt movement thus attempted to avoid both atomism and dualism by considering people as perceiving organisms that respond to whole perceptual fields. The Gestalt experiments uncovered several interesting quirks of perception, such as the phi phenomenon, that had to be included in any later perceptual psychology. The Gestalt psychologists' almost mystical theory, however, did not travel well. It was far too German to do well in England and America, where psychology has been most studied since World War II.


## CONCLUSIONS

### Conceptual Summary: Psychology's First Paradigms

#### Ganzheit Psychology

A paradigm has two components: the disciplinary matrix or set of fundamental assumptions that guide research and theory within the science, and the shared exemplars, the basic methods of the science. What was the disciplinary matrix of Ganzheit psychology? The central assumption of the matrix in which Wundt constructed his psychology was the study of the mind, rather than behavior, and was in particular the study of conscious experience. Thus Ganzheit psychology was avowedly *mentalistic*.

A second consciously held and central assumption was *voluntarism*, that we have control over our minds, at least in the normal state. This voluntary control is seen most clearly in the exercise of apperception and attention. We analyze and synthesize, directing our attention where we will, though in accordance with lawful principles. Apperception lies at the base of the higher mental processes and of our sense of self. As a consequence of the doctrine of apperception Ganzheit psychology was synthetic or *holistic*. There are identifiable mental elements, to be sure, but they are synthesized by apperception into greater wholes.

Finally, Ganzheit psychology is *psychologically explanatory* and *centralistic*. Wundt was not content merely to describe the processes of the mind but wanted instead to explain them, to show how they work and why they come to be. He did this not by reference to brain physiology, but to psychological entities such as apperception. His system was thus not *materialistic* or *reductionistic.* Further, Wundt held that psychological explanation was retrodictive, not predictive. We can explain a mental event after it occurs, but we cannot predict it in advance.

We can summarize the assumptions comprising the disciplinary matrix of Ganzheit psychology as follows: it was mentalistic, voluntaristic, holistic, psychologically explanatory, retrodictive, and centralistic.

When we turn to methodology or the shared exemplars of Wundt's system, we find that two methods were fundamental. First, there was the experimental psychology of the individual using the method of *simple introspection.* The subjects (or observers as they were called in those days because they observed themselves) were asked to react to a stimulus or report a stimulus. They were *not* asked to perform a retrospective analysis of their experiences. Wundt was adamant on this point, and severely criticized those psychologists who engaged in the practice. Wundt's introspection was thus simple, rather than elaborate and analytical as was Titchener's or Külpe's.

The second major method of Wundt's system was the analysis of the collective products of mental life that belonged to *Völkerpsychologie,* the approach Wundt felt was needed in order to penetrate to the higher mental processes that elude individual experimental introspection. Although there was no well-defined method as in individual psychology, Wundt's analysis of language exemplifies the approach. We should also note that although Wundt had no personal interest in child, animal, or abnormal psychology, he was willing to incorporate their results into Ganzheit psychology. Similarly, although he did not himself pursue the application of psychology to human problems, he did not regard it as a perversion of pure science to do so.

### Structuralism

Titchener, like Wundt, was a mentalistic psychologist. He regarded the study of behavior as a part of biology, for it studies animals as behaving organisms, while psychology was the study of human mental experience. In particular, Titchener's structuralism was avowedly *sensationlistic.* His goal as a psychologist was to analyze the contents of experience into its simplest sensational and meaningless elements so as to give a complete description of consciousness. This description was to show how the sensational elements were connected to form larger complexes. Thus Titchener was *atomistic,* for he assumed that experience could be broken down into distinct, enumerable elements, and he was connectionistic (or *associationistic* in the broad sense), for he assumed that these elements are joined together to make up perceptions, images, and so forth. Psychological descriptions were to be supplemented by physiological explanations that referred to the brain processes underlying experience. As we have seen, Titchener rejected Wundt's attempt to explain mind psychologically when he rejected such "theory ridden" terms as apperception.

Titchener's sensationlism and his descriptive, anti-theoretical bent increased as he got older until it became something stronger and more general, namely *positivism*. Ironically, in his last books the arch-mentalist Titchener forcefully stated an extreme Machian positivism, compatible with the Machian positivism of the arch-behaviorist B. F. Skinner. Wrote Titchener in *Systematic Psychology: Prolegemena*: "Science . . . is nothing else than the elaborated product of observation . . . the problem of science may be summed up in the single word 'description' . . . [science has nothing] to do with explanation, with why and because. . . ." Finally, he wrote, "I don't *explain* or *causally relate* at all, at all! In science all the 'explanation' that there is for me is the correlation of a dependent with a[n] independent variable. . . . Causality I regard as mythological,—if you mean by it anything more than correlation."

Titchener's sensationlism has here gone as far as it can go. He rejects all forms of explanation in favor of a purely descriptive account of mind that seeks only correlations and reduces mind to meaningless attributes of sensations. To describe experience in terms of meaningful percepts or ideas such as "book" or "chair" was roundly rejected by Titchener as a lapse into philosophy. The positivism expressed in these statements would be unacceptable to Titchener's teacher, Wundt, but would be, as we shall see, wholly acceptable to B. F. Skinner, whose descriptive behaviorism, like Titchener's descriptive mentalism, seeks only correlations of independent and dependent variables.

Structuralism was also *peripheralistic,* again like extreme forms of behaviorism. Titchener disallows reference to central, deep mental processes such as attention, which he reduced to peripheral sensations such as frowns and body-attitudes.

Thus, we may summarize the assumptions in the disciplinary matrix of structuralism as *mentalism, sensationism, positivism, atomism, connectionism,* and *descriptivism* (against explanations).

In turning to method, we find that Titchener accepted only one: introspection. He rejected (or at least did not practice) *Völkerpsychologie,* which became unnecessary because there were no "deep" mental processes to investigate by any method. In his early years, introspection was analytical introspection, an attempt to isolate the atoms of experience. Later, the method became more purely descriptive or phenomenological. Experience was to be internally scrutinized and described in simple, meaningless terms. No reduction to elements was attempted, only a description of the attributes of experience. In either form, the method was an elaborate form of retrospective introspection rejected by Wundt. With regard to application, Titchener opposed technological psychology even more fervently than did Wundt.

### Gestalt Psychology

Since the Würzburg school was too short-lived to develop a paradigm, we may pass directly to the Gestalt movement, which aspired to be a complete psychology. Its last member, Wolfgang Köhler, who served as president of the American Psychological Association, did not die until 1967. Nevertheless, despite the Gestaltist's years of systematic writing deeply concerned with theoretical psychology, constructing a picture of the Gestalt paradigm is difficult. In fact, it is sometimes said that Gestalt psychologists had no presuppositions, for instead of analyzing experiences they took them as they found them, as do all phenomenologists (Helson, 1973). Given their battles with atomistic associationism, or, as they called it, the bundle-hypothesis, wherever it arose, however, the Gestalt psychologists must have been led by some assumptions however difficult to discover.

Central to the movement, of course, was Wertheimer's "Gestalt vision," the holistic *Weltanschauung*. In 1924 Wertheimer declared that "Gestalt theory is neither more nor less" than the belief that "there are wholes, the behavior of which is not determined by that of their individual elements, but where the part processes are themselves determined by the intrinsic nature of the whole. It is the hope of Gestalt theory to determine the nature of such wholes." So Wundt's half-way holism in which wholes are constructed by the mind was unacceptable to the Gestaltists, and of course Titchener's sensationism was anathema. Beyond this central vision, and its consequent field concept, we are on less sure ground.

To begin with, it is not clear that Gestalt psychology was mentalistic. Its most impressive research was in vision, its phenomenological orientation implies a concern with consciousness, and it battled behaviorism with vigor and deep feeling. On the other hand, Koffka (1963) defined psychology as "the study of behavior in its causal connection with the physical field." Gestalt psychology's isomorphism offered an alternative to the mentalism-behaviorism dichotomy; behavior is to be causally explained in terms of its physical field. There are really two physical fields to be studied: the objective physical field of things, and the physical field of electrical brain processes, which is isomorphic to the physical field. Thus Gestaltists were not mentalists, because they denied the mind's autonomous existence, but they were not behaviorists because they talked about inferred brain processes and attended to the subject's subjective experience which reflects the underlying brain-fields.

Gestalt psychology was thus partly materialistic and reductionistic. They refused to ascribe any active role to mind, preferring to explain behavior in physical terms. Therefore, they saw attention as a mysterious "makeshift" theoretical device used to explain phenomena such as apparent motion, not traceable to peripheral stimulation (Koffka, 1922). These phenomena they explained in physical field terms. On the other hand, however, Wertheimer (1925) argued that traditional psychology, despite its "continued emphasis on consciousness," is far more "materialistic, arid, and spiritless than a living tree which is not conscious." Koffka argued that blind associationism of mental atoms is more machine-like, and "material" than Gestalt psychology's picture of dynamic brain-fields. Moreover, Koffka (1963) pointed out that although consciousness "does not enter into our causal explanations" it is so much part of "the warp and woof" of certain psychological processes that it cannot "be regarded as a mere epiphenomenon," as the behaviorists saw it. So we must conclude that although the Gestalt psychologists sought physiological rather than psychological or conditioning explanations of behavior, their physiological reality was a dynamic field-process in the brain, not mechanical sensorimotor linkages. One Gestalt psychologist, Kurt Lewin, felt that talk of brain-fields was unnecessary. His field theory of social psychology examined only the behavioral field and eschewed physiological speculation.

So far, then, Gestalt psychology differs from Ganzheit psychology in being materialistic rather than mentalistic, explaining behavior by referring to physical fields instead of to voluntarily controlled mental processes, and it is more holistic than Ganzheit psychology. The Gestalt psychologists also were not as opposed to practical application of their principles as was Wundt, and in fact Gestalt psychology became involved in the progressive education movement. The attitude of the Gestaltists to the nature of explanation is unique in psychology. It is clear that they aimed at more than description, but they advocated neither the historical kind of after-the-fact explanation advocated by Wundt, nor the prediction and control advocated by behaviorism. Instead, the Gestaltists looked for the dynamic structure of the behavioral-field and, except for Lewin, of the brain-field. Behavior then results from the changes among the forces in these fields. In this view the self is not a free and active agent, but is pushed and pulled by external and internal field forces.

Turning to shared exemplars of method, we find Gestalt psychology to be unfocused. The only methods they positively eschewed were analytical introspection and experiments in which important factors could not enter the subject's behavioral field. Otherwise, they considered all methods legitimate. Descriptive introspection was used in their perceptual experiments; free association was used in Wertheimer's first research. Köhler investigated ape intelligence through semi-formal experiments, while topics such as memory and thinking were investigated by methods as diverse as recalling drawings to formal experiments with syllogisms. The Gestaltists always opposed eclectic theorizing, but in method they were more eclectic than most. They did favor experimental methods and one finds in Gestalt psychology none of the comparative-historical method of Wundt's *Völkerpsychologie*. This is a natural consequence of the Gestalt focus on present physical and brain-fields, in which "history" acts only in the form of memory-traces in the brain.

### Historical Trends

What happened to the psychology of consciousness? Wundt and Titchener are no more cited by modern psychologists than are Aristotle and Newton by modern physicists. Wundt and Titchener died only about 50 years ago, yet little trace of them remains but the memory of one as founder of psychology the other as a faithful pupil. This question has two sets of answers, for Wundt and Titchener proposed different systems and worked in different contexts.

Ganzheit psychology suffered a number of blows. American students crossed the divide from the English world to the German to take their degrees and become psychologists, but without really assimilating Wundt's system. They returned to America and pursued their "completely American" questions. In Germany, Wundt was abandoned by one of his best students, Oswald Külpe, who found things in the mind Wundt would not admit to, thereby altering the scope and theory of experimental psychology. At the same time Wundt's position was rejected by other Germans even more holistic than he, the Gestalt psychologists. In America, Titchener promulgated a vastly simplified form of Ganzheit psychology that was modified from Wundt's. Structuralism became a straw man for the attacks of functionalists such as William James and behaviorists such as Watson. The *coup de grace* to German psychology was delivered by the Nazis, who destroyed the German intellectual community by expulsion, fear, and intimidation, as well as the general destruction of World War II that they brought down on Germany.

There is, moreover, a deeper reason for the disappearance of Ganzheit psychology. It is often said that nothing is more powerful than an idea whose time has come. Psychoanalysis succeeded for just this reason, but Ganzheit psychology failed because it was an idea whose time had passed.

Wundt and the psychological system he fathered were products of the German Mandarin culture described earlier, a culture which experienced a devastating crisis in the years 1890-1930. It was simply too elitist, too rationalist, too romantic, and too fragile to withstand the rising tide of socialism and democracy, positivism and pragmatism, as well as defeat in World War I and the coming of the Nazis. The rational psychology of consciousness could not compete with the psychology of the irrational and the unconscious of which Freud was only a part. The aloof, arcane, and subjective method of introspection could not compete with the objective study of behavior that held out the promise of Utopia. Americans in particular were deadened and depressed by working with Wundt (Steffens, 1938). As Ganzheit psychology could not compete, it became an unsuccessful variant in the struggle for scientific existence. It carved out an academic niche which was then more successfully occupied by rival psychologies. The birth of psychology was historically inevitable, but Ganzheit psychology was obsolete at birth—the product of a culture that could not last.

What of structuralism? Titchener took Wundt's Ganzheit psychology and reduced it to a sterile sensationlism. He threw away Wundt's explanatory psychology in favor of an introspective dissection of consciousness that never completed its initial task of cataloguing the elements of consciousness. At the end, Titchener and his students produced almost grotesque descriptions of sensations like "the glassy sensation" utterly alien to anything in ordinary awareness. This baroque elaboration of introspection repelled even some of Titchener's students (Washburn, 1930). When he died there was no one to carry on, and structuralism vanished.

Turning to those who revolted against Wundt and Titchener, we find that the Würzburg school simply faded away after Külpe left Würzburg and was gone by the time he died. The fate of Gestalt psychology is more complex. The usual view is to agree with E. G. Boring that Gestalt psychology was simply absorbed into an increasingly eclectic mainstream psychology. There is some support for this view. The Gestalt psychologists completely changed the field of perception. It made the field turn from atomistic sensationism of a Berkeleyan type, to examining, as Koffka (1935) put it, "why things look as they do" in our everyday, unanalyzed experience. They paid attention to problem-solving and other complex behaviors while the behaviorists were running rats in mazes. In both these areas Gestalt demonstrations are a standard part of every text book, even today. Some direct influence on others is also evident. For example, E. C. Tolman looked at maze learning as a process by which a rat constructs a holistic map of its environment, and he even incorporated the term *Gestalt* into his technical vocabulary.

On the other hand, survivors of the Gestalt movement disagree with Boring's conclusion. If we look at Germany, we find that "by the end of World War II, the first generation of young Gestalt psychologists was essentially wiped out," either by death, immigration, or adoption of a different kind of work (Henle, 1977). Koffka came to America in 1927 at the invitation of Americans interested in the Gestalt movement. He was followed in the 1930s by Wertheimer and Köhler, who were fleeing the Nazis.

Therefore the center of Gestalt psychology shifted to America, where they suffered two handicaps. The first was that all three founders obtained academic posts at institutions that gave no graduate degrees, so a new generation of professors and scientists could not be raised. More important, however, was the intellectual gulf between "trader" and "hero" that weakened Wundt's influence. Unlike Wundt, Gestalt psychologists were able to speak for themselves in America, but while they earned respect, their influence was limited. In 1935, Koffka acknowledged not only the difference in intellectual climate, but also noted that when Gestalt psychology was introduced to America, its most German interest (namely the stress on moral values) "was kept in the background." American psychology, moreover, was in the grip of behaviorism, which the Gestaltists saw as fundamentally similar to mentalistic associationism.

As a result, the Gestalt psychologists were holistic prophets of theoretical psychology in an atomistic, relatively atheoretical wilderness. While their demonstrations were impressive, many found their theory obscure. The general American reaction is described by Gordon Bower: "There were always several features to their writings—an experimental or demonstrational part . . . and then a polemical, almost philosophical part in which the ancient elementarism of Titchener's (or Watson's) analyses was flogged to death and some relatively incomprehensible 'field theory' . . . would be advanced" (Hilgard & Bower, 1975). Americans respected good data, but found the German "Gestalt vision" complete unacceptable when it could be understood at all. What revolutionized the study of perception were the new questions and demonstrations proposed by the Gestaltists, not their theory of perception. The same holds true in thinking. Their other work—in memory, association and so on—was generally ignored, while their whole theory was distorted into an easily criticized straw man. Despite the enduring fame of the Gestalt psychologists, their systems could no better cross the Atlantic than Wundt's. But they did at least provide a continuing criticism of behaviorism that modern cognitive psychologists appreciate, even if they do not always agree with it.

So in 1959 we find Wolfgang Köhler, in his presidential address to the American Psychological Association continuing to hold out hope of fruitful collaboration between Americans and Gestalt psychology, while despairing that it would occur. He found Americans to be over-cautious and over-critical, daring nothing, while the promise of mechanical behaviorism caused "in the present speaker a mild, incredulous horror." In 1975 A. S. Luchins, an old Gestaltist, decried the increasing misunderstanding of Gestalt psychology and ignorance of what it had accomplished. He observed that while certain Gestalt terms have been adopted by contemporary psychologists, they fail to see "the main thrust of Gestalt psychology." And in 1977 Mary Henle, a student of Köhler, concluded that Gestalt ideas have not "been given a real hearing." Like Köhler, she expressed hope of a hearing, but doubted it would occur.

None of these systems could survive in America, which became the center of twentieth century psychology. Evolution took hold in America as it did almost nowhere else. American psychologists were interested in the mind in use—in mental, and later behavioral, functioning as adaptive processes. They saw nothing in the psychology of consciousness that would answer evolutionary questions. How does the mind adapt? What are its functions? How can we improve it? These considerations were foreign to Titchener and Wundt, and so the psychology of consciousness was foreign to Americans. They abandoned Ganzheit psychology and structuralism for functionalism, a modern psychology born in the New World, ready to inhabit the niche created by Wundt. It was itself short-lived, being replaced by its aggressive offspring, behaviorism. These developments will occupy us in future chapters.

## SUGGESTED READINGS

There is no one study that encompasses all the psychologies of consciousness. For Wundt, Titchener, and the Gestaltists, there are separate English primary sources which you will find in the references and bibliography. Translated excerpts of the Würzburg studies may be found in George and Jean Mandler's *The Psychology of Thinking: From Association to Gestalt* (John Wiley, 1964).

## REFERENCES

Ben-David, J., & Collins, R. Social factors in the origin of a new science: The case of psychology. *American Sociological Review,* 1966, *31,* 451-465.

Wundt, W. *Lectures on human and animal psychology.* New York: Macmillan, 1896.

Blumenthal, A. L. *Language and psychology: Historical aspects of psycholinguistics.* New York: John Wiley, 1970.

Blumenthal, A. L. A reappraisal of Wilhelm Wundt. *American Psychologist,* 1975, *30,* 1081-1088.

Clark, H. M. Conscious attitudes. *American Journal of Psychology* 1911, *22,* 214-249.

Helson, H. Why did their precursors fail and the Gestalt psychologists succeed? In *Historical Conceptions of Psychology,* M. Henle, J. Jaynes, & J. Sullivan (Eds.). New York: Springer, 1973.

Henle, M. The influence of Gestalt psychology in America. *Annals of the New York Academy of Sciences,* 1977, *291,* 3-12.

Hilgard, E. R., & Bower, G. *Theories of learning* (4th ed.). Englewood Cliffs, N.J.: Prentice-Hall, Inc., 1975.

Keller, F. S. *The definition of psychology.* New York: Prentice-Hall, Inc., 1973.

Koffka, K. Perception: An introduction to *Gestalt Theorie. Psychological Bulletin,* 1922, *19,* 531-585.

Koffka, K. *Principles of gestalt psychology* (1935). New York: Harcourt Brace Jovanovich, Inc., 1963.

Luchins, A. S. The place of gestalt theory in American psychology. In S. Ertel, L. Kemmler, & M. Stadler (Eds.) *Gestalt-theorie in der modernen psychologie.* Darmstadt, Germany: Dietrich Steinkopf Verlag, 1975.

Meyer, A. & Orth, J. Experimental studies of association (1901). Partially reprinted in G. Mandler & J. Mandler (Eds.) *The psychology of thinking: From association to Gestalt.* New York: John Wiley, 1964.

Ogden, R. M. Imageless thought. *Psychological Bulletin,* 1911a, *8,* 183-197.

Ogden, R. M. The unconscious bias of laboratories. *Psychological Bulletin,* 1911b, *8,* 330-331.

Ringer, F. K. *The decline of the German Mandarins: The German academic community 1890-1933.* Cambridge, Mass.: Harvard University Press, 1969.

Steffens, L. *The letters of Lincoln Steffens,* New York: Harcourt, Brace, 1938.

Titchener, E. B. *An outline of psychology.* New York: Macmillan, 1897.

Titchener, E. B. *Experimental psychology: A manual of laboratory practice* (4 vols.). New York: Macmillan, 1901-1905.

Titchener, E. B. *Lectures on the experimental psychology of the thought processes.* New York: Macmillan, 1909.

Titchener, E. B. *Systematic psychology: Prologemena.* Ithaca, N.Y.: Cornell University Press, 1972.

Washburn, M. F. Some recollections. In *History of psychology in autobiography* (Vol. 2). C. Murchison (Ed.). New York: Russell & Russell, 1961.

Wertheimer, M. The general theoretical situation (1922). Reprinted in W. D. Ellis (Ed.) *A sourcebook of Gestalt psychology.* London: Routledge & Kegan Paul, 1938.

Wertheimer, M. Gestalt theory (1925). Reprinted in W. D. Ellis, (Ed.) *A sourcebook of Gestalt psychology.* London: Routledge & Kegan Paul, 1938.

Wertheimer, Michael. Max Wertheimer: Gestalt prophet. Presidential address to Division 26, annual meeting of the American Psychological Association, Toronto, Ontario, August 31, 1978.

Woodworth, R. S. *Experimental psychology.* New York: Holt, Rinehart & Winston, 1938.

Woodworth, R. S. & Schlosberg, H. *Experimental psychology* (2nd ed.). New York: Holt, Rinehart & Winston, 1954.

Wundt, W. M. *Lectures on human and animal psychology.* New York: Macmillan, 1896.

# 8

# The Psychology of the Unconscious Mind
## Sigmund Freud and Psychoanalysis

If greatness may be measured by scope of influence, then Sigmund Freud is without doubt the greatest of psychologists. Scarcely any inquiry into human nature has not felt his touch. His work affected—and affects—literature, philosophy, theology, ethics, aesthetics, political science, sociology, and popular psychology. He revolutionized our thinking about sex. "Freudian slip" is a household word. The modish belief that we all have secret selves with which we must get in touch through the aid of some therapy or belief-system comes from Freud—although he would scorn most such enterprises, for they stress a person's feelings, and Freud valued reason above all else.

Freud, along with Darwin and Marx, is one of the great fathers of twentieth-century Western thought. Freud saw himself as a revolutionary, fighting alone against a condemning world. He explicitly placed himself in the line of Copernicus and Darwin, as one of those who challenged humanity's childish egocentrism and pushed it toward self-sufficient maturity. He was pessimistic about human nature and the dangers of the future, yet his pessimism was hopeful. He wanted us to understand our unconscious, darker nature so that we might subject it to the rule of reason.

## BACKGROUND

### Freud and Academic Psychology

For all Freud's influence on Western culture, the relations between psycho-analysis and academic psychology have been ambivalent. No psychologist can be ignorant of psychoanalysis, and its concepts are discussed even in texts that call them wrong. Academic psychologists have been critical of and even hostile to Freud's ideas (when they have not ignored them), and psychoanalysts have generally remained aloof from experimental psychology.

In Freud's own time and place the major source of disagreement was over the unconscious. Belief in unconscious mental processes is the cornerstone of any "depth" psychology, but for Wundt and other mentalistic psychologists, psychology was the science of consciousness. One can hardly introspect the unconscious, so Wundt dismissed it as a metaphysical "myth." On his side, Freud marshaled clinical evidence in support of his concept of the unconscious and believed that those who refused to accept the unconscious did so on metaphysical rather than scientific grounds. Sometimes Freud read academic psychologists, but he was rarely influenced by them. For example, he cites Wundt several times in *The Interpretation of Dreams,* but never thereafter, for he had less and less use for academic psychologists as psychoanalysis grew and built on itself.

Early American psychology shared some of the European prejudice against psychoanalysis, but it was more willing to listen to Freud. His first public recognition was his 1909 trip to Massachusetts to deliver a series of anniversary lectured at Clark University. But William James, the founding American psychologist, shared Wundt's view of the unconscious; and later on behaviorism rejected both consciousness and the unconscious as useless myths. If the acceptance of psychoanalysis had depended on academic psychology, psychoanalysis would have vanished long ago. But psychoanalysis found its support in psychiatry and clinical psychology, where it began, as well as support and acceptance by many in the humanities and the educated public.

### Intellectual Antecedents

Freud is the most analyzed of psychologists. Because of his wide influence Freud's writings have been scrutinized by everyone from biologists to literary critics. We have available not only Freud's massive published output, but his unpublished drafts, letters revealing his personal and intellectual development, and the recollections of friends, associates, and patients. This mass of material has been attacked by a small industry of Freud scholars; Freud's concepts have been dissected and traced to their roots.

We now know that little Freud said was entirely original, rather it was his synthesis and use of old ideas that was original. For example, his idea of sexual energy—libido—was a combination of Victorian morality and physics. The everyday concept of sex in Victorian times was that a man had allotted him a limited amount of sexual energy to "spend" and that "profligacy" would lead to illness and a run-down nervous system. We find that Freud's sexual theory is replete with economic imagery and he viewed libido as fixed in amount. From the concept of conservation of energy in physics, Freud derived the conservation of libido. Sexual energy may be converted from one form to another, but cannot be created or destroyed. For example, persons who devote themselves to science will engage in sexual activity less frequently than others, for scientists have less libido to spend. Freud's hypothesis appears innocuous, but Freud used it to argue that civilized man is inevitably unhappy because civilization demands that we give up instinctual pleasures, which directly produce pleasure, in order to pursue more civilized ends. Freud's concept of libido thus was not original, but the implications he drew from it are profound.

We will now examine the sources of two of Freud's major concepts: the unconscious and the theory of sexuality.

### The Unconscious

We have already met the concept of unconscious ideas or sensations in the works of Leibniz, Herbart, and Fechner. In the nineteenth century there was a popular book called *The Psychology of the Unconscious* by Eduard von Hartmann (1842-1906). So in arguing the existence of unconscious ideas, Freud was saying nothing new. In fact, Freud was not alone among late nineteenth-century thinkers in assigning to irrational factors beyond our awareness a greater role in human behavior than had been allowed by earlier nineteenth-century social science.

We must distinguish, however, the hypothesis of unconscious ideas from the hypothesis of the unconscious. It is obvious that one is unconscious of one's phone number until the occasion to use it arises. But does the idea continue to exist unseen in a mental place called the unconscious, or is it no longer a mental entity at all, having disappeared into the neural network? Freud followed von Hartmann and Herbart in positing a mental place called the *unconscious* where ideas reside when they are not conscious and from which they can affect behavior without our awareness. Leibniz's and Fechner's conceptions were more purely descriptive, saying that some ideas are conscious while others are not-in-consciousness, or are unconscious. For them, there is no place called "the unconscious"; when an idea is unconscious it exists only physiologically, as a brain trace, not psychologically. Wundt and William James differed on much else, but they both accepted the Leibniz-Fechner description of "unconsciousness" and rejected Herbart's concept of a mental place called "unconsciousness."

In considering the concept of the unconscious, it is also important to distinguish different kinds of unconscious material. Theorists of unconsciousness before Freud, whether they reified the unconscious or not, saw unconsciousness as a state readily overcome, for unconscious ideas are weak. An increase in attention can make an unconscious idea conscious, or an increase in sensation can make a *petite perception* an apperception. Freud, however, distinguished two—and later three— kinds of unconscious material. Freud assigned unconscious but not repressed material to the *preconscious*, indicating that such material, although descriptively unconscious, could easily become conscious. He reserved the term *unconscious* for a more innovative concept, the repository of a second kind of unconscious material that does not have ready access to consciousness because it is *repressed*. This concept is also called the *dynamic unconscious*. Truly unconscious ideas are so unacceptable to consciousness that we deliberately keep them unconscious; we defend our egos against them. However, such ideas remain strong and constantly try to enter consciousness so that repression must be a continuing activity. Freud found the source of dreams, neuroses, behavioral errors, and resistances to therapy in repressed ideas.

This concept was unlike earlier psychological views of the unconscious, but it can be found in German philosophy. Schopenhauer, for example, speaks of the opposition of our Will to "repellent" ideas, whose breakthrough into consciousness may cause insanity. Freud again combined several current ideas into a new synthesis. Freud claimed that some ideas are not just too weak to enter consciousness, but are too threatening to be allowed to enter consciousness. Repressed ideas are not weak; on the contrary, they are strong but repulsive ideas that must be forcibly repressed. This concept also implies the concept of the unconscious as a mental place. Repressed ideas are active, forcing themselves to our attention in dreams and other phenomena. Therefore they must continue to exist and seek expression from some secret place in the mind. The hypothesis of the repressed is a cornerstone of psychoanalysis. Without it the whole system would fall apart, for Freud traced nearly all behavior and mental life to unconscious determinants. Freud's distinctions of conscious, preconscious, and unconscious concern the topography of mind. Another essential concept describes the energy that drives behavior and mental activity.

### The Instincts

Freud believed that all behavior is motivated by one or more innate, physiological instincts. Some behaviors directly satisfy instincts, while others do so only indirectly. In either case, Freud's model is always one of drive reduction, for all behavior must somehow reduce a physiological tension. As is well known, Freud put special emphasis on the sexual instinct, particularly before 1920. At no time did he forget other needs such as hunger and thirst, but he did not find them implicated in neuroses or other human problems. In 1920 Freud placed a death instinct alongside the sexual, or life, instincts; but in his characteristically pessimistic way, Freud never believed in any uniquely human instinct that might separate humans from the animals. Humans have no inherent "higher nature"; whatever in humans is "higher" is the product of cultural repression or reason. In setting humans on the side of the apes, Freud was heir to Darwin.

Antecedents to Freud's views are easily found in nineteenth-century German philosophy. Arthur Schopenhauer shared Freud's pessimistic view of humans' essential nature. Friedrich Nietzsche (1844-1900) even more closely resembled Freud. Both believed that each person has an animal nature of which he or she tries to remain unconscious to satisfy the demands of civilization. Nietzsche always believed in natural human aggression, a view Freud came to share late in life. Both also saw the cultural side of humans as a transformation, or *sublimation*, of their baser nature, setting civilization at war with human animal instinct. In contrast to Freud, however, Nietzsche's answer to this conflict was to transcend civilization.

Schopenhauer and Nietzsche were sources Freud sometimes acknowledged, but some of Freud's ideas on sex can be traced to less obvious, unacknowledged sources. David Bakan has argued that Freud was influenced by the Jewish mystical tradition in theology. For example, a secret Jewish book, the Cabala, presents sex as a powerful force present in both man and God. Sex and knowledge are closely identified by the Cabala—similarly, the Biblical word for sexual intercourse is "know." This indicates that sexual energy may be sublimated to intellectual pursuits. Another unacknowledged influence on Freud was popular Victorian ideas about sex. Victorian pornography, for example, represents female sexuality as a deeply repressed animal nature to be awakened by the right seducer. In his *Three Essays on the Theory of Sexuality*, Freud says almost exactly the same thing about the "average uncultivated woman." Further, Victorians were horrified by masturbation and strove mightily to detect it and stamp it out in their children. Again, in the *Three Essays*, Freud says that abandonment of masturbation is part of "the course of development laid down for civilized men." In many ways, Freud was thoroughly Victorian. Intellectually he tried to free himself from repressive Victorian views, but as he says in a letter, "I stand for an infinitely freer sexual life, although I myself have made very little use of such freedom" (E. Freud, 1960). Freud prescribed sexual liberation for the world at large, but could not follow his own advice.

The aspect of Freud's sexual theories that contemporaries found most shocking was his belief in childhood sexuality. The hypothesis that children are sexual creatures would not have shocked medievals who were merely amused by children's sexual play. By the nineteenth century, however, greater privacy had enabled middle and upper classes to avoid knowledge of it. How Freud arrived at his hypothesis that children have sexual desires is controversial. All agree that Freud always believed in the importance of sexual needs in the causation of neurosis, as his early correspondence makes clear. What is less clear is how he came upon the hypothesis of *infantile* sexuality as the basis for neurosis.

The "orthodox" account of his discovery of childhood sexuality, put forward by Freud and his major biographers, is as follows. Freud found that many of his early patients reported being seduced as children, usually by servants. The patients naturally found the seductions traumatic, and Freud believed their later neuroses originated in the traumatic event and its repression. However, as more data came in, Freud found these events to have an air of unreality about them, and he also found that some non-neurotics had been seduced as children. He was slowly forced to the conclusion that the seductions were fantasies, reflecting the patient's childhood desire to sleep with mother (or father), and that the fantasy was repressed just as a real traumatic seduction might be. This formulation requires that children have sexual feelings that motivate the fantasies. This conclusion contradicted his earlier belief that children had no sexual feelings and that seductions gave them traumatic sexual feelings. Freud was so reluctant to accept this conclusion and admit his seduction error that years passed between private and public changes of view.

The orthodox story has been vigorously challenged, especially by Frank Cioffi. He asks why Freud's patients should tell us of seductions in childhood. Even during the period when he believed in the seductions, Freud wrote that his patients did not believe in them, so that he later concluded that the stories were invented "screen memories" concealing fantasies of incestuous desires for the patients. The first difficulty Cioffi raises is that in his early cases Freud reported no seductions by parents. The second difficulty concerns motivation. Freud held that the stories were fabricated to hide incestuous, Oedipal wishes, yet is it really more acceptable to "remember" sexual abuse during childhood than to "remember" childhood sexual desires? Cioffi suggests that the seduction stories came not from his patients but from Freud himself. Freud was already convinced of the role of sexuality in the neuroses and simply pushed his patients until they "recalled," or accepted from the analyst, a story of a childhood seduction. In *Studies in Hysteria,* a book that preceded the seduction theory period, Freud wrote that the analyst must *insist* that a patient recall the cause of a symptom. The analyst's technique will cause "thoughts to emerge which the patient never recognizes as his own, which he never remembers!" Cioffi argues that Freud's patients simply made up stories to satisfy Freud's demands.

There is also evidence of a cover-up, intentional or unintentional, regarding the seduction error. When he finally confessed the error, Freud justified the change in view by saying that some non-neurotics had also been seduced, so that such trauma cannot cause neurosis, and he asserted that at the time of the seduction error he did not know this fact. However, Freud clearly states in one of the original papers that he did know. Finally, if it is asked where Freud could have got the idea of childhood sexuality in a prudish world, we need look to no crank but to one of the most eminent psychiatrists of the nineteenth century, Richard von Krafft-Ebbing, who wrote in 1886 that any physician familiar with neuroses is aware that the "sexual instinct may occur in very young children."

Cioffi then asks how Freud got himself into such a difficult situation. Freud had to defend his clinical method of scientific investigation—a method in which a patient's unconscious is plumbed by free association by an analyst who knows the patient's mind better than does the patient. The analyst interprets symptoms and, by his superior knowledge, leads the patient to a cure. But the seduction episode raised an ominous possibility. If no seductions took place, then what patients tell their analysts is untrustworthy and cannot be an accurate guide to the unconscious. The obvious alternative to Freud's defense of the seduction error was to believe that the recollections were fabricated to please Freud or were interpolated events forced on the patient by the therapist. Freud consistently maintained that a therapist should be authoritarian, so it is plausible that such interpolation could easily occur. This account undercuts Freud's method as a scientific tool, for if true, it means the therapist is learning nothing about the patient's past or unconscious. Freud resolved this dilemma by saying that the seduction memories were not true childhood memories but were true childhood fantasies, preserving the psychological, if not the historical, accuracy of clinical recollection.

The criticism that Freud's method could lead to false results because of therapists' suggestions was made very early, and the seduction error seemed to confirm it. Freud, however, publicly denied making such suggestions, and the orthodox account of the genesis of the hypothesis of childhood sexuality argues that Freud successfully overcame the seduction error. Cioffi's view holds that Freud fooled himself as well as his patients into believing the suggested seduction stories, whether they are believed to be truth or fantasy, producing confirmation of the sexuality hypothesis and of the Oedipus complex by simply demanding such evidence from patients. Which account of Freud's discovery of childhood sexuality is correct remains debatable, but certain doubts remain about the scientific, if not the therapeutic, value of the psychoanalytic method.

### Social Context

Since Freud's experience was in the clinic treating real human problems, his theory, more than those of experimental psychologists, is erected on social foundations. We therefore need to consider certain social and personal attitudes of Victorian people. "Where should we find that reverence for the female sex, that tenderness towards their feelings, that deep devotion of the heart to them, which is the beautiful and purifying part of love? Is it not certain that all of the delicate, the chivalric which still pervades our sentiments, may be traced to the *repressed,* and therefore hallowed and elevated passion?" So wrote W. R. Greg in 1850. The Victorians did not accept the animal part of their nature, whether sexual or simply sensual. Wrote Greg: "Smoking . . . is liked because it gives agreeable sensations. Now it is a positive objection to a thing that it gives agreeable sensations. An earnest man will expressly avoid what gives agreeable sensations" (Houghton, 1957). (Earnestness was a cardinal virtue to Victorians.) Victorian culture and religion thundered against pleasure, especially sexual pleasure, and Victorians were burdened by an oppressive sense of guilt. Like a medieval saint, British Liberal Prime Minister William Gladstone recorded his least sin and grieved over it. Guilt was heightened by constant temptation. Prostitution was rampant; men and women, boys and girls—all could be had for a price. The anonymous author of *My Secret Life,* a sexual autobiography, supposedly seduced over 2,000 people of all ages and sexual orientations and engaged in every vice. Boys at the finest private schools were sexually abused. The Victorians were caught between stern conscience and compelling temptation; it is no wonder that so many were neurotic.

These two sides of Victorian life emerged in their attitudes toward women, which resemble the medieval attitudes we explored in Chapter 3. Wives and mothers were "angels"—unhuman, holy voices of God, as described by Tennyson in *The Princess*:

> No angel, but a dearer being, all dipt
> In angel instincts, breathing Paradise . . .
> On tiptoe seem'd to touch upon a sphere
> Too gross to tread, and all male minds perforce
> Sway'd to her from their orbits . . .
> Happy he
> With such a mother! faith in womankind
> Beats with his blood. . . .
> He shall not blind his soul with clay.

To feel lust for such a one would obviously bring disgust and repression. Thus it is easy to see why Freud discovered an Oedipus complex. It certainly fit the society he knew, even if it was not as universal as he claimed.

Woman was the guardian of the home, protector of the hearth from the harsh outside world. Emancipation therefore could only degrade, not liberate. Freud himself wrote the following in a letter to his fiancée (E. Freud, 1960). He is commenting on J. S. Mill's "Emancipation of Women," one of the best feminist tracts of the nineteenth century.

> It seems a completely unrealistic notion to send women into the struggle for existence in the same way as men. Am I to think of my delicate, sweet girl as a competitor? . . . Women's delicate natures . . . are so much in need of protection. [Emancipation would take away] the most lovely thing the world has

to offer us: our ideal of womanhood . . . the position of woman cannot be other than what it is: to be an adored sweetheart in youth and a beloved wife in maturity.

Freud was very Victorian.

As in the Middle Ages, on the dark side of the Good Woman and Mother was the Bad Woman. Victorian men went to prostitutes for the sexual pleasure they often could not get, and almost certainly did not want to get, at home. Prostitutes gave pleasure, but for that very reason were not respected; they were fallen women, good only for satiating animal lust. The price was high for the Good Woman who strayed. Lady Ward is a case in point. Her husband did not sleep with her, preferring merely to stare at her naked except for her jewelry. She took a lover, and got pregnant. Both her husband and father threw her out, and she died soon after. No one blamed her husband or her parents (Plumb, 1972). A similar belief in the "Bad Woman" is betrayed in Freud's comment on the "uncultivated" woman, mentioned earlier, who he said was awaiting the right seducer.

There was, however, one Victorian trait Freud rejected, and its rejection is the essence of Freud's revolution. He was not a hypocrite. Victorian men and women knew about sex and pleasure but tried to cover it up in public, as they covered "indecent" piano legs, and tried, often desperately, to repress sexuality in their private lives. What Freud did was call on people to not hide from instincts but rather to face them openly, to confront their darkest secrets and conquer them through reason. Freud told his colleagues that he sought to lift repression—not to liberate sexuality, but to rationally suppress it. Like the Victorians Freud did not want to liberate lust; but unlike them he faced its temptation and power directly.

### Freud's Life (1856-1939)

The story of Freud's life has been told many times by many hands. It would be pointless to add to this list of biographical studies. We will here only comment on his relation to German culture and let him describe his character himself. Freud was an outsider to German and Austrian intellectual life. He was an intellectual but no Mandarin as was Wundt. In his *Future of an Illusion* Freud wrote: "I scorn to distinguish culture and civilization." He prized being an outsider, often judging the correctness of his ideas by how much they offended society. He formed a tightly knit group of analysts bound to a single faith and embarked on a crusade from which heretics were expelled. He identified with Moses and valued his Jewishness. Although he was irreligious, he felt a bond with his Jewish brethren who were much persecuted in Vienna, as well as a bond with the historic experience of Judaism. He felt himself to be beyond nationalistic claims because he was a Jew. When the Nazis seized Austria, Freud and his family narrowly escaped arrest with the help of outsiders. In Nazi Germany, Freudian psychoanalysis and Einsteinian physics were both condemned as "Jewish science."

We may let Freud himself describe his character. The following letter (E.

Freud, 1960) was written in 1886 to his fiancée, while Freud was under the influence of cocaine, which he used as a young man. The letter reveals Freud's state of mind shortly before he began the self-analysis that led to *The Interpretation of Dreams,* his masterpiece.

> There was a time when I was all ambition and eager to learn, when day after day I felt aggrieved that nature had not, in one of her benevolent moods, stamped my face with that mark of genius which now and again she bestows on men. Now for a long time I have known that I am not a genius and cannot understand how I ever could have wanted to be one. I am not even very gifted; my whole capacity for work probably springs from my character and from the absence of outstanding intellectual weaknesses. But I know that this combination is very conducive to slow success, and that given favorable conditions I could achieve more than Nothnagel, to whom I consider myself superior, and might possibly reach the level of Charcot. . . . Breuer told me he had discovered that hidden under the surface of timidity there lay in me an extremely daring and fearless human being. I had always thought so, but never dared tell anyone. I have often felt as though I had inherited all the defiance and all the passions with which our ancestors defended their Temple and could gladly sacrifice my life for one great moment in history. . . .

## MAJOR WORKS

Trying to present Freud's thought is an enormous task, for his writings span almost 50 years and cover everything from memory lapses to neurosis to the nature of civilization. To give a summary of psychoanalysis as a system obscures the tremendous changes Freud made as his thinking advanced. It also takes one far from what Freud said about specific topics or theoretical problems. Here, we will discuss several specific major works in chronological order, to remain close to Freud's concepts as they evolved from 1895 to 1939.

### Laying the Foundations 1895-1899

#### Studies in Hysteria (1895)

Freud started out doing neurological research, but circumstances forced him to become a practicing physician specializing in "neurological" disorders, what today we would recognize as a psychiatrist. The most widespread psychological disorder of Freud's time (it is much rarer now) was *hysteria,* in which some mental disturbance manifests itself as a physical symptom that has no physiological basis. The name *hysteria* comes from the Greek word for womb, for the Greek physicians blamed the ailment on a diseased uterus. In Freud's time, it was still widely believed that only women could become hysterical, since the overwhelming majority of hysterical patients were women.

In 1885 Freud briefly studied hysteria at the clinic of Jean Martin Charcot in Paris. Charcot believed, as did many other physicians, in a close relationship between hysteria and the hypnotic state, since hysteria-like symptoms could be induced by hypnosis, and hypnotic suggestion could be used to remove a hysteric's symptoms. Most important for Freud was Charcot's hypothesis that hysteria was *ideogenic,* that its causation lay in a disturbed mental state that acted on an underlying, inherited predisposition to hysteria. Freud would later abandon hypnotic therapy and minimize the constitutional basis of hysteria while emphasizing its origin in a disturbed mind.

In Vienna, Freud went into practice with Joseph Breuer (1842-1925). Together they developed a new kind of cathartic hypnotic treatment of hysteria, which they presented in *Studies in Hysteria.* At this point, Freud's work was not yet psychoanalytic, but contained the germs of many psychoanalytic ideas.

The book begins with a journal article Breuer and Freud published in 1893 describing their new method. They argued that the cause of hysteria is a traumatic experience in which the generated emotion is not adequately discharged. Then, because the experience was unpleasant, the event and its affect are *repressed,* that is, not allowed into consciousness or remembered. However, the affect is still present, and its undischarged or "strangulated" tension gives rise to the hysterical symptoms. As Breuer and Freud put it: *"Hysterics suffer mainly from reminiscences."* But these are *unconscious* reminiscences; the patient is aware only of his or her symptoms, not of the precipitating event, which is repressed. Breuer and Freud reported that they had been able to cure each hysterical symptom in their patients by hypnotizing them and having them remember the traumatic episode and discharge the pent-up affect. They called this discharge *abreaction* and considered it the key to successful therapy. Remembering the event alone is insufficient; the patient must emotionally *relive* the event to be cured.

In the 1895 book, Breuer and Freud went on to support their views with a series of case histories, the most famous of which was Breuer's case of Anna O. (treated between 1880-1882), which furnished Freud with much food for thought. Anna O. was a young woman with a rich array of hysterical symptoms from paralysis to disorders of vision and hearing to occasional inability to speak anything but English. Her symptoms generally centered around her feelings for her father, and Breuer methodically eliminated each symptom by letting her (under hypnosis) talk about and abreact the events that gave rise to them. Anna called this procedure the "talking cure," a label that has stayed with psychotherapy ever since. The cure went well until Breuer announced he was taking a vacation, whereupon Anna manifested a hysterical pregnancy with a child "fathered" by Breuer himself. Breuer panicked, dropped the case, and left Vienna for two years. Breuer did not report these events in his case history but says only that Anna was restored to health.

By 1895 Breuer and Freud had some differences over the etiology and treatment of hysteria; *Studies* concludes with separate chapters by each author. Breuer contributed a long chapter on the theory of hysteria which elaborated the preliminary theory of 1893 and went on to argue that the precipitating events of hysterical symptoms are experienced during "hypnoid states," which accounts for their unconsciousness and curability by hypnosis; Freud eventually rejected this theory. Freud contributed a chapter on therapy in which he abandoned Breuer's hypnotic method for a method that is closer to classical psychoanalysis. Freud found that, since not all patients could be hypnotized, the usefulness of Breuer's method was limited. Freud therefore insisted that his patients free associate to their symptoms and report anything that entered their minds, no matter how seemingly trivial or irrelevant. Thoughts were not to be censored or arranged in any way, but simply reported. In this way, Freud effected cures by uncovering the ideas underlying the hysteria, but without using hypnosis. Freud saw that in the physician-patient relation lay a key to successful therapy. Breuer had been alarmed by his stormy relationship with Anna O., but Freud instead made it the basis of therapy, saying that the source of the healer's strength lay in the affection the patient has for the therapist. In this way the therapist gains influence and power and effects the cure by insisting on the patient's cooperation. Freud made two more important points. First, he argued that the underlying problem in hysteria is always sexual, as in Anna's feelings for her father—Freud and Breuer broke over this hypothesis. Second, Freud found that hysterics *resist* their cures. They do not want to know, or re-experience, the events that precipitated their symptoms. They are not simply ignorant of the cause; they resist knowing it. Therapeutic success is thus a matter of overcoming resistances by exploiting the therapist's power over the patient.

Although *Studies in Hysteria* is really a pre-psychoanalytic work, we find in it some foundation stones of psychoanalysis. Most important is the claim that hysterics, and probably everyone else, have within them motives that they cannot accept and therefore repress. These motives do not lose their force, however, but manifest themselves as symptoms (or—in Freud's later work—dreams, slips of the tongue, myths, and the like). The key to mental health is to make these unacceptable ideas conscious and deal with them rationally. The first great theme of psychoanalysis is this existence within each person of unconscious, irrational forces that must be conquered by conscious reason. The second great theme announced in *Studies* is the nature of the irrational force. In *Studies*, and until about 1920, Freud saw the irrational force as sex; later he proposed a death wish as an even darker force, controlled by reason, civilization, and sexuality.

In the *Studies* we also find the beginnings of psychoanalysis as a therapy. Charcot had cured hysterics by giving hypnotic commands that their symptoms disappear. Breuer made his patients hypnotically relive traumatic, precipitating events. Freud inaugurated a real "talking cure" in which his patients talked about their problems, feelings, and experiences, while the therapist guided, interpreted, and sometimes commanded compliance. Eventually, patients would unravel their own troubles by reflecting on them and discovering their cure. It was a lengthy procedure that Freud much later said could never really end.

Finally, a recurrent personal theme is evident in the *Studies*, namely Freud's pessimism. Freud tells us that he could not treat anyone who struck him as "low-minded" or "repellent"; later he would say that most people are "worthless."

Freud never had a high opinion of the human race. He was also pessimistic about the limitation of therapy. In his last paragraph he notes an objection made by many patients: Why should I endure this arduous course of cure if you cannot alter the circumstances of life that make me unhappy? Freud replies: "You will be able to convince yourself that much will be gained if we succeed in transforming your hysterical misery into common unhappiness. With a mental life that has been restored to health you will be better armed against that unhappiness." Freud never believed that therapy could bring about human happiness. All it could do was to prepare a person to endure the inevitable hardships of living.

### Project for a Scientific Psychology

At the end of the *Studies in Hysteria,* Freud spoke of restoring a patient's "mental life" to health. It is significant that in editions before 1925 Freud used the phrase "nervous system," not "mental life." Early in his career Freud, trained as a neurologist, was strongly committed to materialistic reductionism, to the view that human behavior was to be scientifically explained by reference only to brain processes. Shortly after the *Studies* appeared, Freud (1895) wrote a manuscript "to furnish a psychology that shall be a material science, that is, to represent psychical processes as quantitatively determinate states of specifiable material particles." Freud never published the manuscript; in fact he tried to prevent its publication late in his life, and it only appeared posthumously.

Because Freud did not wish to publish his *Project,* it would be wrong to consider it a proper part of psychoanalysis. But it does contain, in primitive and broad form, a number of important psychoanalytic concepts. The first of these concepts was Freud's quantitative approach to mental functioning. Unlike academic psychologists, Freud was first of all concerned with human motivation, which he believed comes from the organism's desire to lower its states of tension. According to Freud's quantitative conception, the goal of all mental and behavioral functioning is to discharge built-up quantities of nervous tension, felt as "unpleasure." The need for discharge Freud called the "unpleasure" principle, later changed to the "pleasure principle," an important psychoanalytic concept. The former name is more accurate, for Freud's view of motivation, like Plato's, was negative. What we call pleasure is in fact the discharge of built-up unpleasure—not something desired in its own right.

We also find in the *Project* Freud's characteristic division of the mind into separate components whose conflicts, demands, and regulations underlie human behavior and thinking. In the *Project* Freud proposed three neurological systems based on different modes of synaptic functioning. There is, first, a perceptual system of neurons, second, an unconscious system within which most of our mental life takes place, and third, a system giving rise to consciousness, which regulates behavior by distinguishing real perceptions from hallucinations. Although these systems are not exact forerunners of the id, ego, and superego, we do find in them evidence of Freud's analytic approach of dividing the mind into independent entities.

Freud also made an important functional distinction that does persist, with modifications, into psychoanalysis. Freud wrote of a *primary process* of nervous functioning whose goal is immediate and complete discharge of unpleasurable tension. However, this system is unrealistic, for it seeks its goal through wish-fulfilling fantasy. There is therefore a need for a more realistic mode of functioning, one that operates in accord with reality; Freud called this the *secondary process*. It was also believed to modify primary functioning by seeking to lower tension to a manageable, but not a nonexistent, level. The residual tension provided the rational self with a pool of energy on which it could draw to fuel its own activities.

Finally, both in the *Project* and later, Freud stressed the role of endogenous stimulation in determining mental life. Academic psychologists on the other hand were concerned more with perception of the outside world. Wundt, for instance, wanted to understand how we attend to and understand the world. Kant had set this problem by his contention that psychology should study how consciousness imposes organization on the unknowable noumena. What made Freud special was his attempt to understand how consciousness deals with internal sensation, especially innate instincts, which operate in a confused, unconscious world (later called the *id*) that we sense only indirectly. Wundt looked at the external world through human consciousness; Freud sought to fathom our unconscious inner world. Both the noumena and the unconscious are primordial and formless; Wundt chose to study the former, Freud the latter.

After the *Project*, Freud cast his theory in mental, not physiological terms, as the change in the passage from *Studies in Hysteria* shows. However, he never seems to have abandoned the hope of a psychology that would be purely materialistic, positing nothing beyond atoms and the void. The *Project* was a premature attempt along these lines. However, it indicates the direction of Freud's thinking as he began to write his masterpiece, *The Interpretation of Dreams*.

### Defining Psychoanalysis 1900-1920

In the years after the *Studies* and the *Project*, Freud worked out the system he called psychoanalysis in a long series of writings. He did this largely alone, based on his analysis of patients and his own self-analysis. We will examine now the only two works Freud considered worthy of constant revision as psychoanalysis evolved, *The Interpretation of Dreams* and *Three Essays on the Theory of Sexuality*.

#### The Interpretation of Dreams (1900)

Of all his works, Freud himself believed *The Interpretation of Dreams* to be his greatest. In a letter to Fliess (E. Freud, 1960) he hoped that a plaque would be erected some day saying, "In this House on July 24, 1895 the Secret of Dreams was revealed to Dr. Sigmund Freud." The insight which Freud valued so highly was that a dream is not the meaningless collection of images it appears to be, but is "the royal road to the unconscious": a clue to the innermost recesses of the personality. That dreams have meaning was not a new idea, as Freud acknowledged, but it was out of step with the received academic opinion of his times. Most thinkers, including Wundt, assigned little importance to dreams, believing them to be only confused nighttime versions of waking mental processes. Freud sided instead with supposedly disreputable philosophers and ancient religions in valuing dreams as symbolic statements of a reality unavailable to waking experience.

Freud's basic idea is simple, but its details and ramifications are complex and far-ranging: All of us, whether neurotic or not, carry within us desires that we cannot accept consciously. In fact we deliberately keep these desires unconscious, or *repress* them. Nevertheless, they remain active, precisely because they are repressed and not subject to conscious scrutiny and memory-decay. They constantly press for access to awareness, and hence the control of behavior. In our waking life, our *ego*, or conscious self, represses these wishes; but during sleep consciousness lapses and repression weakens. If our repressed desires ever completely eluded repression, we would awaken and reassert control. Dreaming is a compromise that protects sleep, for dreams are hallucinatory, disguised expressions of repressed ideas. They give partial satisfaction of unacceptable wishes, but in such a way that consciousness and sleep are rarely disturbed.

Freud summarized his view by saying that every dream is a *wish-fulfillment*, that is, a disguised expression (fulfillment) of some unconscious desire, or wish. It is this characteristic of dreams that makes them the royal road to the unconscious: If we can decipher a dream and retrieve its hidden meaning, we will have recovered a piece of our unconscious mental life and be able to subject it to the light of reason. Dreams and hysteria thus have the same origin, for both are symbolic representations of unconscious needs, and both can be understood by tracing them back to their sources. The existence of dreams shows that no sharp line can be drawn between neurotic and normal mental lives. Everyone has needs of which they are unaware and whose realization they would find disturbing. In neurotics, however, the usual means of defense have broken down, and symptoms have taken their place.

The method of decoding is also the same in both hysteria and dreams—the method of free association. Just as hysterical patients were asked to freely talk about their symptoms, so we may understand dreams by free associating to each element of the dream. Freud's assumption was that free association would reverse the process which produced the dream and bring one at last to the unconscious idea embodied in it. In both symptom analysis and dream analysis the goal is the same: to reach rational self-understanding of the irrational unconscious, a step toward mental health.

Freud introduced technical terms as part of his theory of dreams. The actually experienced dream he called the *manifest content* of the dream. The true meaning of the dream, the repressed unconscious desires symbolized by the dream, he called the *latent content*. The process of transformation of latent to manifest content is the *dream work*, performed because of the demands of the *endopsychic censor*, which is the psychic agency which refuses direct expression to anxiety producing desires.

The last chapter of *The Interpretation of Dreams* is a theoretical account of dream production, which appears to be an informal mentalistic version of parts of the *Project*. Freud pictured the mind as a complex structure comprising several independent but related systems. Closest to the world is the *perceptual system* that receives impressions from the environment and conveys them inward, where they leave behind a series of memory-traces. At the other end of this chain of reflexes, for Freud said that all mental processes are ultimately reflexes, is the *motor system*, which produces overt behavior. The motor system is governed by the *preconscious* and its rational *secondary process* thought, which guides realistic action. In the deepest level of the mind resides the *unconscious,* the home of repressed wishes and of the irrational *primary process.* Freud located consciousness in two places. One was the preconscious, for part of it is at any time conscious since it contains only rational and acceptable chains of thought. Consciousness is then the ultimate governor of behavior. We are also conscious of what we perceive, so consciousness is also found in the perceptual system. In the normal course of events, sensations enter the perceptual system, lay down memory-traces, and eventually progress to the preconscious where they may be acted on in the conduct of behavior.

Dreams, however, are regressive. Unacceptable wishes, which live forever in the unconscious, seek expression but are blocked by repression during the waking hours. This control weakens during sleep, and the impulses gain strength. Sleep however, blocks all motor activity, so these impulses cannot become behavior. Instead, they move toward the perceptual system, where they can find hallucinatory fulfillment as mock-perceptions distorted to preserve sleep.

We cannot leave *The Interpretation of Dreams* without discussing Freud's introduction of his most famous, or infamous, concept, the *Oedipus complex.* Freud described a kind of "typical dream," which expresses certain infantile wishes regarding one's parents. These wishes are repressed and persist in the unconscious to later provide latent content for dreams. This infantile complex of wishes is made up of the child's sexual desire for the cross-sex parent and of the child's consequent desire that the same-sex parent, the child's rival, be eliminated. This set of feelings Freud considered universal, and named it the Oedipus complex after the mythical Greek king who unwittingly killed his father and married his mother.

Oedipal feelings are powerful ones, subject to repression, and consequently fertile ground for the formation of neuroses. Indeed, Freud puts the blame on the parents of neurotics for their child's later sickness. If they react badly to the trying Oedipal period, neurosis or even psychosis will ensue. If the storm is weathered, the child will attain a sound personality.

It was said earlier that Freud revised the *Interpretation of Dreams* as his system evolved. The major change was in the means by which dreams may be decoded. In the early editions of the book, the only method was free association, but because of the work of a follower, Wilhelm Stekel, Freud came to believe that dreams could also be interpreted according to a more-or-less uniform set of symbols. That is, in most cases certain objects or experiences could be shown to stand for the same unconscious ideas in everyone's dreams. So, for example, walking up a flight of stairs symbolizes sexual intercourse, a suitcase stands for the vagina, and a hat for the penis.

Such an approach of course simplified the process of dream interpretation. It also made possible a wider application of Freud's insight, namely the interpretation of myths, legends, and works of art. Freud had already engaged in such an analysis in the early versions of the work, treating Sophocles' *Oedipus Rex* and Shakespeare's *Hamlet* as Oedipal stories, and he and other psychoanalysts would go on to do many such analyses. Psychoanalysis was never limited to a mere psychotherapy, but was increasingly used as a general tool for understanding all of human culture. Myth, legend, and religion were seen as disguised expressions of hidden cultural conflicts; art was seen as the expression of the artist's personal conflicts: all share the same mechanism with dreams. The symbol-system helped justify and make possible this extension of psychoanalysis. We cannot put Sophocles, Shakespeare, or a whole culture on the analytic couch and ask them to free associate, but we can search their products for universal clues to the universal human unconscious.

Throughout *The Interpretation of Dreams*, Freud makes clear that all the repressed wishes that we find in dreams have an infantile character, as in the Oedipus complex. It is during childhood that the repressions form that produce the latent material for the dreams of adulthood. The roots of personality should be sought in childhood and especially in the development of the sexual instinct during the early years of life. This brings us to Freud's other classic work, *Three Essays on the Theory of Sexuality*.

### Three Essays on the Theory of Sexuality (1905)

In the popular mind, Freud is best remembered for saying that sexual motivation is the major cause of human behavior. There is no denying that Freud's most revolutionary impact has been on our willingness, in contrast to the Victorians, to accept sexuality as an essential part of being human. It is ironic, therefore, that it is in his theory of sexuality that Freud is most Victorian. As was shown earlier, there are great similarities between Freud's views on sex and the ordinary Victorian view. The virtue of Freud's discussions lies not in the details of his theory, which are anachronistic and culture-bound, but in his lack of shocked hypocrisy. By drawing attention to sexuality, he provoked the research and the culture change that transcended his own concepts.

As the title of the book says, the text consists of three short essays on different aspects of sex: "The Sexual Aberrations," "Infantile Sexuality," and "The Transformations of Puberty." Far more than *The Interpretations of Dreams,* the *Three Essays*—especially the last two—were revised after 1905 as Freud developed his later libido theory.

Freud made two important general points in the first essay, on sexual aberrations. First: "There is indeed something innate lying behind the perversions but . . . it is something innate in *everyone.*" What society calls "perverse" is only a development of one component of the sexual instinct, an activity centering on an erotogenic zone other than the genitals, a zone that plays its part in "normal" sexual activity in foreplay. The second point was that *"neuroses are, so to say, the negative of perversions."* That is, all neuroses have a sexual basis, and arise out of the patient's inability to deal with some aspect of his or her sexuality. Freud went so far as to say that a neurotic's symptoms *are* his or her sex life. The neurotic has symptoms rather than perversions or healthy sexuality.

Freud's second essay, on infantile sexuality, was the most revolutionary. When Freud said that the neurotic has difficulty with sexual needs, he meant that this difficulty began with the child's confrontation with sexual feelings in the first five years of life. Freud's basic claim was that children have sexual feelings. This shocked the Victorians, who looked on childhood as a time free of sexual demands, a view Freud himself had echoed at one point in *The Interpretation of Dreams.*

Freud, however, believed that the child's sexual feelings are different from the adult's in that they are egocentric, or to use his term, a child is *narcissistic.* Children primarily get pleasure from the several *erotogenic zones* distributed about the human body: the mouth, the anus, and the genitals—although Freud believed the entire skin surface could be erotogenic. Pleasure from self-manipulation is narcissistic because the child chooses no other person as the object of desires but gives self-pleasure, as in masturbation or thumb-sucking. Nevertheless, these power-ful feelings should later play their part in foreplay as part of adult, other-directed sexuality. The way in which the child and the parents handle these feelings early on has much to do with adult personality.

Why, Freud asked, do we usually have so little memory of our infantile sexual feelings, or indeed of any experiences before we are about six years old? Freud said that early sexual desires are strongly inhibited, or repressed, so that we do not recall them. This repression is so strong that it spreads to all early experiences and brings on a period of sexual latency, during which sexual desires are dormant, to be later activated at puberty. Freud put great value on this *primal repression* and the ensuing period of latency, for he believed them to be essential to civilization. He was, however, rather obscure as to the reason for the first repression. Although he did not deny that the most obvious source—a culture's moral teachings—may play a role, he seems to have put most emphasis on inherited "disgust" at "perverse" sexual activities and went so far as to claim that many moral taboos are inherited. Freud maintained this position throughout his life, but it was vehemently rejected by almost every later thinker, in or out of the psychoanalytic school.

We also find in the central essay Freud's most notorious error, the concept of *penis envy* and the related *castration complex.* Freud believed that children are curious about the facts of sex and form many peculiar theories as a result of their researches—Victorian parents being loathe to reveal the truth. According to Freud, the most significant of these childish ideas is that girls are castrated boys. In boys this theory leads to fear of castration as a punishment for Oedipal desires and helps bring on latency. Girls, however, are overcome by desire for a penis and wish to be boys themselves. Research has not supported the universality of these notions. It is an interesting example of Freud's Victorianism, for it was then a common belief that women had hidden penises and ejaculated like men. As a physician Freud knew better, but his own male Victorian valuation of the penis caused him to view female clitoral orgasm as just childish imitations of male orgasm. He believed women should put away their hopeless emulation and locate their sexual feelings in their vaginas.

In the last essay, Freud turned to adult sexuality, which begins in puberty when maturational changes reawaken and transmute the dormant sexual instincts. At this time in the healthy person, sexual desire is directed to another person of the opposite sex, and reproductive genital intercourse becomes the goal; the instincts of childhood sexuality now serve genital drives through the kissing and caressing of foreplay that create the arousal necessary to actual coitus. In perverse individuals the pleasure associated with some infantile instinct is great enough to replace genital activity altogether. The neurotic is overcome by adult sexual demands and converts his sexual needs into symptoms.

In 1915 Freud introduced an important theoretical concept, *libido*. He believed that all behavior must be motivated by some instinct, and before 1920 he thought that the most important of these was the sexual instinct—which produces a form of mental energy called *libido*. Libido cannot be destroyed but can only be expressed directly in sexual behavior, or repressed, or indirectly expressed (*displaced*) as a dream, a neurotic symptom, or some other nonsexual behavior. The concept of libido and its displacement allowed Freud to retain the simple tension-reduction model of motivation formulated as early as the *Project,* while being able to explain almost any behavior as an outgrowth of the sexual impulses. It was the libido theory that led critics to assert that Freud saw sex everywhere.

At various places in the *Three Essays*, but especially in the conclusion, Freud introduced a concept that was central to the analysis of culture that occupied his later years. This was the concept of *sublimation,* the most important form of displacement. We may express our sexual desires directly; we may repress them, in which case they may find expression in dreams or neurotic symptoms; or we may employ sexual energy to motivate higher cultural activities, such as art, science, and philosophy. This last process is sublimation, and it diverts animalistic drives to the service of civilization. In the *Three Essays* Freud only discussed sublimation as an option for a person with a constitutionally strong sexual disposition, but in his later works the alternatives of satisfying direct sexual expression, on the one hand, and repression, sublimation, and consequent residual tension on the other, were to pose a dilemma for Freud and—as he saw it—for civilization itself.

Throughout the *Three Essays* only one human drive, sex, is discussed, and it is assigned the central role in determining behavior. However, Freud became dissatisfied with this formulation and began to feel that some other drive was present in humanity besides sex and its associated pleasure principle (the tendency to seek pleasure and avoid pain). His doubts grew and in 1920 crystallized in the aptly named *Beyond the Pleasure Principle.*

*Beyond the Pleasure Principle (1920)*

Freud always represented mental life as a field of battle. Conflict between unacceptable memories or drives, and the ego (or self) produces neurotic symptoms or dreams. This conflict arises from people's incompatible instinctual needs. In his earliest formulation Freud distinguished between sexual impulses unacceptable to the ego and the ego's own instincts for self-preservation. In this approach, ego-instincts provide the ego with energy to repress sexual instincts.

Freud altered his view on the nature of instinctual conflict without ever abandoning the thesis of conflict itself. As he pointed out many times, the theory of instincts and their conflicts was the essence of psychoanalysis. In *Beyond the Pleasure Principle* Freud put forward his final views on instinctual conflict.

Freud pictured the instincts as basically conservative. Their goal is always the restoration of some earlier state of affairs—the reduction of tension to a tension-free state, a view that goes back to the *Project*. In the development of life, the starting point was inorganic matter. Thus the ultimate possible "earlier state of affairs" for a living creature is the non-living state, or as Freud starkly stated: *"The aim of all life is death."* There are thus instincts within each being whose aim is death, the return to non-living, inorganic matter and the *dissolution* of life. Freud called these the *death instincts*.

The sexual instincts, on the other hand, aim at the reproduction and the continuation of life, and Freud argued that in addition they tend to keep the organism whole and functional. Freud now wrote of an expanded sexual instinct, *eros*, the preserver of life, or the life instincts. In this new account of our mental life, conflict arises out of the struggle within each person between the forces of life and death, on seeking a "return" to death, the other seeking longevity and immortality in our offspring.

In *Beyond the Pleasure Principle*, Freud raised an issue that has been debated again in recent years: the origin of human aggression. He traced sexual aggression and sadism to displacements of the death instincts, and in *The Ego and the Id* he stated that all forms of aggression have the same origins. Aggression, then, is an inherent part of human nature. This pessimistic belief is typical of Freud, and it is found, although in a different form, in several modern thinkers, particularly some ethologists such as Konrad Lorenz. Many others, for example the anthropologist M. F. Ashley Montague, share Freud's earlier view that aggression is a perversion of a loving and life-preserving human nature. Thus the debate between the early and late Freud is still with us.

In addition to his revisions of the instinct theory, Freud modified his concepts of the conscious and the unconscious in *Beyond the Pleasure Principle*. Heretofore, the repressing agency, the ego, had been loosely equated with consciousness. Unconscious impulses were unacceptable to consciousness, the ego, and so it repressed them. Now, however, Freud remarked that much of the ego is unconscious. This heralds Freud's complete reexamination of his theory of the unconscious and the conscious and his presentation of an entirely new map of the mind. This change occupied Freud's last major theoretical work, which gave final shape to the mind as seen by Freud.

### The Ego and the Id (1923)

The unconscious is by its very nature unobservable and in consequence presents problems for any science. The terms *unconsciousness* and *unconscious* may be used in three different senses, which Freud disentangles and reformulates in *The Ego and the Id,* a further development of *Beyond the Pleasure Principle.*

Two senses of "unconscious" have already been distinguished, the *descriptive* and the *dynamic*. We can describe as unconscious any idea or sensation of which we are not aware (as did Leibniz, Herbart, or Fechner). What was of greater importance for Freud was the body of ideas or desires that are unconscious because they are repressed; these are dynamically unconscious. They are unconscious because we have a positive aversion to them, not just because they are too weak to cross the threshold of consciousness; indeed, they are powerful, threatening ideas. Reflecting this distinction, Freud distinguished the preconscious, containing ideas readily accessible to consciousness, but not now conscious, from the unconscious, the dynamic unconscious. The distinction was present from Freud's earliest work.

All along, however, Freud tended to use unconscious in a more theoretical sense, designating an active mental system in opposition to the system of consciousness. It is this *systematic* notion of the unconscious that comes to the fore in this work as the *id*, and Freud herein remarks that the old conscious/unconscious dichotomy "begins to lose significance." On the remains of the old system of unconscious-preconscious-conscious, Freud now builds a new system of id-ego-superego.

The primal system is the *id*, wholly unconscious, irrational, home of the pleasure principle and the great reservoir of instinctual energy. During the early months of a child's life the id directs energy at (*cathects*) objects in the environment, especially the parents, particularly the mother. Because the child thus gets to know these objects, they are incorporated into the child's personality and form the nucleus of the ego, the representative of mental life. The *ego* is rational and follows the reality principle, withholding tension reduction until pleasure is realistically attainable. The ego's energy, with which it manages the id and conducts rational thought, is derived from the id. The ego identifies with, and so tries to be like, the objects the id has chosen for libidinal cathexis, the parents. By becoming like the id, the ego itself is cathected by the id, and so it gains energy from the id. Freud calls this state *narcissism,* love of self or ego. It is important to the growth of a healthy personality, for the ego must become strong in order to control the other two systems, to adapt to reality, and to engage in science, art, philosophy, and humanity's other civilized pursuits.

One component of personality remains to be developed; the *superego*, or the inner moral agency. It is formed during the Oedipal period when the child must renounce desire for the cross-sex parent under moral strictures laid down by the parents, especially the father. The fear and rivalry felt by the child creates a new kind of identification with the parents that is moral in nature: the child accepts moral rules enunciated by the parents. These rules now act as an ideal by which the ego is expected to conduct itself, and repression is carried out by the ego at the behest of the superego. Repression sets the stage for neurosis, dreams, slips of the tongue, and other evidences of our unconscious mental life. The Oedipus complex is part of what is repressed, and consequently the superego is itself unconscious. It is also irrational, like the id, except that it is irrational in its moral rather than in its instinctual demands.

In another way, too, the superego is more like the id than the ego, for part of it is innate. This aspect of the superego reveals a Lamarckian side of Freuds' thought. It is one of Freud's more controversial beliefs that experience could become part of one's "archaic heritage" inherited through the genes. Wrote Freud: "Thus, in the id, which is capable of being inherited, are harbored residues of the existence of countless egos; and, when the ego forms the superego out of the id, it may perhaps only be reviving shapes of former egos and bringing them to resurrection." The superego is, then, the internal voice not only of the parents but of ancient moral experiences as well.

It is the interaction of these three systems, whose relations can become complex indeed, that gives rise to conscious mental life and behavior. The id desires and commands the ego to satisfy it; the superego prohibits and commands the ego to repress the id; the ego must compromise these sets of command and also attend to the world and execute realistic actions. Should it fail in its task, mental illness ensues, and psychoanalytic therapy must teach the ego to conquer the id.

A final topic, sublimation, also occupied Freud's attention in *The Ego and the Id*. Sublimation is the conversion of sexual libido into neutral mental energy and is carried out by the child's narcissism. This unbound energy allows the ego to function, but it is an energy that serves both eros and the death instincts. On the one hand, the ego is adaptive and hence enables the person to live; but on the other hand it opposes the id's pleasure principle, as do the death instincts. Thus a dilemma is raised for civilization. Civilized life makes increasing demands on the ego to control the immoral id, and to pursue civilized activities rather than simple animal pleasures. Yet such demands aid death and oppose pleasures, making happiness harder to achieve. The problem of civilization occupied Freud more and more as the years went by and he no longer had to establish psychoanalysis as a movement. In the next two works, Freud analyzed religion, a major carrier of moral demands, and this analysis carried him on to civilization itself.

### The Problem of Civilization

**The Future of an Illusion (1927).** The nineteenth century appears to us to be a religiously secure age. In public, people professed strong belief in religion, holding it to be the bulwark of civilization. However, in private these same believers were often tormented by grave doubts about the validity of what they professed.

They wanted to believe, they tried to believe, they yearned for the simple untroubled faith of their childhoods—but the doubts remained. Doubt was especially frightening precisely because it appeared to be a crack in the bulwark of civilization.

Freud, however, had no doubts; *The Future of an Illusion* is Freud's most polemical and assured work. He said simply that religion *is* an illusion, a massive attempt at wish-fulfillment. Religion is based on nothing more than our infantile feelings of helplessness and the consequent desire to be protected by an all-powerful parent who becomes God. Moreover, to Freud religion is a dangerous illusion, for its dogmatic teachings stunt the intellect, keeping mankind in a childish state. Religion is something to be outgrown as humans develop scientific resources and can stand on their own. The secret religious doubters are people who have outgrown religion but do not know it, and it was to them Freud addressed his work. His goal was, as ever, to assert the "primacy of the intellect" over infantile wishes and emotional needs.

Before turning to religion, Freud made some startlingly pessimistic statements that he took up in *Civilization and Its Discontents,* companion to *Future of an Illusion.* He wrote: "Every individual is virtually an enemy of civilization . . ." and people "feel as a heavy burden the sacrifices which civilization expects of them to make a communal life possible." In a phrase, the topic of *Civilization and its Discontents* is the unhappiness of civilized man.

**Civilization and its Discontents (1930).**    Wrote Freud: "The sense of guilt [is] the most important problem in the development of civilization and . . . the price we pay for our advance in civilization is a loss of happiness through the heightening of a sense of guilt." Each person seeks happiness, and according to Freud the strongest feelings of happiness come from direct satisfaction of our instinctual, especially sexual, desires. Civilization, however, demands that we renounce to large degree such direct gratification and substitute cultural activities in their stead. Such sublimated drives provide us less pleasure than direct gratification. To add to our discontents we also internalize the demands of civilization as harsh superegos, burdening us with guilt for immoral thoughts as well as deeds. Civilized man is consequently less happy than his primitive counterpart, and as civilization grows, happiness diminishes.

On the other hand, civilization has its rewards, and is necessary to human social life. Along with Hobbes, Freud feared that without a means of restraining aggression, society would dissolve into a war of all against all. Civilization is therefore necessary for the survival of all but the strongest, and at least partly serves eros. Moreover, in return for repression, civilization gives us not only security but also art, science, philosophy, and a more comfortable life through technology.

Civilization thus presents a dilemma from which Freud saw no way out. On the one hand civilization is the protector and benefactor of mankind. On the other hand, it demands unhappiness and even neurosis as payment for its benefactions. Near the end of the book, Freud hinted that civilizations may vary in the degree of unhappiness they produce—a question he left for others to consider.

This question has been taken up by many recent thinkers, for *Civilization and its Discontents* has proven to be one of Freud's most provocative works. Some writers, such as Erich Fromm, have argued that Western civilization is neurotic and they anoint some utopia as man's savior, as Fromm does socialism. Others, such as Norman O. Brown, believe the only way out of Freud's dilemma is renunciation of civilization itself and a return to the simple physical pleasures of childhood. Whatever the validity of these claims, Freud's dilemma remains and is acutely felt today when the rebellion against inhibition and guilt that Freud saw beginning in his own time has achieved such large dimensions.


## CONCLUSIONS

### Conceptual Summary: The Freudian Paradigm

A good way to explore the psychoanalytic paradigm is to compare it with Wundt's Ganzheit psychology. We have already noted a number of obvious differences, so we will first look at the similarities.

At the metapsychological level Freud and Wundt agree on the nature of psychological explanation. Wundt held that psychology could not predict a mental event, only explain it after its occurrence. Freud wrote in "The Psychogenesis of a Case of Homosexuality in a Woman": "So long as we trace the development from its final outcome backward . . . we feel we have gained an insight which is completely satisfactory. . . . But if we . . . start from the premises . . . and try to follow these up to the final result, then we no longer get the impression of an inevitable sequence of events which could not have been otherwise determined . . . [T]here might have been another result . . ." equally explicable by psychoanalysis. To both Wundt and Freud, psychology was more like history than physics—it would explain but not predict. Freud himself drew an analogy to archeology, his passionate avocation. Just as the archeologist gradually strips away layers of debris and uncovers strata after strata of human remains, so the psychoanalyst picks through the human mind to its deepest layers. No prediction is possible, for in both cases we start with the present and go backwards through material long since laid down. The psychoanalyst and archeologist can only explain where we have been, not where we are going.

Also, at the metapsychological level, Freud and Wundt agree broadly that the subject matter of psychology is the adult human mind, which should be investigated through introspection. Both were committed to mentalistic psychology and found behaviorism too restrictive, or even not psychological at all. Both used introspection as the primary research tool, although their exact methods differed. Wundt's introspection was controlled, descriptive, and superficial, while Freud used a free association technique that called for the client to let his or her mind wander from idea to idea, ultimately to penetrate the unconscious. Freud did analyze external manifestations of mind such as dreams, slips of the tongues, and symptoms, but always as a jumping-off point for free association. Neither Freud nor Wundt studied children; each believed their techniques of self-observation were inappropriate for children.

The final metapsychological similarity concerns *Völkerpsychologie*. Although Freud had no formal program of cultural and historical analysis, he agreed with Wundt that the modern mind is heir to a long development that it can never understand through introspection alone; congruent with this idea, both accepted the Lamarckian theory of the inheritance of acquired characteristics. Just as Wundt supplemented "physiological" psychology with *Völkerpsychologie*, Freud supplemented analysis of clinical case material with cultural analysis and speculative historical studies.

Conceptual similarities between Wundt and Freud may be quickly summarized. Both believed that mental life was deterministic. Freud was even more committed to meaningful determinism than was Wundt. Wundt found no meaning in dreams while Freud found meaning in all products of mental life, including dreams and mistaken acts. Such determinism does not contradict their belief that psychology cannot predict behavior. Freud and Wundt held that we must wait for determined events to occur before we can explain them. Although Wundt went beyond it, he recognized the role of association in human thought. Freud emphasized association much more strongly, using free association as his main tool. According to Freud, idea leads to idea, ultimately taking therapist and patient to the center of the patient's problem. Freud viewed the mind as a large associative net, but realized that the ego is not a passive victim of fortuitous association. Thinking, for Freud, was the ego directing mental energy along certain associative pathways whose viability as plans for behavior it assessed.

The differences between psychoanalysis and Ganzheit psychology are obvious and have been touched on already. Beginning with metapsychology, the most obvious difference is in the problems Wundt and Freud chose to consider. Wundt was a cognitive psychologist, little concerned with human motives. Although Freud's unpublished *Project* contains the beginnings of a cognitive psychology, Freud chose to devote his life instead to the study of the instincts. Although Freud recognized the need for an ego psychology, he believed it could not be worked out before the instincts were understood. One of the major themes of neo-Freudian psychoanalysis has been the development of theories of ego, or cognitive, functioning. In method, although both Freud and Wundt used introspection, Wundt used it descriptively in an experimental setting while Freud used it in the less controlled clinical setting for deeper exploration of the mind.

Given the different problems Wundt and Freud set themselves, it is not surprising to find that when we turn to technical concepts, psychoanalysis and Ganzheit psychology make little contact with one another. Id, superego, and libido have no place in Wundt's system, as apperception or assimilation have no place in Freud's.

There was always disagreement over the unconscious, as we have seen. Both sides accused the other of making a metaphysical assumption in positing or denying an unconscious. This difference is profound, for each psychology is shaped by its assumption about unconsciousness. Where Freud saw a conflict-ridden mind driven by dark forces largely beyond its conscious control, Wundt saw an entirely conscious mind engaging in orderly conscious activities. For Freud the mind is an almost unfathomable mystery, while for Wundt the surface is all that matters, for below consciousness is only physiology, not an autonomous unconscious. There are many similarities between the two systems, but no one could ever mistake the one for the other; one is a study of consciousness, the other of unconsciousness.

If we place the two paradigms side by side, we find that in large measure they are complementary in metapsychology, method, and concepts. Freud touches us more deeply because he tells us about the most personal part of our lives, while Wundt's dry academic psychology sticks to what we think we know best, our consciousness. Freud, for all his roots in the Victorian past, remains a contemporary, for the problem of our times, after two world wars, after the Jewish holocaust and My Lai, remains the conquest of the dark side of the soul. Wundt, for all his affinities to modern cognitive psychology, remains anchored in the past. The Mandarin culture he accepted, rejected by Freud, seems today at best quaint, at worst insensitive and dehumanizing.

## Historical Trends

### Freud and Psychoanalysis

Freud did not lack followers—disciples in his own time and apostles after his death. He succeeded in founding a self-conscious psychological and psychotherapeutic movement that lives today in psychoanalytic associations and psychoanalytic journals that have never merged with general psychological associations and publications.

Freud kept psychoanalysis close to his concepts while he lived. He had a firm idea of what normal-science psychoanalytic research and theory should look like, and in true Kuhnian fashion (although Freud's model was Moses) he was intolerant of any analyst who violated the paradigm. However, original minds were attracted to psychoanalysis, and original minds challenge established concepts. Freud valued intelligence, and consequently a series of bright people were welcomed to psychoanalysis only to be expelled later on.

As a result, even during Freud's lifetime psychoanalysis experienced schism after schism. Beginning with Alfred Adler (1870-1936) various analysts broke with Freud or were expelled from psychoanalytic circles because of disagreement with the master. The loss Freud felt most deeply was that of Carl Gustav Jung (1875-1961), who rejected Freud's insistence on the primacy of the sexual instinct. Freud prized Jung's discipleship, for he was an established psychiatrist and a gentile, which meant that Jung's arrival was the first sign of recognition from the medical establishment and the non-Jewish world. Freud valued his own Jewishness, and most of the early analysts were Jewish, but Freud wanted his movement to escape the stigma of being an exclusively Jewish science. So Jung was welcomed, at least by

Freud, with open arms and became something of a Crown Prince to Freud's patriarchal father-figure. There were neurotic elements in their relationship, at least on Freud's side. Once, for example, Freud fainted when Jung challenged him on a scientific point. Such challenges were inevitable since Jung had his own ideas about the mind even before joining Freud. For a time Jung was groomed to succeed Freud, but in the end he too had to leave Freud's circle to found his own school, analytic psychology.

Psychotherapy had existed before Freud and after his time the number of therapies multiplied greatly. Many of these new movements, like Adler's individual psychology and Jung's analytic psychology, grew out of psychoanalysis; others arose in opposition to it. Today the number of therapies available to the neurotic, or even to the healthy seeker after self-improvement, is bewilderingly large but still includes orthodox psychoanalysis. Each therapy has its own concepts and methods but few have had significant impact on Western culture or on the human goal of scientific self-understanding, even if they have improved individual lives. We will therefore have little to say about these therapies in future chapters. It should be remembered, however, when we discuss the behaviorist revolution and its dominance of academic psychology, that outside the academy there existed and exists a large, independent movement committed to mentalistic psychology.

### The Reception of Psychoanalysis

Freud liked to measure the worth of his ideas against the resistance they met in the outside world. He reasoned that if resistance hides truth in the neurotic, so it must in society at large. Freud was, therefore, in the interesting position of being able to count as evidence for his concepts their rejection by others. Freud liked to see himself as a lone battler against a hostile world, and Freud's self-image, embodied in friendly biographies, has been widely accepted.

However, recent research has shown that the reaction to psychoanalysis was not uniformly hostile. We must look at two levels of reception, among psychological professionals and among popular writers and the press. At the professional level Freud's theory received a mixed response (Cioffi, 1973). Some writers were horrified, especially at the emphasis on sex. One review of the *Three Essays* called it "pornography gone to seed," while a well-known American psychiatrist whom Freud respected, burned a book of Freud's because it was "filthy." On the other hand, when *Studies in Hysteria* was reviewed by *Brain*, it was seen as nothing new, only the reviving of the old theory of the origin of hysteria in sexual disorders. A distinguished biologist, W. M. Wheeler, compared psychoanalysis favorably to academic psychology on the grounds that it recognized our animal inheritance.

At the popular level, Freud's works were well received, although it was sometimes complained that Freud said nothing poets had not said better. This evaluation Freud would have at least partly accepted. *The Interpretation of Dreams* received almost unanimous praise in the German popular press. Freud's visit to America received favorable coverage in the newspapers. New York society women, who had 500 analysts to choose from by 1916, found psychoanalysis an interesting diversion: "It became an absorbing game to play with oneself, reading one's motives, trying to understand the symbols by which the soul expresses itself" (Cioffi, 1973).

The two levels of response to Freud accounts for the peculiar fact that psychoanalysis has had much more impact on general cultural values and beliefs than on mainstream academic psychology. Since its appearance, psychoanalysis has been subjected to relentless criticism by academic psychology—when it has not been altogether ignored. Behaviorism, the dominant psychological movement since the 1920s has had little use for Freud's mentalistic system. Aside from a brief attempt in the 1940s and early 1950s by some Neobehaviorists to behaviorize psychoanalysis, Freud's theories have been either dismissed as a myth or attacked as a failure.

At the popular level, however, few thinkers have had as much influence on modern Western civilization as Sigmund Freud. The common man's intuitive psychology and childrearing methods would today be very different had there been no psychoanalysis. This is entirely consistent with Freud's own character. He viewed himself not as a genius or even a scientist, but as a conquerer, overcoming cultural resistance to his profound insights. He sought less to persuade the world than to take it by storm. He failed to persuade the professional scientific psychologist, but he did conquer the popular mind.

When Freud's concepts are discussed today, they may be called "wrong," but it is a measure of his enduring influence that his "wrong" ideas must be discussed at all. Freud's scientific hypotheses have not always fared well at the hands of researchers. It is therefore best to see Freud not as a doctor, or a scientist, but ultimately as a philosopher, forced into medicine against his will. As a philosopher he is a modern Stoic, a man who could remain calm in the face of the irrational— confident that a rational order could be found. His commitment to determinism was less a faith in efficient neural causation than a faith in the *Logos* of the universe. Like the Stoics, Freud bids us to abandon repressive civilization not to surrender to the simple joys of the id, but rather to substitute rational self-control for unconscious repression. Freud asks us to face the unconscious in order to conquer it in the name of reason.

## SUGGESTED READINGS

The standard, "orthodox" biography is Ernest Jones' *The Life and Work of Sigmund Freud*, in three volumes, now available in a one-volume abridgement (Basic Books, 1961). A more recent, broad and critical study is Paul Roazen, *Freud and His Followers* (Meridian, 1976). An excellent study of Freud in the context of Western culture and civilization is Philip Rieff, *Freud: Mind of a Moralist* (Anchor Books, 1961).

# REFERENCES

Cioffi, F. Wollheim on Freud. *Inquiry,* 1972, *15,* 172-186.

Cioffi, F. Introduction. In F. Cioffi (Ed.) *Freud: Modern judgments.* London: Macmillan, 1973.

Cioffi, F. Was Freud a Liar? British Broadcasting Corporation Radio 3, no date.

Freud, E. (Ed.) *The letters of Sigmund Freud.* New York: Basic Books, 1960.

Freud, S. Project for a scientific psychology. In *Standard edition of the complete psychological works of Sigmund Freud* (Vol. I). London: Hogarth Press, 1950.

Freud, S. The psychogenesis of a case of homosexuality in a woman. *Collected Papers* (Vol. 2). London: The Hogarth Press, 1953.

Freud, S. *The ego and the id.* New York: Norton, 1960.

Freud, S. *Beyond the pleasure principle.* New York: Norton, 1961a.

Freud, S. *The future of an illusion.* New York: Norton, 1961b.

Freud, S. *Civilization and its discontents.* New York: Norton, 1961c.

Freud, S. *Three essays on the theory of sexuality.* New York: Avon, 1962.

Freud, S. *The interpretation of dreams.* New York: Avon, 1965.

Freud, S. & Breuer, J. *Studies in hysteria.* New York: Avon, 1966.

Houghton, W. E. *The Victorian frame of mind.* New Haven, Conn.: Yale University Press, 1957.

Plumb, J. H. The Victorians unbuttoned. In *In the light of history.* New York: Delta/Dell, 1972.

# 9

# The Psychology
of Adaptation

The last founding psychology we will examine has proved the most valuable and influential in academic psychology. Wundt's psychology of consciousness was an anachronistic product of nineteenth-century German thought, and it survived neither transplantation to other countries nor the destruction of its intellectual ecology by the Nazis and World War II. The same is largely true of Gestalt psychology. Psychoanalysis is a living tradition, having adapted to conditions outside nineteenth-century Vienna, and its influence on modern culture has been greater than that of any other psychology. Nevertheless, psychoanalysis remains primarily a branch of medical psychiatry, and its relations with academic psychology have been ambivalent from Freud's time to our own.

The approach that academic psychologists—first in England and later in America—have found most attractive and useful is a psychology based on evolution, Lamarckian or Darwinian. With the ascendance of American psychology in the twentieth century, the psychology of adaptation in one form or another has dominated academic psychology. It has proved able to produce many conceptual variants, although its ability to select among them has often faltered.

Ignoring for the moment the differences between theories, any theory of evolution raises two questions that can engender psychological research programs. The first we may call the *species question*. If the body and brain are products of organic evolution, then we may ask in what ways this inheritance shapes the thought and behavior of organisms. This question leads to comparative psychology, which studies species differences in mental and behavioral capacities—differences presumably created by evolution. The second psychological question raised by evolution we may call the *individual question.* As the individual creature grows up it can be seen as adapting psychologically to the environment in a way analogous to organic evolution. This question leads to the study of learning, research designed to uncover how the individual adjusts to the environment.

The species question and the individual question are interrelated. If species differences are great, then different psychologies of individual adaptation will be needed for different species. If, on the other hand, species differences are small, then the same laws of individual learning will apply to all individuals, regardless of species. In this chapter we will trace the development of the psychology of adaptation and will soon discover that its proponents adopt the latter line of thought. Gall's phrenology had implied a comparative psychology that looked for species differences in the possession of mental faculties. To a phrenologist, structural differences in the brain meant structural differences in mind. However, by the middle of the nineteenth century the sensorimotor concept of the brain had vanquished phrenology among scientists, while associationism was displacing faculty psychology among philosopher-psychologists. The view of the brain as an intially formless associative machine, and the view of the mind as a *tabula rasa* awaiting associations, will combine to cause psychologists to focus on the individual question and minimize species differences.

# THE BEGINNINGS OF THE
# PSYCHOLOGY OF ADAPTATION IN BRITAIN

## Lamarckian Psychology: Herbert Spencer (1820-1903)

In the summer of 1854 Herbert Spencer began to write a psychology whose "lines of thought had scarcely anything in common with lines of thought previously pursued" (Spencer, 1904). His work appeared the following year, 1855, as *Principles of Psychology*. This book gives Spencer a good claim to be the founder of the psychology of adaptation. Bain had integrated associationism and the sensorimotor conception of brain function, but, although he acknowledged the validity of Darwinian evolution, his psychology remained part of classical, pre-evolutionary associationism. Writing before Darwin, Spencer integrated not only associationism and sensorimotor physiology, but also Lamarckian evolution. Consequently, he anticipated the psychology of adaptation. Furthermore, not only did he raise the two evolutionary questions, but he also answered them in the ways basic to Anglo-American psychology ever since.

Spencer's *Principles of Psychology* was just one part of his all-embracing *synthetic philosophy*. Spencer was the greatest systematizer since Aquinas, although Spencer thought of himself as the new Newton. Another, lengthier, part of his system was the *Principles of Sociology*, and Spencer is regarded as a founder of that field, too. Aquinas organized all philosophy around the Christian God. Spencer organized it around Lamarckian evolution, in which he believed as early as 1852. He referred all questions, metaphysical or otherwise, to the principle of evolution and presented it as a cosmic process, embracing not only organic evolution but also the evolution of mind and societies.

In 1854, Spencer wrote: "If the doctrine of Evolution is true, the inevitable implication is that Mind can be understood only by observing how Mind is evolved." Here is the starting point of the psychology of adaptation. Spencer proceeded to discuss both the evolutionary psychological questions. Considering the individual, Spencer viewed development as a process by which the connections between ideas come to mirror accurately the connections between events prevailing in the environment. The connections between ideas are built up by contiguity. Wrote Spencer (1897): "The growth of intelligence at large depends upon the law, that when any two psychical states occur in immediate succession, an effect is produced such that if the first subsequently recurs there is a certain tendency for the second to follow it." This tendency is strengthened as ideas are more frequently associated together. Like Bain, Spencer attempted to "deduce" the laws of mental association from the sensorimotor constitution of the nervous system and brain. In general, then, Spencer's analysis of the individual mind is that of atomistic associationism. He carried out the "successive decomposition of the more complex phenomena of intelligence into simpler ones ... down to the simplest ... element." What Spencer adds to Bain is the evolutionary conception, viewing the development of the mind as an adaptive adjustment to environmental conditions.

Spencer's conception of the nervous system is clearly empiricistic, the brain being pictured as a sensorimotor associational device. Spencer (1897) stated that "the human brain is an organized register of infinitely numerous experiences." This empiricism has two important consequences. Given the Lamarckian idea of the heritability of acquired characteristics, instinct can be made acceptable to the associationist and empiricist. Following the passage just quoted, Spencer described how the brain accumulates experiences "during the evolution of that series of organisms through which the human organism has been reached." Thus, innate reflexes and instincts are simply associative habits so well learned they became part of a species' genetic legacy. Such habits may not be acquired during an individual's life, but they are still acquired following the laws of association in the life of the species. Innate ideas need no longer terrify the empiricist.

The second consequence of Spencer's integration of evolution and the sensorimotor concept of nervous function is more portentous: Differences in the mental processes of different species reduce to the number of associations the brains are able to make. All brains work the same way, by association, and differ only quantitatively in the richness of their associations. As Spencer (1897) put it, "The impressions received by inferior intelligences, even down to the very lowest, are dealt with after a like model." Thus, his answer to the species question is to deny qualitative differences between species and admit only quantitative, associational differences. This idea extends to differences within, as well as between, species; the "European inherits from twenty to thirty cubic inches more brain than the Papuan," he said. This implies that the "civilized man has also a more complex or heterogeneous nervous system than the uncivilized man," as he wrote in *First Principles*.

Spencer's conclusions are of tremendous importance for the development of the psychology of adaptation. Given his framework, comparative psychology would be directed toward studying species differences in simple associative learning, studies aimed at quantifying a single dimension of "intelligence" along which species can be arranged. Moreover, such studies could be performed in the laboratory, ignoring an organism's native environment. If the brain is no more than an initially empty stimulus-response associating mechanism, then it is irrelevant whether the associations are natural or contrived; in fact, the laboratory offers greater control of the process than naturalistic observation.

It also follows that, if all organisms learn the same way, then the results of studies of simple animal learning, with their precision, replicability, and rigor can be extended without serious modification to human learning. We will find that all of these conclusions are of fundamental importance to behaviorism, the twentieth-century psychology of adaptation. Behaviorists seek laws of learning valid for at least all mammals and assume the extension of animal findings to human psychology—often without supporting data. We will also find that behaviorism pays a high price for ignoring innate, qualitative differences between species and runs into special difficulty over the unique human characteristic: language.

Finally, the quantitative conception of associative mental function would help develop intelligence testing, which purports to assign a number to a person's intelligence. Although it is not demanded by the theory, the connection of associational ability with brain mass and complexity of association would push mental testing in a racist direction. We have already seen Spencer denegrate uncivilized man for having low brain mass and a simple nervous system, and in *First Principles* he implies that the "lower human races" are children: "In the infant European we see sundry resemblances to the lower human races." Such supposedly scientific views helped justify, though they did not solely cause, the "white man's burden" and the exclusion of "inferior races" from the poor, huddled masses admitted to the United States.

## Darwinian Psychology

Spencer's general principles, while inspired by Lamarck, are not inconsistent with Darwin's theory of natural selection. The only new assumption needed is that natural selection has produced the sensorimotor nervous system believed to exist in all animals, which justifies an associationist theory of mind, or later of behavior. Many naturalistic thinkers, including Darwin himself, consciously or unconsciously adhered to the Lamarckian view of progressive evolution, however, and sometimes even accepted the heritability of acquired characteristics. Thus Spencer's Lamarckian psychology shades insensibly into a Darwinian psychology.

### Darwin on Humans

The central challenge of Darwins' *Origin of Species* concerned what Huxley called man's place in nature. In the comprehensive, naturalistic scheme of evolution, humanity was made part of nature, no longer a being who transcended it. Everyone saw this implication immediately whether they agreed with it or not. Yet the *Origin* itself contains very little on human psychology. We know that in his early notebooks, dating back to the 1830s, Darwin was concerned with these topics, but he seems to have set them aside from his initial publication as too troublesome. All his life Darwin projected, but never completed, a master work on evolution in all its facets. In any event, it was not until 1871 that he finally published *The Descent of Man*, which brings human nature within the scope of natural selection.

Darwin's aim in *The Descent of Man* is to show that "man is descended from some lowly organized form," a conclusion that he regretted would "be highly distasteful to many." He broadly compared human and animal behavior and concluded that "the difference in mind between man and the higher animals, great as it is, is certainly one of degree and not of kind. We have seen that the senses and intuitions, the various emotions and faculties, such as love, memory, attention, curiosity, imitation, reason, etc., of which man boasts may be found in an incipient, or even sometimes in a well-developed condition, in lower animals." Even "[t]he ennobling belief in God is not universal with man."

The *Descent* is not primarily a work of psychology; it mainly attempts to incorporate humans fully into nature. Darwin felt that Spencer had already laid the foundations for an evolutionary psychology. Yet Darwin's work contrasts importantly with Spencer's *Principles*. Darwin followed philosophical faculty psychology, relegating association to a secondary factor in thought. Partly as a consequence, Darwin was concerned almost exclusively with the species question, for he assumed that evolution shaped the faculties. He also allowed great scope to the effects of heredity, sounding at times like an extreme nativist: Both virtue and crime may be heritable tendencies; woman is genetically inferior to man in "whatever he takes up." On the other hand, Darwin agreed with Spencer that the nature of species differences is quantitative rather than qualitative and that well-learned habits can become innate reflexes. Lamarckian psychology and Darwinian psychology differ only in emphasis, not in content. The major difference is that Darwin's psychology is only a part of a materialistic, evolutionary biology. Spencer's psychology, in contrast, was part of a grand metaphysics that tended toward dualism and postulated an "Unknowable" forever beyond the reach of science. Darwin sheared off this metaphysical growth from the psychology of adaptation.

### The Spirit of Darwinian Psychology: Sir Francis Galton (1822-1911)

Galton was the most outstanding of that distinct Victorian type, the gentleman dilettante. Independently wealthy, he was able to turn his inventive mind to whatever he chose. He traveled over most of Africa and wrote an unsurpassed manual for travelers in wild lands. He empirically investigated the efficacy of prayer. He pioneered the use of fingerprints for personal identification. He invented composite photographic portraiture. Many of his wide-ranging investigations were psychological or sociological. He once tried to understand paranoia by suspecting everyone he met of evil intentions. He canvassed the female beauty of Great Britain trying to ascertain which county had the most beautiful women in it. He measured boredom at scientific lectures. He applied anthromorphic tests to thousands of individuals visiting a fair in Kensington. However, Galton's researches were so eclectic that they do not add up to a research program. Consequently Galton cannot be considered a psychologist in the same sense as Wundt, Titchener, or Freud.

Nevertheless, Galton made important contributions to the growing psychology of adaptation. He broadened psychology to encompass topics excluded by Wundt. In his *Inquiries into the Human Faculty* (1883) he wrote: "No professor of . . . psychology . . . can claim to know the elements of what he teaches, unless he is acquainted with the ordinary phenomena of idiocy, madness, and epilepsy. He must study the manifestations of disease and congenital folly, as well as those of high intellect." Wundt wanted to understand only the normal, adult mind. Galton inquired into any human mind.

Galton devised a number of important methods used by the psychology of adaptation. He was the first to systematically apply statistics to psychological data, and he invented the correlation coefficient. He studied twins to sort out the contributions of nature and nurture to human character, intellect, and behavior. He tried to use indirect behavioral measures (rate of fidgeting) to measure a mental state (boredom). He invented the free association technique of interrogating memory. He used questionnaires to collect data on mental processes such as mental imagery. He tried to use a psycho-physical method (lifting weights) to measure acuteness of perception, and thus—he thought—intelligence. He tried to directly introspect his higher mental processes, which Wundt had said was impossible. All these techniques found a place in English and American psychology.

Spencer began the psychology of adaptation, but Galton epitomized it. His eclectic attitude concerning both method and subject matter, and his use of statistics, would strongly characterize Darwinian psychology from this point on. Above all, his interest in individual differences points to the future. In German rationalist fashion, Wundt had wanted to describe the transcendent human mind; he quite literally found the study of individual differences to be foreign. Galton, however, was interested in concrete individuals and in all those factors that make people different. The study of individual differences is an essential part of Darwinian science, for without variation there can be no differential selection and no evolutionary improvement of the species.

Improvement of the human species was precisely Galton's aim. Underlying his various investigations was not a research program but rather a social program that Galton (1907) called *eugenics*: "[T]his new animal man . . . ought, I submit, to awake to a fuller knowledge of his relatively great position, and begin to assume a deliberate part in furthering the great work of evolution." Galton saw this involvement as man's "religious duty." He was convinced that the most important individual differences, including those of morals, character, and intellect, are not acquired. His great aim was to demonstrate that these characteristics were innate and then to measure them so that they could inform the procreative behavior of mankind. Eugenics is the selective breeding of human beings to improve the species.

It was in his *Hereditary Genius* (1869) that Galton "propose[d] to show that a man's natural abilities are derived by inheritance, under exactly the same limitations as are the form and physical features of the whole organic world. Consequently, as it is easy, not withstanding these limitations, to obtain by careful selection a permanent breed of dogs or horses gifted with peculiar powers of running, or of doing anything else, so it would be quite practicable to produce a highly gifted race of men by judicious marriages during several consecutive generations." In this work Galton endeavored to show that abilities as different as those required to be a good judge or a good wrestler are innate and heritable, which would make a eugenics program feasible. Galton, like Darwin, was primarily interested in the species question. Galton, however, cared about the improvement of man and thought selective breeding would improve humanity faster than improved education.

This set of assumptions has a long and often ugly history in modern psychology. Galton's most devoted follower, Karl Pearson, who is usually remembered for perfecting Galton's statistical approach to psychology, was also active in the cause of eugenics. He believed, for instance, that tuberculosis was a hereditary disease and therefore was against curing the carriers who would only procreate and thus spread their diseased genes. He consequently opposed the Fight Against Tuberculosis movement in Great Britain. He also maintained that Jewish children were dirtier than Anglo-Saxon ones not because they lived in slums, but that they lived in slums because they were innately dirtier. These kinds of ideas did not disappear in recent times. In 1969, Arthur Jensen, a student of Sir Cyril Burt who furthered Galton's work, wrote a paper called "How much can we boost IQ and scholastic achievement?" in which he concludes, not much. He argues that blacks are, as Galton held, intellectually inferior to whites, and that this difference probably cannot be overcome by programs such as Head Start.* Jensen was followed by William Shockley, a Nobel prize-winning physicist, who advocated tax incentives for the intelligent to have children and for the stupid not to have children. This unfortunate racist, nativist approach to intelligence is also the legacy of Galton.

### The Rise of Comparative Psychology

It is clear that a psychology based on evolution should call forth research aimed at comparing the various abilities of different species of animals. Simple comparison of human and animal abilities goes back to Aristotle, and both Descartes and Hume buttressed their philosophies with such considerations. The Scottish faculty psychologists argued that humans' moral faculty distinguished them from animals. Galton studied animals and people to discover the special mental faculties of each species. The theory of evolution, however, gave comparative psychology a powerful impetus, placing it in a wider biological context and giving it a specific rationale. In the later nineteenth century comparative psychology grew in strength until in the twentieth-century behaviorists studied animals in preference to humans.

Modern comparative psychology may be said to have begun in 1872 with the publication of Darwin's *The Expression of the Emotions in Man and Animals*. The new approach is heralded by Darwin's statement early in the book: "No doubt as long as man and all other animals are viewed as independent creations, an effectual stop is put to our natural desire to investigate as far as possible the causes of Expression." However, he who admits "that the structure and habits of all animals have been gradually evolved, will look at the whole subject in a new and interesting light." In the rest of his book Darwin surveyed the means of emotional expression possessed by humans and animals, noting the continuity between them, and demonstrating their universality among the races of humanity. Darwin's theory is very Lamarckian, it may be noted: "Actions, which were at first voluntary, soon become habitual, and at last hereditary, and may then be performed even in opposition to the will." Darwin's theory was that our involuntary emotive expressions have gone through this development.

Darwin's early work in comparative psychology was systematically carried on by his friend George John Romanes (1848-1894). In *Animal Intelligence* (1883) Romanes surveyed the mental abilities of animals from protozoa to apes. In later

---

*Galton (1925) did concede that one race, the ancient Greeks, was superior to the British.

works such as *Mental Evolution in Man* (1889), Romanes attempted to trace the gradual evolution of mind down the millenia. Romanes died before he could complete his comparative psychology. His literary executor was C. Lloyd Morgan (1852-1936), who in his own *Introduction to Comparative Psychology* (1894) objected to Romanes' overestimation of animal intelligence. Romanes had quite freely attributed complex thinking to animals from analogy to his own thinking. Morgan, in formulating what has since been called *Morgan's canon*, argued that inferences of animal thinking should be no more than absolutely necessary to explain some observed behavior. The last British comparative psychologist was the philosopher Leonard T. Hobhouse (1864-1928), who used the data of comparative psychology to construct a general evolutionary metaphysics. He also carried out some experiments on animal behavior that in some respects anticipated Gestalt work on animal insight and that were designed to undermine the artificiality of behaviorist animal experiments.

These comparative psychologists combined faculty psychology with associationism in their theories of development and collected some interesting facts. The paradigm that informed their efforts was less important than their method, however. What Romanes consciously introduced to psychology was an objective, behavioral method in contrast to the subjective method of introspection since we cannot observe the minds of animals, only their behavior. Nevertheless, the theoretical goal of the British animal psychologists was never merely to describe behavior. Rather they wanted to explain the workings of animal minds, and therefore they attempted to infer mental processes from behavior. The problems involved in this research program importantly affect the development of behaviorism, which was founded by American comparative psychologists.

Methodologically, comparative psychology began with Romanes' *anecdotal method*. He collected vignettes of animal behavior from many correspondents and sifted through them for plausible and reliable information from which to reconstruct the animal mind. The anecdotal method became an object of derision among the experimentally oriented Americans, especially E. L. Thorndike. The method lacked the control available in the laboratory and was felt to overestimate animal intelligence. The anecdotal method did have the virtue, largely unappreciated at the time, of observing animals in natural, uncontrived situations. We will find that animal behaviorism runs into real difficulties in the 1960s because of its exclusive reliance on controlled laboratory methods that overlook the animals' ecological histories.

Theoretically, inferring mental processes from behavior presented difficulties. It is altogether too easy to attribute to animals complex mental processes they may not possess—any simple behavior can be explained (incorrectly) as the result of complex reasoning. Anyone who today reads Romanes' *Animal Intelligence* will feel that he frequently committed this error. Morgan's canon was an attempt to deal with this problem by requiring conservative inferences.

However, no matter how conservatively and carefully mind might be reconstructed from behavior, it remained possible for the skeptic to doubt. As Romanes

(1883) himself put it: "Skepticism of this kind is logically bound to deny evidence of mind, not only in the case of lower animals, but also in that of the higher, and even in that of men other than the skeptic himself. For all objections which could apply to the use of [inference] . . . would apply with equal force to the evidence of any mind other than that of the individual objector." Such skepticism constitutes the essence of the behaviorist revolution. The behaviorist may admit that she or he possesses consciousness, if not mind, but refuses to use mental activity to explain the behavior of animals, or of other human beings.

The psychology of adaptation began in England, where the modern theory of evolution was born. However, it found more fertile ground in one of Britain's former colonies: the United States. There, it became the only psychology, and as the United States came to dominate psychology, so did the psychology of adaptation.

## PSYCHOLOGY IN THE NEW WORLD

### Background

#### General Intellectual and Social Environment

America was new. Its original inhabitants were seen as savages, noble or brutish, who revealed man's original nature untouched by civilization. The original settlers confidently expected to displace the Indians, replacing their primitive state with farms, villages, and churches. The wilderness found by the settlers opened up possibilities of erecting a new civilization in the new world. The Puritans came to establish a "city on a hill," a perfect Christian society and example to be looked up to by the rest of the world. In America there was no feudal hierarchy, no established Church, no ancient universities. Instead, each person could make his or her own way in the wilderness.

This is not to say that the European settlers brought no intellectual baggage. They did, and two traditions are particularly important: evangelical religion and Enlightenment philosophy. America was initially settled by Protestants, not Catholics. In fact, when Catholics first came to America in large numbers they were forced to remain outside the mainstream of American life. Catholics were seen as agents of a dangerous foreign power, the Pope, and anti-Catholic riots and the burning of Catholic churches were not unknown in nineteenth-century America. What emerged most strongly from the dominant American Protestantism was evangelical Christianity. This form of Christianity has little or no theological content, looking instead to the salvation of the individual soul in an emotional conversion experience when the person accepts the will of God.

An important part of the European reaction to the excessive geometric spirit of the Enlightenment was romanticism. In America, however, the reaction against the Age of Reason was religious. America experienced revivals in the colonial period, and another took place shortly after the French Revolution. Romanticism touched

America only briefly, in the transcendental movement. Henry David Thoreau, for example, decried industry's encroachment on romantic nature. However, more important for most people was evangelical Christianity, which rejected the anti-religious skepticism of the Enlightenment.

It is no accident that many early American psychologists, including John B. Watson, the founder of behaviorism, were early intended for the church. The stock in trade of the evangelical preacher is conversion, playing on an audience's emotions to change people from sinners to saints, modifying both soul and behavior. The goal of many American psychologists in both the functionalist and behaviorist periods has been to modify behavior, to make the person of today into the new person of tomorrow. The evangelical preachers wrote about the ways to change souls through preaching; the psychologists wrote about the ways to change behavior through conditioning.

The importance of evangelical Christianity in the developing intellectual life of the United States should not be underestimated. America's tradition of freedom of religion may suggest that the founders did not care especially about religion. The contrary is true. Freedom of religion came into existence because of the demands of evangelical sects afraid of the power of established Churches. Evangelical Christianity acted as a filter for Enlightenment thought, keeping out the radical skepticism and anti-religious attitudes of the late Enlightenment that were unacceptable to most Americans.

In the period before 1800 America did possess some genuine philosophes. There was Benjamin Franklin, whose experiments on electricity were admired in Europe, who charmed France as the "natural man" of the new world, and who was enshrined as one of the leading figures of the Enlightenment, ranking even with Voltaire. Thomas Jefferson, another philosophe, is perhaps the best example of the geometric spirit in America. Jefferson attempted to apply numerical calculation to every subject from crop rotation to human happiness. His Newtonian mechanism even blinded him to biological facts: Arguing against the possibility of Noah's flood, he "proved" from physical calculations that in any flood the waters cannot rise more than about fifty feet above sea-level, and that consequently the fossil sea shells found in the American Appalachian mountains were just unusual rock growths (Wills, 1978). Jefferson, who was skeptical of the claims of Christianity, was probably a Voltairian deist.

Ideas such as these were anathema to evangelical religion, however, and only certain moderate elements of Enlightenment thought became important in America. Foremost among these acceptable ideas were those of the Scottish Enlightenment, which in fact exerted more influence on Jefferson than is commonly supposed. As we have seen, Reid's common-sense philosophy was perfectly compatible with religion. In America's religious colleges, which were the vast majority of American colleges, Scottish philosophy became the established curriculum, dominating every aspect of higher education from ethics to psychology. Scottish philosophy was American orthodoxy.

In considering the intellectual climate of the United States, to the influences of evangelical Christianity and a moderated Englightenment must be added a third element, business, which interacted with the other two in important ways. America came to be a nation of business unlike any other nation on earth. There was no feudal aristocracy, no established Church, and only a distant King. What remained was individual enterprise, and the individual's struggle to survive in confrontation with the wilderness and in competition with other businessmen. The business of America was indeed business.

Out of this unique American mix of ideas, combined with a growing national chauvinism, several important ideas emerged. One was the supreme value placed on useful knowledge. The Enlightenment certainly held that knowledge should serve human needs, should be practical rather than metaphysical. American Protestants came to think of inventions as glorifying the ingenuity of God in creating the clever human mind. *Technology* was an American word. An unfortunate consequence of this attitude was anti-intellectualism. Abstract science was scorned as something European and degenerate. What counted was practical accomplishment that at once enriched the businessman, revealed God's principles, and advanced the American dream. The businessman valued the same hard-headed "common sense" taught in the religious colleges. Common-sense philosophy told the ordinary person that his untutored ideas were basically right, which tended to increase American anti-intellectualism.

In "businessman" the word *man* ought to be stressed. It was the men who struggled for survival in the world of business and who valued clear-headed common sense and practical achievement. Feeling and sentiment were the special province of women, who in the nineteenth century were increasingly removed from the world of work, as such formerly domestic activities as baking, brewing, cheese making, spinning, and weaving became industrialized. This change left women with little economic importance, leaving only the realm of the emotions to female rule. In America, emotions were not romantically inspiring but were instead feminine and weak.

Americans also tended to be radical environmentalists, greatly preferring to believe that peoples' circumstances, not their genes were the primary cause of human characteristics and achievements. They believed that, contrary to the prejudices of Europeans, the American environment was the best in the world and would produce geniuses to surpass Newton. This belief reflects the empiricism of the Enlightenment and the flexible beliefs of the businessman. There would be no bounds on the perfectibility of humans in the new world, no bounds on the achievement of the free individual. Progress was the order of the day. There was even a cult of self-improvement from the early days of the American republic. In the 1830s there was a monthly magazine called *The Cultivator*, "designed to improve the soil and the mind." Not only could a man improve his farm business, but he could improve his mind as well. In fact, it was expected that the good Christian would be a successful businessman or farmer.

All these attitudes—religious, Enlightened, and commercial—are nicely epitomized in the American attitude to the machine: the product of human ingenuity, improver of the world, and enricher of its maker. The builder of a machine became Newton's God, and the machine was made divine by association with the celestial mechanism. A writer named John Pendleton Kennedy visited an early American factory and recorded his reactions (Miller, 1965):

> When I look upon this vast enginery, this infinite complication of wheels, this exquisitely delicate adjustment of parts, and this sure, steady and invariable result shown in the operation of the perfect machine . . . I am lost in admiration of the genius that masters the whole.

One observer of the early American scene recognized these American trends. Alexis de Tocqueville wrote in *Democracy in America* following his visit to America in 1831-1832: "The longer a nation is democratic, enlightened and free, the greater will be the number of these interested promoters of scientific genius, and the more will discoveries immediately applicable to productive industry confer gain, fame and even power." However, Tocqueville worried that "in a community thus organized . . . the human mind may be led insensibly to the neglect of theory." Aristocracies, on the other hand, "facilitate the natural impulse of the highest regions of thought." Tocqueville foresaw well. American psychology since its founding has neglected theory, even being openly hostile to theory at times. While Europeans such as Jean Piaget construct grand, almost metaphysical theories, B.F. Skinner argues that theories of learning are unnecessary.

### Pre-Darwinian Background in Philosophical Psychology

The Puritans brought the medieval faculty psychology with them to America. It perished in the early eighteenth century, however, when America's first great philosopher, Jonathan Edwards (1703-1758), read Locke. His enthusiasm for empiricism was such that his genius carried him independently in the direction of Berkeley and Hume. Like Berkeley, he denied the distinction between primary and secondary qualities and concluded that the mind knows only its perceptions, not the external world. Like Hume, he expanded the role of associations in the operation of the mind, finding as Hume had that contiguity, resemblance, and cause and effect are the laws of association (Jones, 1958). Finally, like Hume, he was driven toward skepticism through his recognition that generalizations about cause cannot be rationally justified, and that emotion, not reason, is the true spring of human action (Blight, 1978). Edwards, however, remained a Christian, as Hume did not, and he may be regarded as more medieval than modern in this respect (Gay, 1969).

Edwards' stress on emotion as the basis of religious conversion helped pave the way for the American form of romanticism and idealism: transcendentalism. Transcendentalism was a New England revolt against what had become a comfortable, stuffy, and dry form of Puritanism. The transcendentalists wanted to return to the lively, emotional religion of Edwards' time, and to the direct, passionate encounter with God that Edwards had believed in. Such an attitude was compatible with both romanticism and post-Kantian idealism. The former prized individual feeling and communion with nature, similar to Thoreau's report of an extended, solitary sojourn in the wilderness in *Walden*. The latter believed Kant's transcendent *noumena* were knowable; similarly, George Ripley, a leading transcendentalist in *A Letter Addressed to the Congressional Church in Purchase Street*, wrote that they "believe in an order of truths which transcend the sphere of the external senses" (White, 1972). Thus, in some respects, transcendentalism was in tune with European romanticism and idealism.

In other respects, however, transcendentalism appears very American. It supported, for example, an evangelical, emotional Christianity that put the individual's feelings and conscience above hierarchical authority. Ralph Waldo Emerson preached "self-reliance," always an American ideal. He derided the radical empiricists as "negative and poisonous." Whether European or American in tone, however, transcendentalism's effect on mainstream American thought was limited. Like romanticism, its chief products were artistic rather than philosophical, and even its great art, such as Melville's *Moby Dick,* was much less popular than other works totally forgotten today. The American intellectual establishment of the colleges viewed transcendentalism, Kant, and idealism with horror, so that budding scientists and philosophers had little contact with the movement.

Instead of any romantic revolt, Scottish common-sense philosophy maintained its grip on American thought. Americans, too, began to produce faculty psychology texts at an accelerating rate as the nineteenth century progressed. There were at least two attempts to integrate German and American psychology. Frederick Rauch (1806-1841) tried to Americanize Hegel in his *Psychology* (1841), only the second book to use *psychology* in its title. The theologian Laurens Perseus Hickock (1798-1888) followed both Wolff and Kant, writing a *Rational Psychology* (c. 1848) and an *Empirical Psychology* (1882). Both reveal the American tendency to make psychology serve religion by "improving" the mind. Rauch concluded his text with a discussion of religion, while Hickock appealed to Christian faith as the source of the noumenal knowledge that Kant thought unattainable. Scottish faculty psychology was so well entrenched, however, that it either overrode or assimilated outside influences.

Academic faculty psychology in America did not add anything original to European faculty psychology. The Americans simply used the Europeans' ideas to improve and indoctrinate students into proper American and religious ways of thinking. More revealing of the American temperament is the popularity of phrenology, or popular faculty psychology. Phrenology enjoyed some popularity in Europe, especially in England, but in America, where it was put on a sound business basis and decked out in the trappings of vaudeville, it became a mania.

Early in the nineteenth century Gall's colleague Spurzheim started on a triumphal tour of the United States, whose rigors took his life after only a few weeks. Spurzheim was followed by the British phrenologist George Combe, who was well received by educators and college presidents. These lectures were too theoretical for American audiences, however, and phrenology fell into the hands of two industrious and businesslike brothers, Orson and Lorenzo Fowler. They minimized the scientific content of phrenology and maximized the practical applications. They set up an office in New York where clients could have their characters read for a fee. They wrote endlessly of the benefits of phrenology and published a phrenological journal that endured from the 1840s to 1911. They traveled around the country, concentrating on the frontiers, giving lectures and challenging skeptics. Like the great magician Houdini, they accepted any kind of test of their abilities, including blindfolded examinations of volunteers' skulls.

What made the Fowler's phrenology so popular was its appeal to the American character. It eschewed metaphysics for practical application. It pretended to tell employers what people to hire and to tell men which wives to take. It was thus the first mental testing movement in America and was Galtonian in its scrutiny of individual differences. Furthermore, it was progressive and reformist. Gall had believed the brain's faculties to be set by heredity. The Fowlers, however, said that weak faculties could be improved by practice and overly strong ones controlled by efforts of will. Many people sought out the Fowlers for advice on how to lead their lives; the Fowlers were the first guidance counselors. They also held out the hope that the nation and the world could be improved if only every person would be "phrenologized." Finally, the Fowlers believed they served religion and morality. They encouraged their clients to improve their moral faculties and believed that the existence of the faculty of Veneration demonstrated the existence of God, because the existence of the faculty implies the existence of its object.

Not only phrenology but also mesmeric magnetism flourished in America, and spiritualism began in America. On his tour of America in the 1840s George Combe reported that mediums ran a flourishing business in New York. In the early twentieth century spiritualism was so widespread that both *Scientific American* and the United States Congress appointed committees to investigate the claims of spiritualism. Animal magnetism arrived in the United States as a music hall turn and then was assimilated to phrenology in phrenomagnetism, which joined phrenology in the business of selling advice. No one could better look out for Number One than the possessor of *Instantaneous Personal Magnetism,* a system that included diets and physical exercises to build the "magnetic mind" capable of outstanding business success.

We will find that all the characteristics that contributed to the success of phrenology and its allied pseudo-sciences, except support for religion, were present in the native American psychology, functionalism. It, too, valued practical application, studied individual differences, and hoped to improve both the individual and society.

### The Arrival of Darwinism

Darwin's theory of evolution was received favorably in America for the most part. There were some attempts to silence Darwin's spokesmen, as in the notorious Scopes trial, but with few exceptions American intellectuals felt little threatened by Darwinism and became important supporters of natural selection. Nor was evolution's impact restricted to academia, for it produced two social movements that influenced the late nineteenth and early twentieth centuries.

### Social Darwinism and Eugenics

One application of the theory of evolution is to see human society as an arena for the struggle for existence. This attitude is called *social Darwinism,* although it began before Darwin with Herbert Spencer. Spencer argued that natural selection should be allowed to take its course on the human species. Government should do nothing to save the poor, weak, and helpless. In nature, poor, weak, helpless animals, and their poor hereditary traits, are weeded out by natural selection. This should be the way in human society as well, said Spencer. Government should leave the cosmic process alone, for it will perfect humanity by the selection of the fittest. To help human failures will only serve to degrade the species by allowing them to have children and thus pass on their hereditary tendency to fail.

When Spencer toured America in 1882 he was lionized. Social Darwinism had great appeal in a *laissez-faire* capitalist society where it could justify even cut-throat competition on the grounds that such competition perfected humanity. Although it promised eventual perfection of the species, social Darwinism was profoundly conservative, for all reform was seen as tampering with nature's laws. The American social Darwinist Edward Youmans complained bitterly about the evils of the robber barons, but when asked what he proposed to do about them replied, "Nothing" (Hofstadter, 1955). Only centuries of evolution could relieve human problems.

Despite their frequent fondness for Spencer, American psychologists had relatively little to do with social Darwinism. They were very active, however, in the other Darwinian social program, eugenics. Galton argued that evolution should not be left to natural selection, but should be helped along by artificial selection. America was ready to heed Galton's advice, and some psychologists were willing to help with the eugenic work. As the eminent American psychologist E.L. Thorndike put it: "In the actual race of life, which is not to get ahead, but to get ahead of somebody, the chief determining factor is heredity" (Pickens, 1968). Heredity should be improved by detecting and selecting the fit, and detecting and selecting out the unfit.

Even before 1859 Americans had suspected that characteristics such as drunkenness, prostitution, and crime were innate, and the coming of Darwinism intensified these fears. Galton's eugenics differed from American eugenics in one major respect, however. Galton had no plans for the unfit, only aiming to encourage the multiplication of the fit. Americans took the opposite course, doing little to inter-marry the fit, but trying to keep the unfit from reproducing, by such means as sterilization.

Eugenic needs did much to encourage the study of individual differences and the development of mental testing, especially intelligence testing. The unfit had to be detected if their genes were to be kept out of circulation. Testing became, and in some respects remains, a national obsession.

The first tests used by American psychologists were either Galton's or Wundt's. The results suggested that criminals, derelicts, prostitutes, and teenage delinquents were all of very low intelligence. The "menace of the feebleminded" haunted many. The ability to test intelligence became more efficient and reliable with the translation of Alfred Binet's (1857-1911) sophisticated instrument. Binet, who invented the *intelligence quotient* (I.Q.), was a French psychologist who devised his tests to spot children in need of special education. Binet viewed intelligence as a collection of intellectual abilities that could be taught. American psychologists adopted and revised Binet's test, but held to Galton's idea that intelligence was hereditary. Thorndike, for example, was a leading exponent of the Galtonian view.

The introduction of Binet's test only deepened the fear of the menace of the feebleminded. The test was used nationwide, and its findings seemed to bear out the earlier results. Psychologists also were active in the Army's testing program during World War I. Army psychologists developed a simplified intelligence test that was used to choose potential officers from the ranks of the draftees. Their findings, however, seemed to show that the feebleminded were even more numerous than previously thought. It was widely quoted that about half American whites, and far more than half American blacks, were "morons." The menace of the feebleminded became the menace of the masses. Psychologists also administered intelligence tests to immigrants and concluded that most of them, especially those from the Orient and Eastern Europe, were feebleminded—possibly because the tests were in English.

The eugenics movement, lead primarily by biologists such as Charles Davenport, pressed for government action and got it. At the end of the nineteenth century, states began to pass laws that allowed judges to sterilize people possessing a wide range of supposedly heritable antisocial traits, including feeblemindedness. Such sterilizations continued at least into the 1960s. The Army tests had reinforced racism by its findings on black intelligence, and laws against black-white intermarriage were adopted or strengthened. Congress seriously accepted this argument against immigration given by the president of the National Institute of Immigration, Broughton Brandenburg: "It is not vain glory when we say that we have bred more than sixty million of the finest people the world has ever seen. Today there is to surpass us, none. Therefore any race that we admit to our body social is certain to be more or less inferior" (Haller, 1963). The result was the passage of immigration quotas strictly limiting the entrance of people from "inferior" nationalities.

It should be pointed out that most psychologists and biologists were not eugenists, and some actively opposed its measures. However, what really killed the eugenics movement was Naziism. Hitler's slaughter of six million Jews showed to what end the desire to eliminate the "unfit" could finally come. In psychology, eugenics was further weakened by behaviorism, which holds that humans are behavioral blank slates shaped by environmental stimuli, rewards, and punishments. Eugenics, however, did not die. Some psychologists still argue that blacks are inherently less intelligent than whites, while in biology genetic counselors attempt to persuade carriers of undesirable traits to have no children. Finally, some of its opponents think the appearance of sociobiology, which maintains that genes influence all human behavior, signals a resurgence of eugenics and social Darwinism.

### The Philosophical Fruits of Darwin: Pragmatism

The first philosophy native to America was pragmatism, which may be viewed as a combination of Hume and Darwin. Hume had argued that all human beliefs are fundamentally only habits. This is precisely the starting point of pragmatism as stated by its founder, Charles Saunders Peirce (1839-1914), a scientist turned philosopher. Peirce (1878) said that "The essence of belief is the establishment of a habit." It was the reduction of belief to habit that distressed Reid and Kant, for it seemed to open the door to skepticism. Peirce argued that the truth is just the opposite. For the truth of a belief wrote Peirce (1905) "lies exclusively in its conceivable bearing upon the conduct of life."

Peirce argued that this definition of a concept allows us to eliminate metaphysical nonsense by giving us a scientific means of getting to the truth of any claim. In the first place, a concept will be meaningless if it has no observable manifestations. This is the natural touchstone of the scientist: "force" is a valid concept because we can measure it, but "angel" is meaningless because "angels" are invisible and intangible. So far Peirce follows Hume, who rejected unobservable metaphysical fictions. However, a second aspect of Peirce's criterion of truth took him beyond Hume. Peirce was greatly influenced by Bain, and therefore brought action into his philosophy. Peirce's criterion referred to the *conduct* of life. A belief or idea must affect our actions to be meaningful. The test of a concept is not passive observation but active experiment. We each act on the world, and we should retain only those concepts that effectively guide our actions and bring us into better contact with the resulting observations. Metaphysical concepts fail to do this, while scientific ones succeed, and so the pragmatic criterion of truth supports not skepticism but realism. It tells us how to find out what things really are, instead of offering us only empty metaphysical verbiage.

The incorporation of human action into epistemology suggests the direction of the development of pragmatism taken by its outstanding spokesman, William James (1842-1910). It seems a little awkward to speak of habits, whether mental or physical, as true or false, but it makes a great deal of sense to ask if they are useful or useless. The agoraphobic person's habitual fear of open spaces is useless, for it keeps the person from places and activities he or she might otherwise enjoy; the good driver's habitual response of braking at red traffic lights is useful, for it enables the person to drive with little effort. At this point the influence of Darwin becomes evident, since usefulness is also the criterion of natural selection. An animal's physical traits, like pragmatic habits, are not true or false, only useful or useless in the struggle for survival. Natural selection retains the former and discards the latter. James extended this evolutionary criterion to the whole of human life. Not only should the agoraphobic person's fear and the driver's reflex be considered habits, but, following Peirce, so should all beliefs and concepts be considered habits, too, all subject to the pragmatic test of usefulness.

Darwin's influence on James was thoroughgoing. James in his book *Pragmatism* contrasted pragmatism and rationalism by saying that while rationalists believe reality is unchanging and eternal, "for Pragmatism it is still in the making, and awaits part of its complexion from the future." There are no Forms, for the universe is continuously evolving; truth thus cannot be a static thing, but is instead an eternally evolving process. Wrote James: "True ideas are those we can assimilate, validate, corroborate and verify. False ideas are those we cannot. . . ." The truth of an idea is not a stagnant property inherent in it, for truth happens to an idea. It *becomes* true, is *made* true by events. Its verity is an event, a process: "the process of . . . its verification." Pragmatism is staunchly a philosophy of becoming.

Thus far, James sounds like a tough-minded empiricist, insisting on observable support for any idea. However, for James the touchstones of truth are far greater than simple, direct observation. He says that ideas "become true just in so far as they help us to get into satisfactory relations with other parts of our experience." Experience here means *all* of our experience without exception. The truth of a belief should not only be tested against observation, but also against its effects on our practical life, its agreement with our prior stock of ideas, and its ability to satisfy us emotionally. An idea that passes these tests is said to be true because it works; one that does not work is false.

James' pragmatism thus rebukes Hume's rejection of metaphysical and religious speculations that refer to what is not observable. As James (1907) wrote, pragmatism's "only test of probable truth is what works best in the way of leading us, what fits every part of life best and combines with the collectivity of experience's demands, nothing being omitted. If theological ideas should do this, if the notion of God, in particular, should prove to do it, how could pragmatism possibly deny God's existence?" What pragmatism seeks is ideas that work in human terms, and in fact pragmatism often presented itself as modern Sophist humanism. Ideas that are useful, satisfying, and in agreement with other beliefs are true, no matter whether they be scientific, metaphysical, or religious. Such attitudes led James to be active in psychical research, which more tough-minded empiricists found disreputable.

The third great Pragmatist was John Dewey (1859-1952), who made pragmatism a philosophy of life and values, deeply concerned with the problems of the real world beyond academia. Whereas James applied the Heraclitean-Darwinian idea of evolutionary flux to reality and truth, Dewey (1957) applied it to life and values: "The process of growth, of improvement and progress, rather than the static outcome and result, becomes the significant thing. . . . The end is no longer a terminus or limit to be reached. It is the active process of transforming the existent situation. Not perfection as a final goal, but the ever-enduring process of perfecting, maturing, refining is the aim in living. . . . Growth itself is the only moral 'end.' " Dewey believed that any philosophy should try to affect public life. Indeed, by the pragmatic criterion, should it fail to do so it would render itself false. Most important to Dewey was education, for he viewed philosophy "as the general theory of education." Dewey is primarily remembered today as the inventor of "progressive" education, founded on pragmatism, that emphasizes learning by doing and engages the child in an active give-and-take with the world, letting the child learn truth by practical experience rather than forcing the child to learn by passive recitation.

Pragmatism is a uniquely American philosophy, as was recognized by its European critics (Russell, 1945), one that judges truth by success and emotional appeal. To the pragmatists truth is what works, what brings success. Eternal progress and improvement replace static eternal Truth. Apparently arcane fields such as philosophy should get involved with the world of affairs. Religious beliefs are to be grounded not in metaphysical reasoning about God, but in the human emotional need for faith, and for its contribution to individual moral behavior. Pragmatism is, as James admitted, anti-intellectualist in its reduction of abstract concepts to agreement with concrete experience and feeling. Such philosophical anti-intellectualism can give comfort to the social anti-intellectualism that justifies by feeling alone any set of beliefs, from evangelical Christianity to romantic revolution against an "oppressive," "bourgeois" state (White, 1972). All these attitudes are typically American. They could lead, as we have seen, to the widespread acceptance of the occult, or to the first native American philosophy.

### Experimental Psychology in America

#### Pragmatism and Psychology

Pragmatic philosophy necessarily runs over into psychology: If all beliefs and concepts are fundamentally habits, then the psychological process of learning needs to be investigated; if beliefs are held because of observation, agreement with previous beliefs, and emotional satisfaction, then these psychological processes must be investigated; if values grow through active experience and education, then the psychological processes of action and child development must be investigated. And, through it all, there runs the theme of evolution, saying that beliefs, truths, and values are all ways people adapt to their surroundings.

Beginning with Peirce, the three major pragmatists were involved with the practice and establishment of experimental psychology in the United States. As early as 1862 Peirce read Wundt and soon began to call for experimental psychology to replace Scottish faculty psychology. He carried out a series of psychophysical investigations of color, reported in 1877 as the first psychophysical study published in America. He continued psychological investigations, and one of his students, Joseph Jastrow, later became President of the American Psychological Association.

Even in 1887, while he was still a Hegelian idealist, Dewey wrote a text, *Psychology*, which argued that psychology "is a central science, for its *subject matter*, knowledge, is involved in them all." His most important contribution to the new American psychology was "The Reflex Arc Concept in Psychology," which appeared in the third volume of *Psychological Review* in 1896 (Dewey, 1970). It contributed an acute attack on the reflex arc, or sensorimotor model of the brain and its allied associationism. The sensorimotor view implies a stimulus-response psychology, made familiar to American philosophers by Chauncey Wright (1830-1875). This sensorimotor, or reflex arc, concept is artificial according to Dewey, for it is not "an organic unity, but a patchwork of disjointed parts." It breaks behavior up into the triad of sensation → idea → response, all viewed as independent entities. According to Dewey, however, behavior is really a series of *acts* coordinated to some end. So, for example, a visual sensation is not the passive registration of a given stimulus but an act of looking and should be treated as just as much an act as a motor response. Motor responses, in turn, act on the environment and so partly determine the next sensation. Thus, behavior is not an arc but a complete circuit of acts and their consequences. Dewey summarized, "There is simply a continuously ordered sequence of acts, all adapted in themselves and in the order of their sequence, to reach a certain objective, end, the reproduction of the species, the preservation of life, locomotion to a certain place" (Dewey, 1970).

Three important tendencies are to be observed in Dewey's paper. First, he incorporated psychology into Darwinism, viewing mind and behavior as adaptive functions by which the organism achieves the ends of individual and species survival. Second, he rejected atomistic associationism and the psychology of content. Associationism divides mental and behavioral activity into artificial units, or atoms, the stages in the reflex arc. The psychology of content fails to recognize that the exact same sensation has different meaning depending on the behavioral context. The exact same sound of a snapping twig, for example, means something different to a hunter, a soldier on guard, and a child on a picnic. Finally, Dewey makes action or behavior the focal point of psychology. This is a natural consequence of pragmatism, which evaluates concepts according to their effect on the conduct of life. This last tendency foreshadows behaviorism, although Dewey's analysis of the reflex arc remained a hidden criticism of S-R psychology.

By far the most important pragmatic contribution to American psychology was James' *Principles of Psychology.* Its date of publication, 1890, is a watershed date in the history of American psychology, for it inspired American students as neither the Scots nor Wundt could, and it set the tone for American psychology from 1890 to 1913. James combined the usual interests of a founding psychologist, physiology and philosophy. He began his academic career with an M.D. and held a variety of posts at Harvard. Beginning as an instructor of physiology, he next saw to the establishment for himself of a Chair in Psychology; he spent his last years as a professor of philosophy. It was in the *Principles* that James began to develop his pragmatic philosophy.

"Psychology is the Science of Mental Life," James told his readers. Its primary method is ordinary introspection, accompanied by the "diabolical cunning" of German experimentalism and by comparative studies of men, animals, and savages. James rejected sensationlistic atomism, the billiard-ball theory also rejected by Wundt. According to James, this theory takes the discernable parts of objects to be enduring objects of experience, falsely chopping up the flow of experience. Wrote James: "Consciousness . . . does not appear to itself chopped up in bits. Such words as 'chain' or 'train' do not describe it fitly, as it presents itself in the first instance. It is nothing jointed; it flows. A 'river' or a 'stream' are the metaphors by which it is most naturally described. *In talking of it hereafter let us call it the stream of thought, of consciousness, or of subjective life."*

In Darwinian fashion, James found that what consciousness contains is less important than what it does; it is function, not content, that counts. The primary function of consciousness is to choose. He wrote (1890): *"It is always interested more in one part of its object than in another, and welcomes and rejects, or chooses, all the while it thinks."* Consciousness creates and serves the ends of the organism, the first of which is survival through adaptation to the environment. For James, however, this adaptation is never passive. Consciousness chooses, acting always toward some end. The ceaseless flow of choices affects perception as well as conduct: "The mind, in short, works on the data it receives very much as a sculptor works on his block of stone." James' mind is not the passive blank slate of the sensationists. It is a "fighter for ends," actively engaged with a practical world of experience.

Although James said psychology is the Science of Mental Life, it must simultaneously be "cerebralist." It is a fundamental assumption that "the brain is the one immediate bodily condition of the mental operation," and the *Principles,* all one thousand three hundred and seventy-seven pages of it, is "more or less of a proof that the postulate is correct." James applies the cerebralist approach throughout his text, and intensifies it in the *Brief Course* (1892). He applauds Hartley's attempt to show that the laws of association are cerebral laws, "and so far as association stands for a *cause*, it is between *processes in the brain*. . . ."

This seems to involve James in a contradiction; the brain-machine must make choices. He has said that consciousness plays a positive role in human and animal life and explicitly rejected mechanism, or what he called the "automaton theory." For James an evolutionary naturalism demands consciousness. A dumb machine knows no direction, it is like "dice thrown forever on a table . . . what chance is there that the highest number will turn up oftener than the lowest?" James argued that consciousness increases the efficiency of the cerebral machine by "loading its dice." Wrote James (*Principles of Psychology*): "Loading its dice would bring constant pressure to bear in favor of *those* of its performances" that serve the "interests of the brain's owner." Consciousness transforms survival from "a mere hypothesis" into an "imperative decree. Survival *shall* occur and therefore organs *must* so work. . . . Every actually existing consciousness seems to itself at any rate to be a *fighter for ends*. . . ." Consciousness thus possesses survival value. Association may depend on cerebral laws, but our will can, through emphasis and reinforcement, direct chains of association to serve our interests, and their direction is "all that the most eager advocate of free will need demand" for by directing association it directs thinking, and hence action, wrote James.

Having thus argued for the causal efficacy of consciousness, James elsewhere seems to make it impossible. In his discussion of the mind-body problem in *Principles of Psychology*, James rejects dualism, and concludes that psychologists must adopt parallelism, "a blank unmediated correspondence, term for term, of the succession of states of consciousness with the succession of total brain processes," at least for the present.

On the one hand James tells us that consciousness directs thought and action, while on the other hand he pictures consciousness as only parallel to the bodily nervous processes that *are* thought and action. We will see in the next chapter that this contradictory view of consciousness proved absolutely fatal to American mentalistic psychology.

In James' *Principles* can be seen the future history of American psychology. His book did more than anything else to launch functionalism. Beyond that, it also points to behaviorism. He tells us in *Principles of Psychology* that "*no mental modification ever occurs which is not accompanied or followed by a bodily change*," and that "the whole neural organism" is "but a machine for converting stimuli into reactions; and the intellectual part of our life is knit up with but the middle or 'central' part of the machine's operations." The first statement opens the door to the basic behaviorist attitude; we cannot see the mind, only the bodily changes, so let us study them alone. The second statement implies the S-R formulation central to most behaviorism, whether peripheralist or mediationist. James even formulated two technical concepts central to S-R theory, the idea that habits can be chained together as series of S-R reflexes, and the habit-family hierarchy, as advocated by Clark Hull. James also anticipated the information processing psychology that succeeded behaviorism. Like them, James distinguished primary, or short term, and permanent memory, and pictured the latter as a network of associated memory-nodes.

Two years after its publication James reflected on his aims in writing the Principles. He tells us in "A Plea for Psychology as a Natural Science" (1892) that psychology "is a mass of phenomenal description, gossip, and myth," not a science, but that "I wished, by treating Psychology *like* a natural science to help her become one." However, he thought the content of the book to be "of small moment" and "wearisome." He maintains that "almost all the fresh life that has come into psychology of recent years has come from the biologists, doctors, and psychical researchers," not from philosophers, and that this new impulse to make psychology into "a branch of biology [is] an unsafe one to thwart." Finally, what people crave, James says, "is a sort of psychological science that will teach them how to *act*," that provides "practical rules." He concludes that a pragmatic psychology is needed: "The kind of psychology which could cure a case of melancholy, or charm a chronic insane delusion away, ought certainly to be preferred to the most seraphic insight into the nature of the soul."

### The New American Psychology: Functionalism

Scottish faculty psychology was moribund after the Civil War, continued only by tradition. A new impulse toward practical and scientific psychology had arisen quite independently of Wundt, whom Americans respected but did not always admire. By 1875, the year Wundt went to Leipzig, James was giving courses in psychology and had established a modest and informal laboratory. He contracted to write the *Principles* in 1878, and chapters appeared as articles before 1890. The American minister and Yale philosopher, G.T. Ladd (1842-1921), produced *Principles of Physiological Psychology* in 1887, which, while drawing on Wundt and Lotze, advocated a funcational view of consciousness. James McKean Cattell (1860-

1944), studied with Wundt and brought his Leipzig degree back to America and founded laboratories at the University of Pennsylvania (1887) and Columbia (1891). His orientation, however, came more from Galton, with whom he had also studied, than from Wundt, who had found his work *"ganz Amerikanisch"* (completely American). In 1890 he described his research at Pennsylvania ss the measurement of mental processes, exactly Galton's goal.

The institutionalization of American psychology was undertaken by G. Stanley Hall (1844-1920). In 1878, at Harvard, he received America's first degree in experimental psychology, although it was nominally in physiology. He established the first official American psychology laboratory in 1883 at Johns Hopkins, and organized the founding of the American Psychological Association in 1892. In 1887 he founded the first lasting journal of psychology in America, the *American Journal of Psychology*, which superseded the earlier *Journal of American Psychology*, which had lasted for only a few issues in 1883-84.

The democratic, evolutionary, practical, pragmatic atmosphere of America insured that scientific psychology there would be different from that in elitist, rationalist, abstract, refined Germany. As E.G. Boring (1950) put it, in American psychology, "the apparatus was Wundt's, but the inspiration was Galton's." No one was better able to detect and describe this new trend than E.B. Titchener. In his "Postulates of a Structural Psychology" (1898) he distinguished two kinds of psychology, and the names he gave them became permanent.

Titchener drew a broad analogy between biology and psychology. In biology, the anatomist tries to describe the structure of the body by accurately locating and describing each organ, gland, and muscle. So, in psychology one may, as Titchener did, seek to accurately locate and describe each sensation in human consciousness; this is structural psychology, or *structuralism*. On the other hand, in biology the physiologist tries to explain the functions of each bodily organ, gland, and muscle. So, in psychology one may, like James, try to say what consciousness does; this is functional psychology, or *functionalism*. Of course, Titchener believed that "the best hope for psychology lies today in a continuance of structural analysis." He found functional psychology to be confused, although ultimately valuable when tamed by experiment. Functional psychology is close to ordinary thought-habits and language, a fact James valued but Titchener deprecated. A year later Titchener (1899) put nicely the exact difference between the two psychologies: "Introspection, from the structural standpoint, is observation of an Is; introspection, from the functional standpoint, is observation of an Is-for."

American psychologists accepted Titchener's distinction, but not his psychology. Americans came to see structuralism as both scientifically and practically sterile, preferring functionalism as the proper and useful approach to mind. The "spying and scraping" of German experimentalism as James put it, was not to the taste of Americans. "The soul of man is no simple equation to be stated in terms of the 'differentiation,' 'aggregation,' 'reintegration' of sensational factors. Its manifold beliefs, fears, hopes, aspirations, and even cognitions, that take hold on what is forever hidden from sense, and yet give support and value to sensation itself, are integral moments in its own being," proclaimed Ladd in 1899.

By 1901, the time had come to openly proclaim the value of functional psychology. In a thoughtful address (1901), Joseph Jastrow, Peirce's collaborator and at the time President of the American Psychological Association, explored "Some currents and undercurrents in psychology." He declared that for him psychology is "the science of mental function," not content. The functional approach arose out of evolution; it "at once cast a blinding light" upon dark areas of psychology long held by "dogmatism, misconception and neglect," and "breathed a new life" into "the dry bones" of psychology. Jastrow correctly observed that although functional psychology pervaded current research, it did not act as the central subject of investigation, but rather gave a distinctive "color tone" to American psychology. Jastrow saw functional psychology as an accepted undercurrent, which he wanted to bring forward as a "main current." Functional psychology is more catholic than structural psychology. It welcomes to psychology the previously excluded topics of comparative psychology, abnormal psychology, mental testing, the study of the average person, and even psychical research, although this last clearly troubled him. Jastrow predicted that functional psychology would prove of more value to practical affairs than structural psychology. Finally, he noted, as we have, that all these trends are characteristically American, and he prophesied that the future would belong to functional, not structural, psychology.

In 1903, James Rowland Angell (1869-1949), a major exponent of functionalism, reversed Titchener's priorities. He argued that any sensation a structuralist might discover "is determined by the demands made upon the organism by the environmental situation, i.e., that it is functionally determined," and that even in biology function is more important than structure. He stated the basic thesis of functionalism, which is Jamesian but also maintains continuity with the Scottish school: "Consciousness is not merely epiphenomenal, but is really an efficient agent in the furtherence of the life activities of the organism (the view of common sense)." In 1904 Angell published his text *Psychology*, which systematized James' ideas in a functionalist manner. This book forcefully brought the new view into the classroom.

Although some attempts were made to reconcile structural and functional psychology, the time when that was possible had passed, and in 1907 Angell laid out the functionalist program in "The province of functional psychology." Angell begins by indicating functional psychology's continuity with Aristotle, Darwin, and Spencer, all biologically oriented psychologists; only functionalism's self-consciousness is new. Structuralism is a chimera, for sensations are not permanent physical entities, according to Angell. What is truly permanent is mental function, for at different times different mental contents may "be called on to perform identical functions." Angell implies that structuralists are unconscious frauds, pretending to investigate mental atoms, while really attacking mental functions by calling their atoms "processes." Angell acknowledges functional psychology's relationship to pragmatism and humanism, tracing both to evolution. The "cue" of the functionalist is "the basal conception" of evolution that "organic structures and functions" exist because "of the efficiency with which they fit into the extant conditions of life. . . ." This implies that psychology is nearer to biology than to philosophy. Structuralism is "sterile" compared to functionalism when it comes to practical application. Moreover, structuralism "appears stiff and rigid and corpselike. It lacks the vital spark" compared to functionalism, which studies the "utilitarian aspects of mental process" in "actual vital service" to the organism. Angell's paper summarizes the functionalist attitude and asserts its sense of superiority to structuralism.

Although it was a characteristically American movement, certain European psychologies show the functional spirit.

### European Psychologies of Functionalist Tendencies

#### James Ward (1843-1925) and British Psychology

The functional point of view arose also in Britain, home of modern evolutionism. Its William James was James Ward, sometimes called the "father of modern British psychology" (Turner, 1974). He was for a time a minister, but after a crisis of faith turned first to physiology, then psychology, and finally philosophy, exactly as James had done. His tremendous influence in British psychology comes from his article on psychology in the *Encyclopaedia Brittanica*'s ninth edition of 1886. It was the first article by that name in the *Encyclopaedia,* and Ward reworked it later into a text. Ward settled at Cambridge University, where he was active in attempts to establish a psychological laboratory.

Like James, Ward rejected atomistic analysis of the continuum of consciousness. Instead of a sensationistic atomism, Ward advocated a functional view of consciousness, the brain, and the whole organism. Ward wrote (1904): "Functionally regarded, the organism is from first to last a continuous whole . . . the growing complexity of psychical life is only parodied by treating it as mental chemistry." To Ward perception is not the passive reception of sensation, but active grasping of the environment. In a passage that resembles James, Ward (1904) wrote that "not mere receptivity but creative or selective activity is the essence of subjective reality. . . ." He struck a Darwinian note when he said (1920): "Psychologically regarded, then, the sole function of perception and intellection is, it is contended, to guide action and subserve volition—more generally to promote self-conservation and betterment."

Ward is clearly expounding the same kind of pragmatic, or functional, psychology that James did. For both, consciousness is an active, choosing entity that adjusts the organism to the environment and so serves the struggle for survival. Ward resembles James in one more way—his *fin de siècle* concern with defending religion against the rising tide of Huxlean naturalism. Ward devoted his last great works to the refutation of naturalism and the support of Christianity.

Ward's influence endured for many years in English psychology. Adoption of his approach helped British psychologists resist behaviorism while remaining committed to an experimental psychology. Britain retained a functionalist, mentalist psychology that provided an orienting point for post-behaviorist cognitive psychology. Ward's anti-atomism also endured, to be picked up by later anti-associationists. A later Cambridge psychologist, Frederick Bartlett, for example, explicitly rejected the attempt to study memory as the acquisition of discrete "bits" of information such as the nonsense syllables used in most memory experiments. Instead, Bartlett studied memory of everyday paragraphs. He argued that running prose is not a set of atomistic ideas, but is rather an embodiment of a larger meaning, which he called a *schema* (compare to Wundt's *Gesamtvorstellung*). Bartlett (1932) showed, for example, that different cultures possess different schemas for organizing their experience, and that consequently systematic distortions are introduced into one culture's member's memory of another culture's stories. In exploring alternatives to behaviorism in the 1960s, Bartlett's schema theory was revived and refined. Thus a variety of Ward's functionalism has continued to the present day.

### Franz Brentano (1878-1917) and Act Psychology

A German, or more precisely Austrian, psychologist recognized by both Titchener and Angell as essentially functionalist was Franz Brentano, a priest turned philosopher. Although Brentano in no way derived his psychology from Locke, the best way to approach him is through Locke's ambiguous use of "idea." For sensationists, such as Titchener, an idea is a mental content, an "Is" as Titchener put it. However, an idea may be interpreted as a mental *act* whereby the mind comes in contact with the world. Brentano took this latter view of mental processes, and his system is therefore called an *act psychology*.

Studying what mind does is fundamental to Brentano's system. All mental processes may be classified as some form of act, as "Ideating (I see, I hear, I imagine)" or as "Judging (I acknowledge, I reject, I perceive, I recall)," or as "Loving-Hating (I feel, I wish, I resolve, I intend, I desire)" (Titchener, 1921). Each of these acts has a content, referring to something beyond mind, for example, "I see a cat." To Brentano, however, the existence of mental content is less important than the mental act that grasps the phenomena. Brentano's psychology is thus functionalist, for, as Titchener (1921) said, he "takes mind as he finds it, and ... he finds it in use; he finds it actively at work in man's intercourse with nature and with his fellow-men, as well as in his discourse with himself."

Although, beginning in 1874, Brentano tried to establish a psychological laboratory in Vienna, he remained primarily a philosopher and preeminently a metaphysician. He was often read with sympathy by functionalists, but his main influence has been in philosophy. His most direct offspring was Edward Husserl's phenomenology, a difficult discipline that has only occasionally impinged on experimental psychology, though clinicians have been more sympathetic to it. In their hands a modified *phenomenology,* or the attempt to understand another's consciousness, would become a rival to behaviorism.

*Hermann Ebbinghaus (1850-1909)*
*and the Study of Memory*

Ebbinghaus was a young doctor of philosophy unattached to any university when he came across a copy of Fechner's *Elements Psychophysics* in a secondhand bookstore. He admired the scientific precision of Fechner's work on perception and resolved to tackle the "higher mental processes" that Wundt had excluded from experimental treatment. Using himself as his only subject, Ebbinghaus set out in 1879 to demonstrate Wundt's error. The result was his *Memory* of 1885, which was hailed as a first-rate contribution to psychology and which helped win him a professorship at the prestigious University of Berlin.

*Memory* represents a necessarily small scale but well thought-out research program. Ebbinghaus decided to investigate the formation of associations by learning serial lists of nonsense syllables, meaningless combinations of three letters invented by Ebbinghaus for the purpose. In electing to memorize nonsense syllables, Ebbinghaus reveals the functionalist cast of his thought. He chose nonsense syllables because they are meaningless, because the sameness of their content would not differentially affect the process of learning. He wanted to isolate and study memory as the pure *function* of learning, abstracting away any effects of content.

Ebbinghaus remained an eclectic rather than a systematic thinker, and his influence derives from his work on memory rather than from any theoretical views. But that influence was wide. In Germany memory studies were carried on by G.E. Müller and his associates, whose distinctions, new procedures, and theories anticipated modern cognitive psychology (Murray, 1976). In America, James praised Ebbinghaus' work in *Principles,* and in 1896 Mary Calkins augmented Ebbinghaus' serial learning method with a paired-associate procedure in which the subject learns specific pairs of words or nonsense syllables. More broadly, Ebbinghaus' *Memory* prefigures the style of twentieth-century psychology. Its subject is learning, the favorite topic of functionalists, behaviorists, and cognitive psychologists. The book minimizes theory while multiplying facts and looking for systematic effects on behavior of independent variables, such as list length. Ebbinghaus strove to quantify his data and apply statistical methods. In short, Ebbinghaus is the empirical, atheoretical, research-oriented, eclectic modern psychologist.


## CONCLUSIONS

### The Paradigm of the Psychology of Adaptation

The creation of the psychology of adaptation was the work of many minds—Spencer, Darwin, Galton, and James. In the first decade of the twentieth-century functionalism, the American form of the psychology of adaptation, seemed about to become a paradigm. As late as 1907, however, Angell conceded that "Functional psychology is at the present little more than a point of view, a program, an ambition." This is but a small advance on Jastrow's statement in 1901 that functional psychology was only an undercurrent giving American color to psychological research.

Functionalism never became more than "a point of view." The vocabulary and problems for research were derived primarily from Wundt, with some additions by Galton. James in his *Principles* and Angell in his *Psychology* consider all the traditional topics: imagination, association, attention, sensation, and so on. The important shift is in point of view, from introspecting the contents (the "Is") of the mind to introspecting its function and purposes (the "Is-fors").

Functionalism's point of view was self-consciously derived from Darwin. It asks how the mind guides the adaptation of the organism to its environment. However, the functionalists asked only the individual evolutionary question, viewing an individual as analogous to a species. They did not pursue Darwin's or Galton's interest in the species-question, that is, how minds are made different by heredity. Eugenics, which dealt with the species-question, was a social movement that rarely penetrated academic discussions of mind. Functionalism reflected instead the American belief in the rough equality of men, and in the ability of the individual to adapt to circumstances and get ahead.

As well as its self-conscious use of evolution, functionalism had another new attitude, its desire to provide a useful and practical psychology, an applied psychology. Application is a natural consequence of the adaptive viewpoint, for if we can understand mental functions we may hope to improve them. "Improvement" of sensational content makes little sense; we can do no more than describe sensations. Therefore, an applied psychology must study more than sensations. As phrenology's popularity showed, the American desire for a practical psychology existed before Spencer or Darwin came on the scene. It was the craving of Americans for a useful psychology that ensured the birth of functionalism, not the reverse.

Functionalism was never more than a paradigm in the making. Its viewpoint was indeed different from that of any other system we have examined, but it had not worked out the details of a new research program. American psychologists were going off in all directions, investigating any and all aspects of mind from the functional point of view, without concentrating on a sustained, normal science effort to solve a few promising problems. The major reason for functionalism's failure to achieve a paradigm, however, was not a want of effort or of numbers, but a new historical trend.

### Historical Trends

Functionalism was mentalistic. It saw psychology as the Science of Mental Life, and its primary tool was introspection. Even from its beginnings, however, there were signs that mind was shortly to be squeezed out of psychology altogether. We have already seen how James' *Principles* implies the construction of a psychology of the bodily manifestations of mind, a psychology of behavior. As action got incorporated into psychology, beginning with Bain and the sensorimotor physiologists, the activities of the organism became more important. Evolution reinforced this trend, for the environment is biologically relevant to an organism whose activities affect its chances of survival. It is an organism's *actions* that are selected by nature for retention or elimination. An idea that leads to no behavior is totally irrelevant to evolution.

The shift from studying inner experience to studying behavior, implicit in James, grew steadily. The study of perception might seem to be immune to this kind of change, for it appears to deal with our conscious sensations. In 1902, however, Thaddeus Bolton, a disciple of James and C.L. Morgan, offered "A biological view of perception." He accused traditional experimental studies of "almost complete failure," and offered a new definition of perception. Perception is not just a set of sensations, but is rather "an attitude toward an object," and "reduced to its lowest terms is an act." To study perception is to study animal activity. Bolton (1902) wrote: "In so far then as animals perceive objects they act in definite ways towards them." Bolton anticipated Skinner's view of perception as behavior under reinforcement control: "Only those objects with life and death possibilities for lower forms of life, and those with pleasure and pain possibilities for higher forms, have interests and are acted toward—consequently perceived." The role of consciousness is thus greatly reduced from James' conception. Bolton denies that it interferes in the chain of nervous processes from stimulus to response, acting only in some indefinite way to "adjust the organism to the environment."

By 1910 the tendency to view psychology as primarily concerned with behavior had become widespread. For the pragmatist H. Heath Bawden, for example, mental processes are no more than "vicarious responses. All thinking and speaking are an abortive or anticipative doing. . . ." The problem of psychology is, "What is the soul in terms of hands and feet, what is mind in terms of motor processes?" From this standpoint, introspection becomes unnecessary, for behavior is visible. Bawden (1910) wrote: "The alleged uniqueness of the so-called introspective method is a figment. . . . It reveals no peculiar facts and no special laws," and is "truly" the study of behavior. C.H. Judd (1910) argued that "To study behavior more completely is the most urgent of our problems." In 1912 Knight Dunlap made "The case against introspection," concluding that "there is, as a matter of fact, not the slightest evidence for the reality of 'introspection' as the observation of 'consciousness.'"

An important source of the drive toward the study of behavior and away from introspection was the expansion of psychological subjects undertaken by functionalists. Bawden (1910) noted "the rapid growth of the allied sciences of animal, child, and social psychology, dealing as they do with the so-called objective manifestations of mind, has introduced an almost entirely new nomenclature into a field in which the introspective method formerly held undisputed sway." Foremost among these "objective" fields was animal psychology, where introspection was impossible. In his "Province," Angell (1907) said that animal psychology's growth "is surely the most pregnant with which we meet in our own generation."

The usual procedure of comparative psychologists in the mentalistic tradition of Romanes and Morgan, carried on in American functionalism, was to reconstruct animal mind from its behavioral manifestation. Some charming descriptions of animal mind ensued, for example in Willard Small's (1901) account of a rat getting used to a maze: "The manner soon became more confident, affective tension was relaxed, and curiosity and the play instinct became unloosed. After [one rat] had eaten and drunk a little he seemed to become thoroughly happy, and, for the nonce quite oblivious of the world of traps and snares . . . investigating all the passages in a sprightly and eager manner."

But younger, more tough-minded investigators were becoming impatient with this approach. E.L. Thorndike (1900) of whom we will say more in the next chapter, attacked Small's work as "anthropomorphic" and poked sarcastic fun at passages such as that quoted above. What Thorndike and others wanted was thoroughly objective procedures that exerted maximal control and minimized the dangers of anthropomorphizing the animal mind. This method came on the American scene in 1909 when R. M. Yerkes and S. Morgulis made American psychologists aware of "The method of Pawlow [Pavlov] in animal psychology."

The appearance of Pavlov's name indicates that a new movement, behaviorism, is about to begin, a movement deep-rooted in functionalism. The functionalists tried to resist the new movement's total rejection of mind, but failed; functionalism was dead after 1913, although its soul lived on. Judd had called the study of behavior the "chief" problem of psychology, but he attempted to retain consciousness as integral to evolution and a necessary part of psychology. He prophesied (1910): "I believe we are on the eve of a newer psychology than we have ever known." His prophesy came true, but he did not expect what happened next.

## SUGGESTED READINGS

There is no good single source on the psychology of adaptation. On American philosophy, an excellent short work is Morton White's *Science and Sentiment in America* (Oxford University Press, 1972). On American psychology, an interesting work is A.A. Roback's *History of American Psychology* (Library Publishers, 1952) which is marred, however, by some factual errors and by his excessive distaste for behaviorism ("Psychology Out of its Mind"). For special topics such as phrenology, social Darwinism, or eugenics, consult the bibliography, and references.

## REFERENCES

Angell, J. R. The province of functional psychology. *Psychological Review,* 1907, *2,* 61-91.

Bartlett, F. C. *Remembering.* Cambridge: Cambridge University Press, 1932.

Bawden, H. H. Mind as a category of psychology. *Psychological Bulletin,* 1910, 7, 221-225.

Blight, J. G. The position of Jonathan Edwards in the history of psychology. Paper presented at the annual meeting of the American Psychological Association, Toronto, Ontario, September 1, 1978.

Bolton, T. A biological view of perception. *Psychological Review,* 1902, *9,* 537-548.

Boring, E. G. *A history of experimental psychology.* Englewood Cliffs, N.J.: Prentice-Hall, 1950.

Darwin, C. *The descent of man and selection in relation to sex.* New York: Appleton & Co., 1896.

Darwin, C. *The expression of emotion in man and animals.* Chicago: Chicago University Press, 1965.

Dewey, J. *Reconstruction in philosophy.* Boston: Beacon, 1957.

Dewey, J. *Psychology.* Carbondale, Ill.: Southern Illinois University Press, 1967.

Dewey, J. The reflex are concept in psychology. Reprinted in H. S. Thayer (Ed.) *Pragmatism: The classic writings.* New York: Mentor, 1970.

Dunlap, K. The case against introspection. *Psychological Review,* 1912, *19,* 404-413.

Ebbinghaus, H. *Memory.* New York: Dover, 1964.

Emerson, R. W. *Selected prose and poetry.* New York: Holt, Rinehart & Winston, 1950.

Galton, F. *Inquiries into the human faculty and its development.* London: J. M. Dent, 1907.

Galton, F. *Hereditary genius.* London: Macmillan, 1925.

Gay, P. The obsolete Puritanism of Jonathan Edwards. Reprinted in J. Opie (Ed.) *Jonathan Edwards and the Enlightenment.* Lexington, Mass.: D. C. Heath, 1969.

Haller, M. *Eugenics: Hereditarian attitudes in American thought.* New Brunswick, N.J.: Rutgers University Press, 1963.

Hofstadter, R. *Social Darwinism in American thought* (Rev. ed.). Boston: Beacon, 1955.

James, W. A plea for psychology as a natural science. *Philosophical Review,* 1892, *1,* 146-153.

James, W. *Principles of psychology* (2 vols.). New York: Dover, 1950.

James, W. *Pragmatism.* New York: Meridian, 1955.

James, W. *Psychology: The briefer course.* New York: Harper & Row, Pub., 1961.

Jastrow, J. Some currents and undercurrents in psychology. *Psychological Review,* 1901, *8,* 1-26.

Jones, A. L. *Early American philosophers.* New York: Ungar, 1958.

Judd, C. H. Evolution and consciousness. *Psychological Review,* 1910, *17,* 77-97.

Ladd, C. T. On certain hindrances to the progress of psychology in America. *Psychological Review,* 1899, *6,* 123-133.

Miller, P. *The life of the mind in America.* New York: Harcourt, Brace & World, 1965.

Murray, D. J. Research on memory in the nineteenth century. *Canadian Journal of Psychology,* 1976, *30,* 201-220.

Peirce, C. S. How to make our ideas clear (1878). Partially reprinted in A. Rorty (Ed.) *Pragmatic Philosophy.* Garden City, N.Y.: Anchor Books, 1966.

Peirce, C. S. What pragmatism is (1905). Reprinted in H. S. Thayer (Ed.) *Pragmatism: The classic writings.* New York: Mentor, 1970.

Pickens, D. *Eugenics and the progressives.* Nashville, Tenn.: Vanderbilt University Press, 1968.

Romanes, G. *Animal intelligence.* New York: Appleton & Co., 1883.

Russell, B. *A history of western philosophy.* New York: Simon & Schuster, 1945.

Small, W. An experimental study of the mental processes in the rat, II. *American Journal of Psychology,* 1901, *12,* 206-309.

Spencer, H. *The principles of psychology,* 3rd ed. New York: Appleton & Co., 1897.

Spencer, H. *An autobiography,* 2 vols. London: Williams & Norgate, 1904.

Spencer, H. *First principles.* London: Watts & Co., 1945.

Thorndike, E. L. Comparative psychology. *Psychological Review,* 1900, *7,* 424-426.

Titchener, E. Postulates of a structural psychology. *Philosophical Review,* 1898, *7,* 449-465.

Titchener, E. Structural and functional psychology. *Philosophical Review,* 1899, *8,* 290-299.

Titchener, E., Brentano and Wundt. Empirical and experimental psychology (1921). Reprinted in L. McAlister (Ed.) *The philosophy of Brentano.* Atlantic Highlands, N.J.: Humanities Press. 1976.

Tocqueville, A. de *Democracy in America.* (Edited and abridged by R. D. Heffner). New York: Mentor, 1956.

Turner, F. M. *Between science and religion.* New Haven: Yale University Press, 1974.

Ward, J. The present problems of general psychology. *Philosophical Review,* 1904, *13,* 603-621.

Ward, J. *Psychological principles.* Cambridge: Cambridge University Press, 1920.

White, L. *Science and sentiment in America.* London: Oxford University Press, 1972.

Wills, G. *Inventing America: Jefferson's Declaration of Independence.* Garden City, N.Y.: Doubleday, 1978.

# Modern
# Psychology

We have already found that functionalism was becoming the objective study of behavior by the early years of the twentieth century, having made the journey from James' original mentalism. Freudian psychology became psychoanalysis, one school of medical psychiatry concerned with the practical cure of mental disorders rather than abstract understanding of the human mind. Psychoanalysts remained aloof from psychologists as the latter focused their attention on the laboratory study of simple behaviors. The dominant academic psychology of the twentieth century was behaviorism, founded by a young animal psychologist named John Broadus Watson in 1913.

Several varieties of behaviorism arose after Watson's initial call to arms, and these varieties defined laboratory psychology for decades. However, after World War II psychologists began to feel less secure in their behaviorism, and several rival movements arose that capitalized on this insecurity. The 1960s in psychology, as in the larger society, were years of revolt and chaos. By 1970 psychology was taking on a new shape in which the mind returned as a legitimate object of study, although introspection as a legitimate method remained suspect.

These developments will occupy us in the next four chapters.

# 10

# Classical Behaviorism
## Origin, Background, and Formulation

Psychology as the behaviorist views it is a purely objective experimental branch of natural science. Its theoretical goal is the prediction and control of behavior. Introspection forms no essential part of its methods, nor is the scientific value of its data dependent upon the readiness with which they lend themselves to interpretation in terms of consciousness. The behaviorist, in his efforts to get a unitary scheme of animal response, recognizes no dividing line between man and brute. The behavior of man, with all of its refinement and complexity, forms only a part of the behaviorist's total scheme of investigation.

John Broadus Watson, "Psychology as the Behaviorist Views It"

## INTRODUCTION

### Revolution or Evolution?

With these dramatic words, a self-conscious new psychological movement was launched by a young animal psychologist trained by Angell at the University of Chicago. Watson resolutely rejected the psychology he found around him in favor of a reformulation of the entire field and its methods—a change widely regarded as revolutionary. David Palermo (1971) has argued that behaviorism was a Kuhnian revolution against structuralism. On the other hand, Joncich (1968) writes that in 1913 behaviorism was "already an adolescent—legitimate, unmiraculous, forseeable." Watson certainly acted like a revolutionary, but we may ask which historical model better fits the change from structuralism and functionalism (Gestalt psychology was never a serious force in America [Henle, 1977]): Kuhn's revolutionary model or Toulmin's evolutionary one.

Let us review the criteria Kuhn lays down for describing a change as revolutionary. First, a period of normal science must precede the revolution. Second, in the course of puzzle-solving, one or more serious anomalies must be discovered. Third, these anomalies must resist solution and precipitate a crisis and a loosening of paradigm restrictions. Fourth, at some point a rival paradigm must emerge, one which can explain the anomalies. Fifth, as the crisis deepens, the new paradigm attracts adherents, mostly younger scientists. Finally, after a period of struggle the field is redefined according to the new paradigm and a new kind of normal science is pursued.

According to Toulmin's account, on the other hand, we should be able to trace a relatively smooth evolution of one kind of science into a new kind, without any apparent gaps between the two. Which of these ideas of change best fits behaviorism's appearance? To find out we must examine the historical context of behaviorism. First, however, we will examine John B. Watson's formulation of classical behaviorism.

### The Classical Behaviorism of John Broadus Watson (1878-1958)

Two broad periods in the growth of behaviorism are usually distinguished: classical behaviorism, associated with Watson and which lasted until around 1930, and neo-behaviorism, associated with many theorists and which may or may not still exist. John Broadus Watson was trained in psychology at the University of Chicago under the functionalist, J.R. Angell, although he had extensive contact with the more radical views of physiologist Jacques Loeb, a strong advocate of reductionism. Watson's field was animal psychology; he tells us himself that he preferred to work with animal rather than human subjects, and that he disliked serving as an introspective subject. Much of Watson's behaviorism flows from this background. Although Watson's dissatisfaction with traditional psychology and the genesis of his behavioristic ideas may go back to his days at Chicago in 1904, it was only in 1913 that he formulated his views in print in "Psychology as the Behaviorist Views It." This date is a turning point in American psychology.

After the trumpet call of his first paragraph, quoted at the beginning of this chapter, Watson proceeded systematically, beginning with a criticism of structuralism. Appropriately enough, his first criticism was that there was no room in structuralism for animal study, because its focus was entirely on human consciousness. What little animal study was done, he called "absurd," because the researcher was forced to construct his subject's consciousness on the basis of behavioral data and analogies to human consciousness, an approach Watson called "false." Watson also noted that researchers had provided no firm criterion for ascribing consciousness to animals, and that in any case experiments were designed without reference to consciousness in animals. Watson's basic point was that ascribing consciousness to animals is wholly unnecessary—that behavioral data alone is sufficient for scientific work.

Watson went on to claim that psychology had failed to become "an undisputed natural science." He ascribed its failure to the method of traditional psychology, introspection, which he argued had produced no progress and never could. Introspection also cuts psychology off from the other sciences, which rely on public data. Therefore "psychology must discard all reference to consciousness," and give up speculation about mind for the objective study of behavior. He lumped together structuralism and functionalism, for both are mentalistic and use introspection. Watson implied that functionalism was worse than structuralism, for in seeking the pragmatic value of consciousness it lapsed into an indefensible interactionism of mind and body, while the structuralists maintained a rigid parallelism. His solution to the mind-body problem was to ignore it by studying behavior alone. He intended to keep his students ignorant of such problems just as physicists are ignorant of them. In neither science should the experimental methods of problem solution be affected by problems of mind. He next turned to the constructive side of his argument. Psychology could be studied without, as he wrote (1913a), "the terms consciousness, mental states, mind, content, introspectively verifiable, and the like. . . . It can be done in terms of stimulus and response . . . habit formation, habit integrations and the like." What behaviorism will study is how the animal, including man, adjusts to his environment, and ultimately "given the response the stimuli can be predicted; given the stimuli the response can be predicted." Such prediction would naturally make it possible to control behavior, and to apply psychology to the practical problems of education, medicine, law, and business. Watson wrote that the lack of an applied psychology helped disenchant him with structuralism.

Watson argued that the methods of this new psychology should be the methods of objective animal psychology applied to humans: the manipulation of the environment (stimuli) and the determination of its effects on behavior (responses), all without reference to mind. As an example, he discussed a behavioral method for determining to what colors an animal may respond by training the animal to discriminate colors, and he showed how the method may be easily applied to humans. His hope for such a behavioral psychology stemmed from the already existing behavioral methods used in biology and in applied psychology, although he criticized these sciences for taking an interest in the machinery of the mind rather than determining solely how a person shapes his or her behavior to fit the environment.

Finally, Watson presented a behaviorist approach to the higher mental processes, or "complex behavior." Here he was at his most radical. He doubted the existence of all mental imagery and argued that even if it exists it is a luxury, not causally connected to behavior. Instead, he proposed that thought is just the "faint reinstatements of . . . muscular acts" chained together into associative serial mechanisms, so that "the reflective processes (are) as mechanical and habit." He also argued that learning is an unconscious process, so that consciousness plays no role in the improvement of thought. Most extremely, he stated that "there are no reflective processes (centrally initiated processes)." All thinking happens in the peripheral musculature. Watson held out little hope for an immediate behaviorist assault on these problems, and argued that psychologists should shelve the "threadbare" questions of cognition until they can lay firm foundations in the study of simpler processes.

We will later summarize classical behaviorism, but now we should note an important theme in Watson's paper—the defining theme of all behaviorism, namely an emphasis on method (Mackenzie, 1977; Koch, 1964). Watson's essential criticism of traditional psychology was the weakness and unreliability of its method, introspection. It is this method that he felt had denied psychology a place in the sciences, a place behaviorism would secure by using a new method, that of objective behavioral study. In this short paper, Watson repeatedly said that methods solve scientific problems. For example, he wrote (1913a): "As our methods become better developed it will be possible to undertake investigations of more and more complex forms of behavior." There was no mention of better developed theory, or even the existence of real theoretical problems; all may be known by good method. This stress on method is characteristic of all behaviorism, but especially of what may be called radical or descriptive behaviorism, founded by Watson and carried on by B. F. Skinner.

In another paper appearing in 1913, "Image and Affection in Behavior," Watson continued his assault on the traditional higher mental processes. He stated that his "principal contention [is] that there are no centrally initiated processes." He proposed again that thought is merely implicit behavior that fills in time between stimulus and response, and that this implicit behavior consists largely of laryngeal habits open to behavioral study. He said that psychologists who believe that the cortex is active in governing behavior are still dominated by religious concerns, for an appeal to the cortex is an appeal to the unknowable. According to Watson, all the cortex does is staple together stimulus and response. Finally, he asserted again that behaviorism aims at a methodological revolution, discarding introspective self-observation in favor of objective methods.

For all his emphasis on objective methods, Watson failed to specify exactly what method or methods should be adopted, for which he was criticized. However, he won many adherents, and was elected President of the American Psychological Association for 1916, and in his Presidential address he fixed on Pavlov's conditioning methods (see later section) as psychology's new tool. This was his second choice. Watson spent some time futilely trying to record the implicit behavior he identified with thought. It was only at the last moment that he decided to present classical conditioning in his address, borrowing from the work of his student Karl Lashley, later a critic of radical behaviorism (Koch, 1964).

Watson applied this method to a human child in a study reported in 1920 called "Conditioned Emotional Reactions" carried out with his assistant and soon-to-be second wife, Rosalie Rayner. Their study is one of the most famous in all psychology, although it is more often misdescribed than not; in fact, often it is seriously distorted (Cornwell & Hobbs, 1976; Harris, 1979). Watson wanted to demonstrate how emotional reactions are learned by classical conditioning based on innate responses. One subject, 9-month-old Albert B., is presented. First, Watson and Rayner determined that Albert showed little fear of anything except having a steel bar struck by a hammer behind his back. Watson and Rayner then established a new fear by classical conditioning. At 11 months Albert was given a white rat, which he enjoyed. At the moment the child touched the rat, Watson clanged the bar. After seven such pairings the same fear was manifested to the rat as to the sound of the bar. Wrote Watson and Rayner (1920): "The instant the rat was shown the baby began to cry. Almost instantly he turned sharply to the left, fell over on left side, and crawled away rapidly." Watson found that the fear was generalized for similar objects, such as rabbits and a Santa Claus beard, and that these fears persisted until he was at least 12½ months old. Contrary to most textbook accounts, Watson never deconditioned the fear, although he had intended to, because Alfred's mother removed him from the hospital where the experiment had taken place. It should be pointed out that this study would be considered unethical by psychologists today.*

Watson made an extended statement of behaviorism in his book *Behaviorism,* which appeared in 1924 with a third edition in 1930. We will only discuss what is new in the book beyond his earlier papers. Watson had attacked both *Gestalt* psychology, for being obscure and introspective, and psychoanalysis for its mentalism, although he respected it as a therapy. In defining behavioristic psychology, he first tied it closely to physiology, spending two chapters on human physiology. Later in the book, however, he severed behaviorism from physiology by asserting that behavior may be scientifically studied in its own right without knowledge of physiological mechanisms. This latter opinion is also characteristic of later radical behaviorism under Skinner.

Watson now said that the goal of psychology should be to learn how to make people act differently than in the past, that is, to control their behavior. The tool of change is classical conditioning, and the knowledge it garners is to be placed at the service of society. Wrote Watson (1930): "It is a part of the behaviorist's scientific job to be able to state what the human machine is good for and to render serviceable predictions about its future capacities whenever society needs such information." In a footnote denouncing free speech, Watson revealed his Utopia: the behaviorist's world will contain people conditioned "so that their speech and their bodily behavior could equally well be exhibited freely everywhere without running afoul of group standards." His Utopia also would contain neither law nor legal process, only police, presumably behavioristically trained. Like Skinner more recently, Watson believed traditional methods of behavior control, such as punishment, to be haphazard and ineffective, and said that behaviorist methods would prove more effective.

Watson's program was made possible by his extreme empiricism, environmentalism, and determinism. He denied the existence of any native character traits or faculties. All that is innate for Watson are a few motor and nonrational reflexes: "All complex behavior is a growth out of simple responses." His stand is clear (1930): "Give me a dozen healthy infants . . . and my own specified world to bring them up in and I'll guarantee to take any one at random and train him to become any type of specialist I might select—doctor, lawyer, artist, merchant-chief, and, yes, even beggar-man and thief; regardless of his talents . . . (etc.) and the race of his ancestors." This position was very progressive. Many eugenically inclined psychologists then believed blacks to be innately inferior to whites. Watson, on the other hand, upheld the equality proclaimed in the Declaration of Independence.

In a more scientific vein, Watson, in *Behaviorism,* essayed a detailed analysis of language and thinking. Wrote Watson (1930): "Language, . . . in spite of its com-

*Watson himself had some qualms about the procedure, but felt finally that its scientific purpose justified his method. Today, no research on children may be performed without obtaining the consent of the parents, who must be informed about the experimental procedures to be used.

plexities, is in the beginning a very simple type of behavior. It is really a manipulative habit." Language is just a chain of sounds linked together by conditioning, aided by imitation, and nothing more. Words are just implicit-behavior substitutes for real objects which make it possible for a person to carry the world around in his or her body. Watson thus adopted James Mill's associationist theory of language, but in terms of vocal movements rather than ideas. Words have no meaning except in the bodily reaction to the object named.

Watson also reduced thinking to implicit behavior, although he now downplayed the special role of laryngeal habits; instead, he now said that we think with the implicit movements of our whole body. He was a bit inconsistent, however, for at one point he also said that thinking is talking to ourselves, but elsewhere he said that in thinking the musculature of our whole body is implicitly involved. Creativity he reduced to the combination of previously learned reflexes into novel combinations. But Watson remained silent on how this combining is done.

### Preliminary Summary of Classical Behaviorism

Watson clearly sought to reformulate the methods, problems, and goals of psychology. For introspection he would substitute classical conditioning. For the problems of attention, feeling, thought, and the description of consciousness he would substitute the problem of learning. For the goal of psychological explanation he would substitute the forward-looking prediction and control of behavior, modeled on physics. In all this he was largely successful.

Watson's behaviorism was the final fruit of the seeds planted by William Ockham and David Hume. Ockham suggested that much thought was habit, while Hume reduced all thinking, causality, and induction to forms of habit. Watson merely substituted behavioral habits for mental ones. As an epistemology, behaviorism maintains the most radical nominalism. Words, names, are nothing but vocal habits that evoke in hearers certain bodily responses. There are no forms, essences, or mental concepts. All philosophical problems are to evaporate into behavioral problems. Even aesthetics may be made behavioral, for art may be evaluated by people's willingness to engage in the behavior of purchase.

Classical behaviorism is empiricist, atomist, peripheralist, associationist, materialist, and determinist. All problems are to be defined in terms of stimulus and response. Its goal is to predict and control human behavior, to adjust people to society. Its orientation is toward practical effects rather than abstract knowledge. It seeks to oust all other forms of psychology and then go on to refashion society in its image.

## THE HISTORICAL CONTEXT OF BEHAVIORISM

Such was Watson's classical behaviorism. He presented it himself as revolutionary, and certainly it brought great change to psychology. However, historical forces were working to produce behaviorism, not just the mind of one man. Many trends merged in the movement called behaviorism. We will now examine the historical context in which Watson acted, keeping an eye on the revolution or evolution question. We may conveniently divide the context into three portions: the social background, the intellectual background, and the personal background.

### The Social Background

The intellectual crisis that began in the nineteenth century (see Chapter 6) deepened in the twentieth century. As William Butler Yeats wrote in his poem, "The Second Coming," in 1920:

> Turning and turning in the widening gyre
> The falcon cannot hear the falconer:
> Things fall apart; the centre cannot hold;
> Mere anarchy is loosed upon the world,
> The blood-dimmed tide is loosed, and everywhere
> The ceremony of innocence is drowned;
> The best lack all conviction, while the worst
> Are full of passionate intensity.
> Surely some revelation is at hand;
> Surely the Second Coming is at hand.
> The Second Coming! Hardly are those words out
> When a vast image out of "Spiritus Mundi"
> Troubles my sight: somewhere in sands of the desert
> A shape with lion body and the head of a man,
> A gaze blank and pitiless as the sun,
> Is moving its slow thighs, while all about it
> Reel shadows of the indignant desert birds.
> The darkness drops again; but now I know
> That twenty centuries of stony sleep
> Were vexed to nightmare by a rocking cradle,
> And what rough beast, its hour come round at last,
> Slouches towards Bethlehem to be born?

1913 was a revolutionary date for art as well as psychology. In New York the famous Armory show, a mammoth exhibition of modern art, opened; in Chicago, cubist art was condemned by teachers as "Nasty, lewd, immoral . . . indecent" and "crazy-guilt art . . . not for children's eyes" (Bailyn, et al., 1977).

Art and psychology were responding to the same crisis described by Yeats that was challenging all culture and society. The nineteenth century had seen all the verities of Western life questioned. The twentieth century spawned many answers, from cubist art to behaviorist psychology to existential philosophy. All were attempts to see old problems in new ways or to eliminate them altogether and build a world view on new principles. Like the cubists, Watson discarded an old mode of perception, introspection, in favor of a new one, observation of behavior. Like the existentialists, Watson discarded the isolation of the laboratory for engagement with real life. None of the answers Watson and the others gave is compelling today, but the crisis remains; Yeats' words are still true.

Three aspects of the social environment require more consideration. First of all, classical behaviorism was very American in its pursuit of utopia. The United States founded itself in a revolution based on a new view of the state, and Americans ever since have sought the perfect society. Watson held out the possibility of a utopia founded on scientific principles discovered in the laboratory but applied to human affairs.

Behaviorism is also the product of progressivism, a widespread political reform movement that began in the 1890s. It sought to displace the old bosses and hack politicians with an elite bureaucracy that would scientifically manage society. It was mildly utopian and its goal was social control: "Long live social control . . not only to enable us to meet the rigorous demands of the war (World War I) but also as a foundation for the peace and brotherhood that is to come" (Bailyn, et al., 1977). Behaviorism seemed to many progressives to provide the scientific tools with which they could rationally and efficiently manage society. Social control through behavioral technology is one of the longest-lived of progressive ideas. Politically, progressivism died after Wilson's presidency in the widespread post-war violence and, finally, the depression. Intellectually, it was undermined by the new philosophies of the irrational (such as Nietzsche, Freud) and anti-realist aesthetics (such as cubism, abstract expressionism).

Finally, behaviorism participated in the American anti-intellectual impulse discussed in the last chapter, turning away from theory in favor of practical concerns. Watson always wanted to improve the practice of education, business, and the like. He told readers of *Behaviorism* that the sole value of a college education lies in its training for success in real life, and that genius is just good work habits. But behaviorism goes beyond mental, or intellectual, utility. It says that consciousness is not useful, that mind does nothing and probably doesn't even exist. Behaviorism, then, denies intellect, reducing it to implicit muscular responses. Mind disappears into body altogether.

### The Intellectual Background

*General Scientific and Philosophical Trends*

The most immediate source of classical behaviorism was Watson's own field of animal psychology, where the usefulness of reference to consciousness was already being questioned. In 1912 Elliot Frost asked "Can biology and physiology dispense with consciousness?" He canvassed leading students of animal behavior who called for objectivism. J. Von Üxküll, for example, said, "Before objective investigation, the memory and thoughts of animals disappeared like fluttering forms of vapor . . . nowhere remained the smallest spot for the psyche of the animal."

A. Bethe said ". . . the objective aspect of psychic phenomena, and that alone, should be the object of scientific investigation" (Frost, 1912). Frost concluded that such workers and others had dismissed any psychology of consciousness, but Frost himself wound up reducing mind to accumulated past experience stored as energy in the brain and activated by a stimulus, which, when released, modifies "the machinery of behavior."

How did this come about? When we left animal psychology Romanes and even the conservative Morgan were inferring mental processes from behavior. Brian MacKenzie (1977) has argued that functionalist analyses of animal mind got into an impossible bind. They wanted to understand animal mind, but restricted themselves solely to animal consciousness, neglecting other aspects of mind. Also, Watson was probably right in pointing to psycho-physical parallelism as a problem. The functionalists wanted to avoid interactionism, but parallelism makes it hard to give consciousness any utility in controlling behavior. As a result, functionalist comparative psychology wound up describing animal consciousness in passive, sensationistic (parallelist) terms. As experiments continued, consciousness, *mind* for the functionalist, seemed to do less and less in the life of the animal. All the real influences seemed to be in the environment. It was therefore an easy step to get rid of reference to consciousness altogether and talk only about environment and behavior. It was a step many before Watson were willing to take.

The impact of the objective approach was being felt outside animal psychology. In 1912 Robert MacDougall noted that the place of mind in all parts of psychology was uncertain. The study of abnormal human minds and of animals, which precludes introspection, made the use of the concept of consciousness strained at best. As well as animal and abnormal psychology, subliminal states, "automatisms," the mentally retarded, and even the fetal mind were being studied. In all these areas data on consciousness are hard to come by. MacDougall (1912) also noted pressures on mentalism from physiology and biology, which may be seen as "the science [s] of behavior, whether behavior be construed in terms of consciousness or not." MacDougall believed that these influences all led to the question, "What is meant by mind?" Like Frost, MacDougall presented an ultimately unsuccessful argument for retaining the concept of mind in psychology.

It was clear even to the functionalist Angell, Watson's teacher, that psychology was moving in the direction of behaviorism. In a remarkable article appearing in 1913, but written before Watson's great paper, Angell noted that consciousness was about to disappear from psychology, a change he welcomed with but little reservation, unlike Frost or MacDougall. In a footnote added in press, Angell proclaimed himself "heartily sympathetic" to Watson's constructive, positive, objective approach to psychology. He remarked on the gradual reduction in the role ascribed to consciousness by functionalists, who were finally seeing it as no more than the middle link in a reflex arc. The step to behaviorism then became easy, for psychologists needed only to drop the hidden mental term. Angell even wondered if psychology was any longer aptly named, since "psyche" was gradually being excluded from the field. He saw psychology moving steadily in the direction of biology and physiology, perhaps to be swallowed up by them, a move his own view made "entirely easy." However, he still believed that a role for mind would inevitably emerge from objective methods. He thought objective descriptions would help him see "just how ideas and feelings embody themselves in action." Angell (1913) concludes: "Let us bid [objective psychology] . . . Godspeed, but let us also counsel it to forego the excesses of youth." The latter exhortation was often repeated and always ignored in the next half-century.

Another source of behaviorism is the mechanical approach to human behavior that goes back at least to the eighteenth century. La Mettrie called for an entirely materialist, mechanistic understanding of human behavior and mental life. Before him Montaigne had minimized the difference between animal and human life, a difference Watson was eager to erase altogether. In physiology, as we have seen, there as a growing body of literature on the sensorimotor, reflexive nature of the nervous system. At the University of Chicago, Watson was attracted to the extreme physioloical reductionist Jacques Loeb, but was kept from close association with him because Loeb was considered "too extreme" by Watson's mentors (Creelan, 1974).

Nor was Watson the first to attack introspection. In 1867, the English psychiatrist Henry Maudsley (1834-1918) wrote "self-consciousness is utterly incompetent to supply the facts for the building up of a truly inductive psychology." Maudsley considered introspection unreliable, for not all people can do it and those who can often produce differing reports of the same process. He also objected that an introspectively caught event is necessarily altered by the act of introspection and so rendered unnatural. Madmen have delusions; is this good introspective data? Introspection reveals nothing of unconscious states or physiological processes. Maudsley made these arguments and more, many of them repeated by Watson.

Another intellectual influence on classical behaviorism was positivism, whose influence was to grow until it virtually defined neo-behaviorism. We have touched on positivism earlier as part of the nineteenth-century intellectual crisis. Auguste Comte had argued for a completely objective approach to the study of humanity. Ernst Mach argued that science is just an ordering, preferably mathematical, of our experience. Any reference to unobserved entities, such as the atom, was inadmissible; only objective data, experience, was acceptable. We should pause and note how similar to Titchener's structuralism that is. Structuralism *was* the analysis of sensations. In any case, the lesson that Watson and the other behaviorists drew from positivism was that the essence of scientific practice—as found in the queen of sciences, physics—was objective observation of public behavior, whether of balls rolling down inclined planes or of animals in mazes. In neither case was reference to the unseen to be allowed Watson believed that as psychology adopted the positivist program it would join the ranks of the sciences and progress as beautifully as had physics.

### Specific Precursors to Behaviorism

In addition to the general trends discussed above, we may discern two specific research programs that provided important foundations for behaviorism. The first was that of Russian objective psychology, culminating in I. P. Pavlov's method of *classical conditioning,* behaviorism's first shared exemplar. The other research program was the connectionism of E.L. Thorndike, whose studies of trial-and-error behavior defined the other shared exemplar, *operant conditioning.* Both programs also led to theoretical orientations compatible with the merging disciplinary matrix of behaviorism.

**Russian Objective Psychology.**   The founder of modern Russian physiology was Ivan Michailovich Sechenov (1829-1905) who studied in some of the best physiological laboratories in Europe, including Helmholtz's, and who brought back their methods and ideas to Russia. Sechenov believed that psychology, which was known to him only as a branch of philosophy, could be scientific only if it were completely taken over by physiology and adopted physiology's objective methods. Introspective psychology he dismissed as akin to primitive superstition. In a passage remarkably similar to Watson's polemics Sechenov (1973) wrote:

> Physiology will begin by separating psychological reality from the mass of psychological fiction which even now fills human mind. Strictly adhering to the principle of induction, physiology will begin with a detailed study of the more simple aspects of psychical life and will not rush at once into the sphere of the highest psychological phenomena. Its progress will therefore lose in rapidity, but it will gain in reliability. As an experimental science, physiology will not raise to the rank of incontrovertible truth anything that cannot be confirmed by exact experiments; this will draw a sharp boundary-line between hypotheses and positive knowledge. Psychology will thereby lose its brilliant universal theories; there will appear tremendous gaps in its supply of scientific data; many explanations will give place to a laconic "we do not know"; the essence of the psychical phenomena manifested in consciousness (and, for the matter of that, the essence of all other phenomena of nature) will remain an inexplicable enigma in all cases without exception. And yet, psychology will gain enormously, for it will be based on scientifically verifiable facts instead of the deceptive suggestions of the voice of our consciousness. Its generalizations and conclusions will be limited to actually existing analogies, they will not be subject to the influence of the personal preferences of the investigator which have so often led psychology to absurd transcendenalism, and they sill thereby become really objective scientific hypotheses. The subjective, the arbitrary and the fantastic will give way to a nearer or more remote approach to truth. In a word, *psychology will become a positive science. Only physiology can do all this, for only physiology holds the key to the scientific analysis of psychical phenomena.*

We should note the similarities between Watson's program and Sechenov's. Psychology is to be positive, concerned with objective, public facts. Starting with the simple it will proceed to the more complex, being cautious and unspeculative. It will ignore consciousness. All this is similar to Watson. Watson, however, did not share Sechenov's reductionism, choosing to base positivistic psychology on objectively observable behavior, not on brain processes.

Sechenov's analyses of behavioral processes also foreshadowed Watson's. Sechenov's great work was *Reflexes of the Brain* (1863), in which he wrote: "All the external manifestations of brain activity can be attributed to muscular move-ment. . . . Billions of diverse phenomena, having seemingly no relationship to each other, can be reduced to the activity of several dozen muscles. . . ." Watson's peri-pheralism is found in Sechenov (1863): "Thought is generally believed to be the cause of behavior . . . [but this is] the greatest of falsehoods: [for] the initial cause of all behavior always lies, not in thought, but in external sensory stimulation. . . ." He also stated that all conscious, voluntary movements are reflexes. Elsewhere, he too adopted the model of language as a chain of vocal responses.

Sechenov's objectivism was popularized by Vladimir Michailovitch Bechterev (1867-1927) who called his system *reflexology,* a name which accurately describes its character. However, the greatest of Sechenov's followers, though not his student, was Ivan Petrovich Pavlov (1849-1936), one of psychology's few household names. Pavlov was a physiologist whose studies of digestion won him the Nobel Prize in 1904. In the course of this work he discovered that stimuli other than food may produce salivation, and this led him to the study of psychology, especially to the concept of the conditioned reflex and its exhaustive investigation.

Pavlov's general attitude was uncompromisingly objective and materialistic. Many of his pronouncements resemble Watson's. He shared Watson's faith in the objective method as the touchstone of natural science, and also shared a consequent rejection of reference to mind. Pavlov (1957) wrote: "For the naturalist everything lies in the method, in the chance of obtaining an unshakable, lasting truth; and solely from this point of view . . . the soul . . . is not only unnecessary but even harmful to his work." Like Watson, Pavlov rejected any appeal to an active inner agency, or mind, in favor of an analysis of the environment: it is possible to explain behavior without reference to a "fantastic internal world," referring only to "the influence of external stimuli, their summation, etc." His analysis of thinking was atomistic, like Watson's, though perhaps without the peripheralism: "The entire mechanism of thinking consists in the elaboration of elementary associations and in the subsequent formation of chains of associations." His criticism of all non-atomistic psychology was unremitting. He carried out replications of Köhler's ape experiments in order to show that "association is knowledge, . . . thinking . . . (and) insight," and devoted many meetings of his weekly Wednesday discussion group to unfriendly analyses of Gestalt concepts. He viewed the Gestaltists as dual-ists who "did not understand anything" of their own experiments. Pavlov's general orientation, then, is consonant with classical behaviorism.

Pavlov's technical contribution to the psychology of learning was consider-able. He discovered classical conditioning and inaugurated a systematic research program to discover all its mechanisms and situational determinants. In the course of his Nobel prize-winning investigation of canine salivation, Pavlov observed that salivation could later be elicited by stimuli present at the time food was presented to an animal. He originally called these learned reactions *psychical secretions* because they were elicited by non-innate stimuli, but later he substituted the term *conditioned response.* *

*This is the English term. However, a more accurate rendering would have been *condi-tional response.*

Following the fully refined paradigm of classical conditioning, one begins with a reflex elicited by some innate stimulus, as salivation is elicited by presentation of food. This connection is between an *unconditioned stimulus* (US) and an *unconditioned response* (UR). Then, while presenting the US one presents some other stimulus that does not elicit the reflex, such as the sound of a metronome. This stimulus is called the *conditioned stimulus* (CS), for after several pairings with the US it will come to elicit the same response (UR) now called the *conditioned response* (CR). This was the method applied by Watson and Rayner to little Albert. There, the US was the sound of the steel bar, which elicited the UR of fear. Watson paired his US with a CS, the rat. After several pairings the CS now elicited fear, a CR (or CER, *conditioned emotional reaction* as Watson and Rayner called it) of fear. It is also possible, although more difficult, to establish a new CS-CR relationship starting with a previously learned CS-CR relationship (for example, pairing a tone with the metronome sound to get the tone to elicit salivation). Such a procedure is known as *higher order conditioning.*

Pavlov systematically investigated conditioned reflexes. He found that conditioned responses will occur to stimuli similar to the original CS; this is called *generalization.* Similarly, Watson found that little Albert's fear spread to objects resembling the rat, the original CS. Further, Pavlov found that one could require that an animal make a CR to one stimulus but not another; this is called *discrimination.* If too-fine discriminations are required of an animal, it displays neurotic-like symptoms. Pavlov also studied how to inhibit conditioned reflexes. If one repeatedly presents the CS without the US, eventually the CR will disappear; this is called *extinction.* However, if one leaves the animal alone for awhile, the CS will again elicit the CR; this is called *spontaneous recovery.* There is also *conditioned inhibition,* in which one presents the CS and some new CS together without the US, although the old CS is still occasionally paired with the US. After a while the new combination will fail to elicit the CR. Pavlov's researches were meticulous and detailed, one of the best examples in psychology of a research program in Lakatos' sense.

Was Pavlov a behaviorist? This is a difficult question to answer. His general attitude was certainly anti-mentalistic, anti-introspectionist, and thoroughly objective. He provided one of the two shared exemplars of behaviorism. On the other hand, Pavlov was often critical of the American behaviorist research he came in contact with. He felt that his views had been simplified in America, and he called the eminent neobehaviorist Edwin Guthrie an idealist. His criticism reveals how he was not behaviorist. American behaviorists, as Pavlov (1957) pointed out, take learning as a fundamental phenomenon used to explain more complex behaviors, but not itself to be explained. Pavlov, on the other hand, saw learning as a phenomenon to be explained by proposing unobserved physiological mechanisms. He was willing, as Watson was not, to speculate about the cerebral processes behind behavior. Another difference concerns values. Recently, B.F. Skinner has attacked the common sense beliefs in human freedom and dignity as unscientific delusions. Pavlov, however, defends human freedom and dignity by arguing that a person is an "autoregulating system," the "supreme creation of nature." His view, he says (1957) enhances "the dignity of man" and retains "everything vital" in "the idea of free will."

### The Connectionism of Edward Lee Thorndike (1874-1949).

Thorndike was attracted to psychology when he read James' *Principles* for a prize competition at his undergraduate school, Wesleyan (Connecticut). When Thorndike went to Harvard for graduate study he eagerly signed up for courses with James and eventually majored in psychology. His first research interest was children and pedagogy but, no child subjects being available, Thorndike took up the study of learning in animals. James gave him a place to work in his basement after Thorndike failed to secure official research space from Harvard. Before completing his work at Harvard, Thorndike was invited to go to Columbia by Cattell; at Columbia, he pursued his animal research. Upon graduation, Thorndike returned to his first love, educational psychology, which—along with psychometrics—Thorndike made his field of study. Thorndike's importance for us is in his methodological and theoretical approach to animal learning and in his formulation of an S-R psychology he called connectionism.

Thorndike's animal researches are summarized in *Animal Intelligence,* which appeared in 1911. It includes his most important work, the report on his graduate studies, "Animal Intelligence: An experimental study of the associative processes in animals," published in 1898. In the introduction to his monograph Thorndike (1911) adopts the usual problem of animal psychology, "to learn the development of mental life down through the phylum, to trace in particular the origin of the human faculty." However, he deprecated the value of previous research, for it relied on the anecdotal method, which Thorndike argued focused only on unusual animal performances, not on the typical. As a substitute, Thorndike argued that the experimental approach is the only way to completely control the animal's situation. Thorndike's goal was by experiment to catch animals "using their minds."

Thorndike placed an animal in one of many "puzzle-boxes," each of which could be opened by the animal in a different way. When the animal escaped it was fed. Thorndike's subjects included cats, chicks, and dogs. Thorndike's setup is an example of what would later be called *operant conditioning* or *learning*: An animal makes some response, and if it is rewarded—in Thorndike's case with escape and food—the response is learned. If the response is not rewarded, it gradually disappears.

Thorndike's results led him to heap scorn on the older view of the anecdotal psychologists that animals reason; animals learn, he said, solely by trial and error, reward and punishment. In a passage that foreshadowed the future, Thorndike wrote that animals may have no ideas at all, no ideas to associate. There is association, but (maybe) not of ideas. Wrote Thorndike (1911): "the effective part of the association (is) a direct bond between the situation and the impulse." In 1898, Thorndike could not quite accept this radical thesis, although he acknowledged its plausibility.

By 1911 however, Thorndike wrote in the introduction to *Animal Intelligence*: Any "of the lower animals is . . . obviously a bundle of original and acquired connections between situation and response." He argued that we should try to study animal behavior, not animal consciousness, because the former problem is easier. He contended that this objective method could be extended to man, for we can study mental states as behavior. He criticized the structuralists for fabricating a wholly artificial and imaginary picture of human consciousness. Like Watson, he also argued that the purpose of psychology should be the control of behavior: "There can be no moral warrant for studying man's nature unless the study will enable us to control his acts." He concluded his introduction by prophesying that psychology would become the study of behavior.

Thorndike proposed two laws of human and animal behavior. The first was the law of effect: "Of several responses made to the same situation, those which are accompanied or closely followed by satisfaction to the animal will, other things being equal, be more firmly connected with the situation, so that, when it recurs, they will be more likely to recur." Punishment, on the other hand, reduces the strength of the connection. Further, the greater the reward or punishment, the greater the change in the connection. Later, Thorndike abandoned the punishment part of the law of effect, retaining only reward. The law of effect is the basic law of operant conditioning, accepted in some form by most behaviorists. Watson, however, considered it too mentalistic, for it refers to an animal's subjective satisfaction. Watson preferred Pavlov's more mechanical classical conditioning. Thorndike's second law is the law of exercise: "Any response to a situation will, all other things being equal, be more strongly connected with the situation in proportion to the number of times it has been connected with that situation, and to the average vigor and duration of the connections." Later, Thorndike had to modify this law, and in any case it was not generally accepted by other learning theorists.

Thorndike contended that these two laws can account for all behavior, no matter how complex: It is possible to reduce "the processes of abstraction, association by similarity and selective thinking to mere secondary consequences of the laws of exercise and effect." He analyzed language in Watsonian terms as a set of vocal responses learned because the parents reward some of a child's sounds but not others. The rewarded ones are acquired and the nonrewarded ones are unlearned, following the law of effect.

Thorndike applied his connectionism to human behavior in *Human Learning,* a series of lectures delivered at Cornell in 1928-1929. He presented an elaborate S-R psychology in which many stimuli are connected to many responses in hierarchies of S-R associations. He attempted to fulfill Watson's goal of prediction. He asserted that each S-R link could be assigned a probability that S will elicit R. For example, the probability that food will elicit salivation is very near 1.00, while before conditioning the probability that a tone will elicit salivation is near 0. Learning is increasing S-R probabilities; forgetting is lowering them. Just as animal learning is automatic, unmediated by an awareness of the contingency between response and reward, so, Thorndike argues, is human learning also unconscious. A person may learn an operant response without being aware that he is doing so. This doctrine is called the *automatic action of reinforcers,* and it will become a prime difficulty for behaviorism in the 1960s. As he did for animals, Thorndike reduced human reasoning to automatism, custom, and habit. Like Watson, Thorndike holds out the promise of a scientific utopia, founded on eugenics and scientifically managed education.

Thorndike recognized a number of difficulties that frequently troubled critics of behaviorism. For example, he admitted that the objective psychologist, who stresses how the environment determines behavior, has a difficult time defining the situation in which an animal acts. Are all stimuli equally relevant to an act? When one is asked, for example, "What is the cube root of 64?" many other stimuli are acting on a person at the same time as this question. Defining the response is equally difficult. One may respond "4," but many other behaviors (such as, breathing) are also occurring. How do we know what S is connected with what R without recourse to subjective, nonphysical meaning? Thorndike admitted that such questions were reasonable and that answers would have to be given eventually. About reading and listening, Thorndike wrote (1911): "In the hearing or reading of a paragraph, the connections from the words somehow cooperate to give certain total meanings." That "somehow" conceals a mystery only partially acknowledged. He realized the complexity of language when he said that the number of connections necessary to understand a simple sentence may be well over 100,000, and he conceded that organized language is "far beyond any description given by associationist psychology." All these difficulties recognized by Thorndike were sometimes acknowledged but rarely tackled in the succeeding half-century of behaviorism until they were revived with extraordinary force by a linguist, Noam Chomsky in 1957.

Was Thorndike a behaviorist? His biographer (Joncich, 1968) says he was, and can cite in support such statements as this: "Our reasons for believing in the existence of other people's minds are our experiences of their physical actions." He did formulate the basic law of operant learning, the law of effect, and the doctrine that consciousness is unnecessary for learning. Unlike Pavlov, he practiced a purely behavioral psychology without reference to physiology. On the other hand, he proposed a principle of "belongingness" that violates a basic principle of classical conditioning, that those elements most closely associated in space and time will be connected in learning. The sentences, "John is a butcher, Harry is a carpenter, Jim is a doctor," presented in a list like this, would make *butcher-Harry* a stronger bond than *butcher-John* if the classical conditioning contiguity theory were correct. However, this is clearly not the case. *John* and *butcher* "belong" together (because of the structure of the sentences) and so will be associated, and recalled, together. This principle of belongingness resembled Gestalt psychology rather than behaviorism. This principle also foreshadowed animal research in the 1960s that showed some S-R connections to be more "natural" than others.

Historically, Thorndike is hard to place. He did not found behaviorism, though he practiced it in his animal researches. His devotion to educational psychology quickly took him outside of the mainstream of academic experimental psychology in which behaviorism developed. Watson, for example, found the law of effect too mentalistic. It might best be concluded that Thorndike was a practicing behaviorist but not a wholehearted one. He was less polemical than Watson and could see difficulties where others did not.

What forces were acting on Watson to make him proclaim behaviorism? These forces were cultural, professional, and personal. As an animal psychologist Watson would have been aware of the general trend among students of animals toward purely objective methods without reference to consciousness. We know he associated with Jacques Loeb at the University of Chicago. He surely knew Thorndike's arguments in the 1898 monograph "Animal Intelligence." The American progressive zeitgeist encouraged a move toward practical, objective psychology, and the success of positivism in presenting physics as the model for scientific psychology was alluring. The arguments with which to propound behaviorism were there for the taking. They constitute the cultural and professional reasons for Watson's views. However, why did Watson seize on them the way he did? Watson was never an original scientific thinker; he contributed nothing of theoretical substance or methodological innovation to the movement he launched. Watson was a brilliant polemicist, and for him at least behaviorism was a revolt. But against what?

Against the former schools of thought, as any revolutionary would say. But Paul Creelan (1974), analyzing Watson's personality, has suggested that he was revolting against much more than worn-out mentalism. Watson was raised by a devout Baptist mother, to be a minister. Before he could go to Princeton Seminary, however, his mother died. Instead he went to the University of Chicago, an urban university and the heart of American functionalism, where he met an entirely different atmosphere. He was interested in psychology but had trouble acting as an introspective subject. Eventually he had a nervous breakdown. After recovering, he preferred animal subjects to human ones. Perhaps, having rebelled against his mother's religion, he preferred to believe that there is no soul, no mind, that only muscular responses are real. Thus there is no hell or heaven. There is instead the prospect of a completely controllable world, a scientific heaven on earth. Watson often insisted that his opponents' mentalism was really clinging to a scientifically impossible soul, an entity that made him profoundly uncomfortable.

Thus, like many moderns, Watson may have been revolting against a no longer believable religion, against maternal puritanism. Possibly the depth of his personal involvement made this natural twentieth-century outgrowth of the nineteenth-century crisis of conscience feel more revolutionary than it really was.

## CONCLUSION

### Was There a Revolution?

To Watson behaviorism was a revolution, led directly against structuralism but indirectly against Calvinist religion. But was it a scientific revolution? Let us ask each Kuhnian question in turn.

*Was there normal science and an established paradigm to revolt against?*

America contained both functionalism and structuralism. Each practiced a kind of normal science, especially Titchener's structuralism. However, to the extent that these two paradigms were in competition, and Titchener at least clearly saw them in competition, they were rival schools in a pre-paradigm science. The two groups criticized each other, and certainly could not agree on fundamental assumptions defining psychology. By Watson's time, functionalism, of an increasingly behavioral sort, was clearly in the ascendant. Watson's attacks on structuralism were in a sense irrelevant. He was an animal psychologist and should have been attacking a dominant animal psychology, but he chose as his main villain introspective structuralism, which had nothing to do with animals. There was really no unified normal science in Kuhn's sense in 1913 for Watson to revolt against, and he attacked the system with which he was least associated.

*Were there anomalies?* In his 1913 paper, Watson lists a number of problems facing structuralism, for example the much discussed question of imageless thought. He seemed to believe they were insoluble. However, were they anomalies? A problem is not an anomaly, but a puzzle to be solved by the normal scientist. Certainly Titchener, Wundt, and Külpe all believed that the imageless thought controversy was resolvable within mentalistic psychology; they did not see it as anomalous. The same may be said of the other "anomalies" on Watson's list. Furthermore, these cannot have been anomalies for Watson in any case, for he was an *animal* psychologist unconcerned with questions in human psychology. Watson lists no empirical problems in animal psychology at all. His only dissatisfaction is with the method of imputing consciousness to animals. In any case, Watson's proposed revolution would not have solved any of the so-called structuralist "anomalies" as a new paradigm should—rather it would dissolve them by eliminating all reference to thought, imageless or not. The answer to this question, of anomalies, then, must be no.

*Was there a crisis?* Given that there were no anomalies, we might expect that the answer here must be no—but it is yes. There was a crisis. The papers by Frost and Elliot, of 1912, clearly reflect a crisis atmosphere, for they are discussions of fundamental issues, not pieces of puzzle-solving research. There are also available a useful series of papers by Edward F. Buchner, which appeared from 1904 to 1913 in *Psychological Bulletin,* each of which summarized the previous year's activity in psychology. In 1905 Buchner noted that 1903-1904 (when Watson was at Chicago) was "chiefly marked by a sudden and widespread reexamination of the aims, methods, and fundamental conceptions of psychology." This crisis centered on the nature of consciousness, with James, for example, arguing that there was no *thing* called consciousness, just various processes of which we are conscious. Although 1905 was a quiet year, in 1907 Buchner described psychology as "transitional," marked by a rebellion against traditional and "almost consecrated" psychological terms such as consciousness, feeling, and sensation. Things quieted down again for a while, but in 1911 he wrote: "Some of us are still struggling at initial clearness as to what psychology is about." He observed that biologists considered psychology to be "crude, inexact and unscientific," and that applied psychology was on the rise. In 1912 he discussed the continuing crisis over the subject matter of psychology, which seemed to be becoming the science of behavior. In 1913, covering the year 1912, Buchner described attacks on introspection as an illegitimate method, or at least of limited value.

There clearly was some sort of continuing crisis, but it cannot have been a Kuhnian crisis because nowhere is there any reference to anomalies. It is a philosophical, pre-paradigm crisis. Psychologists were finding consciousness to be a slippery foundation on which to build psychology. First, they redefined it, then they began to question its existence and the introspective method, with help from the animal psychologists and biologists. There are no empirical problems at the root of the crisis, only a continuing effort to define psychology. We should note that much of psychologists' uncertainty was over whether psychology is truly a science. It is a question that arose frequently in the period and is periodically heard throughout psychology's history. Increasingly in Watson's time psychologists seemed to suspect that it was the introspective method that barred them from a secure sense of scientific status.

*Did a rival paradigm emerge to solve the anomalies?* Clearly a change was coming over American psychology, but it was not of Watson's making, nor was it in response to empirical anomalies. Instead, more and more workers, from Angell to Thorndike, were becoming convinced that only the objective methods expounded by positivism could furnish a scientific psychology. The crisis was over method and subject matter; the response was first to substitute a new method —behavioral study—but retain the old goal, to understand animal or human mind, as Thorndike did in 1898. What Watson did was to make a final break with the past by adopting a new name, a new method, and a new, positivist subject matter. Mind cannot be observed, therefore any reference to it is illegitimate. We must stay entirely at the level of behavioral description, relating observable stimulus to observable response. Watson seized on the evolutionary movement in functionalist psychology from a science of consciousness to a science of behavior, and crystallized it into a self-conscious "ism," a new paradigm for the practice of psychology. But if this is a revolution it is not a Kuhnian revolution, for it was not built on empirical anomalies but on continuing doubts about the goals, methods, and subject matter of psychology. Behaviorism explained no anomalies.

*Did the new paradigm attract adherents?* Obviously it did. In 1915, only two years after the publication of his manifesto, Watson was elected president of the American Psychological Association. Other psychologists stepped forward to be called behaviorists, while some, like Angell, wished the movement "Godspeed" although unable to join it (Larson & Sullivan, 1971).

*Was there a period of struggle?* Yes; many traditional psychologists could not accept behaviorism. We need consider only the most eminent, Titchener, who criticized Watson for misrepresenting structuralism and for being unhistorical in not realizing that proposals to make psychology behavioral are nothing new. Titchener's most interesting point is that behaviorism is simply irrelevant to structuralism. No matter how far behavioral methods are pushed, there must always remain human consciousness to be introspectively explored. Titchener correctly perceived that the basic issue was methodology, and he argued that different methods could not produce results that were incompatible, only different. Titchener also argued against the anomalous character of Watson's proposed problems in introspective psychology. He argued that the problems of reasoning, judgment, and so forth are not "threadbare" as Watson held, but quite fresh and inviting. Titchener made numerous other points against Watson, many of them revived by later critics: behaviorism is irrefutable; it is excessively technological; it has no place for meaning; its problems are all borrowed, for it reacts to questions set by mentalistic psychology but then reduces them to S-R terms, being unable itself to pose creative puzzles. Titchener (1914) remained confident: "Meanwhile introspective psychology ... will go quietly about its task ... declining with the mild persistance of matters of fact—either to be eliminated or ignored." The tone here is remarkably similar to that of B. F. Skinner in the face of challenges from cognitive and humanistic psychology in the 1960s. Titchener's confidence, however, was misplaced. Structuralism died with Titchener.

### Historical Trends: Was Psychology Redefined Under a New Paradigm?

The old introspective psychology was finished. From its founding in 1916, the number of introspective research papers in the *Journal of Experimental Psychology* steadily declined, while the number of purely behavioral ones rose. By 1929 names that were to dominate experimental psychology for a generation began to appear—Tolman, Hull, McGeoch—while Watson disappeared into the world of business, which welcomed him after he was fired from Johns Hopkins University for divorcing his first wife to marry Rosalie Rayner, his collaborator.

However, whether there was a new, unified paradigm in Kuhn's sense is a difficult question. Throughout the next 30 years there continued to be some few psychologists who questioned the validity of behaviorism and held to some rival school, such as Gestalt psychology or psychoanalysis. Furthermore, as early as 1922 there was dissension in the ranks of behaviorists. In 1922 Tolman, for example, wrote "A New Formula for Behaviorism," which questioned Watson's radical formulation. Tolman began by saying, "The idea of Behaviorism is abroad ... spreading like wildfire," but rejected Watson's behaviorism of muscle twitches and glandular secretions for a "molar" description and explanation of behavior, one based on acts larger than muscle movements.

We must postpone answering the last Kuhnian question until the next chapter, for the post-Watsonian behaviorism of Tolman and others, neobehaviorism, is the next topic.

## SUGGESTED READINGS

The best single account of the conceptual origins of behaviorism is Brian Mackenzie's *Behaviorism and the Limits of Scientific Method* (London: Routledge & Kegan Paul, 1977).

# REFERENCES

Angell, J. R. Behavior as a category of psychology. *Psychological Review*, 1913, *20*, 255-270.

Bailyn, B., David D., Donald, D., Thomas, D., Wielse, R., & Wood, C. *The great republic.* Boston: Little Brown, 1977.

Cornwell, D. & Hobbs, S. The strange saga of Little Albert. *New Society*, 1976, *18*, 602-604.

Creelan, P. G. Watsonian Behaviorism and the Calvinist conscience. *Journal of the history of the Behavioral Sciences,* 1974, *10*, 95-118.

Frost, E. P. Can biology and physiology dispense with consciousness? *Psychological Review,* 1912, *3*, 246-252.

Harris, B. Whatever happened to Little Albert? *American Psychologist,* 1979, *34*, 151-160.

Henle, M. The influence of Gestalt psychology in America. In R. Rieber & K. Salzinger (Eds.) *The roots of American psychology. Annals of the New York Academy of Sciences,* 1977, *291*, 1-394.

Joncich, G. *The sane positivist: A biography of Edward L. Thorndike.* Middletown, Conn.: Wesleyan University Press, 1968.

Koch, S. Psychology and emerging conceptions of knowledge as unitary. In T. W. Wann (Ed.) *Behaviorism and phenomenology.* Chicago: Chicago University Press, 1964.

Larson, C. & Sullivan, J. Watson's relation to Titchener. In V. S. Sexton & H. Misiak (Eds.) *Historical perspectives in psychology.* Belmont. Cal.: Brooks/Cole, 1971.

MacDougall, R. Mind as middle term. *Psychological Review,* 1912, *19*, 386-403.

MacKenzie, B. *Behaviorism and the limits of scientific method.* London: Routledge & Kegan Paul, 1977.

Maudsley, H. *The physiology and pathology of the mind* (1867). Excepted in S. Diamond (Ed.) *The roots of psychology.* New York: Basic Books, 1974.

Palermo, D. Is a scientific revolution taking place in psychology? *Science Studies,* 1971, *1*, 135-155.

Pavlov, I. P. *Experimental psychology and other essays.* New York: Philosophical Library, 1957.

Sechenov, I. M. *Reflexes of the brain* (1863). Excerpted in R. J. Herrnstein & E. G. Boring (Eds.) *A source book in the history of psychology.* Cambridge, Mass.: Harvard University Press, 1965.

Sechenov, I. M. *I. M. Sechenov: Biographical sketch and essays.* New York: Arno, 1973.

Thorndike, E. L. *Animal intelligence* (1911). New York: Hafner, 1965.

Thorndike, E. L. *Human Learning.* New York: Johnson Reprint Corp., 1968.

Titchener, E. On "Psychology as the behaviorist views it." *Proceedings of the American Philosophical Society,* 1914, *53*, 1-17.

Watson, J. B. Psychology as the behaviorist views it. *Psychological Review,* 1913a, *20*, 158-177.

Watson, J. B. Image and affection in behavior. *Journal of Philosophy, Psychology, and Scientific Methods,* 1913b, *10*, 421-428.

Watson, J. B. *Behaviorism*. New York: Norton, 1930.

Watson, J. B. Autobiography. In C. Murchison (Ed.) *A history of psychology in autobiography*. New York: Russell & Russell, 1961.

Watson, J. B. & Rayner, R. Conditioned emotional reactions. *Journal of Experimental Psychology*, 1920, *3,* 1-14.

# 11

# Neobehaviorism

## VARIETIES OF NEOBEHAVIORISM

Watson gave behaviorism its first, crude formulation. He wanted to excise the mind from psychology, and behaviorism "spread like wildfire" among younger psychologists who, like Watson, saw the psychology of consciousness as sterile, unscientific, and irrelevant to the prediction and control of human actions. Watson's converts, however, found his classical behaviorism to be too simple, and they sought to refine behaviorism into a truly scientific psychology. Watson had defined behaviorism purely in terms of experimental methods, as the substitution of objective for subjective research procedures. Watson had nothing to say about theory, although theory was obviously an important part of the natural sciences Watson wanted to emulate, and various young psychologists embraced Watson's objective psychology with a view toward developing objective psychological theory as well as experiment. This refined strain of classical behaviorism has come to be called neobehaviorism, for although it builds on the objectivism of Watson, it is less dogmatic and aggressive, and more philosophically sophisticated than classical behaviorism. Three strains of neobehaviorism dominated experimental psychology from 1930 to about 1960, formal behaviorism, radical behaviorism, and informal behaviorism.*

### Formal Behaviorism

Watson had sought the scientific salvation of psychology in sound experimental method. It was application of objective method, he believed, that would unravel all the old problems of psychology. In this he followed the positivism of Ernst Mach, who abjured all theoretical terms for careful description of observable facts. However, such an atheoretical approach was inconsistent with science as it was actually practiced. Physicists needed theory and so did psychologists. Psychologists who recognized this need looked to philosophers of science for guidance about good theoretical method to supplement Watson's objective experimentation. Formal behaviorists believed that rigorously defined experiment and theory together could be used to systematically construct a scientific psychology of equal stature with their model, physics. To understand formal behaviorism, we must begin by examining the philosophy that provided their model: logical positivism.

#### Logical Positivism

Out of the uncertainties of the late Middle Ages and Renaissance, Descartes and Locke constructed new philosophies to put human knowledge on a certain foundation. Similarly, out of the nineteenth-century intellectual crisis and dis-

*The terms *formal behaviorism* and *informal behaviorism* are Don E. Dulany's; taken from private communication.

illusionment of World War I, the logical positivists constructed a philosophy that they believed would put human knowledge on a new and certain foundation. Logical positivism started in Vienna in the early twentieth century, founded by Rudolph Carnap, Moritz Schlick, and Otto Neurath, among others. They sought to revise all of philosophy according to their program. Like Kant before them, they decided that physical science was the most certain knowledge humanity possessed, and so they tried to explicate the nature of scientific knowledge so that it could be taken as a model by other fields. Logical positivism combines the empiricism of Mach with the logical apparatus of Russell's and Whitehead's *Principia Mathematica* with the aim that this union would encompass both scientific method and theory. It was the early logical positivists' rational reconstruction of physical science that formal behaviorists took as the prescription for scientific progress that psychology should follow.

The logical positivists were not very concerned to give a historically accurate description of the development of physics. Rather they wanted to understand what it was about science that made it so successful in producing human knowledge, and then to formalize science's procedures in a rigorous description of final finished scientific systems. Their picture thus provided a goal for other sciences, including psychology, to try to achieve.

The logical positivists divided science into two parts: theory and observation. The positivists were empiricists, saying that direct observation yields factual descriptions of the world and provides the bedrock upon which all other knowledge is based. The value of any scientific theory was to be evaluated according to the observations it was able to successfully predict. Up to this point, the logical positivists adhere to Mach's views. However, every science must refer to unobservable, hypothetical entities, such as force, mass, or atom in physics. Mach had fought against the introduction of hypothetical terms into physics—especially the concept of the atom—for it was conceived as too small to be directly observed. The logical positivists, however, were willing to admit purely theoretical terms into science as long as each term was defined according to some observable manifestation. This is similar to the pragmatic conception of truth discussed in Chapter 9; Peirce drew his analysis of concepts from his scientific training. Thus a term such as *mass* was legitimate, for it could be related to observable manifestations such as weight registered on a scale, while a term such as *God* would be rejected, for it has no observable consequences. The goal was to admit the importance of theory to science, while ensuring that all theory would be firmly tied to experience, the empiricist's arbiter of truth.

Building a scientific theory became akin to constructing a geometrical system. A scientist could invent theoretical terms, and then relate them to one another by writing theoretical sentences, or *axioms*. For example, one might conceive the theoretical ideas of force, mass, and acceleration. No one actually observes any of these in the abstract, but one does experience their consequences—or more scientifically, each may be measured. Further, one might propose a specific interrelation among these terms and say that force varies directly as a product of mass multiplied by acceleration, or F = M x A; this is an axiom. So far, the exercise is purely theoretical, for we have specified no values of force, mass, or acceleration, nor do we have any assurance that the axiom is true. Other possible axioms might be $F = M \times A^2$ or $F = \log M \times A^3$, and so on. In order to achieve scientific knowledge, the axiom must be used to predict the outcome of a specific experiment. In the present example, we could do this by taking an object of known mass, accelerating it to a known degree and measuring the resulting force. The axiom predicts exactly what the force should be. If the measured value of force agrees with the prediction, the axiom and the larger theory of which it is a part are said to be confirmed—to be provisional knowledge. If the prediction is not confirmed, it means that the axiom is incorrect and must be replaced.

Such was the logical positivist's rational reconstruction of science, and it was worked out with a great deal of logical sophistication. The logical positivists failed to remake all philosophy in the image of science, but they did invent the field of philosophy of science, which they dominated until the 1960s. Their program underwent a number of changes after its early days in Vienna, but the single most problematic concept, and the most influential on psychology, was the operational definition.

Given their sharp division between theory and data, and their requirement that each theoretical term be tied to observation, the logical positivists had to provide for the connection between theory and data. Their initial proposal was that each theoretical term in a system had to be explicitly defined in terms of its observable manifestations. A virtually identical concept was proposed independently by a physicist, Percy Bridgman, who called it *operational definition*, the name by which it is known to psychologists. According to the concept of operational (or explicit) definition, any theoretical term must be defined by an empirical operation. For example, *mass* might be defined as the metric weight of an object at sea level. The operation was held to completely define its corresponding concept. There was to be no *surplus meaning*, meaning beyond the specific operation used to define the concept. A psychological concept makes this restriction clearer. We may define *hunger* by the operation of withholding food from an animal for 24 hours. Such an operational definition of hunger excludes the feelings we associate with hunger and its behavior-directing properties. According to the early logical positivists, hunger would be nothing more than observable food deprivation, not a mental or emotional state.

The requirement that theoretical terms be operationally defined was introduced to psychology in the 1930s by the psychophysicist S.S. Stevens (1939), who presented it as an objective method for settling all scientific disputes; it is still widespread today. It is frequently presented by both introductory texts and advanced theoretical papers as a touchstone of good science. However, it was abandoned in the mid-1930s by the logical positivists themselves because it was far too restrictive and did not accurately describe the practice of the queen of the sciences, physics. The reasons for its rejection are quite technical, but suffice it to say that by the 1950s most logical positivists themselves had given up the search for any formal way of tieing theory to observation. Post-positivist philosophers of science have shifted away from formal explications of ideal science to accounts of how science is actually practiced. We have met such philosophies in Chapter 1, and later we will examine their impact on recent psychology. The fact that most psychologists still revere operational definitions, however, indicates that they have been out of touch with philosophical studies of science since 1935.

The immediate impact of logical positivism and operationism on psychology was tremendous. They seemed to promise psychologists that theory could be just as objective and nonmentalistic as the experimental methods of classical conditioning and trial-and-error learning. Before logical positivism, any psychological theory seemed to demand reference to mind, and so smacked of the old psychology. Positivism seemed to show that theoretical terms could be completely defined by observable behavior, while operationism made it possible to expunge surplus mentalistic meanings. The way seemed open for slow and steady progress on the problems of psychology. The orientation of logical positivism is most fully embodied in logical behaviorism.

### Logical Behaviorism

A heroic, highly technical, but ultimately futile attempt (Koch, 1954) to construct a behaviorial psychology was made by Clark Leonard Hull (1884-1952). For Hull, as for Watson, the central problem of psychology was learning: how the organism adapted to its environment. Also like Watson, Hull (1952) believed that "the behavior of all mammals operates according to the same primary laws." Hull's goal (1951) was consequently to establish "the basic laws of mammalian behavior" following what he took to be accepted scientific practice in the natural sciences, as described by the logical positivists. Hull devoted most of his efforts over his career to achieving this goal, although he also worked on other topics such as hypnosis.

Of all learning theories, Hull's is the most extreme in taking the stimulus-response (S-R) point of view. This is a reasonable consequence of the logical positivist orientation, for the observation-terms of objective psychology must refer to the observable environment (stimuli) and an organism's observable behavior (responses). Hull believed that learning was a matter of acquiring the correct responses to certain situations, and as a result his theory is an S-R association theory with similarities to Thorndike's. He sought, however, to explain how and why stimulus and responses get connected, not to merely describe the course of learning. Thus, following the logical positivist program, Hull postulated unobservable theoretical entities that intervened between stimulus and response. Hull was rather vague about the exact nature of his intervening theoretical terms, although he was disposed to believe they represented nervous system processes peripheral to the cortex (Hull, 1951). He was thus a peripheralist, as Watson had been.

Hull's theoretical system was of enormous complexity, as axiom was piled on postulate and corollaries were appended to these. One simplified example will illustrate Hull's logical positivist psychology (Hull, 1943; 1951; 1952). We will define three theoretical terms $_SE_R$, $_SH_R$, and D. $_SE_R$ is called *reaction potential*, "the tendency to produce some reaction under the effect of a stimulus." No one can observe $_SE_R$; it is a theoretical term that intervenes between stimulus and response. Reaction potential finds its empirical definition in an organism's behavior: how strong a response is; how fast it is made after the stimulus is presented; how resistant it is to extinction. The stronger, faster, and more resistant is an R, the greater is its $_SE_R$. Reaction potential is a performance variable, for it relates to the strength of an actual movement or response, already learned or given innately. Learning is represented by another theoretical entity, $_SH_R$, or *habit strength*. As an organism learns, it builds up a particular habit, which gets stronger as learning proceeds. The most important empirical definer of habit strength was number of reinforcements. Hull proposed that the more often a response was reinforced, the stronger was the corresponding habit—although he recognized that there was an upper limit on habit strength.

Behavior is determined not only by an organism's habits, but also by its motivational state, which Hull called its *drive,* or D. A completely satiated animal will behave differently from a hungry one. Drive was empirically defined by some drive-inducing operation carried out on an animal, such as depriving it of food for 24 hours. Drive increases as a consequence of such deprivation until the animal is weakened and drive strength diminishes.

We have now empirically defined three theoretical terms as required by the logical positivist program, and are prepared to write an axiom or postulate interrelating the terms; we will then be in a position to test our axiom. Hull's postulate relating the three entities was $_SE_R = _SH_R \times D$. Although it appears fearsome, it is intuitively obvious. A response will occur, that is $_SE_R$ will be strong enough to instigate behavior, only if that response has been adequately learned ($_SH_R$ is positive) and the organism is motivated to behave (D is positive): $_SE_R = _SH_R \times D = 10 \times 10 = 100$. Obviously, a response cannot occur if it has not been learned no matter how strong drive is: $_SE_R = _SH_R \times D = 0 \times 100 = 0$. It also will not occur if there is no motivation to act regardless of how well it is learned: $_SE_R = _SH_R \times D = 100 \times 0 = 0$.

Testing this axiom in a qualitative way is relatively simple. You could design the following two-factor experiment with three conditions under each. Rats could be taught some habit, such as pressing a lever in a Skinner box to three different degrees of habit strength: low (no reinforced presses), medium (50 reinforced presses), and high (100 reinforced presses). Then you could divide each of these three groups into three sub-groups, each based on drive: low (satiated), medium (12 hours food deprivation) and high (24 hours deprivation). Then each rat from all nine (3 x 3) groups would be put in a Skinner box and it could be determined how long it took each rat to make its first bar press. The shorter the time, the greater the $_SE_R$. If the axiom is correct, all low drive and low habit strength groups should not press the lever at all ($_SE_R = 0$), while the shortest latencies should be recorded by the high-high groups followed by the low-high and high-low groups and the medium-medium group. If the data came out otherwise, the axiom would stand refuted.

However, Hull was not content with a qualitative theory and qualitative experiments. His very use of mathematical equations, such as $_SE_R = {_S}H_R \times D$ indicates that he wanted to establish a precise quantitative theory, that is, to be able to assign exact values to all theoretical terms. An example of Hull's obsession with mathematical precision may be found in his exact definition (1952) of D. D consists of two components, D´ and $\epsilon$. D´ is "an increasing monotonic sigmoid function of h, the number of hours of food privation": D´ = $37.824 \times 10^{-27.496}$ h + 4.001. $\epsilon$ reflects the weakening effects of starvation, and "is a positively accelerated monotonic function of h": $\epsilon = 1 - .00001045h^{2.486}$. Finally, D = D´ $\times$ $\epsilon$.

These numbers appear precise and formidable, but Hull was quite willing to ignore them in order to make his data come out right. During a discussion of maze learning in *A Behavior System* he wrote that the value of $\sigma$, the unit by which $_SE_R$ was measured, should according to theory be 1.00, but that "in order to secure something like usual blind-alley elimination scores" he arbitrarily altered it to 0.3012. Moreover, the entire quantification program was built on a small bed of sand. Only one experiment was carried out to quantify $_SE_R$, which was then used as the basis for quantifying the other theoretical variables. This experiment involved 59 rats pressing bars in a Skinner box. It borrowed a very complex procedure from human psychophysics while violating its assumptions, and produced a distribution of scores at variance with some of Hull's mathematical assumptions (Koch, 1954).

Hull's quantitative theory may have been adequate for this one experiment, but it is clear that whether it could be generalized to all mammalian behavior is highly questionable, and today it is the consensus even among those remaining in the Hullian tradition that Hull's quantitative program was the least important feature of his work (Hilgard & Bower, 1975). However, he took it quite seriously, at least as an ultimate goal if not an accomplished fact, until his death in 1952. We shall postpone further evaluation of logical behaviorism until a later section.

Hull found a close associate in Kenneth Spence (1907-1967) who worked with Hull and carried the system to the University of Iowa, where his rigorous graduate training left *"The Journal of Experimental Psychology* literally yellow with graduate student sweat" (Brewer, 1974). He developed the system while staying close to Hull's own axiomatic formulations and continued to present the logical positivist view of science as the correct one. In this latter task he was aided by his Iowa colleague in philosophy, Gustav Bergmann who aggressively espoused early logical positivism long after its abandonment by other philosophers of science. However, Spence was primarily a technical learning theorist best known for his brilliant work in discrimination learning. On the larger psychological issues with which we are concerned, Spence followed his mentor Hull. Hull also influenced large numbers of psychologists who were attracted by his rigorous scientific stance, but who were not committed to the mathematical method of logical behaviorism. We shall discuss some of them under informal behaviorism.

Although he was the most mathematical, hypothetical-deductive of the formal behaviorists, Hull was not the only learning theorist in the 1930s and 1940s.

The most important rival system, one far less peripheralistic, and far less committed to S-R formulations, was E. C. Tolman's cognitive behaviorism.

### Cognitive Behaviorism

Edward Chace Tolman (1886-1959), although born later than Hull, began his psychological career earlier. We discuss him after Hull because he was a gadfly to Hull for many years, and because his system stands in sharp contrast to Hull's. Tolman was an early and forceful advocate of behaviorism. Like Watson, he asserted in "Operational Behaviorism and Current Trends in Psychology" that "the ultimate interest of psychology is solely the prediction and control of behavior" and eschewed introspection or reference to consciousness. It was he who introduced to psychology the concept of intervening variables, unobserved entities (such as D in Hull's theory) that come between stimulus and response. Like Hull, he thought that operational definitions were the proper way to define the intervening variables. Also like Hull, he sought an entirely general psychology, one capable of explaining all learned behavior in all organisms.

Like Watson, Tolman felt that structuralism was unscientific. He was won over to behaviorism by reading Watson's *Behavior: An Introduction to Comparative Psychology*. Still, he did not share all Watson's views. He wrote (1959): "However, although I was sold on objectivism and behaviorism as *the* method in psychology . . . I rejected the extreme peripheralism and muscle-twitchism of Watson." What is distinctive about Tolman is his rejection of peripheralism in favor of centralism, of S-R formulations in favor of a Gestalt-influenced field approach, and in general his rejection of atomistic, pure behaviorism in favor of a theory that would admit a rat's or a human's mind, if not consciousness, to science. Tolman gave his system many names over the years, but here the title cognitive behaviorism is adopted to convey Tolman's concern with including in behaviorism mental processes, as operationally defined intervening variables.

Tolman's theory is impossible to summarize briefly. He never set down a group of postulates, as Hull did, nor was he as quantitative, despite his logical positivist orientation. He adopted rather awkward terminology for many of his ideas. We will sample his work in a delightful late paper called "Cognitive maps in rats and men," and discuss a sample experiment that contrasts Tolman's cognitive theory with Hull's S-R theory.

Tolman's major experimental paradigm was the rat in the maze. As Tolman described the S-R position (1948): "The maze behavior of rats is a matter of mere stimulus-response connections. Learning . . . consists in the strengthening of some of those connections and in the weakening of others." This is, of course, Hull's S-R position, which says that learning is associating the correct specific response to each choice-point stimulus in a maze. Tolman (1948), however "may be called a field theorist. . . . In the course of learning something like a field map of the environment gets established in the rat's brain." Here Tolman borrowed the Gestalt concept of isomorphism. The S-R school views the central nervous system as "a complicated telephone switchboard," a view we have met in Watson that was also shared by Hull. Field theory, however, sees the central nervous system as "more like a map control room. The stimuli . . . are not connected by just simple one-to-one switches to the outgoing responses . . . but are worked over and elaborated" (Tolman, 1948) into a cognitive map of the environment. The contrast of the two theories is clear.

Now let us consider an example of an experiment which contrasts the cognitive and S-R views. It was actually reported in 1930 (Tolman, 1932), well before the Hull-Tolman debates really got underway, but it is a simpler version of more complex experiments described in "Cognitive Maps in Rats and Men" meant to differentially support Tolman's theory. The maze is shown in Figure 11-1. Rats were familiarized with the entire maze by forcing them to run each path in early training. Having learned the maze, a rat coming out of the start box into the choice point must pick one of the paths. How does he do this?

A Hullian analysis may be sketched. The choice point presents stimuli (S) to which three responses (R's) corresponding to each path have been conditioned during initial training. For a variety of reasons, most obviously the different amounts of running that must be done in each alley, Path 1 is preferred to Path 2, which is preferred to Path 3. That is, connection $S \rightarrow R_1$ is stronger than $S \rightarrow R_2$, which is stronger than $S \rightarrow R_3$. Such a state of affairs may be notated

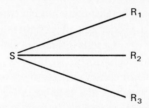

This is called a *divergent habit family hierarchy*. Now, should a block he placed at Point 1, the rat will run into it, back up, and choose Path 2. The connection $S \rightarrow R_1$ is weakened by the block, so that $S \rightarrow R_2$ becomes stronger and is acted on. On the other hand, if the second block is placed, the rat will retreat to the choice point and again choose Path 2 as $S \rightarrow R_1$ is again blocked, and $S \rightarrow R_2$ becomes stronger. However, the block will be met again, $S \rightarrow R_2$ will weaken, and finally $S \rightarrow R_3$ will be strongest and Path 3 will be chosen. This is the Hullian prediction.

The cognitive field theory position denies that what is learned is a set of responses triggered to differing degrees by the stimuli at the choice-point. Instead, it holds that the rat learns a mental map of the maze which guides its behavior. According to this view, the rat encountering the first block will turn around and choose Path 2, as in the S-R account, because Path 2 is shorter than 3. However, if it encounters Block 2 the rat will know that the same block will cut off Path 2 as well as Path 1. Therefore the rat will show "insight": it will return and choose Path 3, ignoring Path 2 altogether. A map displays all aspects of the environment, and is more informative than a set of S-R connections. The two theories diverge

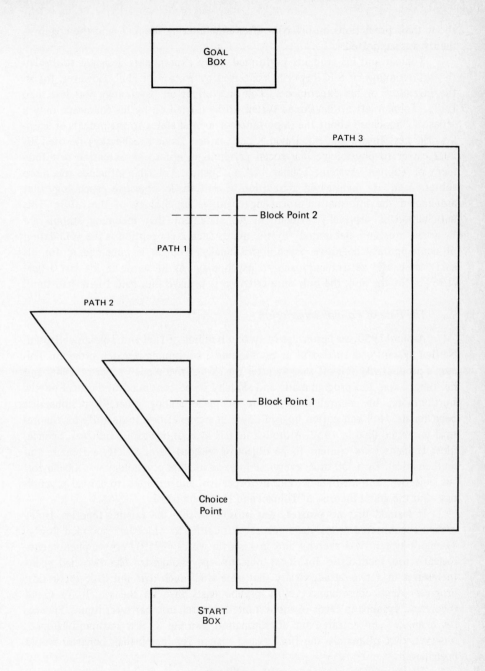

**FIGURE 11-1.**
Tolman-Honzik Maze.

about their predictions on behavior after encountering Block 2, and the cognitive theory was supported.

Tolman and his students performed many experiments designed to display the shortcomings of S-R theory as conceived by Watson or Hull. However, for all the ingenuity of his experiments, Tolman's effect on psychology was less than Hull's. Tolman left no developed system to be carried on by his followers, only a series of "hunches" about the importance of mental states to the process of learning. His best-known student, David Krech (earlier, David Krechevsky), devoted his later career to physiological or social psychology, not to an extension or refinement of Tolman's system; Tolman had no Spence. Tolman's influence was more subterranean. He maintained a tradition of centralistic, objective psychology that anticipated the information-processing cognitive psychology of the future. This anticipation is especially evident in his statement that incoming stimuli are "worked over and elaborated" by the mind. Such a conception is the foundation of contemporary cognitive psychology. Finally, Tolman is remembered for his lively style and zestful approach to psychology. As he wrote in his last article (1959): "In the end, the only sure criterion is to have fun. And I have had fun."

### The Fate of Formal Behaviorism

Around 1950, the heroic age of system building of Hull and Tolman collapsed. Neither system was successful at establishing a continuing research program. Tolman's productivity fell off sharply after the "Cognitive maps" paper of 1948, and his theory was too programmatic and sketchy to be continued by faithful pupils. Furthermore, his centralism was out of place among generally peripheralist behaviorists. Hull had gotten bogged down in arcane efforts to quantify his theoretical terms; he died in 1952. Although he left at least one astute follower, Spence, most Hullians were content to be objective without being strictly axiomatic and mathematical. By 1950 most everyone in experimental psychology was a behaviorist—objective, anti-mentalistic, anti-introspective, and oriented to animal psychology—but the grand theories of Tolman and Hull were passé.

It seemed that no progress was possible within the existing theories. Hull's system encountered numerous empirical difficulties to which he responded slowly. Tolman's system was sketchy and in his own words (1959) "crypto-phenomenological"—too mentalistic for most objective psychologists. The two had spent themselves in a two-decade rivalry that generated much data but little theoretical progress. As a consequence, most psychologists gave up the search for grand theoretical systems in favor of more limited research into narrower topics. Spence, for example, concentrated on discrimination learning. It was commonly hoped, however, that ultimately the final axiom system for mammalian behavior would be achieved.

The formal behaviorists furnish an illuminating lesson by their failure, however. Tolman and Hull sincerely pursued psychology with what they believed was the proper scientific approach. Their belief in objective research they learned from Watson. Their belief in an objective theory they learned from the logical positivists.

Yet, despite their rigorous methods, they failed to produce a psychology any more viable in its details than Titchener's.

Their failure may lie with them, or with positivism. Given the intelligence and diligence of Tolman, Hull, and their students, it is unlikely that they failed through want of effort or intelligence. The failure, then, is probably traceable to logical positivism, which claimed to offer a logical reconstruction of science in its ultimate form. But it ignored the way sciences actually grow and improve, and it ignored the psychological underpinnings of science. Both have been emphasized by recent students of science, such as Toulmin and Kuhn whom we discussed in Chapter 1. There we saw that science is not always logical, that negative results do not always refute a theory, and that a research program rests on a central core of unprovable concepts. None of this is to be found in the logical positivist program of science. It presents a wholly unrealistic picture of the growth of science and hence cannot be a useful model for practicing scientists to follow. Psychologists are perenially insecure about their status as scientists. Logical positivism and operationism seemed to hold out hope that a set of procedures existed that, if followed faithfully, would produce psychological science. Hull and Tolman made every effort to follow these procedures and by 1950 they had come to a dead end. Logical positivism was tried and found wanting. Psychologists continued to be objective and to believe in operationism, but the grand program had failed. Not until the 1960s would philosophy of science exert a comparable influence on psychology.

By 1950 experimental psychologists were ready for a change. Already there were signs that an objective mentalistic psychology was possible, but its fruition lay more than a decade in the future. The immediate past had been dominated by grandiose theories of learning, but in 1950 a radically minded behaviorist reasserted the less formal psychological program of Watson and the simpler positivism of Mach by asking, "Are theories of learning necessary?" and by answering emphatically NO. The reassertion of a simpler, less elaborate, but no less grandiose, psychology was made by B. F. Skinner.

### Radical Behaviorism

Define
And thus expunge
The *ought*
The *should*
* * *
Truth's to be sought
In *Does* and *Doesn't*

B.F. Skinner, *For Ivor Richards* (Skinner, 1971)

By far the best-known and most influential of all the major behaviorists is Burrhus Frederick Skinner (born 1904), whose radical behaviorism, if accepted, would constitute a momentous revolution in humanity's understanding of the human self, demanding as it does no less than the complete rejection of the entire intellectual psychological tradition nurtured in philosophy that we have considered in this book. It would replace this tradition with a scientific psychology grounded in neo-Darwinian evolutionary theory which looks outside humans for the causes of behavior. Every psychological thinker we have considered, from Thales to Wundt, even to Hull and Tolman, intended psychology to be an explication of internal processes, however conceived—processes that produce behavior or conscious phenomena. Skinner follows Watson in placing responsibility for behavior squarely in the environment, however. A person does not act at the behest of moral values, the "ought" and "should," the highest guides to action for Plato. For Skinner, a person deserves neither praise nor blame for anything he "does" or "doesn't." The environment controls behavior so that both good and evil, if such exist, reside there, not in the person. To paraphrase Shakespeare's Julius Caesar: "The fault, dear Brutus, lies in our contingencies of reinforcement, not ourselves."

The heart of radical behaviorism may best be approached by looking at Skinner's attitude to Freud. Skinner discusses Freud more than he does any other psychologist. One convenient single discussion can be found in his paper "A critique of psychoanalytic concepts and theories." For Skinner, Freud's great discovery was that much human behavior has unconscious causes. However, to Skinner Freud's great mistake was in inventing a mental apparatus—id, ego, super-ego—and its attendant mental processes to explain human behavior. Skinner believed that the lesson taught by the unconscious is that mental states are simply irrelevant to behavior. We may observe that a student shows a neurotic subservience to her teachers. The Freudian might explain this by asserting that the student's father was a punitive perfectionist who demanded obedience, and that his child incorporated a stern father image that now affects the student's behavior in the presence of authority figures. Skinner would allow us to explain the current servility by reference to punishments at the hand of a punitive father, but he would insist that the link be direct. The student cowers now because as a child she received punishment from a similar person, not because there is any mental image within her of her father. For Skinner, the inference to an unconscious father-image explains nothing that cannot be explained by simply referring current behavior to the consequences of past behavior. The mental link adds nothing to an account of behavior, according to Skinner, and in fact complicates matters by requiring that the mental link itself be explained. Skinner has extended this criticism of mental entities to encompass all traditional psychologies, rejecting equally the superego, apperception, $_sH_R$, and cognitive maps. All are unnecessary steps in the explanation of behavior.

Skinner's rejection of mental or hypothetical entities as unnecessary fictions is similar to Aristotle's rejection of Plato's Forms. Aristotle argued that the Forms were unseen, fictitious entities introduced into the universe to explain those things that could be seen, but which really add nothing to our understanding of the observable world and which themselves require explaining. Similar, too, was Ockham's rejection of the doctrine of mental faculties. That we remember does not imply the existence of an unobservable faculty of memory. Ockham pointed out that remembering is a mental *act,* not a faculty. Skinner holds that remembering is simply an act, without any reference to mind at all. In Skinner's case, as in Aristotle's and Ockham's, the desire is to simplify our understanding of nature and of the human as a natural creature by eliminating anything not absolutely necessary to scientific explanation, especially any reference to hypothetical unobservable entities. Aristotle did away with the Forms, Ockham the faculties, and Skinner the mind.

Although radical behaviorism represents a sharp break with any traditional psychology, whether scientific or common sense, its intellectual heritage can be located. It stands clearly in the empiricist camp, especially with radical empiricism from Ockham to Francis Bacon to Hume to Mach. As a young man, Skinner read Bacon's works, and he often refers favorably to the great inductivist. Like Bacon, Skinner believes that truth is to be found in observations themselves, in "Does" and "Doesn't," rather than in our interpretations of our observations. Skinner's first psychological paper was an application of Mach's radical descriptive positivism to the concept of the reflex. Skinner concluded that a reflex is not an entity inside an animal but merely a convenient descriptive term for a regular correlation between stimulus and response. This presages his rejection of all hypothetical entities.

Skinner's account of behavior is also heir to Darwin's analysis of evolution, as Skinner himself often suggests, although until recently he considered only the individual evolutionary question. Darwin argued that species constantly produce variant traits and that nature acts on these traits to select those that contribute to survival, eliminating those that do not. Similarly, for Skinner an organism is constantly producing variant forms of behavior. Some of these acts lead to favorable consequences—are reinforced—while others do not. Those that do are strengthened, for they contribute to the organism's survival and are learned. Those that are not reinforced are not learned and disappear from the organism's repertoire, just as weak species become extinct. Both Skinner's analysis of behavior and his values are Darwinian, as we shall see.

Like many innovative scientific thinkers, Skinner received little early training in his discipline. He took his undergraduate degree in English at Hamilton College, intending to be a writer, studying no psychology. However, a biology teacher called his attention to works by Pavlov and the mechanist physiologist Jacques Loeb. The former taught him a concern for the total behavior of an organism, and the latter impressed him with the possibility of careful, rigorous, scientific research on behavior. He learned of Watson's behaviorism from some articles by Bertrand Russell on Watson, whom Skinner then read. After failing to become a writer, Skinner turned to psychology filled with the spirit of Watsonian behaviorism. He initiated a systematic research program on a new kind of behavior, the operant.

The basic goal guiding Skinner's scientific work is stated in his first psychological paper and was inspired by the success of Pavlov's work with conditioned reflexes. Wrote Skinner in "The Concept of the Reflex" (1931) "Given a particular part of the behavior of an organism hitherto regarded as unpredictable (and probably, as a consequence, assigned to non-physical factors), the investigator seeks out the antecedent changes with which the activity is correlated and establishes the conditions of the correlation." The goal of psychology is to analyze behavior by locating the specific determinants of specific behaviors, and to establish the exact nature of the relationship between antecedent influence and subsequent behavior. The best way to do this is by experiment, for only in an experiment can all the factors affecting behavior be systematically controlled. Skinner thus calls his science "the experimental analysis of behavior."

A behavior is explained within this system when the investigator knows all the influences of which the behavior is a function. We may refer to the antecedent influences acting on a behavior as *independent variables,* and the behavior which is a function of them we may call the *dependent variable.* The organism can then be thought of as a *locus of variables.* It is a place where independent variables act together to produce a behavior. There is no mental activity which intervenes between independent and dependent variables, and traditional references to mental entities may be eliminated when independent variables have been understood. Skinner assumes that physiology will ultimately be able to detail the physical mechanisms controlling behavior, but that analysis of behavior in terms of functional relationships among variables is completely independent of physiology. The functions will remain even when the underlying physiological mechanisms are understood.

Thus far, these theories closely follow Mach. Scientific explanation is nothing more than an accurate and precise description of the relationship between observable variables; for Skinner these are environmental variables and behavior variables. Just as Mach sought to exorcise "metaphysical" reference to unobserved causal links in physics, so Skinner sought to exorcise "metaphysical" reference to causal mental links in psychology. In his early work Skinner emphasized the descriptive nature of his work, and it is still sometimes called *descriptive behaviorism.* We may note here the mirror image nature of Skinnerian and Titchenerian psychology. Titchener also followed Mach by seeking only to correlate variables analyzed within an experimental framework, but of course he wanted a description of consciousness, not behavior. Skinner sometimes concedes the possibility of such a study, but dismisses it as irrelevant to the study of behavior as Titchener had dismissed the study of behavior as irrelevant to the psychology of consciousness.

What separates Titchener and Skinner, besides their subject matters, is the importance of control for Skinner. Skinner is Watsonian in wanting not just to describe behavior but to control it. In fact, for Skinner control is the ultimate test of the scientific adequacy of observationally determined functions between antecedent variables and behavior variables. Prediction alone is insufficient, for prediction may result from the correlation of two variables causally dependent on a third, but not on each other. For example, children's toe size and weight will correlate very highly: the bigger a child's toe, the heavier he is likely to be. However, toe size does not "cause" weight, or vice versa, for both depend on physical growth, which causes changes in both variables. According to Skinner an investigator can only be said to have explained a behavior when in addition to being able to predict its occurrence he can also *influence* its occurrence through the manipulation of independent variables. Thus an adequate experimental analysis of behavior implies a technology of behavior, wherein behavior may be engineered for specific purposes, such as teaching. Titchener always vehemently rejected technology as a goal for psychology, but it is a concern of Skinner's that became increasingly pronounced after World War II.

The experimental analysis of behavior is without doubt the closest psychology has come to a normal science research program. It began with Skinner's first psychological book, *The Behavior of Organisms* (1938). This work contains most of the important concepts of the experimental analysis of behavior, and Skinner wrote in 1978 that *The Behavior of Organisms* "has long been out of date . . . but I am continually surprised at how little of the book is actually wrong or no longer relevant." We would expect this in a document that defines a successful paradigm and research program: It laid out the "hard core" of the program, as well as some specific hypotheses in the "protective belt." What is out of date are only the latter; the hard core remains relevant.

In *Behavior of Organisms* Skinner distinguished two kinds of learned behavior, each of which had been studied before but not clearly differentiated. The first category Skinner called *respondent* behavior, or learning, studied by Pavlov. This category is properly called *reflex* behavior, for a respondent is a behavior *elicited* by a definite stimulus, whether unconditioned or conditioned. It loosely corresponds to "involuntary" behavior, such as the salivary responses studied by Pavlov. The second category Skinner called *operant* behavior or learning, which corresponds loosely to "voluntary" behavior. Operant behavior cannot be elicited, but is simply emitted from time to time. However, an operant's probability of occurrence may be raised if its emission is followed by an event called a *reinforcer*; after reinforcement it will be more likely to occur again in similar circumstances. Thorndike's puzzle boxes define an operant learning situation: the imprisoned cat emits a variety of behaviors; one of which, such as pressing a lever, leads to escape, which is *reinforcing.* Placed back in the box, the probability of the correct response is now higher than before; the operant response, lever-pressing, has been strengthened. These three things—the setting in which the behavior occurs (the puzzle box), the reinforced response (lever-pressing), and the reinforcer (escape)—collectively define the *contingencies of reinforcement*. The experimental analysis of behavior consists of the systematic description of contingencies of reinforcement as they occur in all forms of animal or human behavior.

These contingencies are analyzed in Darwinian fashion. Emitted behavior is parallel to random variation in species' traits. Reinforcement from the environment follows some operants and not others; the former are strengthened and the latter are extinguished. The environment's selection pressures select favorable responses through the process of operant learning, just as successful species flourish while others become extinct. Skinner considers the experimental analysis of behavior to be part of biology, concerned with explaining an individual's behavior as the product of the environment resulting from a process analogous to that which produces species. There is no room in either discipline for vitalism, mind, or teleology. All behavior, whether learned or unlearned, is a product of an individual's reinforcement history or his genetic make-up. Behavior is never a product of intention or will.

Skinner's definition of the operant and its controlling contingencies distinguishes him from other behaviorists in three frequently misunderstood ways. First, operant responses are never elicited. Suppose we train a rat to press a lever in a Skinner box (or "experimental space" as Skinner would call it) reinforcing the bar press only when a certain light is on above the bar. The rat will soon come to barpress whenever the light comes on. It may appear that the stimulus of the light elicits the response, but according to Skinner, this is not so. It merely sets the occasion for reinforcement. It enables the organism to discriminate a reinforcing situation from a nonreinforcing situation, and is thus called a *discriminative stimulus*. It does not elicit bar-pressing as an unconditioned stimulus or a conditioned stimulus elicited salivation in Pavlov's dogs. Thus Skinner denies that he is an S-R psychologist, for that formula implies a reflexive link between a response and some stimulus, a link which exists only for respondents. Watson adhered to the S-R formula, for he applied the classical conditioning paradigm to all behavior. The spirit of radical behaviorism is so clearly Watsonian that many critics mistake Watson's analysis of behavior for Skinner's.

There is a second way in which Skinner is not an S-R psychologist. He says that the organism may be affected by controlling variables that need not be considered stimuli. This is clearest with respect to motivation. Motivation was seen by Hullians and Freudians as a matter of drive-stimulus reduction: food deprivation leads to unpleasant stimuli associated with the hunger drive, and the organism acts to reduce them. Skinner sees no reason for the drive-stimuli. They are examples of mentalistic thinking that may be eliminated by directly linking food deprivation to change in behavior. Depriving an organism of food is an observable procedure that will affect an organism's behavior in lawful ways, and there is no gain in speaking of "drives" or their associated stimuli. A measurable variable, although not conceived in stimulus terms, may be causally linked to changes in observable behavior. The organism is truly a locus of variables, and whether or not the variables are stimuli of which the organism is aware is irrelevant, which renders the S-R formulation less applicable to Skinner.

The third important aspect of the operant concerns its definition. Behavior for Skinner is merely movement in space. This definition recalls Democritus' statement that, "Only atoms and the void exist in reality," but Skinner is careful not to define operants as simple movements. To begin with, an operant is not a response; it is a class of responses. The cat in the puzzle box may press the escape lever in different ways on different trials. Each is a different *response* in that its form is different at each occurrence, but all are members of the same *operant*, for each response is controlled by the same contingencies of reinforcement. Whether the cat butts the lever with its head or pushes it with its paw is unimportant—both are the same operant. Similarly, two otherwise identical movements may be instances of different operants if they are controlled by different contingencies. You may raise your hand to pledge allegiance to the flag, to swear to tell the truth in court, or to wave to a friend. The movements may be the same in each case, but each is a different operant, for the setting and reinforcement (the contingencies of reinforcement) are different in each case. This proves to be especially important in explaining verbal behavior: "sock" is at least two operants controlled either by (a) a soft foot covering or (b) a punch in the nose. Earlier behaviorists such as Hull tried to define responses in purely physical terms as movements and were criticized for ignoring the meaning of behavior. A word, it was argued, is more than a puff of air; it has meaning. Skinner agrees, but places meaning in the contingencies of reinforcement, not the speaker's mind.

These are the most important theoretical ideas which guide the experimental analysis of behavior. When Skinner asked "Are theories of learning necessary?" and answered "No," he did not intend to eschew all theory. What he rejected was theory that refers to the unobserved hypothetical entities he considers fictions, be they ego, $_sE_R$, or apperception. He did accept theory in the Machian sense as being a summary of the ways in which observable variables correlate, but no more. But Skinner is additionally guided by theoretical assumptions at the level of the disciplinary matrix, and it is those we have just reviewed.

Skinner also defined an innovative and radical methodology, or shared exemplar, in his *Behavior of Organisms*. First, he chose an experimental situation which preserved the fluidity of behavior, refusing to chop it up into arbitrary and artificial "trials." An organism is placed in a space and reinforced for some behavior which it may make at any time. The behavior may be closely observed as it continuously changes over time, not as it abruptly changes with each trial. Second, the experimenter seeks to exert maximal control over the organism's environment, so that the experimenter may manipulate, or hold constant, independent variables and so directly observe how they change behavior. Third, a very simple, yet somewhat artificial response is chosen for study. In Skinner's own work this has typically been either a rat pressing a lever or a pigeon pecking a key to obtain food or water. Choosing such an operant makes each response unambiguous, easily observed, and easily counted by machines to produce a cumulative record of responses. Finally, Skinner defined rate of responding as the basic datum of analysis. It is easily quantified; it is appealing as a measure of response probability; and it has been found to vary in lawful ways with changes in independent variables. Such a simple experimental situation stands in contrast to the relative lack of control found in Thorndike's puzzle boxes or Hull's and Tolman's mazes. The situation is capable of defining precise puzzles for the investigator, since it imposes so much control on the organism. The investigator need only draw on previous research to select what variables to manipulate and observe their effects on response rate. There is minimal ambiguity about what to manipulate or measure. Skinner provided a well-defined exemplar shared by all who practice the experimental analysis of behavior.

A final methodological point also sets Skinner apart from the other behaviorists. Skinner completely dispenses with statistics or statistically dictated experimental design. He believes statistics are necessary only for those who infer an inner state (such as $_SH_R$) from actual behavior. Such researchers see actual behavior as indirect measures of the inner state, contaminated by "noise," and thus they must run many subjects and treat data statistically to get measures of this hypothetical state. Skinner studies behavior itself, so there can be no "noise." All behavior is to be explained, none may be explained away as irrelevant or as "error variance." His experimental paradigm gives such clear-cut results and allows such control that "noise" does not occur. As a result, those who practice the experimental analysis of behavior run only a few subjects (often for long periods) and do not use statistics. The statistics are unnecessary, for one can see in graphic records of behavior how response-rate changes as variables are altered; no inference is necessary.

The research that results from these guiding assumptions has a clear normal science cast. Skinner asserts that his and his followers' research test no hypotheses but simply extend the experimental analysis of behavior piece by piece into new territory. For Kuhn, the puzzle-solving rather than hypothesis-testing character of normal science is one of its defining features, for normal science research extends the paradigm rather than tests it. The appeal of well-defined normal science is attested by the fact that the experimental analysis of behavior has many practitioners, so many that it has its own division in the American Psychological Association (APA).

Skinner has his own clear picture of the experimental analysis of behavior's paradigm. In commenting on graduate training Skinner remarks that his students would be ignorant of learning theory, cognitive psychology, and most of sensory psychology or mental measurement. On the methodological side they would "never see a memory drum" (Evans, 1968). Scientific training such as this would surely produce the Kuhnian normal scientist we described in Chapter 1. (Interestingly, such a training program was instituted for a while at Columbia University after World War II [Krantz, 1973].)

It should be noted that the practice of a unique normal science within the larger body of psychology exacts a price. The experimental analysts have established their own journals, one in 1958 (*Journal of the Experimental Analysis of Behavior*), and one in 1967 (*Journal of Applied Behavioral Analysis*). A study of citations in articles appearing in the first has shown that from 1958 to 1969 writers in JEAB cited their own journal more and more, and others less and less, indicating a growing isolation of the experimental analysis of behavior from psychology as a whole (Krantz, 1973). The establishment of their own division in the APA underscores this isolation. Like Freud, Skinner undoubtedly views this isolation with equanimity, for he, just as Freud, feels he is on the correct track toward a scientific psychology while everyone else remains trapped in the pre-scientific past.

## CONCEPTUAL SUMMARY

### The Paradigm of Behaviorism

We have now surveyed the three most important revisions of Watson's behaviorism that originated before World War II. Can we find a common core of beliefs that unites all behaviorists from Watson to Skinner? For the first time we must consider a large group of workers rather than a single thinker who could articulate a single paradigm. Therefore, we will propose a set of paradigmatic assumptions that characterize at least parts of behaviorism (Koch, 1964; Brewer, informal communications, 1973), and then inquire about individual schools' adherence to or deviation from the common disciplinary matrix.

The simplest assumption of behaviorism is *physical monism,* the denial of all forms of mind-body dualism. Behaviorists are materialistists, denying the existence of any Cartesian mental substance. Going further, they deny the existence of mind in any form, either as substance or as a conceptual entity controlling behavior. Observable conditions are related to observable behavior, and no reference to mind is made. Psychology is the science of behavior, not mind.

Related to this is the assumption of *peripheralism.* Behaviorists seek to minimize or expunge psychological explanations that refer to central mental or physiological states. Behavior is to be treated as behavior, not as the expression of unobservable states, be they metaphysical mental states or hypothetical brain states.

This behavior is largely learned, a product of an organism's environment rather than of its genetic make-up. Thus behaviorism assumes *empiricism.* Moreover, what is learned is some association between a behavior and a stimulus situation that comes to control it, including reward and punishment as aspects of the environment. This association may be expressed in the formula S-R, where S refers to the controlling environmental stimuli, and R refers to the controlled response. Thus behaviorism adheres to *associationism,* where the association is not between ideas or sensations, as in Wundt, Titchener, or Freud, but between stimuli and responses. This special form of associationism may be (badly) called *S-Rism.*

Given these assumptions, it follows that the best strategy for psychology to adopt is some form of *atomism.* That is, any behavior may be viewed as a set of simple responses under the control of specifiable stimuli. Simple responses may be compounded into extremely complex configurations, but ultimately complex behavior may be analyzed down to its component parts, and perhaps taught to another organism as simple behaviors to be assembled into the complex.

Behaviorists also assume a strong continuity in the way in which behavior is learned and maintained in all animal species. That is, they assume *phylogenetic continuity*. Combined with atomism, this assumption dictates a particular research strategy. One should study simple responses in simple organisms in order to understand the basic processes of learning and behavior control. Principles established at this level may then be extended indefinitely to more complex behavior in more complex organisms, including humans.

Finally, behaviorism adheres to the description of science proposed by *positivism*. Behaviorists study observable behavior and the observable environmental events associated with behavior. They minimize or eliminate reference to the unobservable, and when unobservable entities must be introduced, they are defined by reference to observable behavior or environmental events. Belief in positivism supports many of the other assumptions, most obviously physical monism, peripheralism, and empiricism. The whole spirit of behaviorism is positivistic to the point where it can be said that behaviorism *is* positivistic psychology.

As to shared exemplars, we may designate two, the method of *classical conditioning* devised by Pavlov, and the method of *operant conditioning* used by Skinner (although discovered by Thorndike). In approaching any behavior, the behaviorist investigates how it is learned according to either the arrangements of classical or operant conditioning or both. Methods that involve no learning are not used.

Watson's classical behaviorism clearly makes all the assumptions of the disciplinary matrix. He rejected the existence of mind and analyzed all behavior in terms of peripheral overt or covert muscle movements. His claim that human behavior can be shaped into almost any form displays his empiricism. He analyzed complex behaviors such as language into simpler behavioral atoms associated together in S-R chains. He assumed that animal results would extend to humans and applied Pavlov's animal methods to little Albert. Although Watson did not explicitly argue from positivism, his materialistic spirit anticipated it. On the methodological side, however, he attempted to reduce all behavior to classically conditioned reflexes, including Thorndike's puzzle-box situation. In Watson's time the importance of operant learning had not been demonstrated, while the power of classical conditioning had been shown and argued by Pavlov.

Hull's formal behaviorism also fits the paradigm well, although his positivism was the sophisticated philosophy of logical positivism. Hull was willing to introduce unobservables into psychology as long as they were operationally defined. Otherwise, he clearly denied the existence of mind and believed that behavior was learned S-R associations of simple atomic behaviors, and that studies of animal learning could be applied to human learning. His position on peripheralism is somewhat ambiguous. He formalized the idea of covert stimuli and responses that mediate connections between environmental stimuli and overt responses. In the hands of some of his followers, the mediating stimulus response chains came to refer to central brain processes. However in Hull's own works these mediating responses seemed to remain the same as Watson's peripheral, but covert, muscle twitches or glandular secretions. Thus Hull himself was a peripheralist, but some neo-Hullian formal behaviorists moved toward centralism. We will explore this change in the next chapter. Hull accepted both operant and classical learning methods.

Tolman's cognitive behaviorism diverges sharply from the paradigm at several points. He clearly would have rejected the existence of a mental substance, but his reference to "cognitive maps" makes it unclear if he wholly disbelieved in mind.

Similarly, cognitive maps are central, not peripheral, entities, are non-associationistic, and are not S-R chains or links of atomic behavioral units. On the other hand, he agreed that most behaviors are learned and that animal studies may be generalized to human behavior. Finally, Tolman, like Hull, adhered to logical positivism, especially to operationism, and accepted both classical and operant learning.

Skinner's radical behaviorism is like Watson's classical behaviorism in its crusading and technological spirit, but its adherence to the paradigm is more sophisticated. Like Watson, Skinner rejects mind in all its forms—as substance or hypothetical entity. Skinner does accept, however, the existence and scientific respectability of private events, which Watson did not. Watson questioned the existence of images; Skinner calls them *seeing without an object seen,* a form of behavior. Acceptance of private stimuli appears to preclude acceptance of peripheralism, for conscious stimuli are central. However, Skinner clearly rejects the existence of any *explanatory* central processes such as apperception. Like Titchener, he reduces attention to self-observed bodily states, but adds environmental control. The spirit of radical behaviorism is clearly peripheralistic: a toothache is a stimulus like any other, only it originates inside the human body.

Clearly Skinner believes most behaviors are learned and therefore believes in empiricism. He has little to say about native behaviors. Further, he believes results from animal studies may be extended to human behaviors such as language. Indeed, his acceptance of phylogenetic continuity appears quite radical, for the basis of his book on language, *Verbal Behavior,* was his body of work with rats and pigeons, not human beings. However, Skinner does concede that innate behavior patterns exist, although their significance has become a bone of contention between him and other students of animal behavior. Even if he concedes the existence of some phylogenetically determined behaviors, however, he still asserts the continuity of the basic processes of learning and applies the analysis of behavior into its contingencies to all species without admitting the possibility of emergent behavioral processes.

Although Skinner sometimes speaks of the fluidity of behavior and adopts methods that do not break it up into artificial trials, he accepts atomism. The experimental *analysis* of behavior tries to break down any complex behavior into simple units, each of which may be studied or taught separately. Skinner sees such analysis as a necessary step in any science, as did Titchener. We have seen how Skinner denies he is an S-R psychologist. However, if we do not interpret the formula S-R as indicating a reflex, but only that behavior (R) is a function of environmental forces (S), Skinner may be said to be an *S-R* psychologist in a broad sense. Similarly, the contingencies of reinforcement describe a functional *association* between a response, its setting, and its reinforcer, so that Skinner is associonist. Finally, Skinner prefers the radical descriptive positivism of Ernst Mach to the elaborate trappings of the logical positivism he associates with Hull and Tolman, the methodological behaviorists.

As to method, where Watson saw only classical conditioning, Skinner sees only operant learning. Although he distinguished the two types, in his later writings Skinner sometimes wonders if classical conditioning properly so-called applies to anything but salivation. In any event, Skinner sees operant learning as far more important in scope and controllability than classical learning. Further, he has refined the general concept of operant learning into a very well-specified experimental methodology with rate of response of a simple operant as the basic datum to be explained, eliminating all other forms of reward learning from mazes to memory-drums.

The overall paradigm of behaviorism fits all the behaviorists except Tolman fairly well. Skinner's radical behaviorism is a sophisticated and subtle reformulation of Watson's classical behaviorism, while Hull's formal behaviorism differs from them only over the value of formal theory and the use of hypothetical entities— which is essentially the difference between logical positivism and Machian descriptive positivism.

Tolman's cognitive behaviorism stands out, however. He seems to have been a behaviorist only in the sense that he viewed psychology as the science of behavior, not mind. In other respects his system shows marked mentalism in contrast to the systems of Watson, Hull, and Skinner.

### Historical Trends

The age of foundation in behaviorism was over by 1950. We have already noted the fate of formal and cognitive behaviorism. Radical behaviorism continued and grew through the 1950s and beyond, but its foundations were laid in *The Behavior of Organisms* (1938) and its application to human affairs proclaimed in *Science and Human Behavior* (1953). Even Skinner's own later work builds on, but does not alter, the substance of these works. The years immediately ahead will show three trends: liberalization of formal behaviorism as the aggressive wars fought by founders dim in memory; the continuation, growth, and invention of non-behaviorist systems; and finally direct challenges to the behaviorist paradigm. In the background is the growth of radical behaviorism as other systems change. These trends are the subject of our next chapter.

### SUGGESTED READINGS

An excellent secondary source describing the important neobehaviorist psychologies is *Theories of Learning* by Ernest R. Hilgard and Gordon H. Bower (Prentice-Hall). Its first edition appeared in 1948, and following its changes from 1948 to its most recent edition in 1975 provides an interesting series of documents on changes in experimental psychology in the post-war era. Works by major behaviorists themselves may be found in the bibliography and references.

# REFERENCES

Brewer, W. There is no convincing evidence for operant or classical conditioning in normal, adult human beings. In W. Weimer & D. Palermo (Eds.) *Cognition and the symbolic processes.* Hillsdale, N.J.: Erlbaum, 1974.

Evans, R. I. *B. F. Skinner: The man and his ideas.* New York: Dutton, 1968.

Hilgard, E. & Bower, G. *Theories of learning* (4th ed.). Englewood Cliffs, N.J.: Prentice-Hall, 1975.

Hull, C. L. *Principles of behavior.* New York: Appleton-Century-Crofts, 1943.

Hull, C. L. *Essentials of behavior.* New Haven, Conn.: Yale University Press, 1951.

Hull, C. L. *A behavior system.* New Haven, Conn.: Yale University Press, 1952.

Krantz, D. L. Schools and systems: the mutual isolation of operant and non-operant psychology as a case study. In M. Henle, J. Jaynes, and J. Sullivan (Eds.) *Historical Conceptions of Psychology.* New York: Springer, 1973.

Koch, S. & Clark L. Hull. In W. F. Estes, S. Koch, K. MacCorquodale, R. Meehl, C. Mueller, W. Schoenfeld, & W. Verplanck (Eds.) *Modern learning theory.* New York: Appleton-Century-Crofts, 1954.

Skinner, B. F. *The behavior of organisms.* Englewood Cliffs, N.J.: Prentice-Hall, 1938.

Skinner, B. F. The concept of reflex in the description of behavior. *Journal of General Psychology,* 1931, *5,* 427-458.

Skinner, B. F. A critique of psychoanalytic concepts and theories (1954). Reprinted in *Cumulative record* (3rd ed.). Englewood Cliffs, N.J.: Prentice-Hall, 1972.

Skinner, B. F. A lecture on having a poem (1971). Reprinted in B. F. Skinner *Cumulative Record* (3rd ed.). Englewood Cliffs, N.J.: Prentice-Hall, 1972.

Stevens, S. S. Operationism and logical positivism (1939). Reprinted in M. H. Marx (Ed.) *Theories in contemporary psychology.* New York: Macmillan, 1963.

Tolman, E. C. Operational behaviorism and current trends in psychology (1936). Reprinted in *Behavior and psychological man.* Berkeley: University of California Press, 1951.

Tolman, E. C. Cognitive maps in rats and men. *Psychological Review,* 1948, *55,* 189-208.

Tolman, E. C. Principles of purposive behaviorism. In S. Koch (Ed.) *Psychology: A study of a science* (Vol. 2). New York: McGraw-Hill, 1959.

# 12

# Challenge and Change, 1945-1960

**THE CRISIS OF 1950**

**NEO-HULLIAN PSYCHOLOGY: INFORMAL BEHAVIORISM**

Weakening of Peripheralism: Liberalized S-R Theory

Reversal Shift Learning: A Break in the Phylogenetic Continuum

**THE EXTENSION OF RADICAL BEHAVIORISM TO MAN**

The Problem of Language

Creating a New Society

**ALTERNATIVES TO BEHAVIORISM**

Continuing Non-Behaviorist Psychology

New Movements of the 1950s

Challenges to Behaviorism

**CONCLUSION: THE CRISIS OF 1960**

## THE CRISIS OF 1950

In 1951, Sigmund Koch wrote in the *Psychological Review*: "Since the end of World War II, psychology has been in a long and intensifying crisis . . . its core seems to be disaffection from the theory of the recent past. Never before has it seemed so evident that the development of a science is not an automatic forward movement. . . ." These sentiments obviously describe a science in a state of crisis: certainty is gone, belief in progress has evaporated, continuity with the past has been shattered.

Signs of the searching self-examination typical of a scientific crisis are easily found. In September 1950 a conference on modern learning theory was held to thoroughly examine the scientific merits of the grand theories of neobehaviorism, resulting in some savage criticism of Hull, Tolman, Guthrie, and Skinner (Estes et al., 1954). In 1952 the American Psychological Association decided to conduct an extensive examination of psychology's status as science, a massive undertaking whose first fruits were not born until 1959.

Before World War II, psychologists had felt some confidence in the progressive character of their research. By 1950, however, many were dissatisfied. The Tolman-Hull debates turned into a sort of intellectual tennis match in which each volley of critical experiment was met with a return interpretation. No resolution was in sight, and publications, even those of the principals themselves, became scarcer after the war. Skinner asked whether theories were necessary at all, questioning a cardinal belief of Formal Behaviorism. It was becoming apparent to others that Tolman's and Hull's theories were not theories at all but rival metaphysical programs in search of theories. Assaults were made on other points as well. In 1951 Karl Lashley, at one time Watson's student, attacked the standard S-R chaining theory of complex behaviors, originally proposed by Watson himself. Lashley's critique thus questioned one of the first and most fundamental behaviorist ideas, atomism. Lashley argued on physiological grounds that the process was impossible because of the relatively slow transmission of nervous impulses from receptor to brain and back to effector. Lashley proposed instead that organisms possess central planning functions that coordinate sets of actions as large units, not as chains. Lashley specifically argued that language was organized this way, raising a problem that would increasingly bedevil behaviorism. On another front in 1950, Frank Beach, a student of animal behavior, decried experimental psychologists' increasing preoccupation with rat learning. He asked if psychologists are truly interested in a general science of behavior or in only one topic, learning, in only one species, the Norway rat. Without studies of other behaviors and species, he argued, the generality of laboratory findings must remain suspect. He also pointed out the existence of species-specific behaviors such as imprinting that are not the exclusive result of either learning or instinct. Such behaviors escape all existing learning theories, which sharply divide the learned from the unlearned and then study only the latter. Problems of comparative psychology would increasingly plague the psychology of learning in the 1950s and the 1960s.

Responses to the crisis were diverse. One option was radical behaviorism. It was only after the war that B.F. Skinner began to gather around him like-minded psychologists who avoided the crisis of theory by avoiding theory altogether. Another option was narrow specialization. One could study, for example, animal behavior in itself, making few if any claims for its relevance to humans. The grand claims had been made by Hull, Tolman, and Skinner and were avoided by many later behaviorists. Since in this book psychology is the study of humans, we will have less to say about animal psychology in the future than in the past two chapters.

In this chapter we will examine two other broad classes of response to the crisis. The first are modifications to behaviorism, especially Hullian behaviorism, that blur its paradigmatic assumptions. The second are various alternatives to behaviorism, some of which exist alongside it, but some of which directly challenge it. By 1960 these alternatives had gained momentum, and the crisis had worsened.

## NEO-HULLIAN PSYCHOLOGY: INFORMAL BEHAVIORISM

Hull had many students and followers, such as Kenneth Spence. There were others who carried on a systematic research program of animal learning, but this tradition became more narrowly oriented as time progressed. Others influenced by Hull, however, sought to extend his approach directly to human affairs, including psychotherapy, anthropology, and child development. These psychologists were relatively unaffected by Hull's quantitative program and pursued instead a program that sought qualitative laws of human behavior in a modified positivist framework. Moreover, in attacking the problems of clinic and society they were forced to modify some of the usual behaviorist assumptions. They are thus neo-Hullian, and can be called informal behaviorists because of their reduced concern with atiomatic theory. We will discuss two important facets of informal behaviorism: Neal Miller's "liberalized behaviroism" and the work of Howard and Tracy Kendler on children's discrimination learning.

### Weakening of Peripheralism: Liberated S-R Theory

Neal Miller (born 1909), from his post-graduate days with Hull, had an interest in extending rigorous psychology to problems outside the laboratory. In particular, he was interested in incorporating psychoanalysis (he went through a brief analysis in Vienna with a student of Freud's, Heinz Hartmann) and socialization into a positivist psychology. To this end he collaborated with other researchers, especially with anthropologist Leonard Doob on a series of works giving an objective foundation to psychotherapy (*Personality and Psychotherapy*, 1950), child development

(*Social Learning and Imitation,* 1941), and the problem of aggression (*Frustration and Aggression,* 1939). These works show little of Hull's fine-grained quantitative approach to simple behaviors, being instead an attempt to give an informally axiomatized account of larger human problems. Miller's final "liberalized" S-R theory is found in his contribution to *Psychology: A Study of a Science.*

Miller adopts the logical positivist philosophy of science espoused by Hull, but he uses it in a more flexible, informal way, without Hull's insistence on rigorously stated axiom-sets and quantification, although Miller clearly looks toward such a formulation as a final goal. Miller was at his most positivistic in discussing his work with animals in approach-avoidance situations, in which he set up postulates, deduced consequences, and conducted the appropriate research. He then extended this analysis to human neuroses, which he saw as the products of similar conflicts in people.

He was more informal and less Hullian in his discussion of liberalized S-R theory. There are two important changes he introduced to Hull's system. First, he stopped trying to define stimuli in terms of energy impinging on sensory receptors, and responses as particular muscle movements. Instead, he adopted "functional behavioral definitions" in which a response is anything an organism does, overtly or covertly, that may be functionally connected to a stimulus. A stimulus, in turn, is defined as any event which can be functionally connected to a response. This "liberalizes" S-R theory in that we no longer have to speak of S-R connections in purely physicalistic terms as energies and physical movements. Now, S and R events may be connected together regardless of their physical make-up. Thus Miller could speak of good Gestalts as functional stimuli without trying to reduce them to bundles of energy acting on visual receptor neurons, which loses sight of Gestalt properties as the Gestaltists pointed out. Miller's position brought him closer to Skinner's functional definitions of response and reinforcer, but Miller does not acknowledge this. Despite its liberalization, Miller's theory remained an S-R theory in the strict sense. Even though he changed the definitions of S and R, each response was still said to be elicited by a certain stimulus.

The second and more important change Miller introduced into the Hullian paradigm was a weakening of its peripheralism. For Hull, all stimulus-response connections whether overt (S-R) or covert (r-s) were peripheral. Following Watson, even covert responses were viewed as generally unobserved, but potentially observable, behaviors. Miller was willing to abandon this assumption in order to introduce into behaviorism the old forbidden topic of thinking. Miller argued that central processes may be analyzed as central S-R connections, presumably available for observation only to neurophysiologists. Miller thus extended Watson's old notion of stimulus-response behavior chains to include central s-r connections that mediate between environmental S and overt R. These central associations are thoughts, images, verbal responses, and other "higher mental processes." Miller made what he calls the "key assumption" that the central associations follow exactly the same laws as simpler S-R connections (Miller, 1959). This enables the informal behaviorist to extend existing S-R laws discovered with animals to human thinking.

For example, Dollard and Miller analyzed repression as the learned avoidance of an unpleasant thought, just as a rat learns to avoid a place in which it is regularly shocked.

Again we find Miller liberalizing S-R theory, yet not radically changing it. He remains (Cohen, 1977) unwilling to move all the way to centralism or to Wundt's belief that the inner laws of mind are different from the outer, but only to a modified peripheralism. He acknowledges central processes, but insists they are just like peripheral processes copied weakly in the brain. Miller's position is not unlike Hartley's in the eighteenth century. Hartley viewed brain processes as tiny echoes of nervous vibrations that began in the periphery of the body.

Miller's own description of his position is apt. It is a liberal version of Hull's S-R theory. It is informal, less quantitative, willing to deal with complex problems in human behavior, and less insistent on certain paradigmatic assumptions. Yet it does not radically restructure formal behaviorism or seek to overthrow it. Miller maintained a clear continuity with the past and is no revolutionary. Informal behaviorism was widely influential. It provided a way out of the old Hullian theoretical straightjacket by weakening some assumptions and seeking a *rapprochement* with Tolman's cognitive theory, but at the same time maintained at least the appearance of the scientific rigor for which Hull spoke. It also enabled psychologists to directly attack important human psychological problems, such as socialization and psychotherapy, without waiting for exhaustive laboratory studies of animals learning simple responses. In short, in a time of increased social recognition of psychology, it allowed behaviorists to be at once scientifically respectable and socially relevant.

The influence of informal behaviorism was such that it cannot easily be surveyed, and we shall see later that it provided a bridge to later information processing cognitive psychology, which moved more in the direction of centralism without abandoning behaviorist attitudes. One important line of neo-Hullian research, however, should be described, for it concretely illustrates informal behaviorists' practice, and also weakens another paradigmatic assumption, phylogenetic continuity.

### Reversal Shift Learning: A Break in the Phylogenetic Continuum

Hull's foremost pupil, Kenneth Spence, intensively studied animal discrimination learning, but unlike Hull, he suspected that his theory of animal discrimination learning might not apply to human beings because of their verbal abilities. Some of Spence's students, especially Howard and Tracy Kendler, set out to examine Spence's hunch.

Consider the discrimination problem pictured in Figure 12-1. We may require an organism to discriminate the stimuli shown under Preshift Training, rewarding responses (say, bar-pressing) only to the stimuli marked "+", and not those marked "-." Soon the organism will only press the bar when + stimuli are present and not otherwise. This is so far only simple discrimination learning as described in the last

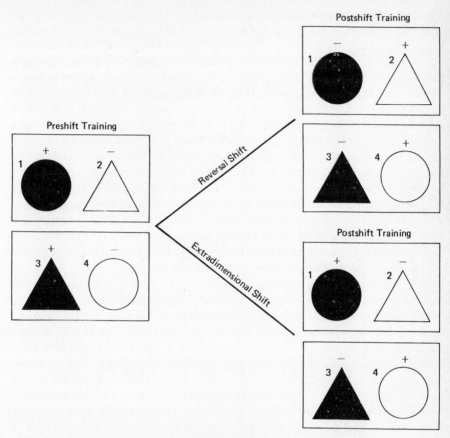

**FIGURE 12-1.**
Discrimination shift learning paradigm involving a comparison
between a reversal (RS) and extradimensional shift (EDS).
For each pair of discriminanda, plus indicates reinforcement:
minus indicates nonreinforcement. A counterbalanced design is
conventionally used so that each cue (*black, white, circle,* and *triangle*)
is correct for one-fourth of the subjects during both the preshift
and postshift problems. (Adapted from Kendler, H., and Kendler, T.
"From discrimination learning to cognitive development," 1975.)

chapter. After this initial learning, we then change the contingencies of reinforcement as shown under Postshift Training in one of two ways, each without informing the organism of the change, but simply requiring a new discrimination to be learned. In either case the reinforced responses are marked +, the nonreinforced ones marked –. The point of the experiment is to find out which kind of shift in contingencies will be more easily learned.

According to Hull's theory, as modified by Spence, what the learner acquires during preshift training is a set of S-R associations. The learner must learn to bar-press (R) to stimuli 1 and 3, but not to bar-press (-R) to stimuli 2 and 4. Four S-R habits are learned: (1) $S_1 \to R$; (2) $S_2 \to -R$; (3) $S_3 \to R$; (4) $S_4 \to -R$. Given these four habits, a learner should find the extradimensional shift easier. For in an extradimensional shift two habits are still correct, (1) $S_1 \to R$ and (2) $S_2 \to -R$, while two habits must be unlearned and replaced: (3) $S_3 \to R$ is incorrect and must be replaced by $S_3 \to -R$, and (4) $S_4 \to -R$ is incorrect and must be replaced by $S_4 \to R$. In a reversal shift, however, all the earlier habits must be unlearned and replaced with new ones.

Research on this problem began during World War II and revealed an interesting pattern. Animals in a discrimination shift procedure behaved as predicted by the simple S-R model, finding extradimensional shifts easier than reversal shifts. However, college students responded to the shifts the opposite way, preferring reversal to extradimensional shifts. Further, when children were the subjects, it was found that the younger the child the more he or she behaved according to S-R theory, that is, like animals. These findings present an anomaly for Hullian theory. Hull's laws of S-R learning are found not to be the same across different species or even across members of the same species at different ages.

In the mid-1950s Howard Kendler proposed a "mediational" analysis of these findings in the spirit of informal behaviorism's moderate centralism. Kendler suggested that the usual S-R laws, now called single-stage S-R laws, applied to animal learning, but that humans possess central and developing cognitive processes—including most importantly language—that modify the laws of learning. These central responses *mediate* between environmental stimuli and overt response. According to this model, an environmental stimulus elicits a central, covert symbolic response: $S \to r$. This central response has covert stimulus properties: $r \to s$. These stimulus properties then control overt behavior: $s \to R$. Thus any cognitively mediated behavior is an associative chain of stimulus-response events some of which are symbolic: $S \to r \to s \to R$. This scheme is in full accord with Miller's working assumption that central responses ($r \to s$) obey the same behavioral laws as overt responses ($S \to R$). According to informal behaviorism the brain functions like the body, only covertly.

The mediational apparatus may be used to explain the apparently anomalous behavior of the college students. The adult subject makes a mediational response (r) to the stimuli to be discriminated. We may regard these responses as implicit labels for the stimuli which categorize them according to the two stimulus dimensions defining the four stimuli. In Figure 12-1, two dimensions, brightness and shape, define the stimuli. The subject learns to make the mediational response "brightness" to the stimuli, because this is the dimension relevant to the preshift training where black figures are reinforced and white ones are not. The mediational association $r_{brightness} - s_{brightness}$ controls the terminal overt response: to press the lever when black stimuli are present. We may write what is learned as follows in S-R language.

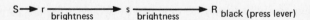

$$S \to r \underset{\text{brightness}}{\longrightarrow} s \underset{\text{brightness}}{\longrightarrow} R \text{ black (press lever)}$$

What happens after each possible shift? In the reversal shift, brightness is still the relevant stimulus dimension, so the mediational response is correct, and all the subject must learn is a new terminal response, pressing the lever when the white stimuli are present:

$$S \longrightarrow r_{\text{brightness}} \longrightarrow s_{\text{brightness}} \longrightarrow R_{\text{white (press lever)}}$$

However, when the shift is extradimensional, the terminal responses are wrong and the mediational response is wrong. Brightness is no longer the relevant stimulus dimension; shape is, so the subject must learn the S-R chain.

$$S \longrightarrow r_{\text{shape}} \longrightarrow s_{\text{shape}} \longrightarrow R_{\text{circle (press lever)}}.$$

There is more to learn in the extradimensional shift case, and so it naturally takes longer.

The Kendlers' analysis of discrimination shift learning is an example of a paradigm successfully responding to anomalous findings. However, the Kendlers and Miller did not leave the paradigm intact, for strong versions of peripheralism and phylogenetic continuity had to be modified to accommodate the demands of the higher mental processes of human beings. We must recognize, however, that these changes were not revolutionary. As Miller stated, S-R theory was liberalized; it was not overthrown. Later on, some would look back and see shift learning as a crisis-inducing anomaly, but it was not. The Kendlers successfully met its challenge within a modified S-R pattern.*

## THE EXTENSION OF RADICAL BEHAVIORISM TO MAN

In his *Behavior of Organisms* Skinner carefully articulated his experimental analysis of behavior as a paradigm for animal research. In the 1950s, while other behaviorists were liberalizing their brands of behaviorism, Skinner began to extend his radical behaviorism to human behavior without changing any of his fundamental concepts. Skinner viewed human behavior as animal behavior not significantly different from the behavior of the rats and pigeons he had studied in the laboratory.

Two particular problems of human psychology were especially important to Skinner. The first was the problem of explaining language, humanity's most obvious unique possession. As a would-be writer Skinner was naturally interested in language, and some of his earliest, albeit unpublished research was on speech perception. His ideas on language were set forth in a series of lectures at Harvard University and then in a book, *Verbal Behavior* (1957). At the same time, Skinner was also concerned with using his radical behaviorism and experimental analysis of

*By 1975, however, the Kendlers recognized that S-R theory had vanished, and they argue that much of cognitive psychology grew out of S-R research such as their own.

behavior as bases for the construction of a Utopian society and the reconstruction of existing society. His first extended treatment of these problems came in *Science and Human Behavior* (1953). It was presaged by Walden II (1948) and followed by a series of articles through the 1950s, culminating in *Beyond Freedom and Dignity* (1971).

### The Problem of Language

Although "most of the experimental work responsible for the advance of the experimental analysis of behavior has been carried out on other species . . . the results have proved to be surprisingly free of species restrictions . . . and its methods can be extended to human behavior without serious modification." So writes Skinner in what he considers his most important work, *Verbal Behavior*. The final goal of the experimental analysis of behavior is a science of human behavior using the same principles first applied to animals. Extension of his analysis to human behavior increasingly preoccupied Skinner after World War II.

The scope and nature of the extension is well conveyed in an interesting paper, "A lecture on 'having' a poem," about how he came to write his only published poem, partially quoted in Chapter 11. In this paper he draws an analogy between "having a baby" and "having a poem": "A person produces a poem and a woman produces a baby, and we call the person a poet and the woman a mother. Both are essential as loci in which vestiges of the past come together in certain combinations." Just as a mother makes no positive contribution to the creation of the baby she carries, so "the act of composition is no more an act of creation than 'having' the bits and pieces" that form the poem. In such case something new is created, but there is no creator. Again we see the hand of Darwin: a baby is a random combination of genes that may be selected for survival or may die. A poem is a collection of bits and pieces of verbal behavior, some of which are selected, some of which are rejected, for appearance in the poem. As Darwin showed that no divine Mind was necessary to explain the production and evolution of natural species, so Skinner seeks to show that no human mind is necessary for the production of verbal behavior or language, man's unique possession according to Descartes.

His argument is worked out in most detail in *Verbal Behavior,* which appeared in 1957. It is a complex and subtle book that defies easy summary. Only a few salient points may be discussed here. It is a work of interpretation only. Skinner reported no experiments, and sought only to establish the plausibility of applying his analysis to language, not its reality. Further, to say he is analyzing language is misleading; the title of his book is *Verbal Behavior,* behavior whose reinforcement is mediated by other persons. The definition includes an animal behaving under the control of an experimenter, who together form a "genuine verbal community." It excludes the listener in a verbal interchange, except insofar as the listener reinforces speech (for example, by replies or compliance with demands) or acts as a discriminative stimulus (one speaks differently to one's best friend and to one's teacher). The definition makes no reference to the process of communication we usually assume takes place during speech. Skinner's account may be contrasted with that of Wundt, who excluded animals from consideration, examined the linguistic processes of both speaker and listener, and attempted to describe the communication of a *Gesamtvorstellung* from the mind of a speaker to the mind of a hearer.

Nevertheless, *Verbal Behavior* is basically about what we ordinarily consider language, or more accurately speech, for Skinner analyzed only real utterances spoken in analyzable environments, not the hypothetical abstract entity "language." Skinner introduced a number of technical concepts in his discussion of verbal behavior. To show the flavor of his analysis, we will briefly discuss his concept of the "tact," because it corresponds roughly to the problem of universals, and because Skinner considers it the most important verbal operant.

We apply the three-term set of contingencies of reinforcement, stimulus, response, and reinforcement. A *tact* is a verbal *operant response* under the *stimulus control* of some part of the physical environment, and correct use of tacts is reinforced by the verbal community. So a child is reinforced by parents for emitting the sound "doll" in the presence of a doll (Skinner, 1957). Such an operant "makes contact with" the physical environment and is called a *tact*. Skinner reduced the traditional notion of reference or naming to a functional relationship between a response, its discriminative stimuli, and its reinforcer. The situation is exactly analogous to the functional relation holding between a rat's bar-press in a Skinner box, the discriminative stimulus that sets the occasion for the response, and the food that reinforces it. Skinner's analysis of the tact is a straightforward extension of the experimental analysis of behavior paradigm to a novel situation.

Skinner extended his analysis to metaphor, metonymy, and the subtleties of "tact" behavior, but we need not pursue them. The essential extension of the paradigm has been shown. Two points deserve further comment. First, Skinner's analysis of the tact is the purest nominalism ever proposed by anyone tackling the problem of universals. A noun is now indeed no more than a puff of air emitted under certain definable contingencies of reinforcement. There is no Platonic Form of cat, no Aristotelian essence of catness, no Ockhamist mental concept of Cat, only a certain verbal habit. Skinner pursues Hume's reduction of knowledge to habit to its final end, substituting purely behavioral for mental habits. The essence of "cat" is no more than the contingencies of reinforcement governing its utterance.

The second point raises an important general aspect about Skinner's treatment of human behavior, his notion of private stimuli. Skinner believes that earlier behaviorists (he calls them methodological behaviorists) such as Tolman and Hull were wrong to exclude private events (such as mental images, toothaches) from behaviorism simply because such events are unobservable. Skinner holds that part of each person's environment includes the world inside her or his skin, those stimuli to which the person has privileged access. Such stimuli may be private but they can control behavior and so must be included in any behaviorist analysis of human behavior. Many verbal statements are under such control, including complex tacts. For example: "My tooth aches" is a kind of tacting response controlled by a certain kind of painful inner stimulation.

This simple analysis implies a momentous conclusion. For how do we come to be able to make such statements as the private tact? Skinner's answer is that the verbal community has trained us to observe our private stimuli by reinforcing utterances which refer to them. It is useful for parents to know what is distressing a child, so they attempt to teach a child self-reporting verbal behaviors. "My tooth aches" indicates a visit to the dentist, not the podiatrist. Such responses thus have Darwinian survival value. It is these self-observed private stimuli that constitute consciousness. It therefore follows that human consciousness is a product of the reinforcing practices of a verbal community. A person raised by a community that did not reinforce self-description would not be conscious in anything but the sense of being awake. The person would have no self-consciousness.

Self-description also allows Skinner to explain apparently purposive verbal behaviors without reference to intention or purpose. For example, "I am looking for my glasses" seems to describe my intentions, but Skinner (1957) argues: "Such behavior must be regarded as equivalent to *When I have behaved in this way in the past, I have found my glasses and have then stopped behaving in this way. . . .*" Intention is a mentalistic term Skinner has reduced to the physicalistic description of one's bodily state.

The last topic discussed in *Verbal Behavior* is thinking, the most apparently mental of all human activities. Skinner continued, however, to exorcise mentalism by arguing that "thought is simply *behavior.*" Skinner rejected Watson's view that thinking is subvocal behavior, for much covert behavior is not verbal, yet can still control overt behavior in a way characteristic of "thinking": "*I think I shall be going* can be translated *I find myself* going," a reference to self-observed, but non-verbal stimuli.

The simplicity of Skinner's argument is hard to grasp. Once one denies the existence of the mind, as Skinner does, all that is left is behavior, so thinking must be behavior under the control of the contingencies of reinforcement. The thought of B.F. Skinner is, in his terms, simply "the sum total of his responses to the complex world in which he lived." "Thought" is simply a tact that we have learned to apply to certain forms of behavior, a tact Skinner would ask us to unlearn, or at least not teach to our children. For Skinner does not merely wish to describe behavior, human or animal, he wants to control it, control being a fundamental part of the experimental analysis of behavior. Skinner believes that current control of human behavior, based as it is on mental fictions, is ineffective at best and harmful at worst.

### Creating a New Society

During World War II, Skinner worked on a behavioral guidance system for air to surface missiles. He trained pigeons to peck at a projected image of the target which the missile they were imprisoned in was to seek out. Their pecking operated controls on the missile so that it followed its target until it struck the target, destroying target and pigeons alike. Skinner achieved such total control of the pigeons' behavior that they could carry out the most difficult tracking maneuvers during simulated attacks. The work impressed him with the possibility of a thorough control of any organism's behavior. Skinner's superiors found the project implausible, and no pigeon-guided missiles ever flew. Shortly afterward, however, Skinner wrote his most widely read book, *Walden II,* a utopian novel based on the principles of the experimental analysis of behavior.

In the book, two characters represent Skinner: Frazier (an experimental psychologist and founder of Walden II, an experimental utopian community) and Burris (a skeptical visitor ultimately won over to membership in Walden II). Near the end Frazier speaks to Burris: "I've had only one idea in my life—a true *idée fixe....* The idea of having my own way. 'Control' expresses it, I think. The control of human behavior, Burris." Frazier goes on to describe *Walden II* as the final laboratory and proving ground of the experimental analysis of behavior: "Nothing short of *Walden II* will suffice." Finally Frazier exclaims: "Well, what do you say to the design of personalities? the control of temperament? Give me the specifications and I'll give you the man! . . . Think of the possibilities! A society in which there is no failure, no boredom, no duplication of effort. . . . Let us control the lives of our children and see what we can make of them."

We have met the *idée fixe* of control before in the history of behaviorism. Frazier's claim to custom-make personalities recalls Watson's claim to custom-make the careers of infants. We have seen how important the desire for social control in progressivism was to the favorable reaction to Watson's behaviorism. Skinner is heir to the progressive desire to scientifically control human lives in the interest of society, more specifically the survival of society, the ultimate Darwinian and Skinnerian value. He is also heir, and consciously so, to the tradition of Enlightenment optimism about human progress. Skinner asks us, in an otherwise disillusioned age, not to give up Rousseau's utopian dream, but to build a Utopia on the principles of the experimental analysis of behavior. If pigeons' behavior can be controlled so that the birds guide missiles to their death, so a human being, whose behavior is likewise determined, can be controlled to be happy, productive, and to feel free and dignified. *Walden II* was Skinner's first attempt to describe his vision.

The control of human behavior is the theme that dominates Skinner's writing after World War II. His general views are spelled out in *Science and Human Behavior* (1953), *Beyond Freedom and Dignity* (1971), and *About Behaviorism* (1974). During the same period he argued for the application of the experimental analysis of behavior to teaching. His work was the major impetus behind the development of teaching machines and programmed learning. There are two important steps in Skinner's argument for the control of human behavior. The first is establishing the ethical and social consequences of environmental determinism for the interpretation of human behavior. The second is establishing the desirability of deliberate self-control.

The consequences of a rigorous determinism for understanding human nature are profound. In general, our own experience and the teachings of our culture tell us there is free will although from time to time philosophers such as Spinoza have argued otherwise. It appears that one chooses to lift one's arm, that one chooses a profession, that one chooses for whom to vote. To accept a rigorous determinism and apply it to one's own behavior is extremely difficult, requiring the overthrow of a lifetime's habits of thought. Yet such a revolution is required when Skinner asks that we give up the traditional notions of freedom and dignity.

As early as his first paper (1931), Skinner wrote of the *"preconceptions of freedom"* that hinder the scientific understanding of behavior. Skinner assumes that all behavior is determined, and that consequently a notion such as freedom is nonsense. In his view a desire for freedom is always a response to punishment. Skinner draws an important distinction between positive reinforcement and punishment. Positive reinforcement effectively controls behavior without undesirable consequences, since it lets you do essentially what you want. Punishment, on the other hand, is generally ineffective and produces unfortunate side effects, since organisms react emotionally to punishment. Organisms seek to avoid, that is to be free from, punishment, but do not avoid positive reinforcement, which is by definition desirable. Historically, governments have tried to control behavior through punishment. One is told what *not* to do, not what to do. As an emotional reaction to punishment, a "literature of freedom" has grown up demanding freedom from punishment, but which has also fostered a belief in freedom as a characteristic of life, a false belief according to the scientific assumption of determinism. Now that the early aims of the literature of freedom have been attained in constitutions and so forth, the illusory notion of freedom stands in the way of further progress, for it rails against the control of behavior by positive reinforcement as well as by punishment.

Skinner argues that if humanistic goals, the goals of human happiness, are to be reached it will be done only by controlling behavior through positive reinforcement, for scientific control is more efficient than the haphazard control exerted by the current social environment. It is important to remember again that Skinner assumes all behavior is always completely determined, that there is never freedom of choice. Therefore, he proposes that we substitute deliberate, systematic control for inefficient control. If the goal is happiness, it will be reached fastest if we apply methodical control, and this cannot be done without first abandoning belief in freedom, which prohibits such control.

The concept of dignity depends on belief in free will. We believe that one deserves praise for freely chosen good acts, and deserves blame for freely chosen wrong acts. However, Skinner, like Spinoza, argues that both praise and blame are equally irrational, since all behavior is determined for Skinner by the contingencies of reinforcement, not by an individual's free will. We do not blame the rain for getting us wet or praise the sun for warming our skin (although ancient religions did); we accept each as a natural occurrence beyond the will of any person. Skinner asks us to view human behavior as we have other natural phenomena, not religiously, but scientifically, recalling Watson's linkage of religion and mentalism. The poet is not to be praised for "having a poem," for the poet is merely the site at which external variables operate. The rapist is not to be blamed for "having a rape," for the rapist, too, is a locus of variables that converge on an act society condemns. Desirable behaviors are to be strenghened by positive reinforcement, while undesirable behaviors will not be learned, at least in a properly engineered society such as Walden II. Both freedom and dignity are outmoded concepts, inconsistent with scientific determinism, which stand in the way of an effective control of human behavior.

To what end are we to be controlled? Skinner's answer is Darwinian. A culture is an experiment in survival, just as a species is an experiment in survival. The ultimate biological value is survival, for the "good" species is the one that survives. Similarly, the "good" society will be the one that survives. Skinner argues that the chances our society will survive will be greatly enhanced should it adopt the methods of the experimental analysis of behavior in pursuit of life, liberty, and the pursuit of happiness. Scientific control is our surest guarantee against both unhappiness and extinction. The technology of behavior must be used, Skinner argues, if humanity is to survive. The old mentalistic scheme of freedom and dignity is outmoded and must be replaced by his science of behavior. Skinner wrote (1972): "The ease with which mentalistic explanations can be invented on the spot is perhaps the best gauge of how little attention we should pay to them. . . . It is science or nothing. . . ."

Skinner stands clearly in the tradition of those who would improve humans by improving their environment. He feels an affinity for Jean-Jacques Rousseau who, although he believed humans are free, located their faults in the environment: "Man is born free but he is everywhere in chains." In *Emile* Rousseau proposes that a teacher's student will be happiest if the student feels free, but is kept under the teacher's subtle control. Skinner's *Walden II* is a Rousseauian Utopia. Control is benign and hidden, so feelings of freedom and dignity remain, even though they have no referents beyond those feelings.

Skinner is, finally, a humanist in the tradition of the Sophists. Science exists to serve human happiness, not such transcendent Platonic ends as Reason and Truth. For Skinner, the human being, at least scientifically understood, is the measure of all things. Reason and logic are arbitrary verbal behaviors whose truth lies only in the contingencies of reinforcement, not in a realm of Ideas. Freedom and dignity are verbal operants, not linguistic expressions of enduring values. The crisis Skinner sets for the modern person is the crisis set for ancient Greeks by the Sophists, and by the Marquis de Sade for eighteenth-century Europeans. Is there anything of value in human affairs beyond feelings, if freedom and dignity mean nothing else? To what can we cling if all tradition is thrown into doubt, if the old center cannot hold? Skinner answers: "the experimental analysis of behavior."

## ALTERNATIVES TO BEHAVIORISM

### Continuing Non-Behaviorist Psychology

Behaviorism was the dominant form of experimental psychology, but it was not the only psychological viewpoint available to psychologists as a whole. Psycho-analysis, a movement independent of psychology, provided a continuing mentalistic alternative to behaviorism and posed an implicit challenge only partially met by liberal behaviorists such as Miller. In this section we will describe two important psychological alternatives to behaviorism which are closer to the science of psychology than is clinical practice. The first is a sub-field of psychology, social psychology, which was not significantly penetrated by behaviorism and which grew in size after World War II. The second alternative is a cognitive approach to child development that during the 1960s attracted many students of developmental and educational psychology.

### Social Psychology

Social psychology is the study of the person as a social being, and so has roots going back to the Greek political thinkers and to Hobbes' first political science. We have said little about it before because as a field it is exceedingly eclectic, unified by no coherent paradigm or vision of humanity. It draws our attention now because during the 1940s and 1950s it remained outside behaviorist control and continued to employ mentalistic concepts, albeit frequently of a common-sense sort. Since social psychology is so eclectic, it is impossible to outline a single version of its mentalism; therefore we will briefly consider one theory widely influential in the 1950s and early 1960s, Leon Festinger's theory of cognitive dissonance. Its name betrays its mentalism.

Festinger's theory is about a person's beliefs and their interaction. He holds that beliefs may agree with one another, or they may clash. When beliefs clash they induce an unpleasant state called *cognitive dissonance,* which the person tries to reduce. For example, a nonsmoker who is persuaded that cigarettes cause lung cancer will feel no dissonance, for her or his belief that smoking causes cancer agrees with and supports her or his refusal to smoke. However, a smoker who comes to believe smoking causes cancer will feel cognitive dissonance, for the decision to smoke clashes with this new belief. The smoker will act to reduce the dissonance, perhaps by giving up smoking. However, it is quite common to manage dissonance in other ways. For example, a smoker may simply avoid antismoking information in order to avoid dissonance.

Festinger's theory provoked much laboratory research. One classic study appears to challenge the law of effect. Festinger and a collaborator, J. Merrill Carlsmith, devised some extremely boring tasks for subjects to perform, such as turning screws for a long time. Then the experimenter got the subject to agree to tell a waiting subject that the task was fun. Some subjects were paid $20 for telling the lie, others were paid only one dollar. According to the theory, the $20 subjects should feel no dissonance: the large payment justified their little lie. However, the $1 subjects should feel dissonance: they were telling a lie for a paltry sum. One way to resolve this dissonance would be to convince one's self that the task was in fact fun, for if one believed this, telling another subject that it was fun would be no lie. After the whole experiment was over, another experimenter interviewed the subjects and discovered that the $1 subjects voted the task significantly more enjoyable than the $20 subjects, as Festinger's theory predicted. The finding appears inconsistent with the law of effect, for we might expect that a $20 reward for saying the experiment was fun would change one's report about the enjoyability of the experiment more than a $1 reward.

What is most important about the theory of cognitive dissonance for our purposes is that it is a cognitive theory—a theory about mental entities, in this case about a person's beliefs. It is therefore a mentalistic and centralistic theory, appealing to unseen central mental processes in order to explain behavior. It is also not an informal behaviorist theory, for Festinger did not conceive of beliefs as mediating responses, but, in common sense terms, as beliefs which control behavior. The theory of cognitive dissonance and other cognitive theories in social psychology constitute a vigorous scientific mentalism outside the orbit of behaviorism. Festinger's 1957 book, *A Theory of Cognitive Dissonance,* makes no reference to behaviorist ideas. Social psychologists rarely challenged behaviorism, but their field was an alternative to it.

### Genetic Epistemology

Although European psychology in the early twentieth century was quiescent, it was by no means extinct. A most important European psychologist was the Swiss thinker Jean Piaget (born 1896). Piaget, like Freud and Wundt before him, had begun with purely biological interests, but eventually found himself practicing an innovative psychology. In Piaget's case the influences that drew him away from biology were threefold. First, he maintained a strong interest in the questions of epistemology, although he believed traditional philosophies to be too speculative and unscientific. Second, he experienced psychoanalysis with one of Freud's pupils, and studied with Jung's mentor, Bleuler, at Zurich. Third, he worked with Alfred Binet's collaborator, Theophile Simon, administering intelligence tests to children. Out of this eclectic background Piaget formulated a unique cognitive psychology. The traditional problems of epistemology are important: What is knowledge, and what is man that he may have knowledge? To Piaget, these questions should admit of a scientific answer based on sound theory and empirical research. In particular, Piaget felt it should be possible to trace the psychological growth of knowledge in children as they grow up by studying their reactions to intellectual situations, as in intelligence tests, followed up by probing questions as in psychoanalysis. Finally, Piaget's biological orientation shines through in his conception of knowledge as a set of cognitive structures that enable a child to adapt to the environment. Piaget calls his field of study *genetic epistemology,* the study of the origins of knowledge in child development.

As one would expect with a European psychologist, Piaget shows strong Kantian influences. The titles of many of his works are the names of Kant's transcendental categories: *The Child's Conception of Space, The Child's Conception of Number, The Child's Conception of Time,* and many more. In other ways, too, Piaget is distinctly European. Like Wundt, Piaget is interested in the general human mind, which Piaget calls the *epistemic subject,* not in individuals or their unique lives. Also like Wundt, Piaget is less interested in applied aspects of his work than are Americans, although he has written on education. The question of whether training can accelerate the course of cognitive growth Piaget calls "The American Question," for he is not asked it in Europe. In true pragmatic fashion Americans want to know how to get knowledge faster and more efficiently.

Piaget began his studies of children's knowledge in the 1920s, but—after a brief flurry of interest—his work was largely ignored in the United States. It was only in the 1960s that his work was rediscovered, in a context to be discussed in the next chapter. From 1930 to 1960 Piaget's thought was clearly out of step with American behaviorism, and his works consequently went unread and untranslated.

The details of Piaget's theory are most complex, but Piaget is no behaviorist. Genetic epistemology is concerned with human knowledge, not human behavior, and Piaget's theory explicitly attempts to characterize the mental structures that guide a child's intelligent adaptation to the environment and that constitute the child's knowledge of the world. Piaget is thus a mentalist and a centralist. Furthermore he rejects associationism and atomism in favor of *structuralism,* a European philosophy that explains human behavior by reference to unobserved, abstract, mathematically describable structures.

During his long intellectual lifetime, Piaget systematically pursued his own research program, paying only occasional attention to behaviorism. Thus, although he was little read before 1960, Piaget and his genetic epistemology constituted a sophisticated alternative to behaviorism ready to be picked up when the behaviorist paradigm faltered. After 1960, as young psychologists became disenchanted with behaviorism, Piaget would be increasingly read, translated, and researched by students of cognitive development.

### New Movements of the 1950s

In addition to older mentalistic psychologies that persisted through the 1950s, the period also witnessed the emergence of some new movements that provided alternatives to traditional or informal behaviorism. Two important examples will be briefly summarized.

#### Jerome Bruner: Perception and Thinking

Jerome Bruner (born 1915) has been active in a variety of psychological fields. He is perhaps best known as an educational theorist, but in the 1950s he was an experimental psychologist who pioneered in two important non-behaviorist areas: perception and thinking.

Bruner was a leader in the "New Look in Perception" movement that began after World War II. He and his colleagues proposed a view of perception in which the perceiver takes an active role, rather than being a passive register of sense data. Bruner and others did a variety of studies to support the idea that a perceiver's personality and social background play a role in affecting what the perceiver sees. The most famous and controversial of these studies concern perceptual defense, which raise the possibility of subliminal perception. Bruner and others in the New Look movement presented words to subjects for brief intervals, as had Wundt in his studies of the span of consciousness. However, these modern researchers varied the emotional content of the words: some were ordinary or "neutral" words, others were obscene or "taboo" words. Bruner and his associates found that longer exposures are required for a subject to recognize a taboo word than to recognize a neutral word. It appears that subjects somehow unconsciously perceive the negative emotional content of a taboo word and then attempt to repress its entry into awareness. Subjects will see the word only when the exposure is so long that they cannot help seeing it.

Research on perceptual defense was extremely controversial for many years, some psychologists arguing that subjects see taboo words as quickly as neutral words, falsely denying the experience as long as possible to avoid embarrassment. The controversy grew heated and has never been fully resolved. What is significant for us is that the New Look in perception was mentalistic. It analyzed perception as an active mental process involving both conscious and unconscious mental activities intervening between a sensation and a person's response to it. The idea of perceptual defense is much closer to psychoanalysis than to behaviorism, a fact in part responsible for the controversy surrounding Bruner's findings. In any event, the New Look was a mentalistic alternative to behaviorism.

In the mid-1950s Bruner was active on another front: thinking. In 1956 he and two collaborators, Jacqueline Goodnow and George Austin, published *A Study of Thinking* that defined a new research area: concept formation. Bruner and his colleagues presented subjects with arrays of geometrical figures defined along many dimensions: shape, size, color, and the like. The subject was then asked to figure out what concept the experimenter had in mind by choosing, or being presented with, examples and nonexamples of the experimenter's concept. For example, the concept to be discovered might be "all red triangles," and the experimenter might begin by pointing out to the subject a large, red, triangle as an example of the concept. The subject would then choose other stimuli from the array and be told whether it was or was not a member of the concept class. For example, if the subject chose a large red square, the subject would be told "No"; and if the subject chose a small red triangle he or she would be told "Yes." The subject would choose instances until he or she was prepared to guess the definition of the experimenter's concept.

Bruner, Goodnow, and Austin did not view the process of concept learning in terms of learning implicit mediational responses, although some informal behaviorists did. Rather, they looked on concept formation as an active, not reactive, process in which the subject's choices are guided by some strategy constructed to solve the problem. Again, the details of the theory are not important for our purposes. What is important is the mentalistic nature of Bruner's theory. The subject is not seen as a passive connector between S and R or even as linking S-r-s-R, or as a locus of variables. Instead, concept formation is an active intellectual process in which a subject constructs and follows certain strategies and decision procedures which guide (or fail to guide) the subject to the correct concept.

*A Study of Thinking* is therefore another mentalistic alternative to behaviorism. Its procedures became enormously popular in the late 1950s and early 1960s, eventually becoming absorbed in the cognitive psychology of the 1960s. Although research on concept formation began to taper off in the 1970s, it is not altogether gone. Bruner, Goodnow, and Austin proposed an experimental paradigm with wide application and appeal and formulated a mentalistic theory to account for their data.

### Computer as Mind; Mind as Computer

During World War II the modern high-speed digital computer was developed, originally for the computation of missile trajectories and other military purposes. After the war, computer science began to grow as an autonomous field, and computer scientists began to wonder if the machines they were designing could be called intelligent. Computers seem to think: information goes in, it is stored and processed, and then the computer "behaves," or produces output. Is this really thinking? Can a computer be as intelligent as a human being?

In 1950, A. M. Turing, an important pioneer in computing theory, proposed a test by which to answer these questions. Imagine a person conversing via teletype with another person and a computer. If the first person cannot distinguish between the human being and the computer on the basis of the interaction with each, then, argued Turing, we will have created an intelligent machine, or artificial intelligence. The field of artificial intelligence grew, and is growing, rapidly, and early scientists foresaw a world in which artificial intelligences would translate languages, conduct psychotherapy, and do other sophisticated tasks. These dreams have not yet been fulfilled except in experimental settings, but today's computers are immensely more sophisticated than those in Turing's time. Nevertheless, no computer has passed the Turing test for more than a few sentences.

Artificial intelligence workers see the computer as a mind potentially equal to a human's, although different. The next logical step was to see a human as a computer. A person may be said to receive information from the environment, store it, process it, and then produce output, or behave. The mind thus can be seen as a computer. The goal of computer simulation is not just to manufacture an intelligence different from a person's, that is, artificial, but to write computer programs which have the same kind of intelligence as a human being.

The first systematic attempt to simulate human intelligence was made by three theorists at Carnegie-Mellon University, Allan Newell, J. C. Shaw, and Herbert Simon, who tackled human problem solving. They studied how people solve a variety of logical and mathematical problems, and then attempted to write computer programs that would solve the same problems in the same ways. In 1958, they presented their General Problem Solver, a general purpose program capable of simulating human performance as a wide variety of problems.

Again, we find a new development outside behaviorism. Computer simulation is necessarily new, for the computer was a product of the 1940s. The General Problem Solver is an objective, sophisticated theory that is not part of orthodox behaviorism. It does not work on the basis of S-R chains or r-s mediational mechanisms. It is not conceived as a locus of variables, for its problem solving procedures are central processes—not directly and externally observable in the human being or computer—that control overt behavior. We may even note that Carnegie-Mellon University is largely a business school, and Simon has always remained active in business economics, winning the 1978 Nobel Prize for Economics. So the General Problem Solver was outside behaviorism in both conception and background.

We will see in the next chapter that this alternative to behaviorism has proved the most important one. For the computer makes possible a sophisticated and precise theory not available to behaviorists or mentalists. By 1970 or so, the computer-inspired paradigm of information processing had replaced behaviorism as the dominant approach in human experimental psychology. In the next chapter we will ask if that replacement was a revolution.

### Challenges to Behaviorism

As early as 1955 we find evidence of a recognition by psychologists of a loosening of the restrictions of the behaviorist paradigm. In May of 1955 a symposium was held at the University of Colorado on the topic of cognition. The symposium's organizers wrote in the volume reporting the proceedings: "Recent years . . . have loosened the hold of narrow operationism and psychologists have felt free, as well as stimulated, to attack . . . less precise but certainly for more interesting and significant problems of human behavior. This is the Zeitgeist that motivated us to arrange a symposium on the topic of cognition" (Bruner et al., 1957).

The symposium brought together a wide range of behaviorists and representatives of alternatives. The informal behaviorist Charles Osgood offered a mediational analysis of language and perception. David Rapaport, a neo-Freudian ego psychologist, presented a clinician's view of cognition. There were also papers by Jerome Bruner, Leon Festinger, Fritz Heider (another cognitively oriented social psychologist) and Egon Brunswik (an associate of Tolman's). That the conference was eclectic was clear to the participants. Osgood recognized that each theorist was using a different psychological language to analyze cognition, and that this would entail complex translation problems if each thinker were to understand the other. However, despite the eclecticism and representation of different schools of thought, there was little feeling of confrontation. Only Rapaport, who harshly criticized Osgood's behaviorist theory of perception as too Humean, struck a discordant note. Otherwise the conference participants simply agreed to disagree. The paradigm was becoming blurred, but there was no attendant sense of crisis, and no one challenged the paradigm in a spirited or effective way.

The eclectic peace was about to be broken by two very different thinkers. Each would take Skinner's radical behaviorism as his point of attack, and each would be concerned with problems of human psychology and environmental control. These attacks did produce a sense of crisis to which psychologists of the 1960s responded. We begin with the more diffuse challenge, that of Carl Rogers and humanistic psychology.

## Humanistic Psychology

Carl Rogers (born 1902) is perhaps the best-known spokesman for a tradition in clinical psychology that derives from the phenomenological tradition in philosophy and psychology dating back to Brentano and Husserl. He and Skinner have engaged in an off-and-on running debate since 1956 when they debated the merits of their respective positions before the American Psychological Association.

Phenomenological psychology is especially appealing to the clinician, for the clinician's stock in trade is empathy, and phenomenology is the study of subjective experience. Rogers distinguishes three modes of knowledge. The first is the objective mode, in which we seek to understand the world as an object. The second and third modes of knowing are subjective. One is each person's own subjective knowledge of personal conscious experience, including each person's intentions and sense of freedom. The other mode of subjective knowledge is the attempt to understand another person's subjective inner world. The clinician, of course, must master this last mode of knowing, for in Roger's view it is only by understanding the client's personal world and subjective self that the clinician can hope to help the client. Rogers believes that personal beliefs, values, and intentions control behavior. He hopes that psychology will find systematic ways to know the personal experience of other people, for then therapy will be greatly enhanced.

Rogers argues that behaviorism limits itself exclusively to the objective mode of knowledge and so constrains psychology within a particular set of allowable techniques and theories. It treats human beings exclusively as objects, not as experiencing subjects in their own right. In specific contradistinction to Skinner, Rogers puts great emphasis on each person's experienced freedom, rejecting Skinner's purely physical causality. Wrote Rogers (1964): "The experiencing of choice, of freedom of choice . . . is not only a profound truth, but is a very important element in therapy." As a scientist he accepts determinism, but as a therapist he accepts freedom; the two "exist in different dimensions."

This position, expounded by Rogers and others (especially Abraham Maslow), since it stresses the importance of the human being and the necessary subjectivity of perception, has come to be called humanistic psychology. Humanistic psychologists accept Protagoras' rule that "Humanity is the measure of all things" in both its perceptual and ethical senses. Humanistic psychology is also called the "Third Force" in psychology, to contrast it with the forces of behaviorism and psychoanalysis (which Rogers calls a pseudo-science). It is therefore a conscious alternative to the behaviorist paradigm.

Further, Rogers explicitly criticizes and challenges behaviorism. But he criticizes it for being too narrow and challenges it to include subjective experience. Rogers does not say behaviorism is wrong, only limited, and he seeks only to go beyond it, not to overthrow it. His attack on behaviorism is diffuse, and his criticisms are not telling. Humanistic psychology has grown as a viewpoint within the general field, yet Rogers did not provide a strident radical voice calling for a revolution. Behaviorism began as a self-conscious movement only after John B. Watson pulled together existing trends in functionalism into a revolutionary standpoint. The movement toward mentalism which we have traced in the 1950s finally found its own revolutionary prophet in a linguist, Avram Noam Chomsky (born 1928).

### Cartesian Linguistics: The Attack on Verbal Behavior

Since the time of Descartes language has been seen as a special problem for any mechanistic psychology. Hull's student Spence suspected that language might render inapplicable to humans laws of learning derived from animals. In 1955 the informal behaviorist Osgood referred to the problems of meaning and perception as the "Waterloo of contemporary behaviorism," and in response attempted to provide a mediational theory of language, applicable only to human beings (Osgood, 1957). The philosopher Norman Malcolm (1964), sympathetic to behaviorism, regards language as "an essential difference between man and the lower animals."

B. F. Skinner, however, was a dissenter from the Cartesian view, shared in part even by fellow behaviorists. The whole point of *Verbal Behavior* was to show that language, while it is a complex behavior, could be explained by reference to only the principles of behavior formulated from animal studies. Skinner therefore denied that there is anything special about language, or verbal behavior, or that there is any fundamental difference between humans and the lower animals. Somewhat as the empiricist Hume raised Kant from his dogmatic slumbers to a defense of the transcendental mind, Skinner's Humean treatment of language roused a rationalist counterattack that said behaviorism was not merely limited, but completely wrong. Further, a rationalist account of language was offered in its place. In the next chapter we will look at the new psycholinguistics; here we will summarize the rationalist attack on *Verbal Behavior*.

In 1959 the journal *Language* carried a lengthy review of Skinner's *Verbal Behavior* by a young and obscure linguist named Noam Chomsky. In his view he was attacking not only Skinner's work, but empiricist ideas in linguistics, psychology, and philosophy generally. Chomsky regarded Skinner's book as a *"reductio ad absurdum* of behaviorist assumptions," and wanted to show it up as pure "mythology" (Jacobovits & Miron, 1967). These are the words of an angry revolutionary, and Chomsky's review is perhaps the single most influential psychological paper published since Watson's behaviorist manifesto of 1913.

Chomsky's basic criticism of Skinner's book was that it is an exercise in equivocation. Skinner's fundamental technical terms—stimulus, response, reinforcement and so on—are well defined in animal learning experiments, but cannot be extended to human behavior without serious modification, as Skinner claims. Chomsky argued that if one attempts to use Skinner's terms in rigorous technical senses, they can be shown not to apply to language, while if the terms are metaphorically extended, they become so vague as to be no improvement on traditional linguistic notions. Chomsky systematically attacked each of Skinner's concepts, but we will consider only two examples: his analysis of stimulus and reinforcement.

Obviously, to any behaviorist proper definitions of the stimuli that control behavior are important. The difficulty of defining "stimulus," however, is a notorious one for behaviorism, noted by Thorndike and even some behaviorists. Are stimuli to be defined in purely physical terms, independent of behavior, or in terms of their effects on behavior? If we accept the former definition, then behavior looks unlawful, for very few stimuli in a situation ever affect behavior. While if we accept the latter definition, behavior is lawful by definition, for then the behaviorist only considers those stimuli that do systematically determine behavior. Chomsky raised this problem and others specific to Skinner's *Verbal Behavior*. First, Chomsky pointed out that to say each bit of verbal behavior is under stimulus control is scientifically empty, for given any response, we can always find *some* relevant stimulus. A person looks at a painting and says "It's by Rembrandt, isn't it?" Skinner would assert that certain subtle properties of the painting determine the response. Yet the person could have said: "How much did it cost?," "It clashes with the wallpaper," "You've hung it too high," "It's hideous!", "I have one just like it at home," "It's forged," and so on, virtually *ad infinitum*. No matter what is said, *some* property could be found that "controls" the behavior. Chomsky argued that there is no prediction of behavior, and certainly no serious control, in this circumstance. Skinner's system is not the scientific advance toward the prediction and control of behavior it pretends to be.

Chomsky also pointed out that Skinner's definition of stimulus becomes hopelessly vague and metaphorical, at a great remove from the rigorous laboratory environment. Skinner speaks of "remote stimulus control," in which the stimulus need not impinge on the speaker at all, as when a recalled diplomat describes a foreign situation. Skinner says the suffix "-ed" is controlled by the "subtle property of stimuli we speak of as action in the past." What physical dimensions define "things in the past"? Chomsky argued that Skinner's usage here is not remotely related to his usage in his bar-pressing experiments, and that Skinner has said nothing new about the supposed "stimulus control" of verbal behavior.

Chomsky next considered reinforcement, another term easily defined in the usual operant learning experiment in terms of delivered food or water. Chomsky argued that Skinner's application of the term to verbal behavior is again vague and metaphorical. Consider Skinner's notion of automatic self-reinforcement. Talking to oneself is said to be automatically self-reinforcing: that is why one does it. Similarly, thinking is also said to be behavior that automatically affects the behaver and is therefore reinforcing. Also consider what we might call remote reinforcement: A writer shunned in his own time may be reinforced by expecting fame to come much later. Chomsky argued (1959) that "the notion of reinforcement has totally lost whatever meaning it may ever have had . . . a person can be reinforced though he emits no response at all [thinking], and have the reinforcing 'stimulus' need not impinge on the 'reinforced person' [remote reinforcement] or need not even exist [an unpopular author who remains unpopular] . . . ."

Chomsky also criticized the behaviorist view of language acquisition and sketched his own position on that and other matters. We shall consider the positive side of Cartesian linguistics in the next chapter. Here, the important thing to note is Chomsky's revolutionary attitude. He is not prepared to accept Skinner's *Verbal Behavior* as a plausible scientific hypothesis. It is clear that he regards *Verbal Behavior* as hopelessly muddled and fundamentally wrong. His acute and unrelenting criticism, coupled with his own positive program, are aimed at the overthrow of behaviorist psychology, not its liberalization as called for by Miller, or its transcendence as called for by Rogers. For Chomsky, behaviorism cannot be built upon, cannot be transcended; it can only be replaced. Just as Watson's polemic inaugurated a profound change in psychology by arguing the overthrow of functionalism and structuralism, so Chomsky's biting review touched off crisis and revolt.

### Who Controls the Controllers?

We have found the pursuit of control to be characteristic of behaviorism from Watson to Skinner. Desire for social control played a large role in the favorable reception of behaviorism among progressives. However, in the second half of the twentieth century people had experienced the fruits of control in Hitler's Germany and Stalin's Russia, and many were disenchanted with the United States' attempt to control Vietnam. Control was less popular and B. F. Skinner's continued espousal of technological control in *Walden II*, and *Beyond Freedom and Dignity* was greeted with horror in many circles.

As early as *Walden II*, many libertarians had found Skinner's proposals frightening. In *Beyond Freedom and Dignity* Skinner discusses his world view without the trappings of fiction, but as achievable with existing technology. Although reviewers as different as radical behaviorists and Christian theologians praised the book, most reaction ranged from mild disagreement to sarcastic denunciation.

For example, Noam Chomsky called the book a "travesty," branded behaviorism a "pseudo-science" in the tradition of racist nineteenth-century anthropology, and implied that Skinner is at best a muddled thinker, and at worst an outright fraud. As in his review of *Verbal Behavior*, much of Chomsky's critique showed that in applying his animal science to human behavior Skinner stretches the meaning of his technical terms so much that they do no more than poorly substitute for ordinary English. Chomsky, like others, argued also that Skinner's own position makes it pointless for him to write the book. Since Skinner says persuasion is a generally ineffective means of behavior change, why should he hope to persuade the reader of *Beyond Freedom and Dignity* to support him?

Other critics feared the possibility of a behavioral tyranny. Skinner, following the tradition of pragmatism, reduces values to their consequences, reinforcement, and makes survival the ultimate value overriding all others, including life, liberty, and the pursuit of happiness. Who then is to say that a fascist state might not be best? Skinner has said that he could design better slot machines, but would not. Presumably some scruples stop him, but why should not another behaviorist do what Skinner refuses to do? Skinner says we must design a culture that makes tyranny impossible, but this pushes the question back one step: Who will design *that* culture?

Finally, various critics, including Chomsky, have pointed out that *Beyond Freedom and Dignity* is full of empty platitudes and tautologies. For example, we are told that punishable behavior may be minimized by creating circumstances in which it is not likely to occur, and that we can cure overpopulation by inducing people to have fewer babies, and cure pollution by inducing people not to pollute. No one could disagree with these aims, but Skinner provides no evidence that radical behaviorism can bring these things to pass any better than conventional procedures. He asserts that the experimental control of animals provides the needed techniques, but he nowhere demonstrates it.

In closing, we may note that in this one area Skinner is heir to Platonic rationalism. Plato envisaged a highly structured, carefully controlled society ruled by the Philosopher King. Only the elite were to be free, and even their behavior was carefully controlled. Skinner, too, believes in a perfect society, in which all behavior is carefully controlled by manipulation of the contingencies of reinforcement. It is to be ruled by the Psychologist King who has discovered the Platonically True principles of conditioning and applies them to fellow persons and self. In many ways radical behaviorism appears to be relativistic: we only behave as we do because of our individual histories of reinforcement which are different for each person. Yet this surface relativism is belied by Skinner's assumption that the principles of learning are as eternal and immutable as the Form of the Good, which of course, for him is survival.

## CONCLUSION: THE CRISIS OF 1960

We leave psychology in 1960 as we found it in 1950, in the grip of crisis, uncertain about its proper subject matter and methods, and about the future of behaviorism. The period from 1950 to 1959 was an eclectic period, marked by divergent but not hostile schools, by a growing interest in mentalistic psychology of one sort or another, and by some realization that language was a trouble area for behaviorism. The quiet and eclectic 1950s ended with Chomsky's blast at *Verbal Behavior*. A new period of confrontation was beginning.

We will close by noting a sign of crisis and revolution occurring not long after Chomsky's review—a crisis which parallels the conference on modern learning theory in the crisis of 1950. This clear sign of crisis was a symposium held in 1963 called *Behaviorism and Phenomenology: Contrasting Bases for Modern Psychology*. The symposium pitted behaviorism, and its spokesperson B. F. Skinner, against phenomenology and its spokespersons Carl Rogers and Robert B. MacLeod. It included a critique of behaviorism by Sigmund Koch, and comments by two philosophers, Norman Malcolm and Michael Scriven.

The atmosphere at this conference, like that at the 1950 conference on learning theory, was clearly one of crisis and confrontation. Koch, who was present at both, said in 1963: "I would be happy to say what we have been hearing could be characterized as the death rattle of Behaviorism . . ." (Wann, 1964). Koch through-out was intemperately critical of behaviorism. He called one of Skinner's answers to a question "quite characteristic" of behaviorism in that "It was an intolerant answer" (Wann, 1964). His own contribution to the symposium was an extended critique of all forms of behaviorism, attacking in particular behaviorism's reliance on early logical positivism, which by 1963 had been both heavily modified and finally given up by most philosophers of science. He also briefly assaulted phenomenology for being an "escape" from psychological problems rather than an answer, and for its unscientific style, its "epigrammatic nuance," and "association-chasing" before a problem is even stated.

At the conference, Skinner and Rogers simply continued their debate, each criticizing the other in familiar terms, while complimenting each other for their contributions. Theirs had become a friendly confrontation, lacking the acrimony of Chomsky or Koch. MacLeod contributed a historical and technical presentation of philosophical phenomenology, concluding that human consciousness can be, and ought to be, systematically studied, but that behaviorism's grip would have to loosen first.

Norman Malcolm was at least partly in accord with Skinner. He noticed some-thing rarely observed by behaviorists and phenomenologists themselves, namely that the positions are quite compatible. Skinner pays attention to private stimula-tion, as we saw in discussing *Verbal Behavior*. A toothache is part of one's private world, and can certainly determine behavior, as both Skinner and Rogers would hold. Further, Rogers requires that scientific psychology must be able to objectify private experience. If this can be done, then behaviorists may happily correlate objective measures of private stimuli with objective behavior, as will the scientific phenomenologist. The two positions converge.

On the other hand, Malcolm called Chomsky's review of *Verbal Behavior* "brilliant," and called Skinner's actual analysis of self-observation "weird." Skinner says the statement "I am looking for my glasses" is based on self-observation: I see myself rummaging around on my desk, looking in drawers, and so forth, and since this has lead in the past to reinforcement, by finding my glasses, I now say "I am looking for my glasses." Malcolm pointed out that if you asked someone to justify this statement, you would naturally think the person either crazy or joking if he or she said "I must be looking for my glasses because I'm opening drawers and lifting papers on my desk."

Scriven concluded the volume with a philosophical reflection on psychology in general and behaviorism and phenomenology in particular. Like Koch, he derided psychology for its reliance on outdated positivism: "I remember the glee with which I discovered that nobody actually produces operational definitions even when they say they do." Scriven also appeared rather pessimistic about the future of psychology. Said Scriven, psychology suffers from limitations not imposed on other sciences (for example, much of it is already anticipated by common sense), and its young scientists are adherents of the wrong philosophy, positivism.

According to Kuhn, when scientists listen to philosophers, it is a sign of crisis.

When there are competing points of view, it is a sign of crisis. When scientists debate fundamental issues, it is a sign of crisis. Each of these signs was present at this symposium.

## SUGGESTED READING

The best volume on the psychology of the 1950s is *Psychology: Study of a Science,* edited by Sigmund Koch, especially Study I (McGraw-Hill, 1959) which contains discussions of central problems and theoretical systems written by leading researchers.

## REFERENCES

Bruner, J. S., Brunswik, E., Festinger, C., Heider, F., Muenzinger, K., Osgood, C., & Rapaport, P. *Contemporary approaches to cognition.* Cambridge, Mass.: Harvard University Press, 1957.

Chomsky, N. Review of *Verbal Behavior* by B. F. Skinner (1959). Reprinted in L. Jakobovits & M. Miron (Eds.) *Readings in the psychology of language.* Englewood Cliffs, N.J.: Prentice-Hall, 1967.

Cohen, D. *Psychologists on psychology.* London: Routledge & Kegan Paul, 1977.

Estes, W. K., Koch, S., MacCorquodale, K., Meehl, P., Mueller, C., Schoenfeld, W., & Verplanck, W. S. *Modern learning theory.* New York: Appleton-Century-Crofts, 1954.

Jakobovits, L. & Miron M. (Eds.) *Readings in the psychology of language.* Englewood Cliffs, N.J.: Prentice-Hall, 1967.

Kendler, H. H. & Kendler, T. S. From discrimination learning to cognitive development: A neo-behavioristic odyssey. In W. K. Estes (Ed.) *Handbook of learning and cognitive processes* (Vol. 1). Hillsdale, N.J.: Erlbaum, 1975.

Koch, S. Theoretical psychology, 1950: An overview. *Psychological Review,* 1951, *58,* 295-301.

Koch, S. Psychology and emerging conceptions of knowledge as unitary. In T. W. Wann (Ed.) *Behaviorism and phenomenology.* Chicago: University of Chicago Press, 1964.

Malcolm, N. Behaviorism as a philosophy of psychology. In T. W. Wann (Ed.) *Behaviorism and phenomenology.* Chicago: University of Chicago Press, 1964.

Miller, N. Liberalization of basic S-R concepts. In S. Koch (Ed.) *Psychology: Study of a science* (Vol. 2). New York: McGraw-Hill, 1959.

Osgood, C. A behaviorist analysis of perception and language as cognitive phenomena. In J. Bruner et al., *Contemporary approaches to cognition.* Cambridge, Mass.: Harvard University Press, 1957.

Rogers, C. Toward a science of the person. In T. W. Wann (Ed.) *Behaviorism and phenomenology.* Chicago: University of Chicago Press, 1964.

Scriven, M. Views of human nature. In T. W. Wann (Ed.) *Behaviorism and phenomenology.* Chicago: University of Chicago Press, 1964.

Skinner, B. F. *Walden II.* New York: Macmillan, 1948.

Skinner, B. F. *Verbal behavior.* Englewood Cliffs, N.J.: Prentice-Hall, 1957.

Skinner, B. F. A lecture on having a poem (1971). Reprinted in *Cumulative record: A selection of papers.* Englewood Cliffs, N.J.: Prentice-Hall, 1972.

Skinner, B. F. *Beyond freedom and dignity.* New York: Bantam, 1972.

Wann, T. W. (Ed.) *Behaviorism and phenomenology.* Chicago: University of Chicago Press, 1964.

# 13

# Revolt and Reform, 1960-1970

## CONTINUED CHALLENGE TO THE BEHAVIORIST PARADIGM

The crisis of 1960 deepened as the decade continued. More challenges and alternatives emerged, as psychologists sought firm foundations on which to reestablish their science. For many, the old answers of neobehaviorism were no longer adequate, but others still chose the radical purity of Skinner's behaviorism. In this section we will examine important empirical and theorietical challenges to the behaviorist paradigm.

### Erosion of the Foundations

Behaviorism was conceptually anchored at two ends: the philosophical and the empirical. The philosophical basis was positivism, which was supposed to have provided a general blueprint for sound scientific research. The empirical basis was composed of studies of animal learning, largely of rat learning, which were supposed to produce general laws of behavior applicable to all animals, including humans. In the 1960s, however, both anchors became less and less secure.

#### The Disappearance of Positivism

The philosophy of positivism, whether Mach's early radical positivism or the sophisticated logical positivism of the Vienna circle, was an attempt to explicate the essential features of science. It claimed to be able to characterize what differentiated science from pseudo-science and metaphysics. Its explication emphasized objective experiment yielding unarguable objective data, and rigorous axiomatic theory yielding testable and concrete hypotheses. Psychologists accepted the positivist image of science, and so behaviorists stressed objective behavioral methods and formal theory (although of course Skinner, following Mach, eschewed the latter).

However, this precise and objective view of science became increasingly suspect in the late 1950s and beyond. Since its founding, logical positivism had undergone continuous change that took it further and further away from the simple logical positivism of the 1920s. For example, in the 1930s it was recognized that theoretical terms cannot be neatly linked to observations by the single step of operational definition, a fact some psychologists acknowledged without abandoning the jargon of operationism. Younger philosophers, though, were less inclined to accept the positivist paradigm even in principle, so that during the 1960s the movement became moribund. It began to be called "The Received View," like a dead theology, and a symposium on "The Legacy of Logical Positivism" was published in 1969.

Although many criticisms of "The Received View" were offered, perhaps the most fundamental was that its explication of scientific practice was false. Historically oriented philosophers of science, such as Thomas Kuhn, Stephen Toulmin, and N. R. Hanson, showed that the supposed objectivity of science was a myth. In Chapter 1 we discussed how science is a human enterprise in which researchers see what they expect to see, investigate some problems and not others as defined by unconscious paradigms, respond to current intellectual demands, and suppress novelty. Positivism's postmortem dissection of science as a logically coherent system consisting of axioms, theorems, predictions, and verifications distorts and falsifies science as a lively, fallible human enterprise.

If positivism is false even as a reconstruction of physics, what kind of guide can it offer to a young science such as psychology? Behaviorism to a large degree proceeded on the premise that the positivist analysis of science was correct, and adopted methods and theories consistent with positivism's precepts. If the analysis is wrong, can the science be right? The crises of behaviorism, especially the learning theory crisis of 1950, can be seen as an empirical refutation of logical positivism. The formal behaviorists, especially Hull, seriously tried to practice positivist psychology. As we have seen, they failed. Hull's theory, despite his best efforts, was never able to conform to positivist precepts, and in the end it became a sterile exercise in quantification. The Hull-Tolman debates produced scholarly feuds, not scientific progress. Kuhn, Toulmin, and others showed that positivism is false to history. Formal behaviorism showed that positivism's recipe for science is impossible to follow.

Kuhn's views have themselves become popular with many psychologists. As cognitive psychology seemed to replace behaviorism in the later 1960s, references to scientific revolutions and paradigm clashes abounded. Kuhn's doctrines seemed to justify a revolutionary attitude: Behaviorism must be overthrown, it cannot be reformed. Many psychologists adopted a kind of scientific revolutionary radical chic paralleling the widespread revolutionary radical political chic of the 1960s. Using *The Structure of Scientific Revolutions* to justify a scientific revolution raises an interesting problem in social psychology. Can the perception of revolution be a self-fulfilling prophecy? Would there have been a revolution against behaviorism without Kuhn's book? Or, more subtly, could belief in Kuhn's ideas have created the appearance of revolution where there was really only conceptual evolution?

We shall return to these questions at the end of the chapter, when we again ask "Was there a revolution?" What is important at present for the fate of behaviorism was that by the later 1960s few, if any, philosophers of science believed positivism to be a credible philosophy of science. Many rejected the social psychological approach of Kuhn, but it was clear that positivism was no longer a viable alternative. Positivism had simply disappeared, and along with it, behaviorism's philosophical foundation.

### Constraints on Animal Learning

At the other end from philosophy, behaviorism was anchored by empirical studies of animal behavior. Watson began his career as an animal psychologist, and Tolman, Hull, and Skinner rarely studied human behavior, preferring the more controlled situations that could be imposed on animals. Animal experiments were expected to yield general behavioral laws applicable to a wide range of species, including humans, with little or no modification. Tolman spoke of cognitive maps in rats and persons, Hull of the general laws of mammalian behavior, and Skinner of the extension of animal principles to verbal behavior. It was believed that the principles that emerged from artificially controlled experiments would illuminate the ways in which all organisms learn regardless of evolutionary conditioning. The assumption of generality was crucial to the behaviorist program, for if laws of learning are species-specific, studies of animal behavior are pointless for understanding humanity, which even Skinner assumes to be the final goal of psychology.

Evidence accumulated in the 1960s, however, that the laws of learning uncovered with rats and pigeons are not general, and that serious constraints exist on what and how an animal learns, constraints dictated by the animal's evolutionary history. This evidence came both from psychology and other disciplines. On the one hand, psychologists discovered anomalies in the application of learning laws in a variety of situations, while on the other hand, ethologists demonstrated the importance of innate factors in understanding an animal's behavior in the natural environment its ancestors evolved in.

In developing the pigeon-guided missile, Skinner worked with a young psychologist, Keller Breland, who was so impressed by the possibilities of behavior control that he and his wife became professional animal trainers. As Skinner put it in 1959: "Behavior could be shaped up according to specifications and maintained indefinitely almost at will . . . Keller Breland is now specializing in the production of behavior as a saleable commodity. . . ." Skinner's claim for Breland resembles Frazier's boast in *Walden II* of being able to produce human personalities to order.

However, in the course of their extensive experience in training many species to perform unusual behaviors, the Brelands found instances in which animals did not perform as they should. In 1961, they reported their difficulties in a paper whose title, "The misbehavior of organisms," puns on Skinner's first book, *The Behavior of Organisms*. For example, they tried to teach pigs to carry wooden coins and deposit them in a piggy bank. Although they could teach the behaviors, the Brelands found that the behavior degenerated in pig after pig. The animals would eventually pick up the coin, drop it on the ground and root it, rather than deposit it in the bank. The Brelands report that they found many instances of animals "trapped by strong instinctive behaviors" that overwhelm learned behaviors. Pigs naturally root for their food, and so they come to root the coins which they have been trained to collect to get food reinforcers. Breland and Breland (1972) conclude that psychologists should examine "the hidden assumptions which led most disastrously to these breakdowns" in the general laws of learning proposed by behaviorism. They are clearly questioning behaviorism's paradigmatic assumptions in the light of experimental anomalies.

They identify three such assumptions: "That the animal . . . (is) a virtual *tabula rasa,* that species differences are insignificant, and that all responses are about equally conditionable to all stimuli." These assumptions are fundamental to empiricism, and statements of them have been made by the major behaviorists.

Although limits on these assumptions had been suggested before (Bitterman, 1960; 1965), the Brelands' paper seemed to open the floodgates to discoveries of more anomalies under more controlled conditions.

We may mention one such line of research, conducted by John Garcia and his associates. Garcia was a student of Krechevsky, Tolman's major pupil. Garcia studied what he called "conditioned nausea," a form of classical conditioning. Standard empiricist assumptions, enunciated by Pavlov, held that any stimulus could act as a conditioned stimulus that through conditioning could elicit any response as a conditioned response. More informally, any stimulus could be conditioned to elicit any response. Empirical studies further indicated that conditioned stimulus and unconditioned stimulus had to be paired within about a half-second of each other for learning to take place.

Using a variety of methods, Garcia let rats drink a novel-tasting liquid, and then made the rats sick over an hour later. The question was whether rats would learn to avoid the place they were sick, the unconditioned stimulus immediately connected with their sickness, or the solution they drank, although it was remote in time from the unconditioned response. The latter uniformly occurred. The usual laws of classical conditioning did not hold. Garcia argued that rats know instinctively that nausea must be due to something they ate, not stimuli present at the time of sickness. This makes good evolutionary sense, for sickness in the wild is more likely to be caused by drinking tainted water than by the bush under which a rat was sitting when it felt sick. Connecting taste with sickness is more biologically adaptive than connecting it with visual or auditory stimuli. It appears, therefore, that evolution constrains what stimuli may be associated with what responses.

Garcia's research was initially greeted with extreme skepticism and was refused publication in the major journals devoted to animal behavior. This skepticism is typical of a paradigm's first response to empirical anomalies. However, studies by other researchers demonstrated for many behaviors that an animal's evolutionary inheritance places distinct limits on what it can learn. Garcia's studies are now considered classics.

Meanwhile, ethologically oriented biologists had maintained a tradition of studying animal's natural behaviors in their evolutionary context. Ethologists stressed the role of instinct in determining behavior, and this tradition never adopted the *tabula rasa* assumptions of behaviorism. Their work, therefore, provided further anomalies for empiricism. For example, Peter Marler and his colleagues have intensively investigated birdsong learning over many years. Song is functionally important to birds in their natural environments, for many birds use distinct calls to establsh territories, attract mates, or warn of danger, all abilities vital to the survival of their species. What Marler found is that some bird species for whom song has functional significance come programmed to learn their own species calls. Birds who hear no song when young grow up without song, so extreme nativism is ruled out. But birds exposed to songs of other species do not learn these songs, even though the songs are within their vocal range. Birds learn their species' songs only when exposed to them as youngsters. This indicates that birds are born with the innate ability to attend to and learn only certain sounds. Again, this makes good evolutionary sense, for a bird which learned to sing the wrong songs, or imitate the sounds of passing cars, would be unable to mate and have offspring. Since adult birds do not teach their young to sing, young birds must have native mechanisms that direct their learning to the appropriate sounds.

Often ethological work presented many instances of natural learning being determined by animals' genetic makeup, casting further doubt on the validity of empiricism and on the belief that the laws of learning discovered in the laboratory could be extended across species without serious modification.

In 1961 the Brelands stated that ethological work had done more to further understanding of animal behavior than behaviorist laboratory studies. By the 1970s, animal psychologists were proclaiming that a revolution had occurred in which the old paradigm was shattered (Bolles, 1975). Although such an assessment is premature, the existence of books and symposia in the 1970s on constraints on learning indicated that the field of animal learning was in crisis, that the old security of the rat lab and the anchor of general learning laws, were gone.

This particular crisis reveals an interesting fact about the influence of Darwin on American psychology. Both functionalists and behaviorists viewed mind and behavior as adaptive processes, adjusting the organism to its environment. We have seen that Skinner's analysis of learning is squarely and consciously based on an extension of natural selection. Yet behaviorism adopted the empiricist assumptions of the *tabula rasa* and species-general laws of learning and ignored the contribution of evolution to behavior. This was the product of another behaviorist assumption, peripheralism. Behaviorists of course recognized that a dog cannot respond to a tone it cannot hear; nor can it learn to fly. These constraints, however, are only on the organism's peripheral sensory and motor abilities. Since behaviorism denied that central processes exist, it could not recognize evolutionary limits on them. Therefore, it had to assume that as long as an organism could sense a stimulus, it could be associated with any response it could physically make.

However, many of the anomalies uncovered by researchers such as the Brelands, Garcia, and Marler seem to involve either tastes or sights or sounds an animal can sense, yet Garcia showed that rats are predisposed to link only certain stimuli and responses, and Marler showed that birds do not learn other species songs they hear and could physically produce. Both findings seem to indicate some central control over learning—central control that is at least partly determined by heredity.

Therefore, although behaviorism, following functionalism, adopted the theory of natural selection as a conceptual tool, it denied the biological implications of evolution because it denied centralism. Peripheralism is a central assumption of behaviorism, the study of observable behavior, and it supported other paradigmatic assumptions. The assumptions of the disciplinary matrix interlocked to produce the expectation of general laws of learning.

We may note, finally, that behaviorism's extreme empiricism denied already established constraints on learning. For example, Thorndike himself found great differences in how easily cats learned to escape from different puzzle boxes. In particular, they had a difficult time learning to lick their paws in order to escape. Such a behavior is not naturally connected to escape, and so cats were slow to discover the connection. Similarly, early students of animal behavior from Darwin to the ethologists had described biologically determined behavior patterns. All of this is consistent with the extension of a normal science paradigm. Certain anomalies are quietly ignored or put down to bad method (for example, the anecdotal method) until they become too serious to ignore, as they did in the 1960s in animal learning.

### The Problem of Language

#### Cartesian Linguistics: Adult Language

Noam Chomsky did not merely criticize B. F. Skinner's *Verbal Behavior*; he proposed his own highly sophisticated analysis of language, especially syntax. He created a new formal method, called *transformational grammar,* for describing a language's grammatical structure. Since transformational grammar is enormously complex, involving formal logic and abstract mathematics, we will only summarize Chomsky's general points.

Chomsky's central insight is that language is creative. Aside from clichés and television reruns, every sentence you hear each day is new to you. As a speaker, nearly every sentence you speak is new. Every human being, in every act of language, is creating new responses and understanding new stimuli. Chomsky believes no behaviorist approach to language can cope with its endless creativity and flexibility. He argues that creativity can only be understood by recognizing that language is a rule governed system. As part of their mental processes, persons possess a set of grammatical rules which allow them to generate new sentences by appropriately combining linguistic elements. Each person can thus generate an infinity of sentences by repeated application of the rules of grammar, just as a person can generate numbers infinitely by repeated application of the rules of arithmetic. Chomsky argues that human language will not be understood until psychology describes the rules of grammar, the mental structures that underlly speaking and hearing. A superficial behaviorist approach, which studies only speech and hearing but neglects the inner rules that govern speech and hearing, is necessarily inadequate.

Like Wundt, Chomsky distinguishes inner and outer language phenomena, but he calls them deep and surface structures. The distinction may be exemplified in the following sentences: (1) John is easy to please; (2) John is eager to please. If we diagram the grammar of these sentences we will discover they are identical: Subject + verb + predicate adjective + infinitive phrase. However, this analysis is of surface structure only, and is false to the deeper logical structure of the sentences. This may be shown by applying the same grammatical operation to the two supposedly identical sentences, by moving "to please" to the front of each sentence. This generates: (1) To please John is easy; and (2) To please John is eager. The first is still an acceptable sentence, the latter is not. We must conclude that the sentences are not grammatically the same. The sentences differ in logical deep structure. In sentence 2, John is the grammatical subject of the sentence, and its logical subject as well: John does the pleasing. However, in sentence 1, John is the grammatical subject but the logical object: John receives pleasing from someone else. The sentences have identical surface grammatical structure, but different deep structures. The reverse relationship may also hold. "The boy hit the ball" and "The ball was hit by the boy" have different surface structures, but the same deep structure, for they mean the same thing. Chomsky believes that behaviorism has limited itself to studying surface structures and cannot handle these deeper relationships.

Chomsky poses other problems for the behaviorist approach. Consider sentences such as: (3) The rabbit is ready to eat; (4) The shooting of the hunters was terrible; or (5) They are cooking apples. Each of these sentences has two meanings. Sentence 3 might be spoken by a chef or a pet owner. Sentence 4 either says the hunters were shot or they made a lot of noise. Sentence 5 either says those apples are to be cooked with, or those people are cooking apples. In each case one may respond in two very different ways to identical stimuli, depending on how one analyzes the sentences grammatically. Different analyses produce different meanings. Chomsky argues that when one hears a sentence one analyzes it using grammatical rules, and that this is an act of *mind*. To study and describe only behavior is inadequate for a scientific understanding of language. Just as theory in physics refers to unobservable entities such as the quark and abstract properties such as a quark's "charm" or "color," so theory in psychology should refer to unobservable mental structures to explain observable behavior.

Chomsky's ideas were enormously influential on psycholinguistics, rapidly and completely eclipsing behaviorist approaches, whether mediational or Skinnerian. Many psychologists became convinced that their behaviorist views were wrong and committed themselves to a renewed study of language along Chomskian lines. Chomsky's technical system, described in *Syntactic Structures* (which appeared in 1957, the year of *Verbal Behavior*), provided a new paradigm around which to design research. Study after study was done, so that in only a few years Chomsky's ideas had generated much more empirical research than had Skinner's. Chomsky's impact is nicely described by George Miller. In the 1950s Miller had adhered to a behaviorist picture of language, but personal contact with Chomsky convinced him the old paradigm had to be abandoned. By 1962, he could write (Miller, 1967) "In the course of my work I seem to have become a very old-fashioned kind of psychologist. I now believe that mind is something more than a four letter, Anglo-Saxon word—human minds exist, and it is our job as psychologists to study them." The mind, exorcized by Watson in 1913, had returned to psychology, brought back by an outsider, Noam Chomsky.

### Cartesian Linguistics: Language Acquisition

Chomsky places himself with rationalism, something quite unusual for an American thinker. He considered his critique of *Verbal Behavior* to be an attack on the inadequacy of any empiricist account of language. Chomsky's rationalism is nowhere more evident than in his theory of language acquisition. Like Descartes, Chomsky views language as the human's unique possession, setting him off sharply from other animals. Like Plato, Descartes, and Leibniz, Chomsky argues that some knowledge—specifically for Chomsky knowledge of language—is at least in part innate.

Chomsky distinguishes linguistic competence from performance. Competence is a person's knowledge of the rules of language; performance is the person's actual use of those rules in speaking or hearing. Performance is only an indirect and often imperfect reflection of competence, as anyone knows who has read unedited transcripts of speech. People have limited memories; they are distractable; they change their minds; and so change their grammar in midstream. Those and other non-linguistic factors help determine language performance. However, each person possesses a sophisticated and unconscious knowledge of the rules of grammar, and this competence seems to be the same for all native speakers of a given language. Where does competence come from?

Chomsky argues that much of it is innate. Competence is not taught. An immigrant's child, for example, easily picks up English on the street, and studies of parent-child interaction show parents to be more interested in the truth of what their 3- or 4-year-old says than in its grammatical form. Since performance only indirectly reflects competence, and since grammatical rules are unobservable, children might be expected to have a hard time figuring out what the rules are—that is, acquiring their competence—which they have largely done by age five. Chomsky believes that this achievement is possible only if each child is born with a general knowledge of what human language is like and of what is relevant and what not. This point is reinforced by the existence of linguistic universals, features of language found in all known languages. Chomsky says they exist because they reflect innate linguistic structures. Chomsky is not arguing that the Chinese child innately knows Chinese, or that the French child innately knows French, but that each human child comes equipped with biologically given structures which make it possible for the child to learn any human language simply by being exposed to it.

We have already met a similar situation in Marler's ethological studies of birdsong learning. Baby birds are equipped with brain structures that enable them to learn their species calls. These structures tell the chick what is birdsong and what isn't, and which birdsongs to learn (its own species'). Marler himself has suggested a similarity between birdsong acquisition and language acquisition. Both sets of communication abilities are functionally important for the organism's survival, for without language one cannot be a part of human society. Therefore, natural selection will have favored the development of biological processes which support language or birdsong acquisition.

As with adult language, Cartesian linguistics has generated enormous amounts of research. Under the behaviorist paradigm studies of language learning had largely been word counts, focusing on what seemed to be the elementary response units strung together by S-R chaining. After Chomsky's proposal, studies of language acquisition became much more numerous, with independent investigators examining child syntax, often reporting almost identical data and writing identical grammars. Unsuspected regularities in child behavior were found only because Chomsky's grammatical system made them significant; they had gone unnoticed by behaviorist researchers. Studies of language acquisition in different cultures were undertaken for the first time, discovering that the early stages of language learning are the same everywhere. All these findings support Chomsky's nativist proposal.

There was also another kind of research performed in an interesting echo of the empiricist response to Descartes' nativism. Investigators now proposed to carry out La Mettrie's old idea of teaching language to an ape. Several such programs began in the 1960s, the most successful being the attempt to teach sign language to chimpanzees. Whether or not any of the linguistic monkeys possess something equivalent to human language is still controversial, although it is clear that they can communicate with their keepers. But as with La Mettrie, the goal has been to show that human language is not as unique as Descartes or Chomsky believed, and that it can be learned like any other non-native behavior.

Unfortunately, La Mettrie's logic is faulty. The fact that a bird fancier can learn birdcalls does not demonstrate that birds do not have innate mechanisms that underlie their own language learning. Similarly, the fact that a chimpanzee can be taught language abilities after prolonged and intensive instruction does not show that the human child in a natural setting learns language without applying innate mechanisms. As with animal learning, what happens in the wild may be quite different from what happens in an artificial laboratory setting.

### Awareness and Human Learning

Behaviorism held that human awareness is generally irrelevant to human behavior, and that therefore control of behavior resides in the environment, not in the individual. This assumption helps justify the application of animal methods to human beings, for it means that introspection cannot find the causes of behavior, which are not mental, so that animals may substitute for humans. However the irrelevance of human awareness to determining human behavior was an assumption directly attacked in the late 1950s and early 1960s.

As early as Thorndike, learning theorists assumed that learning could take place without a person being aware that her or his behavior was being changed. This assumption was important to maintaining the assumption of phylogenetic continuity. Animals learn apparently without awareness of the contingencies of reinforcement, and since people were thought to learn the same way, awareness was considered unnecessary for human learning. Verbalization of the correct contingencies of reinforcement, when it occurred, was held to be a simple byproduct of learning, not its cause. The behaviorist position was forcefully stated by Leo Postman and Julius Sassenrath in 1961: "It is an outmoded and an unnecessary assumption that the modification of behavior must be preceded by a correct understanding of the environmental contingencies."

Some experiments seemed to support the view. The classic experiment was by Joel Greenspoon, reported in 1955. Greenspoon was interested in nondirective psychotherapy, in which the therapist merely says "um-hum" periodically during a session. From the behaviorist perspective, this situation could be analyzed as a learning situation. The patient emits behaviors, some of which are reinforced by "um-hum." Therefore the patient should come to talk about those things that are reinforced, and not others. Greenspoon took this hypothesis to the laboratory. Subjects were brought to an experimental room and induced to say words. Whenever the subject said a plural noun, the experimenter said "um-hum." After a while extinction was begun; the experimenter said nothing. At the end of the session the subject was asked to explain what had been going on. Only 10 of 75 subjects could do so, and interestingly Greenspoon excluded their data from analysis. His results showed that production of plural nouns increased during training and then decreased during extinction—exactly as operant theory predicts— and in the apparent absence of awareness of the connection between plural nouns and reinforcement. Experiments similar to Greenspoon's found similar results.

In the 1960s, however, various researchers disenchanted with behaviorism, and often under Chomsky's influence, challenged the validity of the "Greenspoon effect," or learning without awareness. They argued that Greenspoon's method was inadequate. The questions probing awareness were vague, and they were asked only after extinction, by which time subjects who had been aware of the response-reinforcement contingency could have concluded they had been wrong. Replication of the Greenspoon procedure showed that many subjects held technically incorrect hypotheses that nevertheless led to correct responses. For example, a subject might say "apples" and "pears" and be reinforced, concluding that fruit names were being reinforced. The subject would continue to say fruit names and be rewarded, yet when the subject told the hypothesis to the experimenter, the subject would be called "unaware."

Even behaviorists started turning up anomalies. A paper in the 1961 *Journal of Experimental Analysis of Behavior* found that student experimenters told that "um-hum" would increase the reinforced behavior reported such results, while those told the "um-hum" would lower the reinforced operant reported exactly that! Further, interviews showed that most student experimenters had made up their data. Finally, graduate students, rigorously trained to follow Greenspoon's procedure, completely failed to modify their subject's behavior.

Those who doubted the automatic action of reinforcers carried out extensive experiments to show the necessity of awareness to human learning. One extensive research program was conducted by Don E. Dulany, who constructed a sophisticated axiomatic theory about types of awareness and their effects on behavior. His experiments seemed to show that only subjects aware of the contingencies of reinforcement could learn, and that subject's confidence in their hypotheses was systematically related to their overt behavior.

By 1966 the area of verbal behavior was in a state of crisis which called for another symposium. The organizers of the meeting had optimistically hoped that they could gather psychologists from different backgrounds together to work out a unified S-R theory of verbal behavior. They called together mediationists such as Howard Kendler, workers in the Ebbinghaus verbal learning tradition, colleagues of Noam Chomsky's, and rebellious thinkers such as Dulany. Instead of unanimity the symposium discovered dissent and disenchantment, ranging from mild displeasure with the current state of verbal learning to a formal proof of the inadequacy of the S-R paradigm's theories of language. In closing the book, the editors cited Kuhn, identifying behaviorism as a paradigm in crisis (Dixon & Horton, 1968). The last sentence in the book is: "To us, it appears that a revolution is certainly in the making."

Another Kuhnian point was made by a later writer, William Brewer. As with the anomalies in animal learning, it turns out that evidence against the automatic action of reinforcers existed from early days of the behaviorist paradigm. In an extensive review of the literature going back to 1919, Brewer found that the vast majority of findings indicated that awareness of the contingencies of reinforcement was necessary for human learning. This conclusion holds over a wide range of human behavior from the verbal response studies by Greenspoon and Dulany down to apparently involuntary responses such as the galvanic skin response. As we saw with animal learning, anomalies turned up but were ignored until there was some reason to notice them. Brewer concluded his paper, "There is no convincing evidence for operant or classical conditioning in adult humans" by writing: "S-R psychology has been subjected to powerful attacks from outside of psychology by Chomsky. It now appears that one need not use the abstract phenomenon of language to pull the house down. The conditioning curves of learning were the foundation upon which S-R psychology was built. Now it seems obvious that that foundation was one of sand."

## THREE PARADIGMS FOR COGNITIVE PSYCHOLOGY

By the late 1960s behaviorism was in disarray, attacked on all sides by unfriendly critics and anomalous findings. As the editors of the 1966 conference on verbal behavior sensed, revolution was in the air. But a scientific revolution requires an alternative paradigm around which scientists can reorganize their efforts. The alternatives of psychoanalysis, humanism, and the common-sense psychology of social psychology are inappropriate for experimental psychology. Research in language seemed to call for a renewed study of the mind, as George Miller said in 1962. So the 1960s saw the emergence of cognitive psychology, an experimental psychology willing—unlike behaviorism—to propose unobservable mental entities in order to explain behavior. These new entities, furthermore, did not have to be mediational r-s connections, but could be different processes and structures altogether. Three main alternative cognitive psychologies emerged, although none today has unquestioned paradigmatic status.

### The New Structuralism

The first form of cognitive psychology to emerge was structuralism. This was not a continuation of Titchener's system, with which it shares nothing but the name, but was an independent movement of continental European origin. Structuralism hopes to be a unifying paradigm for all the social sciences, and its adherents range from philosophers to anthropologists. Structuralists believe that any human behavior pattern, whether individual or social, is to be explained by reference to abstract structures, frequently believed to be logical or mathematical in nature. In the realm of social behavior the leading exponent of structuralism is Claude Levi-Strauss, who seeks to explain everything from a culture's myths to its cooking practices by describing a small set of logical structures that underlie these myths and cooking practices.

In psychology, the leading structuralist is Jean Piaget. Piaget was originally trained as a biologist, but his interests shifted to epistemology, to which field he applies his scientific method. He criticizes philosophers for remaining content with armchair speculations about the growth of knowledge when the questions of epistemology can be empirically investigated. Genetic epistemology is his attempt to chart the development of knowledge in children. Piaget divides the growth of intellect into four stages, in each of which occurs a distinct kind of intelligence. Piaget believes intelligence does not grow quantitatively, but undergoes widespread qualitative metamorphosis, so that the 5-year-old not only knows less than the 12-year-old, but also thinks in a different way. Piaget traces these different kinds of intelligence, or ways of knowing the world, to changes in the logical structure of the child's mind. Piaget attempts to describe the thinking of each stage by constructing highly abstract and formal logical models of the mental structures he believes guide intelligent behavior.

Some other psychologists are at least partially structuralists. It is sometimes held that Freud was a structuralist because he attempted to describe the structure of personality, but he lived long before the movement became self-conscious. Noam Chomsky may be regarded as a structuralist for trying to explain language in terms of its formal grammatical structure. In this, Chomsky follows the lead of the French linguist Ferdinand de Saussurre (1857-1913), who many think provided the inspiration for structuralism as a movement.

Structuralism has had enormous influence in continental European philosophy, literary criticism, and social science, including psychology. The leading exponents of structuralism, Levi-Strauss, Michel Foucault, and Piaget are French (or French-speaking), and are carrying on the Platonic-Cartesian rationalist attempt to describe the transcendent human mind. Piaget, for example, limits his interest to "the epistemic subject," the person as abstract knower. He disclaims all interest in the "completely American" topic of individual differences. Also, like Wundt, he cares little for application. He speaks humourously of "The American Question," a question never asked of him in Europe, namely, how can the stages of intellectual development be accelerated by training? Piaget feels it is best not to try, preferring to let natural development take its course.

As one might expect, given the European-rationalist background of structuralism, its impact on American psychology has been limited. Americans have paid great attention to Piaget since 1960, and his theory has generated a good deal of research. However, few American psychologists have adopted his structuralism. His logical models are generally viewed as too abstruse and far removed from behavior to be of any value. Americans are impressed by his findings, but frequently explain them in other terms. Additionally, Americans are interested in individual differences and the effects of experience or training on cognitive development and do not care greatly about Piaget's idealized "epistemic subject." As happened with Wundt, Americans have taken what they value from a rationalist psychology, but have remained securely empiricists.

Chomsky's transformational grammar has suffered a similar fate. After an initial flurry of interest, psychologists came to feel that Chomsky's formal grammar, like Piaget's logical models, had little psychological reality, but merely gave overly complex formal descriptions of behavior. His nativist theory of language acquisition also gained initial acceptance, to be followed only by retreat to more empiricist accounts. After 1965 psycholinguists were prepared to declare themselves separate from, and perhaps superior to, formal linguistics.

In moving away from Chomsky and Piaget, cognitively inclined psychologists came increasingly to adhere to the system spawned by the computer, information processing psychology.

### Man the Machine: Information Processing

The essential idea of the information processing brand of cognitive psychology was stated by E. C. Tolman in 1948 in his "Cognitive maps in rats and men": "Incoming impulses are usually worked over and elaborated in a central control room into a tentative, cognitive-like map of the environment." That is, stimuli do not directly control responses, but are instead processed inside the organism into an organized structure that in turn governs behavior. Tolman's purposive behaviorism, however, was rejected by other behaviorists, particularly Skinner, because Tolman's description seemed to require an implicit little person in the organism's head to read and understand the map before behavior could begin. Tolman's theory fails to explain the behavior of that inner person, unless it, too, has a map-room and map-reader, who must in turn have a map-room and reader and so on forever. Tolman's theory seemed to smuggle in the old Cartesian thinking soul as an inner map-reader and decision-maker whose unexplained purposes control behavior. Skinner preferred to directly connect environment and behavior, eliminating the need for the inner person and map-room.

In short, Tolman's view was too mysterious and unmechanistic to win acceptance. However, developments already taking place outside psychology provided a mechanical explanation of purpose and cognition that required no unseen inner person. The context for this work was the same as for Skinner's pigeon-guided missile, the need in World War II to improve the accuracy of weaponry. The problem of the guided missile is prototypical: how can a missile be designed to track a moving target and hit it? Skinner's answer was his pigeons trained to peck at displays of the targets and control the missile, but other investigators sought a less biological answer. They built electronic devices to detect targets, track them, and guide missiles home without the intervention of an inner person (who would be killed) or even an inner pigeon. The result would be a purposive machine.

In 1943 three researchers (Rosenblueth, Wiener, & Bigelow, 1966) in this area described a mechanical approach to teleology, a subject which had always struck biologists and psychologists as unscientific. They pointed out that a guided missile has a purpose, to strike its target, and this purpose mechanically controls behavior. A more homely (and peaceable) example is a thermostat. You set your thermostat at 70°F. This defines the purpose of the thermostat, to maintain the house temperature at 70° or so. If the temperature falls, a thermometer in the thermostat detects the change, and starts the furnace. As the temperature rises, the thermometer senses when it reaches 70°, and stops the furnace. In this way the thermostat regulates the behavior of the furnace. No mysterious inner agent is needed, only the idea of *informational feedback*. The thermostat is in touch with the environment through the information provided by its thermometer, which tells the thermostat about the effect of the furnace's behavior on room temperature. The system's own behavior feeds information back to the thermostat, which thereby changes its behavior, which alters the feedback and so on. In its simple way a thermostat, or a guided missile, is an intelligent, purposive machine. Digital computers, also developed during World War II, can provide even more sophisticated purposive and intelligent behaviors.

Around the computer, then, grew up a sophisticated field called *cybernetics,* the study of such feedback control systems. We have already touched on some aspects of this field in discussing artificial intelligence and computer simulation in the last chapter. Around 1958, and growing rapidly thereafter, Tolman's purposive cognitive psychology, supported by the mechanical account of purposive thinking provided by cybernetics, became a reality. Psychologists began to draw a general parallel between computers and human beings. The computer receives input—information from the environment—it processes and stores that information, and then uses it to produce planful, goal-directed output. Human beings may also be looked at in this way. They receive information through the senses; it is processed and stored by the brain, which uses it to execute planful, goal-directed behavior. The computer is a well-understood, deterministic "organism" that is nevertheless to some degree intelligent. It was an attractive idea to apply human understanding of computer intelligence to human intelligence. La Mettrie's *L'Homme Machine* was realized by calling mind a computer.

In the last chapter we have already mentioned the first fruits of the new information processing psychology: artificial intelligence and the computer simulation of human problem solving. The same year the General Problem Solver was presented to psychologists, 1958, saw the appearance of a similar effort in England, though without the simulation. In his *Perception and Communication* Donald Broadbent exploited information processing language as an alternative language for discussing the behaviorist topic of learning and the mentalist topic of attention. Broadbent showed that the cybernetic view provided a tough-minded, scientific approach to psychology that was more flexible than S-R language and more specific and rigorous than introspective mentalism.

The most influential of the early statements of the information processing viewpoint, and the first classic in the new cognitive psychology, was *Plans and the Structure of Behavior* by George Miller, Eugene Galanter, and Karl Pribram, appearing in 1960. The senior author, Miller, was one of those converted away from behaviorism by Noam Chomsky, and we have already met him as psychology's most earnest spokesman for Chomsky's psycholinguistics. In their book, Miller and his colleagues try to show, in a general nontechnical way, that the cybernetic information feedback model may be applied to human behavior. For example, they analyze the simple behavior of hammering a nail in feedback terms. You begin with a current state of affairs—the nail resting in the wood, but not driven home—and a goal—to make the nail flush to the wood's surface. By visual inspection you see that the nail is still up, and so strike it with the hammer. Again, you look at the nail; if it is still up, you strike again; if it has become flush, you stop. As with the thermostat, this is purposive behavior explained in mechanical terms; it is human behavior rendered deterministic and mechanical, void of the Cartesian soul, and therefore acceptable to the tough-minded behaviorist.

Computers solve problems purposely, and the programs that let them do this we conveniently think of as equivalent to the human mind, in a kind of dual aspect answer to the mind-body problem. A computer's program and its wiring are not identical, for we may have alternate programs for the same computer. Mere inspection of the blueprints of a particular IBM model cannot tell us whether the machine is used to process a university's grades, guide robots on Mars, or simulate the world economy; only inspection of the program can do that. Similarly, the same program may be given to different physical machines yet behave the same in each. Therefore, as Aristotle argued centuries ago, a computer program, or mind, may be separately discussed from its physical embodiment, just as a form and its material embodiment may be conceptually separated. Information processing psychology is the analysis of the human program.

Although the information processing approach began with an analysis of purpose and problem solving, it has been most widely applied to the traditional behaviorist problem of learning. Computers store information, and so they learn. Thus the idea of computer memory may be applied to human memory, or learning. The study of human learning began with Ebbinghaus' and Müller's separate studies of memory, and the verbal-learning tradition has maintained itself in one form or another since their beginnings. During the dominance of behaviorism it was looked on as serial or paired associate learning in which a subject builds up bonds between stimulus word and response word. It was a favorite topic of informal mediational behaviorists who explored the effects of different kinds of covert mediational links between stimulus and response words. With the advent of the information processing approach the mediational framework could be reformed and expanded. It was now possible to abandon discussion of covert r-s chains in favor of reference to "memory nodes," places in a computer memory bank that stored word-concepts, and the associative links between those nodes.

One classic theory illustrates the new view (Collins & Quillian, 1969). It is possible to think of our knowledge of word meanings as a structured set of concepts, as in Mill's tinker-toy theory of the mind. So, for example, one fragment of our knowledge might look like Figure 13-1.

Our knowledge of kinds of animals is a set of hierarchically organized concepts. We know a canary is a type of bird, which is a type of animal, for example. Further, we know certain facts about each concept. All canaries sing. All birds have feathers. All animals eat. Finally, let us assume that the process of understanding a concept is a matter of knowing its associated concepts and items of information. So, someone who knows the meaning of "canary" knows it is a yellow songbird. If this is true, then an experiment is possible. The fact of a canary singing is directly associated with the concept, while the facts of having feathers or eating are only indirectly, and increasingly remotely associated with the concept "canary." Similarly, the concept "bird" is directly linked to "canary" while "animal" is indirectly linked, via "bird." Therefore, it should take a person longer to respond "Yes" to "Is a canary an animal?" than to "Is a canary a bird?," and longer still to respond to "Does a canary eat?" This experiment has been done, and these predictions (though not some others) confirmed.

Many models of memory along similar lines have been proposed, and the study of human memory has moved from nonsense syllables learned in S-R fashion to studies of memory for words, sentences, and prose. Out of the studies of memory, attention and problem solving has arisen a new cognitive psychology, complex, sophisticated and highly technical, all organized around the idea of people as information processing devices similar to computers. However, not all cognitive psychologists are structuralists or information processors. Some are traditional mentalists.

### Mentalism

As the dominance of behaviorism weakened and alternatives such as structuralism and information processing psychology were being explored, a small group of cognitive psychologists influenced by pre-behaviorist mentalism has arisen.

**FIGURE 13-1.**
The structure of semantic memory according to Collins and Quillian
(Adapted from A. M. Collins and M. R. Quillian, Retrieval time
from semantic memory, *Journal of Verbal Learning and Verbal Behavior,*
1969, *8*, 240-247).

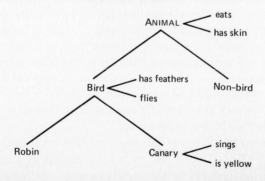

Psychologists of this extremely loose camp have resurrected some very old theory and research, as two examples will show.

The Würzburg psychologists did experiments on the memorization of proverbs which showed that people frequently remember not what a proverb says, but what it means. In recent research, William F. Brewer has replicated the Würzburg finding with ordinary sentences. For example, when read "The bullet struck the bull's-eye" most people later recall "The bullet hit the bull's-eye." More strikingly, "The absent-minded professor didn't have his car keys" is often "recalled" as "The absent-minded professor forgot his car keys." Brewer argues that subjects store in memory not a string of word-concepts but the global idea described by a sentence. When the idea is recalled, the idea may be expressed differently, as in the first sentence. Sometimes the stored idea is not exactly what was said, as the second sentence shows. Brewer's ideas are partially based on Wundt's similar analysis of language, in which complex ideas, *Gesamtvorstellungen,* are spoken and reconstructed, sometimes incorrectly, by the hearer. Practical implications of the theory have also been explored. Jurors, for example, may recall not what a witness actually said but rather recall their own reconstructions of what the witness meant and so distort the findings of a court.

Another example of new mentalism is the work of John C. Bransford and his colleagues. They have constructed paragraphs describing such processes as washing clothes in terms so vague that the hearer cannot tell what the passage is about unless told. The passages are not gibberish; each sentence is grammatical and each word meaningful, but the whole paragraph is ambiguous. Bransford has found that subjects who hear the passage without knowing the topic remember almost nothing, while those who are told the topic show good recall. To explain these results, Bransford calls on Bartlett's old idea of the *schema,* a central idea around which memory is organized. Bransford believes his findings challenge the more associative information processing view of memory as structured concept-modes. According to the information processing account, a person who does not know the topic should be able to store each concept word and its associated material and so remember the passage. The results, however, show that this is not the case. Bransford argues that cognitive psychologists should include nonassociative factors such as the schema in their studies of memory.

Like the Gestalt psychologists, proponents of mentalism find themselves with some interesting demonstrations and provocative ideas, but with no acceptable paradigm to give them structure. The mentalists are a small and eclectic group, swamped, to their dissatisfaction, by the larger information processing school.

## CONCLUSION: WAS THERE A REVOLUTION?

As when behaviorism replaced functionalism, we now appear to be confronted with a scientific revolution. A new paradigm, in this case cognitive psychology, is replacing a worn-out one, behaviorism. Many cognitive psychologists themselves believe that there has been a revolution, and rhetoric borrowed from Kuhn has been widely used. It is possible to find frequent references to "revolution," "paradigm clash," and "paradigm shift" by cognitive psychologists. One long article has asked "Is a scientific revolution taking place in psychology?", answering itself "Yes" (Palermo, 1971). However, as with behaviorism, we must look closely at the evidence and ask the correct questions.

*Did behaviorism constitute normal science?* There can be no doubt that behaviorism was the major force in academic psychology for many years, especially 1930-1955, but whether it practiced true normal science is more open to debate. According to Kuhn, debate over fundamental issues by rivals of different schools should not occur in normal science. Instead, puzzle-solving, directed at well-defined empirical problems, is the work of normal science. If we examine the *Psychological Review*, American psychology's most prestigious theoretical journal, from 1930 to 1958, we find the former description more accurate. We may note a few relevant articles. In 1932, H. M. Johnson calls psychology "thoroughly muddled." In 1936, E. J. Varon commends Alfred Binet for rejecting associationism. In 1940, A. G. Balz wrote a paper trying to define psychology's subject matter. In 1945 E. Heidbreder wrote "Toward a dynamic theory of cognition." In 1950 B. F. Skinner asked "Are theories of learning necessary?" In 1954 J. R. Maze asked "Do intervening variables intervene?" Finally, in 1958 Newell, Shaw and Simon published their "Elements of a theory of problem solving," describing the General Problem Solver.

All these titles testify to a lack of unanimity among psychologists on important issues such as the definition of psychology, the nature of explanation, the value of theory, as well as continuing debate over important theoretic concepts such as association and cognition. Kuhn argues that such debates are characteristic of pre-paradigm science or crisis science. Hence, either psychology was still pre-paradigmatic during the supposed reign of behaviorism, or it was in a continuing state of crisis. It is clear that there was no normal science. Instead, schools of psychology both inside and outside behaviorism—schools clearly perceived by psychologists themselves—struggled at least as much with each other to control the field, as with nature to understand human behavior. The debates between Tolman, Hull, and Skinner, not to mention between Skinner and Rogers admirably illustrate this.

The teaching of psychology in these years supports the view of psychology as being still pre-paradigm. Very few texts present a single theoretical picture of psychology, in contrast to texts in physics and chemistry, which speak with one voice. Furthermore, psychology students read a great deal of original literature by "classic" psychologists beginning almost with their first course. According to Kuhn advanced science has no "classics," and students do not read anything but texts until they begin their thesis research as graduate students.

*Were there anomalies?* It now becomes necessary to separate animal and human psychology, for by the 1950s investigators in each field were fairly separate. In the field of animal learning the early 1960s did see the appearance of a number of empirically discovered phenomena which were at odds with the expectations of learning psychologists (such as the findings of Breland and Breland). They fit the definition of anomaly given by Kuhn. These findings were discovered by behaviorists themselves in the course of their ordinary research; they were at first disbelieved to the extent of being unpublishable in the best journals, but eventually they sparked similar research which brought about a crisis as various psychologists failed to explain them in conventional terms. As a result of the crisis workers in animal learning moved away from traditional S-R explanations to more cognitive ones, often incorporating ideas from human information processing psychology. The recent history of animal psychology, therefore, seems to fit Kuhn's model of revolution, although the shape of the new paradigm is unclear. Even in animal psychology, however, the revolution is not unanimous. For there is a continuing line of radical behaviorism in animal psychology, rather isolated from the rest of psychology but lively and growing nonetheless. There have been at least two schools of animal psychology over the last decade—the Skinnerian and the neocognitive—agreeing on too little to constitute a single paradigm.

In human psychology the existence of Kuhnian anomalies is highly questionable. Some discrepant findings, such as Festinger's cognitive dissonance, were largely ignored as irrelevant social, and therefore nonexperimental, nonscientific, psychology. Others, such as reversal shift versus extradimensional shift learning were successfully incorporated into liberalized S-R theory. One general topic, language, seemed to pose a special problem, but even so behaviorists investigated language confident that behaviorism could explain it, elusive though such an explanation might be. We should also note that there were no empirical phenomena associated with language that constituted anomalous findings. Formal research on language was usually consistent with behaviorist principles, as in Greenspoon's verbal conditioning study. It was not until Chomsky established a different point of view that empirical anomalies for behaviorism began to be recognized. But in such a case the anomalous research was created by the revolutionary paradigm; it did not lead to revolution.

*Was there a crisis?* Just as with the behaviorist "revolution," we must recognize that there was a crisis around 1960, but that it was not caused by anomalous data. Instead, the crisis was created by the forceful statement of a rationalist psychology by an outsider, Noam Chomsky. Like Watson, Chomsky preached a fiery doctrine, denouncing rivals as unscientific failures, pointing out their failings with vigor, and proposing a bold new scheme for understanding human behavior. Either personally or through his writing Chomsky convinced many psychologists that what they had been doing was wrong, and the resulting feeling of crisis and desire for change spread through much of human experimental psychology. Consequently, alternatives to behaviorism were sought in Chomsky's linguistics, in Piaget's cognitive development, in the intelligent computer, and sometimes as far afield as humanistic psychology.

This was a crisis, but it was created by an outside attack. Furthermore, the attack found a psychology already divided over basic pre-paradigm issues, ready to respond to a new stimulus. Finally, psychologists responded not by creating new purely psychological theories but by borrowing outside ideas, even those of the attacker himself.

*Did a new paradigm emerge?* We have already discussed how in the 1960s psychology apparently rediscovered the human mind in forming cognitive psychology. We must ask now if the new cognitive approaches are sufficiently different from behaviorism to constitute radical and revolutionary alternatives to it.

Chomskian structuralism is almost certainly such a radical alternative. Chomsky himself traces its roots to Cartesian rationalism, and he opposes himself to empiricist linguistics. Chomsky is very much interested in an abstract human mind divorced from environmental control. He pays no attention to individual or group differences in language. He refuses to speculate on how language evolved, even though he is a nativist, and therefore does not consider the adaptive value of language. He is thus not in the tradition of the psychology of adaptation out of which behaviorism grew. However, Chomsky's very radicalism has caused many who acknowledge the justice of his criticisms of behavior to shun his positive alternative. He has stirred many psychologists from their dogmatic slumbers, but upon arising they have followed another banner than his.

Piagetian structuralism is a less radical alternative. Piaget has always asked what intelligence and knowledge are good for, seeing them as organs of adaptation to the environment. Therefore Piaget's theory may be viewed as a psychology of adaptation. His structuralist description of the mind is less congenial to American functionalism or behaviorism, however. Piaget's influence has thus been mixed, as has Chomsky's. American students of development have marveled at the new phenomena he uncovered, and the new tasks he invented, but they have been less willing to adopt his theory in any but general terms.

The mentalists are a small and diverse group with no general alternative paradigm to offer; they therefore often have no secure rallying point for dissaffected behaviorists. They have acted more as gadflies to associationism than as systematic theorists.

The remaining cognitive psychology, information processing, was by 1970 clearly the most popular among American and British experimental psychologists, and it is, not unexpectedly, the least different from behaviorism. If we refer back to the opening paragraph of Watson's proclamation of behaviorism we will find little with which the information processing psychologist would disagree. For both, psychology is an objective branch of natural science, taking as its subject matter human behavior. Like Watson, the information processing psychologist places no special value on introspective report, relying instead on careful descriptions of human behavior. Furthermore, both seek to predict and control behavior instead of seeking to explain human consciousness. With the application of information processing language to animal behavior, no sharp dividing line between man and animal is recognized.

Statements by information processing psychologists confirm their continuity with behaviorism. Herbert Simon (1969) wrote: *"A man, viewed as a behaving system, is quite simple. The apparent complexity of his behavior over time is largely a reflection of the complexity of the environment in which he finds himself."* Simon, like Skinner, views human beings as largely the products of the environment that shapes them, since they themselves are simple. In the same work, Simon follows Watson in dismissing the validity of mental images, reducing them to lists of facts and sensory properties associatively organized. Simon also argues that complex behaviors are assemblages of simpler behaviors. Information processing psychologists thus share an important portion of the behaviorist paradigm: the assumptions of atomism, associationism, and empiricism. On the philosophical side it espouses materialism, holding that there is no independent Cartesian soul, and positivism, continuing to insist on operationalizing all theoretical terms (Simon, 1969). Proponents of this position are made uncomfortable by Chomsky's nativism and his abstract analysis of language. They believe his linguistics confuses formal logical description of grammar with the concrete psychological processes which in fact produce grammatical speech.

What information processing psychologists reject of behaviorism is peripheralism. They believe that complex processes intervene between stimulus (input) and response (output). Unlike Watson or Skinner, information processing cognitive psychologists are willing to infer central mental processes from observable behavior. However, although peripheralism was part of Watson's, Hull's, and Skinner's behaviorisms, it was not shared by Tolman or informal behaviorism. We have already seen that Tolman gave early expression to the information processing viewpoint, and that informal behaviorism willingly abandoned Hull's peripheralism in order to incorporate complex forms of human behavior. The information processing adherents do not believe central processes are covert versions of S-R associations, but their theory is not far removed from Tolman's, except in complexity and sophistication.

If Tolman was correct in calling himself a behaviorist, and he was one of behaviorism's earliest proselytizers, then information processing psychology is also a form of behaviorism. It represents a continuing conceptual evolution in the psychology of adaptation, for it views cognitive processes as adaptive behaviorial functions, and is in a sense a reassertion of earlier American functionalism. The functionalists saw the mind as adaptive, but were trapped by the limited metaphysics of the nineteenth century into espousing at the same time a strict mind-body parallelism, engendering a conflict exploited by Watson in establishing behaviorism. The cybernetic analysis of purpose, and its mechanical realization in the computer, however, vindicated the functionalist attitude by showing that purpose and cognition were not necessarily mysterious, and need not involve dualism.

Watson's and Skinner's behaviorisms were extreme statements of the psychology of adaptation that attempted to circumnavigate the inaccessible—and therefore potentially mythical—reaches of the human mind. The information processing view follows the steps of William James and E. C. Tolman in seeing, beneath behavior, cognitive processes to be investigated and explained. Behaviorism was one response by the psychology of adaptation to crisis; information processing is another, but in both we see a deeper continuity under the superficial changes. Perhaps to those involved, the revolt against S-R psychology is a scientific revolution, but viewed against the broader framework of history, the revolt is a period of rapid evolutionary change, not a revolutionary jump.

In this chapter we have pressed up against the present, and so cannot discuss historical trends except as informed predictions. We will reserve these for the last chapter, in which we inquire into psychology's future.

## SUGGESTED READINGS

The ferment of the years after 1959 is captured in no single work. A good anthology of conflicting views on human language is *Readings in the Psychology of Language*, edited by L. Jakobovits and M. Miron (Prentice-Hall, 1967). It includes statements by behaviorists of every type and reprints Chomsky's review of Skinner's *Verbal Behavior*. Hilgard and Bower's *Theories of Learning* (Prentice-Hall) includes chapters on Piaget and the information-processing framework in its fourth (1976) edition. The diligent reader will be rewarded by W. K. Estes' (ed.) *Handbook of Learning and Cognitive Processes* (Hillsdale, N.J.: Erlbaum, 1975), which surveys recent developments in all areas of human and animal psychology.

## REFERENCES

Bitterman, M. Toward a comparative psychology of learning. *American Psychologist,* 1960, *15*, 704-712.

Bitterman, M. The evolution of intelligence. *Scientific American,* 1965, *212*, 92-100.

Bolles, R. C. Learning motivation, and cognition. In W. K. Estes (Ed.) *Handbook of learning and the cognitive processes* (Vol. 1). Hillsdale, N.J.: Erlbaum, 1973.

Breland, K., and Breland, M. The misbehavior of organisms. Reprinted in M. Seligman and J. Hager (Eds.) *Biological boundaries of learning.* New York: Appleton-Century-Crofts, 1972.

Brewer, W. There is no convincing evidence for operant or classical conditioning in normal, adult human beings. In W. Weimer & D. Palermo (Eds.) *Cognition and the symbolic processes.* Hillsdale, N.J.: Erlbaum, 1974.

Collins, A. & Quillian, M. Retreival time from semantic memory. *Journal of Verbal Learning and Verbal Behavior,* 1969, *8*, 240-247.

Dixon, T. R. & Horton, D. C. (Eds.) *Verbal behavior and general behavior theory.* Englewood Cliffs, N.J.: Prentice-Hall, 1968.

Miller, G. Some psychological studies of grammar (1962). Reprinted in L. Jakobovits and M. S. Miron (Eds.) *Readings in the psychology of language.* Englewood Cliffs, N.J.: Prentice-Hall, 1967.

Postman, L. & Sassenrath, J. The automatic action of verbal rewards and punishments. *Journal of General Psychology,* 1961, *65*, 109-136.

Rosenblueth, A., Wiener, N., & Bigelow, J. Behavior, purpose, and teleology (1943). Reprinted in J. V. Canfield (Ed.) *Purpose in nature.* Englewood Cliffs, N.J.: Prentice-Hall, 1966.

Simon, H. *The science of the artificial.* Cambridge: M.I.T. Press, 1969.

Skinner, B. F. Principles of purposive behaviorism. In S. Koch (Ed.) *Psychology: A study of a science* (Vol. 2). New York: McGraw-Hill, 1959.

Tolman, E. C. Cognitive maps in rats and men. *Psychological Review,* 1948, *55,* 189-208.

# Retrospect and Prospect

Having reached contemporary times, we should stop and reflect on psychology's past, present, and future. Has psychology made progress? What is its current situation? What are its prospects? No definitive, final answers can be given to these questions, but they deserve to be asked. The two chapters that follow are intended to be provocative. I offer my own assessment of psychology's past accomplishments and future prospects, but you are free to disagree. History is made by the clash of opinions and personalities, and no one's word is dogma.

# 14

# Retrospect
## Psychology – Science of Crisis

We have now completed our 2,500-year journey from the first philosophical speculations about mind to the sophisticated experiments and theory of contemporary psychology. How should we sum it up? As an attempt to understand humans, psychology was invented by the Greek philosophers, although they were preceded by centuries of less organized speculation recorded in myth. Four fundamental attitudes toward philosophy and psychology emerged from the work of the Greek philosophers. One was rationalism, committed to eternal values and truths, having little faith in sense perception, enshrining logic, and searching for the transcendent human mind. The other was empiricism, committed to studying the behavior of particular individuals in particular cultures, doubting the power of logic and the existence of transcendent values, and basing its work on the evidence of our senses. Intertwined with rationalism and empiricism are the ideas of being and becoming. Around these broad attitudes clustered a set of specific theses, often at war with one another. Is the mind a unified whole or a set of sensations? Is experience, reason, or innate endowment our guide to wisdom? Is humanity eternally and everywhere the same or does it change with time and place? Are truths and moral values eternally fixed or forever becoming?

The attitudes of rationalism, empiricism, and their various permutations were pursued down through the centuries, producing a variety of psychological systems that combined different aspects of mind and behavior, each system stressing different aspects. At no time has there been a single psychology shared by all learned people. The history of philosophical psychology is a history of strife. Platonist versus Aristolelian, Eipcurean versus Stoic, Augustinian Christianity versus Aquinian Christianity, modern rationalist versus empiricist, hero versus trader.

During the Enlightenment the possibility of a scientific psychology began to be recognized, although it was not until the late nineteenth century that the possible became the actual. The first psychology of consciousness was born in rationalist, romantic Germany and sought to know the eternal laws of the normal, human adult mind through a mixture of laboratory experiments and comparative historical study. At least in partial reaction to rationalism, a psychology of the unconscious arose, which used the concrete, clinical investigation of the abnormal to understand the full range of human motivation and thinking. In the empiricist, English-speaking world, supported by continental skepticism and materialism, the psychology of adaptation was born, a psychology focusing on the adaptive behavior of the unique individual. Ultimately, this psychology came to doubt the existence of mind, whether conscious or unconscious. Scientific psychology, then, has seen little more agreement than philosophical psychology.

Periodically, psychology has been wracked with crises in which the very possibility or value of a systematic study of mind has been doubted. These crises have been precipitated by forces outside psychology that seemed to challenge the value of reason in all forms. The end of the classical world drove philosophers to prescribe for human happiness rather than to investigate mind and world in new ways. Many people then sought refuge in mysticism and mystery religions. The crisis of late medieval and Renaissance Europe created philosophies in which God and eternal values were proclaimed unknowable, and the possibility of knowledge itself doubted. Again, many looked to numerous schismatic sects for the certainty lost by the Church.

Modern science and philosophy again produced a measure of confidence for a time. Then Hume's revolutionary skepticism, Enlightenment atheism, romanticism and revolution, again drove many to seek truth in feeling and the occult rather than in reason. Kant was roused from his dogmatic slumbers by Hume to reassert the value of reason. Wundt's psychology sought to bring the human mind within the purview of science, which after Newton had marched forward largely unaffected by philosophical and social crisis.

In the nineteenth century humanity again put on a self-confident face, apparently secure in Church, Country, and Newton. However, underneath the facade were cracks of doubt. The Newtonian world of science, so triumphantly successful, really did little to support Church and Country so in need of defense from atheists and revolutionaries. The growth of Socialism and Communism, the revolutions of 1848 and Darwin's theory brought the crisis into the open and smashed the facade. A wealth of philosophies and revolutionary movements arose, many stressing emotion and personal commitment over the rule of reason, and the rule of becoming triumphed. From this crisis came the psychology of the unconscious, asserting the fundamental irrationality of man, and the psychology of adaptation, which eventually eliminated the categories of reason and being altogether. Even Newtonian science failed to escape the crisis, being replaced first by Einstein's physics, in which observation is relative to the observer, and then by quantum physics, in which nothing can be known with certainty.

Looking more narrowly at scientific psychology, we see within it the same cycles of crisis. Around 1900 various psychologists began to question the possibility of a subjective science of unobservable mental entities. Watson seized the moment to propound a new certainty, the objective study of behavior. He was followed by other behaviorists who added the objective construction of theory. After World War II, however, the fruitfulness of the standard behaviorist approaches was questioned, and again, a crisis over aims and methods ensued. Alternatives abounded, whether as rediscovered old psychologies, or new movements within and without behaviorism. Attack from the outside, by a linguist, precipitated a more severe crisis, producing a shift to cognitive psychologies. We will find, however, that crisis continues.

Psychology seems, therefore, to be a science of perpetual crisis. It has never been able to get entirely past what Kuhn calls the pre-paradigm phase of science. Psychologists have never ceased to debate basic issues about the nature, goals, methods, and definitions of their field. Only within schools has there ever been much agreement on these problems, and even the schools usually contain warring factions.

Perhaps psychology can never be a science, in the same way English literature can never be a science. English literature defines a field of study in which one can pursue ideas in a rigorous fashion, in which truth is debated in rational, organized, institutional frameworks. Yet no one calls the study of English literature a science. Could the same be true of psychology?

Kuhn himself sees an essential difference between the social and natural sciences. In fact, it was hearing social scientists debate big issues such as the nature of humanity while natural scientists debated small technical details that led him to propose the concept of the paradigm, a possession of natural but not social scientists. Another philosopher of science, Stephen Toulmin also believes that science is not a "compact" discipline, since it is organized around fragmented schools and sub-fields that frequently do not even acknowledge one another's existence (Toulmin, 1972). At a more mundane level, too, psychology is not seen as a real science. The person in the street thinks of a psychologist as a bumbling clinician, knowing little of experimental psychology. Psychiatrists think of psychologists as second-rate psychiatrists, arguing that psychologists' clients should not receive help from insurance companies, and that ideally the clinical psychologist should be directed by a psychiatrist. In academic circles the scientific standing of psychologists is always in doubt among their natural science colleagues.

Some eminent psychologists have also concluded that psychology is not, and probably cannot be, a science. No one has done more to study the foundations of modern psychology than Sigmund Koch, whom we have met several times already. Koch has forcefully argued in recent years that the belief that psychology is a science, or can even hope to be an integral discipline is "an illusion." Koch (1974) bases his arguments on both history and philosophy of science. Historically, psychology has failed to become a science. It was invented out of awe for physics, in the hope that natural science methods could be applied to the ordinarily speculative study of humans. However, and as we have seen in this book, the subsequent history of psychology shows a series of approaches each radically different from the other, each defining psychology in a different way, with no sign of progress within or between approaches. Koch argues that the label "science" functions for psychologists as a kind of security blanket, desperately clutched as a talisman against doubt. Koch next argues that in principle psychology's domain is too large to be encompassed by any single methodological or theoretical system, for it includes everything from sensation to psychosis. The analytic pattern of science is too restrictive to be applied to the complexity of the human organism. Positively, Koch believes psychology can be tough-minded and empirical, but must acknowledge that it is closer to the humanities than the sciences in overall functioning. He calls for psychology to admit its variety of schools and sub-fields, rather than try to argue them away. "Psychology" should be replaced by the "psychological studies," a phrase open to pluralism and presupposing no specific method.

Koch's arguments are part of the continuing crisis of psychology we will examine in the next chapter. The lesson he draws from history is that humanity *necessarily* eludes the best efforts of scientists to predict and control it, and that a looser, more open approach is called for. It is certainly true that psychology has not changed in a way characteristic of scientific change, and that it is marked by less consensus than established sciences. Further, it is possible, even probable, that psychology in the broadest sense seen as the study of mind or behavior is too large to be an integral discipline. However, neither history nor size show that psychology's fields cannot be sciences, even if they are not sciences at present. Since scientific status is a future prospect, we will defer its consideration to the next chapter.

The last question to ask history is, has psychology progressed since Greek times? B.F. Skinner, for one, does not think so, and is distressed by students reading Plato and Aristotle as if they were moderns. Skinner's own experimental analysis of behavior would be incomprehensible to them, and to lay society, which Skinner feels establishes its progress over ancient wisdom and common sense.

In a purely technical sense psychology has progressed since 1879. Our knowledge of the physiological functioning of brain and body is more precise and general than ever. Simple forms of learning have been exhaustively researched, and if there are anomalies they have emerged against the background of otherwise well-established findings and principles. Many of the basic phenomena of human memory are clear, even though their significance is not. Aspects of children's thinking that would surprise any parent have been discovered by Piaget's research.

However, in a broader, conceptual sense progress is harder to demonstrate. The most modern psychology, information processing cognitive psychology, is remarkably similar to Aristotle's account of mind. Both view the acquisition of knowledge as the internalization and processing of information about the environment which is then stored in some form of memory. Where Aristotle distinguished between the personal, particular knowledge of the memory faculty and the knowledge of universals in the passive mind, the information processing psychologist distinguishes "episodic memory" for personal experiences from "semantic memory" for universal terms (Tulving, 1972). Chomsky traces his linguistics to Descartes, Piaget his genetic epistemology to Kant.

The stock of concepts laid down by the classical world have been, and are being, used over and over in new guises and new combinations by each psychological system. The concepts of atomism, associationism, empiricism, nativism, and the others we studied in Chapter 2, still serve to define the psychological paradigms of scientific psychology. It can be argued that the last conceptual advance was made by Darwin and the other evolutionists, calling attention to the adaptive aspects of mind that philosophers had usually overlooked. Out of evolution came the psychology of adaptation, less traditionally philosophical than the psychology of consciousness. Nevertheless, the concepts used by the psychology of adaptation were still continuous with traditional philosophy, as our analyses of functionalism and behaviorism have shown. In its technical reaches radical behaviorism may be incomprehensible to ancient philosophers, as Skinner claims, but the general image of humanity it upholds is not.

So if psychology is a science of perpetual crisis, it is also a science of continuity. Each psychological system is different, and if there has been no linear progress there has been at least a succession of points of view that illuminates humankind from different angles. Each perspective contributes something unique, and if each perspective is limited, and no advance on its predecessors, nevertheless, viewing them as a whole paints a larger and more complete portrait of human nature than any one alone can give. To help paint that picture was one aim of this book.

Having taken stock of psychology's past, we will now conclude by surveying its present and assessing its prospects for the future.

## SUGGESTED READING

Gordon Westland, *Current Crises of Psychology* (Heinemann, 1978).

## REFERENCES

Koch, S. Psychology as an integral discipline: The history of an illusion. And Conceptual sweep *vs.* knowledge: Thoughts towards a feasible future for psychology. Papers presented at the annual meeting of the American Psychological Association, New Orleans, Louisiana, August 30 and Sept. 2, 1974.

Toulmin, S. *Human Understanding* (Vol. 1). Princeton, N.J.: Princeton University Press, 1972.

Tulving, E. Episodic and semantic memory. In E. Tulving and W. Donaldson (Eds.) *Organization of Memory*. New York: Academic Press, 1972.

# 15

# Prospects

## The Future of Psychology

**THE CURRENT STATE OF THE FIELD**

The State of the Systems

Psychology and Society

**HAS PSYCHOLOGY A FUTURE?**

In this last chapter we shall briefly try to assess the current state of psychology, and then to foretell psychology's future. We will look at the major surviving psychological systems, alternatives to them, signs that psychology is again experiencing a crisis, and at the sometimes strained relations of psychology and society.

## THE CURRENT STATE OF THE FIELD

### The State of the Systems

*Psychoanalysis, Humanistic Psychology, and Related Movements*

Psychoanalysis since the 1970s has become in some instances a "zany" field in which some who call themselves analysts cannot accept others who share the same label (R. Evans, 1976). Not only are there conflicting neo-psychoanalytic schools—Jungian, Rankian, Adlerian, Eriksonian, and so on—there are even different schools claiming to be loyal to Freud's version of psychoanalysis. This splintering of the psychoanalytic movement began in Freud's lifetime and has continued to the point where there is nothing close to an analytic paradigm.

Psychologists' criticism of psychoanalysis and psychiatry has continued for decades. Freud's views are still discussed in most psychology texts, but he is given less space than before and his views are described as at best narrow and at worst completely false. Behaviorists have accepted Skinner's criticisms of Freudian theory as a metaphysical myth, and have gone on to attack all psychiatries which attribute unhappiness to defective mental states. They largely reject psychiatrists' attempts to categorize "mental illnesses," preferring to see supposedly unitary "dissociative reactions" or "anxiety reactions" (forms of neurosis) as collections of learned but maladaptive behaviors to be unlearned by the application of conditioning principles. This new form of therapy is called *behavior modification.*

The behaviorist's rejection of "mental illness" as a myth perpetuated by the psychiatric establishment finds an echo from more radical psychiatrists who accept the mind but dismiss mental "diseases." The best known of such thinkers, themselves psychiatrists, are R. D. Laing and Thomas Szasz. Laing believes that many forms of so-called mental illness, especially schizophrenia, are best understood as attempts by a person to cope with impossible personal situations. There may be method in madness, a strategy for adapting to bizarre circumstances which create bizarre behavior. In any case, there is no disease. Laing places himself in the Greek skeptical tradition as one who tries to view mind and behavior without presuppositions. Szasz focuses on Western Society's response to psychotics. He believes that "schizophrenia" is a derogatory label applied to people whose behavior society does not approve of. Society gives certain persons, psychiatrists, the right to persecute and incarcerate so-called "psychotic" deviants. Szasz draws a parallel between late medieval witch persecutions and modern treatment of the insane. In both cases, Szasz argues, there is no ailment, spiritual or mental. Instead, society manufactures "witchcraft" or "madness" as a rationalization for its harsh treatment of behavioral deviants. Psychiatrists thus need the "mentally ill" more than the "mentally ill" need psychiatrists, and the psychiatrists fight jealously to guard their economic and social positions.

Humanistic, or "Third Force" psychology continued strongly through the 1960s and 1970s. During the counterculture years of the Vietnam war it appealed to students who disliked mechanistic behaviorism and wanted a person-centered psychology that believed in human freedom and dignity. One of the humanistic psychologists, Abraham Maslow (1968), in his later years envisioned a "fourth psychology, transpersonal, transhuman, centered in the cosmos rather than human needs and interest. . . ."

*Transpersonal psychology*, as the new movement came to be called, seeks to perfect humanity through transcendent experiences. Some of its researchers use LSD to promote awareness of a Universal Mind, while others use biofeedback. meditation, or other exotic techniques. Although transpersonal psychologists consciously look toward Oriental religions and philosophies for guidance, transpersonal psychology may be seen as a reassertion of the old mystical neoplatonic stream of Western thought. They seek, as did Plotinus, direct experience of a "Universal Mind" (compare with Plotinus' "Intelligence"), searching for experiences of people and objects that are "timeless, spaceless, universal, absolute, ideal" (compare with Plato's Forms) (Roberts, 1977).

It is fair to say that the areas of psychology centered on human pesonality and its improvement are extremely diverse at present, with many contending schools. The field includes everyone from behavioristically inclined behavior modifiers to social psychologists who deny the existence of personality, to orthodox psychoanalysts, to seekers of personal transcendence. Despite claims by each school to be the wave of the future, the prospects for psychology here are mysterious.

### Behaviorism

The current state of behaviorism is complex. The systems of Tolman and Hull are almost entirely gone, effaced by eclecticism or absorbed into other movements such as information processing. Skinner's experimental analysis of behavior is very much alive, however, and Skinner is today the major spokesman for behaviorism, both within psychology and through his popular works to the world at large.

Animal behaviorists are still digesting the various "misbehaviors of organisms" that came to light in the 1960s, and apart from a general desire to somehow include ethology within the science of animal behavior, reactions have been diverse. In Chapter 13 we noted that some believe a revolution is at hand, toward a cognitive animal psychology. A conservative response has been to abandon behaviors "contaminated" by evolution, such as the pigeon's key peck, to study still more artibrary behaviors, such as pigeon's lever-press (Rosenthal, 1978). A student of Skinner's, R.J. Herrnstein, argues that evolution determines what an organism finds reinforcing, and that apparently instinctive behaviors should be explained not as innately programmed but as shaped by self-reinforcement. So, for instance, a cat stalks a mouse because stalking is self-reinforcing, not because the behavior itself is pre-programmed. Skinner finds this line of argument too environmentalistic. He asserts that he has been widely misunderstood as a radical environmentalist, while in fact he accepts the existence of pre-programmed phylogenic behaviors, such as the cat's stalk or salmon swimming upstream to spawn (Herrnstein, 1977; 1977b; Skinner 1977). The final outcome of these controversies is unclear, but it is apparent that many in the area of operant learning are abandoning Skinner's radical inductionism and are willing to discuss theoretical issues whether genetic, physiological, or cognitive. Many operant researchers also want to integrate their work with that of other experimentalists, rather than maintain the almost complete isolation of the 1960s (Honig & Staddon, 1977).

As a method, operant conditioning has proved a tremendous success. Investigators in the fields of psychopharmacology and brain damage, for example, use it to precisely measure the effects on behavior of drugs and brain damage. However, the present and future role of behaviorism as a paradigm in these areas is cloudy. Use of a technique need imply no committment to theoretical principles. In clinical psychology, the days of behavior modification narrowly defined seem numbered. Many behavior modifiers have themselves argued that most clinical behavior modification techniques are not in fact extensions of behaviorism at all, in some cases even conflicting with it. They maintain that behavior modification, and clinical psychology generally, have all along been eclectic, technological fields pragmatically committed only to what works, not to abstract learning principles and that this fact should be faced and valued (London, 1976; Lazarus, 1977). The current trends among clinical psychologists seem to be toward therapies based on understanding and changing a client's cognitions rather than just his or her behavior (Mahoney, 1977; Meichenbaum, 1977).

On another front, behaviorism and humanistic psychology seem to be groping for a rapproachment. On the behaviorist side, some behaviorists recognize that the automatic action of reinforcers is incorrect and are willing to incorporate cognitive, especially information processing, factors in accounting for behavior (Bandura, 1976). On the humanist side, some humanists see that their mode of psychotherapy is at many points similar to the practices of behavior modifiers and have searched for more general accord. Some humanists have argued that behaviorism and humanistic psychology are not really competing, as was believed in the early 1960s (recall the 1963 *Behaviorism and Phenomenology* symposium) but are so different as to be complementary and potentially cooperative. Other humanists and behaviorists maintain the view that their respective schools are clashing paradigms (Wandersman, Poppen, & Ricks, 1976). Again, the prospects for this continuing debate are vague, although clearly much of the acrimony that accompanied earlier meetings of behaviorism and humanistic psychology has abated.

It was in the area of language that behaviorism, especially radical behaviorism, was most violently and successfully attacked in the late 1950s and early 1960s. The behaviorist answer took a long time to develop and combines both animosity and gestures of reconciliation. Some purist radical behaviorists have maintained Skinner's analysis of verbal behavior. Stephen Winokur (1976) has written a simplified version of Skinner's *Verbal Behavior* 20 years after its publication. Winokur reasserts Skinner's views, including an explicit peripheralism and commitment to chaining that recall Watson: "Thinking is caused by real muscle movements, not just the brain or nervous system", and "Many so-called mental acts are covert behavior chains." Winokur's teacher, Kenneth MacCorquodale, in 1970 provided the reply to Chomsky that Skinner never made. MacCorquodale argues that Chomsky misunderstood, and therefore misrepresented everything Skinner had to say, compounding the error by confusing Skinner's views with those of older, outdated behaviorists. He asserts that Skinner's system is the true fruit of the natural science approach and by implication that Chomsky's is not. MacCorquodale does admit that Chomsky's review was enormously influential.

Between Skinner and his closest followers on the one hand and Chomsky on the other is the clearest example of a paradigm clash to be found in psychology. The former insist that Chomsky's structuralism is not scientific, while Chomsky says (Cohen, 1977) that Skinner's approach ". . . struck me at once as a curious sort of mysticism. . . . It was very foreign to the spirit of the sciences . . . putting psychology in [a] wierd straitjacket. . . ." MacCorquodale takes several facets of *Verbal Behavior* that distressed Chomsky to be virtues, not defects. MacCorquodale also accuses Chomsky of not seeing the competence-performance distinction, although he uses different terms. There seems to be no future to this debate. The rise of information processing cognitive psychology, which embodies neither structuralism nor radical behaviorism, has rendered their arguments irrelevant to the current development of the psychological study of language. Chomsky's theory generated much research in the 1960s, but almost none continues today. Neither Winokur nor MacCorquodale cite research generated by *Verbal Behavior*. Both Chomsky and Skinner represent faded paradigms.

Some behaviorists have been more conciliatory to Chomskian psycholinguistics, and, as with humanistic psychology, have sought grounds for agreement. Attempts have been made to "translate" generative grammar into behavioral equivalents (Catania, 1972). A call has been issued for both camps to abandon involvement with grand theory and get involved with inductive, empirical research (Whitehurst, 1976), echoing Skinner's own rebuke to Tolman and Hull. A behavioral, empiricist alternative to Chomsky's nativist theory of language acquisition has been proposed, although it allows for mediated associations (Robinson, 1972). Finally, a broad analysis of Skinner's and Chomsky's accounts has been made which concludes that in many places they are simply discussing different problems, and that where they tackle the same topic, they agree. The author (Segal, 1977) argues for a mix of behaviorist, Chomskian, and information processing research and optimistically says "Psychology seems to be emerging, at last, into a science. The balkanization of psychology into doctrinaire schools, each with its own special language spoken only by initiates, is giving way to a unified conception of problems, methods and theories."

Such optimistic claims have been made before, both on behalf of eclecticism and of particular schools. Given the history of psychology, and its breadth today we may entertain doubts about the accuracy of this forecast. However, if one trend does exist, it lies in the increasing strength of cognitive psychology, especially the information processing brand.

### Cognitive Psychology

Cognitive psychology seems to be flourishing. In particular, the information processing approach seems to be ousting its ecological competitors structuralism and mentalism. After a brief fling with Chomsky's Cartesian linguistics, psychologists have returned to the more empiricist, and therefore familiar, psychology of information processing. Criticisms of Chomsky's views have appeared that are so aggressively self-confident that Chomsky (1976) has replied ". . . such astonishing dogmatism about matters so poorly understood can hardly be imagined in the natural sciences." The sentiment recalls his attitude to Skinner. Perusal of journals in developmental psychology indicates that Piaget's influence is waning, while that of information processing waxes. Even Piaget's associates admit to "information processing tendencies" (Inhelder, 1972). Mentalists still lack a coherent theory to aid them in their struggle for conceptual existence.

Yet, even inside the information processing camp there are evidences of strain. Allen Newell (1973), one of the founders of the approach, prefaced some comments on symposium papers this way: "Half of me is half distressed and half confused. Half of me is quite content and clear on where we are going." After citing the high quality of the symposium's papers, and foreseeing more of the same from each author, he asks, given all that future good work, ". . . *where will psychology then be*? Will we have achieved a science of man adequate in power and commensurate with his complexity? And if so, how will this have happened via these papers. . . ?"

The specific source of Newell's half-distress is the proliferation of methods and low-level issues in human experimental psychology. Newell enumerates at least 59 recently investigated phenomena and 24 issues defined around competing views (such as nature versus nurture). He argues that no issue is ever resolved, no clarity achieved, instead, things just get "muddier." Each issue of each journal seems to report some experimental result that is allowed to challenge a large theoretical edifice. No one ever puts all the results together. Newell's proposed remedy is more complete processing models engaging complex, not simple, tasks.

Newell's description is, unknowingly, of a science in search of a paradigm. His survey of the field turns up random fact-gathering and dispute over basic issues. In particular, two faults are evident. First, the information processing approach defines just that, an *approach*, not an articulated theory with definite claims. The information processing view's disciplinary matrix is, at least at present, too ill-formed and conflicted to guide normal research, since each investigator may formulate her or his own version and tackle any question she or he chooses. Secondly, a shared exemplar is missing. Newell listed 59 basic phenomena, not the single one on which Skinner's research program, for instance, is based. The shared exemplar is a vital part of a paradigm, for it defines the basic situation about which specific hypotheses will make claims. If each scientist chooses his or her own exemplar, then the community of scientists simply cannot, by definition, discuss the same problems and find a common ground for agreement. The prospect is for much research, but little progress, as Newell fears.

We may also diagnose in information processing increased evidence of behaviorism, in its doubts about the importance of consciousness. Currently fashionable theories of attention view consciousness not as the gateway to memory and behavior, but as their product (Deutsch & Deutsch, 1963). Echoing Watson, Zenon Pylyshyn (1973) has argued that mental imagery plays no causal role in behavior. He believes imagery can be reduced to propositional information encoded in long term memory. Again echoing Watson, J. Evans (1976) fears that a re-introduction of introspective methods "might lead us to abandon experimental psychology and regress to the methods of nineteenth century introspectionists." A more general attack on the usefulness of consciousness has been mounted by Richard Nisbett and Timothy Wilson (1977), who argue that consciousness only rationalizes behavior caused by unknown forces, playing no role in determining behavior. They argue that the common sense belief in conscious control of behavior is a myth warding off the "frightening [belief] that one has no more certain knowledge of the workings of one's own mind than would an outsider with intimate knowledge of one's history and the current situation," a statement Skinner would heartily endorse.

These attitudes reflect the behaviorist belief that consciousness has nothing to do with behavior, and therefore is unworthy of study. They also remind us of Freud's conviction, which may have led him into the seduction mistake, that a scientifically trained observer knows her or his subjects' (or patients') minds better than the subjects do themselves. One of the counts against behaviorism in the early 1960s was that people consciously control their actions and that the automatic action of reinforcers was a myth. In the 1970s, information processing psychologists are returning to the behaviorist view that consciousness does not count.

The usefulness of the computer metaphor and its application in psychology have become centers of controversy. Hubert Dreyfus (1972), a phenomenologist, has argued that artificial intelligence is an unreachable goal. Dreyfus argues that no disembodied machine can rival human consciousness, because it lacks the intimate developmental involvement with the world characteristic of every human being. Dreyfus even argues against the possibility of an information processing cognitive psychology. Precisely because information processors assert the introspective inaccessibility of cognitive processes, Dreyfus argues they are inventing a realm of psychology that does not exist. According to Dreyfus, psychological terms should refer either to consciousness or to physiology, for there is nothing in between. Dreyfus' view recalls the Wundt-James position on the unconscious. There is no

such place; a mental element is either in consciousness or it exists only physiologically, with no realm of "the unconscious" for it to disappear into when not
conscious. Dreyfus is similar to Titchener, as well, arguing for a science of human
consciousness that makes no reference to hypothetical entities, only conscious
elements and their physiological substrata.

Joseph Weizenbaum, a pioneer in artificial intelligence, has become distressed
at some of the applications of his and others' work. He believes that regardless of
what computers can be made to do, there are some things they morally ought not
do. For example, it has been proposed that computers can be made into psycho-
therapists, if only as adjuncts to human therapists. Weizenbaum (1976) calls this
kind of proposal "simply obscene . . . [its] very contemplation ought to give rise
to feelings of disgust in every civilized person."

Such criticisms have, of course, provoked replies from advocates of information processing, artificial intelligence, and computer simulation. The most extended
defense is given by the philosopher Margaret Boden (1977), who argues that only
the information processing approach, of all approaches to psychology, offers the
precision and testability needed by scientific psychology. Dreyfus' critiques are
seen as mistaken or outdated by more recent programs. She agrees with Weizen-
bum that artificial intelligence could be misused, but believes safeguards are
possible. She sees information processing as a potentially scientific version of
humanistic psychologies in that they treat of the mind without reducing it either
to psychology or S-R connections.

Despite its critics, artificial intelligence and computer simulation have
produced programs of sophistication and power unknown a few years ago, although
all fall far short of passing Turing's test (Boden, 1977). As psychological theories,
however, their present status and future prospects are mixed. The information processing trend has gained momentum, not only in human experimental psychology,
but in animal, clinical, and social psychology as well. It seems to be the wave of the
near future. Yet Newell's nagging doubt remains. For all the fine research, is there
progress? Technically, the information processors are light years ahead of Aristotle,
yet in broad conceptual outline, they only repeat him. And as Newell pointed out,
each technical advance belongs only to a single investigator, not to the field as a
whole. Once again, the prospect is unclear.

### Alternatives and Crisis

The decade 1965-1975 saw the proliferation of alternative psychologies
beyond the four identified by Maslow: psychoanalysis, behaviorism, humanistic
psychology, and transpersonal psychology. The self-consciously revolutionary
fervor of the new movements is captured in the following "Manifesto" of dialectical
psychology written by Klaus Riegel (1976), openly modeled on Marx's and Engel's
*Communist Manifesto*: "A specter is haunting western psychology: the specter of
scientific dialectics. The scaffold of the academic world is shaking; the time for its
transformation is near. . . . You have nothing to lose but the respect of vulgar

mechanists and pretentious mentalists." Riegel is obviously eager for a Kuhnian revolution.

Riegel was not the only psychologist to challenge the foundations of mid-twentieth century scientific psychology. Ludwig von Bertalanffy (1968) argued against the prevailing psychological atomism in favor of a more holistic approach, general systems theory. That at least social psychology was an eclectic, non-paradigmatic field was recognized by one of its leading figures (Newcomb, 1975). The failure of psychology to achieve maturity as a science equal to physics and chemistry, Hume's "science of human nature," was attributed to psychologists' inability or unwillingness to critically examine their basic theoretical concepts (Rozeboom, 1974). Such were the rebellious voices raised within academic psychology.

One interesting alternative arose outside psychology, when some biologists claimed that their field could encompass psychology. Their claim is based on a Darwinian biological analysis of animals' social behavior, defining the new field called "sociobiology" (Wilson, 1975). Sociobiologists argue that such social behaviors as aggression and altruism are biologically adaptive traits, acquired by natural selection, and rooted in the individual's genes. E. O. Wilson, sociobiology's founder, writes (1975): "Let us now consider man in the free spirit of natural history as though we were zoologists from another planet. . . . In this macroscopic view the humanities and social sciences shrink to specialized branches of biology. . . ." More polemically he claims "Only when the machinery [of the brain] can be torn down on paper at the level of the cell will the properties of emotion and ethical judgment become clear" and neurobiology will "cannibalize" psychology. Finally, "When we have progressed enough to explain ourselves in these mechanistic terms . . . the social sciences [will] come to full flower."

Wilson's sociobiology represents the confluence of three strains of psychological thinking. Two are traceable to Descartes. The first is nativism, for sociobiology holds that much of human and animal nature is innate; the second is mechanism, the reduction of mind to the mechanical operation of the brain. The third strain is Darwin's theory of evolution, which provides the theoretical groundwork for claims about inherited traits. Sociobiology is a powerful and forceful doctrine, and has aroused a great deal of argument from empiricists.

The future of all alternative psychologies is cloudy, despite their revolutionary rhetoric and claims on the future. However, their very existence shows that psychology now faces another crisis. Other evidence of this crisis has been cited, especially Koch's argument against the possibility of a scientific psychology. A gradual disenchantment with training in rigorous experimental psychology can be seen, for example, in the ideas of Liam Hudson (1972), who proposes instead a more humanistic but still scientific psychology based on personal acquaintance with another's life. In this same questioning vein, it has been argued that psychology cannot hope to find laws that transcend human cultures (Diaz-Guerra, 1977). Trends such as these have prompted at least one traditional information processing psychologist to a defense of tough-minded science against tender-hearted humanism.

Donald Broadbent (1974) accuses a whole spectrum of thinkers—from Chomsky to Hudson—of undermining scientific psychology in their pursuit of unscientific, fuzzy-minded notions such as "innate grammar."

Further evidence of the crisis of psychology in the 1970s could be cited, but it should be clear that psychologists had no firm agreement on anything, from the definition of psychology (should it stick to behavior or accept transcendental mystical altered states of consciousness?) to its methods (Skinner box or LSD?), to its theories (contingencies of reinforcement or Buddhistic *chakras*?). The present crises should remind us of earlier crises which were not provoked by empirical anomalies. Riegel says, "A specter is haunting psychology," but the specter is not dialectics but the continued fear, returned in acute form, that psychology is not a science, and worse, cannot be. Some defend the old ways, some look for a new scientific salvation including scientific humanism, while others choose a nonscientific humanism or even neoplatonism.

Perodically these concerns and battles become more acute, though they are never absent. This is one such time, and as so often before, it is part of larger unheavals in society.

### Psychology and Society

Present day relations between psychology and society run in two directions: the effect of psychology on society and that of society on psychology. An excellent illustration of this ambiguity is America's reaction to Skinner's behaviorism and his utopian proposals. Watson's system of control was welcomed by the progressive elite as a means to control the masses. Today, however, Skinner is denounced by conservative politicians and established humanist philosophers, while alienated youth, who usually fear manipulation, establish Walden II communities. We thus find paradoxically that those who usually advocate social control oppose radical behaviorism, which preaches control, while those who are attempting to overthrow or escape control, and who usually believe in freedom, support radical behaviorism, which denies freedom.

Another area that has become a topic of heated controversy is psychology's involvement in education, which has been continuous since its earliest days. Psychologists such as Thorndike, Skinner, Dewey, and Rogers have all at least advised society how to run its schools, and educational psychological research has long been a growth industry in academia. Nevertheless, although educators often adopt techniques advocated by psychologists, from Skinnerian teaching machines to Piagetian open classrooms, parents frequently resist innovations. They decry the breakdown of standards and push for return to basics. Another area of ambiguous interactions is testing. Many psychologists advocate removing traditional psychological tests, especially IQ tests, from the schools on the grounds that early testing may label a child "retarded" or "neurotic," a label the child will find hard to overcome and which may bias teachers against the child. They propose this at a time when the public takes some tests, notably the college entrance tests, more seriously than ever and pushes for competency testing to ensure that children are being educated.

The use of tests has also become involved in American race relations. Arthur Jensen argued in 1969 that results of IQ tests support the idea that blacks are genetically less intelligent than whites, and that consequently compensatory education programs can do little, if any, good for blacks. This proposal touched off a storm of controversy within psychology, some denouncing Jensen as a racist ignorant of genetics who distorts research findings (Hirsch, 1976), while others, such as Richard Herrnstein, rush to his defense (Cohen, 1977). Attempts were made to prevent Jensen from speaking on some college campuses, while any research into genetics and IQ became suspect. The controversy has arisen again in legal challenges to all ability testing.

Psychotherapy has had a mixed reception. More people than ever are seeking psychological help, and its forms proliferate yearly. To many, psychotherapy has become a secular religion, offering comfort and advice in time of trouble and a framework for every day living. However, voices of complaint are heard. Conservatives are often bothered by some of the more outlandish modes of therapy just as they were bothered by Freud's preoccupation with sex. People of various persuasions are disturbed by the "me-ism" promoted by some psychologists who teach a person to look out for himself first and who elevate egoistic feelings over reason. As an industry, psychotherapy must be counted a success, with a secure future, but it has not yet won the full acceptance of society.

The effect of society on psychology has been diffuse and varied. During the late 1960s, against the background of the Vietnam war, many people began to feel profound doubts about Western rationalism and its most important offspring, science. Science and technology were used to kill in what increasing numbers of Americans saw as an unjust war pursued by hard men of reason, "the best and the brightest" (Halberstam, 1972). A reaction against scientism and the Western preoccupation with the mind over the body set in. The mechanization of the world picture had gone too far. Psychology, as a science and a technology concerned with mind and behavior, was naturally affected. The impact was most dramatic in psychotherapy and related fields, for in this period irrational, physical, or emotional approaches to therapy grew rapidly, mysticism, meditation, and drugs were all tried. Freud's colder, more intellectual, form of therapy became less popular.

Effects on experimental psychology are harder to pin down. Chomsky, who started a cognitive revolt in psychology, was also a prominent critic of the war in Vietnam, so his lectures attracted both students of language and political dissidents, regardless of whether he spoke on language or the war. As the war and dissent from it grew, so did disaffection with traditional behaviorism. As the rhetoric of crisis and revolution against the political establishment grew, so did Kuhnian rhetoric of crisis and revolution grow in experimental psychology. There was no rejection of reason or an apotheosis of emotion in experimental psychology. Cartesian linguistics and information processing are both highly austere intellectual systems. But there was a heady spirit of change, as the Establishment of the past withered away or converted to the new view. As so often before, psychological views of humanity changed along with larger social movements.

So, psychology and society have had a varied relationship. It is probably a closer relationship than is the case with the physical sciences. While physics and chemistry may be denounced or applauded for their impact on life and the world, they have become so technical and substantively remote that the ordinary person cannot challenge them or feel them personally. The person in the street has no opinions about quarks and quasars. It is quite otherwise with psychology and the other social sciences. Psychology is about mind and behavior, and everyone has opinions about mind and behavior. When a psychologist challenges common sense no one believes it, and when a psychologist supports common sense, she or he is criticized for discovering the obvious. It is probably for this reason that when congressmen attack waste in government sponsored research, they usually pick on social science projects. They believe we know all that we need to know about love, and so they attempt to ridicule research on love—yet the value of a piece of high-energy physics research is beyond common sense or ridicule.

The intimate relationship of each person to his or her own mind and behavior, and the existence of common sense beliefs about them have thus made for a stormy, uneven relationship of common sense with the science of mind and behavior. The prospect is for no change in the pattern, though no one can tell where the next controversy or fad will appear.

## HAS PSYCHOLOGY A FUTURE?

> The history of modern psychology is a record, not of scientific advance, but of intellectual retreat.
>
> R. B. Joynson, "The Breakdown of Modern Psychology"

Joynson (1976) renders a harsh judgment on psychology, one that bodes ill for its future, and Joynson is not alone. J. J. Gibson (1967), a great perceptual psychologist, states in his autobiography that psychology is "ill founded" and its gains "puny." Sigmund Koch (1974) asserts that psychology is breaking up. Jacob Bronowski (1973) fears the entire West has lost its nerve; perhaps psychology's "retreat" is just part of it. We have frequently heard optimistic assertions that psychology is, or is about to become a real, coherent science, most recently from one who expected to reconcile Chomskian and Skinnerian psycholinguistics. It is not clear that psychology has a future, if it is breaking up, or in retreat despite claims by the optimists who have been proven wrong by crisis after crisis. What prospects await psychology? What lies beyond the current crisis?

As an institution, no one can doubt that psychology will survive for a very long time. Psychologists make too many contributions to society, from industry to psychotherapy, from education to psychological warfare. Further, psychology is well entrenched among other disciplines in universities, in academic and scientific organizations, in fund-granting institutions, and in government. Society may not always be comfortable with psychology, but psychology will not, and cannot, go away. This means the futures of psychologists are secure, although perhaps in fewer numbers than in recent years.

What is more important, however, is the future of psychology as a disciplined, scientific attempt by humanity to understand our nature. Textbooks define psychology as "the science of. . . ." Implicit in the statement, particularly in the use of the words *the science,* is a belief that psychology is or should be one unified, coherent science, that all psychologists should use the same methods and aim at a single theoretical account of human mind and behavior. Each psychological system struggles to become that account, that paradigm. Such an assumption is most clearly true of behaviorism, which sought (and with Skinner still seeks) to write a set of laws that would account at least for all mammalian behavior, including humans'. All facets of human behavior from perception to psychosis were to be subsumed in a single framework. This assumption also may be found in Wundt and Titchener who sought a complete human (though not animal) psychology; in Gestalt psychology, which ascribed insight to apes and people; in Freud, who saw psychoanalysis as the psychology of the future; in functionalism, behaviorism's forerunner; and in information processing, which attempts to trace information completely from input to output, and which is extending itself into child development and animal behavior.

The assumption seems to be that one day someone will give a synthesis of the laws of behavior, just as Newton synthesized the laws of physics. But the assumption may be questioned. Can a Newtonian synthesis of psychology be made?

Outside observers have noted psychology's diversity. For example, Stephen Toulmin (1972) says that psychology is not a "compact discipline." It is, rather, "diffuse" because psychology consists, and always has consisted of warring sects (Johnson, 1934; Husband, 1932), each with its own methods, ideals, and viewpoints, all highly inbred and represented by journals which express only one sect's point of view. Constant squabbling between the sects and ideological pronouncements have stalled psychology. Each sect believes it has *the* best method and rejects everything else. Proponents of a Newtonian synthesis view this state with misgiving, but believe one viewpoint (their own) is correct, and must, if psychology is to be a science, banish the others. And so the long struggle goes on. However, after nearly a century of psychology, whose gains indeed may be "puny," a different strategy may be in order.

The background to Newton's own triumph is instructive. Medieval physicists wanted to explain all forms of change in nature, not just change in the position of heavenly bodies. So they believed that one set of laws could be given for physical motion, heating and cooling, maturation and aging, and so on (Toulmin, 1972). Progress was made only when this grand ambition was abandoned, and natural philosophy was replaced by distinct sciences, each defined around its own subject matter, methods, theories, and goals. Each science was different; they did not compete. So Newton did not try to explain change in general, the old ideal of the medievals, but a particular kind of change, motion of physical objects. It is also important to realize how limited Newton's synthesis was; he made drastically simplifying assumptions, could never mathematically explain the motion of more than two bodies in empty space at a time, and attributed some phenomena he could not handle to angels or God.

Psychology's century of failing to produce its grand synthesis ought to convince us not that psychology needs a Newton, but rather that the goal of a unified psychology is chimerical. Why should a single science with a single set of principles seek to embrace both visual illusions and lever-pressing? There is no reason to believe the two phenomena have the same explanation. Of course, they are connected, for a rat must see the lever to press it. Similarly, a plant needs sunlight to grow, but we do not expect the laws of botany and solar fusion to be the same.

Perhaps psychology is breaking up, and if it is, perhaps we should be glad. If psychologists can define separate subject matters, and tackle each alone in the way it requires—without the grandiose belief that they can explain everything eventually—then psychology may progress. Natural philosophy progressed only after its break-up, so the future of psychology may lie in its breaking up. Then, there will be no single science of psychology, but sciences of psychology. Texts will have to begin "Psychology is a collection of sciences of. . . ."

Sigmund Koch (1974) draws a more radical conclusion, that the break up means most of psychology *cannot* be scientific. In one respect, however, he too is tied to the Newtonian ideal, for he defines a science after the fashion of Newtonian physics. This is too narrow, for geology is a science and in no way resembles mathematical classical physics. We should return to our definition of Chapter 1: Science is an effort by man to bring a public, empirically based order out of the chaos of sense perceptions. No stronger requirement should be made before calling a field a science, although some sciences may achieve more than others in precision, scope, mathematical elegance, and other attributes. These characteristics, however, must not be made fetishes for all sciences to worship.

Psychology has a long past, a short history, and an uncertain future. Perhaps it has retreated in modern times, owing to the delusion of a Newtonian synthesis. Today it prospers as a popular and useful field. Tomorrow we may hope that it will break up, leaving each section free to advance in its own way. The final judge will be history.

## SUGGESTED READINGS

A good survey of the present state of psychology, reflections on its recent past, and prognostications for its future is *Theories in Contemporary Psychology*, 2nd Ed., (Macmillan) edited by Melvin Marx and Felix Goodson (1976). The interested reader might like to compare it to the first edition (1963) edited by Marx alone. The changes over thirteen years are stunning.

# REFERENCES

Bandura, A. Behavior theory and the models of man. In A. Wandersman *et al.* (Eds.) *Humanism and behaviorism: Dialogue and growth.* Oxford: Pergamon Press, 1976.

Bertalanffy, L. von *General systems theory.* New York: George Braziller, 1968.

Boden, M. *Artificial intelligence and natural man.* New York: Basic Books, 1977.

Broadbent, D. *In defense of empirical psychology.* London: Methuen, 1974.

Bronowski, J. *The ascent of man.* Boston: Little, Brown, 1973.

Catania, A. Chomsky's formal analysis of natural languages: A behaviorial translation. *Behaviorism,* 1972, *1,* 1-15.

Chomsky, N. On the biological basis of language capacities. In R. W. Rieber (Ed.) *The neuropsychology of language.* New York: Plenum, 1976.

Cohen, D. *Psychologists on psychology.* London: Routledge & Kegan Paul, 1977.

Deutsch, J. & Deutsch, D. Attention: Some theoretical considerations. *Psychological Review,* 1963, *70,* 80-90.

Diaz-Guerrero, R. A Mexican psychology. *American Psychologist,* 1977, *32,* 934-944.

Dreyfus, H. *What computers can't do.* New York: Harper & Row, Pub., 1972.

Evans, J. St. B. T. A critical note on Quinton and Fellows' observation of reasoning strategies. *British Journal of Psychology,* 1976, *67,* 517-518.

Evans, R. I. *The making of psychology.* New York: Knopf, 1976.

Gibson, J. J. Autobiography. In E. G. Boring & G. Lindzey (Eds.) *A history of psychology in autobiography* (Vol. 5). New York: Appleton-Century-Crofts, 1967.

Halberstam, D. *The best and the brightest.* New York: Random House, 1972.

Herrnstein, R. The evolution of behaviorism. *American Psychologist,* 1977a, *32,* 593-603.

Herrnstein, R. Doing what comes naturally! A reply to Professor Skinner. *American Psychologist,* 1977b, *32,* 1013-1016.

Hirsch, J. Jensenism: The bankruptcy of science without scholarship. *Educational theory,* 1976, *25,* 3-27.

Honig, W. & Staddon, J. (Eds.) *Handbook of operant behavior.* Englewood Cliffs, N.J.: Prentice-Hall, 1977.

Hudson, L. *The cult of the fact.* New York: Harper & Row, Pub., 1972.

Husband, R. W. Can an eclectic position be sound? *Psychological Review,* 1934, *41,* 368-380.

Inhelder, B. Information processing tendencies in recent experiments in cognitive learning—Empirical studies. In S. Farnham - Diggory (Ed.) *Information processing in children.* New York: Academic Press, 1972.

Johnson, H. M. Some follies of "emancipated" psychology. *Psychological Review,* 1932, *39,* 293-323.

Joynson, R. B. Breakdown of modern psychology (1970). Reprinted in M. Marx & F. Goodson (Eds.) *Theories in contemporary psychology.* New York: Macmillan, 1976.

Koch, S. Psychology as an integral discipline: the history of an illusion. And Conceptual sweep vs. knowledge: thoughts toward a feasible future for psychology.

Papers presented at the annual meeting of the American Psychological Association, New Orleans, Louisiana, September, 1974.

**Lazarus, A.** Has behavior therapy outlived its usefulness? *American Psychologist,* 1977, *32,* 550-554.

**London, P.** The end of ideology in behavior modification (1972). Reprinted in M. Marx & F. Goodson (Eds.) *Theories in contemporary psychology.* New York: Macmillan, 1976.

**MacCorquodale, K.** On Chomsky's review of B. F. Skinner's *Verbal Behavior. Journal of the Experimental Analysis of Behavior,* 1969, *12,* 831-841.

**Mahoney, M. J.** Reflections on the cognitive-learning trend in psychotherapy. *American Psychologist,* 1977, *32,* 5-13.

**Maslow, A. H.** *Toward a psychology of being* (2nd Ed.). Princeton: Van Nostrand, 1968.

**Meichenbaum, D.** *Cognitive-behavior modification: An integrative approach.* New York: Plenum, 1977.

**Newcomb, T.** A macro-sketch of social psychology. Paper presented at the annual meeting of the American Psychological Association, Washington, D. C., August, 1975.

**Newell, A.** You can't play 20 questions with nature and win. In W. Chase (Ed.) *Visual Information Processing.* New York: Academic Press, 1977.

**Nisbett, R. & Wilson, T.** Telling more than we can know: Verbal reports on mental processes. *Psychological Review,* 1973, *84,* 231-259.

**Pylyshyn, Z.** What the mind's eye tells the mind's brain: A critique of mental imagery. *Psychological Bulletin,* 1973, *80,* 1-24.

**Riegel, K.** The dialectics of human development. *American Psychologist,* 1976, *31,* 689-700.

**Roberts, T.** Education and transpersonal relations: A research agenda. *Simulation & Games,* 1977, *8,* 7-28.

**Robinson, G.** Procedures for the acquisition of syntax. In W. Honig & J. Staddon (Eds.) *Handbook of operant behavior.* Englewood Cliffs, N.J.: Prentice-Hall, 1977.

**Rosenthal, R. L.** Auditory stimulus control of treadle pressing in pigeons. Paper presented at the annual meeting of the Eastern Psychological Association, Washington, D.C., April, 1977.

**Rozeboom, W.** Metathink: A radical alternative. Paper presented to the annual meeting of the American Psychological Association, New Orleans, Louisiana, 1974.

**Segal, A.** Toward a coherent theory of language. In W. Honig & J. Staddon (Eds.) *Handbook of Operant Behavior.* Englewood Cliffs, N.J.: Prentice-Hall, 1977.

**Skinner, B. F.** Herrnstein and the evolution of behaviorism. *American Psychologist,* 1977, *32,* 1006-1012.

**Toulmin, S.** *Human understanding* (Vol. 1). Princeton, Princeton University Press, 1972.

**Wandersman, A., Poppen, P. & Ricks, P.** (Eds.) *Humanism and behaviorism: Dialogue and growth.* Oxford: Pergamon, 1976.

**Weizenbaum, J.** *Computer power and human reason.* San Francisco: W. H. Freeman & Co., 1976.

**Whitehurst, G.** Communication and language. Paper presented at the annual meeting of the American Psychological Association, Washington, D. C., September, 1976.

Wilson, E. O. *Sociobiology.* Cambridge, Mass.: Harvard University Press, 1975.

Winokur, S. *A primer of verbal behavior: An operant view.* Englewood Cliffs, N.J.: Prentice-Hall, 1976.

# Bibliography

## GENERAL INTELLECTUAL HISTORIES

Baumer, F. L. *Modern European thought.* New York: Macmillan, 1977.

Brinton, C. *The shaping of modern thought.* Englewood Cliffs, N.J.: Prentice-Hall, 1950.

Bronowski, J. & Mazlish, B. *The Western Intellectual Tradition.* New York: Harper & Row, Pub., 1960.

Copleston, F. C. *A history of philosophy* (9 vols.) Garden City, N.Y.: Image Books, 1962-1977.

Mason, S. *A history of the sciences.* New York: Collier Books, 1962.

Russell, B. *A history of western philosophy.* New York: Simon & Schuster, 1945.

Thorndike, L. *History of magic and experimental science* (8 vols.) New York: Columbia University Press, 1923-1958.


## CHAPTER 1
## INTRODUCTION

Burian, R. More than a marriage of convenience: On the inextricability of history and philosophy of science. *Philosophy of Science,* 1977, *44,* 1-42.

Crane, D. *Invisible colleges.* Chicago: University of Chicago Press, 1972.

Feyerabend, P. *Against method.* London: New Left Books, 1975.

Scheffler, I. *Science and subjectivity.* Indianapolis: Bobbs-Merrill, 1967.

Shapere, D. The structure of scientific revolutions. *Philosophical Review,* 1964, *73,* 384-394.


## CHAPTER 2
## THE CLASSICAL WORLD

Brehier, E. *The philosophy of Plotinus.* Chicago: University of Chicago Press, 1958.

Burnet, J. *Early Greek philosophy* (4th ed.) New York: Collins Publishers, 1957.

Hamilton, E. & Cairns, H. (Eds.) *The collected dialogues of Plato.* Bollingen Series LXXI. New York: Pantheon, 1961.

Kirk, G. & Raven, J. *The presocratic philosophers.* Cambridge, England: Cambridge University Press, 1971.

Long, A. *Hellenistic philosophy: Stoics, Epicureans, Skeptics.* London: Duckworth, 1974.

Marshack, A. *The roots of civilization.* New York: McGraw-Hill, 1972.

McKeon, R. (Ed.) *The basic works of Aristotle.* New York: Random House, 1941.

Nash, R. *The light of the mind; St. Augustine's theory of knowledge.* Lexington, Ken.: The University Press of Kentucky, 1969.

Raven, J. *Plato's thought in the making.* Cambridge, England: Cambridge University Press, 1965.

Robinson, T. *Plato's psychology.* Toronto: Toronto University Press, 1970.

Ross, D. *Aristotle.* London: Methuen, 1966.

Snell, B. *The discovery of the mind: The Greek origins of European thought.* New York: Harper & Row, Pub., 1960.

## CHAPTER 3
## THE MEDIEVAL WORLD

Aquinas, T. *The pocket Aquinas.* New York: The Washington Square Press, 1960.

Augustine. *Confessions.* Harmondsworth, England: Penguin, 1961.

Bark, W. C. *Origins of the medieval world.* Stanford, Calif.: Stanford University Press, 1958.

Brandt, W. *The shape of medieval history.* New York: Schocken Books, 1973.

Cantor, J. *Medieval history* (2nd ed.) New York: Macmillan, 1969.

Colish, M. *The mirror of language.* New Haven, Conn.: Yale University Press, 1968.

Dales, R. *The scientific achievement of the middle ages.* Philadelphia: University of Pennsylvania Press, 1973.

Duns Scotus, J. *Philosophical writings: A selection.* Indianapolis: Library of Liberal Arts, 1962.

Fakhry, M. *A history of Islamic philosophy.* New York: Columbia University Press, 1970.

Harvey, E. *The inward wits: Psychological theory in the middle ages and Renaissance.* London: The Warburg Institute, Survey VI, 1975.

Huizinga, J. *The waning of the middle ages.* New York: Doubleday, 1954.

Knowles, D. *The evolution of medieval thought.* New York: Vintage, 1962.

Kristeller, P. *Renaissance thought.* New York: Harper & Row, Pub., 1961.

Leff, G. *William of Ockham.* Manchester: Manchester University Press, 1975.

Leff, G. *The dissolution of the medieval outlook.* New York: Harper & Row, Pub., 1976.

Moody, E. *Studies in medieval philosophy, science, and logic.* Berkeley: University of California Press, 1975.

Morris, C. *The discovery of the individual 1050 - 1200.* New York: Harper & Row, Pub., 1972.

Nicholas of Autrecourt. *The universal treatise.* Milwaukee: Marquette University Press, 1971.

Ockham, W. *Philosophical writings: A selection.* Indianapolis: Library of Liberal Arts, 1964.

Russell, J. *Witchcraft in the middle ages.* Ithaca, N.Y.: Cornell University Press, 1972.

Wallace, K. *Francis Bacon on the nature of man.* Urbana, Ill.: University of Illinois Press, 1967.

Weinberg, J. *A short history of medieval philosophy.* Princeton, N.J.: Princeton University Press, 1964.

Wilcox, D. *In search of God and self: Renaissance and Reformation thought.* Boston: Houghton Mifflin, 1975.


## CHAPTER 4
## THE SEVENTEENTH CENTURY

Bullough, V. (Ed.) *The Scientific Revolution.* New York: Holt, Rinehart & Winston, 1970.

Descartes, R. *The philosophical works of Descartes* (2 vols.) Cambridge, England: Cambridge University Press, 1972.

Leibniz, G. *Selections.* P. P. Wiener (Ed.) New York: Scribner's, 1951.

Locke, J. *The Locke reader.* Compiled by J. W. Yolton. Cambridge, England: Cambridge University Press, 1977.

Spinoza, B. *Works of Spinoza* (2 vols.) Translated by R. H. M. Elwes. New York: Dover, 1955.

Tipton, I. C. (Ed.) *Locke on human understanding.* Oxford: Oxford University Press, 1977.

Willey, B. *The seventeenth century background.* Garden City, N.Y.: Doubleday, 1953.

Williams, B. *Descartes: The project of pure inquiry.* Harmondsworth, England: Pelican, 1978.

Yolton, J. *Locke and the compass of human understanding.* Cambridge, England: Cambridge University Press, 1970.


## CHAPTER 5
## THE EIGHTEENTH CENTURY

Berkeley, G. *Works on vision.* C. M. Turbayne (Ed.) Indianapolis: Bobbs-Merrill, 1963.

Berkeley, G. *A treatise concerning the principles of human knowledge,* and *Three dialogues between Hylas and Philonus.* In A. J. Ayer (Ed.) *British Empirical Philosophers.* London: Routledge & Kegan Paul, 1952.

Brown, T. *Sketch of a system of the philosophy of the human mind.* Edinburgh: Bell and Bradfute, Manners and Miller, 1820.

Condillac, E. B. de *Treatise on sensations.* Partially reprinted in B. Rand (Ed.) *The classical psychologists.* Gloucester, Mass.: Peter Smith, 1974.

Gay, P. (Ed.) *The Enlightenment: A comprehensive anthology.* New York: Simon and Schuster, 1973.

Hartley, D. *Observations on man, his frame, his duty and his expectations.* London and Bath: James Leake and Wm. Frederick, 1749.

Kant, I. *Critique of pure reason.* Translated by N. K. Smith. New York: St. Martin's Press, 1929.

Passmore, J. *Hume's intentions.* New York: Basic Books, 1968.

**Rappaport, D.** *The history of the concept of association of ideas.* New York: International Universities Press, Inc., 1974.

**Stewart, D.** *Elements of the philosophy of the mind.* London: A. Strahan and T. Cadell, 1792.

**Stock, G. J.** *Berkeley's analysis of perception.* The Hague: Mouton, 1972.

**Tagliacozzo, G. & Verene, D. P.** (Eds.) *Giambattista Vico's science of humanity.* Baltimore: John Hopkins University Press, 1976.


## CHAPTER 6
## THE NINETEENTH CENTURY


**Anonymous.** Physical puritanism. *Westminster Review,* 1852, *57,* 405-442.

**Bain, A.** *Mental science.* New York: D. Appleton & Co., 1868.

**Bamler, P.** Malthus, Darwin and the concept of struggle. *Journal of the History of Ideas,* 1976, *37,* 631-650.

**Berlin, I.** *Karl Marx.* New York: Oxford University Press.

**Bernheim, H.** *Hypnosis and suggestion in psychotherapy.* New York: Jason Aronson, 1973.

**Blackmore, J.** *Ernst Mach.* Berkeley: University of California Press, 1972.

**Buranelli, V.** *The wizard from Vienna.* New York: Coward, McCann, & Geoghegan, 1975.

**Burke, E.** *The philosophy of Edmund Burke.* L. Bredvold & G. Ross (Eds.). Ann Arbor, Mich.: The University of Michigan Press, 1960.

**Carlyle, T.** *On heroes, hero-worship and the heroic in history.* Lincoln, Neb.: University of Nebraska Press, 1966.

**Clark, E. & Dewhurst, K.** *An illustrated history of brain function.* Berkeley: University of California Press, 1972.

**Colquhoun, J.** *Report on the experiments on animal magnetism.* Edinburgh, Scotland: Robert Cadell, 1833.

**Comte, A.** *A general view of Positivism.* New York: Robert Speller & Sons, 1975.

**Crookes, W.** *Crookes and the spirit world.* R. C. Medhurst, (Ed.). New York: Taplinger, 1972.

**Darwin, C. & Wallace, A.** *Evolution by natural selection.* Cambridge, England: Cambridge University Press, 1958.

**Darnton, R.** *Mesmerism and the end of the Enlightenment in France.* New York: Schocken Books, 1968.

**Davies, J.** *Phrenology: Fad and science.* New Haven, Conn.: Yale University Press, 1955.

**Donders, F. C.** On the Speed of Mental Processes. In W. G. Foster (Trans. & Ed.) *Attention and performance II. Acta Psychologica,* 1969, *30,* 412-431.

**Dunkel, H. B.** *Herbart and Herbartism.* Chicago: University of Chicago Press, 1970.

**Dupotet de Sennevoy, J.** *An introduction to the study of animal magnetism.* London: Saunders & Utley, 1838.

**Eisley, L.** *Darwin's century.* Garden City, N.Y.: Doubleday, 1958.

**Fechner, G. T.** (1860-1966). *Elements of psychophysics* (Vol. 1). New York: Holt, Rinehart & Winston, 1966.

Feuer, L. S. (Ed.) *Marx and Engels: Basic writings on politics and philosophy.* Garden City, N.Y.: Doubleday, 1959.

Fromm, E. *Marx's concept of man.* New York: Ungar, 1966.

Ghiselin, M. *The triumph of the Darwinian method.* Berkeley: University of California Press, 1969.

Glass, B., Temkin, O., and Straus, W. L. (Eds.) *Forerunners of Darwin: 1745-1859.* Baltimore: The John Hopkins Press, 1959.

Greenway, A. P. The incorporation of action into associationism. *Journal of the History of the Behavioral Sciences,* 1973, *9,* 42-52.

Hearnshaw, L. *A short history of British psychology 1840-1940.* New York: Barnes & Noble Books, 1964.

Helmholtz, H. *A treatise on physiological optics.* Partially reprinted in T. Shipley (Ed.) *Classics in psychology.* New York: Philosophical Library, 1961.

Herbart, J. F. *A textbook of psychology.* New York: D. Appleton & Co., 1891.

Himmelfarb, C. *Darwin and the Darwinian revolution.* New York: Norton & Co., 1959.

Houdini, H. *Houdini: A magician among the spirits.* New York: Harper & Row, Pub., 1924.

Hull, D. L.*Darwin and his critics.* Cambridge, Mass.: Harvard University Press, 1973.

Leary, D. E. The historical foundation of Herbart's mathematization of psychology. Paper presented at the annual convention of the American Psychological Association, Toronto, Canada, August 30, 1978.

Lotze, H. *Outlines of psychology.* Boston: Ginn & Co., 1886.

Mach, E. *The analysis of sensations.* New York: Dover, 1959.

Passmore, J. *A hundred years of philosophy* (rev. ed.). New York: Basic Books, 1966.

Simon, W. M. *European positivism in the nineteenth century.* Ithaca, N.Y.: Cornell University Press, 1963.

Wallace, A. R. *Miracles and modern spiritualism.* London: George Redway, 1896.

Walsh, A. Is Phrenology foolish? *Journal of the History of the Behavioral Sciences,* 1970, *6,* 358-361.

Webb, J. (Ed.) *The mediums and the conjurours.* New York: Arno Press, 1976.

CHAPTER 7
THE PSYCHOLOGY OF CONSCIOUSNESS

Angell, J. R. Imageless thought. *Psychological Review,* 1911, *18,* 295-323.

Bringmann, W., Balance, W., & Evans, R. Wilhelm Wundt, 1832-1920: A brief biographical sketch. *Journal of the History of the Behavioral Sciences,* 1975, *11,* 287-297.

Henle, M. (Ed.) *Documents of Gestalt psychology.* Berkeley: University of California Press, 1961.

Hochberg, J. Organization and the Gestalt tradition. In E. Carterette & M. Friedman (Eds.) *Handbook of perception* (Vol. 1) *Historical and philosophical roots of perception.* New York: Academic Press, 1974.

Humphrey, G. *Thinking.* New York: Science Editions, 1963.

Köhler, W. *The mentality of apes.* New York: Liveright, 1938.

Köhler, W. *Gestalt psychology.* New York: Mentor, 1947.

Köhler, W. *The selected papers of Wolfgang Köhler.* New York: Liveright, 1971.

Lewin, E. *Principles of topological psychology.* New York: McGraw-Hill, 1936.

Lindenfield, D. Oswald Külpe and the Würzburg school. *Journal of the History of the Behavioral Sciences,* 1978, *14,* 132-141.

Mischel, T. Wundt and the conceptual foundations of psychology. *Philosophical and Phenomenological Research,* 1970, *31,* 1-26.

Titchener, E. B. *Experimental psychology: A manual of laboratory practice* (4 vols.). New York: Macmillan, 1901-1905.

Titchener, E. B. *Lectures on the elementary psychology of feeling and attention.* New York: Macmillan, 1908.

Titchener, E. B. The past decade in experimental psychology. *American Journal of Psychology,* 1910, *21,* 404-421.

Titchener, E. B. The scheme of introspection. *American Journal of Psychology,* 1912, *23,* 485-508.

Titchener, E. B. *A text-book of psychology.* New York: Macmillan, 1913.

Titchener, E. B. Experimental psychology: A retrospect. *American Journal of Psychology,* 1925, *36,* 313-323.

Wertheimer, M. *Productive thinking,* enlarged edition. New York: Harper & Row, Pub., 1959.

Woodworth, R. S. Imageless thought. *The Journal of Philosophy, Psychology and Scientific Methods,* 1906, *3,* 701-708.

Wundt, W. *Outlines of psychology.* Leipzig: Englemann, 1897; reprinted: St. Clair Shores, Mich.: Scholarly Press, 1969.

Wundt, W. *Principles of physiological psychology* (Vol. 1). New York: Macmillan, 1910.

Wundt, W. *An introduction to psychology.* London: George Allen, 1912.

Wundt, W. *Elements of folk psychology.* London: Allen & Unwin, 1916.

Wundt, W. *The language of gestures.* The Hague: Mouton, 1973.

## CHAPTER 8
## PSYCHOLOGY OF THE UNCONSCIOUS MIND

Alaya, F. Victorian science and the "Genius" of woman. *Journal of the History of Ideas,* 1977, *38,* 261-280.

Bakan, D. *Sigmund Freud and the Jewish mystical tradition.* Princeton, N.J.: D. Van Nostrand, 1958.

Decker, Hannah S. The interpretation of dreams: Early reception by the educated German public. *Journal of the History of the Behavioral Sciences,* 1975, *11,* 129-141.

Ellenberger, Henri F. *The discovery of the unconscious.* New York: Basic Books, 1970.

Fisher, S. and Greenberg, R. P. *The scientific credibility of Freud's theories and therapy.* New York: Basic Books, 1977.

Freud, S. *The psychopathology of everyday life.* New York: Mentor, 1920.

Freud, S. *Totem and taboo.* New York: Vintage, 1918.

Freud, S. *A general introduction to psychoanalysis.* New York: Washington Square Press, 1952.

Freud, S. *New introductory lectures on psychoanalysis.* New York: Norton, 1965.

Freud, S. *An outline of psychoanalysis.* New York: W. W. Norton & Co., 1949.

Hale, N. G. *Freud and the Americans.* New York: Oxford University Press, 1971.

Hughes, H. *Consciousness and society.* New York: Vintage, 1962.

Jupp, V. L. Freud and pseudo-science. *Philosophy,* 1977, *52,* 441-453.

Klein, D. B. *The unconscious: Invention or discovery?* Santa Monica, Calif.: Goodyear, 1977.

Marcus, S. *The other Victorians.* New York: Meridian, 1964.

McGuire, W. (Ed.) *The Freud/Jung letters.* Princeton, N.J.: Princeton University Press, 1974.

Mujeeb-ur-Rahman, Md. (Ed.) *The Freudian paradigm.* Chicago: Nelson-Hall, 1977.

Roazen, P. *Freud: Political and social thought.* New York: Knopf, 1968.

Wollheim, R. (Ed.) *Freud: A collection of critical essays.* New York: Doubleday, 1974.

Wollheim, R. *Sigmund Freud.* New York: Viking, 1971.

## CHAPTER 9
## THE PSYCHOLOGY OF ADAPTATION

Angell, J. R. The relations of structural and functional psychology to philosophy. *Philosophical Review,* 1903, *12,* 243-270.

Anonymous. Psychology in American universities. *American Journal of Psychology,* 1892, *3,* 275-286.

Baldwin, J. M. Sketch of the history of psychology. *Psychological Review,* 1905, *12,* 144-165.

Blum, J. M. *Pseudo-science and mental ability.* New York: Monthly Review Press, 1978.

Brentano, F. *Psychology from an empirical standpoint.* New York: The Humanities Press, 1973.

Cadwallader, T. Charles S. Peirce: The first American experimental psychologist. *Journal of the History of the Behavioral Sciences,* 1974, *10,* 191-198.

Commager, H. *The empire of reason.* Garden City, N.Y.: Doubleday, 1978.

Dolby, R. The transmission of two new scientific disciplines from Europe to North America in the late nineteenth century. *Annals of Science,* 1977, *34,* 287-310.

Douglas, A. *The feminization of American culture.* New York: Knopf, 1977.

Dunlap, K. The case against introspection. *Psychological Review,* 1912, *19,* 404-413.

**Ebbinghaus, H.** *Memory.* New York: Dover, 1964.

**Ebbinghaus, H.** *Psychology.* Boston: D.C. Heath, 1908.

**Fay, J. W.** *American psychology before William James.* New York: Octagon Books, 1966.

**Feibleman, J. K.** *An introduction to the philosophy of Charles S. Peirce.* Cambridge, Mass.: MIT Press, 1946.

**Forest, F.** *Francis Galton.* New York: Taplinger, 1974.

**Fowler, O. S.** *Phrenology proved, illustrated, and applied* (4th ed.). Philadelphia: Fowler and Brevoort, 1839.

**Fulcher, J. R.** Puritans and the passions: The faculty psychology in American Puritanism. *Journal of the History of the Behavioral Sciences,* 1973, *9*, 123-139.

**Galton, F.** *Natural inheritance.* London: Macmillan & Co., 1889.

**Gruber, H. E.** *Darwin on man.* New York: Dutton, 1974.

**Hamlyn, D. W.,** Bradley, Ward, and Stout. In B. Wolman (Ed.) *Historical roots of contemporary psychology.* New York: Harper & Row, Pub., 1968.

**Harms, E.** America's first major psychologist: Laurens Perseus Hickock. *Journal of the History of the Behavioral Sciences,* 1972, *8*, 120-123.

**Hickock, L. P.** *Empirical psychology* (rev. ed.). Boston: Ginn and Co., 1882.

**Hofstadter, R.** *Anti-intellectualism in American life.* New York: Vintage, 1962.

**Kamin, L.** *The science and politics of I.Q.* Hillsdale, N.J.: Erlbaum, 1974.

**Kevles, D.** *The physicists.* New York: Knopf, 1977.

**Kuklick, B.** *The rise of American philosophy.* New Haven, Conn.: Yale University Press, 1977.

**May, H.** *The Enlightenment in America.* Oxford: Oxford University Press, 1976.

**Miller, P.** *Errand into the wilderness.* New York: Harper & Row, Pub., 1956.

**Miller, P.** *Jonathan Edwards.* New York: Meridian, 1959.

**Morgan, C. L.** *An introduction to comparative psychology.* London: Walter Scott, 1894.

**Morris, C. W.** *Six theories of mind.* Chicago: Chicago University Press, 1932.

**Nathanson, J.** *John Dewey.* New York: Scribner's, 1951.

**Nye, R. B.** *Society and culture in America 1830-1860.* New York: Harper & Row, Pub., 1974.

**Peel, J.** *Herbert Spencer.* New York: Basic Books, 1971.

**Romanes, G.** *Mental evolution in man.* New York: D. Appleton and Co., 1889.

**Rosenberg, C.** Charles Benedict Davenport and the irony of American eugenics. In C. Rosenberg (Ed.) *No other gods.* Baltimore: The John Hopkins University Press, 1978.

**Schneider, H. W.** *History of American philosophy.* New York: Columbia University Press, 1963.

**Spencer, H.** The comparative psychology of man. *Mind,* 1876, *1*, 7-20.

**Stern, M. B.** *Heads and headlines: The phrenological Fowlers.* Norman, Okla.: University of Oklahoma Press, 1971.

**Wiener, P. P.** *Evolution and the founders of pragmatism.* Cambridge, Mass.: Harvard University Press, 1949.

**Yerkes, R. & Morgulis, S.** The method of Pavlov in animal psychology. *Psychological Bulletin,* 1909, *6*, 257-273.

## CHAPTER 10
## CLASSICAL BEHAVIORISM

Birnbaum, L. Behaviorism: John Broadus Watson and American social thought, 1913-1933. Unpublished doctoral dissertation, University of California at Berkeley, 1964.

Burnham, J. C. On the origins of behaviorism, *Journal of the History of the Behavioral Sciences*, 1968, *4*, 143-152.

Marshall, H. R. Is psychology evaporating? *Journal of Philosophy, Psychology, and Scientific Methods*, 1913, *10*, 710-716.

Pavlov, I. P. *Conditioned reflexes*. New York: Dover, 1960.

Pavlov, I. P. *Lectures on conditioned reflexes* (2 vols.). London: Lawrence & Wishart, 1963.

Ruckmich, C. A. The last decade of psychology in review. *Psychological Bulletin*, 1916, *13*, 109-120.

Singer, E. A. Mind as an observable object. *Journal of Philosophy, Psychology, and Scientific Methods*, 1911, *8*, 180-186.

Thorndike, E. L. Autobiography. In C. L. Murchison (Ed.) *A history of psychology in autobiography* (Vol. III). Worchester: Clark University Press, 1930.

Washburn, M. F. Some thoughts on the last quarter century in psychology. *Philosophical Review*, 1917, *27*, 46-55.

Watson, J. B. The place of the conditioned reflex in psychology. *Psychological Review*, 1916, *23*, 89-116.

Watson, J. B. *Psychological Care of Infant and Child*. New York: W. W. Norton & Co., 1928.

Weiss, A. P. The relation between structural and behavioral psychology. *Philosophical Review*, 1917a, *24*, 302-317.

Weiss, A. P. The relation between functional and behavioral psychology. *Psychological Review*, 1917b, *24*, 353-368.

Woodbridge, F. J. The belief in sensations. *Journal of Philosophy, Psychology, and Scientific Method*, 1913, *10*, 599-608.

## CHAPTER 11
## NEO-BEHAVIORISM

Bergmann, G. The logic of psychological concepts. *Philosophy of Science*, 1951, *18*, 93-110.

Putnam, H. Review of *Philosophy of science* by G. Bergmann. *Philosophical Review*, 1960, *69*, 276-277.

Skinner, B. F. *Contingencies of reinforcement*. Englewood Cliffs, N.J.: Prentice-Hall, 1969.

Skinner, B. F. *About behaviorism*. New York: Knopf, 1974.

Skinner, B. F. *Particulars of my life*. New York: Knopf, 1976.

Skinner, B. F. Autobiography. In E. G. Boring and G. Lindsey (Eds.) *A history of psychology in autobiography*. New York: Appleton-Century-Crofts, 1967.

Skinner, B. F. The steep and thorny way to a science of behavior. In R. Harre (Ed.) *Problems of scientific revolution.* Oxford: Oxford University Press, 1975.

Spence, K. Historical and modern conceptions of psychology. In E. H. Maddon (Ed.) *The structure of scientific thought.* Boston: Houghton-Mifflin, 1956.

Tolman, E. C. *Purposive behavior in animals and men.* New York: Irvington, 1967.

Watson, J. B. *Behavior: An introduction to comparative psychology.* New York: Holt, 1914.


## CHAPTER 12
## 1945-1960

Beach, F. A. The snark was a boojum. *American Psychologist,* 1950, *5,* 115-124.

Bruner, J., Goodnow, J. J., & Austin, G. A. *A study of thinking.* New York: John Wiley, 1956.

Chomsky, N. The case against B. F. Skinner. *New York Review of Books,* 1971, *17,* (December 30), 18-24.

Dollard, J., & Miller, N. *Personality and psychotherapy.* New York: McGraw-Hill, 1950.

Erdelyi, H. A new look at the new look. *Psychological Review,* 1974, *81,* 1-25.

Festinger, L. *A theory of cognitive dissonance.* Stanford, Calif.: Stanford University Press, 1957.

Festinger, L. & Carlsmith, J. M. Cognitive consequences of forced compliance. *Journal of Abnormal and Social Psychology,* 1959, *58,* 203-210.

Ginsberg, H. & Opper, S. *Piaget's theory of intellectual development.* Englewood Cliffs, N.J.: Prentice-Hall, 1969.

Kendler, H. H. & D'Amato, M. F. A comparison of reversal shifts and non-reversal shifts in human concept formation behavior. *Journal of Experimental Psychology,* 1955, *49,* 165-174.

Kendler, H. H. & Kendler, T. S. Vertical and horizontal processes in problem-solving. *Psychological Review,* 1962, *69,* 1-16.

Lashley, K. S. The problem of serial order in behavior. In L. A. Jeffress (Ed.) *Cerebral mechanisms in behavior.* New York: John Wiley, 1951.

Miller, N. & Dollard, J. *Social learning and imitation.* New Haven, Conn.: Yale University Press, 1941.

Newell, A., Shaw, J. C., & Simon, H. A. Elements of a theory of problem solving. *Psychological Review,* 1958, *65,* 151-166.

Ripple, E. & Rockcastle, V. (Eds.) *Piaget rediscovered.* Ithaca, N.Y.: Cornell University Press, 1964.

Turing, A. M. Computing machinery and intelligence. In E. A. Feigenbaum, & J. Feldman (Eds.) *Computers and thought.* New York: McGraw-Hill, 1963.

Wheeler, H. (Ed.) *Beyond the punitive society.* San Francisco: W. H. Freeman, 1973.


## CHAPTER 13
## THE 1960s

Bower, G. H. Cognitive psychology: An introduction. In W. K. Estes (Ed.) *Handbook of learning and the cognitive processes* (Vol. 1). Hillsdale, N.J.: Erlbaum, 1975.

Briskman, L. B. Is a Kuhnian analysis applicable to psychology? *Science Studies,* 1972, *2,* 87-97.

Chomsky, N. *Syntactic structures.* The Hague: Mouton, 1957.

Chomsky, N. *Language and mind* (enlarged ed.). New York: Harcourt Brace Jovanovich, Inc., 1972.

Chomsky, N. Recent contributions to the theory of innate ideas. *Synthese,* 1967, *17,* 2-11.

Feigenbaum, E. and Feldman, J. (Eds.) *Computers and thought.* New York: McGraw-Hill, 1963.

Hays, J. R. (Ed.) *Cognition and the development of language.* New York: John Wiley, 1970.

Hinde, R. A. and Stevenson-Hinde, T. (Eds.) *Constraints on learning.* New York: Academic Press, 1973.

Hook, S. (Ed.) *Language and philosophy.* New York: New York University Press, 1969.

Piaget, J. with B. Inhelder. *The psychology of the child.* London: Routledge and Kegan Paul, 1969.

Piaget, J. *Structuralism.* New York: Basic Books, 1970.

Premack, A. and Premack, D. Teaching language to an ape. *Scientific American,* 1972, *227,* 92-99.

Segal, E. M. and Lachman, R. Complex behavior or higher mental processes: Is there a paradigm shift? *American Psychologist,* 1972, *27,* 46-55.

Simon, H. A. and Newell, A. Human problem solving: The state of the theory in 1970. *American Psychologist,* 1970, *25,* 145-159.

Spielberger, L. D. and DeNike, L. Descriptive behaviorism versus cognitive theory in verbal operant conditioning. *Psychological Review,* 1966, *73,* 306-326.

Verplanck, W. S. The operant, from rat to man. *Transactions of the New York Academy of Sciences,* Series II, 1955, *17,* No. 8, 594-601.

Warren, N. Is a scientific revolution taking place in psychology? Doubts and reservations. *Science Studies,* 1971, *1,* 407-413.

Weimer, W. and Palermo, D. (Eds.) *Cognition and the symbolic processes.* Hillsdale, N.J.: Erlbaum, 1974.

## CHAPTER 15
## PROSPECT

Allport, D. A. Critical notice. The state of cognitive psychology. *Quarterly Journal of Experimental Psychology,* 1975, *27,* 141-152.

Andreski, S. *Social sciences as sorcery.* London: Andre Deutsch, 1972.

Breck, A. D. and Yourgrav, W. (Eds.) *Biology, history and natural philosophy.* New York: Plenum, 1972.

Dawkins, R. *The selfish gene.* New York: Oxford University Press, 1976.

Jensen, A. How much can we boost I.Q. and scholastic achievement? *Harvard Educational Review,* 1969, *39,* 1-123.

Kosslyn, S. M. and Pomerantz, J. R. Imagery, propositions, and the form of internal representations. *Cognitive Psychology,* 1977, *9,* 52-76.

MacCorquodale, K. B. F. Skinner's *Verbal behavior*: A retrospective appreciation. *Journal of the Experimental Analysis of Behavior,* 1969, *12,* 831-841.

Pylyshyn, Z. W. Minds, machines and phenomenology: Some reflections on Dreyfus' *What computers can't do. Cognition,* 1974, *3,* 20-42.

# Index